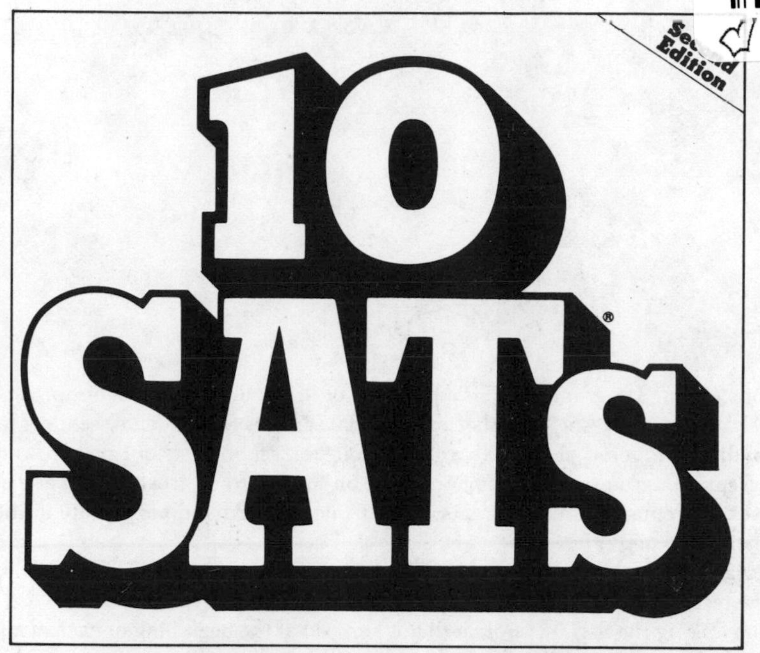

THE ACTUAL AND COMPLETE
SCHOLASTIC APTITUDE TEST®
PLUS ADVICE FROM THE COLLEGE BOARD
ON HOW TO PREPARE FOR IT

COLLEGE ENTRANCE EXAMINATION BOARD
NEW YORK

The Admissions Testing Program (ATP) is a program of the College Board, a nonprofit membership organization that provides tests and other educational services for students, schools, and colleges. The membership is composed of more than 2,500 colleges, schools, school systems, and education associations. Representatives of the members serve on the Board of Trustees and advisory councils and committees that consider the programs of the College Board and participate in the determination of its policies and activities.

This book was prepared and produced by Educational Testing Service (ETS), which develops and administers the tests of the Admissions Testing Program for the College Board. The text of this book is adapted from *Taking the SAT,* a booklet that is shipped at the beginning of each academic year to secondary schools for free distribution to students who plan to register for the SAT. (Copies of *Taking the SAT* can be purchased for $4.00 each; 50 or more, $2.00 each).

The College Board and Educational Testing Service are dedicated to the principle of equal opportunity, and their programs, services, and employment policies are guided by that principle.

Cover design by Bob Silverman

Library of Congress catalog card number: 85-07338

Printed in the United States of America
9 8 7 6 5 4 3 2 1

Contents

Introduction

The College Board knows that some people are uncomfortable when they are faced with the prospect of taking any test, but that there is even greater anxiety before taking national standardized tests such as the Scholastic Aptitude Test (SAT). One reason that people worry about how they will do on the SAT is that they don't know what will be on the test, what it measures, and how the results will be used.

This book enables students to get better acquainted with the SAT and, thus, alleviate some of that anxiety. The following topics, as well as 10 previously administered editions of the SAT, are included:

- What the SAT is designed to measure
- The format of the test as a whole
- The kinds of questions on the test
- How to mark the answer sheet
- How each question is scored
- Rules of good test-taking practice
- How scores are reported and used
- How to use sample tests for practice and self-scoring

This information and one sample test are also available in the booklet *Taking the SAT*, which students planning to take the test receive free of charge from their schools. In addition, the College Board also makes public an average of five editions of the SAT each year as part of its ongoing program to provide full public information about these tests. Ten of these editions, all of which have been administered in the past few years, are included in this book.

Other than to help students become familiar with the test, use of all 10 tests in preparing for the SAT probably will be of limited value. These tests illustrate the range of questions and topics on any SAT test; however, research offers no evidence that extensive drill or practice on these particular tests will increase scores. The soundest preparation for the SAT continues to be serious application to regular school studies, with emphasis on academic courses and plenty of outside reading.

Although this book has been written for students and others who are planning to take the SAT, it also may be useful to parents, teachers, and individuals who have an interest in the SAT and who use its results.

How the Tests Are Developed

Many people are involved in the development of every new edition of the Scholastic Aptitude Test (SAT) and the Test of Standard Written English (TSWE). Questions are written by high school and college teachers and by test specialists at Educational Testing Service. Questions then are placed in an equating section of the SAT to be tried out under standard testing conditions by representative samples of students. The responses to each question are analyzed statistically for usefulness and may be revised if necessary. Satisfactory questions become part of a pool of questions from which new editions of the SAT are assembled.

In developing a new edition of the SAT, test specialists and a test editor review each question and reading selection on which questions are based for accuracy and to ensure balanced content of the test as a whole. Each reviewer prepares a list of answers that is compared with other reviewers' lists to verify agreement on the correct answer for each question. In addition, trained "sensitivity" reviewers eliminate any references in the test material that might be unfair or offensive to some student groups because of stereotyping, sex bias, or meaning that could produce negative feelings.

After the new edition has been assembled, the SAT and TSWE Committees, composed of high school teachers, college faculty, and educational administrators, review the test a final time before it is given to students. In addition to reviewing all new tests, these committees also are responsible for determining overall test specifications, recommending related research, and advising the College Board on policy matters related to the tests.

SAT Committee 1985-86

James R. Buch, University of Oregon, Eugene, Oregon, *Chair*

Dorothy H. Dillon, Kent Place School, Summit, New Jersey

Susan H. Ehringhaus, University of North Carolina at Chapel Hill, Chapel Hill, North Carolina

Joella H. Gipson, Wayne State University, Detroit, Michigan

Alberta E. Meyer, Trinity University, San Antonio, Texas

Paul M. Pressly, Savannah Country Day School, Savannah, Georgia

Maria C. Ramirez, New York State Education Department, Albany, New York

David M. Smith, Milton Academy, Milton, Massachusetts

Robert L. Trinchero, Jr., California State University, Hayward, California

Frank Womer, University of Michigan, Ann Arbor, Michigan

TSWE Committee 1985-86

Marjorie G. Roemer, University of California at Santa Barbara, Santa Barbara, California, *Chair*

Kris D. Gutierrez, University of Colorado, Boulder, Colorado

Jeanette P. Morgan, University of Houston — University Park, Houston, Texas

Jacqueline J. Royster, Spelman College, Atlanta, Georgia

Aaron C. Stander, Oakland Schools, Pontiac, Michigan

About the Tests

The SAT

The SAT is a multiple-choice test made up of verbal and math sections. The verbal questions test your vocabulary, verbal reasoning, and understanding of what you read. The math questions test your ability to solve problems involving arithmetic, elementary algebra, and geometry. These verbal and mathematical abilities are related to how well you will do academically in college. The SAT does not measure other factors and abilities — such as creativity, special talents, and motivation — that may also help you do well in college.

SAT scores are useful to college admissions officers in comparing the preparation and ability of applicants from different high schools which may vary widely in their courses and grading standards. Colleges also consider your high school record and other information about you in making admissions decisions. Your high school record is probably the best single indicator of how you will do in college, but a combination of your high school grades and test scores is an even better indicator.

The TSWE

The TSWE is a multiple-choice test given at the same time as the SAT, but it has a different purpose. The TSWE is intended to be used to help the college you attend choose an English course appropriate for your ability. The questions in it measure your ability to recognize standard written English, the language that is used in most college textbooks and that you will probably be expected to use in the papers you write in college.

How the Tests Are Organized

The SAT and TSWE are included in the same test book. Each test book is divided into six sections:

- 2 SAT-verbal sections,
- 2 SAT-math sections,
- 1 TSWE section, and
- 1 section of equating questions (verbal, math, or TSWE).

The questions in the equating section do not count toward your score. They are used for two purposes: First, representative questions from earlier editions are given again in order to set the SAT on the 200 to 800 scale. Repeating these questions makes it possible to compare fairly scores earned at different administrations. Second, the equating section is used to try out questions for future use in the SAT. Trying out questions in advance makes it possible to assemble each edition of the SAT with the same mix of easy and hard questions. Thus, the unscored equating section is used to assemble SATs of comparable difficulty so that college admissions officers can compare SAT scores equitably.

You will be given 30 minutes to work on each section. The six sections are not in the same order in every test book. Later in this booklet you will find detailed explanations of each type of question as well as tips on how to make the best use of the testing time.

How to Register

The *Registration Bulletin* contains a registration form and directions on how to register for the test and how to have your scores reported. The *Bulletin* also describes other tests and services of the Admissions Testing Program (ATP), such as the Achievement Tests, the Student Descriptive Questionnaire (SDQ), and the Student Search Service (SSS).

The SAT is administered on a regular schedule (six times a year in most states) at thousands of test centers throughout the world. To avoid late fees, you must send in your registration form at least five weeks before the test date you have chosen.

A supply of the *Registration Bulletin* is sent to all high schools each year. High school students can pick up a copy of the *Bulletin* at their school guidance or counseling office. Test candidates who are not currently in high school may obtain a copy by writing to the address below.

If you want to write or call. . .

Address
College Board ATP
CN 6200
Princeton, NJ 08541-6200

Phone Numbers (Monday-Friday)

Princeton, NJ	Berkeley, CA
(609) 771-7600	**(415) 849-0950**
8:30 a.m. to 9:30 p.m.	8:15 a.m. to 4:30 p.m.
Eastern time	Pacific time

How to Prepare for the Test

Know What to Expect

The best way to prepare for the test is to familiarize yourself with its organization, the types of questions that will appear on it, and what will be expected of you on the test day. To make sure you are prepared for the test you should:

- **Read this book or *Taking the SAT*.** They have the information you will need to become familiar with all aspects of the test. Be sure you understand how the test is organized and how it will be scored. The information in these books will help you learn the answers to such questions as "Should I guess?" "Do difficult questions get more credit than easy ones?" "Should I memorize mathematical formulas?"
- **Study the sample questions and explanations.** The sample questions and explanations that begin on page 12 will give you a good idea of the kinds of questions that are on the test. The more familiar you are with the sample questions, the more comfortable you'll feel when you see the questions in your test book on the day of the test.
- **Study and understand the test directions.** The directions in this book for answering the questions are exactly the same as in the test book. If you study them now, you will spend less time reading and figuring out the directions on the test day and have more time for answering the questions.
- **Take at least one sample test.** Try to take a practice test under conditions similar to those of the test day. (Suggestions for doing so are on page 34, just before the sample test.) Make sure you use one of the answer sheets provided. That way, you'll already have been through a "dry run" before you take the test.

The Day Before the Test

Learning as much as you can about the test is something you'll want to do several weeks before the day you plan to take the test. Following are some suggestions for what to do on the day or evening before the test:

- **Spend an hour or so reviewing the sample questions and explanations in this book.** Hours of intense study the night before probably will not help your performance on the test and might even make you more anxious. But a short review of the information you highlighted earlier probably will make you feel more comfortable and prepared.
- **Get your testing materials together and put them in a place that will be convenient for you in the morning.** Use this checklist:
  - ✓ Admission ticket
  - ✓ Acceptable identification (You won't be admitted to the test center without it. See the *Registration Bulletin.*)
  - ✓ Two No. 2 pencils with erasers
  - ✓ Directions to the test center if you need them
  - ✓ All the materials you will need to register as a standby, if you have not preregistered (See the *Registration Bulletin.)*
- **Spend the rest of the evening relaxing.** You'll accomplish little by worrying about the next day. Read a book, watch a television program you enjoy, or do anything you find relaxing.
- **Get a good night's sleep.** You'll want to feel your best when you take the test, so try to be well rested and refreshed. Get to bed early, set your alarm early enough to avoid having to rush, and feel satisfied that you've prepared yourself well for the test day.

Special Preparation

If you or your parents have been thinking about special preparation for the SAT outside your regular classroom activities, consider the following points:

- This book (or *Taking the SAT*) and the *Registration Bulletin* are the best sources of information about the SAT. All the questions in these books, including those in the sample test, are taken from SATs that have been administered during the past few years.
- The SAT measures developed verbal and mathematical reasoning abilities that are involved in successful academic work in college; it is not a test of some inborn and unchanging capacity.
- Scores on the SAT can change as you develop your verbal and mathematical abilities both in and out of school.
- Your abilities are related to the time and effort spent; short-term drill and cramming are likely to have little effect; longer-term preparation that de-

velops skills and abilities can have greater effect. One kind of longer-term preparation is the study of challenging academic courses.

- While drill and practice on sample test questions generally result in little effect on test scores, preparation of this kind can familiarize you with different question types and may help to reduce anxiety about what to expect. You can help yourself to become familiar with the test by using the explanations and sample tests in this book.

- Whether longer preparation, apart from that available to you in your regular high school courses, is worth the time, effort, and money is a decision you and your parents must make for yourselves; results seem to vary considerably from program to program, and for each person within any one program. Studies of special preparation programs carried on in many high schools show various results averaging about 10 points for the verbal section and 15 points for the mathematical over and above the average increases that would otherwise be expected. In other programs, results have ranged from no improvement in scores to average gains of 25-30 points for particular groups of students or particular programs. Recent studies of commercial coaching have shown a similar range of results. You should satisfy yourself that the results of a special program or course are likely to make a difference in relation to your college admissions plans.

- Generally, the soundest preparation for the SAT is to study widely with emphasis on academic courses and extensive outside reading. Since SAT score increases of 20-30 points result from about three additional questions answered correctly, your own independent study in addition to regular academic course work could result in some increase in your scores.

Test-Taking Tips

Think of the number of things you do easily every day that would seem mysterious or difficult if you didn't know how to approach them. When you go to school each morning, you know that you have to turn left at one corner or right at another. And you have a good idea of how far away your school is and how long it will take you to get there. But if you hadn't learned these things at one time or another and received tips from others on shortcuts and new routes, your trip to school would seem like a journey to a far-off land!

Taking the SAT and TSWE does not have to be a mysterious experience. You have already read about how to prepare for the tests in general. Here are some specific test-taking tips that will help when you take the tests.

- Within each group of questions of the same type, the easier questions are usually at the beginning of the group and the more difficult ones are at the end. (An exception to this is the reading comprehension questions. The reading passages are usually ordered easiest to hardest, but the questions that follow each passage are ordered according to the logic and organization of the passage.)
- If you're working on a group of questions of a particular type and find that the questions are getting too difficult for you, quickly read through the rest of the questions in that group and answer only those you think you know. Then go on to the next group of questions in that section. (Again, this is not necessarily true of the questions about a reading passage. A difficult reading comprehension question might be followed by an easier one.)
- You get just as much credit for correctly answering easy questions as you do for correctly answering hard ones. So make sure you answer all the questions that seem easy to you before you spend time thinking about the questions that seem difficult.
- You *can* guess. If you know that one or more of the choices for a question are definitely wrong, then it's generally to your advantage to guess from the remaining choices. But because of the way the test is scored, random guessing is unlikely to increase your score.
- You *can* omit questions. Many students who do well on the SAT omit some questions. You can always return to questions you've omitted if you finish before time is up for that section.
- You don't have to answer every question correctly to score well. In fact, many students who receive average or slightly above-average scores answer only 40-60 percent of the questions correctly.
- You get credit for each question you answer correctly. You lose a *fraction* for each question you answer incorrectly. You neither gain nor lose credit for questions you omit. (See page 61 for more detailed information on scoring.)
- Use the test book for scratchwork and to mark questions you omitted, so you can go back to them if you have time. You will not receive credit for any responses written in the test book. You must mark all your responses to test questions on the separate answer sheet.
- Do *not* make extra marks on the answer sheet. They may be misread as answers by the scoring machine. If the scoring machine reads what looks like two answers for one question, that will be considered an omitted question. So it's in your best interest to keep your answer sheet free of any stray marks.
- Any four-choice mathematics question (see page 58) for which you mark the fifth answer oval, E, will be treated as an omitted question. You will not receive credit for that question.
- Do not omit an entire section of the test. If you do not respond to at least three SAT-verbal, SAT-math, or TSWE questions, you will receive the minimum score for that part.

Sample Questions and Explanations

Following are sample questions and explanations for each type of question that appears on the SAT. Pay special attention to the sample directions. You'll see them again on the test.

Verbal Sections of the SAT

The verbal sections of the SAT contain four types of questions:

- 25 antonyms,
- 20 analogics,
- 15 sentence completions, and
- 25 questions based on reading passages.

The antonyms usually take the least time per question, followed by analogies, sentence completion questions, and, finally, the reading comprehension questions. Individual students spend varying amounts of time working on the different types of questions. Some students can answer two or three antonyms a minute, but the same students may take more than seven minutes to read a 400-word passage and answer five questions on it.

Your answers to the 85 questions in the verbal sections make up your total verbal score. (See page 62.) The score report you receive will also show two subscores: (1) a vocabulary subscore, based on the antonym and analogy questions, and (2) a reading subscore, based on the sentence completions and the questions on the reading passages.

A careful balance of reading materials and words drawn from a variety of subject-matter fields helps ensure that the test is fair to students with different interests. However, no specialized knowledge in science, social studies, literature, or other fields is needed.

Antonyms (opposites)

Antonym questions primarily test the extent of your vocabulary. The vocabulary used in the antonym questions includes words that you are likely to come across in your general reading, although some words may not be the kind you use in everyday speech.

Directions: Each question below consists of a word in capital letters, followed by five lettered words or phrases. Choose the word or phrase that is most nearly opposite in meaning to the word in capital letters. Since some of the questions require you to distinguish fine shades of meaning, consider all the choices before deciding which is best.

EXAMPLE:

GOOD: (A) sour (B) bad (C) red (D) hot (E) ugly

Ⓐ ● Ⓒ Ⓓ Ⓔ

You can probably answer this example without thinking very much about the choices. However, most of the antonyms in the verbal section require more careful analysis. When you work on antonym questions, remember that:

1. Among the five choices offered, you are looking for the word that means the *opposite* of the given word. Words that have exactly the same meaning as the given word are not included among the five choices.

2. You are looking for the *best* answer. Read all of the choices before deciding which one is best, even if you feel sure you know the answer. For example:

   SUBSEQUENT: (A) primary (B) recent (C) contemporary (D) prior (E) simultaneous

   Subsequent means "following in time or order; succeeding." Someone working quickly might choose (B) *recent* because it refers to a past action and *subsequent* refers to an action in the future. However, choice (D) *prior* is the best answer. It is more nearly the opposite of *subsequent* than is *recent*.

3. Few words have exact opposites, that is, words that are opposite in all of their meanings. You should find the word that is *most nearly* opposite. For example:

   FERMENTING: (A) improvising (B) stagnating (C) wavering (D) plunging (E) dissolving

   Even though *fermenting* is normally associated with chemical reactions, whereas *stagnating* is normally associated with water, *fermenting* means being agitated and *stagnating* means being motionless. Therefore, choice (B) *stagnating* is the best of the five choices.

4. You need to be flexible. A word can have several meanings. For example:

   DEPRESS: (A) force (B) allow (C) clarify (D) elate (E) loosen

   The word *depress* can mean "to push down." However, no word meaning "to lift up" is included among the choices. Therefore, you must consider another meaning of *depress*, "to sadden or discourage." Option (D) *elate* means to fill with joy or pride. The best answer is (D) *elate*.

5. You'll often recognize a word you have encountered in your reading but have never looked up in the dictionary. If you don't know the dictionary meaning of a word but have a feeling for how the word should be used, try to make up a short phrase or sentence using the word. This may give you a clue as to which choice is an opposite, even though you may not be able to define the word precisely.

   INCUMBENT: (A) conscious (B) effortless (C) optional (D) improper (E) irrelevant

   You may remember *incumbent* used in a sentence such as, "It is incumbent upon me to finish this." If you can think of such a phrase, you may be able to recognize that *incumbent* means "imposed as a duty" or "obligatory." Of the five choices, (A), (B), and (D) are in no way opposites of *incumbent* and you can easily eliminate them. Choice (E) means "not pertinent" and choice (C) means "not compulsory." Although choice (E) may look attractive, choice (C) *optional* is more nearly an exact opposite to *incumbent*. Choice (C), therefore, is the answer.

Some General Tips for Answering Antonym Questions

Answering antonyms depends on knowing the uses as well as the meanings of words, so just memorizing word lists is probably of little use. You're more likely to improve your performance on antonyms and other kinds of verbal questions by doing things that help you to think about words and the way they are used. So, it would be a good idea to:

- ✓ Read some good books or magazines on subjects with which you're not already familiar. This will give you a better idea of how even familiar words can have different meanings in different contexts.
- ✓ Use a dictionary when you come across words that you don't understand in your reading. This will help to broaden your vocabulary and consequently could improve your performance on the tests.

Analogies

Analogy questions test your ability to see a relationship in a pair of words, to understand the ideas expressed in the relationship, and to recognize a similar or parallel relationship.

Directions: Each question below consists of a related pair of words or phrases, followed by five lettered pairs of words or phrases. Select the lettered pair that best expresses a relationship similar to that expressed in the original pair.

EXAMPLE:
YAWN : BOREDOM : : (A) dream : sleep (B) anger : madness (C) smile : amusement (D) face : expression (E) impatience : rebellion

The first step in answering an analogy question is to establish a precise relationship between the original pair of words (the two capitalized words) before you examine the five answer choices. In the example above, the relationship between *yawn* and *boredom* can best be stated as "(first word) is a physical sign of (second word)," or "(first word) is a facial expression of (second word)." The second step in answering an analogy question is to decide which of the five pairs given as choices best expresses a similar relationship. In the example above, the answer is choice (C): a (smile) is a physical sign of (amusement), or a (smile) is a facial expression of (amusement). None of the other choices shares a similar relationship with the capitalized pair of words: a *dream* is something that occurs when you are asleep, but it is not usually thought of as being a sign of *sleep* as, for example, closed eyes or a snore might be; *anger* denotes strong displeasure and *madness* can refer to rage or insanity, but neither word is a physical sign of the other; an *expression* is something that appears on a *face*, but a *face* is not a sign of an *expression*; *impatience* may lead to *rebellion* or be characteristic of a rebellious person, but *impatience* is not a physical sign of *rebellion*.

For the analogy below, just state the relationship between the original pair of words and then decide which pair of words from choices (A)–(E) has the same relationship.

SUBMISSIVE : LED : : (A) wealthy : employed (B) intolerant : indulged (C) humble : humiliated (D) incorrigible : taught (E) inconspicuous : overlooked

The relationship between *submissive* and *led* can be expressed as "to be submissive is to be easily led." Only choice (E) has the same relationship: "to be inconspicuous is to be easily overlooked."

To be *intolerant* is not to be easily *indulged*, to be *humble* is not to be easily *humiliated*, and to be *incorrigible* (or incapable of being reformed) is not to be easily *taught*. With regard to choice (A), although the wealthy may find it easier to get employment than do the poor, the statement "to be wealthy is to be easily employed" is an expression of opinion and not an expression of the relationship between the words according to their dictionary meanings.

Practice describing verbal relationships. Below are some examples of the kinds of relationships that could be used.

SONG : REPERTOIRE : : (A) score : melody (B) instrument : artist (C) solo : chorus (D) benediction : church (E) suit : wardrobe

The best answer is choice (E). The relationship between the words can be expressed as "several (first word) make up a (second word)." Several (songs) make up a (repertoire) as several (suits) make up a (wardrobe).

REQUEST : ENTREAT : : (A) control : explode (B) admire : idolize (C) borrow : steal (D) repeat : plead (E) cancel : invalidate

The best answer is choice (B). Although both of the capitalized words have similar meanings, they express different degrees of feeling; to (entreat) is to (request) with strong feeling as to (idolize) is to (admire) with strong feeling.

To answer analogy questions, you must think carefully about the precise meanings of words. For instance, if you thought the word "entreat" meant only "to ask" instead of "to ask urgently," you would have trouble establishing the correct relationship between *request* and *entreat*.

FAMINE : STARVATION : : (A) deluge : flood (B) drought : vegetation (C) war : treaty (D) success : achievement (E) seed : mutation

The best answer is choice (A). The relationship can be stated as (famine) results in (starvation) as a (deluge) results in a (flood). None of the other pairs of words expresses a causal relationship. Choice (C) is close, since a *treaty* often follows after a *war*, but we do not think of a war "causing" a treaty in the same way that a famine "causes" starvation.

AMPLIFIER : HEAR : : (A) turntable : listen (B) typewriter : spell (C) platter : eat (D) camera : feel (E) microscope : see

The best answer is choice (E). An (amplifier) magnifies in order to help a person (hear) in the same way that a (microscope) magnifies in order to help a person (see). Note that, in (A), while a *turntable* is part of a larger mechanism that allows a person to *listen*, the choice is not as good an answer as (E) because a *turntable* does not magnify anything. Choice (D) is also wrong for a similar reason: a *camera* produces pictures that may make a person *feel* something, but a *camera* does not magnify in order to help a person to *feel*.

Some choices may have relationships that are close but not parallel to the relationship in the original pair. Most of the pairs of words listed in the choices have relationships that can be stated; however, the correct answer has *most nearly* the same relationship as the original pair. Look at the following example.

KNIFE : INCISION : : (A) bulldozer : excavation (B) tool : operation (C) pencil : calculation (D) hose : irrigation (E) plow : agriculture

On the most general level, the relationship between *knife* and *incision* is that the object indicated by the first word is used to perform the action indicated by the second word. Since "a (knife) is used to make an (incision)," "a (bulldozer) is used to make an (excavation)," and "a (hose) is used for (irrigation)," there appear to be two correct answers. You need to go back and state the relationship more precisely. Some aspect of the relationship between the original pair exists in only one of the choices. A more precise relationship between *knife* and *incision* could be expressed as: "a knife cuts into something to make an incision" and "a bulldozer cuts into something to make an excavation." This relationship eliminates *hose : irrigation* as a possible answer. The best answer is choice (A).

Remember that a pair of words can have more than one relationship. For example:

PRIDE : LION : : (A) snake : python (B) pack : wolf (C) rat : mouse (D) bird : starling (E) dog : canine

A possible relationship between *pride* and *lion* might be that "the first word describes a characteristic of the second (especially in mythology)." Using this reasoning, you might look for an answer such as *wisdom : owl*, but none of the given choices has that kind of relationship. Another relationship between *pride* and *lion* is "a group of lions is called a pride"; therefore, the answer is (B) *pack : wolf*, since "a group of wolves is called a pack."

Some General Tips for Answering Analogy Questions

- State the relationship between the two capitalized words in a sentence or phrase as clearly in your mind as you can. Next, find the pair of words that has the most similar or parallel relationship.
- Always compare the relationship between the pair of capitalized words to the relationships between the pairs of words in each of the choices. Don't try to set up a relationship between the first word in the original pair and the first word in each of the five choices.

✓ Think carefully about the meanings of words. The words in analogy questions are used according to their dictionary definitions or meanings closely related to their dictionary definitions. The better you know the precise meanings of words, the less trouble you'll have establishing the correct relationships between them.

✓ Don't be misled by relationships that are close but not parallel to the relationship in the original pair. The correct answer has a relationship that is most nearly parallel to the relationship between the capitalized words.

Sentence Completion Questions

Sentence completion questions test your ability to recognize relationships among parts of a sentence. Each question has a sentence with one or two words missing. Below the sentence, five words or pairs of words are given. You must choose the word or set of words that best fits with the other parts of the sentence. In sentence completion questions, you have to know the meanings of the words offered as choices and you also have to know how to use those words properly in the context of a sentence. The sentences are taken from published material and cover a wide variety of topics. You'll find that even if you're not familiar with the topic of a sentence, there's enough information in the sentence for you to find the correct answer from the context of the sentence itself.

Directions: Each sentence below has one or two blanks, each blank indicating that something has been omitted. Beneath the sentence are five lettered words or sets of words. Choose the word or set of words that best fits the meaning of the sentence as a whole.

> **EXAMPLE:**
> **Although its publicity has been ····, the film itself is intelligent, well-acted, handsomely produced, and altogether ····.**
> **(A) tasteless . . respectable (B) extensive . . moderate (C) sophisticated . . amateur (D) risqué . . crude (E) perfect . . spectacular**
>
> ● Ⓑ Ⓒ Ⓓ Ⓔ

The word *although* suggests that the publicity gave the wrong impression of the movie, so look for two words that are more or less opposite in meaning. Also, the second word has to fit in with "intelligent, well-acted, handsomely produced." Choices (D) and (E) are not opposites. The words in Choice (B) are somewhat opposite in meaning, but do not logically fulfill the expectation set up by the word *although*. Choice (C) can't be the correct answer, even though *sophisticated* and *amateur* are nearly opposites, because an "intelligent, well-acted, handsomely produced" film isn't amateurish. Only choice (A), when inserted in the sentence, makes a logical statement.

For a better understanding of sentence completion questions, read the following sample questions and explanations.

Nearly all the cultivated plants utilized by the Chinese have been of ···· origin; even rice, though known in China since Neolithic times, came from India.

(A) foreign (B) ancient (C) wild (D) obscure (E) common

To answer this question, you need to consider the entire sentence — the part that comes after the semicolon as well as the part that comes before it. If you only consider the first part of the question, all five choices seem plausible. The second part of the sentence adds a specific example — that rice came to China from India. This idea of origin supports and clarifies the "origin" mentioned in the first part of the sentence and eliminates (C), (D), and (E) as possible answers. The mention of Neolithic times makes (B) harder to eliminate, but the sentence is not logical when (B) is used to fill in the blank because the emphasis in the second part of the sentence — country of origin — is inconsistent with that in the first — age. Only choice (A) produces a sentence that is logical and consistent.

The excitement does not ···· but ···· his senses, giving him a keener perception of a thousand details.

(A) slow . . diverts (B) blur . . sharpens (C) overrule . . constricts (D) heighten . . aggravates (E) forewarn . . quickens

Since the sentence has two blanks to be filled, you must make sure that both words make sense in the sentence. If you look for grammatical clues within the sentence, you will see that the word *but* implies that the answer will involve two words that are more or less opposite in meaning. If you keep this in mind, you can eliminate all of the choices except for (B) *blur . . sharpens*. Only the words in choice (B) imply opposition. Also, "sharpens his senses" is consistent with the notion that he has a "keener perception of a thousand details."

They argue that the author was determined to ···· his own conclusion, so he ···· any information that did not support it.

(A) uphold . . ignored (B) revise . . destroyed (C) advance . . devised (D) disprove . . distorted (E) reverse . . confiscated

The logic of the sentence makes it fairly easy to eliminate choices (B), (D), and (E). The first word in choice (A), *uphold*, and the first word in (C), *ad-*

vance, seem all right. However, the second word in choice (C), *devised,* does not make sense in the sentence. Why would an author who wished to advance his theory devise information that did not support it? Only choice (A) makes a logically consistent sentence.

She is a skeptic, ... to believe that the accepted opinion of the majority is generally ....

(A) prone . . infallible (B) afraid . . misleading (C) inclined . . justifiable (D) quick . . significant (E) disposed . . erroneous

The words to be inserted in the blank spaces in the question above must result in a statement that is consistent with the definition of a skeptic. Since a skeptic would hardly consider the accepted opinion of the majority as *infallible, justifiable,* or *significant,* you can eliminate choices (A), (C), and (D). A skeptic would not be afraid that the accepted opinion of the majority is misleading; a skeptic would believe that it was. Therefore, choice (B) is not correct. Only choice (E) *disposed. . erroneous* makes a logical sentence.

Some General Tips for Answering Sentence Completion Questions

- Read the entire sentence carefully; make sure you understand the ideas being expressed.
- Don't select an answer simply because it is a popular cliché or "sounds good."
- In a question with two blanks, the right answer must correctly fill both blanks. A wrong answer choice often includes one correct and one incorrect word.
- After choosing an answer, read the entire sentence to yourself and make sure that it makes sense.
- Consider all the choices; be sure you haven't overlooked a choice that makes a better and more accurate sentence than your choice does.

Reading Comprehension Questions

The reading comprehension questions on the SAT test your ability to read and understand a passage. The test will have one or more passages taken from any of the following categories:

Narrative:	(novels, short stories, biographies, essays)
Biological Science:	(medicine, botany, zoology)
Physical Science:	(chemistry, physics, astronomy)
Humanities:	(art, literature, music, philosophy, folklore)
Social Studies:	(history, economics, sociology, government)
Argumentative:	(the presentation of a definite point of view on some subject)

Each passage contains all the information you'll need to answer the questions that follow it.

Several types of questions are asked about the passage. Some ask about the main idea of a passage. Some questions ask about those ideas that are stated directly in the passage. Some ask you to recognize applications of the author's principles or opinions. In some questions you must make an inference from what you have read. And in others you must evaluate the way the author develops and presents the passage.

Following are a sample passage, sample questions, and explanations of each of the questions.

Directions: The passage below is followed by questions based on its content. Answer all questions following the passage on the basis of what is stated or implied in that passage.

Any survey of medieval town life delights in the color of guild organizations: the broiders and glovers, the shipwrights and upholsters, each with its guild hall, its distinctive livery, and its elaborate set of rules. But if life in the guilds and at the fairs provides a sharp contrast with the stodgy life on the manor, we must not be misled by surface resemblances into thinking that guild life represented a foretaste of modern life in medieval dress. It is a long distance from guilds to modern business firms, and it is well to fix in mind some of the differences.

In the first place, the guild was much more than just an institution for organizing production. Whereas most of its regulations concerned wages and conditions of work and specifications of output, they also dwelt at length on noneconomic matters: on a member's civic role, on his appropriate dress, and even on his daily deportment. Guilds were the regulators not only of production but of social conduct.

Between guilds and modern business firms there is a profound gulf. Unlike modern firms, the purpose of guilds was not first and foremost to make money. Rather, it was to preserve a certain orderly way of life — a way which envisaged a decent income for the master craftsmen but which was certainly not intended to allow any of them to become "big" businessmen. On the contrary, guilds were specifically designed to ward off any such outcome of an uninhibited struggle among their members. The terms of service and wages were fixed by custom. So, too, were the terms of sale: a guild member who cornered the supply of an item or bought wholesale to sell at retail was severely punished. Competition was strictly limited and profits were held to prescribed

levels. Advertising was forbidden, and even technical progress in advance of one's fellow guildsmen was considered disloyal.

Surely the guilds represent a more "modern" aspect of feudal life than the manor, but the whole temper of guild life was still far removed from the goals and ideals of modern business enterprise. There was no free competition and no restless probing for advantage. Existing on the margin of a relatively moneyless society, the guilds were organizations that sought to take the risks out of their slender enterprises. As such, they were as drenched in the medieval atmosphere as the manors.

Following are sample questions about this passage. You may be asked to identify the main idea or primary focus of the passage. For example:

1. The author is primarily concerned with

(A) analyzing the origins of the guild system
(B) explaining the relationships between manors, fairs, and modern business firms
(C) depicting the weaknesses of the guilds' business practices
(D) stressing the historical evolution of guilds to modern business firms
(E) discussing some differences between medieval and modern business practices

The answer to the question is (E). The passage compares medieval business practices, as represented by the guilds, with modern business practices. The author describes the guilds and suggests some ways in which they differ from contemporary business organizations. The most concise statement of what the author intends to discuss in the passage is made at the end of the first paragraph, in lines 8-10. Choice (A) is incorrect because the passage does not mention the origins of the guild system. Choice (B) is unacceptable because the author's main comparison is not between manors, fairs, and modern business firms, even though all are mentioned in the passage. Choices (C) and (D) are slightly harder to eliminate. Readers who think that the author is criticizing the guilds by pointing out the ways in which they differ from modern business enterprise are mistaken; there is no evidence in the passage to suggest that the author wants either to praise or to criticize the guilds. Choice (D) mentions the author's main concerns — guilds and modern business firms — but is incorrect because the passage does not deal with the evolution from medieval to modern practices.

Another type of question asks about details stated in the passage. Sometimes this type of question asks about a particular phrase or line; at other times, the part or parts of the passage referred to are not as precisely identified. For example:

2. According to the passage, modern business enterprises, compared to the medieval guilds, are

(A) more concerned with increasing profits
(B) influenced more by craftsmen than by tradesmen
(C) more subordinate to the demands of consumers
(D) less progressive in financial dealings
(E) less interested in quantity than quality

To answer this question, locate the parts of the passage that compare guilds and modern business — the beginnings of the third and fourth paragraphs. Lines 19-20 suggest that the foremost purpose of modern firms is to make money. Lines 35-38 indicate that "free competition" and "restless probing for advantage" are central to modern business enterprise. Choice (A) is the most appropriate answer among the choices given. There is no justification in the passage for any of the other choices. Some people might argue from their own experience or opinion that (C) is a possible answer. However, since the question says, "According to the passage ...," the answer must be based on what is stated in the passage.

Some questions ask you to make inferences based on the passage. For example:

3. It can be inferred that the guilds were organized as they were because

(A) life on the manors was boring and drab
(B) technical improvements were still improbable
(C) they stressed preservation and stability, not progress
(D) people in medieval times were interested in advancing individual liberty
(E) social status was determined by income

This question is not answered simply and directly in the passage itself, but the passage gives you information to draw on. In the third paragraph, the author notes that the purpose of guilds "was to preserve a certain orderly way of life" and that guilds were specifically designed "to ward off...uninhibited struggle among their members." In the fourth paragraph, the author states that the guilds "were organizations that sought to take the risks out of their slender enterprises." From these statements and the comparisons between guilds and modern business firms that the author makes elsewhere in the passage, choice (C) is the most reasonable conclusion to draw. Choice (A) is stated in the passage, but is not related to the purpose of the organization of the guilds. The statement about technical progress made in lines 31-33 weakens the plausibility of the inference in (B). The passage doesn't provide enough information to justify the inferences made in (D) and (E). This is a fairly easy and straightforward inference question. You may be asked others that will require somewhat more sophisticated reasoning processes.

Other types of questions ask you to apply information in the passage to situations that are not specifically mentioned in the passage or to evaluate the author's logic, organization, attitude, tone, or language. Following is an example of one type of question that asks you to apply information given in the passage.

4. According to the passage, which of the following would LEAST likely be found in a guild handbook?

(A) The fees a master guildsman should charge
(B) The bonus a member would receive for record sales
(C) The maximum number of hours a guildsman would be expected to work
(D) The steps a new shipwright would follow to become a master craftsman
(E) The organizations to which a member should contribute as an upstanding citizen

To answer this question, you must decide which of the five choices is least likely to have been included in a guild handbook. The passage does not mention a handbook, but it does provide enough information about the areas of business and personal life that the guilds attempted to regulate to enable you to make reasoned judgments. The passage suggests that (A), (C), and (E) would definitely be included in such a handbook and that (D) would be a logical area of concern and regulation for a guild. Choice (B) seems to be the least likely area of regulation and is, therefore, the correct answer. In fact, the statements made in the passage about the purpose of the guilds — to enable all master craftsmen to earn a decent income and to discourage ruthless competition among members — suggest that offering a bonus for record sales would indeed be an unlikely activity for a guild to engage in.

The question below is another type of evaluation question.

5. With which of the following statements concerning modern business firms would the author be most likely to agree?

(A) They make rules concerning appropriate business practices for employees.
(B) They permit the free play of price in terms of service and sales.
(C) Their main concern is the stability of profit levels.
(D) Their aim is to discourage competition among independent manufacturers.
(E) They are organized in such a way that cooperating monopolies will develop.

Paragraphs three and four provide information about the author's characterization of modern business practices and support choice (B) as the correct response. Choices (A), (C), and (D) are more true of guilds than of modern business firms. There is little or nothing in the passage to support (E) as the answer; the author stresses the competition rather than cooperation of modern businesses. When answering such questions, remember to read the question carefully and to look for evidence in the passage to support your choice. In this question, for example, you are not asked which of the statements about modern business is true or which of the statements you agree with, but which one the author is most likely to agree with based on what he or she has written in the passage. Sometimes questions that ask for the most likely or least likely answer require you to make careful distinctions between choices that are partly correct and those that are more complete or more accurate.

Some General Tips for Answering Reading Comprehension Questions

- Read each passage closely and attentively. Follow the author's reasoning; notice how each piece of information relates to the ideas being presented. Notice attitude, tone, and general style.
- You may want to mark an important fact or idea, but don't waste too much time underlining or making notes in the margin of the test book. Try to get a sense of the principal ideas, facts, and organization of the passage.
- A passage with a subject that is familiar to you or in which you are interested may be easier for you. If you find a passage that seems too difficult for you, you might want to skip it and go on. You would be omitting only a few questions and saving yourself time. You can always return to that passage if you finish before time is up for that section of the test.
- You might want to read the questions before you read the passage so that you have a sense of what to look for. But if the content of the passage is familiar to you, looking at the questions before you read the passage might be a waste of time. Try both methods when taking the sample test in this booklet and see if one approach is more helpful to you than the other.
- Answer questions on the basis of what is stated or implied in the passage. Don't answer questions on the basis of your personal opinion or knowledge.
- Read all of the choices before you choose your answer.
- Answer the question that is asked. Don't pick one of the choices simply because you know it's a true statement.

- ✓ Make sure the answer you choose is the best among the choices given. Don't be misled by choices that are partially true.
- ✓ In answering main idea questions, don't be distracted by statements that are true according to the passage but that are secondary to the central point.

Mathematical Sections of the SAT

Some questions in the mathematical sections of the SAT are like the questions in your math textbooks. Other questions ask you to do original thinking and may not be as familiar to you. The questions are designed for students who have had a year of algebra and some geometry. Many of the geometric ideas involved are usually taught in the elementary and junior high years, but a few of the questions involve topics that are first taught in high school geometry. Most of the questions are classified as arithmetic, algebra, or geometry, and there is approximately an equal number of each type.

When you take the SAT, remember to use the available space in the test book for scratchwork. You are not expected to do all the reasoning and figuring in your head.

Following is a review of some specific words, phrases, and concepts you should know. Sample questions and explanations follow the review. The two types of questions that appear in the mathematical sections are explained separately.

Mathematics Review

Some Mathematical Concepts with Which You Should Be Familiar

Arithmetic — simple addition, subtraction, multiplication, and division; percent; average; odd and even numbers; prime numbers; divisibility (for example, 24 is divisible by 8 but not by 5)

Algebra — negative numbers; simplifying algebraic expressions; factoring; linear equations; inequalities; simple quadratic equations; positive integer exponents; roots

Geometry — area (square, rectangle, triangle, and circle); perimeter of a polygon; circumference of a circle; volume of a box and cube; special properties of isosceles, equilateral, and right triangles; 30°–60°–90° and 45°–45°–90° triangles; properties of parallel and perpendicular lines; locating points on a coordinate grid

Words and Phrases You Should Know

When You See:	Think:
Positive Integers	**1, 2, 3, 4, . . .**
Negative Integers	**$-1, -2, -3, -4, \ldots$**
Integers	**$\ldots, -4, -3, -2, -1, 0, 1, 2, 3, 4, \ldots$**
Odd Numbers	**$\pm 1, \pm 3, \pm 5, \pm 7, \pm 9, \ldots$**
Even Numbers	**$0, \pm 2, \pm 4, \pm 6, \pm 8, \ldots$**
Consecutive Integers	**$n, n + 1, n + 2, \ldots$ (n = an integer)**
Prime Numbers	**2, 3, 5, 7, 11, 13, 17, 19, . . .**

Arithmetic and Algebraic Concepts You Should Know

Odd and Even Numbers

Addition:	Multiplication:
even + even = even	**even × even = even**
odd + odd = even	**even × odd = even**
even + odd = odd	**odd × odd = odd**

Percent

Percent means hundredths or number out of 100, so that $\frac{40}{100}$ = 40 percent and 3 is 75 percent of 4 (because $\frac{3}{4} = \frac{75}{100}$ = 75 percent).

Some Percent Equivalents

$\frac{1}{10} = 0.1 = 10\%$

$\frac{1}{5} = 0.2 = 20\%$

$\frac{1}{2} = 0.5 = 50\%$

$\frac{1}{1} = 1.0 = 100\%$

$\frac{2}{1} = 2.0 = 200\%$

Note: To convert a fraction or decimal to percent, multiply by 100.

General Method of Converting a Fraction $\frac{a}{b}$ to a Percent:

$\frac{a}{b} = \frac{x}{100}$

$x = 100\left(\frac{a}{b}\right)$

Example: $\frac{3}{4} = \frac{x}{100}$

Therefore, $x = 100\left(\frac{3}{4}\right) = 75$

$\frac{3}{4} = \frac{75}{100} = 75\%$

Percents Greater Than 100

Problem: 5 is what percent of 2?

Solution 1: $\frac{5}{2} = \frac{x}{100}$

$x = \frac{500}{2} = 250$

Therefore, 5 is 250 percent of 2.

Solution 2: "5 is what percent of 2?" is equivalent to

$$5 = \frac{x}{100} \cdot 2 = \frac{2x}{100}$$

$$500 = 2x$$

$$x = 250$$

This solution is a fairly direct translation of the question into an algebraic statement as follows:

$$\underset{\downarrow}{5} \text{ is } \overbrace{\text{what percent}}^{} \text{ of } \underset{\downarrow}{2}?$$

$$5 = \frac{x}{100} \cdot 2$$

Note that saying 5 is 250 percent of 2 is equivalent to saying that 5 is $2\frac{1}{2}$ times 2.

Problem: Sue earned $10 on Monday and $12 on Tuesday. The amount earned on Tuesday was what percent of the amount earned on Monday?

An equivalent question is "$12 is what percent of $10?"

Solution: $\frac{12}{10} = \frac{x}{100}$

$x = \frac{1{,}200}{10} = 120$

So, $\frac{12}{10} = \frac{120}{100} = 120\%$

Percents Less Than 1

Problem: 3 is what percent of 1,000?

Solution: $\frac{3}{1{,}000} = 0.003 = 0.3\%$ or $\frac{3}{10}$ of 1 percent

Problem: Socks are $1.00 a pair or 2 pairs for $1.99. The savings in buying 2 pairs is what percent of the total cost at the single pair rate?

Solution: At the single pair rate, 2 pairs would cost $2.00, so the savings is only $0.01. Therefore, you must answer the question "$0.01 is what percent of $2.00?" Because $\frac{0.01}{2.00} = \frac{0.5}{100}$, the savings is 0.5% or $\frac{1}{2}$ of 1 percent.

Average

The most common mathematical meaning of the word *average* is the arithmetic mean. The average (arithmetic mean) of a set of *n* numbers is the sum of the numbers divided by *n*. For example, the average of 10, 20, and 27 is

$$\frac{10 + 20 + 27}{3} = \frac{57}{3} = 19$$

Unless otherwise indicated, the term *average* will be used on the mathematical portion of the SAT to denote the arithmetic mean. Questions involving the average can take several forms. Some of these are illustrated below.

Finding the Average of Algebraic Expressions

Problem: Find the average of $(3x + 1)$ and $(x - 3)$.

Solution: $\frac{(3x + 1) + (x - 3)}{2} = \frac{4x - 2}{2} = 2x - 1$

Finding a Missing Number if Certain Averages Are Known

Problem: The average of a set of 10 numbers is 15. If one of these numbers is removed from the set, the average of the remaining numbers is 14. What is the value of the number removed?

Solution: The sum of the original 10 numbers is $10 \cdot 15 = 150$. The sum of the remaining 9 numbers is $9 \cdot 14 = 126$. Therefore, the value of the number removed must be $150 - 126 = 24$.

Finding a Weighted Average

Problem: In a group of 10 students, 7 are 13 years old and 3 are 17 years old. What is the average of the ages of these 10 students?

Solution: The solution is *not* the average of 13 and 17, which is 15. In this case the average is

$$\frac{7(13) + 3(17)}{10} = \frac{91 + 51}{10} = 14.2 \text{ years}$$

The expression "weighted average" comes from the fact that 13 gets a weight factor of 7 whereas 17 gets a weight factor of 3.

Finding the Average Speed in Distance-Rate-Time Problems

Problem: Jane traveled for 2 hours at a rate of 70 kilometers per hour and for 5 hours at a rate of 60 kilometers per hour. What was her average speed for the 7-hour period?

Solution: In this situation, the average speed is:

$$\frac{\text{Total Distance}}{\text{Total Time}}$$

The total distance is 2 (70) + 5 (60) = 440 km. The total time is 7 hours. Thus, the average speed was $\frac{440}{7} = 62\frac{6}{7}$ kilometers per hour. Note that in this example the average speed, $62\frac{6}{7}$, <u>is not the average</u> of the two separate speeds, which would be 65.

Squares of Integers

n	1	2	3	4	5	6	7	8	9	10	11	12
n^2	1	4	9	16	25	36	49	64	81	100	121	144

n	−1	−2	−3	−4	−5	−6	−7	−8	−9	−10	−11	−12
n^2	1	4	9	16	25	36	49	64	81	100	121	144

Signed Number Properties

positive × positive = positive
negative × negative = positive
negative × positive = negative
$-(a - b) = b - a$
$(-x)^2 = x^2$
If $x < 0$, $x^2 > 0$

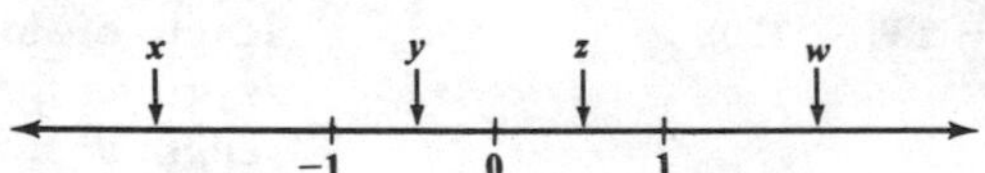

On the number line above:

$x < y$	For example, $-2 < -\frac{1}{2}$
$y^2 > 0$	
$z^2 < z$	For example, $(\frac{1}{2})^2 < \frac{1}{2}$
$x^2 > z$	For example, $(-2)^2 > \frac{1}{2}$
$z^2 < w$	
$x + z < 0$	
$y - x > 0$	

<u>Note</u>: Unless otherwise indicated, in all questions involving number lines, the numbers on the number line increase from left to right. Similarly, in questions involving the x− and y− axes, numbers to the right of the y− axis are positive and numbers above the x− axis are positive.

Factoring

$x^2 + 2x = x(x + 2)$
$x^2 - 1 = (x + 1)(x - 1)$
$x^2 + 2x + 1 = (x + 1)(x + 1) = (x + 1)^2$
$x^2 - 3x - 4 = (x - 4)(x + 1)$

Geometric Figures

Figures that accompany problems on the test are intended to provide information useful in solving the problems. They are drawn as accurately as possible EXCEPT when it is stated in a particular problem that the figure is not drawn to scale. Lines that appear to be straight may be assumed to be straight. Several examples to illustrate the way figures can be interpreted are given below.

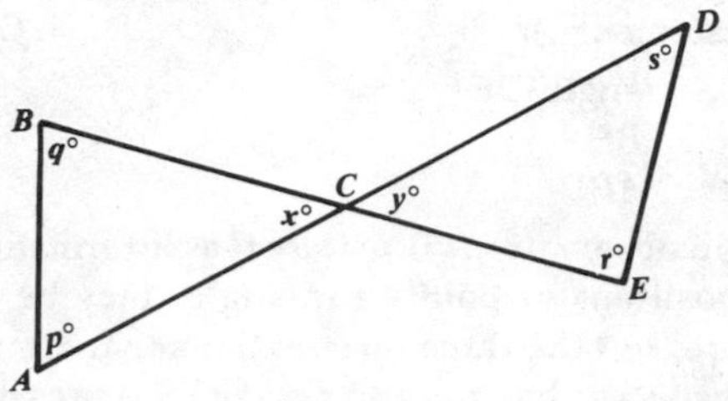

In this figure, you may assume that AD and BE are line segments that intersect at C. You should <u>not</u> assume that $AC = CD$, $p = 60$, or $r = 90$, even though they might look that way. Since $\angle ACB$ and $\angle DCE$ are vertical angles, you can conclude that $x = y$.

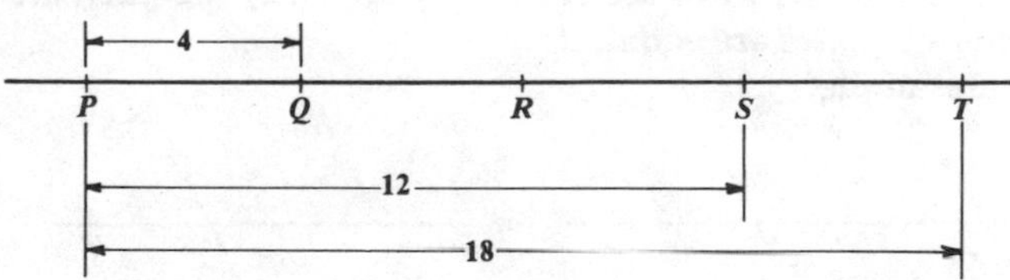

<u>Note:</u> Figure not drawn to scale.

Although the note indicates the figure is not drawn to scale, you may assume that points P, Q, R, S, and T are on line PT. You may also assume that Q is between P and R, that R is between Q and S, and that S is between R and T. You may *not* assume PQ, QR, RS, and ST are of equal length. In fact, since the lengths of PT and PS are shown to be 18 and 12, respectively, the length of ST is 6 while PQ has length 4. In general, even when a figure is not drawn to scale, points on lines may be assumed to be in the order shown, but specific lengths (for example, PQ and ST) might not be accurately represented. In such cases, your answer should be based on other information given about the figure such as the specific lengths shown.

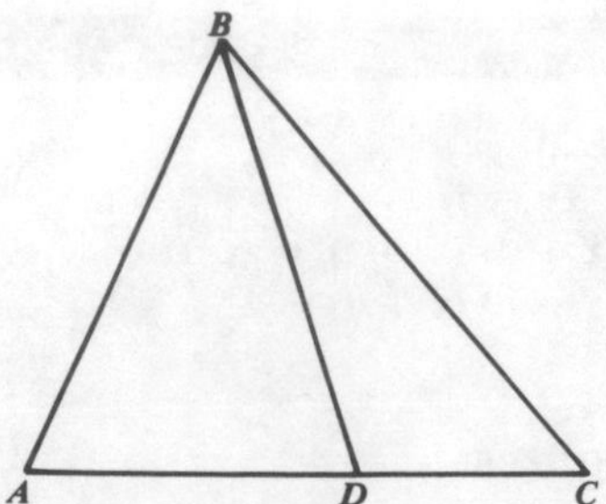

<u>Note:</u> Figure not drawn to scale.

This figure is also not drawn to scale. However, you may assume that ABC, ABD, and DBC are triangles, and that D is between A and C. The following are *valid* observations:

(1) length $AD <$ length AC
(2) $\angle ABD < \angle ABC$
(3) Area $\triangle ABD <$ Area $\triangle ABC$

The following observations are *not* valid. (These may or may not be true statements.):

(1) length $AD >$ length DC
(2) $\angle BAD = \angle BDA$
(3) $\angle DBC < \angle ABD$

The three valid observations illustrate that information about the relative positions of points and angles may be assumed from the figure, but the three observations that are *not* valid illustrate that specific lengths and degree measures might not be accurately shown.

Geometric Skills and Concepts

Properties of Parallel Lines

1. If two parallel lines are cut by a third line, the alternate interior angles are equal.
   For example:

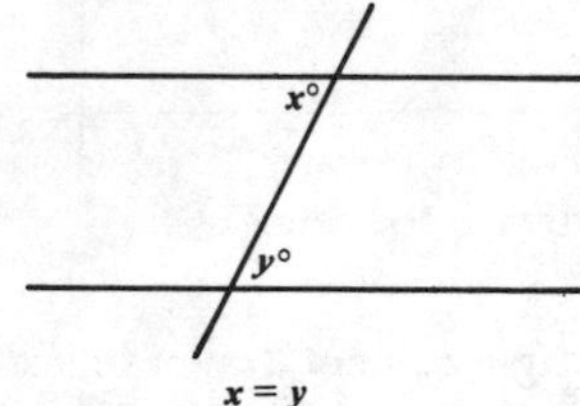

$x = y$

or

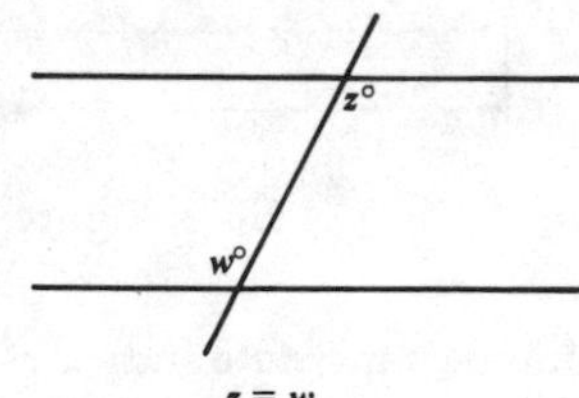

$z = w$

2. If two parallel lines are cut by a third line, the corresponding angles are equal.
   For example:

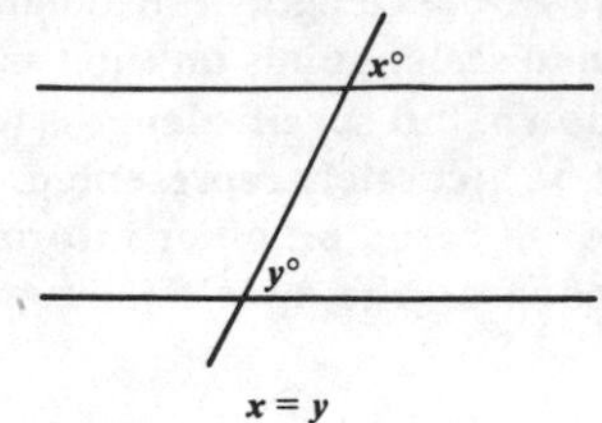

$x = y$

or

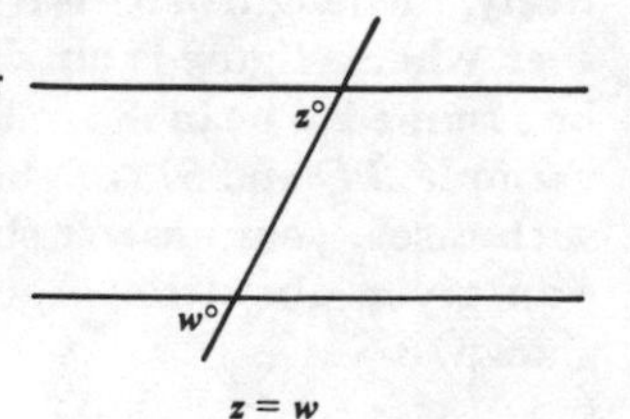

$z = w$

<u>Note:</u> Words like "alternate interior" or "corresponding" are generally <u>not</u> used on the test, but you do need to know which angles are equal.

Angle Relationships

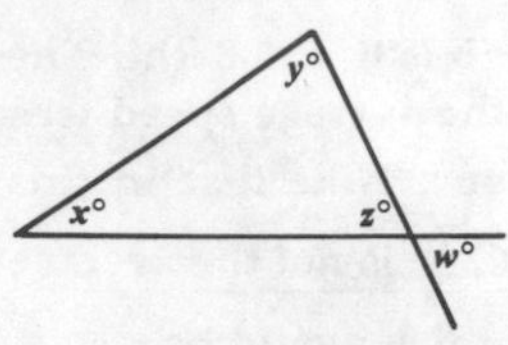

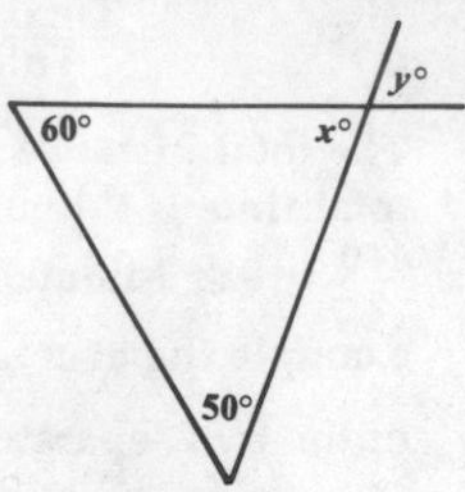

$x + y + z = 180$
(Because the sum of the interior angles of a triangle is 180°)

$z = w$
(When two straight lines intersect, vertical angles are equal.)

$y = 70$
(Because x is equal to y and $60 + 50 + x = 180$)

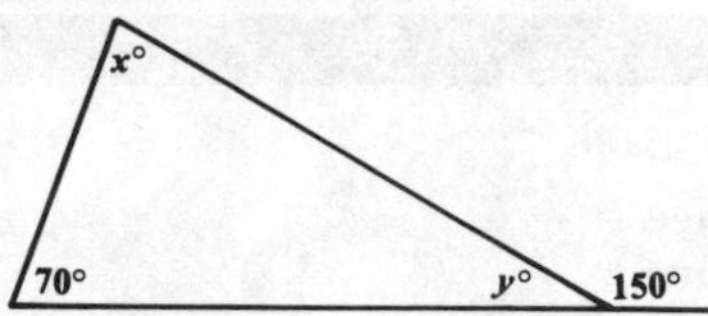

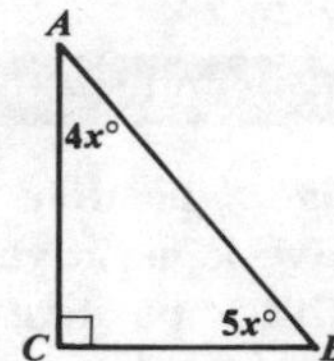

$y = 30$
(Because a straight angle is 180°, $y = 180 - 150$)

$x = 80$
(Because $70 + 30 + x = 180$)

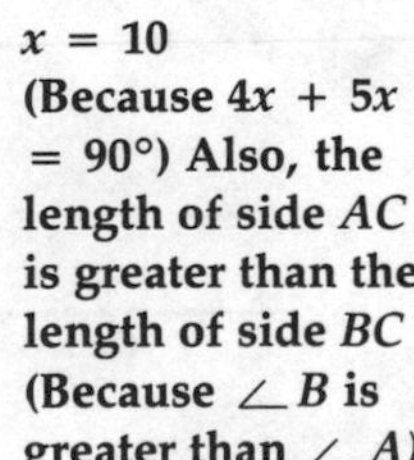

$x = 10$
(Because $4x + 5x = 90°$) Also, the length of side AC is greater than the length of side BC (Because $\angle B$ is greater than $\angle A$)

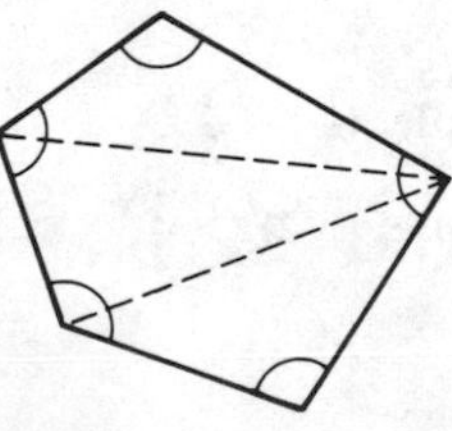

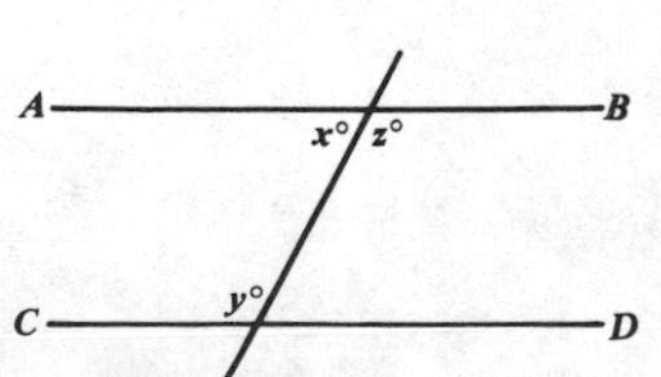

The sum of all angles of the polygon above is 3 (180°) = 540° because it can be divided into 3 triangles, each containing 180°.

If AB is parallel to CD, then $x + y = 180$ (Because $x + z = 180$ and $y = z$)

Side Relationships

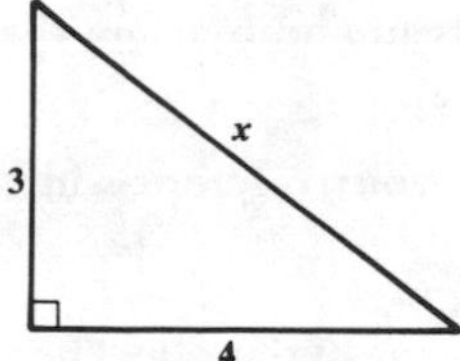

$x = 5$
(By the Pythagorean Theorem,
$x^2 = 3^2 + 4^2$
$x^2 = 9 + 16$
$x^2 = 25$
$x = \sqrt{25} = 5$)

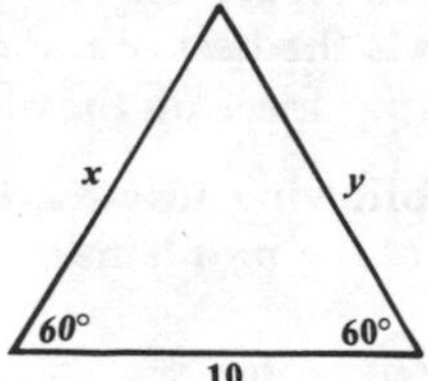

$x = y = 10$
(Because the unmarked angle is 60°, all angles of the triangle are equal, and, therefore, all sides of the triangle are equal)

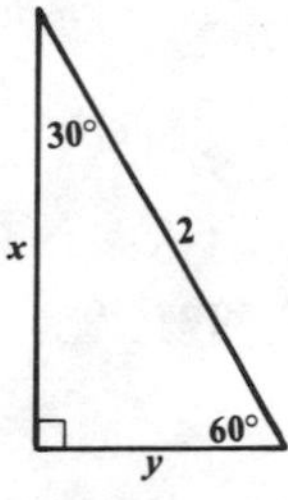

$y = 1$
(Because the length of the side opposite the 30° angle in a right triangle is half the length of the hypotenuse)

$x = \sqrt{3}$
(By the Pythagorean Theorem,
$x^2 + 1^2 = 2^2$
$x^2 = 3$
$x = \sqrt{3}$)

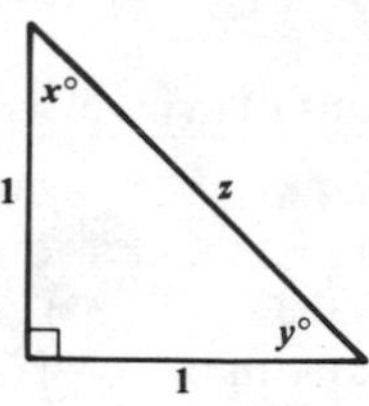

$x = y = 45°$
(Because two sides are equal, the right triangle is isosceles and angles x and y are equal. Also, $x + y = 90$ which makes both angles 45°)
$z = \sqrt{2}$
(Because $1^2 + 1^2 = z^2$)

Area and Perimeter Formulas

Area of a rectangle = length × width = $L \times W$
Perimeter of a rectangle = $2(L + W)$
Examples:

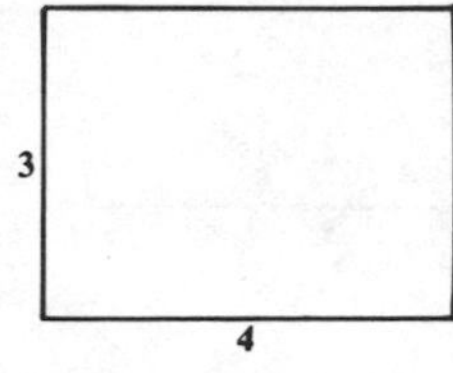

Area = 12

Perimeter = 14

Area = $(x - 3)(x + 3) = x^2 - 9$

Perimeter = $2[(x + 3) + (x - 3)] = 2(2x) = 4x$

Area of a circle = πr^2 (where r is the radius)
Circumference of a circle = $2\pi r = \pi d$ (where d is the diameter)
Examples:

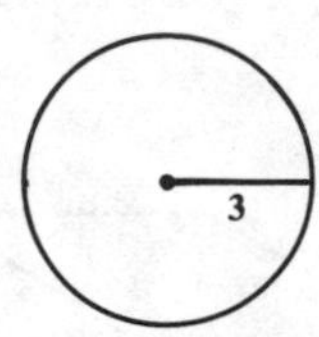

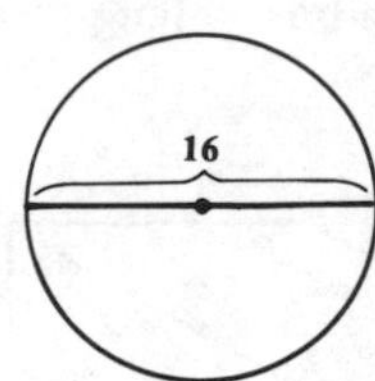

Area = $\pi(3^2) = 9\pi$
Circumference = $2\pi(3) = 6\pi$

Area = $\pi(8^2) = 64\pi$
Circumference = $\pi(16) = 16\pi$

Area of a triangle = $\frac{1}{2}$ (base × altitude)

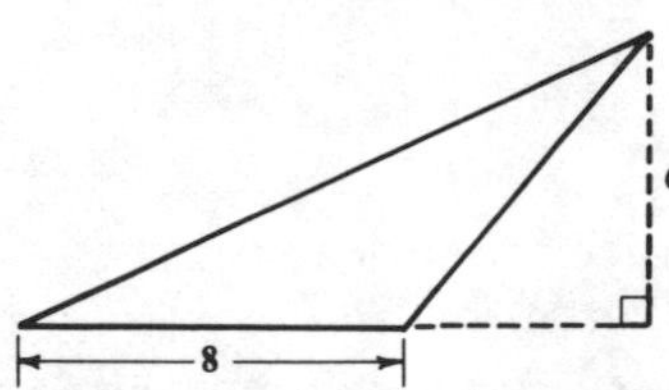

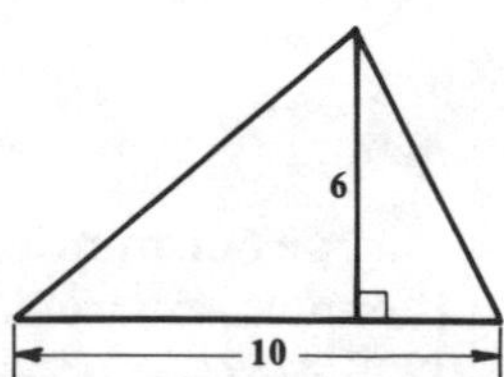

Area = $\frac{1}{2} \cdot 8 \cdot 6 = 24$

Area = $\frac{1}{2} \cdot 10 \cdot 6 = 30$

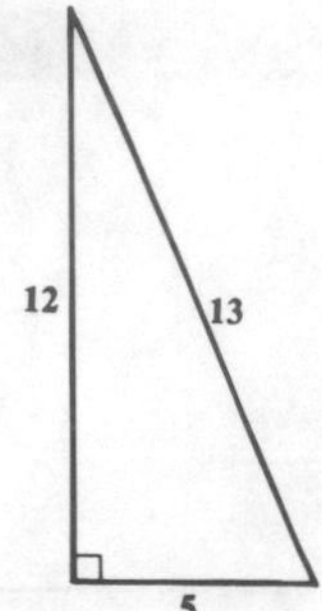

Area $= \frac{1}{2} \cdot 5 \cdot 12 = 30$

Perimeter $= 12 + 5 + 13 = 30$

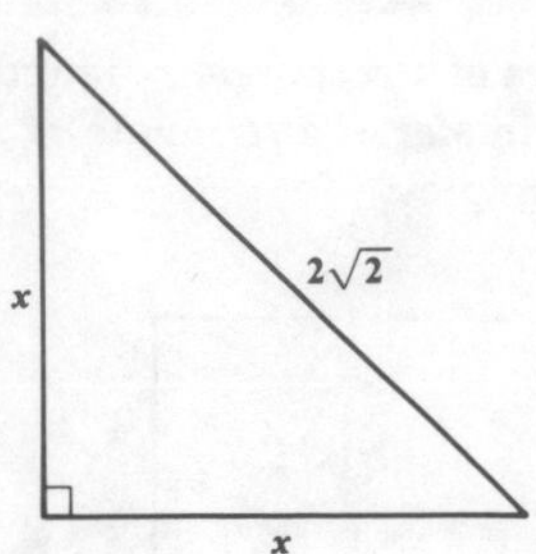

$x = 2$

(Because $x^2 + x^2 = (2\sqrt{2})^2$

$2x^2 = 4 \cdot 2$

$x^2 = 4$

$x = 2$)

Area $= \frac{1}{2} \cdot 2 \cdot 2 = 2$

Perimeter $= 2 + 2 + 2\sqrt{2}$
$= 4 + 2\sqrt{2}$

Volume of a Rectangular Solid (box)

Volume of a box = length × width × height = L • W • H
Examples:

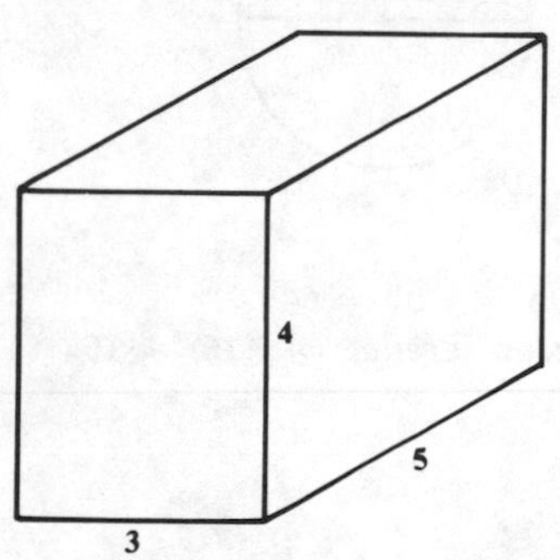

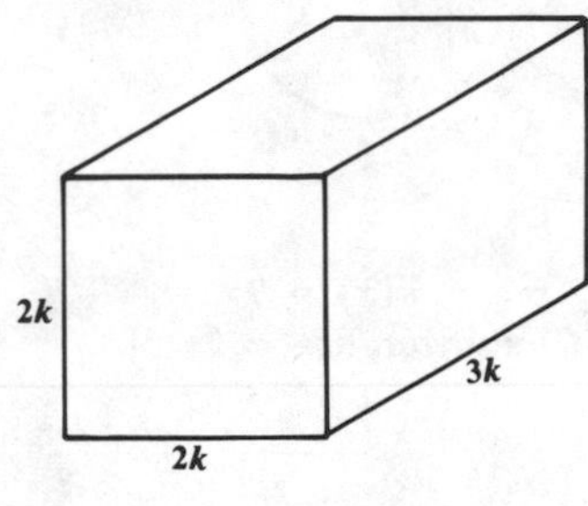

Volume $= 5 \cdot 3 \cdot 4 = 60$ **Volume $= (3k)(2k)(2k) = 12k^3$**

Two types of multiple-choice questions are used in the mathematical sections of the SAT:

1. Standard multiple-choice questions (approximately two-thirds of the math questions)
2. Quantitative comparison questions (approximately one-third of the math questions)

The formulas and symbols given in the directions that follow appear in the test book. Learning them now will help you when you take the actual test.

Standard Multiple-Choice Questions

Directions: In this section solve each problem, using any available space on the page for scratchwork. Then decide which is the best of the choices given and blacken the corresponding space on the answer sheet.

The following information is for your reference in solving some of the problems.

Circle of radius r:
Area $= \pi r^2$;
Circumference $= 2\pi r$
The number of degrees of arc in a circle is 360.
The measure in degrees of a straight angle is 180.

Triangle: The sum of the measures in degrees of the angles of a triangle is 180.

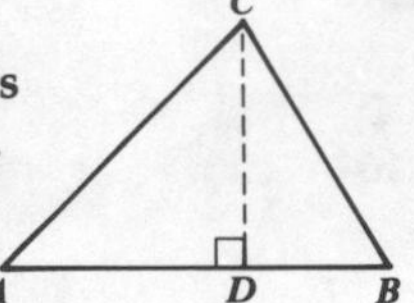

If $\angle CDA$ is a right angle, then
(1) area of $\triangle ABC = \frac{AB \times CD}{2}$
(2) $AC^2 = AD^2 + DC^2$

Definitions of symbols:

= is equal to	**≦ is less than or equal to**
≠ is unequal to	**≧ is greater than or equal to**
< is less than	**‖ is parallel to**
> is greater than	**⊥ is perpendicular to**

Note: Figures which accompany problems in this test are intended to provide information useful in solving the problems. They are drawn as accurately as possible EXCEPT when it is stated in a specific problem that its figure is not drawn to scale. All figures lie in a plane unless otherwise indicated. All numbers used are real numbers.

The problems that follow will give you an idea of the type of mathematical thinking required. First, try to answer each question yourself. Then read the explanation, which may give you new insights into solving the problem or point out techniques you'll be able to use again. Note that the directions indicate that you are to select the *best* of the choices given.

1. If $2a + b = 5$, then $4a + 2b =$

(A) $\frac{5}{4}$ (B) $\frac{5}{2}$ (C) 10 (D) 20 (E) 25

This is an example of a problem that requires realizing that $4a + 2b = 2(2a + b)$. Therefore, $4a + 2b = 2(2a + b) = 2(5) = 10$. The correct answer is (C).

2. If $16 \cdot 16 \cdot 16 = 8 \cdot 8 \cdot P$, then $P =$

(A) 4 (B) 8 (C) 32 (D) 48 (E) 64

This question can be solved by several methods. A time-consuming method would be to multiply the three 16s and then divide the result by the product of 8 and 8. A quicker approach would be to find what additional factors are needed on the right side of the equation to match those on the left side. These additional factors are two 2s and a 16, the product of which is 64. Yet another method involves solving for P as follows:

$$P = \frac{\overset{2}{\cancel{16}} \cdot \overset{2}{\cancel{16}} \cdot 16}{\cancel{8} \cdot \cancel{8}} = 2 \cdot 2 \cdot 16 = 64$$

The correct answer is (E).

3. The town of Mason is located on Eagle Lake. The town of Canton is west of Mason. Sinclair is east of Canton, but west of Mason. Dexter is east of Richmond, but west of Sinclair and Canton. Assuming all these towns are in the United States, which town is farthest west?

(A) Mason (B) Dexter (C) Canton
(D) Sinclair (E) Richmond

For this kind of problem, drawing a diagram may help. In this case, a line can be effectively used to locate the relative position of each town. Start with the statement "The town of Canton is west of Mason" and, using abbreviations, draw the following:

W ——+————————+—— E
C M

From the remaining information, place the other towns in their correct order:

W —+—+—+————+————+—— E
R D C S M

The final sketch shows that the town farthest west is Richmond (R) and the correct answer is (E).

4. If the average of seven x's is 7, what is the average of fourteen x's?

(A) $\frac{1}{7}$ (B) $\frac{1}{2}$ (C) 1 (D) 7 (E) 14

Don't get caught up in the wording of this problem, which might lead you to choose (E) 14. The average of any number of equal numbers such as x is always x. Since you are given that the average of seven x's is 7, it follows that $x = 7$ and that the average of fourteen x's is also 7. The correct answer is (D).

5. If the symbol ∇ between two expressions indicates that the expression on the right exceeds the expression on the left by 1, which of the following is (are) true for all real numbers x?

I. $x(x + 2) \nabla (x + 1)^2$
II. $x^2 \nabla (x + 1)^2$
III. $\frac{x}{y} \nabla \frac{x + 1}{y + 1}$

(A) None (B) I only (C) II only
(D) III only (E) I and III

This kind of problem involves working with a newly defined symbol. One approach is to check the statements one at a time. Statement I reduces to $x^2 + 2x \nabla x^2 + 2x + 1$, so the expression on the right does exceed the expression on the left by 1. Therefore, statement I is true. Statement II reduces to $x^2 \nabla x^2 + 2x + 1$, so the right expression exceeds the left expression by $2x + 1$, which is not equal to 1 except when $x = 0$. This makes statement II false. Statement III is more difficult to check, but you can verify by subtraction or by substituting numbers (for example, $x = 3$, $y = 5$), that the expression on the right does not exceed the expression on the left by 1. Therefore, statement III is false. The only true statement is I, so the correct answer is (B).

In a problem of this kind, if you are able to decide about only one or two statements, you can still eliminate some choices and guess among those remaining. For example, if you can conclude that I is true, then the correct answer is either (B) or (E) because these choices contain statement I.

6. If a car travels X kilometers of a trip in H hours, in how many hours can it travel the next Y kilometers at this rate?

(A) $\frac{XY}{H}$ (B) $\frac{HY}{X}$ (C) $\frac{HX}{Y}$ (D) $\frac{H + Y}{X}$ (E) $\frac{X + Y}{H}$

You can solve this problem by using ratios or by using the distance formula.

Using the ratio method, X kilometers is to H hours as Y kilometers is to $\square$ hours, where $\square$ represents the amount of time required to travel Y kilometers:

$$\frac{X}{H} = \frac{Y}{\square}$$

$$X\square = HY$$

$$\square = \frac{HY}{X}$$

The correct answer is (B).

7. If 90 percent of P is 30 percent of Q, then Q is what percent of P?

(A) 3% (B) 27% (C) 30% (D) 270% (E) 300%

Writing an algebraic equation for this percent problem not only simplifies the work, it also helps you organize your thoughts. "90 percent of P is 30 percent of Q" can be written as $0.90P = 0.30Q$ (or $\frac{9}{10}P = \frac{3}{10}Q$). "$Q$ is what percent of P" tells you to find $\frac{Q}{P}$ and express it as a percent. $\frac{Q}{P} = 3$ and, therefore, Q is 300 percent of P and the correct answer is (E). (See pages 15-16 for a review of percent.)

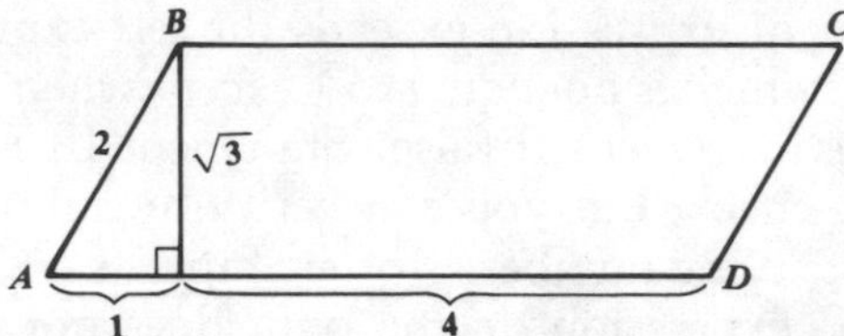

8. The figure above shows a piece of paper in the shape of a parallelogram with measurements as indicated. If the paper is tacked at its center to a flat surface and then rotated about its center, the points covered by the paper will be a circular region of diameter

(A) $\sqrt{3}$ (B) 2 (C) 5 (D) $\sqrt{28}$ (E) $\sqrt{39}$

The first step in solving the problem is to realize that the center of the parallelogram is the point of intersection of the two diagonals; thus, the diameter you are looking for is the length of the longer diagonal AC. One way to find AC is to think of the additional lines drawn as shown below.

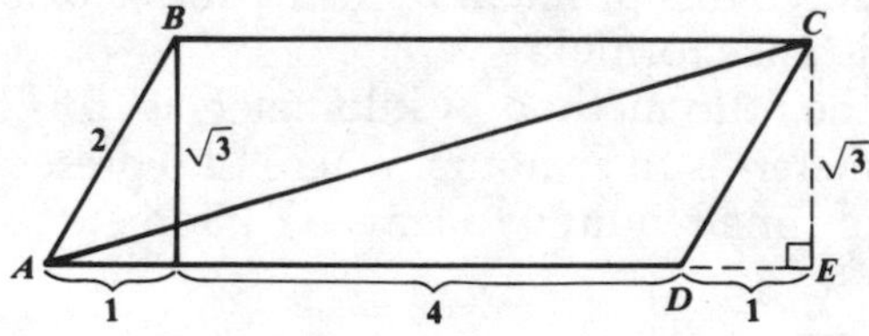

The triangles at each end are congruent (equal in size and shape), so the lengths of DE and CE are 1 and $\sqrt{3}$, respectively. AEC is a right triangle; therefore, the Pythagorean Theorem can be used in solving the problem:

$$AC^2 = CE^2 + AE^2$$
$$AC^2 = (\sqrt{3})^2 + (6)^2 = 3 + 36 = 39$$

The diameter AC is $\sqrt{39}$ and the correct answer is (E).

9. A number is divisible by 9 if the sum of its digits is divisible by 9. Which of the following numbers is divisible by 45?

(A) 63,345
(B) 72,365
(C) 99,999
(D) 72,144
(E) 98,145

It would be very time-consuming to divide each choice by 45. In order for a number to be divisible by 45 it must be divisible by both 9 and 5. Choices A, B, and E are divisible by 5, but choices C and D are not. So you can eliminate choices C and D immediately. You are given that a number is divisible by 9 if the sum of its digits is divisible by 9. The sums of the digits in choices A, B, and E are 21, 23, and 27, respectively.

Of these choices only 27 is divisible by 9. The correct answer is (E). Your scratchwork for this problem might appear as follows:

(A) 63,345 ~~21~~
(B) 72,365 ~~23~~
(C) ~~99,999~~
(D) ~~72, 144~~
(E) 98,145 (27)

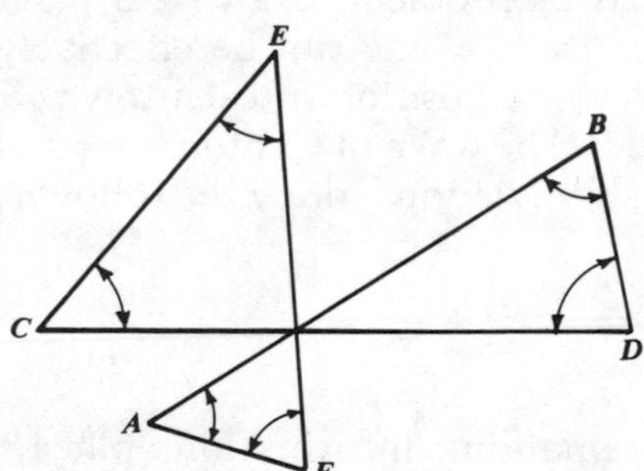

10. In the triangles above, if AB, CD, and EF are line segments, what is the sum of the measures of the six marked angles?

(A) 180° (B) 360° (C) 540° (D) 720°
(E) It cannot be determined from the information given.

This problem requires a creative problem-solving approach. One solution involves recognizing that the sum of the three unmarked angles in the triangles is 180°.

This can be seen from the figure at the top of page 27:

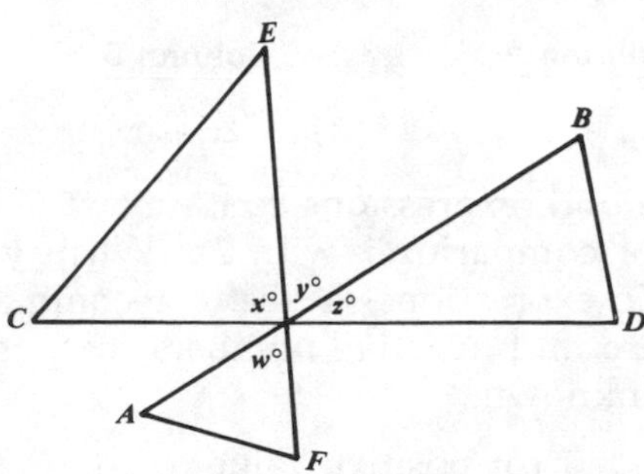

Because *CD* is a line segment, the sum of angles x, y, and z is 180°. Also, $y = w$ because they are vertical angles. Therefore, $x + w + z = 180$. Since the sum of the measures of all angles in the three triangles is 540° (3 • 180°) and the sum of the unmarked angles of the triangles in the original figure equals 180°, it follows that the sum of the marked angles is 540° − 180° = 360°. The correct answer is (B). With this type of problem, if you don't reach a solution in a minute or so, go on to the next problem and go back to it if you have time.

Quantitative Comparison Questions

Quantitative comparison questions emphasize the concepts of equalities, inequalities, and estimation. They generally involve less reading, take less time to answer, and require less computation than regular multiple-choice questions. Quantitative comparison questions may not be as familiar to you as other types of questions. Therefore, give special attention to the directions ahead of time. Be careful not to mark answer option E when responding to the four-choice quantitative comparison questions.

Directions: Each of the following questions consists of two quantities, one in Column A and one in Column B. You are to compare the two quantities and on the answer sheet blacken space

A if the quantity in Column A is greater;
B if the quantity in Column B is greater;
C if the two quantities are equal;
D if the relationship cannot be determined from the information given.

AN E RESPONSE WILL NOT BE SCORED.

Notes: 1. In certain questions, information concerning one or both of the quantities to be compared is centered above the two columns.
2. In a given question, a symbol that appears in both columns represents the same thing in Column A as it does in Column B.
3. Letters such as x, n, and k stand for real numbers.

	EXAMPLES Column A	Column B	Answers	Explanations:
E1.	2×6	$2 + 6$	● Ⓑ Ⓒ Ⓓ Ⓔ	(The answer is A because 12 is greater than 8.)
E2.	x° y° $180 - x$	y	Ⓐ Ⓑ ● Ⓓ Ⓔ	(The answer is C because $x + y = 180$, thereby making $180 - x$ equal to y.)
E3.	$p - q$	$q - p$	Ⓐ Ⓑ Ⓒ ● Ⓔ	(The answer is D because nothing is known about either p or q.)

To solve a quantitative comparison problem, you compare the quantities in the two columns and decide whether one quantity is greater than the other, whether the two quantities are equal, or whether the relationship cannot be determined from the information given. Remember that your answer should be:

A if the quantity in Column A is greater;
B if the quantity in Column B is greater;
C if the two quantities are equal;
D if the relationship cannot be determined from the information given.

Problems are clearly separated and the *quantities to be compared are always on the same line as the number of the problem*. (See example 2 on page 24.) Figures and additional information provided for some problems appear *above* the quantities to be compared. The following are some practice problems with explanations to help you understand this type of question.

	Column A	Column B
1.	$(37)\left(\frac{1}{43}\right)(58)$	$(59)\left(\frac{1}{43}\right)(37)$

Because the numbers in this problem are fairly large, it may save time to study the multipliers first before attempting the calculations. Note that (37) and $\left(\frac{1}{43}\right)$ appear in both quantities; thus, the only numbers left for you to compare are 58 and 59. Since 59 > 58, the quantity on the right is greater and the correct answer is (B).

Figures are also included in some questions that appear in the quantitative comparison format.

Column A	Column B

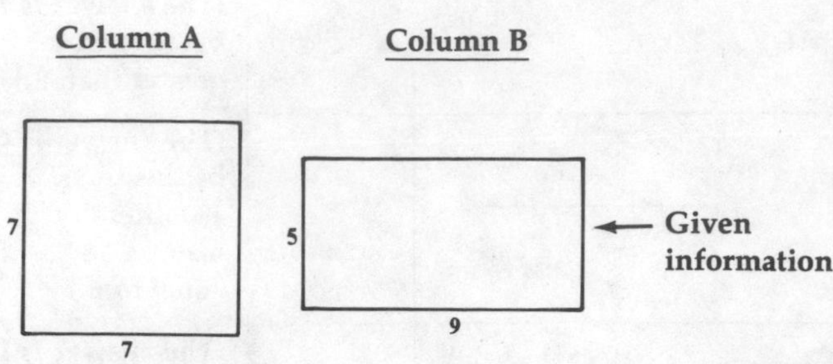

2. The perimeter of the square | **The perimeter of the rectangle** ← **Quantities to be compared**

It can be assumed that the units used to indicate measures in a given problem are the same in all figures in that problem unless otherwise stated. The correct answer is (C) because the perimeter of the square is $4 \cdot 7 = 28$ units and the perimeter of the rectangle is $(2 \cdot 5) + (2 \cdot 9) = 28$ units.

Column A	Column B

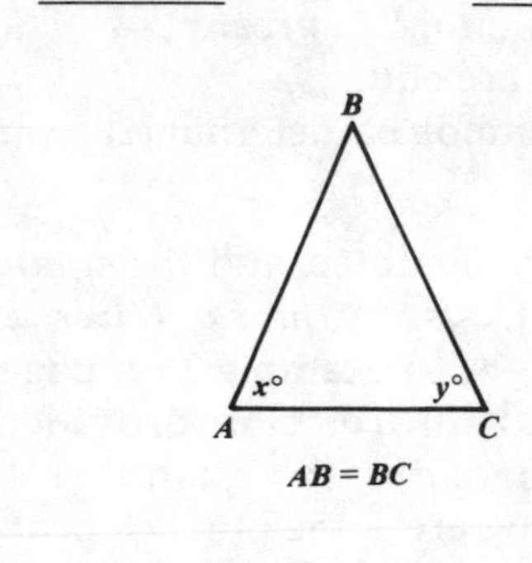

	Column A	Column B
3.	x	y

Since $AB = BC$, the angles opposite AB and BC are equal and, therefore, $x = y$. The correct answer is (C).

	Column A	Column B
4.	$\sqrt{2} - 1$	$\sqrt{3} - 1$

For any positive number x, the symbol $\sqrt{x}$ denotes the positive square root of x. The fact that $\sqrt{3} > \sqrt{2}$ leads to the conclusion that $\sqrt{3} - 1 > \sqrt{2} - 1$. The correct answer is (B). Note that $x^2 = 9$ has two solutions, $x = 3$ or $x = -3$. However, $\sqrt{9} = 3$, not ± 3.

	Column A	Column B
5.	$x + 1$	$2x + 1$

Because both expressions contain a "1," the problem is one of comparing x with $2x$. When you compare algebraic expressions, a useful technique is to consider zero and negative numbers for possible values of the unknown.

$2x > x$ for positive values of x
$2x = x$ for $x = 0$
$2x < x$ for negative values of x

The correct answer is (D), as the relationship cannot be determined from the information given. If you had been given that x was positive (that is, $x > 0$), the correct answer would have been (B) because $2x$ would be greater than x.

Column A	Column B

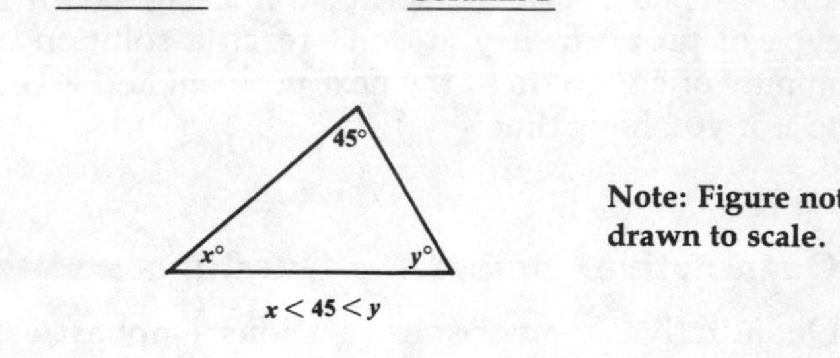

6.	y	**90**

Because the sum of the angles of a triangle is 180, $x + y + 45 = 180$ or $x + y = 135$. Since $x < 45$, it follows that $y > 90$. The answer is (A). In this problem you should not try to determine the answer from the appearance of the figure because the note indicates that the figure is not drawn to scale.

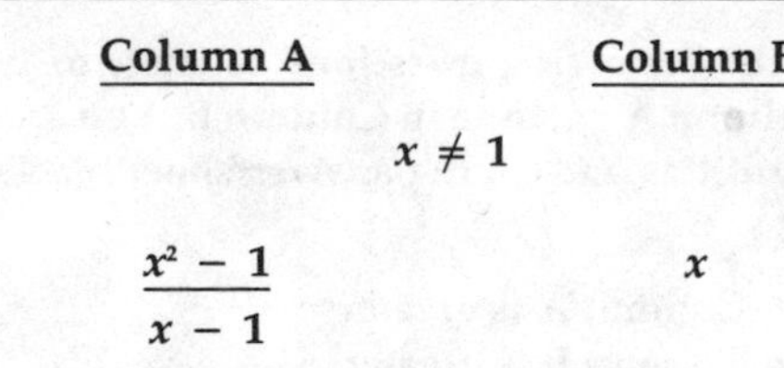

	Column A	Column B
	$x \neq 1$	
7.	$\frac{x^2 - 1}{x - 1}$	x

The condition $x \neq 1$ (read x is not equal to 1) is given because the algebraic fraction in Column A is not defined for $x = 1$ (the denominator becomes zero). The solution of this problem involves simplifying the fraction in Column A as follows:

$$\frac{x^2 - 1}{x - 1} = \frac{(x + 1)(x - 1)}{x - 1} = x + 1$$

Therefore, the quantity in Column A is equal to $x + 1$. Since $x + 1$ is always greater than x, the answer is (A).

Column A	Column B
8. Area of a triangle with altitude 4	**Area of a triangle with base 5**

To answer this question, you need to know how to find the area of a triangle. To find the area of a triangle, you need to know the length of a base and the altitude to that base. You can't find the "area of a triangle with altitude 4" without knowing the base, so the area of such a triangle could be any number depending on the length of the base. Likewise, you can't find the "area of a triangle with base 5" without knowing the length of the altitude. Since you can't tell anything about the two areas, the correct answer is (D).

The Test of Standard Written English

The questions on the TSWE measure skills that are important to the kind of writing you will do in most college courses. In particular, the questions test your ability to recognize the kind of language essential to a finished piece of writing — writing that would be considered acceptable by most educated readers and writers of American English.

The TSWE is made up of 50 questions of two types: usage questions and sentence correction questions. The test is arranged in the following way:

- 25 usage questions,
- 15 sentence correction questions, and
- 10 more usage questions.

The questions in the TSWE ask you to recognize several different types of language problems.

- *Use of basic grammar* — for example, subject-verb agreement, agreement of pronouns with the nouns to which they refer, and the correct use of a verb tense
- *Sentence structure* — for example, distinguishing between complete and incomplete sentences and recognizing when the connections between parts of a sentence are clear and when they are not
- *Choice of words* — for example, recognizing when words or phrases should be revised to make the meaning of a sentence clear or to make the language consistent with that normally expected of educated writers.

You will not be asked to define or to use grammatical terms. No questions test spelling or capitalization. In a few questions, punctuation marks like the semicolon or apostrophe are important in arriving at the correct answer, but these questions primarily test the structure in which the punctuation appears.

The best way to prepare for the TSWE is to get regular practice in writing and rewriting your own prose, paying particular attention to clarity and effectiveness of expression. You should also try to gain experience in reading the prose of skilled writers on a variety of subjects, noticing especially how the writers use language to create meaning. As with the SAT, reading the sample questions and explanations and taking the sample test provided in this booklet will help you prepare for the TSWE. After you've taken and scored the sample test, look carefully at the questions you missed. Talk over those questions with your teachers and other students and look up the portions of your textbooks that discuss writing and problems in wording and sentence structure.

Usage Questions

The questions in this section measure skills that are important to writing well. In particular, they test your ability to recognize and use language that is clear, effective, and correct according to the requirements of standard written English, the kind of English found in most college textbooks.

Directions: The following sentences contain problems in grammar, usage, diction (choice of words), and idiom.

Some sentences are correct.

No sentence contains more than one error.

You will find that the error, if there is one, is underlined and lettered. Assume that elements of the sentence that are not underlined are correct and cannot be changed. In choosing answers, follow the requirements of standard written English.

If there is an error, select the one underlined part that must be changed to make the sentence correct and blacken the corresponding space on your answer sheet.

If there is no error, blacken answer space Ⓔ.

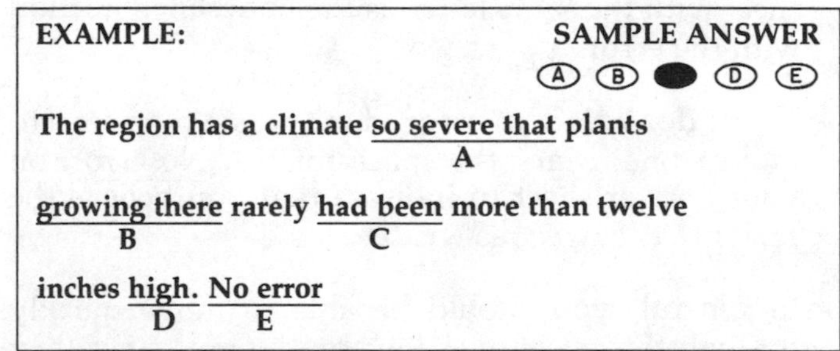
EXAMPLE: **SAMPLE ANSWER** Ⓐ Ⓑ ● Ⓓ Ⓔ

The region has a climate so severe that (A) plants growing there (B) rarely had been (C) more than twelve inches high. (D) No error (E)

As you can see from the example, a usage question consists of a sentence in which four short portions of the sentence are underlined and lettered, and a fifth underline, "No error," follows. Sometimes the underlined portion of the sentence is only a single word, as in (D) above. In other cases it is a group of words or a phrase, as in (A), (B), and (C).

For each question, you must decide whether one of the underlined portions must be changed to make the sentence acceptable in standard written English. In the example above, the underlined portion lettered (C) must be changed because the verb *has* earlier in the sentence leads the reader to expect *are* or possibly *have been*. The tense of the verb at (C) must be changed to be consistent with the tense of *has*. Therefore, the correct answer to the example is (C).

It is true that changes could be made in the other underlined portions of the sentence in the example, but none of those changes is necessary to make the sentence acceptable. It is also true that the sentence could be corrected by changing *has* in the first part of the sentence to *had*, but in this type of question the change must be made in a portion of the sentence that is underlined. Notice that if none of the underlined portions needed to be changed, the correct answer would be (E). By choosing (E) as the answer, you would be indicating that the sentence was correct as written.

Most usage questions test your ability to recognize problems in basic grammatical structure or in choice of words. Some usage questions also test problems in sentence structure. To give you a better sense of the variety of problems tested by usage questions, a few more sample questions follow. Keep in mind the following suggestions as you work through the sample questions.

- ✓ For each question, read the entire sentence carefully but quickly.
- ✓ Go back over the sentence, looking at each underlined portion to see whether anything needs to be changed to make the sentence correct.
- ✓ If you find an error, mark the space on your answer sheet with the same letter as the underlined portion with the error.
- ✓ If you don't find an error, don't waste time searching for one. Mark the space for (E), No error, on your answer sheet to indicate that you believe the sentence is correct as written.
- ✓ In general, you should be able to move quickly through the usage questions on the test, since they do not involve much reading. If you mark the usage questions you want to return to, you will be more likely to allow enough time for the sentence correction questions, which probably will take more time per question.

The four sample questions that follow originally appeared in the TSWE. They are arranged in order of increasing difficulty. Together, the example question and the four samples should give you a sense of the difficulty level of the questions you will be asked.

1. One of the goals of women's organizations
A

is to encourage projects that will make life easier for
B C D

working mothers. No error
E

Probably the first impression you get from reading the sentence is that nothing is really wrong with it. But before you make a final decision, you should look at the sentence again, especially at the underlined portions. The (A) portion, *goals of*, seems correct; *of* is the appropriate preposition for the context. The (B) portion, *is to encourage*, is a little more complicated but also seems correct; *is* is the appropriate verb to use with *one* and *to encourage* is all right following *is*, even though *encouraging* might be nearly as good. In (C), *make* is appropriate with the subject *projects* and is idiomatic in the expression *make life easier*. In (D), *easier* is a comparative form of *easy* and is used correctly, and *for* is the preposition that should follow it for the meaning intended.

Even though your analysis probably would not be as extensive as this, you should do something fairly similar, quickly checking each underlined portion of the sentence to make sure that each is acceptable as written. For some portions, you might have been able to think of another way of writing the sentence, even a way of improving it a little, but you probably decided that no changes were necessary in the underlined portions. At this point, you should have been able to decide on (E), No error, as the correct answer. Keep in mind that some usage questions are correctly answered with (E).

2. Probably the best-known baseball player of all time,
A B

Babe Ruth established a record for lifetime home runs that

has only recently been broke. No error
C D E

You may have noticed when you read the question for the first time that *broke* in (D) should be changed to *broken*. But if you didn't see the error immediately, or if you were not sure of it, you should have looked at the sentence again, especially at the underlined portions. In (A), *probably* is the appropriate adverb, in (B) *of all time* is an acceptable idiom and is used correctly, and in (C) the adverbs *only* and *recently* are acceptable together, with *only* modifying *recently*. But at (D), *broke* is clearly incorrect and needs to be changed to make the sentence acceptable in standard written English. The complete and correct verb for this part of the sentence is *has been broken*. With *has been*, the only possible form of the verb *break* that can be used is *broken*. The correct answer is (D).

3. Many travelers claim having seen (A) the Abominable Snowman, but (B) no one has proved that such a creature (C) actually (D) exists. No error (E)

The answer is (A). In the context of this sentence, the verb *claim* requires the expression *to have seen; claim having seen* is not idiomatic in American English and is therefore not acceptable. The word *but* at (B) provides a link between the two major parts of the sentence and appropriately suggests a contrast between the ideas they present. The expression at (C), *such a creature*, and the adverb *actually* at (D) are correct, although other expressions and adverbs could be substituted.

4. The administration's statements on (A) economic policy indicates (B) that the elimination of (C) hunger will be given (D) first priority. No error (E)

This question is more difficult than any of the others, so you may not immediately see the error in it. For a question as difficult as this one, you should be sure to look carefully at the underlined portions when you reread the sentence. In (A), *on* is correct and idiomatic, though the word *about* could possibly be substituted. Similarly, the preposition *of* is idiomatic with *elimination* in (C), and *elimination* is itself the right word for the meaning implied by the rest of the sentence. In (D), *will be given* is correct in tense and uses the correct form of the verb *give*. But *indicates* at (B) is incorrect; it is a singular verb and should not be used with the plural subject *statements*. The singular noun *policy* before (B) may appear at first to be the subject of the sentence, but a good writer would eventually see that the real subject *statements* is plural and therefore requires the plural verb *indicate*. The correct answer is (B).

Sentence Correction Questions

Directions: In each of the following sentences, some part or all of the sentence is underlined. Below each sentence you will find five ways of phrasing the underlined part. Select the answer that produces the most effective sentence, one that is clear and exact, without awkwardness or ambiguity, and blacken the corresponding space on your anwer sheet. In choosing answers, follow the requirements of standard written English. Choose the answer that best expresses the meaning of the original sentence.

Answer (A) is always the same as the underlined part. Choose answer (A) if you think the original sentence needs no revision.

EXAMPLE: **SAMPLE ANSWER**

Ⓐ ● Ⓒ Ⓓ Ⓔ

Laura Ingalls Wilder published her first book and she was sixty-five years old then.
(A) and she was sixty-five years old then
(B) when she was sixty-five years old
(C) at age sixty-five years old
(D) upon reaching sixty-five years
(E) at the time when she was sixty-five

Sentence correction questions present you with a sentence and four possible revisions of it — (B), (C), (D), or (E). The (A) version is always a repetition of the underlined portion of the original sentence. The underline in the original sentence tells you how much of the sentence will be revised in the other versions that are presented to you.

The example question above is a sentence in which the connection between the two major ideas is weak. The use of *and* to join the two clauses suggests that the ideas are of equal importance in the sentence, but the wording and the ideas in the clauses themselves suggest that the first idea should actually be the major point of the sentence and that the second should be secondary to it. Versions (B), (C), (D), and (E) all begin with more appropriate connecting words, but (B) is the only one in which the second idea of the sentence is clearly, concisely, and idiomatically expressed. Therefore, (B) is the correct answer.

The directions for the sentence correction questions tell you to look for the most effective sentence. In some questions you may find a version of the original sentence that has no grammatical errors, but that does not express the ideas of the sentence as effectively as another version. For other questions you may be able to think of a version you consider better than any of the choices given, but you should select the version that is the *best* of those presented.

Sentence correction questions are primarily concerned with problems of sentence structure. But you'll also need to consider basic principles of grammar and word choice to decide which of the versions makes the clearest and most effective sentence. For example, some versions will be grammatically incorrect or the ideas in the sentence will be presented so awkwardly or imprecisely that they cannot be considered acceptable. You'll get a sense of the problems tested in the sentence correction questions from the discussion of the sample questions provided here. You'll also have an idea of the range of difficulty found in the questions, since the sample questions given here are arranged in order of increasing difficulty. To learn as much as possible from the sample questions, you should read carefully the directions that appear before the example question above and approach the questions with the following suggestions in mind.

- In each question, read the original sentence carefully but quickly. Note the underlined portion of the sentence because that is the portion that may need to be revised. Remember that the portion with no underline stays the same.
- Keep in mind the portion of the original sentence that stays the same when you read through each of the versions presented.
- Decide which version seems best. If you can't decide between two choices, go back and read each version you have chosen in the context of the entire sentence.
- If you still feel uncertain about your answer, put a mark next to that question in your test book and note which versions you thought might be correct. You can return to the question later if you have time.

1. Althea Gibson was the first Black American to win major tennis championships and played in the 1950s.

(A) Althea Gibson was the first Black American to win major tennis championships and played in the 1950s.
(B) Althea Gibson, being the first Black American to win major tennis championships, and playing in the 1950s.
(C) Althea Gibson, playing in the 1950s, being the first Black American to win major tennis championships.
(D) Althea Gibson, who played in the 1950s, was the first Black American to win major tennis championships.
(E) Althea Gibson played in the 1950s, she was the first Black American to win major tennis championships.

Here the original sentence is entirely underlined, so you can expect the versions that follow to be revisions of the whole sentence.

This question is fairly easy. You may have been able to decide which version of the sentence was best simply by reading through all of the choices. However, to help you feel more certain of your choice and to help you understand more fully how the decision can be made, it's worth looking separately at each version. The (A) version, the same as the original sentence, has a problem similar to the one in the previous example: *and* does not adequately convey the relationship between the two clauses in the sentence. The (B) version has the same problem and an additional one: the use of *being* and *playing* makes it an incomplete sentence. In the (C) version, *playing* seems at first to have corrected the original problem of relationship between parts of the sentence, but the use of *being* gives the second idea no more importance than the first and also makes this version an incomplete sentence. In (E), you can see that a comma is used improperly as a means of connecting two independent clauses. Thus, (D) is the only acceptable version. In (D), the major point appears in the main part of the sentence and receives most emphasis, while the less important point appears in the *who* clause and so is emphasized less.

You won't need to analyze most of the sentence correction questions in this much detail. You'll be able to make your decisions by reading through each version and looking closely at one or two of them. But you should use this approach for the questions that are most difficult for you, especially the ones you miss on the sample TSWE.

2. After placing the meatballs in a pan, the cook sautéed them until they were brown and then let them simmer in the sauce.

(A) and then let them simmer
(B) then they were simmered
(C) and then simmering it
(D) then letting them simmer
(E) and then the simmering was done

You should have read the original sentence quickly, noting that the entire portion preceding the underline as well as the short phrase after the underline will be the same in all versions of the sentence. The original sentence and choice (A) may have seemed plausible, but you should have gone on to the other versions before making a final decision. In the (B) version, the unexpected shift from the *cook* as subject to *they* (the meatballs) is awkward and somewhat confusing. The (C) version uses *simmering* where *simmered* is needed to parallel *sautéed*. Furthermore, the pronoun *it* does not seem to refer back to anything named earlier in the sentence. In the (D) version, the use of *letting* rather than *let* again neglects the parallel with *sautéed*. The (E) version is wordy and, like the (B) version, involves a shift in which a passive construction replaces a more appropriate active one and in which the action is described without reference to the person responsible for it. Therefore, the best version of the sentence in this case is the original one, so the correct answer is (A).

3. Being as it was a full moon, the tides were exceptionally high when the storm struck.

(A) Being as it was a full moon
(B) With the moon as full
(C) Due to there being a full moon
(D) The moon was full
(E) Because the moon was full

The problems most immediately apparent in this question are problems in wording. The (A) version, like the underlined portion in the original sentence, uses *Being as*, an expression that is not considered acceptable in standard written English. In addition, the indirect *it was* construction introduces unnecessary wordiness. The (B) version seems acceptable in itself, but leads the reader to expect a construction ("as it was") different from the one that follows in the rest of the sentence. In the (C) version, *due to* is used in a manner that is generally considered unacceptable usage, and *there being* introduces unnecessary wordiness. The (D) version is acceptable in its wording but, when combined with the rest of the sentence, results in the unacceptable joining of two independent clauses with a comma. What is needed in this sentence is an expression that is acceptable in good written English and that accurately reflects the relationship between the first and second parts of the sentence. Version (E) solves the problem—the word *because* indicates that the fullness of the moon was causally related to the high tides described in the second part of the sentence. Therefore, (E) is the correct answer.

4. The Dutch had been trading with the Orient since the sixteenth century, their ships have visited Persia and Japan.

(A) century, their ships have visited
(B) century while their ships had visited
(C) century, but their ships had been visiting
(D) century, when their ships visited
(E) century, where their ships were visiting

The original sentence and the (A) version present two problems. First, two independent statements are joined by a comma, with no indication of the relationship between them. Second, the tense of the verb *have visited* is not consistent with the tense of *had been trading* earlier in the sentence. The (B) version may appear to be acceptable, but the relationship between the ideas in the sentence is not the one implied by *while* and the use of *while* makes the sentence illogical. Similarly, the (C) version appears plausible, but the contrast implied by *but* is not appropriate to the relationship between the two parts of the sentence. The (D) version corrects both of the problems presented in the original sentence and is more logical than either (B) or (C). Notice that the tense of *visited* is consistent with the earlier verb *had been trading*. It suggests that Dutch ships had traveled to Persia and Japan in the sixteenth century, and that such travel was part of a process of Dutch trade with the Orient that continued until some later, unspecified time. Version (E) resembles (D), except that *where* is substituted for *when* and *were visiting* for *visited*. Since the connection with *century* is clearly one of time rather than place, the use of *where* is not appropriate. Futhermore, the use of *were visiting* would imply emphasis on visits occurring over a period of time. Such emphasis is not called for, because the purpose in this part of the sentence is to describe the point at which the Dutch began trading with the Orient. Therefore, (D) expresses most effectively the ideas in the two parts of the sentence as well as the relationship between them. The correct answer is (D).

The Sample Tests

The first SAT in this book (pages 38-60) was given on May 7, 1983 (except for section 3, the TSWE, which was given on June 6, 1981). The equating section has been omitted because it contains questions that may be used in future editions of the test. The sample test will be most helpful if you take it under conditions as close as possible to those of the test.

- To complete the first sample test in one sitting, you will need two and one-half hours because this test has a TSWE as well as two verbal and two math sections. The other sample tests omit the TSWE; therefore, allow only two hours for them.
- Sit at a desk with no other papers or books. You can't take a calculator, a dictionary, other books, or notes into the test room.
- Allow yourself only 30 minutes for each section of the test. Have a kitchen timer or clock in front of you for timing yourself on the sections.
- Tear out the sample answer sheet on page 35 and fill it in just as you will on the day of the test.
- Read the instructions on page 37. They are reprinted from the back cover of the test book. When you take a test, you will be asked to read them before you begin answering questions.
- After you finish the practice test, read "How To Score the Sample Test," on page 61.

Reviewing Your Performance

Although you're probably most interested in your scores, you should spend some time after you take a practice test reviewing your mistakes on questions and also your overall approach to the test. Ask yourself these questions:

- Did you finish most of the questions in each section? Although the last few questions in each section usually are very difficult and are omitted by many students, you might want to adjust your pacing if you didn't get to a large number of questions at the end of each section.
- Did you make a lot of careless mistakes? Perhaps you were rushing and should slow your pace.
- Did you spend too much time on particular questions? Perhaps you should have moved on after marking them in your test book (not the answer sheet) and returned to them if you had time at the end of the section.
- Did you guess after you had eliminated some of the choices but still weren't sure of the answer? (Remember, although wild guessing probably won't affect your scores, you shouldn't be too cautious either.)
- Were there particular types of questions that gave you more difficulty than others? If so, you might want to review the descriptions of those questions in the beginning of this book and then practice again on one of the other sample tests in this book.
- Did you spend so much time reading directions that you took time away from answering questions? If you become thoroughly familiar with the test directions printed in this book, you won't have to spend as much time reading them during the test.
- Look at the specific questions you missed. Did you get caught by a choice that was only partly correct? Figure out what step you overlooked in your reasoning.

For most students, practice on one or two sample tests is enough. However, if you still feel uneasy about a particular type of question (or if you happen to enjoy taking tests), you can work on some of the other tests in this book. Whatever you do, don't memorize answers. It's highly unlikely that any of these questions will be on a test you will take. But whenever you run across a word or an idea that's new to you, be sure you learn what it means and how to use it.

COLLEGE BOARD — SCHOLASTIC APTITUDE TEST and Test of Standard Written English Side 1

Use a No. 2 pencil only. Be sure each mark is dark and completely fills the intended oval. Completely erase any errors or stray marks.

1. YOUR NAME: (Print) ______ Last ______ First ______ M.I.

SIGNATURE: ______ **DATE:** ___ / ___ / ___

HOME ADDRESS: (Print) ______ Number and Street

______ City ______ State ______ Zip Code

CENTER: (Print) ______ City ______ State ______ Center Number

IMPORTANT: Please fill in these boxes exactly as shown on the back cover of your test book.

FOR ETS USE ONLY

2. TEST FORM

3. FORM CODE

0	A	J	S	0	0	0
1	B	K	T	1	1	1
2	C	L	U	2	2	2
3	D	M	V	3	3	3
4	E	N	W	4	4	4
5	F	O	X	5	5	5
6	G	P	Y	6	6	6
7	H	Q	Z	7	7	7
8	I	R		8	8	8
9				9	9	9

4. REGISTRATION NUMBER (Copy from your Admission Ticket.)

0	0	0	0	0	0	0
1	1	1	1	1	1	1
2	2	2	2	2	2	2
3	3	3	3	3	3	3
4	4	4	4	4	4	4
5	5	5	5	5	5	5
6	6	6	6	6	6	6
7	7	7	7	7	7	7
8	8	8	8	8	8	8
9	9	9	9	9	9	9

5. YOUR NAME

First 4 letters of last name				First Init.	Mid. Init.
A–Z	A–Z	A–Z	A–Z	A–Z	A–Z

6. DATE OF BIRTH

Month	Day		Year	
Jan.				
Feb.				
Mar.	0	0	0	0
Apr.	1	1	1	1
May	2	2	2	2
June	3	3	3	3
July		4	4	4
Aug.		5	5	5
Sept.		6	6	6
Oct.		7	7	7
Nov.		8		8
Dec.		9		9

7. SEX

Female

Male

8. TEST BOOK SERIAL NUMBER

(Cut here to detach.)

Start with number 1 for each new section. If a section has fewer than 50 questions, leave the extra answer spaces blank.

SECTION 1

1	A	B	C	D	E	26	A	B	C	D	E
2	A	B	C	D	E	27	A	B	C	D	E
3	A	B	C	D	E	28	A	B	C	D	E
4	A	B	C	D	E	29	A	B	C	D	E
5	A	B	C	D	E	30	A	B	C	D	E
6	A	B	C	D	E	31	A	B	C	D	E
7	A	B	C	D	E	32	A	B	C	D	E
8	A	B	C	D	E	33	A	B	C	D	E
9	A	B	C	D	E	34	A	B	C	D	E
10	A	B	C	D	E	35	A	B	C	D	E
11	A	B	C	D	E	36	A	B	C	D	E
12	A	B	C	D	E	37	A	B	C	D	E
13	A	B	C	D	E	38	A	B	C	D	E
14	A	B	C	D	E	39	A	B	C	D	E
15	A	B	C	D	E	40	A	B	C	D	E
16	A	B	C	D	E	41	A	B	C	D	E
17	A	B	C	D	E	42	A	B	C	D	E
18	A	B	C	D	E	43	A	B	C	D	E
19	A	B	C	D	E	44	A	B	C	D	E
20	A	B	C	D	E	45	A	B	C	D	E
21	A	B	C	D	E	46	A	B	C	D	E
22	A	B	C	D	E	47	A	B	C	D	E
23	A	B	C	D	E	48	A	B	C	D	E
24	A	B	C	D	E	49	A	B	C	D	E
25	A	B	C	D	E	50	A	B	C	D	E

SECTION 2

1	A	B	C	D	E	26	A	B	C	D	E
2	A	B	C	D	E	27	A	B	C	D	E
3	A	B	C	D	E	28	A	B	C	D	E
4	A	B	C	D	E	29	A	B	C	D	E
5	A	B	C	D	E	30	A	B	C	D	E
6	A	B	C	D	E	31	A	B	C	D	E
7	A	B	C	D	E	32	A	B	C	D	E
8	A	B	C	D	E	33	A	B	C	D	E
9	A	B	C	D	E	34	A	B	C	D	E
10	A	B	C	D	E	35	A	B	C	D	E
11	A	B	C	D	E	36	A	B	C	D	E
12	A	B	C	D	E	37	A	B	C	D	E
13	A	B	C	D	E	38	A	B	C	D	E
14	A	B	C	D	E	39	A	B	C	D	E
15	A	B	C	D	E	40	A	B	C	D	E
16	A	B	C	D	E	41	A	B	C	D	E
17	A	B	C	D	E	42	A	B	C	D	E
18	A	B	C	D	E	43	A	B	C	D	E
19	A	B	C	D	E	44	A	B	C	D	E
20	A	B	C	D	E	45	A	B	C	D	E
21	A	B	C	D	E	46	A	B	C	D	E
22	A	B	C	D	E	47	A	B	C	D	E
23	A	B	C	D	E	48	A	B	C	D	E
24	A	B	C	D	E	49	A	B	C	D	E
25	A	B	C	D	E	50	A	B	C	D	E

I.N. 574006—110VV25P3015

COLLEGE BOARD — SCHOLASTIC APTITUDE TEST and Test of Standard Written English Side 2

Use a No. 2 pencil only. Be sure each mark is dark and completely fills the intended oval. Completely erase any errors or stray marks.

Start with number 1 for each new section. If a section has fewer than 50 questions, leave the extra answer spaces blank.

	SECTION 3	SECTION 4	SECTION 5	SECTION 6
1	A B C D E	A B C D E	A B C D E	A B C D E
2	A B C D E	A B C D E	A B C D E	A B C D E
3	A B C D E	A B C D E	A B C D E	A B C D E
4	A B C D E	A B C D E	A B C D E	A B C D E
5	A B C D E	A B C D E	A B C D E	A B C D E
6	A B C D E	A B C D E	A B C D E	A B C D E
7	A B C D E	A B C D E	A B C D E	A B C D E
8	A B C D E	A B C D E	A B C D E	A B C D E
9	A B C D E	A B C D E	A B C D E	A B C D E
10	A B C D E	A B C D E	A B C D E	A B C D E
11	A B C D E	A B C D E	A B C D E	A B C D E
12	A B C D E	A B C D E	A B C D E	A B C D E
13	A B C D E	A B C D E	A B C D E	A B C D E
14	A B C D E	A B C D E	A B C D E	A B C D E
15	A B C D E	A B C D E	A B C D E	A B C D E
16	A B C D E	A B C D E	A B C D E	A B C D E
17	A B C D E	A B C D E	A B C D E	A B C D E
18	A B C D E	A B C D E	A B C D E	A B C D E
19	A B C D E	A B C D E	A B C D E	A B C D E
20	A B C D E	A B C D E	A B C D E	A B C D E
21	A B C D E	A B C D E	A B C D E	A B C D E
22	A B C D E	A B C D E	A B C D E	A B C D E
23	A B C D E	A B C D E	A B C D E	A B C D E
24	A B C D E	A B C D E	A B C D E	A B C D E
25	A B C D E	A B C D E	A B C D E	A B C D E
26	A B C D E	A B C D E	A B C D E	A B C D E
27	A B C D E	A B C D E	A B C D E	A B C D E
28	A B C D E	A B C D E	A B C D E	A B C D E
29	A B C D E	A B C D E	A B C D E	A B C D E
30	A B C D E	A B C D E	A B C D E	A B C D E
31	A B C D E	A B C D E	A B C D E	A B C D E
32	A B C D E	A B C D E	A B C D E	A B C D E
33	A B C D E	A B C D E	A B C D E	A B C D E
34	A B C D E	A B C D E	A B C D E	A B C D E
35	A B C D E	A B C D E	A B C D E	A B C D E
36	A B C D E	A B C D E	A B C D E	A B C D E
37	A B C D E	A B C D E	A B C D E	A B C D E
38	A B C D E	A B C D E	A B C D E	A B C D E
39	A B C D E	A B C D E	A B C D E	A B C D E
40	A B C D E	A B C D E	A B C D E	A B C D E
41	A B C D E	A B C D E	A B C D E	A B C D E
42	A B C D E	A B C D E	A B C D E	A B C D E
43	A B C D E	A B C D E	A B C D E	A B C D E
44	A B C D E	A B C D E	A B C D E	A B C D E
45	A B C D E	A B C D E	A B C D E	A B C D E
46	A B C D E	A B C D E	A B C D E	A B C D E
47	A B C D E	A B C D E	A B C D E	A B C D E
48	A B C D E	A B C D E	A B C D E	A B C D E
49	A B C D E	A B C D E	A B C D E	A B C D E
50	A B C D E	A B C D E	A B C D E	A B C D E

9. SIGNATURE: ______________________

FOR ETS USE ONLY	VTR	VTFS	VRR	VRFS	VVR	VVFS	WER	WEFS	M4R	M4FS	M5R	M5FS	MTFS
	VTW	VTCS	VRW	VRCS	VVW	VVCS	WEW	WECS	M4W		M5W		MTCS

YOUR NAME (PRINT) ______________________________
LAST FIRST MI

TEST CENTER ______________________________
NUMBER NAME OF TEST CENTER ROOM NUMBER

IMPORTANT: The following codes are unique to your testbook. Copy them on your answer sheet exactly as shown.

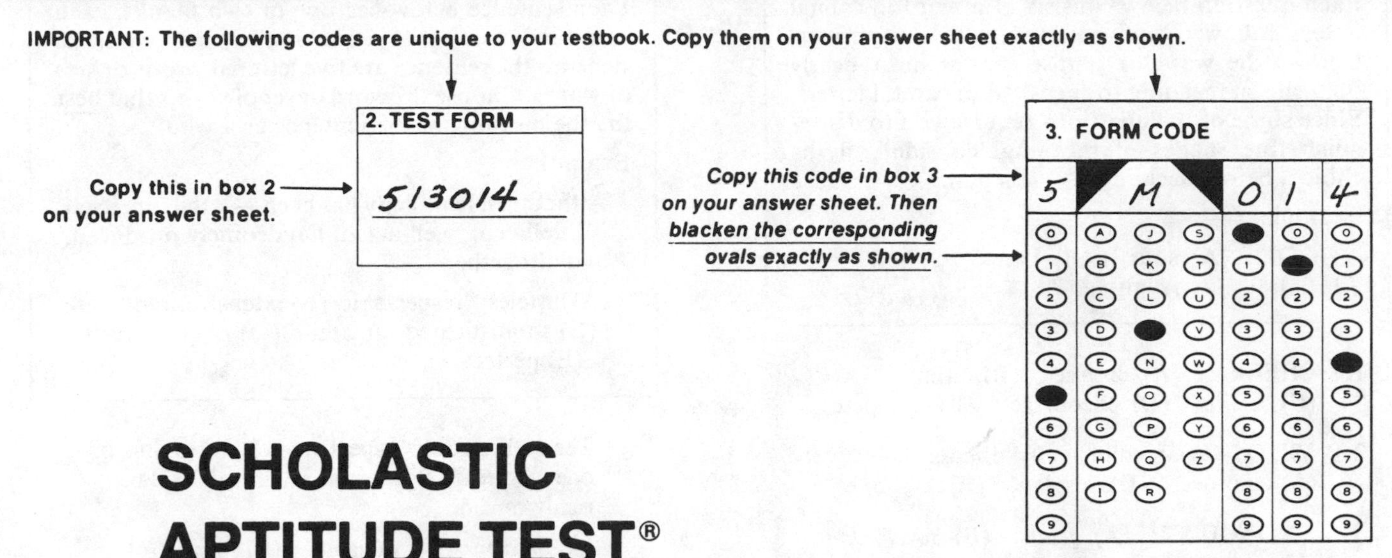

2. TEST FORM
Copy this in box 2 on your answer sheet.
513014
3. FORM CODE
Copy this code in box 3 on your answer sheet. Then blacken the corresponding ovals exactly as shown.
5 M 0 1 4

SCHOLASTIC APTITUDE TEST®

and Test of Standard Written English

You will have three hours to work on the questions in this test book, which is divided into six 30-minute sections. The supervisor will tell you when to begin and end each section. If you finish before time is called, you may check your work on that section, but you are not to work on any other section.

Do not worry if you are unable to finish a section or if there are some questions you cannot answer. Do not waste time puzzling over a question that seems too difficult for you. You should work as rapidly as you can without sacrificing accuracy.

Students often ask whether they should guess when they are uncertain about the answer to a question. Your test scores will be based on the number of questions you answer correctly minus a fraction of the number you answer incorrectly. Therefore, it is improbable that random or haphazard guessing will change your scores significantly. If you have some knowledge of a question, you may be able to eliminate one or more of the answer choices as wrong. It is generally to your advantage to guess which of the remaining choices is correct. Remember, however, not to spend too much time on any one question.

Mark all your answers on the separate answer sheet. Mark only one answer for each question. Since the answer sheet will be machine scored, be sure that each mark is dark and that it completely fills the answer space. In each section of the answer sheet, there are spaces to answer 50 questions. When there are fewer than 50 questions in a section of your test, mark only the spaces that correspond to the question numbers. Do not make stray marks on the answer sheet. If you erase, do so completely, because an incomplete erasure may be scored as an intended response.

You may use the test book for scratchwork, but you will not receive credit for any responses written there.

(The passages for this test have been adapted from published material. The ideas contained in them do not necessarily represent the opinions of the College Board or Educational Testing Service.)

DO NOT OPEN THIS BOOK UNTIL THE SUPERVISOR TELLS YOU TO DO SO.

SECTION 1

Time—30 minutes
45 Questions

For each question in this section, choose the best answer and blacken the corresponding space on the answer sheet.

Each question below consists of a word in capital letters, followed by five lettered words or phrases. Choose the word or phrase that is most nearly opposite in meaning to the word in capital letters. Since some of the questions require you to distinguish fine shades of meaning, consider all the choices before deciding which is best.

Example:

GOOD: (A) sour (B) bad (C) red (D) hot (E) ugly

Ⓐ ● Ⓒ Ⓓ Ⓔ

1. CHERISH: (A) despise (B) utilize (C) aspire (D) encourage (E) compete
2. VETO: (A) predict (B) discuss (C) approve (D) display (E) evaluate
3. EXTINGUISH: (A) graze (B) revive (C) correct (D) intrude (E) exceed
4. CEREMONIOUS: (A) active (B) enjoyable (C) permanent (D) informal (E) widespread
5. SYMMETRY: (A) exclusion (B) imbalance (C) isolation (D) immensity (E) validity
6. DOCUMENT: (A) edit (B) withhold (C) reproduce in full (D) write for pay (E) leave unsupported
7. HARBOR: (A) enlighten (B) burden (C) permit (D) prepare for (E) turn away
8. BREADTH: (A) rarity (B) mobility (C) complexity (D) narrowness (E) roughness
9. NOXIOUS: (A) diffuse (B) unique (C) beneficial (D) latent (E) static
10. REPREHENSIBLE: (A) matchless (B) praiseworthy (C) interesting (D) difficult to control (E) seldom recognized
11. SCANTY: (A) adept (B) copious (C) prosaic (D) candid (E) mellow
12. ADULATION: (A) initiation (B) vilification (C) injustice (D) purification (E) deliverance
13. PRODIGIOUS: (A) questionable (B) approximate (C) ultimate (D) adjacent (E) minuscule
14. TENSILE: (A) inelastic (B) genuine (C) tough (D) sympathetic (E) inharmonious
15. AMITY: (A) strife (B) irrelevance (C) realism (D) topicality (E) unseemliness

Each sentence below has one or two blanks, each blank indicating that something has been omitted. Beneath the sentence are five lettered words or sets of words. Choose the word or set of words that best fits the meaning of the sentence as a whole.

Example:

Although its publicity has been ----, the film itself is intelligent, well-acted, handsomely produced, and altogether ----.

(A) tasteless..respectable (B) extensive..moderate (C) sophisticated..amateur (D) risqué..crude (E) perfect..spectacular

● Ⓑ Ⓒ Ⓓ Ⓔ

16. The ambassador's papers are not ---- reading, but one who reads slowly and attentively will be richly repaid.

    (A) petty (B) valuable (C) insightful (D) easy (E) plausible

17. It is inaccurate to describe Hopkins as a crusader for progressive reforms, for, although he debunks certain popular myths, he is not really ---- of change.

    (A) an advocate (B) a censor (C) an adversary (D) a caricature (E) a descendant

18. He was lonely and might have considered himself miserable were it not for a kind of hysterical ----, which he could neither account for nor ----.

    (A) depression. .enhance
    (B) apathy. .tolerate
    (C) contentment. .enjoy
    (D) merriment. .conquer
    (E) sorrow. .comprehend

19. Occasionally ---- strain of the bacteria appears, changed by some molecular misprint from what was once only ---- into a life-taking poison.

    (A) a new. .an epidemic
    (B) a deficient. .a derivative
    (C) an erratic. .a rudiment
    (D) a virulent. .a nuisance
    (E) an advanced. .a disease

20. The discussions were often ----, degenerating at times into name-calling contests.

    (A) lofty (B) auspicious (C) acrimonious (D) lethargic (E) pragmatic

Each passage below is followed by questions based on its content. Answer all questions following a passage on the basis of what is stated or implied in that passage.

I agree that children need to be—and usually want very much to be—taught right from wrong. But I believe that realistic fiction for children is one of the very hardest media in which it can be done. It is hard not to get entangled in simplistic moralism, and all you end up with are the "baddies" and the "goodies" you had hoped to avoid. Or you can trot out the cliché that "there's a little bit of bad in the best of us and a little bit of good in the worst of us," a dangerous trivialization of the fact that there is tremendous potential for good and for evil in every one of us. Or you can try the "problem books." The problem of drugs, of divorce, of prejudice, and so on—as if evil were merely a problem, something that can be solved, that has an answer, like a problem in fifth-grade arithmetic. That is escapism, that posing of evil as a "problem," instead of what it is: all the pain and suffering and injustice we will meet throughout our lives, and must admit, in order to live human lives at all.

But what, then, is the writer for children to do? Can one present the child with evil as an insoluble problem—something neither the child nor any adult can do anything about at all? To give the child a picture of a land haunted by famines or the cruelties of a brutal parent, and say, "Well, this is how it is. What are you going to make of it?" —that is surely unethical. If you suggest that there is a solution to these monstrous facts, you are lying to the child. If you insist that there is not, you are overwhelming the child with a burden that he or she is not strong enough yet to carry.

Children do need protection and shelter. But they also need the truth. And it seems to me that the way you can speak absolutely honestly and factually about both good and evil to children is to talk about themselves, their inner selves. That is something they can cope with; indeed, their job in growing up is to become themselves. They cannot do this if they feel the task is hopeless or if they are led to think there is no task.

Fantasy is the language of the inner self. I personally find it the appropriate language in which to tell stories to children—and others. I make that statement with some confidence, having behind me the authority of a very great poet, who put it much more boldly. "The great instrument of moral good," Shelley said, "is the imagination."

21. The author's primary goal in the passage is to do which of the following?
    (A) Criticize children's literature for being unrealistic
    (B) Demonstrate that morality is not a fit subject for children's literature
    (C) Argue that imaginative fiction is more suitable than realistic fiction for teaching morality to children
    (D) Propose a solution for the problem of evil in children's literature
    (E) Describe the way in which fantasy puts children in touch with the inner selves that they must obey

22. The author's attitude toward children appears to be one of
    (A) concern for the development of their moral integrity
    (B) idealization of their inexperience and vulnerability
    (C) contempt for their inability to accept unpleasant facts
    (D) exaggerated sympathy for their problems in daily life
    (E) envy of their willingness to learn about morality

23. According to the author, it is the duty of children's literature to
    (A) protect children from learning about anything unpleasant or distressing
    (B) simplify moral issues so that children can understand them
    (C) force children to deal with the facts of pain and suffering
    (D) reassure children that every problem has a solution
    (E) present truth in a way that children can accept and understand

24. In the passage the author indicates that much of human experience is
    (A) wretched and unbearable
    (B) difficult and unfair
    (C) routine and boring
    (D) unpredictable and meaningless
    (E) pleasant and secure

25. In presenting the argument, the author does all of the following EXCEPT
    (A) define a term
    (B) resolve a problem
    (C) refer to an authority
    (D) illustrate through an analogy
    (E) cite a psychological study

GO ON TO THE NEXT PAGE

One important facet of colonial America's early development was the role played by slave artisans from Africa. Slave art was an art of anonymity—an art that rose from slavery in the form of skilled handicrafts—an art descended from African imagery and later rechanneled as a functional aesthetic, finding its way to the wrought iron balconies of New Orleans and to the magnificent ornamentation on the mansions of Charleston, South Carolina. Although they received little credit for their labor, slave artisans accomplished necessary work in preindustrial America and became one of the first classes of technical experts in the New World.

Afro-American arts and crafts originated on the west coast of Africa where they were important in all aspects of communal life. Unlike the Europeans, who tended to perceive art objects only as "curios," Africans viewed the arts as functional and art objects were created for specific use in ceremonies as well as in numerous domestic activities. Many Africans were master artisans, demonstrating various skills and great proficiency in the fashioning of wood, bone, and ivory, in weaving, in pottery-making, and in the making of clothes, tools, and other implements. There is also strong evidence that some African groups were skilled in the building trades, whereas others proved skillful in developing exquisite sculptured objects of bronze through new casting techniques.

The major factors surrounding the development of the slave-artisan class included the diversification of farming and industry and the scarcity of labor to meet the needs of colonial America. As a solution to this problem, slaves were employed in every conceivable fashion. The diversity of occupations held by slave artisans is a clear example of why skilled slaves became very important agents in the rise of manufacturing.

Although research concerning slave artisans is lacking, certain general conclusions are apparent. Black artisans constituted a specialized labor force in colonial America. Without their achievements it is difficult to imagine how the colonists would have survived and prospered. As producers of goods, contributors to the building trades, manufacturers of furniture, and designers of household objects and decor, slave artisans also aided America in its aesthetic development. Their creativity and cleverness laid the foundation for furthering the development of the Afro-American artist.

26. The author is primarily concerned with
    (A) describing the slave artisans' response to the limited opportunities for creative expression in colonial America
    (B) discussing the slaves' artistic heritage and the role their skills played in preindustrial America
    (C) depicting the specific talents of slave artisans in the areas of decoration and design
    (D) noting that contemporary Black art emerged from the work of slave artisans
    (E) praising the long history of the artistic tradition of Africa

27. It can be inferred that one reason slave art was "an art of anonymity" (line 3) was that the slave artisans
    (A) received inadequate fees for their work
    (B) were believed to do stylized work
    (C) did not receive individual credit for their work
    (D) were required to work only on specifically assigned projects
    (E) relied on the artistic techniques of their ancestors

28. With which of the following statements regarding artisans in Africa would the author most likely agree?
    (A) They were the most respected members of their societies.
    (B) They were rewarded for their contributions to the community.
    (C) Their skills related primarily to manufacturing activities.
    (D) All members of a society were considered artisans.
    (E) They played a vital role in communal life.

29. According to the passage, slave artisans were important to colonial America because they
    (A) helped meet the needs of its preindustrial society
    (B) persuaded the colonists to diversify farming and industry
    (C) recognized the need for new and more complex manufacturing procedures
    (D) taught other slaves skills that led to greater freedom
    (E) helped to develop plantations into self-sufficient communities

30. The author cites specific examples of the work of slave artisans primarily to
    (A) show that they had mastered basic craft skills
    (B) indicate the conventional and imitative nature of their work
    (C) explain why they were considered technical experts rather than artists
    (D) attest to the quality and variety of their work
    (E) emphasize the limited opportunities granted to them

Select the word or set of words that <u>best</u> completes each of the following sentences.

31. Many sportswriters have been caught up in the activities about which they write and have become advocates and ---- when they ought to have been ----.

(A) promoters. .colleagues
(B) participants. .collaborators
(C) apologists. .critics
(D) opponents. .antagonists
(E) disputants. .defenders

32. His inability to fathom the latest trends in art led him to fear that his critical faculties had ---- during his long absence.

(A) diversified (B) atrophied (C) converted (D) predominated (E) multiplied

33. Though her lecture contained ideas that were provocative and systematically presented, her style of delivery was so ---- that I actually dozed off.

(A) galling (B) pungent (C) desultory (D) soporific (E) theatrical

34. Fuentes' subtly persuasive arguments for continuity in Latino culture ---- readers to recognize that their future cannot be ---- from the way they treat their past.

(A) implore. .deciphered
(B) condition. .inferred
(C) invite. .divorced
(D) command. .projected
(E) inspire. .elicited

35. Like most ---- literature, this moving remembrance of the poet's parents primarily expresses lamentation for their deaths.

(A) dogmatic (B) elegiac (C) abstract (D) dramatic (E) striking

Each question below consists of a related pair of words or phrases, followed by five lettered pairs of words or phrases. Select the lettered pair that <u>best</u> expresses a relationship similar to that expressed in the original pair.

Example:

YAWN:BOREDOM :: (A) dream:sleep (B) anger:madness (C) smile:amusement (D) face:expression (E) impatience:rebellion

Ⓐ Ⓑ ● Ⓓ Ⓔ

36. JUDGE:COURTHOUSE :: (A) physician:hospital (B) clergyman:library (C) farmer:house (D) visitor:hotel (E) mathematician:computer

37. MUMBLE:INDISTINCT :: (A) relent:gentle (B) stumble:graceful (C) enunciate:clear (D) define:difficult (E) grunt:shrill

38. COLORS:SPECTRUM :: (A) experiments:laboratory (B) panes:glass (C) guests:party (D) letters:alphabet (E) leaves:tree

39. TADPOLE:FROG :: (A) stream:river (B) acorn:oak (C) politician:diplomat (D) negative:photograph (E) student:graduate

40. ABODE:VAGRANT :: (A) ship:pirate (B) fort:sentry (C) faith:prophet (D) costume:eccentric (E) community:outcast

41. CREDITS:MOVIE :: (A) selections:album (B) by-lines:newspaper (C) reviews:journal (D) reruns:television (E) cartoons:government

42. AMORPHOUS:SHAPE :: (A) amorous:trust (B) temporal:patience (C) enticing:guile (D) bland:zest (E) classical:harmony

43. EVIL:MALEFACTOR ::

(A) selfishness:hermit
(B) talent:virtuoso
(C) benevolence:miser
(D) mischief:benefactor
(E) friendliness:thief

44. DIGRESS:SPEECH :: (A) dissemble:truth (B) meander:travel (C) narrate:climax (D) deter:progress (E) circumnavigate:globe

45. PLAINTIVE:SORROW :: (A) systematic:brevity (B) elusive:eloquence (C) confident:defeat (D) distasteful:pessimism (E) contemptuous:disdain

IF YOU FINISH BEFORE TIME IS CALLED, YOU MAY CHECK YOUR WORK ON THIS SECTION ONLY. DO NOT WORK ON ANY OTHER SECTION IN THE TEST. **STOP**

SECTION 2 Time—30 minutes 25 Questions

In this section solve each problem, using any available space on the page for scratchwork. Then decide which is the best of the choices given and blacken the corresponding space on the answer sheet.

The following information is for your reference in solving some of the problems.

Circle of radius r: Area $= \pi r^2$; Circumference $= 2\pi r$

The number of degrees of arc in a circle is 360.

The measure in degrees of a straight angle is 180.

Definitions of symbols:

$=$ is equal to	$\leqq$ is less than or equal to
$\neq$ is unequal to	$\geqq$ is greater than or equal to
$<$ is less than	$\parallel$ is parallel to
$>$ is greater than	$\perp$ is perpendicular to

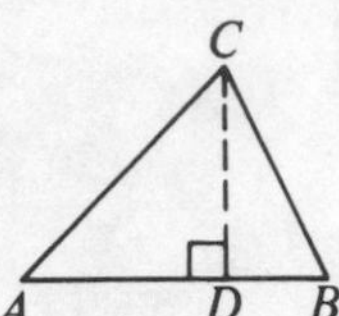

Triangle: The sum of the measures in degrees of the angles of a triangle is 180.

If $\angle CDA$ is a right angle, then

(1) area of $\triangle ABC = \frac{AB \times CD}{2}$

(2) $AC^2 = AD^2 + DC^2$

Note: Figures that accompany problems in this test are intended to provide information useful in solving the problems. They are drawn as accurately as possible EXCEPT when it is stated in a specific problem that its figure is not drawn to scale. All figures lie in a plane unless otherwise indicated. All numbers used are real numbers.

1. If $x - 7 = 5 - x$, then $x =$

(A) −6 (B) −1 (C) 1 (D) 6 (E) 12

2. A gymnast competed in a meet and received the following scores for three events: 9.5 for bars, 8.7 for balance beam, and 8.8 for floor routine. What is the average (arithmetic mean) of these three scores?

(A) 8.9
(B) 9.0
(C) 9.1
(D) 9.2
(E) 9.3

3. On a number line, if point P has coordinate −3 and point Q has coordinate 5, what is the length of segment PQ ?

(A) 2 (B) 4 (C) 5 (D) 8 (E) 64

4. 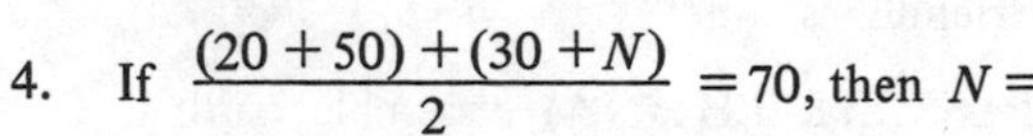
If $\frac{(20+50)+(30+N)}{2} = 70$, then $N =$

(A) 30
(B) 40
(C) 50
(D) 60
(E) 70

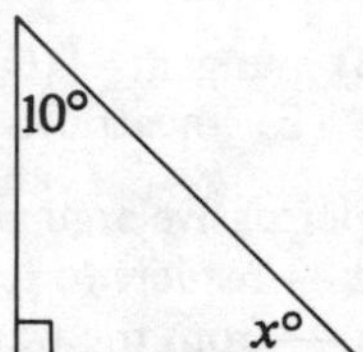

Note: Figure not drawn to scale.

5. In the right triangle above, $x - 10 =$

(A) 60
(B) 70
(C) 80
(D) 90
(E) 100

6. If $(x+3)^2 = (x-3)^2$, then $x =$

(A) 0 (B) 1 (C) 3 (D) 6 (E) 9

GO ON TO THE NEXT PAGE

7. Ms. Jones borrowed $1,000 for a year. The cost of the loan was 6 percent of the amount borrowed, to be paid back together with the loan at the end of the year. What was the total amount needed to pay off the loan?

(A) $1,000.60
(B) $1,006.00
(C) $1,060.00
(D) $1,600.00
(E) $6,000.00

8. If $\frac{5}{x} = 1$ and $\frac{y}{2} = 3$, then $\frac{3+x}{y+3} =$

(A) $\frac{5}{6}$

(B) $\frac{8}{9}$

(C) 1

(D) $\frac{9}{8}$

(E) $\frac{6}{5}$

Candidate	Number of Votes Received
A	20
B	45
C	102
D	x
E	y

9. In a class of 300 students, 5 students were running for the position of student representative. If every student in the class voted for exactly one candidate and the distribution of votes is given in the table above, what is the maximum possible value of x ?

(A) 60 (B) 133 (C) 167
(D) 233 (E) 300

10. If $\underline{\rfloor x \lfloor}$ is defined by the equation $\underline{\rfloor x \lfloor} = \frac{\sqrt{x}}{2}$ for all whole numbers x, which of the following equals 5 ?

(A) $\underline{\rfloor 10 \lfloor}$ (B) $\underline{\rfloor 20 \lfloor}$ (C) $\underline{\rfloor 25 \lfloor}$
(D) $\underline{\rfloor 50 \lfloor}$ (E) $\underline{\rfloor 100 \lfloor}$

11. To the nearest thousand, what is the number of seconds in a 24-hour day?

(A) 8,000
(B) 9,000
(C) 86,000
(D) 87,000
(E) 90,000

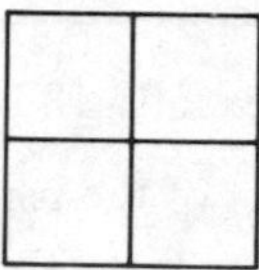

12. The figure above is a square divided into four equal smaller squares. If the perimeter of the large square is 1, then the perimeter of a small square is

(A) $\frac{1}{16}$ (B) $\frac{1}{8}$ (C) $\frac{1}{6}$ (D) $\frac{1}{4}$ (E) $\frac{1}{2}$

13. If $\frac{5}{6} = \frac{x}{5}$, then $x =$

(A) $\frac{6}{25}$ (B) $\frac{6}{5}$ (C) $\frac{25}{6}$ (D) 6 (E) 25

GO ON TO THE NEXT PAGE

14. A jar contains 10 pencils, some sharpened and some unsharpened. Each of the following could be the ratio of sharpened to unsharpened pencils EXCEPT

(A) 1 : 1
(B) 3 : 2
(C) 4 : 1
(D) 5 : 1
(E) 9 : 1

15. Cube X has a volume of 27. If point C is the center of one face of cube X and point D is the center of the opposite parallel face, what is the length of line segment CD ?

(A) 3
(B) $3\sqrt{2}$
(C) 6
(D) $6\sqrt{2}$
(E) 9

16. Initially, there are exactly 18 bananas on a tree. If one monkey eats $\frac{1}{3}$ of the bananas and another monkey eats $\frac{1}{3}$ of the bananas that are left, how many bananas are still on the tree?

(A) 4
(B) 6
(C) 8
(D) 10
(E) 16

17. If $\frac{a}{b} + \frac{c}{d} = 4$, what is the value of $\frac{b}{a} + \frac{d}{c}$?

(A) $\frac{1}{4}$ (B) 1 (C) $\frac{4}{3}$ (D) 4

(E) It cannot be determined from the information given.

18. Which of the following is the greater of two numbers whose product is 220 and whose sum is 10 more than the difference between the two?

(A) 5 (B) 10 (C) 22 (D) 44 (E) 55

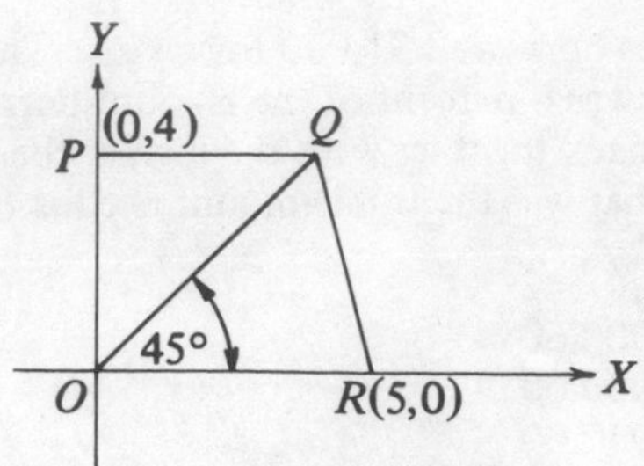

19. In the figure above, if $PQ \parallel OR$, what is the area of quadrilateral $PQRO$?

(A) 9 (B) 14 (C) 18 (D) 36

(E) It cannot be determined from the information given.

20. On the last day of a one-week sale, customers numbered 149 through 201 were waited on. How many customers were waited on that day?

(A) 51 (B) 52 (C) 53 (D) 152 (E) 153

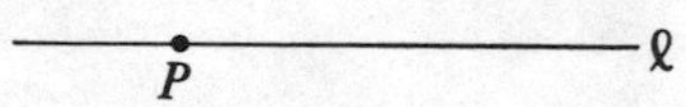

21. If two points, Q and R, are each placed to the right of point P on line ℓ above so that $2PQ = 3PR$, what will be the value of $\frac{RQ}{PR}$?

(A) $\frac{1}{2}$ (B) $\frac{2}{5}$ (C) $\frac{2}{3}$ (D) $\frac{3}{2}$

(E) It cannot be determined from the information given.

GO ON TO THE NEXT PAGE

X	Y
1	4
2	5
3	6

22. If x is a number from column X and y is a number from column Y in the table above, how many different values are possible for $x + y$?

(A) Nine (B) Eight (C) Seven
(D) Six (E) Five

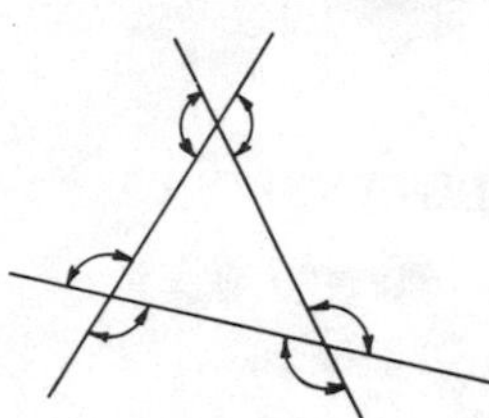

23. Three lines intersect as shown in the figure above. What is the sum of the degree measures of the marked angles?

(A) 360° (B) 540° (C) 720° (D) 900°
(E) It cannot be determined from the information given.

24. If $x^7 = 3$ and $x^6 = \frac{2}{y}$, what is the value of x in terms of y ?

(A) $\frac{3}{2}y$

(B) $\frac{2}{3}y$

(C) $\frac{1}{3}y$

(D) $3y$

(E) $3 - \frac{2}{y}$

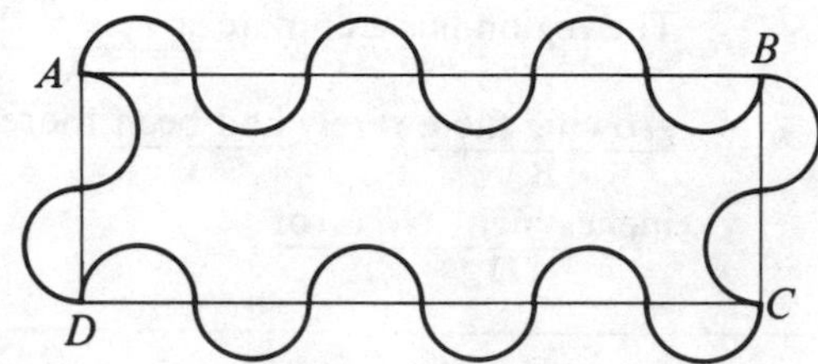

25. In the figure above, $ABCD$ is a rectangle and the curved path is made up of 16 semicircles of equal diameter. If the total length of this curved path is 32π, then the area of rectangle $ABCD$ is

(A) 24 (B) 32 (C) 48 (D) 64 (E) 192

IF YOU FINISH BEFORE TIME IS CALLED, YOU MAY CHECK YOUR WORK ON THIS SECTION ONLY. DO NOT WORK ON ANY OTHER SECTION IN THE TEST. **STOP**

SECTION 3 Time—30 minutes 50 Questions

The questions in this section measure skills that are important to writing well. In particular, they test your ability to recognize and use language that is clear, effective, and correct according to the requirements of standard written English, the kind of English found in most college textbooks.

Directions: The following sentences contain problems in grammar, usage, diction (choice of words), and idiom.

Some sentences are correct.
No sentence contains more than one error.

You will find that the error, if there is one, is underlined and lettered. Assume that elements of the sentence that are not underlined are correct and cannot be changed. In choosing answers, follow the requirements of standard written English.

If there is an error, select the one underlined part that must be changed to make the sentence correct and blacken the corresponding space on your answer sheet.

If there is no error, blacken answer space Ⓔ.

EXAMPLE:

The region has a climate so severe that (A) plants growing there (B) rarely had been (C) more than twelve inches high (D). No error (E)

SAMPLE ANSWER

Ⓐ Ⓑ ● Ⓓ Ⓔ

1. A few scientists claim that food additives not only (A) improve the quality of (B) foods but also made (C) them (D) safer. No error (E)

2. It is rumored that (A) the names of them (B) to be promoted (C) will be announced tomorrow, but I believe the choices have not been made (D) yet. No error (E)

3. In 1957, the appearance of the first (A) Soviet satellite has created (B) a panic in the United States that continued for (C) nearly (D) a decade. No error (E)

4. In appreciation about (A) her work, the committee presented its (B) retiring director with, among other (C) gifts, a plaque describing (D) her accomplishments. No error (E)

5. For many people (A), hang-gliding, an increasingly (B) popular sport, seems satisfying (C) the urge to fly (D). No error (E)

6. Despite (A) much research, there are (B) still certain elements in (C) the life cycle of the cicada that are not fully understood (D). No error (E)

7. Louise's fair skin was (A) sunburned so badly (B) that she looked as if (C) she had fell into (D) a bucket of red paint. No error (E)

8. Whenever (A) we hear of a natural disaster, even in (B) a distant part of the world, you (C) feel sympathy (D) for the people affected. No error (E)

GO ON TO THE NEXT PAGE

9. Late in the war, the Germans, retreating (A) in haste (B), left many (C) of their (D) prisoners go free. No error (E)

10. In many states (A), there seems (B) to be a belief, openly (C) expressed by educators, that the methods of teaching reading should be changed (D). No error (E)

11. Throughout (A) the Middle Ages women work (B) beside (C) men, knowing that the efforts of men and women alike were essential to (D) survival. No error (E)

12. Without hardly a doubt (A), the novels of Thomas Pynchon are (B) more complex (C) than the novels of many other (D) contemporary writers. No error (E)

13. The leading roles in the widely acclaimed (A) play, a modern (B) version of an Irish folktale, were performed (C) by Jessica and he (D). No error (E)

14. In the reserve section of the library, there is (A) two volumes of (B) essays by James Baldwin on (C) the relation of the Black artist and intellectual to (D) society. No error (E)

15. Many studies have tried to (A) determine whether or not (B) seeing violence on television makes (C) children behave more violent (D). No error (E)

16. Between ten and (A) twenty per cent of the textbook appears to be (B) new; the rest is (C) a revision of (D) the previous edition. No error (E)

17. Some people seem remarkably (A) insensitive to physical pain, and (B) this insensitivity does not mean (C) that they are able (D) to endure other kinds of pain. No error (E)

18. During the meeting (A), Congresswoman Barbara Jordan stressed that (B) educators and legislators must cooperate where (C) the goal of equal opportunity is (D) to be reached. No error (E)

19. The population of American alligators, dangerously (A) small a few years ago, are (B) now estimated at (C) more than (D) one million. No error (E)

20. Such (A) novels as *Heidi* and *Little Women* have long been considered (B) by young and old alike (C) to be a classic of (D) children's literature. No error (E)

21. Anyone who (A) gathers mushrooms for the purpose of eating them (B) must distinguish carefully (C) between (D) poisonous and nonpoisonous species. No error (E)

22. In regards to (A) the energy crisis, the President urged (B) all homeowners to keep (C) their (D) thermostats at sixty-five degrees in winter. No error (E)

23. Long ago, well before (A) the invention of (B) the printing press, poets often sung (C) their (D) poetry to small, interested audiences. No error (E)

24. Because of (A) extreme weather conditions, starvation exists (B) in some countries where they (C) must struggle every day to stay alive (D). No error (E)

25. The energy question, along with several other (A) issues, are going (B) to be discussed (C) at (D) the next meeting of the state legislature. No error (E)

GO ON TO THE NEXT PAGE

Directions: In each of the following sentences, some part or all of the sentence is underlined. Below each sentence you will find five ways of phrasing the underlined part. Select the answer that produces the most effective sentence, one that is clear and exact, without awkwardness or ambiguity, and blacken the corresponding space on your answer sheet. In choosing answers, follow the requirements of standard written English. Choose the answer that best expresses the meaning of the original sentence.

Answer (A) is always the same as the underlined part. Choose answer (A) if you think the original sentence needs no revision.

EXAMPLE:

Laura Ingalls Wilder published her first book and she was sixty-five years old then.

(A) and she was sixty-five years old then
(B) when she was sixty-five years old
(C) at age sixty-five years old
(D) upon reaching sixty-five years
(E) at the time when she was sixty-five

SAMPLE ANSWER

26. Freud's complex theory based on the death instinct is, for most people, one that is with difficult understanding.

(A) with difficult understanding
(B) difficult to understand
(C) to understand difficultly
(D) having difficulty being understood
(E) difficult for understanding

27. In the nineteenth century, trains were more than machines they were expressions of the greatness of the United States.

(A) machines they were
(B) machines and were
(C) machines; they were
(D) machines, although they were
(E) machines, but were

28. In the sunlight, the cherry blossoms that burst out everywhere, like foam on breaking waves.

(A) blossoms that burst
(B) blossoms bursting
(C) blossoms, which are bursting
(D) blossoms burst
(E) blossoms, which burst

29. When Dorothy Richardson decided to become a novelist, she knew that her writing would leave her little time for other work.

(A) When Dorothy Richardson decided to become
(B) After the decision was made by Dorothy Richardson to become
(C) After the decision by Dorothy Richardson to become
(D) When Dorothy Richardson decides to become
(E) When Dorothy Richardson decided about becoming

30. The difference between the twins is that one is humorous; the other, serious.

(A) one is humorous; the other, serious
(B) of one being humorous, the other is serious
(C) one is humorous; the other being serious
(D) one is humorous, although the other is more serious
(E) of a humorous one and one that is serious

31. The United States did not go on the gold standard until 1900, it went off it thirty-three years later.

(A) until 1900, it went off it thirty-three years later
(B) until 1900; however, going off after thirty-three years
(C) until 1900, although going off in thirty-three years
(D) until 1900, it was thirty-three years later when it went off it
(E) until 1900 and went off it thirty-three years later

32. Many memos were issued by the director of the agency that had an insulting tone, according to the staff members.

(A) Many memos were issued by the director of the agency that
(B) Many memos were issued by the director of the agency who
(C) The issuance of many memos by the director of the agency which
(D) The director of the agency issued many memos that
(E) The director of the agency, who issued many memos that

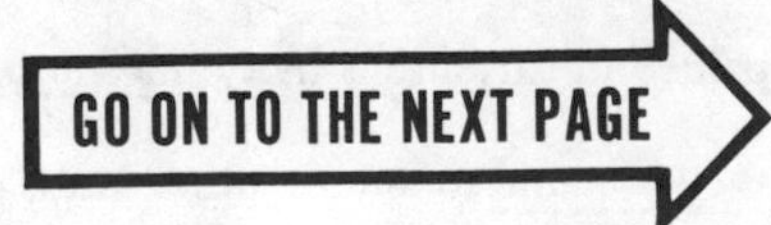

33. The widespread slaughter of buffalo for their skins profoundly shocked and angered Native Americans.

(A) shocked and angered Native Americans
(B) shocked Native Americans, angering them
(C) shocked Native Americans, and they were also angry
(D) was a shock and caused anger among Native Americans
(E) was shocking to Native Americans, making them angry

34. Consumers are beginning to take notice of electric cars because they are quiet, cause no air pollution, and gasoline is not used.

(A) cause no air pollution, and gasoline is not used
(B) air pollution is not caused, and gasoline is not used
(C) cause no air pollution, and use no gasoline
(D) causing no air pollution and using no gasoline
(E) air pollution is not caused, and no gasoline is used

35. Because she was a woman was why Sharon Frontiero, a lieutenant in the United States Air Force, felt that she was being treated unfairly.

(A) Because she was a woman was why Sharon Frontiero, a lieutenant in the United States Air Force, felt that she was being treated unfairly.
(B) Sharon Frontiero, a lieutenant in the United States Air Force, felt that she was being treated unfairly because she was a woman.
(C) Because she was a woman, Sharon Frontiero felt that this was why she was being treated unfairly as a lieutenant in the United States Air Force.
(D) Sharon Frontiero, a lieutenant in the United States Air Force, feeling that she was being treated unfairly because she was a woman.
(E) A woman, Sharon Frontiero, felt that because she was a lieutenant in the United States Air Force, that she was being treated unfairly.

36. A major difference between people and apes is brain size, a person's brain is three times as large as the brain of an ape.

(A) size, a person's brain is
(B) size, with a person's brain being
(C) size; a person's brain is
(D) size; a person's brain, it is
(E) size, in that it is

37. The process of how European immigrant groups being absorbed into American society is complex.

(A) of how European immigrant groups being absorbed
(B) for European immigrant groups being absorbed
(C) where European immigrant groups were absorbed
(D) by which European immigrant groups have been absorbed
(E) whereby the absorption of European groups has been

38. Mr. Howe's class has organized a special program for our school; the purpose being to help us increase our understanding of Japanese culture.

(A) school; the purpose being to
(B) school and the purpose is to
(C) school, the purpose is to
(D) school, being to
(E) school to

39. Light reaching earth from the most distant stars originated billions of years ago.

(A) reaching earth from the most distant stars
(B) which reaching earth from the most distant stars
(C) from the most distant stars reaching earth
(D) that is from the most distant stars and reaches earth
(E) reaching earth which is from stars that are most distant

40. Joseph Conrad was born and educated in Poland and he wrote all of his novels in English.

(A) Joseph Conrad was born and educated in Poland and he
(B) Joseph Conrad, being born and educated in Poland,
(C) Although being born and educated in Poland, Joseph Conrad
(D) Although Joseph Conrad was born and educated in Poland, he
(E) Being from Poland, where he was born and educated, Joseph Conrad

GO ON TO THE NEXT PAGE

Note: The remaining questions are like those at the beginning of the section.

Directions: For each sentence in which you find an error, select the one underlined part that must be changed to make the sentence correct and blacken the corresponding space on your answer sheet.

If there is no error, blacken answer space (E).

EXAMPLE:

The region has a climate so severe that plants
A
growing there rarely had been more than twelve
B C
inches high. No error
D E

SAMPLE ANSWER

41. If you find that it is difficult to concentrate
A B
in noisy surroundings, one should try to find a
C D
quiet place to study. No error
E

42. The speaker claimed that no other modern
nation devotes so small a portion of its wealth
A B C
to public assistance and health as the United States
D
does. No error
E

43. The thought of trying to persuade their three-year-
A B
old to sit in a high chair did not appeal to either the
C
mother nor the father. No error
D E

44. The bright fiberglass sculptures of Luis Jiménez
A
has received critical acclaim not only in his home
B C
state, New Mexico, but also in New York. No error
D E

45. Doctors see a connection between increased amounts
A B
of leisure time spent sunbathing and the increased
C
number of cases of skin cancer. No error
D E

46. Whether or not credit card companies should prevent
A
their customers to acquire substantial debts was the
B C
issue discussed at the meeting. No error
D E

47. The board's final recommendations included hiring
A
additional personnel, dismissing the head of research,
B C
and a reorganized marketing division. No error
D E

48. Some people prefer attending movies to television
A B
because they dislike the frequent interruptions of
C D
programs for commercials. No error
E

49. Like many factory workers of a century ago,
A B
women today are developing organizations to
C
represent their interests. No error
D E

50. In a prominent city newspaper, they claim that the
A
number of unregistered participants in this year's
B C
marathon was half that of last year's. No error
D E

IF YOU FINISH BEFORE TIME IS CALLED, YOU MAY CHECK YOUR WORK ON THIS SECTION ONLY. DO NOT WORK ON ANY OTHER SECTION IN THE TEST. **STOP**

SECTION 4 | Time—30 minutes 40 Questions | For each question in this section, choose the best answer and blacken the corresponding space on the answer sheet.

Each question below consists of a word in capital letters, followed by five lettered words or phrases. Choose the word or phrase that is most nearly opposite in meaning to the word in capital letters. Since some of the questions require you to distinguish fine shades of meaning, consider all the choices before deciding which is best.

Example:

GOOD: (A) sour (B) bad (C) red (D) hot (E) ugly

Ⓐ ● Ⓒ Ⓓ Ⓔ

1. RECALL: (A) oppose (B) forget (C) injure (D) assist (E) quiet
2. INTERCEDE: (A) render harmless (B) stand aside (C) direct incompetently (D) protect publicly (E) convene hastily
3. GRANDIOSE: (A) attractive (B) unhealthy (C) bright and shiny (D) small and unimpressive (E) soft and manageable
4. UNNERVE: (A) warn (B) release (C) evaluate (D) strengthen (E) believe
5. RUFFIANISM: (A) gentle behavior (B) cold disdain (C) false piety (D) ignorant statement (E) wishful thinking
6. PALPABLE: (A) retroactive (B) decorative (C) imperturbable (D) not tangible (E) not trustworthy
7. MIRED: (A) dismissed (B) corrected (C) unsound (D) unhampered (E) unregulated
8. DISPARAGE: (A) praise profusely (B) surrender silently (C) fraternize (D) exorcise (E) reprieve
9. DISSONANCE: (A) practicality (B) agreement (C) probability (D) loyalty (E) cheerfulness
10. CAJOLE: (A) animate (B) browbeat (C) measure up to (D) work intensively (E) determine rapidly

Each sentence below has one or two blanks, each blank indicating that something has been omitted. Beneath the sentence are five lettered words or sets of words. Choose the word or set of words that best fits the meaning of the sentence as a whole.

Example:

Although its publicity has been ----, the film itself is intelligent, well-acted, handsomely produced, and altogether ----.

(A) tasteless..respectable (B) extensive..moderate (C) sophisticated..amateur (D) risqué..crude (E) perfect..spectacular

● Ⓑ Ⓒ Ⓓ Ⓔ

11. Medieval kingdoms did not become constitutional republics overnight; on the contrary, the change was ----.

    (A) unpopular (B) unexpected (C) advantageous (D) sufficient (E) gradual

12. This carefully researched book is useful because it ---- the ---- concerns and influences that have connected women writers over three centuries.

    (A) omits..essential
    (B) distorts..ephemeral
    (C) charts..underlying
    (D) dispels..unimpeachable
    (E) foresees..documented

13. The reef's fragile surface of living polyps is probably more ---- to wounds and infection than a child's skin; indeed, merely brushing against living coral ---- its delicate protoplasm.

    (A) resistant..revives (B) susceptible..enhances (C) immune..imperils (D) vulnerable..damages (E) attractive..impairs

GO ON TO THE NEXT PAGE

14. Though discrepant popular belief makes the findings appear to be ----, recent behavioral studies suggest that most teen-agers are actually happy.

(A) discriminating (B) heretical
(C) anticipated (D) obligatory
(E) depressing

15. The validity of her experimental findings was so ---- that even the most ---- investigators could not refrain from extolling her.

(A) enigmatic. .officious
(B) fallacious. .credulous
(C) unassailable. .disputatious
(D) inevitable. .convivial
(E) dubious. .skeptical

Each question below consists of a related pair of words or phrases, followed by five lettered pairs of words or phrases. Select the lettered pair that best expresses a relationship similar to that expressed in the original pair.

Example:

YAWN:BOREDOM :: (A) dream:sleep
(B) anger:madness (C) smile:amusement
(D) face:expression (E) impatience:rebellion

Ⓐ Ⓑ ● Ⓓ Ⓔ

16. HEIGHT:MOUNTAIN :: (A) depth:trench
(B) shade:tree (C) weight:age
(D) speed:highway (E) mineral:mine

17. CENSUS:POPULATION ::
(A) election:government (B) criterion:judgment
(C) inventory:stock (D) drought:thirst
(E) recipe:cake

18. POET:WORDS :: (A) sculptor:stone
(B) painter:artistry (C) sailor:ocean
(D) physician:care (E) philosopher:book

19. CONTEMPLATION:THINKER ::
(A) corrosion:chemist (B) construction:builder
(C) sullenness:fighter (D) hesitation:liar
(E) pain:soldier

20. RIDDLED:HOLES :: (A) untangled:knots
(B) wrinkled:materials (C) flawed:repairs
(D) pitted:indentations (E) sharpened:injuries

21. MUSE:INSPIRATION :: (A) editor:personality
(B) model:criticism (C) epic:superstition
(D) plot:characterization (E) patron:support

22. VEHEMENT:ENERGY ::
(A) domineering:caution
(B) compassionate:sympathy
(C) dauntless:fear
(D) ruthless:suspicion
(E) amiable:apathy

23. FLAGRANT:OBSERVER ::
(A) blaring:listener
(B) monotonous:speaker
(C) mischievous:prankster
(D) temporary:visitor
(E) aggressive:attacker

24. ASTUTE:INSIGHT :: (A) dutiful:efficiency
(B) affable:friendliness (C) gullible:dependence
(D) zealous:nobility (E) proud:ambition

25. LABOR:RESPITE :: (A) opinion:dissent
(B) commitment:betrayal (C) action:resentment
(D) error:erasure (E) debate:lull

GO ON TO THE NEXT PAGE

Each passage below is followed by questions based on its content. Answer all questions following a passage on the basis of what is stated or implied in that passage.

However one chooses to define weather and climate, there is a simple practical distinction between them: weather is a matter of everyday experience, whereas climate is a statistical generalization of that experience. Weather is what usually interests us, but to interpret it correctly we must first determine what the underlying climate is in general; otherwise, we have no yardstick for comparison. In a sense, climate is like the carrier wave in radio broadcasting on which the irregular signals of programming–weather–are superimposed. We have to study the "normal" distribution of the meteorological elements before we can begin to understand the "variability around the norm" that constitutes weather.

Of all the climatic elements, solar radiation is the most basic. The intensity and duration of sunshine is a partial indication of this radiation, but there are also invisible parts of the radiation that have not by any means been as closely studied. Cloud cover is possibly the next most important because it determines both how much solar radiation reaches the ground and how much is radiated back into space from the Earth's surface. Temperature, which depends on radiation, influences cloud cover and controls humidity, and is obviously important in itself. Winds and pressure are interdependent, the latter representing the weight of the atmosphere, the former representing the air movement that ensues when adjacent vertical columns of the atmosphere have different weights. Humidity indicates the amount of water in vapor form in the atmosphere; precipitation measures the amount of water in its liquid or solid phase that falls to the Earth's surface.

26. Which of the following is the best title for the passage?

(A) Weather and Its Consequences
(B) Technology and Climate
(C) Can Weather Be Controlled?
(D) Climate: A Mixed Blessing
(E) The Components of Climate

27. Which of the following comparisons most closely parallels the relationship between weather and climate described in the first paragraph?

(A) A particular game to a team's season record
(B) A heat-seeking missile to a fighter plane
(C) A bacterium to its colony
(D) An element to a compound
(E) A waterfall to a lake

28. It can be inferred from the passage that the definition of precipitation includes which of the following?

I. Water vapor
II. Rain and snow
III. Hail and sleet

(A) II only (B) I and II only (C) I and III only (D) II and III only (E) I, II, and III

GO ON TO THE NEXT PAGE

"It seems very odd, very sad," Margaret returned, "that you can never act unselfishly in society affairs. If I wished to go and see those girls just to do them a pleasure, and perhaps because they're new in town and lonely, I might do them good, even—but it would be impossible."

"Quite," said her aunt. "Such a thing would be quixotic. Society doesn't rest upon any such basis. It can't; it would go to pieces if people acted from unselfish motives."

"Then it isn't society at all!" said the girl. "All its favors are really bargains. Its gifts are for gifts back again."

"Yes, that is true," said Mrs. Horn, with no more sense of a judgment in the fact than the political economist has in the fact that wages are the measure of necessity and not of merit. "You get what you pay for. It's a matter of business." She satisfied herself with this formula, but she did not dislike her niece's revolt against it. That was part of Margaret's originality, which pleased her aunt in proportion to her own conventionality; she was really a timid person, and she liked the show of courage which Margaret's magnanimity often reflected upon her. She thought that she set bounds to the girl's originality because she recognized them. Margaret understood this better than her aunt and knew that she had consulted her about going to see the girls out of deference and with no expectation of luminous instruction.

29. Mrs. Horn would most likely consider which of the following a good example of the way society actually works?

(A) A celebrity lavishly supports a charity organization solely to obtain favorable publicity.
(B) A city government intervenes to halt construction of a shopping center in a residential district.
(C) A parent provides a child with high ideals but cannot translate theory into practice.
(D) A building contractor secretly replaces expensive materials with shabby and inadequate goods.
(E) A doctor receives a prestigious award for the discovery of a cure for a dangerous disease.

30. According to the passage, Margaret asked Mrs. Horn's opinion because she

(A) wished to emulate her aunt's behavior in society
(B) could not choose a suitable course of action
(C) thought she would receive good advice
(D) needed to bolster her aunt's self-confidence
(E) wanted to show respect for her aunt

31. According to the passage, Mrs. Horn sees her relationship with Margaret as one in which she

(A) protects Margaret from the natural evil of society
(B) consoles Margaret in her disillusionment and loss of innocence
(C) enlightens Margaret by pointing out limitations of her ideas
(D) humiliates Margaret through constant proof that she is wrong
(E) irritates Margaret by frequent intrusions into her personal life

GO ON TO THE NEXT PAGE

Rodents are the largest order of mammals, both in number of species and in individuals, outnumbering all other warm-blooded quadrupeds and bipeds combined. There is considerable variation in this order, which includes beavers, porcupines, rats, lemmings, badgers, and the familiar cage pets, gerbils and hamsters. Rodents are ubiquitous, inhabiting almost every continent, either as natives or as immigrants. Most are hypertense and forever on the alert for predators, since rodents are the principal item on the menus of most furred and feathered carnivores. The common denominator among rodents is their teeth—oversize, chisel-like incisors that grow constantly throughout their lives and that are kept sharp and trimmed by constant chewing on wood, nuts, plaster walls, or other hard matter. Untrimmed, their teeth will grow into inward-curving tusks that can seriously injure or even kill them.

The most familiar rodents are rats and mice, whose usefulness as laboratory animals and as important links in the food chain is virtually unrivaled. In laboratories all over the world, domesticated rats and mice are the prime subjects of scientific experiments and research projects that aim to cure human diseases and determine the effects of myriad drugs on human beings. Because rodents are similar to humans in the adaptability of their eating habits, rats and mice are invaluable to scientists doing studies on diet and nutrition. Another asset is the rodents' life span; in the wild, rats and mice rarely live longer than one year because they are preyed on by a large number of animals, including snakes, dogs, cats, owls, and hawks, but in captivity they may live as long as three years. Such a period is just right for studies on aging, growth, and heredity. In addition, rats and mice are a perfect size to house and handle with ease in laboratories. In the United States alone, scientific studies use some 18 million rats each year. It is the rare person who has not reaped, directly or indirectly, the benefits of the medical and psychological research done with these adaptable rodents.

To most people, the destructiveness and havoc rats and mice wreak on the environment far outweigh any of their virtues. Yet the vast majority of rodents are actually beneficial and essential to the overall balance of nature; they furnish food for other animals and prey on insects, whose numbers they keep in check. These rodents should never be confused with the true villains of the order: the brown or Norway rat, the black rat, and the innocent-looking house mouse. As carriers of plague, typhus, and other epidemic diseases, this trio has inflicted death and misery on the world since prehistoric times. The Black Death, the most catastrophic plague in history, killed approximately one-quarter of the population of medieval Europe and was almost certainly spread by rats, which serve as hosts for plague-bearing fleas.

32. The author states that the laboratory rodents' life span is especially helpful to scientists studying
(A) the effect of captivity on laboratory animals
(B) means of controlling the rodent population
(C) population distribution and predatory patterns
(D) genetic characteristics and growth patterns
(E) the social habits of rodents

33. The passage mentions all of the following facts about rodents EXCEPT that they
(A) eat insects
(B) are amphibious
(C) are easy to handle
(D) chew constantly
(E) can eat a variety of foods

34. It can be inferred that the author thinks rodents are useful for all of the following reasons EXCEPT that they
(A) tend to be very alert
(B) can make excellent laboratory animals
(C) are similar to humans in some ways
(D) are a source of food for other animals
(E) are an important part of the balance of nature

35. According to the author, which of the following is (are) true of rodents?
I. They are a staple in the diets of many predators.
II. Many laboratory rodents live longer than wild rodents do.
III. Most species spread devastating diseases.
(A) I only
(B) II only
(C) III only
(D) I and II only
(E) II and III only

36. Which of the following best describes the development of this passage?
(A) Major points, minor points
(B) Statement of problem, examples, proposed solution
(C) Introduction, positive factors, negative factors
(D) Introduction, cause, results
(E) Thesis, analogy, antithesis

GO ON TO THE NEXT PAGE

"What if all scientists were to publish anonymously?" I was asked this question recently by Dr. Lester Green. "Don't you think," he continued, "that scientific literature would be far less cluttered with nearly useless and carelessly produced articles were the authors to receive no public credit for their contributions? We might, in fact, be able to achieve that great nirvana in which science would be practiced for its own sake, rather than for fame and fortune."

What lies at the heart of the notion pondered by Green is the idea that individual and community interests are necessarily separate entities. Does Green seriously believe that the best interests of society would be served by depersonalizing science? Would he suggest that artists not sign their paintings?

"The highest form of vanity is love of fame," wrote George Santayana. But is an ambition for fame the worst reason for practicing science? Dr. Samuel Johnson said, "None but a blockhead ever wrote except for money." We scientists might paraphrase him, "None but a blockhead ever published a scientific article except for recognition."

Furthermore, anonymity leads to secrecy and secrecy in science is deplorable. Even when countries are at war, recognition of individual performance is necessary. True, scientists have, during periods of crisis such as the Second World War, sacrificed public recognition. In time, however, most of the important breakthroughs were credited to their discoverers.

37. The author's purpose in the passage is apparently to

(A) trace the history of an idea
(B) merge two differing views of an issue
(C) discredit the majority of research scientists
(D) argue against a proposed change
(E) demand a new set of standards

38. It can be inferred that Dr. Green is dissatisfied with the

(A) desire for anonymity among noted scientists
(B) overall quality of articles appearing in scientific literature
(C) small number of articles published by scientists
(D) recent emphasis on secrecy in the scientific community
(E) lack of recognition given to scientists who publish articles

39. Which of the following best describes the author's attitude toward the "nirvana" (line 8) mentioned by Dr. Green?

(A) Excited enthusiasm
(B) Indulgent tolerance
(C) Fascinated curiosity
(D) Cautious skepticism
(E) Disapproving dismissal

40. The author implies that an artist who did not sign his or her painting should be regarded as

(A) a fool (B) a martyr (C) an egotist (D) a conformist (E) a pioneer

IF YOU FINISH BEFORE TIME IS CALLED, YOU MAY CHECK YOUR WORK ON THIS SECTION ONLY. DO NOT WORK ON ANY OTHER SECTION IN THE TEST. STOP

SECTION 5 Time—30 minutes 35 Questions

In this section solve each problem, using any available space on the page for scratchwork. Then decide which is the best of the choices given and blacken the corresponding space on the answer sheet.

The following information is for your reference in solving some of the problems.

Circle of radius r: Area $= \pi r^2$; Circumference $= 2\pi r$
The number of degrees of arc in a circle is 360.
The measure in degrees of a straight angle is 180.

Definitions of symbols:

$=$ is equal to	$\leqq$ is less than or equal to
$\neq$ is unequal to	$\geqq$ is greater than or equal to
$<$ is less than	$\parallel$ is parallel to
$>$ is greater than	$\perp$ is perpendicular to

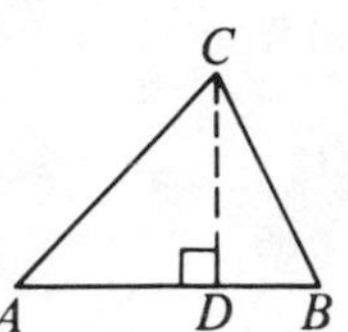

Triangle: The sum of the measures in degrees of the angles of a triangle is 180.

If $\angle CDA$ is a right angle, then

(1) area of $\triangle ABC = \dfrac{AB \times CD}{2}$

(2) $AC^2 = AD^2 + DC^2$

Note: Figures that accompany problems in this test are intended to provide information useful in solving the problems. They are drawn as accurately as possible EXCEPT when it is stated in a specific problem that its figure is not drawn to scale. All figures lie in a plane unless otherwise indicated. All numbers used are real numbers.

1. A man's grocery bill is \$8, but the store deducts \$1.50 from his bill for coupons. If the man gives the grocery clerk \$10, how much change should he get?

(A) \$8.50
(B) \$6.50
(C) \$5.50
(D) \$4.50
(E) \$3.50

2. Which of the following numbers is divisible by 3 and 5, but not by 2 ?

(A) 955
(B) 975
(C) 990
(D) 995
(E) 999

3. The members of a club decided to wash cars in order to earn money for the club. Each member of the club washed 3 cars and charged \$2 per car. When they had finished, their receipts totalled \$66, which included \$6 in tips. How many members were in the club?

(A) 9
(B) 10
(C) 11
(D) 20
(E) 22

4. If x and y are positive integers such that $x^2 + y^2 = 13$ and $x > y$, then $x - y =$

(A) 1 (B) 2 (C) 3 (D) 4 (E) 5

5. If the perimeter of a rectangular garden plot is 80 meters, which of the following could be the length of one of its sides?

I. 30 meters
II. 40 meters
III. 50 meters

(A) I only (B) II only (C) III only
(D) I and II (E) II and III

6. A wire of uniform diameter and composition that weighs 32 pounds is cut into two pieces. One piece is 90 yards long and weighs 24 pounds. What was the length, in yards, of the original wire?

(A) 60
(B) 120
(C) 135
(D) 270
(E) 360

7. If $\frac{1}{2}$ of a number is 2 more than $\frac{1}{3}$ of the number, what is the number?

(A) 2
(B) 6
(C) 12
(D) 20
(E) 24

GO ON TO THE NEXT PAGE

Questions 8-27 each consist of two quantities, one in Column A and one in Column B. You are to compare the two quantities and on the answer sheet blacken space

A if the quantity in Column A is greater;
B if the quantity in Column B is greater;
C if the two quantities are equal;
D if the relationship cannot be determined from the information given.

AN E RESPONSE WILL NOT BE SCORED.

EXAMPLES

	Column A	Column B	Answers
E1.	2×6	$2 + 6$	● Ⓑ Ⓒ Ⓓ Ⓔ
E2.	$180 - x$	y	Ⓐ Ⓑ ● Ⓓ Ⓔ
E3.	$p - q$	$q - p$	Ⓐ Ⓑ Ⓒ ● Ⓔ

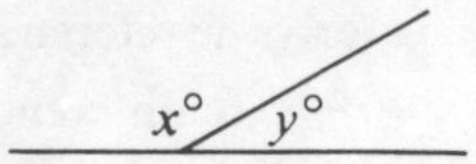

Notes:
1. In certain questions, information concerning one or both of the quantities to be compared is centered above the two columns.
2. In a given question, a symbol that appears in both columns represents the same thing in Column A as it does in Column B.
3. Letters such as x, n, and k stand for real numbers.

	Column A	Column B
8.	$\frac{1}{3} - \frac{1}{5}$	$\frac{2}{15}$

n is a negative integer.

9.	$n \times n \times n \times n$	$n + n + n + n$

$P = \{1, 2, 3, 4\}$
$Q = \{1, 2, 3, 4, 5\}$

10.	The number that is a member of set Q but not of set P	A number that is a member of both sets P and Q

$x = \frac{1}{4}$

$y = \frac{1}{2}$

11.	$\frac{x}{y}$	$\frac{y}{x}$
12.	The number of edges of a cube	The number of faces of a cube

n is an integer.

13.	The remainder when n is divided by 9	The remainder when n is divided by 6

	Column A	Column B
14.	Average (arithmetic mean) of −9, −8, 8, and 9	Average (arithmetic mean) of −7, −6, 0, 6, and 7

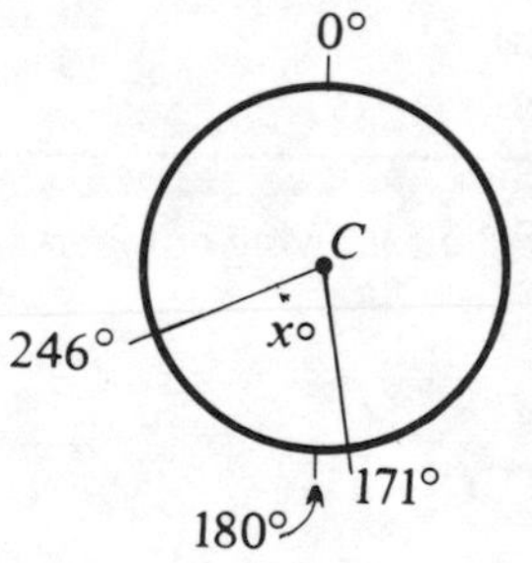

C is the center of the circle.
$x > 0$

15.	x	66

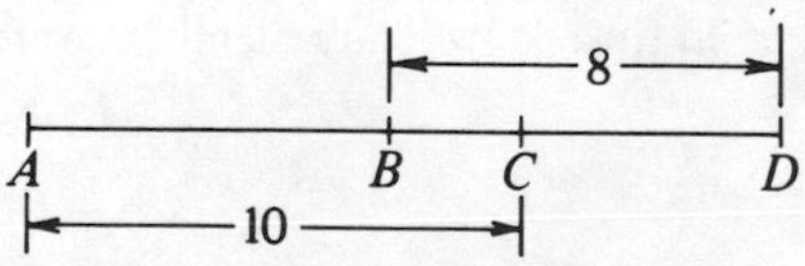

16.	Length of AD	18

GO ON TO THE NEXT PAGE

SUMMARY DIRECTIONS FOR COMPARISON QUESTIONS

Answer:
- A if the quantity in Column A is greater;
- B if the quantity in Column B is greater;
- C if the two quantities are equal;
- D if the relationship cannot be determined from the information given.

AN E RESPONSE WILL NOT BE SCORED.

	Column A	Column B
	$-5 < x < -3$ $-7 < y < -5$ x and y are even integers.	
17.	x	y

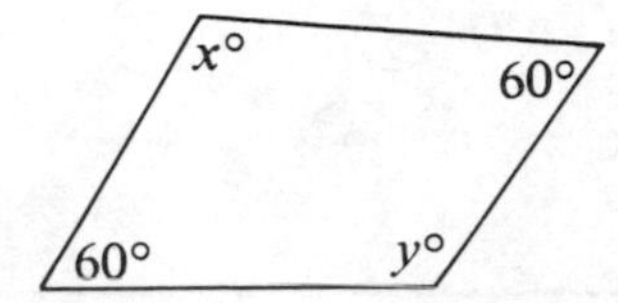

Note: Figure not drawn to scale.

	Column A	Column B
18.	x	y

$x - 2 = y$

	Column A	Column B
19.	$x - 4$	v
20.	$\frac{4}{\sqrt{2}}$	$2\sqrt{2}$

$x = 501$
$y = 500$

	Column A	Column B
21.	$(x + y)(x - y)$	1,000

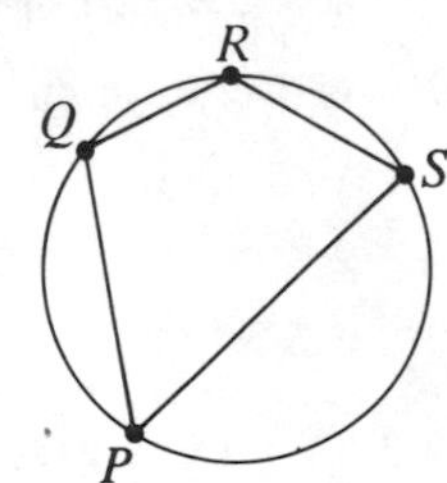

The diameter of the circle is 1.
P, Q, R, and S are on the circumference of the circle.

	Column A	Column B
22.	Perimeter of quadrilateral $PQRS$	4

A fair six-sided die with faces numbered 1 through 6 is to be rolled twice.

	Column A	Column B
23.	The probability of obtaining a 6 on the top face on the first roll and a 5 on the top face on the second roll	The probability of obtaining a 5 on the top face on both the first and second rolls

x and y are consecutive terms of a sequence whose terms alternate, $1, -2, 1, -2, 1, -2$, etc.

	Column A	Column B
24.	$x + y$	$x - y$

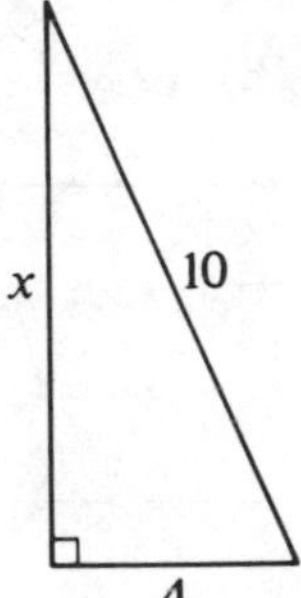

	Column A	Column B
25.	x	9
26.	$0.7x + 0.9y$	$0.7(x + y)$

a, b, and c are positive.

	Column A	Column B
27.	Average (arithmetic mean) of a, b, and c	Average (arithmetic mean) of a^2, b^2, and c^2

Solve each of the remaining problems in this section using any available space for scratchwork. Then decide which is the best of the choices given and blacken the corresponding space on the answer sheet.

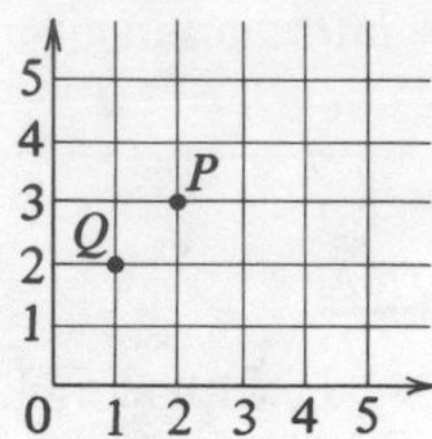

28. Which of the following points, when plotted on the grid above, will be twice as far from $P(2, 3)$ as from $Q(1, 2)$?

(A) (0, 1) (B) (0, 3) (C) (1, 3)
(D) (3, 4) (E) (3, 5)

29. If 15 kilograms of pure water is added to 10 kilograms of pure alcohol, what percent by weight of the resulting solution is alcohol?

(A) $66\frac{2}{3}\%$ (B) 40% (C) 25%
(D) 15% (E) 10%

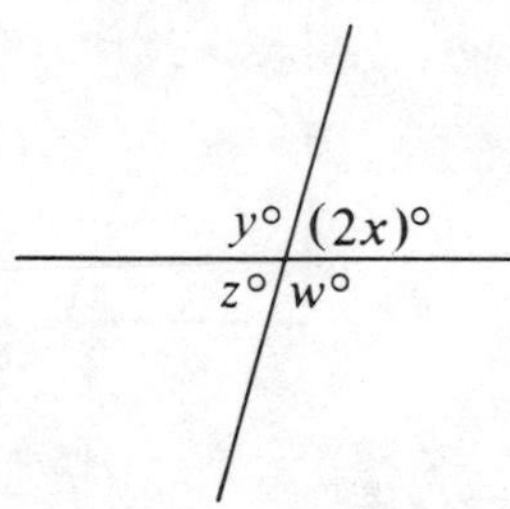

30. In the figure above two lines intersect. Which of the following must equal $180 - x$?

(A) $x + y$ (B) $x + z$ (C) $y + z$
(D) $y + w$ (E) $z + w$

31. If $s = 1 + \frac{1}{2} + \frac{1}{4} + \frac{1}{8} + \frac{1}{16} + \frac{1}{32}$ and $t = 1 + \frac{1}{2}s$, then t exceeds s by

(A) $\frac{1}{4}$ (B) $\frac{1}{8}$ (C) $\frac{1}{16}$ (D) $\frac{1}{32}$ (E) $\frac{1}{64}$

Questions 32-33 refer to the following definition.

For all positive integers n,

let $\textcircled{n} = \frac{1}{2}n$ if n is even;

let $\textcircled{n} = 2n$ if n is odd.

32. If y is a prime number greater than 2, then $\textcircled{y} =$

(A) $\frac{1}{4}y$ (B) $\frac{1}{2}y$ (C) y (D) $2y$ (E) $4y$

33. $\textcircled{5} \cdot \textcircled{10} =$

(A) $\textcircled{15}$ (B) $\textcircled{30}$ (C) $\textcircled{50}$
(D) $\textcircled{100}$ (E) $\textcircled{200}$

34. In the figure above, the radius of the smaller circle is half the radius of the larger circle. If the circles have the same center O, what is the ratio of the area of the shaded region to the area of the larger circle?

(A) 4:5 (B) 3:4 (C) 1:2
(D) 1:4 (E) 1:8

35. If the operation Δ is defined for all positive x and y by $x \Delta y = \frac{xy}{x + y}$, which of the following must be true for positive x, y, and z?

I. $x \Delta x = \frac{1}{2}x$

II. $x \Delta y = y \Delta x$

III. $x \Delta (y \Delta z) = (x \Delta y) \Delta z$

(A) I only (B) I and II only (C) I and III only
(D) II and III only (E) I, II, and III

IF YOU FINISH BEFORE TIME IS CALLED, YOU MAY CHECK YOUR WORK ON THIS SECTION ONLY. DO NOT WORK ON ANY OTHER SECTION IN THE TEST. **STOP**

How to Score the Sample Test

Before you can find out what your scores are on the College Board 200 to 800 scale, you need to determine your verbal, mathematical, and TSWE raw scores. The steps for doing so for each section of the test and a scoring worksheet are provided below and on page 62. Use the table on page 63 to determine your correct and incorrect answers for each section.

Determining Your Raw Scores

SAT-Verbal Sections 1 and 4

Step A: Count the number of correct answers for section 1 and record the number in the space provided on the worksheet. Then do the same for the incorrect answers. (Do not count omitted answers.) To determine subtotal A, use the formula:

$$\text{number correct} - \frac{\text{number incorrect}}{4} = \text{subtotal A}$$

Step B: Count the number of correct answers and the number of incorrect answers for section 4 and record the numbers in the spaces provided on the worksheet. To determine subtotal B, use the formula:

$$\text{number correct} - \frac{\text{number incorrect}}{4} = \text{subtotal B}$$

Step C: To obtain C, add subtotal A to subtotal B, keeping any decimals. Enter the resulting figure on the worksheet.

Step D: To obtain D, your raw verbal score, round C to the nearest whole number. (For example, any number from 44.50 to 45.49 rounds to 45.) Enter the resulting figure on the worksheet.

SAT-Mathematical Sections 2 and 5

Step A: Count the number of correct answers and the number of incorrect answers for section 2 and record the numbers in the spaces provided on the worksheet. To determine subtotal A, use the formula:

$$\text{number correct} - \frac{\text{number incorrect}}{4} = \text{subtotal A}$$

Step B: Count the number of correct answers and the number of incorrect answers for the *five-choice questions (questions 1 through 7 and 28 through 35)* in section 5 and record the numbers in the spaces provided on the worksheet. To determine subtotal B, use the formula:

$$\text{number correct} - \frac{\text{number incorrect}}{4} = \text{subtotal B}$$

Step C: Count the number of correct answers and the number of incorrect answers for the *four-choice questions (questions 8 through 27)* in section 5 and record the numbers in the spaces provided on the worksheet. To determine subtotal C, use the formula:

$$\text{number correct} - \frac{\text{number incorrect}}{3} = \text{subtotal C}$$

Note: Do not count any E responses to questions 8 through 27 as correct or incorrect. Because these four-choice questions have no E answer choices, E responses to these questions are treated as omits.

Step D: To obtain D, add subtotal A, subtotal B, and subtotal C, keeping any decimals. Enter the resulting figure on the worksheet.

Step E: To obtain E, your raw mathematical score, round D to the nearest whole number. (For example, any number from 44.50 to 45.49 rounds to 45.) Enter the resulting figure on the worksheet.

TSWE: Section 3

Step A: Count the number of correct answers for section 3 and record the number in the space provided on the worksheet. Then do the same for the incorrect answers. (Do not count omitted answers.) To determine your unrounded raw score, use the formula:

$$\text{number correct} - \frac{\text{number incorrect}}{4} = \text{total unrounded raw score}$$

Step B: To obtain B, your raw TSWE score, round A to the nearest whole number. (For example, any number from 34.50 to 35.49 rounds to 35.) Enter the resulting figure on the worksheet.

SCORING WORKSHEET FOR THE SAMPLE TEST

SAT-Verbal Sections

A. Section 1: ________ − 1/4 (________) = ________
no. correct — no. incorrect — subtotal A

B. Section 4: ________ − 1/4 (________) = ________
no. correct — no. incorrect — subtotal B

C. Total unrounded raw score (Total A + B) ________ C

D. Total rounded raw verbal score (Rounded to nearest whole number) ________ D

SAT-Mathematical Sections

A. Section 2: ________ − 1/4 (________) = ________
no. correct — no. incorrect — subtotal A

B. Section 5: Questions 1 through 7 and 28 through 35 (5-choice) ________ − 1/4 (________) = ________
no. correct — no. incorrect — subtotal B

C. Section 5: Questions 8 through 27 (4-choice) ________ − 1/3 (________) = ________
no. correct — no. incorrect — subtotal C

D. Total unrounded raw score (Total A + B + C) ________ D

E. Total rounded raw math score (Rounded to nearest whole number) ________ E

TSWE

A. Section 3: Total unrounded raw score ________ − 1/4 (________) = ________
no. correct — no. incorrect — A

B. Total rounded raw TSWE score (Rounded to nearest whole number) ________ B

ANSWERS TO SAMPLE TEST QUESTIONS AND PERCENTAGE OF STUDENTS ANSWERING EACH QUESTION CORRECTLY

Section 1—Verbal

Question number	Correct answer	Percentage of students answering the question correctly
1	A	94%
2	C	97
3	B	89
4	D	87
5	B	80
6	E	63
7	E	66
8	D	42
9	C	49
10	B	36
11	B	30
12	B	27
13	E	32
14	A	20
15	A	24
16	D	79
17	A	64
18	D	31
19	D	32
20	C	40
21	C	47
22	A	87
23	E	83
24	B	68
25	E	47
26	B	79
27	C	55
28	E	69
29	A	68
30	D	49
31	C	35
32	B	36
33	D	31
34	C	20
35	B	18
36	A	88
37	C	70
38	D	71
39	B	56
40	E	28
41	B	41
42	D	31
43	B	32
44	B	22
45	E	23

Section 2—Mathematical

Question number	Correct answer	Percentage of students answering the question correctly
1	D	78%
2	B	93
3	D	88
4	B	87
5	B	64
6	A	81
7	C	76
8	B	82
9	B	75
10	E	64
11	C	70
12	E	43
13	C	65
14	D	63
15	A	44
16	C	40
17	E	39
18	D	37
19	C	22
20	C	23
21	A	18
22	E	22
23	C	18
24	A	18
25	E	14

Section 3—TSWE

Question number	Correct answer	Percentage of students answering the question correctly
1	C	86%
2	B	91
3	B	81
4	A	84
5	C	87
6	E	90
7	D	77
8	C	78
9	C	71
10	E	78
11	B	82
12	A	74
13	D	73
14	A	91
15	D	50
16	E	68
17	B	60
18	C	57
19	B	65
20	D	52
21	E	79
22	A	44
23	C	62
24	C	39
25	B	67
26	B	94
27	C	68
28	D	83
29	A	79
30	A	50
31	E	65
32	D	63
33	A	82
34	C	69
35	B	90
36	C	54
37	D	70
38	E	40
39	A	60
40	D	44
41	D	76
42	E	70
43	D	68
44	B	59
45	E	59
46	C	53
47	D	62
48	B	50
49	E	46
50	A	45

Section 4—Verbal

Question number	Correct answer	Percentage of students answering the question correctly
1	B	89%
2	B	83
3	D	76
4	D	65
5	A	64
6	D	41
7	D	34
8	A	35
9	B	25
10	B	24
11	E	90
12	C	74
13	D	84
14	B	22
15	C	18
16	A	89
17	C	84
18	A	72
19	B	62
20	D	49
21	E	37
22	B	35
23	A	35
24	B	22
25	E	17
26	E	77
27	A	49
28	D	46
29	A	62
30	E	23
31	C	61
32	D	80
33	B	61
34	A	64
35	D	60
36	C	69
37	D	26
38	B	44
39	E	13
40	A	50

Section 5—Mathematical

Question number	Correct answer	Percentage of students answering the question correctly
1	E	92%
2	B	75
3	B	79
4	A	69
5	A	70
6	B	62
7	C	70
8	C	80
9	A	80
10	A	82
11	B	74
12	A	80
13	D	59
14	C	78
15	A	59
16	B	75
17	A	71
18	D	26
19	B	60
20	C	56
21	A	83
22	B	36
23	C	38
24	D	22
25	A	56
26	D	25
27	D	14
28	A	56
29	B	44
30	A	32
31	E	27
32	D	45
33	D	16
34	B	16
35	E	10

Notes: The percentages for the SAT-verbal and SAT-mathematical sections are based on the analysis of the answer sheets for a random sample of juniors and seniors who took this test in May 1983 and whose mean scores were 438 on the SAT-verbal sections and 481 on the SAT-mathematical sections.

The percentages for TSWE are based on the analysis of the answer sheets for a random sample of all students who took this test in June 1981 and whose mean score was 43.

SCORE CONVERSION TABLE
Sample SAT and TSWE

Raw Score	College Board Scaled Score		Raw Score	College Board Scaled Score		Raw Score	College Board Scaled Score
	SAT-Verbal	SAT-Math		SAT-Verbal	SAT-Math		TSWE
85	800		40	460	610		
84	780		39	450	600		
83	770		38	450	590		
82	760		37	440	580		
81	750		36	430	570	50	60 +
80	740		35	430	560	49	60 +
79	730		34	420	550	48	60 +
78	720		33	420	540	47	60 +
77	710		32	410	530	46	59
76	700		31	400	520	45	58
75	690		30	400	510	44	57
74	680		29	390	500	43	56
73	670		28	380	490	42	55
72	660		27	380	480	41	54
71	660		26	370	470	40	53
70	650		25	360	460	39	52
69	640		24	360	450	38	51
68	630		23	350	450	37	50
67	630		22	340	440	36	49
66	620		21	340	430	35	48
65	610		20	330	420	34	47
64	600		19	320	410	33	46
63	600		18	320	400	32	45
62	590		17	310	390	31	44
61	580		16	300	380	30	43
60	580	800	15	290	380	29	42
59	570	780	14	290	370	28	41
58	570	770	13	280	360	27	40
57	560	760	12	270	350	26	39
56	550	750	11	270	340	25	38
55	550	740	10	260	340	24	37
54	540	740	9	250	330	23	36
53	530	730	8	240	320	22	35
52	530	720	7	240	310	21	34
51	520	710	6	230	310	20	33
50	520	700	5	220	300	19	32
49	510	690	4	220	290	18	31
48	510	680	3	210	280	17	30
47	500	670	2	200	280	16	29
46	490	660	1	200	270	15	28
45	490	660	0	200	260	14	27
44	480	650	−1	200	250	13	26
43	480	640	−2	200	250	12	25
42	470	630	−3	200	240	11	24
41	460	620	−4	200	230	10	22
			−5	200	220	9	21
			−6	200	210	8	20
			−7	200	210	or below	
			−8 or below	200	200		

Finding Your College Board Scores

Use the table on page 64 to find the College Board scores that correspond to your raw scores on this edition of the SAT. For example, if you received a raw verbal score of 32 on this edition of the test, your College Board score would be 410. If your raw mathematical score were 22, your raw score would be 440 for this edition. If your raw TSWE score were 31, your College Board score would be 44 for this edition.

Because some editions of the SAT may be slightly easier or more difficult than others, statistical adjustments are made in the scores to ensure that each College Board score indicates the same level of performance, regardless of the edition of the SAT you take. A given raw score will correspond to different College Board scores, depending on the edition of the test taken. A raw score of 40, for example, may convert to a College Board score of 460 on one edition of the SAT, but might convert to a College Board score of 480 on another edition of the test. When you take the SAT, your score is likely to differ somewhat from the score you obtained on the sample test. People perform at different levels at different times, for reasons unrelated to the test itself. The precision of any test is also limited because it represents only a sample of all the possible questions that could be asked.

Reviewing Your Performance on the Sample Test

After you have scored your sample test by following the directions on page 61 and above, analyze your performance.

Asking yourself these questions and following the suggestions can help:

- Did you omit questions because you ran out of time before you reached the end of a section? Reread pages 12 through 33. The suggestions in them may help you pace yourself better.
- Did you spend so much time reading directions that you took time away from answering questions? If you become thoroughly familiar with the test directions printed in this book, you won't have to spend as much time reading them when you take the actual test.
- Look at the specific questions you missed. Did you get caught by a choice that was only partly correct? Figure out what step you overlooked in your reasoning.

How Difficult Were the Questions?

The table on page 63 gives the percentages of a sample of students who chose the correct answer for each question. (These students obtained a mean SAT-verbal score of 438, mean SAT-mathematical score of 481, and mean TSWE score of 43.) These percentages will give you an idea of how difficult each question was.

For example, 80 percent of this group of students answered question 5 in verbal section 1 correctly. However, only 36 percent selected the correct answer for question 10 in section 1. In other words, question 5 was easier than question 10 for the students who took this edition of the SAT.

After the Test

Receiving Your Score Report

About six weeks after you take the SAT and TSWE, you will receive your College Planning Report, which will include your scores, your percentile ranks, and interpretive information. With this report, you'll receive a booklet, *Using Your College Planning Report.* This booklet provides advice on how to use your scores and other information to help you with your college planning.

SAT Question-and-Answer Service

If you take the SAT on one of the dates for which the SAT Question-and-Answer Service is available, you may order the service anytime up to five months after the test. You will receive a copy of your test questions and answer sheet, a list of the correct answers, and scoring instructions. See *Using Your College Planning Report* for additional information and an order form. This service does not apply to the TSWE.

A Sample Score Report

A sample score report for a fictional student is provided on pages 68-69. The report has six major parts:

1. Identification Information
   This is the information that will be used to identify your record, which is stored at Educational Testing Service. If you have any questions about your report, call or write to the College Board's Admissions Testing Program at the address given on page 8.
2. Test Scores
   The next section shows your most recent test scores. SAT scores are shown both as specific numbers and as score ranges to help illustrate that the test cannot measure your abilities with perfect accuracy (see "How Precise Are Your Scores," below).
3. Summary of Test Scores
   This section summarizes your test scores and includes all of your scores from any Admissions Testing Program tests (SAT or Achievement Test) that you have taken at any time while in high school.
4. Educational Background
   This information comes from the Student Descriptive Questionnaire (SDQ), which you fill out when you register to take the test. It describes your high school coursework, summarizes your grades, and gives your grade point average and class rank.
5. Plans for College
   This section includes information about your plans for future study that you reported in the Student Descriptive Questionnaire.
6. Colleges and Scholarship Programs That Received a Score Report
   This is information about the institutions to which you have your scores sent. It includes addresses, telephone numbers, application and financial aid deadlines, and the basis for admissions decisions.

SAT and TSWE Scores

SAT scores are reported on a scale of 200 to 800. You receive separate scores for the verbal and math sections of the SAT. SAT-verbal subscores (reading comprehension and vocabulary) are on a scale of 20 to 80. TSWE scores are reported from 20 to 60+. The tests have no passing or failing scores, and they are not scored on a curve — that is, the scores of other students who took the test with you had no effect on your score.

What Do Your Percentile Ranks Mean?

The percentile ranks on your score report allow you to compare your scores with those of other students. A percentile rank tells you the percentage of students in a given group whose scores were below yours. Remember that the same score can have a different percentile rank for different groups, depending on the ability of the group. (For example, a runner whose time ranks in the 80th percentile when compared with the junior varsity track team might rank in the 50th percentile when compared with the varsity team, which usually has faster runners.)

Percentile ranks on your score report compare your scores with those of "College-bound Seniors/National": all seniors who took the test any time while in high school, and with "College-bound Seniors/State": all seniors in your state who took the test any time while in high school. Your verbal and math scores also are compared with a "National High School Sample," a representative sample of all high school students in the United States who took the PSAT the previous year. Students in the sample were not limited to those considering college or planning to take the SAT.

How Precise Are Your Scores?

When you consider your scores, keep in mind that no test can measure your abilities with perfect accuracy. If you took a different edition of a test or the same edition on different days, your score probably would be different each time. If you were to take a test an infinite number of times, your scores would tend to cluster about an average value. Testing specialists call this average your "true score," the score you would get if a test could measure your ability with perfect accuracy. To measure how much students' obtained scores vary from their true scores, an index called the standard error of measurement (SEM) is used.

For the SAT, the SEM is about 30 points. About

two-thirds of those taking the test score within 30 points (or one SEM) of their true score. If your true score is 430, for example, the chances are about 2 out of 3 that you will score between 400 and 460 (430 plus or minus 30).

You should think of your scores in terms of score ranges rather than precise measurements — a 400 SAT score, for example, should be thought of as being in the 370 to 430 range. This will help you realize that a small difference between your score and another student's on the same test does not indicate any real difference in ability. College admissions officers also are advised to look at scores this way.

Will Your Scores Go Up if You Take the Test Again?

As indicated above, you are not likely to get exactly the same score on a test twice. Improving your score a great deal also is unlikely. Some students who repeat tests do improve their scores, but, on the average, these increases are small.

The *average* increase for a junior who takes the SAT again when a senior is about 15 points for the verbal score and 15 points for the math score. About two out of three students who retake the test improve their scores, but the scores of about one student in three go down. About one student in 20 gains 100 or more points, and about one in 100 loses 100 or more points. Students whose first SAT scores are low are more likely to achieve score gains. Students whose initial scores are high are less likely to achieve score gains.

If you repeat a test, your earlier scores will still appear on your score report. Colleges evaluate multiple scores on the same test in different ways. Some look at all the scores on your report; others use just the highest, most recent, or an average.

Who Receives Your Scores?

A score report will be sent to your high school if you provide your high school code number when you register for the test. Reports also will be sent to all colleges and scholarship programs whose code numbers you give.

The College Board may use your scores and descriptive information for research, but no information that can be identified with you is ever released without your consent.

How Do Colleges Use Your Score Report?

Your SAT scores give college admissions officers an idea of how well you have developed some of the abilities you will need to do well in college courses. The scores also help them to compare you with students from schools with different grading standards. Admissions people know that although your high school grades are the best *single* indicator of your readiness to do college work, a combination of your high school grades and your SAT scores provides a better indicator than either one alone.

Some colleges also use Achievement Tests in making admissions decisions or for course placement, or both. The TSWE is a placement test designed to identify students who may need help in developing their writing skills. Your college may use it to help place you in the freshman English course that is right for you.

Colleges vary in the way they use test scores, but few, if any, make admissions decisions based on scores alone. Therefore, low or high scores should neither discourage you nor make you overconfident. Admissions officers usually consider the descriptive information on your score report as well as other information sent by you and your school.

Different colleges value different qualities in applicants: One college may be looking for leadership potential, while another may place more weight on various extracurricular activities. Some colleges have open admissions policies and admit almost all applicants. Some will admit students who have particular qualities, even if the students' grades and scores indicate they will have to make an extra effort. Whatever your scores, remember that probably there are many colleges that could meet your needs and where you would be happy.

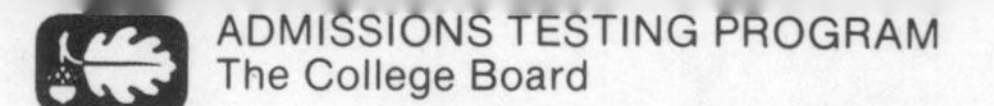

COLLEGE PLANNING REPORT

SCORE REPORT FOR MARGARET K WRIGHT 60600

Sex	Birth Date	Social Security No.	Telephone No.	Registration No.	Ethnic Group	U.S. Citizen	Report Date
F	3/15/68	123-45-6789	111-222-3333	7654321	White	Yes	12/15/85

High School Name and Code	First Language	Religion
JEFFERSON MEMORIAL HIGH SCHOOL 555555	English only	Lutheran Church in America

TEST SCORES — NOVEMBER 1985 SCHOLASTIC APTITUDE TEST

Test	Score	Score Range (200–800)	Percentiles: College-bound Seniors National	College-bound Seniors State	National H.S. Sample
SAT V	480	<<<>>>	67	56	83
SAT MATH	500	<<<<>>>>	59	43	78
TSWE	49		66	53	

See the reverse side of this report for more information about these scores.

SUMMARY OF TEST SCORES

Test Date	Grade Level	SAT Verbal	SAT Verbal Subscores: Reading	SAT Verbal Subscores: Vocabulary	SAT Math	TSWE
Nov 85	12th	480	45	49	500	49
May 84	11th	460	44	47	480	46

Achievement Tests

Test Date	Grade Level	1	2	3
Jun 84	11th	EN 450	BY 500	M1 550

Average of All Reported Achievement Tests 500

EDUCATIONAL BACKGROUND (REPORTED ON STUDENT DESCRIPTIVE QUESTIONNAIRE 11/85)

Courses	Years	Honors	Average Grade	Coursework and Experience
ARTS AND MUSIC	4	Yes	A	Acting/Play Production,Dance,Drama App, Perform Music,Photography/Film,Studio Art
ENGLISH	4	Yes	B	Amer Lit,Comp,Grammar,Other Lit, Speaking/Listening
FOREIGN LANGUAGES	2		B	French
MATHEMATICS	4+	Yes	A	Algebra,Geometry,Trigonometry,Calculus, Computer math
NATURAL SCIENCES	2		B	Biology,Chemistry
SOCIAL SCIENCES	4		A	U.S. Hist,U.S. Govt,European Hist,World Hist, Other
COMPUTER EXPERIENCE				Programming,Math Problems,Word Processing

Grade Point Average A- Class Rank Second tenth

PLANS FOR COLLEGE (REPORTED ON STUDENT DESCRIPTIVE QUESTIONNAIRE 11/85)

Degree Goal	First Choice of Major	Certainty of First Choice
Bachelor's	Arts: Visual and Performing	Very certain

Other Majors Listed	Requested Services
Dramatic arts Art (painting, drawing, sculpture) Engineering/Engineering Technologies	Educational planning Part-time job

Preferred College Characteristics	College Programs and Activities
Type: 4 yr,Public,Private Size: Up to 1,000,10,000 to 20,000, Over 20,000 Setting: Large city,Suburban Distance from home: Undecided Other: Coed,On-campus housing	Art Dance Drama/Theater

Advanced Placement or Exemption Plans

Art,Math

 I.N. 305327

Colleges and Scholarship Programs That Received a Score Report

FOR THE NOVEMBER 1985 TEST ADMINISTRATION

A score report has been sent to the colleges and scholarship programs listed below. The information about the colleges is from *The College Handbook*. For more information about these and other schools, consult the *Handbook* or other materials available in your high school or library and talk with your counselor. Contact the colleges for application materials and additional information.

If you want to have your scores sent to other colleges and scholarship programs, complete an Additional Report Request Form. You received one of these forms with your Admission Ticket. Your high school counselor has additional forms.

1234
City College of Art
3030 West Street
Hill, California 90512
(213) 123-4567

BASIS FOR ADMISSION DECISION: School achievement record is very important. Interview, school and community activities and recommendations are considered.

ADMISSION APPLICATION DEADLINE: Closing date is August 27. Notification is on a continuous rolling basis.

FINANCIAL AID APPLICATION DEADLINE: No closing date; priority date is March 1. Notification is on a rolling basis starting on April 1.

1489
State University
89 Central Street
Center City, Texas 34567
(901) 678-9534

BASIS FOR ADMISSION DECISION: School achievement record, test scores and recommendations are important. Interview and school community activities are considered.

ADMISSION APPLICATION DEADLINE: Closing date is August 1. Applications received by April 1 are given priority. Notification is on a continual rolling basis.

FINANCIAL AID APPLICATION DEADLINE: Closing date is April 1. Notification is on a rolling basis beginning January 30.

7632
St. Michael's College
110 Hilford Street
Bankster, Ohio 06010
(101) 987-6734

BASIS FOR ADMISSION DECISION: School achievement record and test scores are very important. School and community activities and recommendations are important. Interview is considered. Achievement Tests are required of all applicants.

ADMISSION APPLICATION DEADLINE: Closing date is February 1. Notification begins on or about April 15.

FINANCIAL AID APPLICATION DEADLINE: Closing date is February 1. Notification date is April 1.

1920
Alma Mater
645 Southwest Street
Deerfield, New York 10310
(904) 272-6243

BASIS FOR ADMISSION DECISION: School achievement record and test scores are very important. School and community activities and recommendations are important. Interview and school community activities are considered.

ADMISSION APPLICATION DEADLINE: Closing date is January 15. Notification date is April 15.

FINANCIAL AID APPLICATION DEADLINE: Closing date is April 1. Notification date is April 10.

MARGARET K WRIGHT
1234 TIGERLILY LANE
CHICAGO IL 60600

Test 2
SAT *Form Code 1Y*

COLLEGE BOARD — SCHOLASTIC APTITUDE TEST and Test of Standard Written English Side 1

Use a No. 2 pencil only. Be sure each mark is dark and completely fills the intended oval. Completely erase any errors or stray marks.

1.
YOUR NAME: (Print) ____ Last ____ First ____ M.I.

SIGNATURE: ____ DATE: __/__/__

HOME ADDRESS: (Print) ____ Number and Street

____ City ____ State ____ Zip Code

CENTER: (Print) ____ City ____ State ____ Center Number

IMPORTANT: Please fill in these boxes exactly as shown on the back cover of your test book.

FOR ETS USE ONLY

2. TEST FORM

3. FORM CODE

0–9; A–Z

4. REGISTRATION NUMBER (Copy from your Admission Ticket.)

0–9

5. YOUR NAME

First 4 letters of last name | First Init. | Mid. Init.

A–Z

6. DATE OF BIRTH

Month	Day	Year
Jan.		
Feb.		
Mar.		
Apr.		
May		
June		
July		
Aug.		
Sept.		
Oct.		
Nov.		
Dec.		

7. SEX

Female

Male

8. TEST BOOK SERIAL NUMBER

(Cut here to detach.)

Start with number 1 for each new section. If a section has fewer than 50 questions, leave the extra answer spaces blank.

SECTION 1

1–50: A B C D E

SECTION 2

1–50: A B C D E

Q1362-04

I.N. 574006—110VV25P3015

COLLEGE BOARD — SCHOLASTIC APTITUDE TEST and Test of Standard Written English Side 2

Use a No. 2 pencil only. Be sure each mark is dark and completely fills the intended oval. Completely erase any errors or stray marks.

Start with number 1 for each new section. If a section has fewer than 50 questions, leave the extra answer spaces blank.

	SECTION 3	SECTION 4	SECTION 5	SECTION 6
1	A B C D E	A B C D E	A B C D E	A B C D E
2	A B C D E	A B C D E	A B C D E	A B C D E
3	A B C D E	A B C D E	A B C D E	A B C D E
4	A B C D E	A B C D E	A B C D E	A B C D E
5	A B C D E	A B C D E	A B C D E	A B C D E
6	A B C D E	A B C D E	A B C D E	A B C D E
7	A B C D E	A B C D E	A B C D E	A B C D E
8	A B C D E	A B C D E	A B C D E	A B C D E
9	A B C D E	A B C D E	A B C D E	A B C D E
10	A B C D E	A B C D E	A B C D E	A B C D E
11	A B C D E	A B C D E	A B C D E	A B C D E
12	A B C D E	A B C D E	A B C D E	A B C D E
13	A B C D E	A B C D E	A B C D E	A B C D E
14	A B C D E	A B C D E	A B C D E	A B C D E
15	A B C D E	A B C D E	A B C D E	A B C D E
16	A B C D E	A B C D E	A B C D E	A B C D E
17	A B C D E	A B C D E	A B C D E	A B C D E
18	A B C D E	A B C D E	A B C D E	A B C D E
19	A B C D E	A B C D E	A B C D E	A B C D E
20	A B C D E	A B C D E	A B C D E	A B C D E
21	A B C D E	A B C D E	A B C D E	A B C D E
22	A B C D E	A B C D E	A B C D E	A B C D E
23	A B C D E	A B C D E	A B C D E	A B C D E
24	A B C D E	A B C D E	A B C D E	A B C D E
25	A B C D E	A B C D E	A B C D E	A B C D E
26	A B C D E	A B C D E	A B C D E	A B C D E
27	A B C D E	A B C D E	A B C D E	A B C D E
28	A B C D E	A B C D E	A B C D E	A B C D E
29	A B C D E	A B C D E	A B C D E	A B C D E
30	A B C D E	A B C D E	A B C D E	A B C D E
31	A B C D E	A B C D E	A B C D E	A B C D E
32	A B C D E	A B C D E	A B C D E	A B C D E
33	A B C D E	A B C D E	A B C D E	A B C D E
34	A B C D E	A B C D E	A B C D E	A B C D E
35	A B C D E	A B C D E	A B C D E	A B C D E
36	A B C D E	A B C D E	A B C D E	A B C D E
37	A B C D E	A B C D E	A B C D E	A B C D E
38	A B C D E	A B C D E	A B C D E	A B C D E
39	A B C D E	A B C D E	A B C D E	A B C D E
40	A B C D E	A B C D E	A B C D E	A B C D E
41	A B C D E	A B C D E	A B C D E	A B C D E
42	A B C D E	A B C D E	A B C D E	A B C D E
43	A B C D E	A B C D E	A B C D E	A B C D E
44	A B C D E	A B C D E	A B C D E	A B C D E
45	A B C D E	A B C D E	A B C D E	A B C D E
46	A B C D E	A B C D E	A B C D E	A B C D E
47	A B C D E	A B C D E	A B C D E	A B C D E
48	A B C D E	A B C D E	A B C D E	A B C D E
49	A B C D E	A B C D E	A B C D E	A B C D E
50	A B C D E	A B C D E	A B C D E	A B C D E

9. SIGNATURE: ______________________

FOR ETS USE ONLY	VTR	VTFS	VRR	VRFS	VVR	VVFS	WER	WEFS	M4R	M4FS	M5R	M5FS	MTFS	
	VTW	VTCS	VRW	VRCS	VVW	VVCS	WEW	WECS	M4W		M5W		MTCS	

FORM CODE 1Y

1

SECTION 1

Time—30 minutes

45 QUESTIONS

For each question in this section, choose the best answer and blacken the corresponding space on the answer sheet.

Each question below consists of a word in capital letters, followed by five lettered words or phrases. Choose the word or phrase that is most nearly opposite in meaning to the word in capital letters. Since some of the questions require you to distinguish fine shades of meaning, consider all the choices before deciding which is best.

Example:

GOOD: (A) sour (B) bad (C) red (D) hot (E) ugly

Ⓐ ● Ⓒ Ⓓ Ⓔ

1. CALM: (A) disable (B) disapprove (C) dishearten (D) disoblige (E) disturb

2. AMATEUR: (A) spectator (B) professional (C) genius (D) outsider (E) entrepreneur

3. SPIRITUAL: (A) effervescent (B) significant (C) adaptable (D) felicitous (E) worldly

4. EXERTION: (A) innocence (B) inactivity (C) indecisiveness (D) incompetence (E) indifference

5. KNOTTY: (A) youthful (B) newfangled (C) moist (D) easy to solve (E) known to be true

6. LUNGE: (A) abort (B) intercept (C) resist (D) revert (E) recoil

7. NULLIFY: (A) use wisely (B) take seriously (C) perform easily (D) make effective (E) cause annoyance

8. CHAMPION: (A) recline (B) struggle (C) regulate (D) persecute (E) accompany

9. CAPRICIOUS: (A) tardy (B) vindictive (C) predictable (D) alluring (E) erroneous

10. LITHE: (A) restrained (B) inflexible (C) distraught (D) complacent (E) imprecise

11. ELUCIDATE: (A) disconnect (B) avoid (C) confuse (D) appear (E) fasten

12. PERIPHERAL: (A) essential (B) fatuous (C) discursive (D) sectarian (E) persuasive

13. EXEMPLARY: (A) vulnerable (B) uncertain (C) foreign (D) contemptible (E) heedless

14. DISAPPROBATION: (A) coercion (B) sanction (C) negligence (D) exemption (E) restriction

15. CALLOW: (A) barren (B) brave (C) mature (D) strict (E) generous

Each sentence below has one or two blanks, each blank indicating that something has been omitted. Beneath the sentence are five lettered words or sets of words. Choose the word or set of words that best fits the meaning of the sentence as a whole.

Example:

Although its publicity has been ----, the film itself is intelligent, well-acted, handsomely produced, and altogether ----.

(A) tasteless. .respectable (B) extensive. .moderate (C) sophisticated. .amateur (D) risqué. .crude (E) perfect. .spectacular

● Ⓑ Ⓒ Ⓓ Ⓔ

16. The instructor added the restriction that all projects had to be ----: no student could research an area that had been investigated previously by anyone else.

(A) acceptable (B) useful (C) extensive (D) authoritative (E) original

17. Just as congestion plagues every important highway, so it ---- the streets of every city.

(A) delimits (B) delays (C) clogs (D) obviates (E) destroys

18. Some microbiologists believe that the attempt to kill the microbes that live on or in our bodies is a mistake and that the use of antiseptics cannot always be ----.

(A) justified (B) spurious (C) rejected (D) estimated (E) anticipated

19. Although we know that our adversaries' pace is ---- compared to our own, we would be foolish to be ----.

(A) languid. .vigilant (B) torpid. .complacent (C) rapid. .callous (D) accelerated. .prudent (E) dilatory. .pessimistic

20. The ---- theory of the nature of art is vulnerable to the ---- that much art makes no attempt to create likenesses of objects.

(A) abstract. .rebuttal
(B) aesthetic. .criticism
(C) expression. .challenge
(D) modern. .hypothesis
(E) imitation. .objection

GO ON TO THE NEXT PAGE

Each passage below is followed by questions based on its content. Answer all questions following a passage on the basis of what is stated or implied in that passage.

African art is one of the fountainheads of modernist style in contemporary art; this happy accident has saved what otherwise might have been a lost cultural heritage for Afro-Americans. Lack of continuity with traditional African culture and its arts had left premodern Afro-American artists with no advantage, other than sentimental, in either its use or understanding. Their modern counterparts, however, cannot escape the African influence that has since become an integral part of modern art idioms. The tradition of African art, if it is properly understood and assimilated, should and can have even greater influence on the work of black artists today.

In the 1920's, when many young black artists first became aware of this heritage, a sudden and hectic interest flared up. The artistic results, however, suggest that these artists had a relatively superficial understanding; African art could yield little through direct imitation. Having already exerted its primary influence on modern art, to bear fresh fruit, it must be restudied and approached not so much through the mannerisms of its style as through its basic principles. The latter still have rich inspiration to offer to any artist, but especially to artists who may sense a close spiritual kinship with African art. Sound analysis of African art, then, should teach lessons of vigorous simplicity and vitality. On the cultural side, these lessons are those of art for use, of art with a sound and vital rooting in its own cultural soil, and of art not for restricted audiences but for wide popular appreciation. On the technical side, there is the even more important lesson of originality itself, and of the subordination of technique to complete harmony with the artistic idea. For black artists, particularly, there should come from the study of their own ancient and distinctive art tradition a sense of artistic independence and freedom from timid cultural indebtedness.

African art belongs in two native categories—ritualistic and craft art, both more basic than our idea of "fine art." Most African masks and statuettes serve a ceremonial function, and their primary significance is symbolic. They serve to evoke a mood, to enhance the dignity and authority of priest, witch doctor, or chieftain, to symbolize the ancestors or lineage and supernatural attributes of the gods. As talismans, they often serve additionally to control the supernatural spirits by sympathetic magic. Yet closely allied with all this is an appreciation of their artistic beauty and technical skill.

21. The passage primarily concerns the
(A) symbolic importance of ritualistic African art
(B) significance of African art for Afro-American artists today
(C) techniques employed in the creation of original African art
(D) way African art was used in Africa
(E) differences between African art and the work of black artists in America

22. According to the passage, one of the cultural lessons taught by African art is that art should
(A) combine many divergent points of view
(B) reflect the personality of its creator
(C) attempt to reform social injustice
(D) appeal to great numbers of people
(E) intrigue its audience with its complexity

23. The author's attitude toward African art is primarily one of
(A) puzzlement
(B) skepticism
(C) nostalgia
(D) exasperation
(E) admiration

24. Which of the following titles best summarizes the content of the passage?
(A) How African Art Developed Its Unique Style
(B) What African Art Can Teach
(C) Techniques Used by Black Artists
(D) The Future of Art in Africa
(E) The Universal Appeal of Art

25. According to the information in the passage, an artist inspired by the basic principles of African art would most likely have produced which of the following?
(A) A detailed copy of an ancient statuette
(B) An original carving of a dancer in a technique that fully complements the image
(C) An abstract sculpture of a warrior comprehensible only to a few
(D) A complex panorama representing the history of blacks in America
(E) A realistic reproduction of an African mask

GO ON TO THE NEXT PAGE

(This passage was written in 1929.)

Suppose that a rod is moving at very high speed. At first it is oriented perpendicular to its line of motion. Then it is turned through a right angle so that it is along the line of motion. The rod contracts. This contraction, known as the FitzGerald contraction, is exceedingly small under ordinary circumstances. The size of the contraction does not depend at all on the material of the rod, but only on its speed.

It may seem surprising that the dimensions of a moving rod can be altered merely by pointing it different ways. But what rod is being considered? If the rod is thought of as continuous substance, extending in space because it is the nature of substance to occupy space, then there seems to be no valid cause for a change of dimensions. But the rod is really a swarm of electrical particles moving about and widely separated from one another. The marvel is that such a swarm should tend to preserve any definite extension. The particles, however, exert electrical forces on one another, and the volume they fill corresponds to a balance between the forces drawing them together and the diverse motions tending to spread them apart. When the rod is set in motion, these electrical forces change.

There is really nothing mysterious about the FitzGerald contraction. It is an entirely natural property of particles that are held in a delicate balance by electromagnetic forces and that occupy space by buffeting away anything that tries to enter. Or you may look at it this way: your expectation that the rod will keep its original length presupposes that it receives no unfair treatment and is not subjected to any new stresses. But a rod in motion is subjected to a new magnetic stress as a necessary consequence of its own electrical constitution; and under this stress the contraction occurs. Perhaps you will think that if the rod were rigid enough it might be able to resist the compressing force. That is not so; the FitzGerald contraction is the same for a rod of steel and for a rod of rubber. The degree of rigidity and the compressing stress are bound up in the electrical constitution of the rod in such a way that if the degree of rigidity is great so also is the stress. It is necessary to rid our minds of the idea that this failure to keep a constant length is an imperfection of the rod. The FitzGerald contraction is not an imperfection but a fixed and characteristic property of matter, like inertia.

26. The major purpose of the author is to

(A) demonstrate a method
(B) compare evidence
(C) raise a question
(D) debate a point
(E) describe a phenomenon

27. The author feels that the occurrence of the FitzGerald contraction in a rod is less surprising than the fact that the

(A) rod is moving at high speed
(B) degree of the contraction is small
(C) rod maintains any definite shape
(D) particles in the rod are held together by electromagnetic forces
(E) length of the rod decreases when the rod is perpendicular to its line of motion

28. According to the passage, the occurrence of the FitzGerald contraction is most directly related to

(A) the stress exerted on the particles in an object
(B) the material from which an object is made
(C) the direction in which an object is moving
(D) the forces that the particles in an object exert on other objects
(E) an imperfection in the structure of an object

29. It can be inferred that the author considers the occurrence of the FitzGerald contraction to be

(A) unexplainable in terms of present scientific knowledge
(B) unexpected in view of common-sense notions about physical objects
(C) irrelevant to the consideration of other problems in physics
(D) undetectable by any method now known
(E) inconsistent with other physical properties of matter

30. When the author refers to the idea that a solid rod is "continuous substance" (lines 13-14), he implies that this idea is which of the following?

I. A common conception of the nature of solid matter
II. A concept that is not particularly useful for explaining the FitzGerald contraction
III. An accurate description of some kinds of matter

(A) I only (B) III only (C) I and II only
(D) II and III only (E) I, II, and III

GO ON TO THE NEXT PAGE

Select the word or set of words that best completes each of the following sentences.

31. In order to make the best use of available human resources, we must first ---- and then ---- human talents.
(A) educate. .equalize (B) decompose. .rebuild (C) revitalize. .discern (D) discover. .develop (E) produce. .accrue

32. Eastlake is a colorful and ---- commentator, equally at home in high art, folk rock, theology, and economics.
(A) obtuse (B) austere (C) insipid (D) versatile (E) provincial

33. Ms. Wilton urged patience and ---- in dealing with the protesters rather than the unyielding attitude the administration had adopted.
(A) obstinacy (B) desperation (C) arrogance (D) compromise (E) retaliation

34. His subjection bred a longing for self-direction, all the stronger for his underlying sense of the ---- of ever achieving it.
(A) irrevocability (B) impossibility (C) inevitability (D) credibility (E) predictability

35. Unfortunately, certain aspects of democratic government sometimes put pressure on politicians to take the easy way out, allowing ---- to crowd out ----.
(A) exigencies. .necessities
(B) immediacies. .ultimates
(C) responsibilities. .privileges
(D) principles. .practicalities
(E) issues. .problems

Each question below consists of a related pair of words or phrases, followed by five lettered pairs of words or phrases. Select the lettered pair that best expresses a relationship similar to that expressed in the original pair.

Example:

YAWN : BOREDOM :: (A) dream : sleep
(B) anger : madness (C) smile : amusement
(D) face : expression (E) impatience : rebellion
Ⓐ Ⓑ ● Ⓓ Ⓔ

36. HANGAR : AIRPLANE :: (A) stable : horse (B) canal : ship (C) lobby : administrator (D) junkyard : automobile (E) bed : river

37. VANE : WIND DIRECTION ::
(A) thermometer : mercury
(B) speedometer : pedal
(C) hourglass : sand
(D) barometer : heat
(E) sundial : time

38. ANONYMOUS : NAME ::
(A) colorful : hue (B) enormous : size (C) shapeless : form (D) brief : significance (E) precise : measurement

39. SYMPATHY : EMOTION ::
(A) sorrow : happiness
(B) friendship : relationship
(C) pride : punishment
(D) criticism : guilt
(E) harshness : helpfulness

40. HABIT : CUSTOMARY ::
(A) response : coordinated
(B) impulse : corrective
(C) reflex : involuntary
(D) concern : commendatory
(E) performance : descriptive

41. THREAT : HOSTILITY ::
(A) plea : clemency
(B) promise : benevolence
(C) lampoon : praise
(D) capitulation : malice
(E) compliment : admiration

42. MAGNET : IRON :: (A) tank : fluid (B) hook : net (C) sunlight : plant (D) spray : tree (E) flame : bird

43. ARDENT : INTERESTED ::
(A) depressed : cheerful (B) bored : curious (C) shy : listless (D) incensed : annoyed (E) wise : detached

44. VOGUE : ACCEPTED :: (A) ferment : coalesced (B) transition : unchanged (C) jeopardy : voided (D) abundance : desired (E) disrepute : shunned

45. HYPERBOLE : LANGUAGE ::
(A) prodigality : spending
(B) whimsicality : poetry
(C) idiom : slang
(D) repetition : behavior
(E) ambition : working

S T O P

IF YOU FINISH BEFORE TIME IS CALLED, YOU MAY CHECK YOUR WORK ON THIS SECTION ONLY. DO NOT WORK ON ANY OTHER SECTION IN THE TEST.

SECTION 2

Time—30 minutes

25 QUESTIONS

In this section solve each problem, using any available space on the page for scratchwork. Then decide which is the best of the choices given and blacken the corresponding space on the answer sheet.

The following information is for your reference in solving some of the problems.

Circle of radius r: Area $= \pi r^2$; Circumference $= 2\pi r$
The number of degrees of arc in a circle is 360.
The measure in degrees of a straight angle is 180.

Definitions of symbols:

$=$	is equal to	$\leq$	is less than or equal to
$\neq$	is unequal to	$\geq$	is greater than or equal to
$<$	is less than	$\parallel$	is parallel to
$>$	is greater than	$\perp$	is perpendicular to

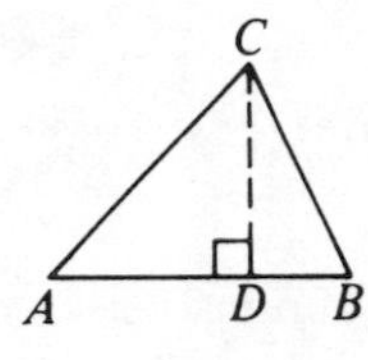

Triangle: The sum of the measures in degrees of the angles of a triangle is 180.

If $\angle CDA$ is a right angle, then

(1) area of $\triangle ABC = \frac{AB \times CD}{2}$

(2) $AC^2 = AD^2 + DC^2$

Note: Figures which accompany problems in this test are intended to provide information useful in solving the problems. They are drawn as accurately as possible EXCEPT when it is stated in a specific problem that its figure is not drawn to scale. All figures lie in a plane unless otherwise indicated. All numbers used are real numbers.

---

1. If $22 \times 3 \times Q = 6$, then $Q =$

(A) $\frac{1}{11}$ (B) $\frac{1}{10}$ (C) 10 (D) 11 (E) 20

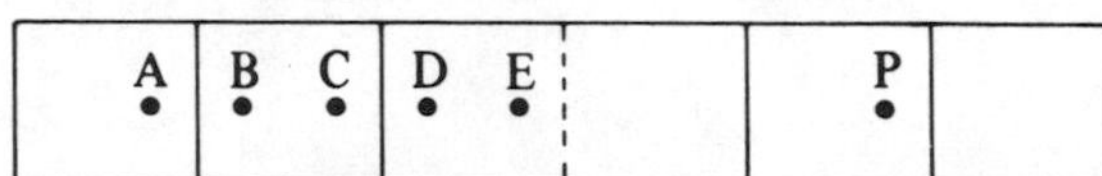

2. All the boxes in the strip above are of equal size. When the strip is folded together along the dotted line, point P is most likely to coincide with point

(A) A (B) B (C) C (D) D (E) E

3. How many tenths of a mile will a car travel on a 100-mile trip?

(A) 1,000
(B) 100
(C) 10
(D) 1
(E) $\frac{1}{10}$

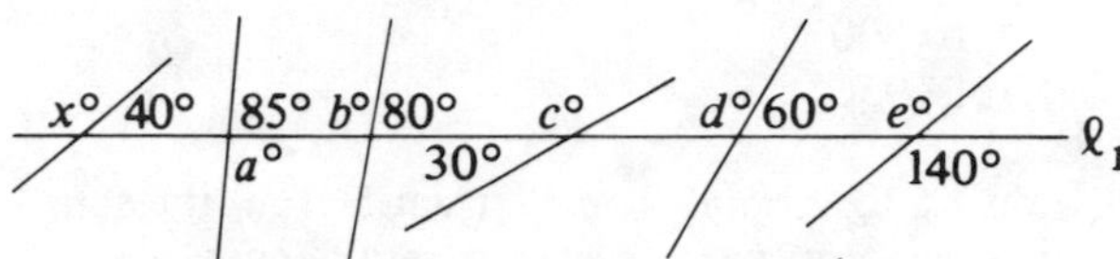

4. In the figure above, six segments intersect line ℓ_1. Which of the degree measures, a, b, c, d, or e, is equal to x?

(A) a (B) b (C) c (D) d (E) e

5. A grocer has 100 apples, 100 oranges, and 100 pears. If he packs 1 apple, 2 oranges, and 1 pear in a bag, then the maximum number of bags he can fill in this manner is

(A) 20
(B) 25
(C) 50
(D) 75
(E) 100

GO ON TO THE NEXT PAGE

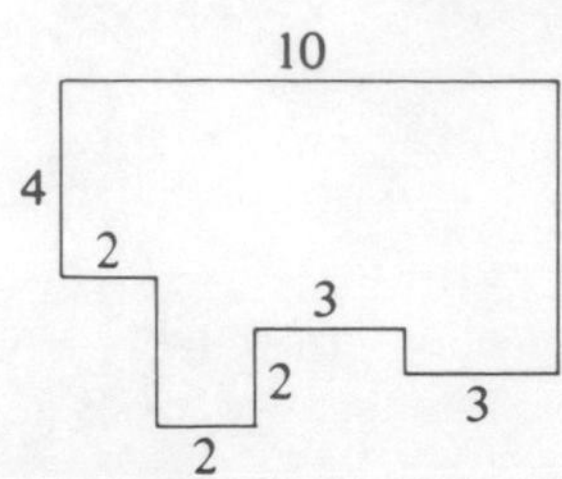

Note: Figure not drawn to scale.

6. What is the perimeter of the figure above?

(A) 15 (B) 20 (C) 26 (D) 32
(E) It cannot be determined from the information given.

---

7. $(45)^2 + 2(45)(55) + (55)^2 =$

(A) 5,050
(B) 9,100
(C) 9,900
(D) 10,000
(E) 14,950

8. Add $8x$ to $2x$ and then subtract 5 from the sum. If x is a positive integer, the result must be an integer multiple of

(A) 2
(B) 5
(C) 8
(D) 10
(E) 15

9. A line segment containing the points (0, 0) and (12, 8) will also contain the point

(A) (2, 3)
(B) (2, 4)
(C) (3, 2)
(D) (3, 4)
(E) (4, 2)

10. If $x < 2$, which of the following is NOT true?

(A) $2 + x < 2 + 2$

(B) $x - 2 < 2 - 2$

(C) $x(2) < 2(2)$

(D) $2 - x < 2 - 2$

(E) $\frac{x}{2} < \frac{2}{2}$

11. If $2\frac{3}{8} = 1 + \frac{x}{24}$, then $x =$

(A) 9
(B) 27
(C) 30
(D) 33
(E) 57

```
     2 3 5
   × 4 △ 7
   -------
   1 6 4 5
 1 □ 1 0
 9 4 0
 ---------
 1 0 ⊗ 7 4 5
```

12. In the multiplication problem above, if △, □, and ⊗ represent digits, what digit does □ represent?

(A) 2
(B) 3
(C) 4
(D) 5
(E) 6

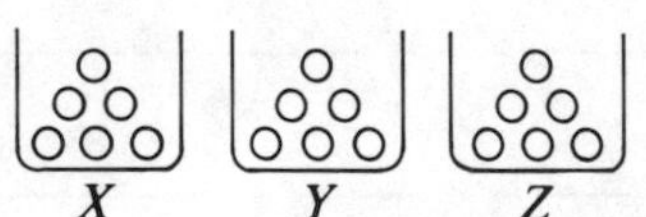

13. Each jar above contains 6 marbles. What is the LEAST number of marbles that must be transferred to make the ratio

marbles in X : marbles in Y : marbles in Z = 3 : 2 : 1 ?

(A) 6 (B) 5 (C) 4 (D) 3 (E) 2

GO ON TO THE NEXT PAGE

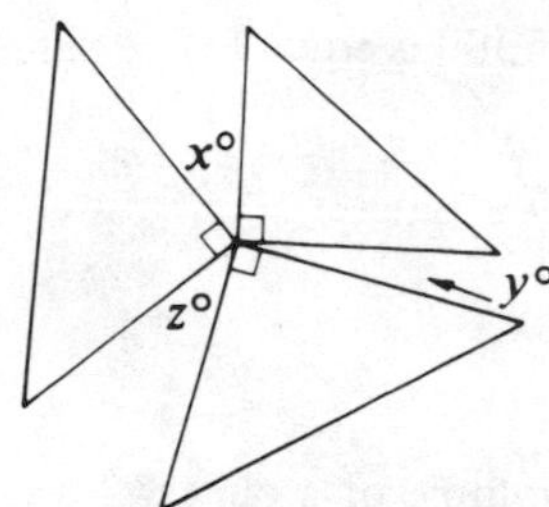

14. In the figure above, three right triangles have a common vertex. $x + y + z =$

(A) 90 (B) 120 (C) 135
(D) 180 (E) 270

15. If $x \neq 0$, which value(s) of p satisfy the equation $px = p^3x$?

(A) 0 only (B) 1 only (C) 1 or −1 only
(D) 0 or 1 only (E) 0, 1, or −1

16. Sue ate $\frac{1}{3}$ of a sandwich at noon and then $\frac{1}{2}$ of the remainder at supper. What part of the sandwich remained uneaten?

(A) $\frac{1}{6}$ (B) $\frac{1}{5}$ (C) $\frac{1}{3}$ (D) $\frac{1}{2}$ (E) $\frac{2}{3}$

17. If the diameter of a bicycle wheel is 0.5 meter, how many meters has the center of the wheel traveled when the wheel has made 3 complete revolutions along a straight road?

(A) $\frac{3\pi}{2}$

(B) 3π

(C) 12π

(D) $\frac{25\pi}{2}$

(E) 25π

18. If S is the sum of 7, 5, 2, 4, and x, what must be the value of x in order for x to equal $\frac{1}{4}S$?

(A) 4
(B) 4.5
(C) 6
(D) 18
(E) 24

	Carson	Greco	Polo	Rand
Carson	0	5	5	1
Greco	5	0	10	4
Polo	5	10	0	6
Rand	1	4	6	0

19. The chart above shows distances in kilometers between four towns that are located along a straight road. Which of the following could be a correct order relationship for these towns along the road?

(A) Carson, Polo, Rand, Greco
(B) Carson, Rand, Greco, Polo
(C) Greco, Carson, Rand, Polo
(D) Polo, Carson, Rand, Greco
(E) Rand, Carson, Polo, Greco

20. If $3 < x < 7$ and $4 < y < 7$, which of the following best describes $x - y$?

(A) $-4 < x - y < 3$
(B) $0 < x - y < 4$
(C) $3 < x - y < 4$
(D) $3 < x - y < 7$
(E) $4 < x - y < 7$

GO ON TO THE NEXT PAGE

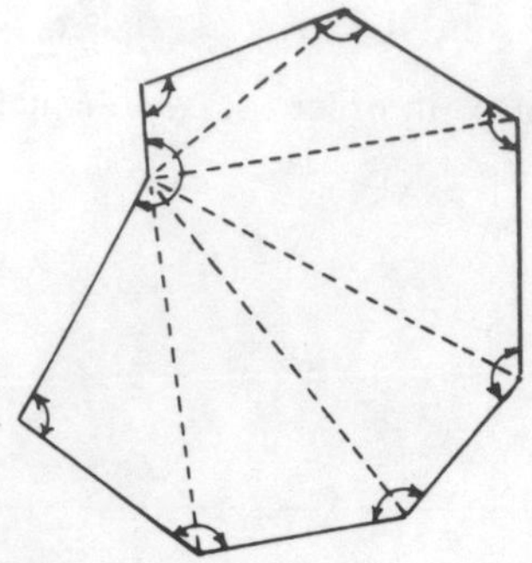

21. In the figure above, what is the average (arithmetic mean) degree measure of the 8 marked angles?

(A) 180 (B) 135 (C) 120 (D) 90
(E) It cannot be determined from the information given.

---

22. For which of the following pairs of numbers is the square of one of the numbers the reciprocal of the other number?

I. 0.25, 2
II. 1, 1
III. 0.5, 4

(A) I only (B) II only (C) III only
(D) I and II only (E) I, II, and III

23. 25 percent of 300 is equal to 7.5 percent of

(A) 10
(B) 75
(C) 90
(D) 100
(E) 1,000

24. What is the volume of a cube with surface area $54x^2$?

(A) $9x^2$ (B) $27x^3$ (C) $81x^2$
(D) $81x^3$ (E) $729x^3$

25. A woman drove to work at an average speed of 40 miles per hour and returned along the same route at 30 miles per hour. If her total traveling time was 1 hour, what was the total number of miles in the round trip?

(A) 30

(B) $30\frac{1}{7}$

(C) $34\frac{2}{7}$

(D) 35

(E) 40

S T O P

IF YOU FINISH BEFORE TIME IS CALLED, YOU MAY CHECK YOUR WORK ON THIS SECTION ONLY. DO NOT WORK ON ANY OTHER SECTION IN THE TEST.

SECTION 3

Time—30 minutes

40 QUESTIONS

For each question in this section, choose the best answer and blacken the corresponding space on the answer sheet.

Each question below consists of a word in capital letters, followed by five lettered words or phrases. Choose the word or phrase that is most nearly opposite in meaning to the word in capital letters. Since some of the questions require you to distinguish fine shades of meaning, consider all the choices before deciding which is best.

Example:

> GOOD: (A) sour (B) bad (C) red (D) hot (E) ugly
> Ⓐ ● Ⓒ Ⓓ Ⓔ

1. HARMONIOUS: (A) appreciative (B) discordant (C) fastidious (D) elementary (E) unworthy

2. PROLONG:
(A) remain intact
(B) assume responsibility
(C) decrease in duration
(D) fluctuate in value
(E) reduce in volume

3. SUPERB: (A) wild (B) insecure (C) impractical (D) extremely scarce (E) grossly inferior

4. CURB: (A) demean (B) repudiate (C) improve (D) urge forward (E) deny information

5. DISENTANGLE: (A) prepare (B) lengthen (C) return (D) reprove (E) enmesh

6. RESERVE: (A) compassion (B) irascibility (C) incoherence (D) lack of restraint (E) lack of strength

7. CONFLUENCE: (A) disparagement (B) disturbance (C) diffidence (D) divination (E) divergence

8. INNOCUOUS: (A) durable (B) identical (C) swift (D) dangerous (E) changeable

9. RIBALD: (A) well-liked (B) high-minded (C) tightfisted (D) farsighted (E) aboveboard

10. UPSHOT: (A) initial step (B) quick descent (C) severe punishment (D) complete silence (E) total destruction

Each sentence below has one or two blanks, each blank indicating that something has been omitted. Beneath the sentence are five lettered words or sets of words. Choose the word or set of words that best fits the meaning of the sentence as a whole.

Example:

> Although its publicity has been ----, the film itself is intelligent, well-acted, handsomely produced, and altogether ----.
>
> (A) tasteless. .respectable (B) extensive. .moderate (C) sophisticated. .amateur (D) risqué. .crude (E) perfect. .spectacular
> ● Ⓑ Ⓒ Ⓓ Ⓔ

11. Alice was annoyed that, although Edgar accepted the ---- of her argument, he would not ---- that her conclusion was correct.
(A) logic. .concede (B) absurdity. .require (C) sequence. .predict (D) existence. .preclude (E) feasibility. .dispute

12. Although the designers have not yet been able to solve the emission problems in the new automobile, their lack of ---- so far cannot be interpreted as final ----.
(A) continuity. .suspension
(B) motive. .rejection
(C) success. .failure
(D) alternatives. .bafflement
(E) concern. .defeat

13. A truly ---- historian of science, Meyer neither ---- the abilities of the scientists she presents nor condescends to them.
(A) unbiased. .scrutinizes
(B) objective. .inflates
(C) impressionable. .patronizes
(D) reverent. .admires
(E) analytic. .evaluates

GO ON TO THE NEXT PAGE

14. By studying ----, psychologists have learned to understand the workings of the healthy mind; similarly, it is in the most ---- instances that the mechanism of many normal processes may be revealed most clearly.

(A) madness. .bizarre
(B) statistics. .unique
(C) genius. .commonplace
(D) animals. .significant
(E) illusion. .real

15. The more knowledge, the fewer ----; wisdom has always been ----.

(A) unknowns. .questionable
(B) certitudes. .elusive
(C) lies. .controversial
(D) benefits. .attainable
(E) aberrations. .subjective

Each question below consists of a related pair of words or phrases, followed by five lettered pairs of words or phrases. Select the lettered pair that best expresses a relationship similar to that expressed in the original pair.

Example:

YAWN : BOREDOM :: (A) dream : sleep
(B) anger : madness (C) smile : amusement
(D) face : expression (E) impatience : rebellion

Ⓐ Ⓑ ● Ⓓ Ⓔ

16. STUDIO : ARTIST ::
(A) play : dramatist
(B) cathedral : architect
(C) blackboard : professor
(D) laboratory : chemist
(E) quarry : sculptor

17. RIPPLE : TIDAL WAVE :: (A) breeze : hurricane
(B) blizzard : avalanche (C) valley : earthquake
(D) puddle : downpour (E) rock : waterfall

18. EDUCATION : IGNORANCE ::
(A) book : knowledge
(B) door : entrance
(C) reason : philosophy
(D) medicine : disease
(E) work : recreation

19. BOW : VIOLIN :: (A) music : piano
(B) brass : trumpet (C) note : flute
(D) string : guitar (E) drumstick : drum

20. DUMBFOUND : ASTONISHMENT ::
(A) exasperate : frustration
(B) domineer : rebellion
(C) evaluate : incompetence
(D) err : punishment
(E) repulse : admiration

21. ORBIT : PLANET :: (A) course : ship
(B) rotation : axis (C) destination : plane
(D) tail : comet (E) current : river

22. BENEFACTOR : GIFT :: (A) performer : applause
(B) advisor : counsel (C) contestant : regulation
(D) enthusiast : objectivity (E) inquirer : answer

23. RAZE : BUILDING :: (A) launch : boat
(B) fell : tree (C) adorn : clothing
(D) invade : territory (E) cultivate : garden

24. NERVOUS : EQUANIMITY ::
(A) miserly : greediness
(B) realistic : foresight
(C) pious : grace
(D) gullible : discernment
(E) conscientious : sociability

25. MILL : PENNY :: (A) silver : quarter
(B) currency : nickel (C) dime : dollar
(D) check : cash (E) wallet : money

GO ON TO THE NEXT PAGE

Each passage below is followed by questions based on its content. Answer all questions following a passage on the basis of what is stated or implied in that passage.

The world of the great forests is a veritable paradise for those who will read its mysteries. Enveloped by towering walls of greenery, like a microbe in a pile carpet, I found never-ending comfort in this safe retreat from the glare of the world. Perhaps these unconventional reactions to an environment hated and feared by many were somehow connected with my upbringing as a city-dweller. Life in great cities is not unlike that in the primeval forests. One passes from one burrow to another along canyons that are only a little lighter, and breadth of vision is everywhere excluded by towering battlements palpitating with the lives hidden behind them. Always there is life around one, but it is hardly visible; imagination must work overtime to formulate its progress, lest one pass forever through the dense crowds utterly alone.

26. The author mentions which of the following as experiences common to visitors in the forests and dwellers in the cities?

    I. They are constantly surrounded by other living creatures.
    II. Obstructions block their view of vast expanses.
    III. They live in fear of attack by hidden enemies.

    (A) I only (B) II only (C) I and II only
    (D) I and III only (E) I, II, and III

27. The author uses the phrase "towering battlements" (line 13) to describe

    (A) ranger towers in a forest
    (B) wild animals
    (C) remote castles
    (D) archaeological excavations
    (E) skyscrapers

GO ON TO THE NEXT PAGE

We Americans have steeped ourselves so thoroughly in the practical and the empirical that we take to political theory with reluctance. We do not like to reason things out in advance. We would rather meet situations as they arise and dispose of them with a domestic blend of precedent and rule of thumb. But the situations we now judge vital to our national welfare will not "arise." They will have to be induced; and since democracy draws no distinction between ends and means, if the situations are to conform with democratic ends they will have to be induced by democratic means. The whole prospect calls for meticulous attention to first principles every step of the way. We can no longer afford to say one thing and do another, to talk free enterprise and tolerate monopoly, to maintain an antitrust law on our books and provide more ways of evading than of enforcing it. This is worse than inconsistency. It is an admission of failure that is already being used against democracy with telling effect by its critics and enemies. We can no longer indulge in the cynicism that interprets first principles as mere myths. The opening sentences of *Bulfinch's Mythology* show us the end of that trail: "The religions of ancient Greece and Rome are extinct. The so-called divinities of Olympus have not a single worshiper among living men." If democracy is to survive, we must believe in it, not as myth but as reality.

28. Which of the following is the best interpretation of "a domestic blend of precedent and rule of thumb" (lines 6-7)?

(A) A pattern of behavior derived from a study of American history
(B) A combination of tradition and rough calculation based on previous experience
(C) A system of principles based on a study of current American political behavior
(D) A judicious mixture of theory and practical know-how
(E) A blend of the opinions of respected Americans both living and dead

29. In reference to the survival of democracy, the passage conveys primarily a sense of

(A) urgency (B) despair (C) hope (D) indifference (E) irrationality

30. Which of the following best expresses the meaning of the phrase "interprets first principles as mere myths" (lines 23-24)?

(A) Recognizes that the philosophical basis of democracy comes to us from the remote past
(B) Believes that early conceptions of democracy were erroneous
(C) Considers democratic ideals to be unrealistic
(D) Treats democratic beliefs with religious veneration
(E) Treats political activities as secondary and unimportant

31. The quotation from *Bulfinch's Mythology* is introduced primarily to show that

(A) religious belief is essential to national welfare
(B) beliefs that are not expressed through action will die out
(C) the power of religion is declining
(D) myths cannot survive the attacks of cynics
(E) Greece and Rome failed to survive because they subscribed to the wrong religions

GO ON TO THE NEXT PAGE

"The boat sails on Saturday, Katie, and I want you and the boy to come home with me," said Uncle George.

"I don't want Charlie to leave," Kate said.

"He wants to leave—don't you, Charlie? And I want you to come, too, Katie. It's your home, and you've only got one. The trouble with you, Katie, is that when you were a kid they used to make fun of you in Krasbie, and you just started running, that's all, and you never stopped."

"I want to go home, Mama," Charlie said. "I'm homesick."

"How could you possibly be homesick for America?" Her voice was sharp. "You've never seen it. This is your home."

"How do you mean?"

"Your home is with your mother," Kate said.

"There's more to it than that, Mama. I feel strange here all the time. Everybody on the street is speaking a language that isn't mine."

"You've never even tried to learn the language here."

"Even if I had, it wouldn't make any difference. It would still sound strange. I mean it would still remind me that it wasn't my language. I just don't understand the people, Mama. I like them all right, but I just don't understand them. I never know what they're going to do next. Sometimes you're homesick, too, I know. I can tell by the way you look."

"Homesickness is nothing," Kate said angrily. "It is absolutely nothing. Fifty per cent of the people in the world are homesick all the time. But I don't suppose you're old enough to understand. When you're in one place and long to be in another, it isn't as simple as taking a boat. You don't really long for another country. You long for something in yourself that you don't have or haven't been able to find."

"It's crazy, Katie," said Uncle George. "You come home with me and Charlie. You and Charlie can live in the other half of my house, and I'll have a nice American kitchen put in for you."

"We'll all be happier, Mama," Charlie said. "We'll all be happier if we have a nice clean house and lots of friends and a nice garden and kitchen and stall shower."

Kate said loudly, "No stall shower or anything else will keep me from wanting to see the world and the different people who live in it." Then she turned to her son and spoke softly. "You are going to miss this country, Charlie."

32. Uncle George believes that Kate's reluctance to go to America is based on her

(A) scorn for modern American conveniences
(B) unpleasant memories of her life in America
(C) fear that her son's education will suffer there
(D) awareness that she has no other relative living in America
(E) belief that she no longer has anything in common with Americans

33. For which of the following reasons does Charlie say he feels strange in the country in which he is living?

I. Everyone speaks a language other than his own.
II. He does not understand the behavior of the people.
III. He misses the friends he had in America.

(A) I only (B) III only (C) I and II only (D) I and III only (E) I, II, and III

34. It can be inferred that Kate cites the figure of "Fifty per cent of the people in the world" (lines 32-33) in order to

(A) use an established fact to support her position about travel
(B) convince Charlie that homesickness is good for a person
(C) take advantage of the fact that her son has respect for a majority opinion
(D) elicit sympathy and concern for other people from her son and Uncle George
(E) fabricate a defense of her disinclination to return home

35. Which of the following does Kate appear to value LEAST?

(A) Personal dignity
(B) Her present way of life
(C) Her relationship to her son
(D) Material possessions
(E) Learning about new places and people

36. Which of the following definitions of "home" is closest to Kate's view of home as presented in the passage?

(A) Home is where you feel safest and most secure.
(B) Home is the place that you never want to leave.
(C) Home is the place you are always seeking but can only find in your own soul.
(D) Home is not where you live but where everyone understands you.
(E) Home is the place where you were brought up and where your relatives live.

GO ON TO THE NEXT PAGE

What we call science today is not the first attempt to introduce order into nature; it is merely the first attempt to introduce a particular kind of order. In medieval times people lived in an orderly universe, a universe in some ways more orderly than our own. But the order they discovered or imported was obtained by employing interpretative concepts quite different from ours. Their chief concept was that of universal purposefulness. People were at the center of a dependent universe; everything that existed and everything that happened did so in order to be useful to them, even if only in order to teach them moral lessons. Nature was part of a larger scheme in which the central fact was humanity and humanity's immortal destiny. The "material universe" was merely a setting within which a moment of this destiny was being worked out; and phenomena were explained in terms of their supposed purposes. The why of phenomena, not the how of phenomena, was the question that interested the medieval mind.

The basic assumption that was needed to support this medieval position was that nature as a whole is rational, that order can be found in it. The general medieval outlook made this assumption reasonable. Since both nature and human beings had the same author and since nature was designed to forward human destiny, it was not unreasonable to suppose that the workings of nature should proceed in a manner intelligible to the human mind. The modern scientific outlook retains this belief in the rationality of nature, but, since the theory of universal purposefulness has been discarded, contemporary scientists can base their assumptions upon nothing but a pure act of faith. Thus the scientific belief in the rationality of nature is seen to be, historically, an inheritance from a system of thought of which the other terms have been discarded.

37. With which of the following statements would the author be most likely to agree?

(A) The universe is not in fact orderly.
(B) Different concepts can be used to explain the same phenomena.
(C) The medieval concept of order has been disproved.
(D) Modern science should reconsider discarded medieval concepts.
(E) The how of phenomena is of no interpretive value.

38. It can be inferred that the phenomenon of birds gathering food for their young would probably have been interpreted in medieval times as

(A) an instructive example of industriousness
(B) an illustration of imitative action in animal life
(C) an example of the universal operation of instincts
(D) a purposeless and therefore uninteresting phenomenon
(E) a purposeless and therefore unintelligible phenomenon

39. According to the passage, modern science has retained from medieval thought the belief that

(A) nature is part of a larger, eternal scheme
(B) the how of phenomena best reveals the rationality of nature
(C) nature operates according to intelligible principles
(D) all human effort should be directed toward the improvement of human welfare
(E) there are many possible ways to explain natural phenomena

40. On the basis of the passage, modern scientific belief would be in agreement with which of the following statements?

I. Universal order has been verified empirically.
II. The concept of order can exist independent of philosophical justification.
III. The object of science is to explain why things happen.

(A) II only (B) III only (C) I and II only (D) II and III only (E) I, II, and III

S T O P

IF YOU FINISH BEFORE TIME IS CALLED, YOU MAY CHECK YOUR WORK ON THIS SECTION ONLY. DO NOT WORK ON ANY OTHER SECTION IN THE TEST.

5

SECTION 5

Time—30 minutes

35 QUESTIONS

In this section solve each problem, using any available space on the page for scratchwork. Then decide which is the best of the choices given and blacken the corresponding space on the answer sheet.

The following information is for your reference in solving some of the problems.

Circle of radius r: Area $= \pi r^2$; Circumference $= 2\pi r$
The number of degrees of arc in a circle is 360.
The measure in degrees of a straight angle is 180.

Definitions of symbols:

$=$	is equal to	$\leq$	is less than or equal to
$\neq$	is unequal to	$\geq$	is greater than or equal to
$<$	is less than	$\parallel$	is parallel to
$>$	is greater than	$\perp$	is perpendicular to

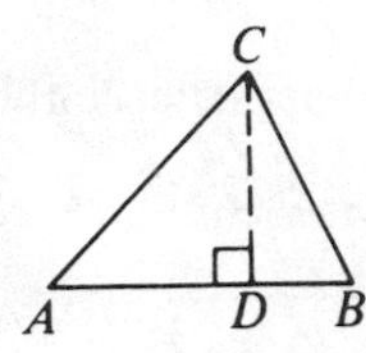

Triangle: The sum of the measures in degrees of the angles of a triangle is 180.

If $\angle CDA$ is a right angle, then

(1) area of $\triangle ABC = \dfrac{AB \times CD}{2}$

(2) $AC^2 = AD^2 + DC^2$

Note: Figures which accompany problems in this test are intended to provide information useful in solving the problems. They are drawn as accurately as possible EXCEPT when it is stated in a specific problem that its figure is not drawn to scale. All figures lie in a plane unless otherwise indicated. All numbers used are real numbers.

---

1. $22{,}222 + (5 \times 10^3) =$

(A) 22,722
(B) 25,222
(C) 27,222
(D) 52,222
(E) 72,222

2. A gasoline tank on a certain tractor holds 16 gallons of gasoline. If the tractor requires 7 gallons to plow 3 acres, how many acres can the tractor plow with a tankful of gasoline?

(A) $6\frac{6}{7}$ (B) $7\frac{1}{6}$ (C) $7\frac{1}{3}$

(D) $10\frac{2}{3}$ (E) $37\frac{1}{3}$

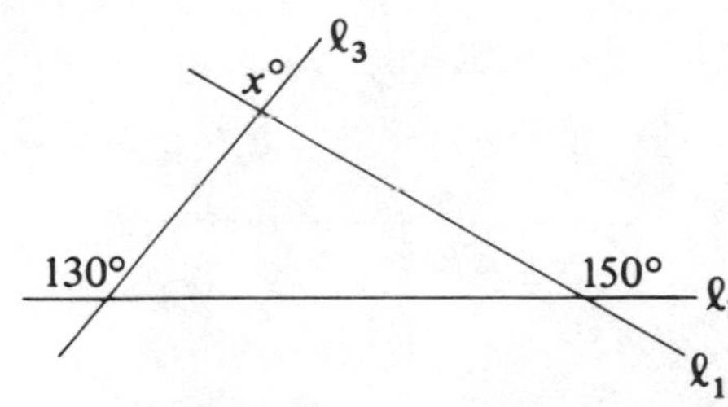

3. If ℓ_1, ℓ_2, and ℓ_3 intersect as shown above, then $x =$

(A) 30 (B) 50 (C) 60 (D) 90 (E) 100

4. What is the maximum possible number of digits in the product of two whole numbers each having two digits?

(A) 3 (B) 4 (C) 5 (D) 6 (E) 7

Questions 5-6 refer to the following definition:

Let $D \overset{A}{\underset{C}{\times}} B$ be defined as

$$D \overset{A}{\underset{C}{\times}} B = (A \times C) - (B \times D).$$

5. If $x \overset{5}{\underset{x}{\times}} 3 = 10$, then $x =$

(A) 2 (B) 3 (C) 4 (D) 5 (E) 6

6. $y \overset{x}{\underset{3}{\times}} 2 \; + \; 4 \overset{1}{\underset{x}{\times}} y \; - \; y \overset{x}{\underset{2}{\times}} 0 \; =$

(A) $y \overset{x}{\underset{2}{\times}} 1$ (B) $6y \overset{2x}{\underset{1}{\times}} 1$ (C) $4 \overset{6x}{\underset{1}{\times}} 2y$

(D) $5 \overset{2}{\underset{x}{\times}} y$ (E) $3 \overset{3}{\underset{2x}{\times}} 2y$

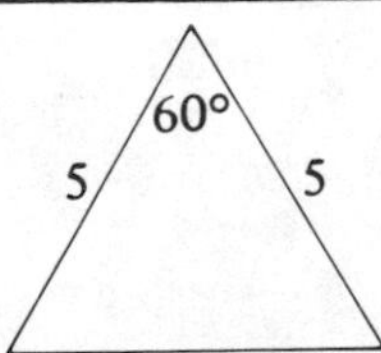

7. The perimeter of the triangle above is

(A) $5\sqrt{2}$ (B) 10 (C) 12.5
(D) 15 (E) 25

GO ON TO THE NEXT PAGE

5

Questions 8-27 each consist of two quantities, one in Column A and one in Column B. You are to compare the two quantities and on the answer sheet blacken space

A if the quantity in Column A is greater;
B if the quantity in Column B is greater;
C if the two quantities are equal;
D if the relationship cannot be determined from the information given.

Notes: 1. In certain questions, information concerning one or both of the quantities to be compared is centered above the two columns.
2. In a given question, a symbol that appears in both columns represents the same thing in Column A as it does in Column B.
3. Letters such as x, n, and k stand for real numbers.

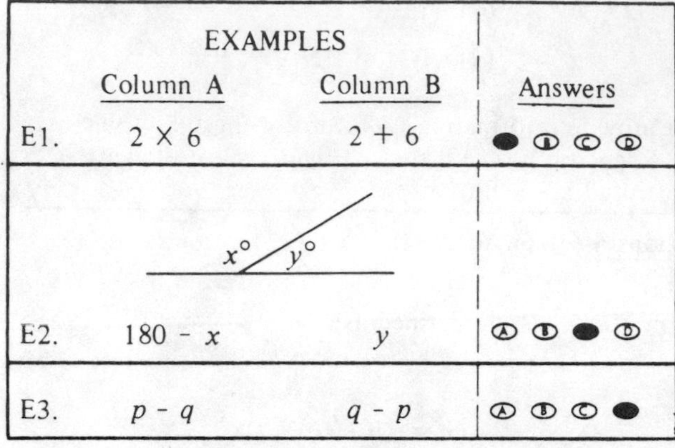

EXAMPLES

	Column A	Column B	Answers
E1.	2×6	$2 + 6$	● Ⓑ Ⓒ Ⓓ
E2.	$180 - x$	y	Ⓐ Ⓑ ● Ⓓ
E3.	$p - q$	$q - p$	Ⓐ Ⓑ Ⓒ ●

	Column A	Column B
8.	$\frac{2}{3} \times N$	$\frac{1}{3} \times 2N$

$17\overline{)3536}$ with quotient x

x is the quotient.

9.	28	x
10.	Average speed, in kilometers per hour, required to travel a distance of 100 kilometers in 2 hours	Average speed, in kilometers per hour, required to travel a distance of 100 kilometers in one-half hour

$n \leqq 12$

11.	$4 + 5 + n$	$4 + 5 + 12$

Column A | Column B

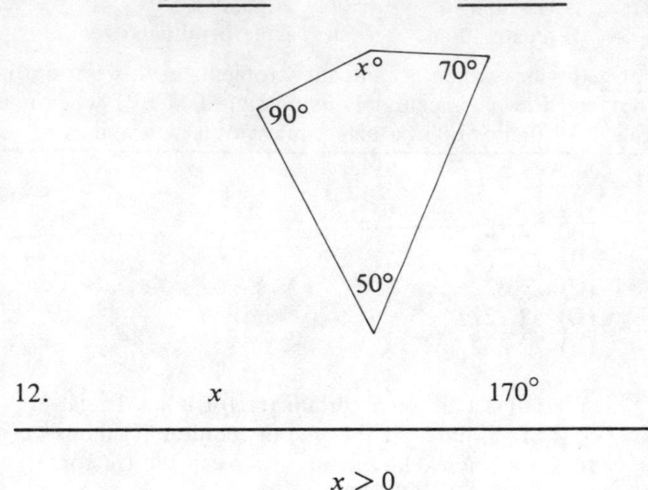

	Column A	Column B
12.	x	$170°$

$x > 0$

13.	$\frac{x^2 + 2x}{x}$	2

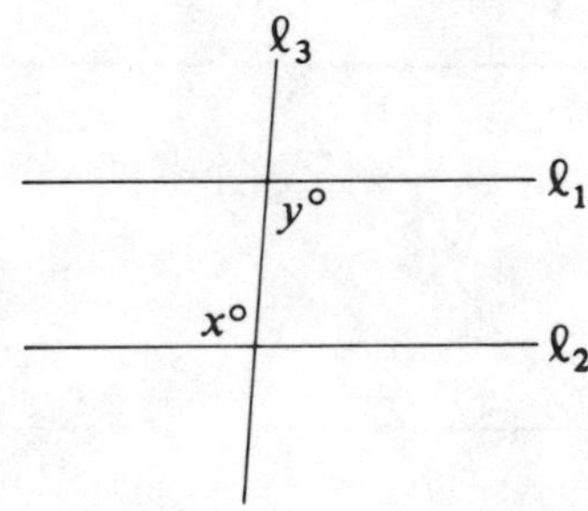

Line ℓ_3 intersects parallel lines ℓ_1 and ℓ_2.

14.	$x + y$	$2x$

GO ON TO THE NEXT PAGE

SUMMARY DIRECTIONS FOR COMPARISON QUESTIONS

Answer: A if the quantity in Column A is greater;
B if the quantity in Column B is greater;
C if the two quantities are equal;
D if the relationship cannot be determined from the information given.

	Column A	Column B

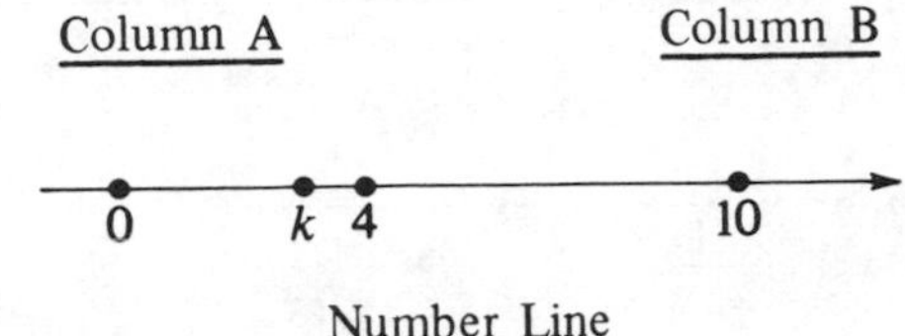

Number Line

	Column A	Column B
15.	k	$10 - k$

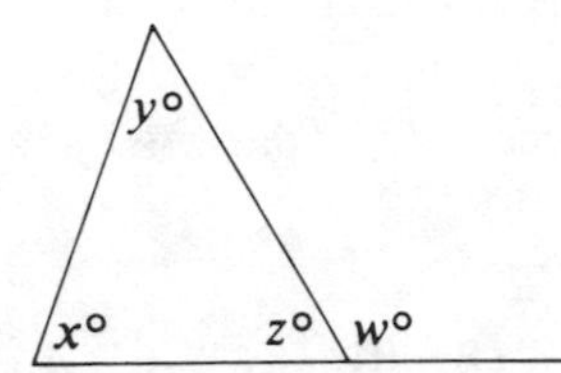

$w = 120$ and $x > y$

16.	y	z

$2x < 12 < 3x$ and
x is an integer.

17.	x	4

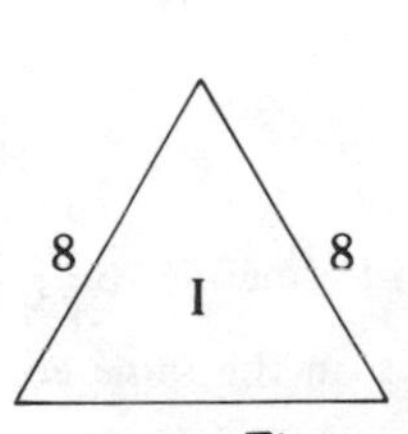

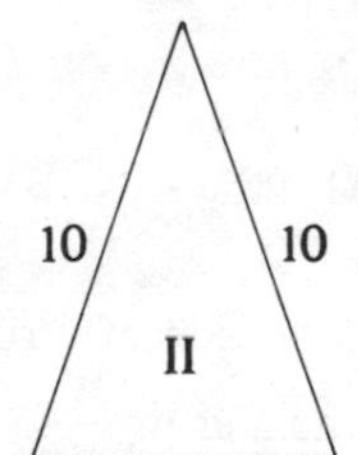

Note: Figures not drawn to scale.

18.	Area of triangle I	Area of triangle II

$$\frac{0.8}{0.04} = \frac{0.04}{x}$$

19.	x	0.002

$p > 0 > n$

20.	p	$n + p$

	Column A	Column B
21.	The number of distinct positive integer divisors of 12	The number of distinct positive integer divisors of 16

For all real numbers x and y, let $\odot$ be defined as $x \odot y = (x + y)^2$.

22.	$p \odot q$	$p \odot (-q)$

$(x + y)z = 0$
$(x + y) - z = x$

23.	y	z
24.	$\dfrac{\frac{2}{3}}{\frac{3}{2}}$	1
25.	15% of 2,000	2,000% of 15

x and y are integers
and $x > y > 1$.

26.	x^y	y^x

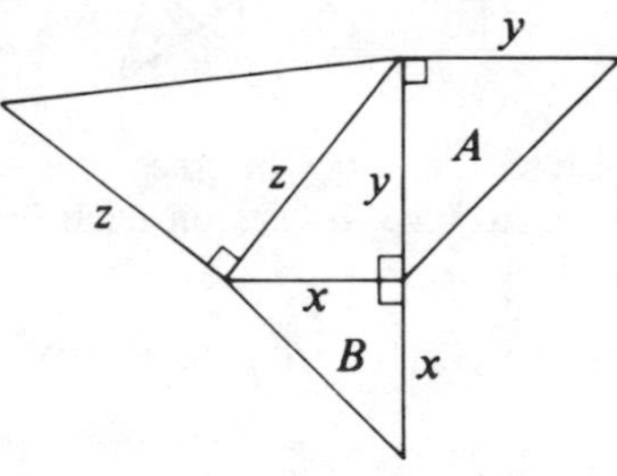

27.	Sum of the areas of triangles A and B above	$\dfrac{z^2}{2}$

GO ON TO THE NEXT PAGE

Solve each of the remaining problems in this section using any available space for scratchwork. Then decide which is the best of the choices given and blacken the corresponding space on the answer sheet.

28. If the average (arithmetic mean) of x and $3x$ is 8, then $x =$

(A) 2
(B) 4
(C) 8
(D) 10
(E) 12

29. If n is an integer greater than 2, which of the following CANNOT be an even integer?

(A) n^2 (B) $n(n - 1)$ (C) $n - 1$
(D) $3n + 1$ (E) $4n + 3$

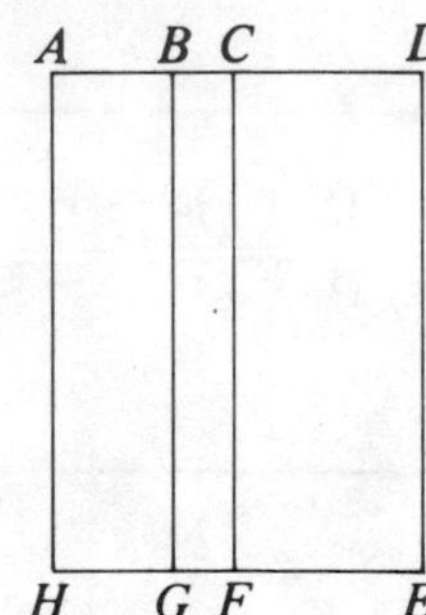

30. In rectangle $ADEH$ above, BG and CF are parallel to AH. Given lengths $AB = 2, BC = 1$, $CD = 3$, and the length of DH, not shown, is equal to 10, what is the area of the small rectangle $BCFG$?

(A) 8 (B) 10 (C) 16 (D) 24 (E) 48

31. The LEAST number of trees one would need in order to arrange 4 trees on each line of the plan above is

(A) 5 (B) 10 (C) 14 (D) 15 (E) 20

32. If $\dfrac{1}{1 + \frac{1}{x}} = k$, which of the following equals $2k$?

(A) $\dfrac{2}{2 + \frac{2}{x}}$ (B) $\dfrac{2}{1 + \frac{2}{x}}$ (C) $\dfrac{1}{\frac{1}{2} + \frac{1}{2x}}$

(D) $\dfrac{1}{1 + \frac{1}{2x}}$ (E) $\dfrac{1}{2 + \frac{1}{2x}}$

33. Given four distinct lines, exactly two of which are parallel, which of the following could be the number of points where at least two of the lines intersect?

I. Three
II. Four
III. Five

(A) I only (B) III only (C) I and II only
(D) I and III only (E) I, II, and III

34. If B is 125 percent of C, then C is what percent of B?

(A) 50%

(B) $66\frac{2}{3}\%$

(C) 75%

(D) 80%

(E) 90%

35. If one side of a ruler is to be marked in $\frac{1}{8}$-inch units and in $\frac{1}{10}$-inch units on the same edge, how many different such marks are needed from the 1-inch mark to the 2-inch mark, including the end points?

(A) 16 (B) 17 (C) 18 (D) 19 (E) 20

S T O P

IF YOU FINISH BEFORE TIME IS CALLED, YOU MAY CHECK YOUR WORK ON THIS SECTION ONLY. DO NOT WORK ON ANY OTHER SECTION IN THE TEST.

Correct Answers for Scholastic Aptitude Test Form Code 1Y

VERBAL		MATHEMATICAL	
Section 1	Section 3	Section 2	Section 5
1. E	1. B	1. A	1. C
2. B	2. C	2. B	2. A
3. E	3. E	3. A	3. E
4. B	4. D	4. E	4. B
5. D	5. E	5. C	5. D
6. E	6. D	6. E	6. B
7. D	7. E	7. D	7. D
8. D	8. D	8. B	*8. C
9. C	9. B	9. C	*9. B
10. B	10. A	10. D	*10. B
11. C	11. A	11. D	*11. D
12. A	12. C	12. C	*12. B
13. D	13. B	13. D	*13. A
14. B	14. A	14. A	*14. C
15. C	15. B	15. E	*15. B
16. E	16. D	16. C	*16. B
17. C	17. A	17. A	*17. A
18. A	18. D	18. C	*18. D
19. B	19. E	19. D	*19. C
20. E	20. A	20. A	*20. A
21. B	21. A	21. B	*21. A
22. D	22. B	22. E	*22. D
23. E	23. B	23. E	*23. C
24. B	24. D	24. B	*24. B
25. B	25. C	25. C	*25. C
26. E	26. C		*26. D
27. C	27. E		*27. C
28. A	28. B		28. B
29. B	29. A		29. E
30. C	30. C		30. A
31. D	31. B		31. B
32. D	32. B		32. C
33. D	33. C		33. D
34. B	34. E		34. D
35. B	35. D		35. B
36. A	36. C		
37. E	37. B		
38. C	38. A		
39. B	39. C		
40. C	40. A		
41. E			
42. C			
43. D			
44. E			
45. A			

*Indicates four-choice questions. (All of the other questions are five-choice.)

The Scoring Process

Machine-scoring is done in three steps:

- *Scanning.* Your answer sheet is "read" by a scanning machine and the oval you filled in for each question is recorded on a computer tape.
- *Scoring.* The computer compares the oval filled in for each question with the correct response. Each correct answer receives one point; omitted questions do not count toward your score. For each wrong answer, a fraction of a point is subtracted to correct for random guessing. For questions with five answer choices, one-fourth of a point is subtracted for each wrong response; for questions with four answer choices, one-third of a point is subtracted for each wrong response. The SAT-verbal test has 85 questions with five answer choices each. If, for example, a student has 44 right, 32 wrong, and 9 omitted, the resulting raw score is determined as follows:

  $$44 \text{ right} - \frac{32 \text{ wrong}}{4} = 44 - 8 = 36 \text{ raw score points}$$

  Obtaining raw scores frequently involves the rounding of fractional numbers to the nearest whole number. For example, a raw score of 36.25 is rounded to 36, the nearest whole number. A raw score of 36.50 is rounded upward to 37.
- *Converting to reported scaled score.* Raw test scores are then placed on the College Board scale of 200 to 800 through a process that adjusts scores to account for minor differences in difficulty among different editions of the test. This process, known as equating, is performed so that a student's reported score is not affected by the edition of the test taken nor by the abilities of the group with whom the student takes the test. As a result of placing SAT scores on the College Board scale, scores earned by students at different times can be compared. For example, an SAT-verbal score of 400 on a test taken at one administration indicates the same level of developed verbal ability as a 400 score obtained on a different edition of the test taken at another time.

How to Score the Test

You can verify the College Board SAT scores reported to you recently by using the information in this booklet along with the copy of your answer sheet. *Before you begin, check that the first two characters (number and letter) of the form code you marked in item 3 on your answer sheet are the same as the form code printed on the front of this booklet.* Compare the responses shown on the copy of your answer sheet with the list of correct answers.

SAT-Verbal Sections 1 and 3

Step A: Count the number of correct answers for *section 1* and record the number in the space provided on the worksheet on the next page. Then do the same for the incorrect answers. (Do not count omitted answers.) To determine subtotal A, use the formula:

$$\text{number correct} - \frac{\text{number incorrect}}{4} = \text{subtotal A}$$

Step B: Count the number of correct answers and the number of incorrect answers for *section 3* and record the numbers in the spaces provided on the worksheet. To determine subtotal B, use the formula:

$$\text{number correct} - \frac{\text{number incorrect}}{4} = \text{subtotal B}$$

Step C: To obtain C, add subtotal A to subtotal B, keeping any decimals. Enter the resulting figure on the worksheet.

Step D: To obtain D, your raw verbal score, round C to the nearest whole number. (For example, any number from 44.50 to 45.49 rounds to 45.) Enter the resulting figure on the worksheet.

Step E: To find your reported SAT-verbal score, look up the total raw verbal score you obtained in step D in the conversion table on page 96. Enter this figure on the worksheet.

SAT-Mathematical Sections 2 and 5

Step A: Count the number of correct answers and the number of incorrect answers for *section 2* and record the numbers in the spaces provided on the worksheet. To determine the subtotal A, use the formula:

$$\text{number correct} - \frac{\text{number incorrect}}{4} = \text{subtotal A}$$

Step B: Count the number of correct answers and the number of incorrect answers for the *five-choice questions (questions 1 through 7 and 28 through 35) in section 5* and record the numbers in the spaces provided on the worksheet. To determine the subtotal B, use the formula:

$$\text{number correct} - \frac{\text{number incorrect}}{4} = \text{subtotal B}$$

Step C: Count the number of correct answers and the number of incorrect answers for the *four-choice questions (questions 8 through 27) in section 5* and record the numbers in the spaces provided on the worksheet. To determine the subtotal C, use the formula:

$$\text{number correct} - \frac{\text{number incorrect}}{3} = \text{subtotal C}$$

Step D: To obtain D, add subtotal A, subtotal B, and subtotal C, keeping any decimals. Enter the resulting figure on the worksheet.

Step E: To obtain E, your raw mathematical score, round D to the nearest whole number. (For example, any number from 44.50 to 45.49 rounds to 45.) Enter the resulting figure on the worksheet.

Step F: To find your reported SAT-mathematical score, look up the total raw mathematical score you obtained in E in the conversion table on page 96. Enter this figure on the worksheet.

SAT SCORING WORKSHEET

FORM CODE 1Y

SAT-Verbal Sections

A. Section 1: ________ (no. correct) − ¼ (________ no. incorrect) = ________ subtotal A

B. Section 3: ________ (no. correct) − ¼ (________ no. incorrect) = ________ subtotal B

C. Total unrounded raw score (Total A + B) ________ C

D. Total rounded raw score (Rounded to nearest whole number) ________ D

E. SAT-verbal reported scaled score (See the conversion table on the back cover.) [ ] SAT-verbal score

SAT-Mathematical Sections

A. Section 2: ________ (no. correct) − ¼ (________ no. incorrect) = ________ subtotal A

B. Section 5: Questions 1 through 7 and 28 through 35 (5-choice) ________ (no. correct) − ¼ (________ no. incorrect) = ________ subtotal B

C. Section 5: Questions 8 through 27 (4-choice) ________ (no. correct) − ⅓ (________ no. incorrect) = ________ subtotal C

D. Total unrounded raw score (Total A + B + C) ________ D

E. Total rounded raw score (Rounded to nearest whole number) ________ E

F. SAT-mathematical reported scaled score (See the conversion table on the back cover.) [ ] SAT-math score

Score Conversion Table
Scholastic Aptitude Test
Form Code 1Y

Raw Score	College Board Reported Score		Raw Score	College Board Reported Score	
	SAT-Verbal	SAT-Math		SAT-Verbal	SAT-Math
85	800		40	470	620
84	790		39	460	610
83	780		38	460	600
82	770		37	450	590
81	760		36	440	580
80	760		35	430	570
79	750		34	430	560
78	740		33	420	550
77	740		32	410	550
76	730		31	410	540
75	720		30	400	530
74	710		29	390	520
73	710		28	380	510
72	700		27	380	500
71	690		26	370	490
70	690		25	360	480
69	680		24	360	480
68	670		23	350	470
67	660		22	340	460
66	660		21	330	450
65	650		20	330	440
64	640		19	320	430
63	640		18	310	420
62	630		17	300	410
61	620		16	300	410
60	610	800	15	290	400
59	610	790	14	280	390
58	600	780	13	280	380
57	590	770	12	270	370
56	590	760	11	260	360
55	580	750	10	250	350
54	570	740	9	250	340
53	560	730	8	240	330
52	560	720	7	230	330
51	550	710	6	230	320
50	540	700	5	220	310
49	530	690	4	210	300
48	530	690	3	200	290
47	520	680	2	200	280
46	510	670	1	200	270
45	510	660	0	200	260
44	500	650	−1	200	260
43	490	640	−2	200	250
42	480	630	−3	200	240
41	480	620	−4	200	230
			−5	200	220
			−6	200	210
			−7 or below	200	200

Test 3
SAT *Form Code 1E*

(Cut here to detach.)

COLLEGE BOARD — SCHOLASTIC APTITUDE TEST and Test of Standard Written English

Side 1

Use a No. 2 pencil only. Be sure each mark is dark and completely fills the intended oval. Completely erase any errors or stray marks.

1. YOUR NAME: (Print) ____________________ Last ____________________ First ____________________ M.I.

SIGNATURE: ____________________ **DATE:** ___/___/___

HOME ADDRESS: (Print) ____________________ Number and Street

____________________ City ____________________ State ____________________ Zip Code

CENTER: (Print) ____________________ City ____________________ State ____________________ Center Number

IMPORTANT: Please fill in these boxes exactly as shown on the back cover of your test book.

FOR ETS USE ONLY

2. TEST FORM

3. FORM CODE

(0)	(A)	(J)	(S)	(0)	(0)	(0)
(1)	(B)	(K)	(T)	(1)	(1)	(1)
(2)	(C)	(L)	(U)	(2)	(2)	(2)
(3)	(D)	(M)	(V)	(3)	(3)	(3)
(4)	(E)	(N)	(W)	(4)	(4)	(4)
(5)	(F)	(O)	(X)	(5)	(5)	(5)
(6)	(G)	(P)	(Y)	(6)	(6)	(6)
(7)	(H)	(Q)	(Z)	(7)	(7)	(7)
(8)	(I)	(R)		(8)	(8)	(8)
(9)				(9)	(9)	(9)

4. REGISTRATION NUMBER
(Copy from your Admission Ticket.)

(0)	(0)	(0)	(0)	(0)	(0)	(0)
(1)	(1)	(1)	(1)	(1)	(1)	(1)
(2)	(2)	(2)	(2)	(2)	(2)	(2)
(3)	(3)	(3)	(3)	(3)	(3)	(3)
(4)	(4)	(4)	(4)	(4)	(4)	(4)
(5)	(5)	(5)	(5)	(5)	(5)	(5)
(6)	(6)	(6)	(6)	(6)	(6)	(6)
(7)	(7)	(7)	(7)	(7)	(7)	(7)
(8)	(8)	(8)	(8)	(8)	(8)	(8)
(9)	(9)	(9)	(9)	(9)	(9)	(9)

5. YOUR NAME

First 4 letters of last name				First Init.	Mid Init.
(A)	(A)	(A)	(A)	(A)	(A)
(B)	(B)	(B)	(B)	(B)	(B)
(C)	(C)	(C)	(C)	(C)	(C)
(D)	(D)	(D)	(D)	(D)	(D)
(E)	(E)	(E)	(E)	(E)	(E)
(F)	(F)	(F)	(F)	(F)	(F)
(G)	(G)	(G)	(G)	(G)	(G)
(H)	(H)	(H)	(H)	(H)	(H)
(I)	(I)	(I)	(I)	(I)	(I)
(J)	(J)	(J)	(J)	(J)	(J)
(K)	(K)	(K)	(K)	(K)	(K)
(L)	(L)	(L)	(L)	(L)	(L)
(M)	(M)	(M)	(M)	(M)	(M)
(N)	(N)	(N)	(N)	(N)	(N)
(O)	(O)	(O)	(O)	(O)	(O)
(P)	(P)	(P)	(P)	(P)	(P)
(Q)	(Q)	(Q)	(Q)	(Q)	(Q)
(R)	(R)	(R)	(R)	(R)	(R)
(S)	(S)	(S)	(S)	(S)	(S)
(T)	(T)	(T)	(T)	(T)	(T)
(U)	(U)	(U)	(U)	(U)	(U)
(V)	(V)	(V)	(V)	(V)	(V)
(W)	(W)	(W)	(W)	(W)	(W)
(X)	(X)	(X)	(X)	(X)	(X)
(Y)	(Y)	(Y)	(Y)	(Y)	(Y)
(Z)	(Z)	(Z)	(Z)	(Z)	(Z)

6. DATE OF BIRTH

Month	Day		Year	
( ) Jan.				
( ) Feb.				
( ) Mar.	(0)	(0)	(0)	(0)
( ) Apr.	(1)	(1)	(1)	(1)
( ) May	(2)	(2)	(2)	(2)
( ) June	(3)	(3)	(3)	(3)
( ) July		(4)	(4)	(4)
( ) Aug.		(5)	(5)	(5)
( ) Sept.		(6)	(6)	(6)
( ) Oct.		(7)	(7)	(7)
( ) Nov.		(8)		(8)
( ) Dec.		(9)		(9)

7. SEX

( ) Female

( ) Male

8. TEST BOOK SERIAL NUMBER

Start with number 1 for each new section. If a section has fewer than 50 questions, leave the extra answer spaces blank.

SECTION 1

1	(A)	(B)	(C)	(D)	(E)	26	(A)	(B)	(C)	(D)	(E)
2	(A)	(B)	(C)	(D)	(E)	27	(A)	(B)	(C)	(D)	(E)
3	(A)	(B)	(C)	(D)	(E)	28	(A)	(B)	(C)	(D)	(E)
4	(A)	(B)	(C)	(D)	(E)	29	(A)	(B)	(C)	(D)	(E)
5	(A)	(B)	(C)	(D)	(E)	30	(A)	(B)	(C)	(D)	(E)
6	(A)	(B)	(C)	(D)	(E)	31	(A)	(B)	(C)	(D)	(E)
7	(A)	(B)	(C)	(D)	(E)	32	(A)	(B)	(C)	(D)	(E)
8	(A)	(B)	(C)	(D)	(E)	33	(A)	(B)	(C)	(D)	(E)
9	(A)	(B)	(C)	(D)	(E)	34	(A)	(B)	(C)	(D)	(E)
10	(A)	(B)	(C)	(D)	(E)	35	(A)	(B)	(C)	(D)	(E)
11	(A)	(B)	(C)	(D)	(E)	36	(A)	(B)	(C)	(D)	(E)
12	(A)	(B)	(C)	(D)	(E)	37	(A)	(B)	(C)	(D)	(E)
13	(A)	(B)	(C)	(D)	(E)	38	(A)	(B)	(C)	(D)	(E)
14	(A)	(B)	(C)	(D)	(E)	39	(A)	(B)	(C)	(D)	(E)
15	(A)	(B)	(C)	(D)	(E)	40	(A)	(B)	(C)	(D)	(E)
16	(A)	(B)	(C)	(D)	(E)	41	(A)	(B)	(C)	(D)	(E)
17	(A)	(B)	(C)	(D)	(E)	42	(A)	(B)	(C)	(D)	(E)
18	(A)	(B)	(C)	(D)	(E)	43	(A)	(B)	(C)	(D)	(E)
19	(A)	(B)	(C)	(D)	(E)	44	(A)	(B)	(C)	(D)	(E)
20	(A)	(B)	(C)	(D)	(E)	45	(A)	(B)	(C)	(D)	(E)
21	(A)	(B)	(C)	(D)	(E)	46	(A)	(B)	(C)	(D)	(E)
22	(A)	(B)	(C)	(D)	(E)	47	(A)	(B)	(C)	(D)	(E)
23	(A)	(B)	(C)	(D)	(E)	48	(A)	(B)	(C)	(D)	(E)
24	(A)	(B)	(C)	(D)	(E)	49	(A)	(B)	(C)	(D)	(E)
25	(A)	(B)	(C)	(D)	(E)	50	(A)	(B)	(C)	(D)	(E)

SECTION 2

1	(A)	(B)	(C)	(D)	(E)	26	(A)	(B)	(C)	(D)	(E)
2	(A)	(B)	(C)	(D)	(E)	27	(A)	(B)	(C)	(D)	(E)
3	(A)	(B)	(C)	(D)	(E)	28	(A)	(B)	(C)	(D)	(E)
4	(A)	(B)	(C)	(D)	(E)	29	(A)	(B)	(C)	(D)	(E)
5	(A)	(B)	(C)	(D)	(E)	30	(A)	(B)	(C)	(D)	(E)
6	(A)	(B)	(C)	(D)	(E)	31	(A)	(B)	(C)	(D)	(E)
7	(A)	(B)	(C)	(D)	(E)	32	(A)	(B)	(C)	(D)	(E)
8	(A)	(B)	(C)	(D)	(E)	33	(A)	(B)	(C)	(D)	(E)
9	(A)	(B)	(C)	(D)	(E)	34	(A)	(B)	(C)	(D)	(E)
10	(A)	(B)	(C)	(D)	(E)	35	(A)	(B)	(C)	(D)	(E)
11	(A)	(B)	(C)	(D)	(E)	36	(A)	(B)	(C)	(D)	(E)
12	(A)	(B)	(C)	(D)	(E)	37	(A)	(B)	(C)	(D)	(E)
13	(A)	(B)	(C)	(D)	(E)	38	(A)	(B)	(C)	(D)	(E)
14	(A)	(B)	(C)	(D)	(E)	39	(A)	(B)	(C)	(D)	(E)
15	(A)	(B)	(C)	(D)	(E)	40	(A)	(B)	(C)	(D)	(E)
16	(A)	(B)	(C)	(D)	(E)	41	(A)	(B)	(C)	(D)	(E)
17	(A)	(B)	(C)	(D)	(E)	42	(A)	(B)	(C)	(D)	(E)
18	(A)	(B)	(C)	(D)	(E)	43	(A)	(B)	(C)	(D)	(E)
19	(A)	(B)	(C)	(D)	(E)	44	(A)	(B)	(C)	(D)	(E)
20	(A)	(B)	(C)	(D)	(E)	45	(A)	(B)	(C)	(D)	(E)
21	(A)	(B)	(C)	(D)	(E)	46	(A)	(B)	(C)	(D)	(E)
22	(A)	(B)	(C)	(D)	(E)	47	(A)	(B)	(C)	(D)	(E)
23	(A)	(B)	(C)	(D)	(E)	48	(A)	(B)	(C)	(D)	(E)
24	(A)	(B)	(C)	(D)	(E)	49	(A)	(B)	(C)	(D)	(E)
25	(A)	(B)	(C)	(D)	(E)	50	(A)	(B)	(C)	(D)	(E)

Q1362-04

I.N. 574006—110VV25P3015

COLLEGE BOARD — SCHOLASTIC APTITUDE TEST and Test of Standard Written English **Side 2**

Use a No. 2 pencil only. Be sure each mark is dark and completely fills the intended oval. Completely erase any errors or stray marks.

Start with number 1 for each new section. If a section has fewer than 50 questions, leave the extra answer spaces blank.

	SECTION 3	SECTION 4	SECTION 5	SECTION 6
1	A B C D E	A B C D E	A B C D E	A B C D E
2	A B C D E	A B C D E	A B C D E	A B C D E
3	A B C D E	A B C D E	A B C D E	A B C D E
4	A B C D E	A B C D E	A B C D E	A B C D E
5	A B C D E	A B C D E	A B C D E	A B C D E
6	A B C D E	A B C D E	A B C D E	A B C D E
7	A B C D E	A B C D E	A B C D E	A B C D E
8	A B C D E	A B C D E	A B C D E	A B C D E
9	A B C D E	A B C D E	A B C D E	A B C D E
10	A B C D E	A B C D E	A B C D E	A B C D E
11	A B C D E	A B C D E	A B C D E	A B C D E
12	A B C D E	A B C D E	A B C D E	A B C D E
13	A B C D E	A B C D E	A B C D E	A B C D E
14	A B C D E	A B C D E	A B C D E	A B C D E
15	A B C D E	A B C D E	A B C D E	A B C D E
16	A B C D E	A B C D E	A B C D E	A B C D E
17	A B C D E	A B C D E	A B C D E	A B C D E
18	A B C D E	A B C D E	A B C D E	A B C D E
19	A B C D E	A B C D E	A B C D E	A B C D E
20	A B C D E	A B C D E	A B C D E	A B C D E
21	A B C D E	A B C D E	A B C D E	A B C D E
22	A B C D E	A B C D E	A B C D E	A B C D E
23	A B C D E	A B C D E	A B C D E	A B C D E
24	A B C D E	A B C D E	A B C D E	A B C D E
25	A B C D E	A B C D E	A B C D E	A B C D E
26	A B C D E	A B C D E	A B C D E	A B C D E
27	A B C D E	A B C D E	A B C D E	A B C D E
28	A B C D E	A B C D E	A B C D E	A B C D E
29	A B C D E	A B C D E	A B C D E	A B C D E
30	A B C D E	A B C D E	A B C D E	A B C D E
31	A B C D E	A B C D E	A B C D E	A B C D E
32	A B C D E	A B C D E	A B C D E	A B C D E
33	A B C D E	A B C D E	A B C D E	A B C D E
34	A B C D E	A B C D E	A B C D E	A B C D E
35	A B C D E	A B C D E	A B C D E	A B C D E
36	A B C D E	A B C D E	A B C D E	A B C D E
37	A B C D E	A B C D E	A B C D E	A B C D E
38	A B C D E	A B C D E	A B C D E	A B C D E
39	A B C D E	A B C D E	A B C D E	A B C D E
40	A B C D E	A B C D E	A B C D E	A B C D E
41	A B C D E	A B C D E	A B C D E	A B C D E
42	A B C D E	A B C D E	A B C D E	A B C D E
43	A B C D E	A B C D E	A B C D E	A B C D E
44	A B C D E	A B C D E	A B C D E	A B C D E
45	A B C D E	A B C D E	A B C D E	A B C D E
46	A B C D E	A B C D E	A B C D E	A B C D E
47	A B C D E	A B C D E	A B C D E	A B C D E
48	A B C D E	A B C D E	A B C D E	A B C D E
49	A B C D E	A B C D E	A B C D E	A B C D E
50	A B C D E	A B C D E	A B C D E	A B C D E

9. SIGNATURE:

FOR ETS USE ONLY	VTR	VTFS	VRR	VRFS	VVR	VVFS	WER	WEFS	M4R	M4FS	M5R	M5FS	MTFS
	VTW	VTCS	VRW	VRCS	VVW	VVCS	WEW	WECS	M4W		M5W		MTCS

FORM CODE 1E

SECTION 1

Time—30 minutes

45 QUESTIONS

For each question in this section, choose the best answer and blacken the corresponding space on the answer sheet.

Each question below consists of a word in capital letters, followed by five lettered words or phrases. Choose the word or phrase that is most nearly opposite in meaning to the word in capital letters. Since some of the questions require you to distinguish fine shades of meaning, consider all the choices before deciding which is best.

Example:

GOOD: (A) sour (B) bad (C) red (D) hot (E) ugly   Ⓐ ● Ⓒ Ⓓ Ⓔ

1. SUMMON: (A) shorten (B) enclose (C) delight (D) send away (E) pull apart
2. TERMINATE: (A) obey (B) begin (C) assist (D) combine (E) illuminate
3. BLAND: (A) airy (B) golden (C) spicy (D) quick (E) distant
4. DEPLETE: (A) prefer (B) wrinkle (C) restore (D) allow (E) surface
5. BIZARRE: (A) underhanded (B) commonplace (C) sincere (D) polite (E) competitive
6. DISARRAY: (A) contemplation (B) friendliness (C) advocation (D) orderliness (E) happiness
7. RIGOR: (A) laxity (B) secrecy (C) immensity (D) tardiness (E) originality
8. DISTANT: (A) cordial (B) graceful (C) scholarly (D) diligent (E) sizable
9. AUDACITY: (A) justice (B) interior (C) silence (D) usefulness (E) meekness
10. AVARICE: (A) intelligence (B) generosity (C) curiosity (D) hypocrisy (E) guilt
11. RESPLENDENT: (A) brief (B) dim (C) isolated (D) inaudible (E) irrational
12. PROSAIC: (A) imaginative (B) agreeable (C) committed (D) successful (E) descriptive
13. RUMINATE: (A) consider fleetingly (B) shout angrily (C) gaze admiringly (D) speak convincingly (E) advance mincingly
14. PARSIMONY: (A) plainness (B) cowardice (C) prodigality (D) formality (E) punctuality
15. FETID: (A) silent (B) refrigerated (C) solidified (D) animated (E) aromatic

Each sentence below has one or two blanks, each blank indicating that something has been omitted. Beneath the sentence are five lettered words or sets of words. Choose the word or set of words that best fits the meaning of the sentence as a whole.

Example:

Although its publicity has been ----, the film itself is intelligent, well-acted, handsomely produced, and altogether ----.

(A) tasteless. .respectable (B) extensive. .moderate (C) sophisticated. .amateur (D) risqué. .crude (E) perfect. .spectacular   ● Ⓑ Ⓒ Ⓓ Ⓔ

16. Ballet is known to be ----; once you go, you are likely to find yourself going again and again, loving the performances more each time.

    (A) addictive (B) erratic (C) expendable (D) anticlimactic (E) interminable

17. American technology borrowed its ideas and methods from the British Industrial Revolution, but soon the natural ---- of Americans became evident and they quickly outstripped their teachers.

    (A) inventiveness (B) stubbornness (C) forgetfulness (D) indifference (E) imitativeness

18. Although they are ---- by traps, poison, and shotguns, predators ---- to feast on flocks of sheep.

    (A) lured. .refuse (B) destroyed. .cease (C) impeded. .continue (D) encouraged. .attempt (E) harmed. .hesitate

19. Because even the briefest period of idleness bored and exasperated her, she worked ---- at some project or activity.

    (A) constantly (B) reluctantly (C) occasionally (D) cynically (E) languidly

20. Meteors become ---- only after they enter the atmosphere, for it is then that they begin to burn and leave their luminous trails.

    (A) incandescent (B) invisible (C) illusionary (D) reflective (E) elemental

Each passage below is followed by questions based on its content. Answer all questions following a passage on the basis of what is stated or implied in that passage.

"I should like," said Mrs. Cantlop in her crooning voice (it was always a croon except when it was a wail), "to add my mite of welcome, Mr. Swyndle. And so, if he were here, would Keturah's father." Here Mrs. Cantlop's voice faltered, and Mrs. Velindre eyed her with contemptuous interest.

The gentleman alluded to was Mr. Cantlop. He was not, as might be supposed, defunct. He was, to use his wife's words, "looking for gold in the wickedest place in the world." He had been thus engaged for the past thirty years, but so far there was no indication of his having found any. In their early married life he had set up as a tea merchant at Dormer. He did not make a living. Mr. Darke, a very arbitrary old gentleman, rated him soundly and told him if he couldn't make gold he'd better "go and scrat for it." As Mr. Cantlop afterwards told his wife, "Incompetence was mentioned, and the name of California." It was useless for Mr. Cantlop to say he did not want gold, or for Mrs. Cantlop to say she wanted Mr. Cantlop. Public opinion was too strong for them. They tried to be cheerful.

"My dear," said Mr. Cantlop, "I'll seek it. I'll find it. I'll bring it." He had a gift for terse and energetic expression; but there it usually stopped. Under the stern eye of Mr. Darke the poor little man did really set out with a carpet bag and a red pocket-handkerchief and eyes even redder from the parting with Amelia, and a ticket provided by the rector. Mystery had flung her curtains over his doings after this, though from his yearly letters it was known that he had arrived in California. In these letters he always spoke of the gold as being just at hand. Mrs. Cantlop nearly always alluded to him as "Keturah's father," seeming to feel that his personality, taken alone, was rather misty. Keturah had ceased to exist a few hours after she began her earthly race (during the tea period) so her personality was, at best, doubtful. But taken together, rolled into a ball and shaped by her imagination, they became quite intimidating and attained a kind of ghostly awfulness, a spook-like majesty. With them—or, rather, with it, for Mrs. Cantlop had made out of two nonentities an entity—the timid old lady was even able to enter the lists with autocratic Mrs. Velindre.

21. In the passage, Mr. Cantlop is portrayed most specifically as

(A) ineffectual (B) adventurous (C) discreet (D) shiftless (E) affectionate

22. The narrator suggests that, in addressing Mr. Swyndle, Mrs. Cantlop speaks of her husband as if he were

(A) stupid (B) dead (C) remarkable (D) famous (E) sick

23. The fact that in his letters Mr. Cantlop "always spoke of the gold as being just at hand" (line 34) expresses primarily what aspect of Mr. Cantlop's character?

(A) His defeatism (B) His diligence (C) His faithfulness (D) His optimism (E) His honesty

24. Why did Mrs. Cantlop always speak of her husband as "Keturah's father"?

(A) She was afraid of Mr. Cantlop's ghost.
(B) It upset her too deeply to say his name.
(C) People could remember Keturah more easily than Mr. Cantlop.
(D) Keturah was more important than Mr. Cantlop in her eyes.
(E) Giving him a distinctive attribute increased his substance.

25. One trait common to all of the members of the Cantlop family described in the passage is

(A) the lack of a strong personality
(B) a financial dependence on others
(C) an active imagination
(D) a thirst for material gain
(E) a fear of Mr. Darke

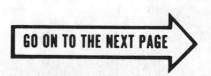

GO ON TO THE NEXT PAGE

The United States civil rights movement in its most important sense is as old as the introduction of human slavery in the New World. From the beginning, the essential conflict of the civil rights movement was inherent in the contradiction between, on the one hand, the practical economic advantages and social status associated with slavery and racial oppression and, on the other hand, the Judeo-Christian ideals of love and brotherhood and their translation into the democratic ideology of equality and justice. The presence of African slaves, visibly different from their owners in culture and color of skin, intensified this contradiction.

One could read the early history of the United States as an attempt to resolve the conflict by continuing slavery while making grudging concessions to religious and democratic ideology. The effort to try to convert some of the African slaves to Christianity and to teach some to read English could be interpreted as the first "victory" of the civil rights movement, but at the same time it paradoxically intensified the conflict. It would have been more consistent logically to leave the African slaves unconverted and uneducated if they were to be kept in slavery. Even the economic demands of slavery, however, required that the slaves be skilled, adaptable, and efficient. The fact that such skills were being developed called attention to the humanity of the African and the beginning of the end of human slavery in a society committed to social and political democracy.

The dynamics of the contemporary civil rights movement continue to reflect this same struggle between the desire to deny Black people full and unqualified status as human beings and the unquestioned evidence that such denial cannot be based on fact. Once the Civil War and Reconstruction were past, signs of a civil rights renaissance did not emerge until the 1940's, when Black resentment mounted against segregation in the armed services and discrimination in employment. A new period of overt and sustained protest had begun. In 1941, A. Philip Randolph threatened a march on Washington to force President Roosevelt to issue the first executive order compelling fair employment of Black people. Testimony to the depth of the ambivalence of the American nation on civil rights was the fact that Roosevelt, himself generally considered one of the most liberal and farseeing Presidents in United States history, only reluctantly issued this order. This conflict between Roosevelt and Randolph marked the beginning of a new militance and assertiveness on the part of Black people that has been sustained in different ways by different leaders ever since.

26. The first two paragraphs of the passage are primarily concerned with which of the following?

(A) Challenging the value of an established point of view
(B) Drawing conclusions based on newly discovered evidence
(C) Presenting the details of a solution to a problem
(D) Stating reasons why existing conditions must be improved
(E) Discussing the historical foundation of a problem

27. According to the author, an example of the "essential conflict" (lines 3-4) of the United States civil rights movement is the conflict between

(A) Black and White religious beliefs about love and brotherhood
(B) the economic benefits derived from slavery and the cost of teaching slaves skills
(C) the usefulness of cheap labor and the unfairness of human enslavement
(D) Judeo-Christian ideals and the moral ideology of a democratic nation
(E) the need to educate slaves and the religious principles of their owners

28. According to the passage, some citizens early in United States history dealt with the issues of slavery and racial oppression by

(A) arguing that slavery was portrayed in the religious writings of both Jews and Christians and was, therefore, acceptable
(B) depriving slaves of all training in an attempt to prevent their assimilation into society
(C) keeping Black people enslaved but granting them the right to practice the religion of their choice
(D) converting slaves to Christianity and educating them while still attempting to maintain the institution of slavery
(E) denying the humanity of the slaves by claiming that they were unable to learn, to adapt, or to work efficiently

29. The passage suggests that the civil rights movement in the United States was LEAST eventful during which of the following ten-year periods?

(A) 1855-1864 (B) 1865-1874 (C) The 1920's
(D) The 1940's (E) The 1960's

30. The passage suggests that A. Philip Randolph's confrontation with President Roosevelt was significant because it

(A) resulted in an executive order ending segregation in the armed forces
(B) represented a turning point in the methods used by those involved in the United States civil rights movement
(C) marked the first time that a Black civil rights leader had dealt personally with a United States President
(D) revealed the willingness of minority groups in the United States to adjust their demands for the good of the nation
(E) offered evidence of the shrewdness and progressiveness of the President of the United States

GO ON TO THE NEXT PAGE

1

Select the word or set of words that best completes each of the following sentences.

31. The superficiality of his calmness was ---- by the tremor of his hands as he tried to pick up the paper.

(A) intensified (B) betrayed (C) imposed (D) secured (E) unchanged

32. The article claimed that, unlike words, which can be ---- context, the essential expressions of music are unchanging, no matter in what musical context they appear.

(A) devoid of (B) transformed by (C) indicative of (D) compatible with (E) unaltered by

33. When the ruthless and authoritarian emperor was overthrown, the act was hailed as a ---- of sanity over ---- despotism.

(A) victory. .benign
(B) tyranny. .cruel
(C) celebration. .reasoned
(D) domination. .courageous
(E) triumph. .murderous

34. Polls are so ---- in our society that it is almost impossible to go out in public without being ---- by an opinion-seeker.

(A) impertinent. .solicited
(B) explicit. .manipulated
(C) gratifying. .cajoled
(D) pervasive. .accosted
(E) ominous. .distracted

35. Luard implies that rising state centralization is ---- as well as detestable and, so, nowhere sets out a strategy for ---- it.

(A) unfortunate. .modifying
(B) intriguing. .evaluating
(C) offensive. .opposing
(D) inevitable. .resisting
(E) momentous. .confronting

Each question below consists of a related pair of words or phrases, followed by five lettered pairs of words or phrases. Select the lettered pair that best expresses a relationship similar to that expressed in the original pair.

Example:

YAWN : BOREDOM :: (A) dream : sleep (B) anger : madness (C) smile : amusement (D) face : expression (E) impatience : rebellion

Ⓐ Ⓑ ● Ⓓ Ⓔ

36. BABBLE : SPEAK :: (A) mutter : hear (B) scribble : write (C) jabber : whisper (D) quibble : ask (E) cuddle : touch

37. FILAMENT : LIGHT BULB :: (A) meteor : trajectory (B) ashes : fireplace (C) wick : candle (D) food : body (E) thread : cloth

38. SHIN : KNEE :: (A) foot : hip (B) tendon : wrist (C) ear : forehead (D) forearm : elbow (E) knuckle : fist

39. ANTIDOTE : POISON :: (A) fertilizer : irrigation (B) sedative : relaxation (C) lubricant : friction (D) radar : frequency (E) fuel : motion

40. EMBEZZLER : FUNDS :: (A) poacher : game (B) traitor : enemy (C) instigator : disturbance (D) opportunist : luck (E) convict : sentence

41. SAVORY : TASTE :: (A) obnoxious : smell (B) slippery : touch (C) blurred : vision (D) melodious : hearing (E) elusive : memory

42. COMMISERATE : SYMPATHY :: (A) surrender : hostility (B) confide : suspicion (C) discuss : admiration (D) revere : devotion (E) free : coercion

43. DIN : CACOPHONOUS :: (A) discordance : peaceful (B) silence : continuous (C) drone : monotonous (D) music : staccato (E) sound : harmonious

44. MATERIALISM : OBJECTS ::
(A) plagiarism : ideas
(B) cynicism : falsehood
(C) hedonism : pleasure
(D) liberalism : education
(E) metamorphism : change

45. STUBBORN : VACILLATION ::
(A) poised : embarrassment
(B) subtle : maneuverability
(C) doubtful : concern
(D) hopeful : decisiveness
(E) immune : healthiness

S T O P

IF YOU FINISH BEFORE TIME IS CALLED, YOU MAY CHECK YOUR WORK ON THIS SECTION ONLY. DO NOT WORK ON ANY OTHER SECTION IN THE TEST.

SECTION 2

Time—30 minutes

25 QUESTIONS

In this section solve each problem, using any available space on the page for scratchwork. Then decide which is the best of the choices given and blacken the corresponding space on the answer sheet.

The following information is for your reference in solving some of the problems.

Circle of radius r: Area $= \pi r^2$; Circumference $= 2\pi r$
The number of degrees of arc in a circle is 360.
The measure in degrees of a straight angle is 180.

Definitions of symbols:

$=$	is equal to	$\leq$	is less than or equal to
$\neq$	is unequal to	$\geq$	is greater than or equal to
$<$	is less than	$\parallel$	is parallel to
$>$	is greater than	$\perp$	is perpendicular to

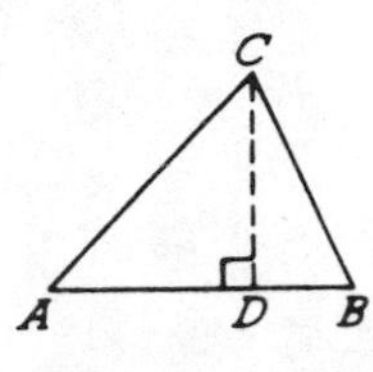

Triangle: The sum of the measures in degrees of the angles of a triangle is 180.

If $\angle CDA$ is a right angle, then

(1) area of $\triangle ABC = \dfrac{AB \times CD}{2}$

(2) $AC^2 = AD^2 + DC^2$

Note: Figures which accompany problems in this test are intended to provide information useful in solving the problems. They are drawn as accurately as possible EXCEPT when it is stated in a specific problem that its figure is not drawn to scale. All figures lie in a plane unless otherwise indicated. All numbers used are real numbers.

---

1. If $5x - 3 = 2a$, then $\dfrac{5x-3}{2} =$

   (A) $\frac{a}{4}$ (B) $\frac{a}{2}$ (C) a (D) $2a$ (E) $4a$

2. A train traveling 60 miles per hour for 1 hour covers the same distance as a train traveling 30 miles per hour for how many hours?

   (A) 3 (B) 2 (C) 1 (D) $\frac{1}{2}$ (E) $\frac{1}{3}$

3. The container above has a rectangular base with sides that are perpendicular to the base. If a cut is made along each of the four vertical edges and the sides folded out flat, which of the following patterns results?

(A)
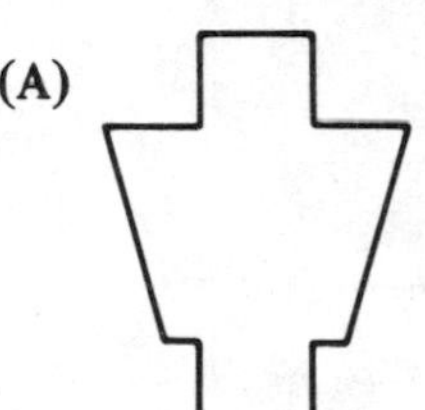

(B)

(C)
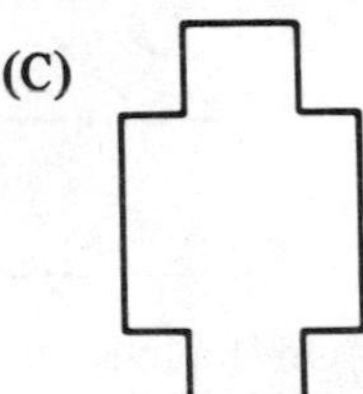

(D) (E)
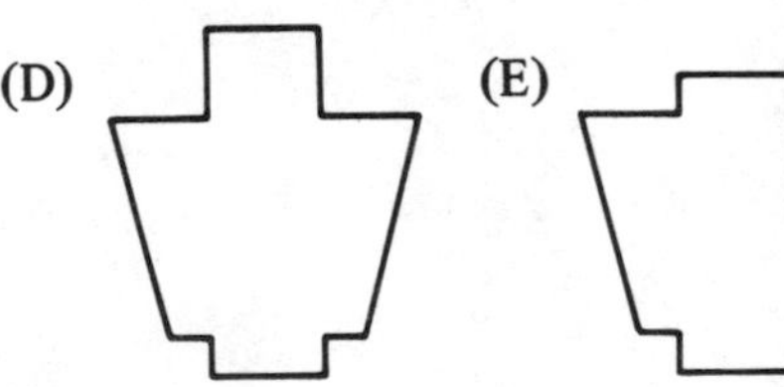

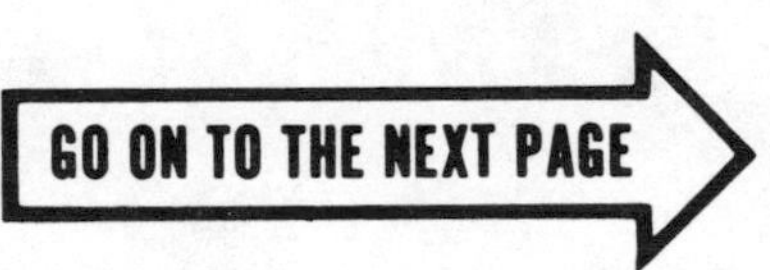

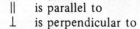

4. What is the sum of 5 consecutive integers if the middle one is 70 ?

(A) 14 (B) 75 (C) 272 (D) 330 (E) 350

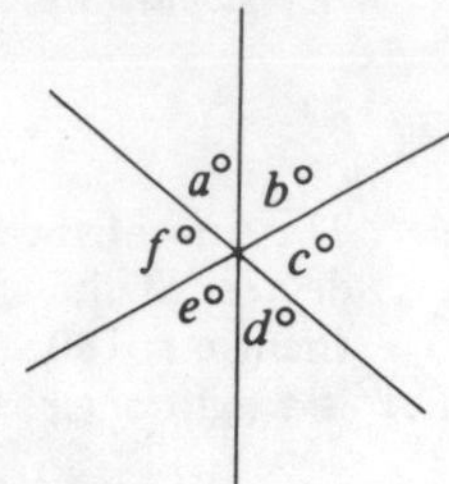

5. In the figure above, if the three lines intersect at a point as shown, then $a + b$ must be equal to which of the following?

I. $d + e$
II. $c + f$
III. $e + f$

(A) I only (B) II only (C) III only
(D) II and III only (E) I, II, and III

6. This question was not counted in computing scores.

A B C D E

7. On the line above, if $AB < BC < CD < DE$, which of the following must be true?

(A) $AC < CD$
(B) $AC < CE$
(C) $AD < CE$
(D) $AD < DE$
(E) $BD < DE$

8. In a basket of 120 apples, exactly 6 were rotten. What percent of the apples were rotten?

(A) 5% (B) 6% (C) 10%
(D) 20% (E) 25%

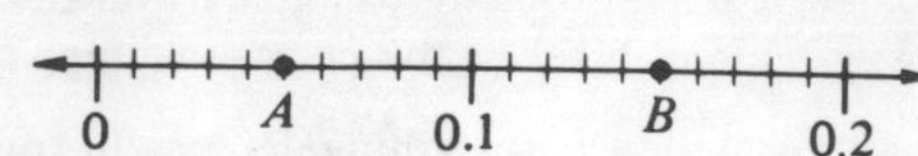

9. In the figure above, what is the length of AB ?

(A) 1.00
(B) 0.50
(C) 0.15
(D) 0.10
(E) 0.05

10. For any sentence J, the expression $N_t(J)$ is defined to mean the number of times the letter "t" appears in J. If J is the sentence "All cats are good luck," then $N_t(J) =$

(A) 0 (B) 1 (C) 2 (D) 3 (E) 4

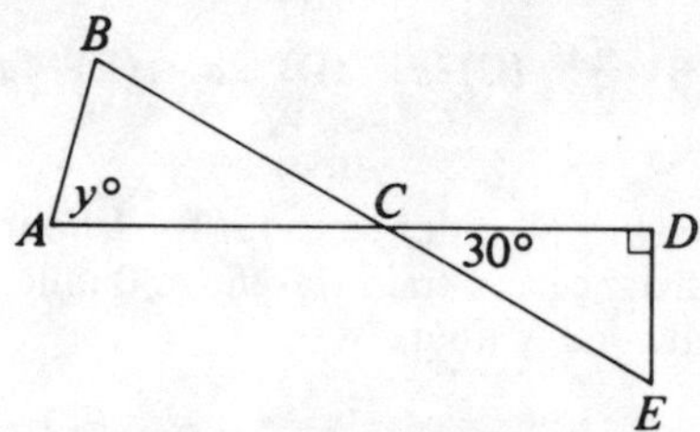

11. In the figure above, if $BC = CA$, then $y =$

(A) 15
(B) 60
(C) 75
(D) 150
(E) 165

12. If 44 is the average (arithmetic mean) of x, x, x, 35, and 65, then $x =$

(A) 40
(B) 42
(C) 44
(D) 48
(E) 50

GO ON TO THE NEXT PAGE

13. If a sports outfit consisting of a jacket, slacks, and hat can be made up from any of 3 different jackets, 4 different pairs of slacks, and 2 different hats, then the total number of different such sports outfits possible is

(A) 4 (B) 9 (C) 12 (D) 24 (E) 36

$3x + 4$

$5x$

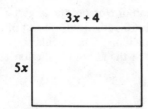

14. What is the perimeter of the rectangle above?

(A) $8x + 4$
(B) $8x + 8$
(C) $15x + 4$
(D) $16x + 4$
(E) $16x + 8$

15. In a relay race, 4 runners each ran 400 meters in 51.0 seconds, 53.2 seconds, 50.8 seconds, and 49.7 seconds, respectively. Their total running time exceeded 3 minutes by how many seconds?

(A) 14.7
(B) 23.3
(C) 24.3
(D) 24.7
(E) 34.7

16. How many shares of stock must be bought at $31\frac{1}{4}$ dollars per share and sold at $31\frac{3}{8}$ dollars per share in order to make a profit of \$100 ? (Ignore fees and taxes.)

(A) 1,000
(B) 800
(C) 400
(D) 80
(E) 40

17. If $x + y = 3$ and $x - y = 5$, then $x^2 - y^2 =$

(A) 4 (B) 8 (C) 15 (D) 16 (E) 64

Questions 18-19 refer to the following definition.

$<x>$ is defined as 1 less than the number of digits in the integer x. For example, $<100> = 3 - 1 = 2$.

18. If x is a positive integer less than 1,000,001, then $<x>$ is at most

(A) 5 (B) 6 (C) 7
(D) 999,999 (E) 1,000,000

19. If x has 1,001 digits, then what is the value of $<<<x>>>$?

(A) 997
(B) 1
(C) 0
(D) -1
(E) It cannot be determined from the information given.

20. In a lottery, a green ticket costs 2 dollars more than a red ticket and a red ticket costs 2 dollars more than a blue ticket. If 12 blue tickets cost $2x$ dollars, what is the price, in dollars, of 5 green tickets and 7 red tickets?

(A) $2x + 24$
(B) $2x + 34$
(C) $2x + 48$
(D) $12x + 24$
(E) $24x + 34$

GO ON TO THE NEXT PAGE

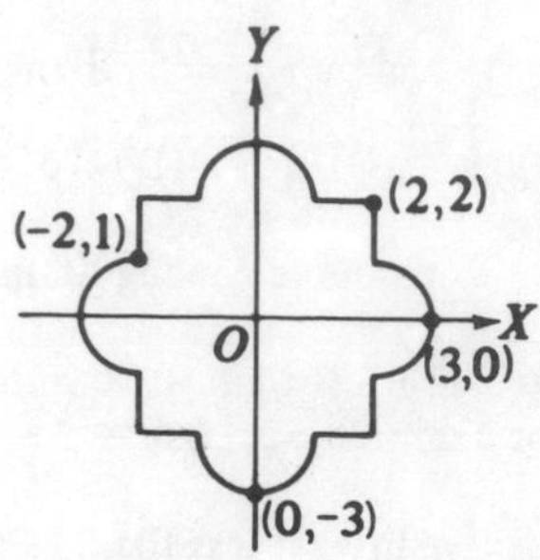

21. In the figure above, the two axes divide the enclosed region into four regions that have the same size and shape. Of the following, which is closest to the area of the entire enclosed region?

(A) 7 (B) 10 (C) 19 (D) 22 (E) 29

22. At Central High School, the math club has 15 members and the chess club has 12 members. If a total of 13 students belong to only one of the two clubs, how many students belong to both clubs?

(A) 2
(B) 6
(C) 7
(D) 12
(E) 14

23. From which of the following statements must it follow that $x > y$?

(A) $x = 2y$
(B) $2x = y$
(C) $x + 2 = y$
(D) $x - 2 = y$
(E) None of the above

24. The population of Norson, the largest city in Transitania, is 50 percent of the rest of the population of Transitania. The population of Norson is what percent of the entire population of Transitania?

(A) 20% (B) 25% (C) 30%

(D) $33\frac{1}{3}$% (E) 50%

25. When 30 gallons of water is poured into a cylindrical tank whose sides are perpendicular to a flat base, the water level rises 0.5 foot. If 7.5 gallons of water occupies 1 cubic foot of space, then the base of the tank has an area of how many square feet? (volume of the tank = height × area of base)

(A) 37.5 (B) 8 (C) 4.5 (D) 4

(E) It cannot be determined from the information given.

S T O P

IF YOU FINISH BEFORE TIME IS CALLED, YOU MAY CHECK YOUR WORK ON THIS SECTION ONLY. DO NOT WORK ON ANY OTHER SECTION IN THE TEST.

SECTION 4

Time—30 minutes

40 QUESTIONS

For each question in this section, choose the best answer and blacken the corresponding space on the answer sheet.

Each question below consists of a word in capital letters, followed by five lettered words or phrases. Choose the word or phrase that is most nearly opposite in meaning to the word in capital letters. Since some of the questions require you to distinguish fine shades of meaning, consider all the choices before deciding which is best.

Example:

GOOD: (A) sour (B) bad (C) red (D) hot (E) ugly

Ⓐ ● Ⓒ Ⓓ Ⓔ

1. IGNITE: (A) snuff out (B) balance carefully (C) clarify immediately (D) stretch over (E) dig up

2. ABRUPT: (A) safe and familiar (B) slow and gentle (C) good and innocent (D) useful (E) decisive

3. INCOHERENCE: (A) prying, rude questioning (B) clear, orderly expression (C) flattery (D) vigilance (E) permanence

4. CONTEST: (A) deflate (B) insert (C) think positively (D) accept without dispute (E) escape without detection

5. FLAMBOYANT: (A) unfamiliar (B) unappealing (C) plain (D) amusing (E) unkempt

6. TREPIDATION: (A) honesty (B) devotion (C) affluence (D) fearlessness (E) talkativeness

7. SEQUESTER: (A) pacify (B) facilitate (C) discuss angrily (D) ward off danger (E) allow to mingle freely

8. MALINGER: (A) discuss rationally (B) depart angrily (C) listen attentively (D) admit readily (E) perform dutifully

9. NEFARIOUSNESS: (A) hilarity (B) insularity (C) tactfulness (D) wondrousness (E) righteousness

10. COALESCENCE: (A) fragmentation (B) fumigation (C) solubility (D) distortion (E) divulgence

4

Each sentence below has one or two blanks, each blank indicating that something has been omitted. Beneath the sentence are five lettered words or sets of words. Choose the word or set of words that best fits the meaning of the sentence as a whole.

Example:

> Although its publicity has been ----, the film itself is intelligent, well-acted, handsomely produced, and altogether ----.
>
> (A) tasteless. .respectable (B) extensive. .moderate (C) sophisticated. .amateur (D) risqué. .crude (E) perfect. .spectacular
>
> ● Ⓑ Ⓒ Ⓓ Ⓔ

11. Although the media has certainly ---- its coverage of newsworthy events in the Black community, some Black groups maintain that the quality of this coverage is still ----.

    (A) curtailed. .declining
    (B) extolled. .excellent
    (C) condemned. .dreadful
    (D) increased. .inadequate
    (E) revived. .unsurpassable

12. He was suddenly thrown into a fit of despair, his faith in himself infirm, his self-confidence ----.

    (A) shattered (B) soaring (C) unassailable (D) inflated (E) delayed

13. Anthropologists have learned that no single one of the tribes could ---- the ---- of Native American cultures found in the plains, desert, and mountain areas of the West.

    (A) reduce. .organization (B) serve. .integrity (C) emulate. .level (D) approach. .types (E) represent. .diversity

14. In poetry intended for presentation to large audiences with ---- expectations, there can be no place for ---- or for strained subtleties of any kind.

    (A) emotional. .controversy (B) limited. .candor (C) political. .duplicity (D) humorous. .levity (E) unsophisticated. .preciosity

15. Although the more benign advertising slogans are designed merely to sell products and the more insidious are ---- that set goals for behavior and achievement, they both serve to interfere with self-acceptance and to ---- discontent.

    (A) deterrents. .inhibit (B) queries. .suspend (C) auguries. .challenge (D) mandates. .banish (E) imperatives. .engender

Each question below consists of a related pair of words or phrases, followed by five lettered pairs of words or phrases. Select the lettered pair that best expresses a relationship similar to that expressed in the original pair.

Example:

> YAWN : BOREDOM :: (A) dream : sleep (B) anger : madness (C) smile : amusement (D) face : expression (E) impatience : rebellion
>
> Ⓐ Ⓑ ● Ⓓ Ⓔ

16. ATOM : MOLECULE :: (A) portrait : masterpiece (B) electron : void (C) nail : hammer (D) element : compound (E) vegetable : mineral

17. KNIT : EYEBROWS :: (A) shake : hands (B) purse : lips (C) walk : legs (D) stoop : knees (E) squirm : body

18. JUDGE : JUSTICE :: (A) guest : invitation (B) doctor : hospital (C) actor : entertainment (D) chef : recipe (E) lawyer : trial

19. MARATHON : ENDURANCE :: (A) race : track (B) hike : guide (C) hurdle : victory (D) line : length (E) sprint : speed

20. CONGRATULATION : SUCCESS :: (A) diligence : wealth (B) immunization : infection (C) condolence : sorrow (D) envy : fame (E) responsibility : burden

21. COFFER : VALUABLES :: (A) cistern : water (B) ocean : tide (C) lawn : grass (D) asylum : refuge (E) pyramid : stone

22. CIRCUMLOCUTORY : SPEECH :: (A) humorous : joke (B) meandering : path (C) tactless : remark (D) successful : attack (E) logical : conclusion

23. STRUT : OSTENTATIOUS :: (A) vacillate : modest (B) cringe : servile (C) flinch : indolent (D) waiver : arrogant (E) sputter : fastidious

24. ASCETIC : SELF-DENIAL :: (A) lunatic : violence (B) miser : frugality (C) investigator : suspicion (D) zealot : participation (E) hermit : selfhood

25. READ : PERUSE :: (A) examine : ignore (B) anticipate : complete (C) express : denounce (D) free : enclose (E) reprove : condemn

Each passage below is followed by questions based on its content. Answer all questions following a passage on the basis of what is stated or implied in that passage.

Many contemporary cosmologists hold that the universe began in a cataclysmic explosion, or "big bang." Evidence for the initial fireball comes primarily from observations of galaxies out beyond our Milky Way. Kinematic studies of such objects show them to be receding from us at a rate proportional to their distance. That is, those galaxies most distant from us have larger recessional velocities. Now, because of the finite speed with which light (a type of radiation) travels, the most distant objects are seen as they were when the light we receive first left them. These most distant galaxies, having the greatest velocities of expansion, provide us with information about the early universe.

In the past decade, the discovery of a weak hiss of radio radiation has given support to the big-bang model for the origin of the universe. This low-level static, observed coming from every direction in space, is regarded as a cool relic of the initial fireball. At the very beginning, the temperature of the fireball was unimaginably hot. But as the universe expanded to fill a larger volume, it also began to cool. It can be shown mathematically that the remnant of the initial fireball, after about 15 to 20 billion years of expansion, should have cooled substantially to the value now measured isotropically (in all directions) by large radio telescopes.

26. The main point of the passage is to

(A) delineate various theories about the origin of the universe
(B) show how scientists derived the age of the universe
(C) consider one major use of the radio telescope
(D) discuss some evidence for one theory of the origin of the universe
(E) prove the existence of galaxies other than our own

27. In order to support the validity of the big-bang theory, the author utilizes which of the following?

I. Studies measuring the different speeds of various types of radiation
II. The discovery of low-level radio radiation
III. The composition of the initial fireball

(A) I only (B) II only (C) III only (D) I and II only (E) I, II, and III

28. The tone of the passage can best be described as

(A) inquisitive
(B) argumentative
(C) aggressive and dogmatic
(D) conciliatory and apologetic
(E) instructional and explanatory

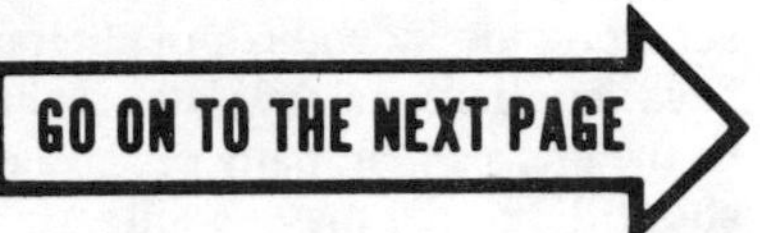

Writers often become the medium through which the future is forecast. Just like other artists, they are often especially sensitive to the new tendencies at work in the society and are active in disseminating images of new goals. These may kindle in the readers' minds emotional drives that lead to the setting up of new patterns of conduct and new social structures. As the history of literature reminds us, again and again writers have set forth such scathing revelations of the life about them or have created such attractive images of ways of life different from those accepted by their times, that they have helped to introduce new standards, new modes of sensibility, new possibilities of behavior, and new social ideals.

However, the typical conservative fear that literary works may incite young people to rush into all sorts of new and untried modes of behavior is a decidedly unrealistic view. Victorian critics often seemed to believe that the mere reading about particular actions in a book would in itself lead to the performance of the same actions in life. They mistakenly thought of the reader as a blank photographic plate upon which was projected the series of images offered by a literary work. But there are many factors that make the individual reader anything but such a blank photographic plate. In the interplay of forces acting on the individual, the literary work will probably have very little weight if its emphasis is directly opposed to the images that many of the agencies in the society about the reader may be reiterating.

29. In the passage, the author claims that those critics who compare the reader of a literary work to a blank photographic plate are wrong because
   (A) the influence of literature is much more subtle than that of the visual arts
   (B) the degree of influence exerted by a literary work is determined by the intelligence and prestige of those who read it
   (C) not all readers respond to the same stimulus in the same way
   (D) the same reader can be as strongly influenced by art and music as by literature
   (E) literary influences represent but one of the many influences which combine to shape an individual's actions

30. Which of the following is the most valid comment on the organization of the passage?
   (A) The second paragraph contradicts the main idea of the first paragraph.
   (B) The second paragraph is an example used to clarify the basic idea of the first paragraph.
   (C) The second paragraph qualifies the first paragraph and detracts from the drama of its claims.
   (D) The second paragraph reinforces and strengthens the first paragraph.
   (E) The second paragraph is only indirectly related to the first paragraph.

31. According to the second paragraph, the typical conservative fear of injurious effects of literature on young people is unrealistic because
   (A) literary influences are effective mainly when they reinforce current social trends
   (B) much that would have shocked people a hundred years ago is universally accepted today
   (C) beneficial influences are at least as common as harmful ones
   (D) literary influences are usually too transitory to result in lasting harm
   (E) modern adolescents are rarely exposed to the harmful influences that were prevalent in the Victorian era

The most fruitful areas for the growth of the sciences are those neglected areas between the various established fields. Since Leibniz, there has perhaps been no one who has had a full command of all the intellectual activity of the day. Increasingly, science has become the task of specialists, in fields which show a tendency to grow progressively narrower. Yet it is the boundary regions of science which offer the richest opportunities to the qualified investigator. At the same time, these regions are most refractory to the accepted techniques of mass attack and the division of labor.

If the difficulty of a physiological problem is mathematical in essence, ten physiologists ignorant of mathematics will get precisely as far as one physiologist ignorant of mathematics, and no further. However, if a physiologist who knows no mathematics works together with a mathematician who knows no physiology, the one will be unable to state a problem in terms that the other can manipulate, and the second will be unable to put the answers in any form that the first can understand. A proper exploration of these blank spaces on the map of science can only be made by a team of scientists, each a specialist in one field, but each possessing a thoroughly sound and trained acquaintance with the other fields. In addition, all must be in the habit of working together, of knowing one another's intellectual customs, and of recognizing the significance of a colleague's new suggestion before it has taken on a full formal expression. The mathematician need not have the skill to conduct a physiological experiment, but must have the skill to understand one, to criticize one, to suggest one. The physiologist need not be able to prove a certain mathematical theorem, but must be able to describe what is needed to the mathematician.

32. It can be inferred from the passage that the explanation for the lack of successful exploration in the boundary regions of science is the

(A) shortage in all fields of scientific specialists
(B) lack of interest accorded this problem by the public
(C) reluctance of scientists to avail themselves of a humanistic education
(D) suspicion with which specialists view these border areas
(E) inability of research teams as presently organized to solve these problems

33. In general, the passage may be interpreted as urging changes in the

(A) number of specialists who work in science
(B) definition of "boundary region" in science
(C) distinction between mathematics and science
(D) education of scientists for research in the boundary regions
(E) use of mass attack and division of labor in the established fields

34. The author most probably cites the example of Leibniz' comprehensive knowledge of the intellectual life of his time in order to

(A) demonstrate that it is necessary for scientists of today to possess such an understanding
(B) establish Leibniz' reputation as the precursor of the modern scientist
(C) indicate the magnitude of the changes that have occurred since the time of Leibniz
(D) contrast the simplicity of Leibniz' mind with the complexity of that of the contemporary scientist
(E) soften the criticism leveled at modern scientific research methods

35. According to the author, which of the following should an individual member of a research team possess?

I. Sensitivity to the thought processes of colleagues
II. Ability to design experiments in several fields
III. Specialization in one field and a working knowledge of the fields of colleagues

(A) I only (B) II only (C) III only
(D) I and II only (E) I and III only

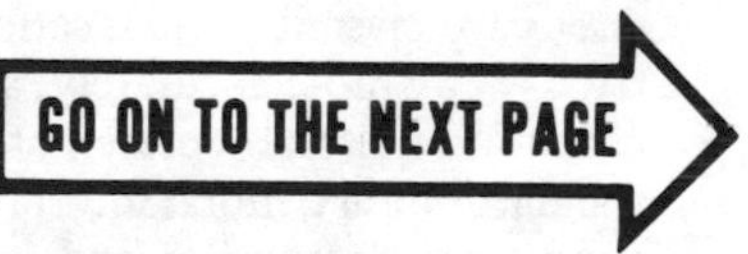

If the origin of art had to wait for somebody's conception of an inner meaning, and on the intention of that person to express it, then our poor addle-brained race would probably never have produced the first artistic creation. We see significance in things long before we know what we are seeing, and it takes some other interest, practical or emotional or superstitious, to make us produce an object which turns out to have expressive virtue as well. We cannot conceive significant form in a vacuum; we can only find it and create something in its image; but when someone has seen the "significant form" in a thing, the copy of that thing is given certain emphasis, not by measure, but by the selective, interpretive power of an intelligent eye.

This insight is not the function of formal education. Apparently the earliest people in most societies have had a vegetative period of artistic activity, as they have had of linguistic and mythological and ritual growth. A pre-Athenian peasant makes a bust of Hermes for the protection of a home and produces a statue of classic beauty. An early Native American carves a totem pole and achieves a composition, or fashions a canoe or molds a water jar and creates a lovely form. The model is the human body, the tree trunk, the curled dry leaf floating, the shell or skull or coconut used for drinking.

But in the imitation of such models for practical ends, those with special vision see more than the utilitarian import of such shapes; they see the reflection of human feeling, the dynamic laws of life, power, and rhythm, in forms on which their attention is focused; they see things they cannot name—magical imports, rightness of line and mass; their hands unwittingly express and even overdraw what they see, and the product amazes and delights them and looks "beautiful." But they do not "know," in discursive terms, what they are expressing, or why they deviate from the model to make the form more "significant." As a society emerges and takes discursive reasoning more seriously, these "artists" try to copy more accurately; and that ambition for naturalistic, literal representation, for rational standards of art, moral interpretations, and so forth, confuses their intuition and endangers their visual apprehension.

36. The implication of the first paragraph is that art is primarily the product of

(A) desire for recognition
(B) self-understanding
(C) exact imitation
(D) reason
(E) intuition

37. Which of the following would be an example of deviating "from the model to make the form more 'significant' " (lines 40-41) ?

(A) Exaggerating the whorl shapes in molding a shell-shaped jar
(B) Including several animal or human forms in a single totem pole
(C) Elevating human importance by making gods look like people
(D) Attaching moral significance to the most beautiful object one makes
(E) Covering a canoe frame with birch bark rather than with sealed dry leaves

38. Which of the following assumptions does the author make about art?

(A) Art is dependent on the development of language and ritual for its existence.
(B) Artistic vision is ultimately of less significance than artistic technique.
(C) Art must come purely from a desire to create something beautiful.
(D) Artistic ability is an innate trait.
(E) Beauty should have objective criteria.

39. The central thought of the passage is most clearly expressed in which of the following lines?

(A) 1-5
(B) 5-10
(C) 18-21
(D) 38-41
(E) 41-43

40. Which of the following best describes the author's technique in this passage?

(A) Presenting highly emotional ideas in a cooly detached tone
(B) Discussing art in a patronizing tone while elevating artists
(C) Offering highly intellectual theories in a stridently anti-intellectual tone
(D) Stating facts in an objective tone in order to debunk the mystery of art
(E) Developing reasons for an assertion in a tone that is explanatory yet not pedantic

S T O P

IF YOU FINISH BEFORE TIME IS CALLED, YOU MAY CHECK YOUR WORK ON THIS SECTION ONLY. DO NOT WORK ON ANY OTHER SECTION IN THE TEST.

SECTION 5

Time—30 minutes

35 QUESTIONS

In this section solve each problem, using any available space on the page for scratchwork. Then decide which is the best of the choices given and blacken the corresponding space on the answer sheet.

The following information is for your reference in solving some of the problems.

Circle of radius r: Area $= \pi r^2$; Circumference $= 2\pi r$
The number of degrees of arc in a circle is 360.
The measure in degrees of a straight angle is 180.

Definitions of symbols:

$=$	is equal to	$\leq$	is less than or equal to
$\neq$	is unequal to	$\geq$	is greater than or equal to
$<$	is less than	$\parallel$	is parallel to
$>$	is greater than	$\perp$	is perpendicular to

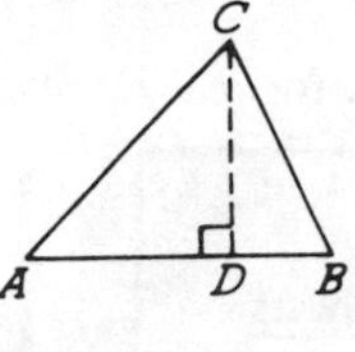

Triangle: The sum of the measures in degrees of the angles of a triangle is 180.

If $\angle CDA$ is a right angle, then

(1) area of $\triangle ABC = \dfrac{AB \times CD}{2}$

(2) $AC^2 = AD^2 + DC^2$

Note: Figures which accompany problems in this test are intended to provide information useful in solving the problems. They are drawn as accurately as possible EXCEPT when it is stated in a specific problem that its figure is not drawn to scale. All figures lie in a plane unless otherwise indicated. All numbers used are real numbers.

---

1. Adding one to which digit of the number 12,345 increases the number by one hundred?

(A) 1
(B) 2
(C) 3
(D) 4
(E) 5

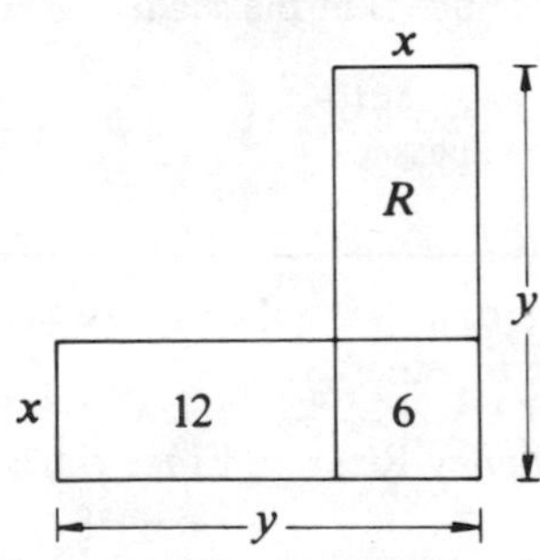

2. In the figure above, if two identical rectangles overlap to form three regions with areas 12, 6, and R, respectively, then $R =$

(A) 6 (B) 12 (C) 15 (D) 18 (E) 24

3. A person bought 12 cards for 30 cents. If the next day the price of the cards was 5 cents each, how much did the person save per card by buying at the earlier price?

(A) 2¢ (B) $2\frac{1}{2}$¢ (C) 3¢ (D) $3\frac{1}{2}$¢ (E) 5¢

$$\begin{array}{r} 5\triangle 2 \\ \times \quad 9 \\ \hline 5{,}2\square 8 \end{array}$$

4. In the correctly computed multiplication problem above, if $\triangle$ and $\square$ are different digits, then $\triangle =$

(A) 1 (B) 5 (C) 6 (D) 7 (E) 8

5. Of the following, which is greater than $\frac{1}{2}$?

(A) $\frac{3}{7}$ (B) $\frac{4}{9}$ (C) $\frac{5}{11}$ (D) $\frac{7}{13}$ (E) $\frac{8}{17}$

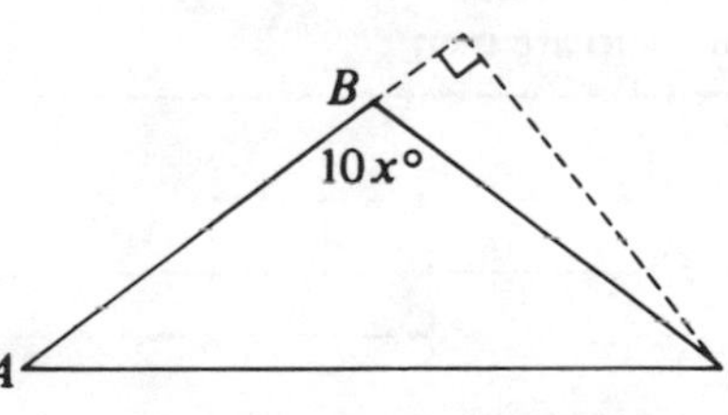

6. In $\triangle ABC$ above, which of the following could be a value of x ?

(A) 12 (B) 8 (C) 4 (D) 2 (E) 1

7. Carol has twice as many books as Beverly has. After Carol gives Beverly 5 books, she still has 10 more books than Beverly has. How many books did Carol have originally?

(A) 20 (B) 25 (C) 30 (D) 35 (E) 40

GO ON TO THE NEXT PAGE

Questions 8-27 each consist of two quantities, one in Column A and one in Column B. You are to compare the two quantities and on the answer sheet blacken space

A if the quantity in Column A is greater;
B if the quantity in Column B is greater;
C if the two quantities are equal;
D if the relationship cannot be determined from the information given.

Notes: 1. In certain questions, information concerning one or both of the quantities to be compared is centered above the two columns.
2. In a given question, a symbol that appears in both columns represents the same thing in Column A as it does in Column B.
3. Letters such as x, n, and k stand for real numbers.

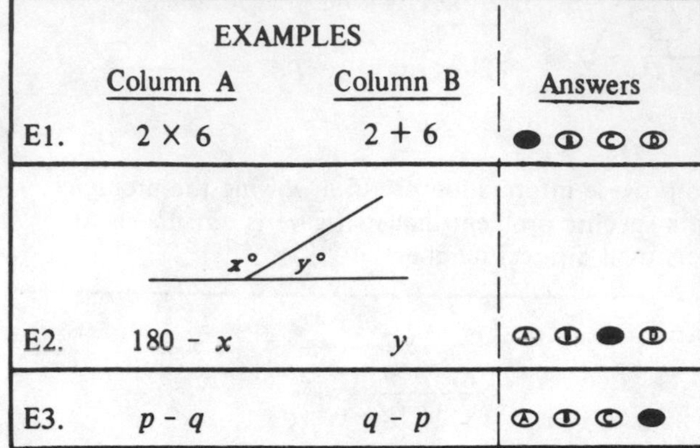

EXAMPLES

	Column A	Column B	Answers
E1.	2×6	$2 + 6$	● Ⓑ Ⓒ Ⓓ
E2.	$180 - x$	y	Ⓐ Ⓑ ● Ⓓ
E3.	$p - q$	$q - p$	Ⓐ Ⓑ Ⓒ ●

	Column A	Column B
8.	333,733	$10 \times 33{,}373$

Of the 100 members of a law school class, exactly 55 are women.

	Column A	Column B
9.	Percent of the class members who are men	55%

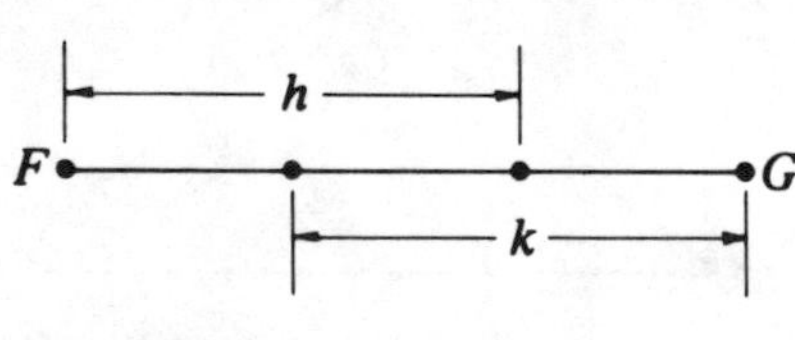

	Column A	Column B
10.	Length FG	$h + k$

A 3-liter bottle of solution P costs \$9.66 and a 4-liter bottle of solution Q costs \$12.88.

	Column A	Column B
11.	The average cost per liter of solution P	The average cost per liter of solution Q
12.	$1 - 0.0001$	$1 - 0.0011$

Column A | Column B

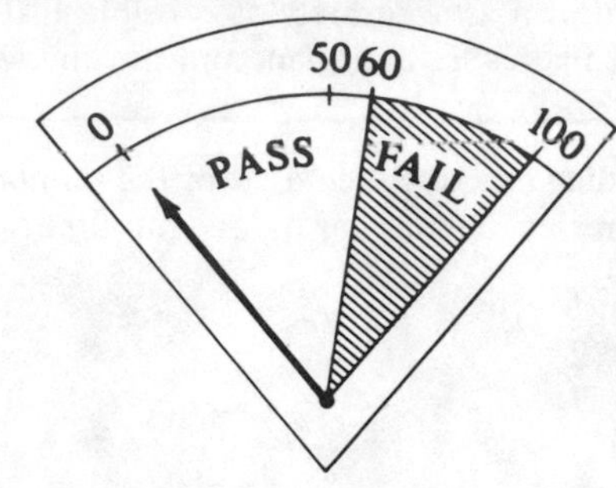

An automobile fails a pollution test if the reading on the meter above is in the shaded region.

	Column A	Column B
13.	The reading for an automobile that has passed the test	65

Rita has more than twice the money that Frank and Lisa have together.

	Column A	Column B
14.	Amount of money Rita has	Three times the amount Lisa has

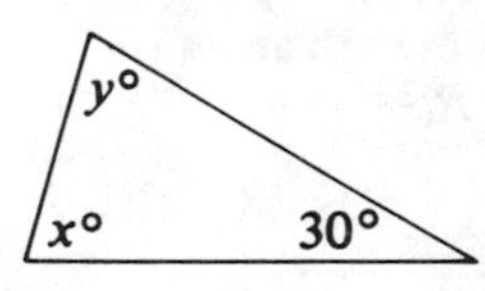

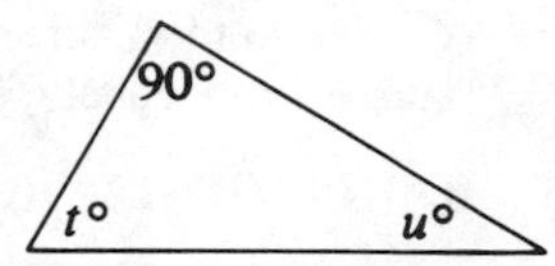

	Column A	Column B
15.	$x + y$	$t + u$

$$xy = 6$$
$$x^2 + y^2 = 13$$

	Column A	Column B
16.	$(x + y)^2$	18

GO ON TO THE NEXT PAGE

SUMMARY DIRECTIONS FOR COMPARISON QUESTIONS

Answer: A if the quantity in Column A is greater;
B if the quantity in Column B is greater;
C if the two quantities are equal;
D if the relationship cannot be determined from the information given.

	Column A	Column B

The three-digit number 6 ■ 5 is divisible by 5.

17.	■	5

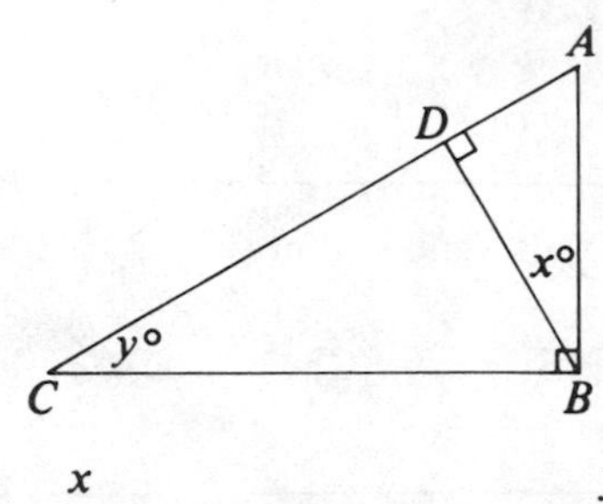

18.	x	y

Questions 19-20 refer to the following definition.

For $x \neq 0$, let ⓧ be defined by ⓧ $= x + \frac{1}{x}$.

19.		-4
20.	(2)	

List A	List B
6	17
13	24
19	11
8	16
14	19

21.	The sum of 3 different numbers from list A	The sum of 3 different numbers from list B

	Column A	Column B
22.	$x(x+y) - z(x+y)$	$(x-z)(x+y)$

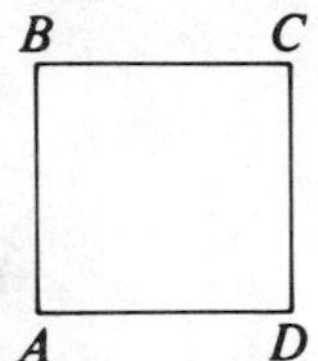

In square $ABCD$, X is the midpoint of side CD, and Y is the midpoint of segment AX.

23.	Length AY	Length CY

x is 10% of y.

24.	The percent that y is of x	100%

$y^2 - 1 > x^2 - 1$

25.	x	y

S is the sum and k is the average (arithmetic mean) of the consecutive positive integers from 1 to n, inclusive.

26.	S	nk

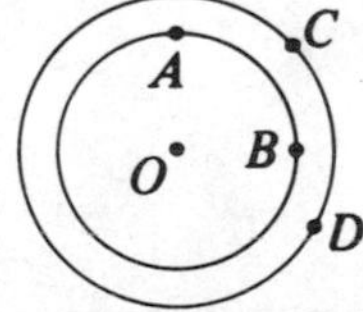

Note: Figure not drawn to scale.

Minor arcs AB and CD have equal length and each lies on a different circle with center O.

27.	Degree measure of minor arc AB	Degree measure of minor arc CD

GO ON TO THE NEXT PAGE

Solve each of the remaining problems in this section using any available space for scratchwork. Then decide which is the best of the choices given and blacken the corresponding space on the answer sheet.

28. If p is an odd integer, which of the following is an even integer?

(A) $p - 2$
(B) p^2
(C) $p^2 - 2$
(D) $(p - 2)^2$
(E) $p^2 - p$

29. The circle above has center P. Given segments of the following lengths, which is the length of the longest one that can be placed entirely inside this circle?

(A) 6.99
(B) 7.00
(C) 7.99
(D) 8.10
(E) 14.00

30. A machine can insert letters in envelopes at the rate of 120 per minute. Another machine can stamp the envelopes at the rate of 3 per second. How many such stamping machines are needed to keep up with 18 inserting machines of this kind?

(A) 9
(B) 12
(C) 15
(D) 24
(E) 27

31. For all numbers $x, y,$ and z, if the operation ϕ is defined by the equation $x \phi y = x + xy$, then $x \phi (y \phi z) =$

(A) $x + xy + xyz$
(B) $x + xyz$
(C) $x + xy + x + xz$
(D) $x + y + yz$
(E) $x + y + xyz$

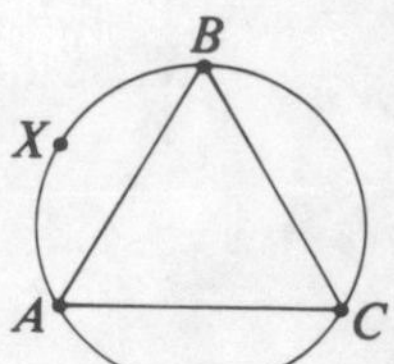

32. In the figure above, inscribed $\triangle ABC$ is equilateral. If the radius of the circle is r, then the length of arc AXB is

(A) $\frac{2\pi r}{3}$ (B) $\frac{4\pi r}{3}$ (C) $\frac{3\pi r}{2}$

(D) $\frac{\pi r^2}{3}$ (E) $\frac{2\pi r^2}{3}$

33. If $x + 2x$ is 5 more than $y + 2y$, then $x - y =$

(A) -5 (B) $-\frac{5}{3}$ (C) $\frac{3}{5}$ (D) $\frac{5}{3}$ (E) 5

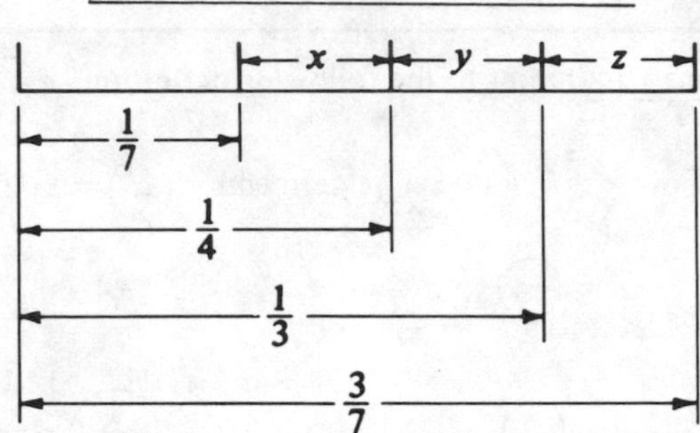

Note: Figure not drawn to scale.

34. In the figure above, if $x, y,$ and z are the lengths indicated, what is an arrangement of $x, y,$ and z in order of increasing length?

(A) x, y, z
(B) z, x, y
(C) y, x, z
(D) z, y, x
(E) y, z, x

35. If $(x + y)^2 = x^2 + y^2$, which of the following statements must also be true?

I. $x = 0$
II. $(x - y)^2 = x^2 + y^2$
III. $xy = 0$

(A) None (B) I only (C) II only

(D) III only (E) II and III

S T O P

IF YOU FINISH BEFORE TIME IS CALLED, YOU MAY CHECK YOUR WORK ON THIS SECTION ONLY. DO NOT WORK ON ANY OTHER SECTION IN THE TEST.

Correct Answers for Scholastic Aptitude Test
Form Code 1E

VERBAL		MATHEMATICAL	
Section 1	**Section 4**	**Section 2**	**Section 5**
1. D	1. A	1. C	1. C
2. B	2. B	2. B	2. B
3. C	3. B	3. D	3. B
4. C	4. D	4. E	4. E
5. B	5. C	5. A	5. D
6. D	6. D	6. †	6. A
7. A	7. E	7. B	7. E
8. A	8. E	8. A	*8. A
9. E	9. E	9. D	*9. B
10. B	10. A	10. B	*10. B
11. B	11. D	11. C	*11. C
12. A	12. A	12. A	*12. A
13. A	13. E	13. D	*13. B
14. C	14. E	14. E	*14. D
15. E	15. E	15. D	*15. A
16. A	16. D	16. B	*16. A
17. A	17. B	17. C	*17. D
18. C	18. C	18. B	*18. C
19. A	19. E	19. C	*19. B
20. A	20. C	20. B	*20. C
21. A	21. A	21. D	*21. D
22. B	22. B	22. C	*22. C
23. D	23. B	23. D	*23. B
24. E	24. B	24. D	*24. A
25. A	25. E	25. B	*25. D
26. E	26. D		*26. C
27. C	27. B		*27. A
28. D	28. E		28. E
29. C	29. E		29. C
30. B	30. C		30. B
31. B	31. A		31. A
32. B	32. E		32. A
33. E	33. D		33. D
34. D	34. C		34. E
35. D	35. E		35. E
36. B	36. E		
37. C	37. A		
38. D	38. D		
39. C	39. B		
40. A	40. E		
41. D			
42. D			
43. C			
44. C			
45. A			

†Not scored

*Indicates four-choice questions. (All of the other questions are five-choice.)

The Scoring Process

Machine-scoring is done in three steps:

- *Scanning.* Your answer sheet is "read" by a scanning machine and the oval you filled in for each question is recorded on a computer tape.
- *Scoring.* The computer compares the oval filled in for each question with the correct response. Each correct answer receives one point; omitted questions do not count toward your score. For each wrong answer, a fraction of a point is subtracted to correct for random guessing. For questions with five answer choices, one-fourth of a point is subtracted for each wrong response; for questions with four answer choices, one-third of a point is subtracted for each wrong response. The SAT-verbal test has 85 questions with five answer choices each. If, for example, a student has 44 right, 32 wrong, and 9 omitted, the resulting raw score is determined as follows:

  $$44 \text{ right} - \frac{32 \text{ wrong}}{4} = 44 - 8 = 36 \text{ raw score points}$$

  Obtaining raw scores frequently involves the rounding of fractional numbers to the nearest whole number. For example, a raw score of 36.25 is rounded to 36, the nearest whole number. A raw score of 36.50 is rounded upward to 37.
- *Converting to reported scaled score.* Raw test scores are then placed on the College Board scale of 200 to 800 through a process that adjusts scores to account for minor differences in difficulty among different editions of the test. This process, known as equating, is performed so that a student's reported score is not affected by the edition of the test taken nor by the abilities of the group with whom the student takes the test. As a result of placing SAT scores on the College Board scale, scores earned by students at different times can be compared. For example, an SAT-verbal score of 400 on a test taken at one administration indicates the same level of developed verbal ability as a 400 score obtained on a different edition of the test taken at another time.

How to Score the Test

You can verify the College Board SAT scores reported to you recently by using the information in this booklet along with the copy of your answer sheet. *Before you begin, check that the first two characters (number and letter) of the form code you marked in item 3 on your answer sheet are the same as the form code printed on the front of this booklet.* Compare the responses shown on the copy of your answer sheet with the list of correct answers.

SAT-Verbal Sections 1 and 4

Step A: Count the number of correct answers for *section 1* and record the number in the space provided on the worksheet on the next page. Then do the same for the incorrect answers. (Do not count omitted answers.) To determine subtotal A, use the formula:

$$\text{number correct} - \frac{\text{number incorrect}}{4} = \text{subtotal A}$$

Step B: Count the number of correct answers and the number of incorrect answers for *section 4* and record the numbers in the spaces provided on the worksheet. To determine subtotal B, use the formula:

$$\text{number correct} - \frac{\text{number incorrect}}{4} = \text{subtotal B}$$

Step C: To obtain C, add subtotal A to subtotal B, keeping any decimals. Enter the resulting figure on the worksheet.

Step D: To obtain D, your raw verbal score, round C to the nearest whole number. (For example, any number from 44.50 to 45.49 rounds to 45.) Enter the resulting figure on the worksheet.

Step E: To find your reported SAT-verbal score, look up the total raw verbal score you obtained in step D in the conversion table on page 122. Enter this figure on the worksheet.

SAT-Mathematical Sections 2 and 5

Step A: Count the number of correct answers and the number of incorrect answers for *section 2* and record the numbers in the spaces provided on the worksheet. To determine the subtotal A, use the formula:

$$\text{number correct} - \frac{\text{number incorrect}}{4} = \text{subtotal A}$$

Step B: Count the number of correct answers and the number of incorrect answers for the *five-choice questions (questions 1 through 7 and 28 through 35) in section 5* and record the numbers in the spaces provided on the worksheet. To determine the subtotal B, use the formula:

$$\text{number correct} - \frac{\text{number incorrect}}{4} = \text{subtotal B}$$

Step C: Count the number of correct answers and the number of incorrect answers for the *four-choice questions (questions 8 through 27) in section 5* and record the numbers in the spaces provided on the worksheet. To determine the subtotal C, use the formula:

$$\text{number correct} - \frac{\text{number incorrect}}{3} = \text{subtotal C}$$

Step D: To obtain D, add subtotal A, subtotal B, and subtotal C, keeping any decimals. Enter the resulting figure on the worksheet.

Step E: To obtain E, your raw mathematical score, round D to the nearest whole number. (For example, any number from 44.50 to 45.49 rounds to 45.) Enter the resulting figure on the worksheet.

Step F: To find your reported SAT-mathematical score, look up the total raw mathematical score you obtained in E in the conversion table on page 122. Enter this figure on the worksheet.

SAT SCORING WORKSHEET

FORM CODE 1E

SAT-Verbal Sections

A. Section 1:	______ no. correct	− ¼	(______) no. incorrect	=	______ subtotal A
B. Section 4:	______ no. correct	− ¼	(______) no. incorrect	=	______ subtotal B
C. Total unrounded raw score (Total A + B)					______ C
D. Total rounded raw score (Rounded to nearest whole number)					______ D
E. SAT-verbal reported scaled score (See the conversion table on the back cover.)					[ ] SAT-verbal score

SAT-Mathematical Sections

A. Section 2:	______ no. correct	− ¼	(______) no. incorrect	=	______ subtotal A
B. Section 5: Questions 1 through 7 and 28 through 35 (5-choice)	______ no. correct	− ¼	(______) no. incorrect	=	______ subtotal B
C. Section 5: Questions 8 through 27 (4-choice)	______ no. correct	− ⅓	(______) no. incorrect	=	______ subtotal C
D. Total unrounded raw score (Total A + B + C)					______ D
E. Total rounded raw score (Rounded to nearest whole number)					______ E
F. SAT-mathematical reported scaled score (See the conversion table on the back cover.)					[ ] SAT-math score

Score Conversion Table
Scholastic Aptitude Test
Form Code 1E

Raw Score	College Board Reported Score		Raw Score	College Board Reported Score	
	SAT-Verbal	SAT-Math		SAT-Verbal	SAT-Math
85	800		40	450	600
84	790		39	450	590
83	780		38	440	580
82	770		37	430	570
81	760		36	430	560
80	750		35	420	550
79	740		34	410	550
78	730		33	410	540
77	720		32	400	530
76	710		31	390	520
75	700		30	380	510
74	690		29	380	500
73	680		28	370	490
72	670		27	360	490
71	670		26	360	480
70	660		25	350	470
69	650		24	340	460
68	650		23	340	450
67	640		22	330	440
66	630		21	320	430
65	630		20	320	430
64	620		19	310	420
63	610		18	300	410
62	610		17	300	400
61	600		16	290	390
60	590		15	280	380
59	580	800	14	270	370
58	580	780	13	270	370
57	570	770	12	260	360
56	560	760	11	250	350
55	560	750	10	250	340
54	550	740	9	240	330
53	540	730	8	230	320
52	540	710	7	230	310
51	530	700	6	220	310
50	520	690	5	210	300
49	520	680	4	210	290
48	510	670	3	200	280
47	500	660	2	200	270
46	490	650	1	200	260
45	490	640	0	200	250
44	480	630	− 1	200	250
43	470	620	− 2	200	240
42	470	610	− 3	200	230
41	460	600	− 4	200	220
			− 5	200	210
			− 6 or below	200	200

Test 4
SAT *Form Code 1F*

(Cut here to detach.)

COLLEGE BOARD — SCHOLASTIC APTITUDE TEST and Test of Standard Written English

Side 1

Use a No. 2 pencil only. Be sure each mark is dark and completely fills the intended oval. Completely erase any errors or stray marks.

1. YOUR NAME: (Print) ______ Last ______ First ______ M.I.

SIGNATURE: ______ **DATE:** ___/___/___

HOME ADDRESS: (Print) ______ Number and Street

______ City ______ State ______ Zip Code

CENTER: (Print) ______ City ______ State ______ Center Number

IMPORTANT: Please fill in these boxes exactly as shown on the back cover of your test book.

FOR ETS USE ONLY

2. TEST FORM

3. FORM CODE

0	A	J	S	0	0	0
1	B	K	T	1	1	1
2	C	L	U	2	2	2
3	D	M	V	3	3	3
4	E	N	W	4	4	4
5	F	O	X	5	5	5
6	G	P	Y	6	6	6
7	H	Q	Z	7	7	7
8	I	R		8	8	8
9				9	9	9

4. REGISTRATION NUMBER (Copy from your Admission Ticket.)

0	0	0	0	0	0	0
1	1	1	1	1	1	1
2	2	2	2	2	2	2
3	3	3	3	3	3	3
4	4	4	4	4	4	4
5	5	5	5	5	5	5
6	6	6	6	6	6	6
7	7	7	7	7	7	7
8	8	8	8	8	8	8
9	9	9	9	9	9	9

5. YOUR NAME

First 4 letters of last name				First Init.	Mid. Init.
A	A	A	A	A	A
B	B	B	B	B	B
C	C	C	C	C	C
D	D	D	D	D	D
E	E	E	E	E	E
F	F	F	F	F	F
G	G	G	G	G	G
H	H	H	H	H	H
I	I	I	I	I	I
J	J	J	J	J	J
K	K	K	K	K	K
L	L	L	L	L	L
M	M	M	M	M	M
N	N	N	N	N	N
O	O	O	O	O	O
P	P	P	P	P	P
Q	Q	Q	Q	Q	Q
R	R	R	R	R	R
S	S	S	S	S	S
T	T	T	T	T	T
U	U	U	U	U	U
V	V	V	V	V	V
W	W	W	W	W	W
X	X	X	X	X	X
Y	Y	Y	Y	Y	Y
Z	Z	Z	Z	Z	Z

6. DATE OF BIRTH

Month	Day		Year	
Jan.				
Feb.				
Mar.	0	0	0	0
Apr.	1	1	1	1
May	2	2	2	2
June	3	3	3	3
July		4	4	4
Aug.		5	5	5
Sept.		6	6	6
Oct.		7	7	7
Nov.		8		8
Dec.		9		9

7. SEX

Female

Male

8. TEST BOOK SERIAL NUMBER

Start with number 1 for each new section. If a section has fewer than 50 questions, leave the extra answer spaces blank.

SECTION 1

1 A D C D F
2 A B C D E
3 A B C D E
4 A B C D E
5 A B C D E
6 A B C D E
7 A B C D E
8 A B C D E
9 A B C D E
10 A B C D E
11 A B C D E
12 A B C D E
13 A B C D E
14 A B C D E
15 A B C D E
16 A B C D E
17 A B C D E
18 A B C D E
19 A B C D E
20 A B C D E
21 A B C D E
22 A B C D E
23 A B C D E
24 A B C D E
25 A B C D E
26 A B C D E
27 A B C D E
28 A B C D E
29 A B C D E
30 A B C D E
31 A B C D E
32 A B C D E
33 A B C D E
34 A B C D E
35 A B C D E
36 A B C D E
37 A B C D E
38 A B C D E
39 A B C D E
40 A B C D E
41 A B C D E
42 A B C D E
43 A B C D E
44 A B C D E
45 A B C D E
46 A B C D E
47 A B C D E
48 A B C D E
49 A B C D E
50 A B C D E

SECTION 2

1 A B C D E
2 A B C D E
3 A B C D E
4 A B C D E
5 A B C D E
6 A B C D F
7 A B C D E
8 A B C D E
9 A B C D E
10 A B C D E
11 A B C D E
12 A B C D E
13 A B C D E
14 A B C D E
15 A B C D E
16 A B C D E
17 A B C D E
18 A B C D E
19 A B C D E
20 A B C D E
21 A B C D E
22 A B C D E
23 A B C D E
24 A B C D E
25 A B C D E
26 A B C D E
27 A B C D E
28 A B C D E
29 A B C D E
30 A B C D E
31 A B C D E
32 A B C D E
33 A B C D E
34 A B C D E
35 A B C D E
36 A B C D E
37 A B C D E
38 A B C D E
39 A B C D E
40 A B C D E
41 A B C D E
42 A B C D E
43 A B C D E
44 A B C D E
45 A B C D E
46 A B C D E
47 A B C D E
48 A B C D E
49 A B C D E
50 A B C D E

Q1362-04

I.N. 574006—110VV25P3015

COLLEGE BOARD — SCHOLASTIC APTITUDE TEST
and Test of Standard Written English — Side 2

Use a No. 2 pencil only. Be sure each mark is dark and completely fills the intended oval. Completely erase any errors or stray marks.

Start with number 1 for each new section. If a section has fewer than 50 questions, leave the extra answer spaces blank.

SECTION 3	SECTION 4	SECTION 5	SECTION 6
1 (A) (B) (C) (D) (E)	1 (A) (B) (C) (D) (E)	1 (A) (B) (C) (D) (E)	1 (A) (B) (C) (D) (E)
2 (A) (B) (C) (D) (E)	2 (A) (B) (C) (D) (E)	2 (A) (B) (C) (D) (E)	2 (A) (B) (C) (D) (E)
3 (A) (B) (C) (D) (E)	3 (A) (B) (C) (D) (E)	3 (A) (B) (C) (D) (E)	3 (A) (B) (C) (D) (E)
4 (A) (B) (C) (D) (E)	4 (A) (B) (C) (D) (E)	4 (A) (B) (C) (D) (E)	4 (A) (B) (C) (D) (E)
5 (A) (B) (C) (D) (E)	5 (A) (B) (C) (D) (E)	5 (A) (B) (C) (D) (E)	5 (A) (B) (C) (D) (E)
6 (A) (B) (C) (D) (E)	6 (A) (B) (C) (D) (E)	6 (A) (B) (C) (D) (E)	6 (A) (B) (C) (D) (E)
7 (A) (B) (C) (D) (E)	7 (A) (B) (C) (D) (E)	7 (A) (B) (C) (D) (E)	7 (A) (B) (C) (D) (E)
8 (A) (B) (C) (D) (E)	8 (A) (B) (C) (D) (E)	8 (A) (B) (C) (D) (E)	8 (A) (B) (C) (D) (E)
9 (A) (B) (C) (D) (E)	9 (A) (B) (C) (D) (E)	9 (A) (B) (C) (D) (E)	9 (A) (B) (C) (D) (E)
10 (A) (B) (C) (D) (E)	10 (A) (B) (C) (D) (E)	10 (A) (B) (C) (D) (E)	10 (A) (B) (C) (D) (E)
11 (A) (B) (C) (D) (E)	11 (A) (B) (C) (D) (E)	11 (A) (B) (C) (D) (E)	11 (A) (B) (C) (D) (E)
12 (A) (B) (C) (D) (E)	12 (A) (B) (C) (D) (E)	12 (A) (B) (C) (D) (E)	12 (A) (B) (C) (D) (E)
13 (A) (B) (C) (D) (E)	13 (A) (B) (C) (D) (E)	13 (A) (B) (C) (D) (E)	13 (A) (B) (C) (D) (E)
14 (A) (B) (C) (D) (E)	14 (A) (B) (C) (D) (E)	14 (A) (B) (C) (D) (E)	14 (A) (B) (C) (D) (E)
15 (A) (B) (C) (D) (E)	15 (A) (B) (C) (D) (E)	15 (A) (B) (C) (D) (E)	15 (A) (B) (C) (D) (E)
16 (A) (B) (C) (D) (E)	16 (A) (B) (C) (D) (E)	16 (A) (B) (C) (D) (E)	16 (A) (B) (C) (D) (E)
17 (A) (B) (C) (D) (E)	17 (A) (B) (C) (D) (E)	17 (A) (B) (C) (D) (E)	17 (A) (B) (C) (D) (E)
18 (A) (B) (C) (D) (E)	18 (A) (B) (C) (D) (E)	18 (A) (B) (C) (D) (E)	18 (A) (B) (C) (D) (E)
19 (A) (B) (C) (D) (E)	19 (A) (B) (C) (D) (E)	19 (A) (B) (C) (D) (E)	19 (A) (B) (C) (D) (E)
20 (A) (B) (C) (D) (E)	20 (A) (B) (C) (D) (E)	20 (A) (B) (C) (D) (E)	20 (A) (B) (C) (D) (E)
21 (A) (B) (C) (D) (E)	21 (A) (B) (C) (D) (E)	21 (A) (B) (C) (D) (E)	21 (A) (B) (C) (D) (E)
22 (A) (B) (C) (D) (E)	22 (A) (B) (C) (D) (E)	22 (A) (B) (C) (D) (E)	22 (A) (B) (C) (D) (E)
23 (A) (B) (C) (D) (E)	23 (A) (B) (C) (D) (E)	23 (A) (B) (C) (D) (E)	23 (A) (B) (C) (D) (E)
24 (A) (B) (C) (D) (E)	24 (A) (B) (C) (D) (E)	24 (A) (B) (C) (D) (E)	24 (A) (B) (C) (D) (E)
25 (A) (B) (C) (D) (E)	25 (A) (B) (C) (D) (E)	25 (A) (B) (C) (D) (E)	25 (A) (B) (C) (D) (E)
26 (A) (B) (C) (D) (E)	26 (A) (B) (C) (D) (E)	26 (A) (B) (C) (D) (E)	26 (A) (B) (C) (D) (E)
27 (A) (B) (C) (D) (E)	27 (A) (B) (C) (D) (E)	27 (A) (B) (C) (D) (E)	27 (A) (B) (C) (D) (E)
28 (A) (B) (C) (D) (E)	28 (A) (B) (C) (D) (E)	28 (A) (B) (C) (D) (E)	28 (A) (B) (C) (D) (E)
29 (A) (B) (C) (D) (E)	29 (A) (B) (C) (D) (E)	29 (A) (B) (C) (D) (E)	29 (A) (B) (C) (D) (E)
30 (A) (B) (C) (D) (E)	30 (A) (B) (C) (D) (E)	30 (A) (B) (C) (D) (E)	30 (A) (B) (C) (D) (E)
31 (A) (B) (C) (D) (E)	31 (A) (B) (C) (D) (E)	31 (A) (B) (C) (D) (E)	31 (A) (B) (C) (D) (E)
32 (A) (B) (C) (D) (E)	32 (A) (B) (C) (D) (E)	32 (A) (B) (C) (D) (E)	32 (A) (B) (C) (D) (E)
33 (A) (B) (C) (D) (E)	33 (A) (B) (C) (D) (E)	33 (A) (B) (C) (D) (E)	33 (A) (B) (C) (D) (E)
34 (A) (B) (C) (D) (E)	34 (A) (B) (C) (D) (E)	34 (A) (B) (C) (D) (E)	34 (A) (B) (C) (D) (E)
35 (A) (B) (C) (D) (E)	35 (A) (B) (C) (D) (E)	35 (A) (B) (C) (D) (E)	35 (A) (B) (C) (D) (E)
36 (A) (B) (C) (D) (E)	36 (A) (B) (C) (D) (E)	36 (A) (B) (C) (D) (E)	36 (A) (B) (C) (D) (E)
37 (A) (B) (C) (D) (E)	37 (A) (B) (C) (D) (E)	37 (A) (B) (C) (D) (E)	37 (A) (B) (C) (D) (E)
38 (A) (B) (C) (D) (E)	38 (A) (B) (C) (D) (E)	38 (A) (B) (C) (D) (E)	38 (A) (B) (C) (D) (E)
39 (A) (B) (C) (D) (E)	39 (A) (B) (C) (D) (E)	39 (A) (B) (C) (D) (E)	39 (A) (B) (C) (D) (E)
40 (A) (B) (C) (D) (E)	40 (A) (B) (C) (D) (E)	40 (A) (B) (C) (D) (E)	40 (A) (B) (C) (D) (E)
41 (A) (B) (C) (D) (E)	41 (A) (B) (C) (D) (E)	41 (A) (B) (C) (D) (E)	41 (A) (B) (C) (D) (E)
42 (A) (B) (C) (D) (E)	42 (A) (B) (C) (D) (E)	42 (A) (B) (C) (D) (E)	42 (A) (B) (C) (D) (E)
43 (A) (B) (C) (D) (E)	43 (A) (B) (C) (D) (E)	43 (A) (B) (C) (D) (E)	43 (A) (B) (C) (D) (E)
44 (A) (B) (C) (D) (E)	44 (A) (B) (C) (D) (E)	44 (A) (B) (C) (D) (E)	44 (A) (B) (C) (D) (E)
45 (A) (B) (C) (D) (E)	45 (A) (B) (C) (D) (E)	45 (A) (B) (C) (D) (E)	45 (A) (B) (C) (D) (E)
46 (A) (B) (C) (D) (E)	46 (A) (B) (C) (D) (E)	46 (A) (B) (C) (D) (E)	46 (A) (B) (C) (D) (E)
47 (A) (B) (C) (D) (E)	47 (A) (B) (C) (D) (E)	47 (A) (B) (C) (D) (E)	47 (A) (B) (C) (D) (E)
48 (A) (B) (C) (D) (E)	48 (A) (B) (C) (D) (E)	48 (A) (B) (C) (D) (E)	48 (A) (B) (C) (D) (E)
49 (A) (B) (C) (D) (E)	49 (A) (B) (C) (D) (E)	49 (A) (B) (C) (D) (E)	49 (A) (B) (C) (D) (E)
50 (A) (B) (C) (D) (E)	50 (A) (B) (C) (D) (E)	50 (A) (B) (C) (D) (E)	50 (A) (B) (C) (D) (E)

9. SIGNATURE: ______________________

FOR ETS USE ONLY	VTR	VTFS	VRR	VRFS	VVR	VVFS	WER	WEFS	M4R	M4FS	M5R	M5FS	MTFS	
	VTW	VTCS	VRW	VRCS	VVW	VVCS	WEW	WECS	M4W		M5W		MTCS	

SECTION 1

Time—30 minutes

45 QUESTIONS

For each question in this section, choose the best answer and blacken the corresponding space on the answer sheet.

Each question below consists of a word in capital letters, followed by five lettered words or phrases. Choose the word or phrase that is most nearly opposite in meaning to the word in capital letters. Since some of the questions require you to distinguish fine shades of meaning, consider all the choices before deciding which is best.

Example:

GOOD: (A) sour (B) bad (C) red (D) hot (E) ugly
Ⓐ ● Ⓒ Ⓓ Ⓔ

1. FRET: (A) explain (B) watch (C) relax (D) plan (E) invite

2. DISHEARTEN: (A) enroll (B) mislead (C) distort (D) prepare (E) encourage

3. LUXURIANT: (A) scanty (B) unskilled (C) reverent (D) shameful (E) unpredicted

4. HINDRANCE: (A) expression (B) preference (C) assistance (D) enjoyment (E) emphasis

5. INANIMATE: (A) somber (B) valiant (C) supportive (D) hidden (E) alive

6. ANONYMOUS: (A) synonymous (B) signed (C) modern (D) proven (E) temporary

7. ATYPICAL: (A) favorable (B) emotional (C) factual (D) usual (E) moral

8. CONCEIT: (A) self-effacement (B) self-sufficiency (C) ill repute (D) ill humor (E) unreceptiveness

9. RANT: (A) hold together (B) happen seldom (C) work diligently (D) speak softly (E) step lightly

10. WOODEN: (A) lucky (B) haughty (C) trustworthy (D) graceful (E) proper

11. ACQUIESCE: (A) combine (B) gain (C) panic (D) protect (E) object

12. ADROIT: (A) impure (B) harmless (C) secretive (D) abstract (E) inept

13. MUNIFICENT: (A) judicious (B) obedient (C) miserly (D) determined (E) suggestive

14. UNDERSTATE: (A) placate (B) insinuate (C) embroider (D) dissemble (E) rebound

15. VIRULENT: (A) sectarian (B) defensible (C) comparable (D) cowardly (E) innocuous

Each sentence below has one or two blanks, each blank indicating that something has been omitted. Beneath the sentence are five lettered words or sets of words. Choose the word or set of words that best fits the meaning of the sentence as a whole.

Example:

Although its publicity has been ----, the film itself is intelligent, well-acted, handsomely produced, and altogether ----.

(A) tasteless. .respectable (B) extensive. .moderate (C) sophisticated. .amateur (D) risqué. .crude (E) perfect. .spectacular
● Ⓑ Ⓒ Ⓓ Ⓔ

16. Historical buildings in many American cities, rather than being destroyed, are now being ----.
(A) constructed (B) condemned (C) described (D) renovated (E) designed

17. Sadly, many tropical rain forests are so ---- by agricultural and industrial overdevelopment that they may ---- by the end of the century.
(A) isolated. .separate
(B) threatened. .vanish
(C) consumed. .expand
(D) augmented. .diminish
(E) rejuvenated. .disappear

18. Like all reformers, Wood is ---- who believes that the world can be changed by good people promoting right deeds.
(A) a statistician (B) a prodigal (C) a legislator (D) an opportunist (E) an optimist

19. The ---- of the Navajos is reflected in the fact that many have retained their language and ancient customs.
(A) diversity (B) adaptability (C) modernization (D) cohesiveness (E) creativity

20. I am astounded that the author of such heretofore ---- articles could generate such spritely prose and maintain such an original narrative.
(A) memorable (B) pedestrian (C) perceptive (D) enthralling (E) effervescent

GO ON TO THE NEXT PAGE

Each passage below is followed by questions based on its content. Answer all questions following a passage on the basis of what is stated or implied in that passage.

(This passage was written in 1959.)

Although at least one school of thought supports the thesis that the people of African descent in the Western world have no African heritage to reclaim, I am not of that school. Many writers, both Black and White, have pointed to a rich and ancient heritage which, in my opinion, we must affirm resolutely if Black Americans in general and Black writers in particular are ever to be reconciled with their roots.

As far back as 1881, the renowned scholar, Dr. Edward Blyden, sounded the note for the organized teaching of African culture and civilization. In 1883 George W. Williams, the first Black member of the Ohio legislature and the person responsible for the first organized African studies in the United States, devoted 125 pages of his *History of the Negro Race in America* to background information about African culture and society. The field of research in African history was widened later under the leadership of three men in particular: Dr. W. E. B. Du Bois, Dr. Jesse E. Moorland, and Dr. Carter G. Woodson. Black America's mission to reclaim its lost African heritage was well underway.

What is this heritage? In the first place, the history, art, and folklore of West Africa, the ancestral home of most Black Americans, offer proof that Black people built great nations and an advanced culture hundreds of years before their first appearance in Jamestown, Virginia, in 1619. During the period when Timbuktu was the great intellectual center of the Songhai empire, African scholars enjoyed a renaissance known and respected throughout most of Africa and parts of Europe. Further, long before the European colonial period, independent nations were already established in Africa; many of them possessed long and glorious histories. For example, during the reign of Askia the Great, who came to power a year after Columbus discovered America, the nations of West Africa enjoyed a standard of life equal to, and often higher than, that of other nations of the world.

Historically, Africa and its peoples have been viewed mainly through European eyes and measured by European standards. The entire history of Africa must be rewritten in a manner that challenges and reverses long-held European concepts. This task is singularly the responsibility of Black writers. An abundance of material on African life awaits their attention. They would do well to consider using as a guide two sentences from John W. Vandercook's book *Tom-Tom.*

> A race is like a man. Until it uses its own talents, takes pride in its own history, and loves its own memories, it can never fulfill itself completely.

21. With which of the following statements regarding African culture would the author most likely agree?
    (A) Africans had highly developed cultures long before their first contact with Europeans.
    (B) African culture will not flourish again until Black Americans reclaim it.
    (C) The work of European historians provides a sound basis for further research in African cultural history.
    (D) The scarcity of material on African life has hindered the efforts of Black Americans to reclaim their heritage.
    (E) The cultural significance of the art, history, and folklore of Africa was not universally acknowledged until the 1880's.

22. The author cites Du Bois, Moorland, and Woodson for their
    (A) strong community leadership
    (B) political achievements
    (C) teaching activities
    (D) scholarly investigations of African history
    (E) benevolence toward West Africa

23. The author suggests that European accounts of African history have been
    (A) culturally biased
    (B) avidly read
    (C) systematically suppressed
    (D) adequately refuted
    (E) extensively researched

24. It can be inferred that the author expects Vandercook's quoted statement to be regarded as
    (A) evidence of the rich and ancient heritage of Black Americans
    (B) consistent with European attitudes regarding African history
    (C) a source of inspiration for Black historians and writers
    (D) a stylistic model that will be imitated by fledgling writers
    (E) a tribute to the literary accomplishments of Black writers to date

25. Which of the following best describes the purpose of the passage?
    (A) To describe the influence of African culture on the Western world
    (B) To defend the validity of African studies programs in United States universities
    (C) To encourage Americans of African descent to reclaim their ancestry
    (D) To investigate the origin of the European concept of African history
    (E) To outline appropriate methods for the documentation of Africa's cultural development

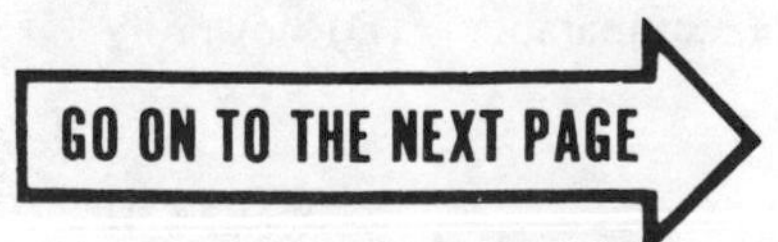

Three main forms of epidemiological investigation are descriptive, analytical, and experimental. Descriptive epidemiology describes events in terms of the persons affected, the place at which the event occurred, and the time frame under consideration. An example of how a descriptive study shows the distribution of disease is the routine surveillance of infections in a hospital. Descriptive epidemiological data obtained from surveillance of hospital-acquired infection may provide information for early recognition of problems, either by detecting an excessive number of cases or, as on several occasions, by identifying the presence of a rare microorganism.

To find the cause of a disease or other problem, investigators follow the techniques of one of the two general types of analytic epidemiological study: cohort and case-control. A cohort study examines two groups–those with and those without an attribute suspected to have some relation to the disease. None of the individuals is a "case" at the outset. A cohort study determines whether or not the group displaying a certain characteristic develops the disease more often than does the group without the characteristic.

A case-control study asks whether the people who have the disease display certain characteristics more frequently than do those who are not affected. "Cases" are defined as those individuals who already have the disease. "Controls," used for comparison, are individuals without the disease. A case-control study is retrospective. The disease or condition has already developed, and researchers look for factors that preceded it. Retrospective studies are faster, less expensive, and better suited to analysis of rare diseases than are prospective studies, which follow a disease-free cohort over time, awaiting the occurrence of the disease. Since not all those exposed to it will develop the disease, large numbers of persons must be included in the prospective study population.

In experimental epidemiology the investigator deliberately manipulates a population, exposing part to the proposed risk or benefit factor and leaving another part unexposed. Risk or benefit factors are those that are thought to be causally related to a condition. (Epidemiologists often prefer the term "condition" to "disease" because an epidemiologist, in contrast to a physician or therapist, focuses interest on subclinical conditions and even on healthy members of the group under study.) Experimental studies are not difficult to justify when the intervention is relatively safe or when the patient is already at risk. However, performing such experimental studies is unacceptable in certain circumstances.

26. The main purpose of the passage is to

(A) compare and contrast different statistical theories
(B) explain common epidemiological research methods
(C) provide historical background on epidemiology
(D) describe specific infection-control practices
(E) emphasize the importance of sound research techniques

27. It can be inferred from the passage that descriptive epidemiology allows an investigator to answer routinely which of the following questions?

(A) What differences exist between the experimental and control groups?
(B) What steps are being taken to control the disease?
(C) How many people in a particular area have the disease?
(D) What specific factors prevented certain people from contracting the disease?
(E) How much information is needed to describe future effects of the disease?

28. According to the passage, a cohort study is one that

(A) gathers retrospective data
(B) is based at its outset on persons who have not yet contracted a given disease
(C) involves treatment of populations
(D) compares those who already have a given disease with those who do not
(E) is an example of descriptive epidemiology

29. The passage implies that an experimental epidemiological study is most likely to focus on a comparison between which of the following?

(A) The number of people in an untreated population who recover from a disease and the number who do not
(B) The occurrence of a disease among those who have and those who do not have a given attribute
(C) The number of people over a certain age with a disease and the number under that age without the disease
(D) The infection rates after treating part of a group with one procedure and the other part with another procedure
(E) The patient population in one area and that in another area

30. According to the passage, an epidemiologist would consider an attribute to be a risk factor if it were thought to be

(A) a result of a disease
(B) a cause of a disease
(C) a symptom of a disease
(D) indicative of an incurable disease
(E) unrelated to the disease under study

GO ON TO THE NEXT PAGE

1

Select the word or set of words that best completes each of the following sentences.

31. Hoping to ---- the angry customer, the manager of the store courteously offered a refund on the purchase.

    (A) pique (B) upbraid (C) embolden (D) conciliate (E) compliment

32. Even those who ---- the aphorism "history repeats itself" must now ---- the fact that certain events bear marked resemblances to incidents of earlier history.

    (A) reject. .doubt
    (B) deny. .acknowledge
    (C) defend. .perceive
    (D) ignore. .forget
    (E) heed. .admit

33. Scientific research has become so ---- that even leading scientists are now expected to ---- their work in order to obtain grants.

    (A) expensive. .justify (B) vital. .propose (C) popular. .belittle (D) exact. .minimize (E) esoteric. .falsify

34. My plea is not for drab and ---- technical writing about music but for pertinent information conveyed with as much ---- as possible.

    (A) repetitive. .redundancy
    (B) obscure. .felicity
    (C) inscrutable. .ambivalence
    (D) euphonious. .harmony
    (E) provocative. .exhilaration

35. Ms. Warner supplements her selection of Queen Victoria's drawings with a text as idiosyncratic as it is ----, for she can be ---- as well as a scholarly writer.

    (A) professional. .a rigorous
    (B) perplexing. .a popular
    (C) unique. .a conscientious
    (D) entertaining. .a traditional
    (E) accurate. .an unconventional

Each question below consists of a related pair of words or phrases, followed by five lettered pairs of words or phrases. Select the lettered pair that best expresses a relationship similar to that expressed in the original pair.

Example:

> YAWN : BOREDOM :: (A) dream : sleep (B) anger : madness (C) smile : amusement (D) face : expression (E) impatience : rebellion
>
> Ⓐ Ⓑ ● Ⓓ Ⓔ

36. INTRODUCTION : CONCLUSION ::
    (A) announcement : news
    (B) greeting : farewell
    (C) birth : marriage
    (D) arrival : salutation
    (E) friendship : termination

37. STRIKE : WORK :: (A) postpone : cancel (B) censor : learn (C) incorporate : merge (D) detour : trespass (E) boycott : purchase

38. SCALPEL : SURGEON :: (A) razor : barber (B) weed : gardener (C) recipe : chef (D) medicine : patient (E) compass : engineer

39. PREPOSTEROUS : COMMON SENSE ::
    (A) illegal : law (B) chronic : pain (C) indelible : error (D) justifiable : logic (E) hilarious : laughter

40. CLASH : COLOR :: (A) intensity : sensation (B) glimpse : vision (C) pebble : texture (D) dissonance : sound (E) absurdity : perception

41. FORMIDABLE : FEAR :: (A) intolerable : patience (B) grateful : regret (C) sickening : disgust (D) generous : pity (E) dismal : cheer

42. BASTION : DEFENSE ::
    (A) arsenal : storage
    (B) anchorage : supply
    (C) citadel : concealment
    (D) asylum : embarkation
    (E) pavilion : fortification

43. SAGA : LENGTHY :: (A) proverb : pithy (B) eulogy : candid (C) poem : humorous (D) play : short-lived (E) novel : acclaimed

44. BIRDS : AVIARY :: (A) bees : garden (B) cows : herd (C) apes : jungle (D) quails : bevy (E) sheep : fold

45. LASSITUDE : VIGOR ::
    (A) dedication : employment
    (B) greed : possessions
    (C) indigence : funds
    (D) rehearsal : performance
    (E) repudiation : theory

S T O P

IF YOU FINISH BEFORE TIME IS CALLED, YOU MAY CHECK YOUR WORK ON THIS SECTION ONLY. DO NOT WORK ON ANY OTHER SECTION IN THE TEST.

SECTION 2

Time—30 minutes

25 QUESTIONS

In this section solve each problem, using any available space on the page for scratchwork. Then decide which is the best of the choices given and blacken the corresponding space on the answer sheet.

The following information is for your reference in solving some of the problems.

Circle of radius r: Area $= \pi r^2$; Circumference $= 2\pi r$
The number of degrees of arc in a circle is 360.
The measure in degrees of a straight angle is 180.

Definitions of symbols:

$=$	is equal to	$\leq$	is less than or equal to
$\neq$	is unequal to	$\geq$	is greater than or equal to
$<$	is less than	$\parallel$	is parallel to
$>$	is greater than	$\perp$	is perpendicular to

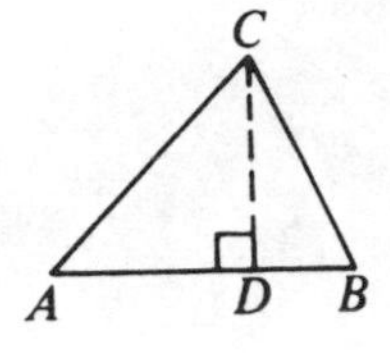

Triangle: The sum of the measures in degrees of the angles of a triangle is 180.

If $\angle CDA$ is a right angle, then

(1) area of $\triangle ABC = \dfrac{AB \times CD}{2}$

(2) $AC^2 = AD^2 + DC^2$

Note: Figures which accompany problems in this test are intended to provide information useful in solving the problems. They are drawn as accurately as possible EXCEPT when it is stated in a specific problem that its figure is not drawn to scale. All figures lie in a plane unless otherwise indicated. All numbers used are real numbers.

---

1. If $\dfrac{1}{N} + \dfrac{1}{N} = 6$, then $N =$

   (A) $\dfrac{1}{6}$

   (B) $\dfrac{1}{3}$

   (C) $\dfrac{1}{2}$

   (D) 2

   (E) 3

2. If $x = 1$ and $y = -2$, then $2x - 3y =$

   (A) −7 (B) −4 (C) −1 (D) 5 (E) 8

3. In a senior class there are 200 boys and 300 girls. If 40 percent of the senior boys and 50 percent of the senior girls bought class rings, how many seniors bought class rings?

   (A) 200
   (B) 225
   (C) 230
   (D) 250
   (E) 275

4. If, in the figure above, $BCDE$ is a square and $AB = AE = DE$, then $x =$

   (A) 15 (B) 30 (C) 45 (D) 60 (E) 90

5. Last year Mr. Brown received 5 percent interest on an investment of \$32,000. How much interest did he receive on this investment?

   (A) \$160 (B) \$640 (C) \$1,600
   (D) \$6,400 (E) \$16,000

6. The sum, product, and average (arithmetic mean) of three integers are equal. If two of the integers are 0 and −5, the third integer is

   (A) −5
   (B) 0
   (C) 2
   (D) 5
   (E) 10

GO ON TO THE NEXT PAGE

Questions 7-9 refer to the following definition.

A	B
C	D

A block sum is a figure, like the one above, that has the following properties:

1. $A, B, C,$ and D are digits from 1 to 9 inclusive.
2. $A + B = 10C + D$.

For example,

5	8
1	3

is a block sum because 1, 3, 5, and 8 satisfy property 1 and $5 + 8 = 13$ satisfies property 2.

A	B
1	2

7. If the figure above is a block sum, what is the value of $A + B$?

(A) 12 (B) 3 (C) 2 (D) 1
(E) It cannot be determined from the information given.

9	7
C	D

8. If the figure above is a block sum, what digit does D represent?

(A) 1 (B) 3 (C) 6 (D) 16
(E) It cannot be determined from the information given.

A	B
1	1

9. If the figure above is a block sum, what is the value of A?

(A) 1 (B) 2 (C) 9 (D) 11
(E) It cannot be determined from the information given.

10. $90 + 6 + \frac{2}{5} + \frac{3}{50} =$

(A) 90.623
(B) 90.646
(C) 96.046
(D) 96.23
(E) 96.46

11. A mechanic can install carburetors in 3 cars every 4 hours. At that rate, how long will it take the mechanic to install carburetors in 5 cars?

(A) 6 hr. 20 min.
(B) 6 hr. 40 min.
(C) 7 hr. 15 min.
(D) 7 hr. 30 min.
(E) 7 hr. 45 min.

12. If Joe is now x years old and Marie is 6 years older than Joe, which of the following gives Marie's age 8 years ago?

(A) $x - 14$ (B) $x - 6$ (C) $x - 2$
(D) $6x - 8$ (E) $x + 14$

13. In flying a plane, a standard rate turn is one in which the rate of turning is 3 degrees per second. A heading is the number of degrees in a clockwise direction from north to the path of the plane. If a plane has a heading of 246° and makes a standard rate turn to a heading of 171°, what is the least number of seconds required for the turn?

(A) 15
(B) 25
(C) 57
(D) 82
(E) 95

GO ON TO THE NEXT PAGE

14. Every student who studies art in a certain school receives exactly one of the grades A, B, C, or D. If $\frac{1}{5}$ of the students receive A's, $\frac{1}{4}$ receive B's, $\frac{1}{2}$ receive C's, and 10 students receive D's, how many students in the school study art?

(A) 50
(B) 60
(C) 90
(D) 100
(E) 200

P	Q	R
2	3	6
4	6	12
6	9	18
8	12	24
10	15	30
12	18	36

15. In the figure above, if p, q, and r are numbers from columns P, Q, and R respectively, then the greatest possible value of $\frac{p+r}{q}$ is

(A) $2\frac{2}{3}$ (B) $10\frac{2}{3}$ (C) 16 (D) 18 (E) 22

16. If $a \neq 0$, then $\frac{(-2a)^3}{-2a^3} =$

(A) −4 (B) −1 (C) 1 (D) 3 (E) 4

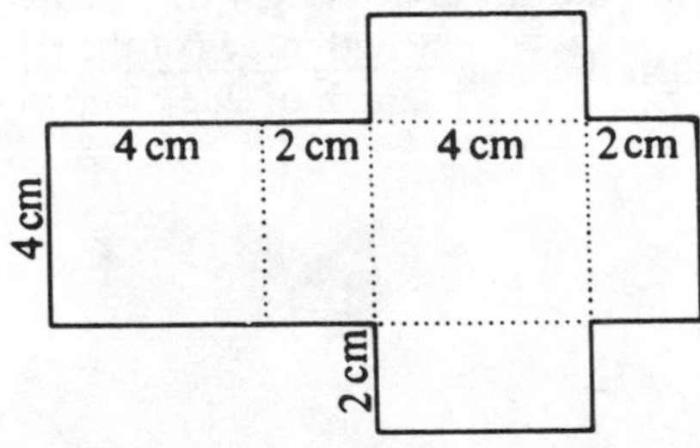

17. A closed rectangular box is formed by folding the figure above along the dotted lines. What is the volume of the box in cubic centimeters?

(A) 8 (B) 16 (C) 32 (D) 64 (E) 128

18. In a certain sequence of numbers, each number except the first is 5 plus twice the previous number. If the third number is 7, what is the first number?

(A) $-\frac{23}{4}$ (B) $-\frac{7}{2}$ (C) −2 (D) 1 (E) 43

19. If $y = 3x$, then the average (arithmetic mean) of x and y, in terms of x, is equal to

(A) x (B) $2x$ (C) $3x$ (D) $4x$ (E) $6x$

20. In a certain lawn-mower factory, 0.06 percent of all mowers produced are defective. On the average, there will be 3 defective mowers out of how many produced?

(A) 5,000
(B) 2,000
(C) 500
(D) 200
(E) 20

GO ON TO THE NEXT PAGE

21. If a square and an isosceles right triangle have equal areas, then the ratio $\frac{\text{length of leg of the triangle}}{\text{length of side of the square}} =$

(A) $\frac{1}{4}$

(B) $\frac{1}{2}$

(C) $\frac{\sqrt{2}}{2}$

(D) $\frac{1}{1}$

(E) $\frac{\sqrt{2}}{1}$

22. If $a = 2d + 3$ and $b = 4d^2$, what is b in terms of a?

(A) $(a - 3)^2$

(B) $2(a - 3)^2$

(C) $\frac{(a - 3)^2}{4}$

(D) $\frac{(a + 3)^2}{4}$

(E) $a + 3$

23. If the length and width of rectangle A are 10 percent less and 30 percent less, respectively, than the length and width of rectangle B, the area of A is equal to what percent of the area of B?

(A) 63%
(B) 60%
(C) 40%
(D) 6%
(E) 3%

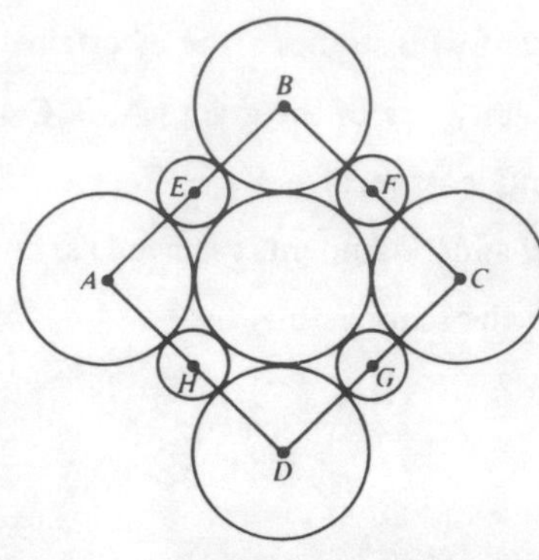

24. Four circles of radius 2 with centers A, B, C, and D are arranged symmetrically around another circle of radius 2, and four smaller equal circles with centers E, F, G, and H each touch three of the larger circles as shown in the figure above. What is the radius of one of the small circles?

(A) $\sqrt{2} - 2$ (B) $\sqrt{2} - 1$ (C) $2\sqrt{2} - 2$
(D) 1 (E) $3\sqrt{2} - 1$

25. To make an orange dye, 3 parts of red dye are mixed with 2 parts of yellow dye. To make a green dye, 2 parts of blue dye are mixed with 1 part of yellow dye. If equal amounts of green and orange are mixed, what is the proportion of yellow dye in the new mixture?

(A) $\frac{3}{16}$

(B) $\frac{1}{4}$

(C) $\frac{11}{30}$

(D) $\frac{3}{8}$

(E) $\frac{7}{12}$

S T O P

IF YOU FINISH BEFORE TIME IS CALLED, YOU MAY CHECK YOUR WORK ON THIS SECTION ONLY. DO NOT WORK ON ANY OTHER SECTION IN THE TEST.

SECTION 3

Time—30 minutes

40 QUESTIONS

For each question in this section, choose the best answer and blacken the corresponding space on the answer sheet.

Each question below consists of a word in capital letters, followed by five lettered words or phrases. Choose the word or phrase that is most nearly opposite in meaning to the word in capital letters. Since some of the questions require you to distinguish fine shades of meaning, consider all the choices before deciding which is best.

Example:

GOOD: (A) sour (B) bad (C) red (D) hot (E) ugly

Ⓐ ● Ⓒ Ⓓ Ⓔ

1. DETERIORATION: (A) haste (B) diversity (C) evasion (D) development (E) concealment

2. DRASTIC: (A) inconsistent (B) accidental (C) creative (D) familiar and pleasing (E) mild and ineffective

3. FORMALITY: (A) lack of variation (B) lack of ceremony (C) lack of emphasis (D) solitude (E) insignificance

4. ASTRONOMICAL: (A) unclouded (B) occasional (C) very small (D) outwardly calm (E) approximately equal

5. BUSTLE: (A) forget (B) dawdle (C) protect (D) correct (E) garble

6. PRODIGY: (A) proclamation (B) maneuver (C) vague suggestion (D) ordinary occurrence (E) foolish explanation

7. STOKE: (A) deny (B) release (C) smother (D) tighten (E) stiffen

8. SUBLIMINAL: (A) debased (B) superlative (C) easily excited (D) consciously perceived (E) brightly colored

9. POTABLE: (A) unable to react (B) unfit to drink (C) irreplaceable (D) agreeable (E) immeasurable

10. EFFRONTERY: (A) need for change (B) show of solidarity (C) diffidence (D) fairness (E) meticulousness

Each sentence below has one or two blanks, each blank indicating that something has been omitted. Beneath the sentence are five lettered words or sets of words. Choose the word or set of words that best fits the meaning of the sentence as a whole.

Example:

Although its publicity has been ----, the film itself is intelligent, well-acted, handsomely produced, and altogether ----.

(A) tasteless. .respectable (B) extensive. .moderate (C) sophisticated. .amateur (D) risqué. .crude (E) perfect. .spectacular

● Ⓑ Ⓒ Ⓓ Ⓔ

11. Chameleons, since they move quickly and adopt the color of their surroundings, are so difficult to ---- that even a careful observer can ---- their presence.

(A) eradicate. .notice (B) detect. .overlook (C) ignore. .misjudge (D) discern. .recognize (E) miss. .deduce

12. A ---- politician, Andrews worked hard and made so few mistakes that her opponents seemed to be ---- by contrast.

(A) shrewd. .sages (B) slothful. .drones (C) canny. .blunderers (D) dynamic. .firebrands (E) conscientious. .geniuses

13. Despite China's 2,000-year-old ---- medicinal plants, there was a period in Chinese history when the art of herbal medicine was almost ----.

(A) expertise in. .lost
(B) bewilderment over. .thwarted
(C) ignorance of. .eliminated
(D) affection for. .encouraged
(E) disapproval of. .censured

14. The author's tales of political chicanery might be taken as ---- were there not so much daily evidence of such tricks in this year's campaign.

(A) censorship (B) atonement (C) endorsement (D) mimicry (E) hyperbole

15. The committee warned that if its suggestions were not implemented, the problems would be ---- and eventually rendered insoluble.

(A) exacerbated (B) insurmountable (C) obliterated (D) vindicated (E) rebutted

GO ON TO THE NEXT PAGE

3

Each question below consists of a related pair of words or phrases, followed by five lettered pairs of words or phrases. Select the lettered pair that best expresses a relationship similar to that expressed in the original pair.

Example:

YAWN : BOREDOM :: (A) dream : sleep
(B) anger : madness (C) smile : amusement
(D) face : expression (E) impatience : rebellion
Ⓐ Ⓑ ● Ⓓ Ⓔ

16. BIRD : MIGRATION :: (A) parrot : imitation
(B) ranger : conservation (C) bear : hibernation
(D) lawyer : accusation (E) traveler : location

17. RACQUET : TENNIS :: (A) springboard : diver
(B) horse : polo (C) glove : boxing
(D) club : golf (E) gun : hunting

18. OIL : LUBRICATE :: (A) adhesive : bond
(B) speedometer : accelerate (C) nail : hammer
(D) knife : sharpen (E) jacket : button

19. DESOLATE : INHABITANTS ::
(A) spacious : expanse (B) barren : vegetation
(C) shallow : hazards (D) residential : homes
(E) stagnant : permanence

20. HEAVY : WEIGHT :: (A) ancient : age
(B) warlike : force (C) brief : clarity
(D) bulky : strength (E) fertile : diversity

21. KERNEL : CORN :: (A) salt : pepper
(B) stem : flower (C) rind : orange
(D) grain : rice (E) trunk : tree

22. ANARCHY : ORDER ::
(A) ignorance : enlightenment
(B) skepticism : science
(C) hierarchy : statue
(D) autocracy : leader
(E) orthodoxy : tradition

23. PRESCRIPTIVE : RULE :: (A) imaginative : fact
(B) narrative : reader (C) symbolic : advice
(D) proverbial : adage (E) concrete : word

24. GIBE : SCORN :: (A) confess : punishment
(B) smile : awe (C) rebuff : friendship
(D) twitch : fury (E) chortle : exultation

25. DIGNITARY : AUGUST ::
(A) ingenue : sporting (B) rustic : abject
(C) zealot : solitary (D) parasite : modest
(E) penitent : contrite

Each passage below is followed by questions based on its content. Answer all questions following a passage on the basis of what is stated or implied in that passage.

The resolution he had deliberately formed of not speaking to Sylvia on the subject of his love till he could announce to her parents the fact of his succession to Foster's business, and till he had patiently worked his way into her regard, was set aside during the present walk. He would speak to her of his passionate attachment before he left for an uncertain length of time and the certain distance of London. And all the modification on this point which his judgment could obtain from his impetuous and excited heart was that he would watch her words and manner well when he announced his approaching absence, and, if in them he read the slightest token of tender regretful feeling, he would pour out his love at her feet, not urging her to make any return or to express the feelings of which he hoped the germ was already budding in her. He would be patient with her; he could not be patient with himself. His heart beating, his busy mind rehearsing the probable coming scene, he turned onto the field-path that led to Haytersbank. Coming along it, and so meeting him, advanced Daniel Robson in earnest talk with Charley Kinraid. Kinraid, then, had been at the farm; Kinraid had been seeing Sylvia, her mother away. The thought of poor dead Annie Coulson flashed into Philip's mind. Could Kinraid be playing the same game with Sylvia? Philip set his teeth and tightened his lips at the thought of it.

26. The major subject of the passage is

(A) Philip's recent success in business
(B) Kinraid's motives for seeing Sylvia
(C) Philip's thoughts and feelings about Sylvia
(D) Annie Coulson's role in Philip's life
(E) the nature of Sylvia's feelings for Philip

27. The passage implies which of the following about Sylvia?

(A) She is trying hard to conceal her budding feelings for Philip.
(B) She is likely to fall for a person like Charley Kinraid.
(C) She prefers Philip's overtures to those of Charley Kinraid.
(D) She has not expressed love for Philip.
(E) She is sure to regret Philip's imminent departure for London.

28. Which of the following best expresses the author's attitude toward Philip?

(A) Reluctant approval
(B) Detached sympathy
(C) Cold objectivity
(D) Veiled disdain
(E) Clear distaste

GO ON TO THE NEXT PAGE

(This passage was written in 1963.)

Many recent advances in engineering--high-strength alloys and plastics no less than fluorescent lamps, transistors, and ferrites—are based on what we know about the structure of atoms. Even in the study of the phenomena of life, the stage has been reached where we examine effects of single atoms on living organisms. For these reasons alone it is clear that the study of atoms and their components is of great importance, but physicists have another strong incentive: curiosity. They just want to know what the world is made of, what the smallest particles are and how they behave. Therefore they are always ahead of practical applications; there always exists some knowledge about which people can ask, "What is it good for?" It is true that at the moment nobody can see any use for the "newer" particles--mesons and hyperons—yet in the past many new discoveries have, within a few decades, found some practical uses, or at least have become such indispensable parts of our knowledge that many practical advances would have been impossible without them. I do not foresee meson guns or hyperon boilers, but if applications for these particles are ever found, it is unlikely that even the most imaginative of present science-fiction writers will have envisaged them correctly.

29. The author mentions fluorescent lamps and transistors (lines 2-3) as examples of

(A) engineering devices that aid physicists in their research
(B) developments dependent on high-strength alloys
(C) inventions whose value was originally questioned by the public
(D) products of slightly less value than plastics and high-strength alloys
(E) applications derived from studies of atomic structure

30. The author apparently assumes that the question, "What is it good for?" (line 15), is usually asked in a tone of

(A) disdain (B) relief (C) enthusiasm (D) reverence (E) apprehension

31. The author's attitude toward physicists' curiosity is one of

(A) cautious skepticism
(B) apologetic embarrassment
(C) admiring support
(D) amused irritation
(E) reluctant tolerance

32. The passage as a whole is best described as a

(A) summary of recent advances derived from research on atomic particles
(B) challenge for physicists to find practical applications for the results of research
(C) prediction of future uses for the latest discoveries by atomic physicists
(D) defense of physicists' pursuit of knowledge about fundamental particles
(E) reminder to physicists that the world is impatient for new information about atoms

GO ON TO THE NEXT PAGE

As the manifestation of capitalism, the factory system led to a rise in the standard of living, to rapidly falling urban death rates and decreasing infant mortality, and to an unprecedented population explosion. In 1749, only one in four London children survived to a fifth birthday; by 1829, two out of three lived to a fifth birthday. England's population doubled from six million in 1750 to twelve million in 1820.

One is both morally unjust and historically inaccurate to blame capitalism for the condition of children during the Industrial Revolution; in fact, capitalism brought enormous improvement over their condition in the preceding age. The sources of the inaccurate perceptions of capitalism were ill-informed, emotional novelists and poets like Dickens and Mrs. Browning; fanciful medievalists like Southey; political tract writers like Engels and Marx, posturing as economic historians. All painted vague, rosy pictures of a lost "golden age" of the working classes, an age that they claimed was destroyed by the Industrial Revolution. Historians have not supported their assertions. Investigation and common sense have deglamorized prefactory domestic industry. In that system, the worker made a costly initial investment in, or paid heavy rentals for, a loom or frame; thus, the worker had to bear the speculative risks involved. His diet was drab and meager, and he was forced to enlist the labor of his wife and children. There was nothing romantic or enviable about a family living and working together in a badly lighted, improperly ventilated, poorly constructed cottage.

33. The author includes statistical information specifically to

(A) dispute the cause-and-effect relationship between the development of the factory system and the growth in population
(B) support the claim that life in preindustrial England was worse than life in the industrial age
(C) emphasize the unfortunate plight of children in the 1800's
(D) prove that Engels and Marx were not economic historians
(E) demonstrate that the Industrial Revolution had ended in England by 1829

34. It can be inferred from the passage that the author's attitude toward the factory system is one of

(A) dismay at the way it separated workers from their families
(B) fear of the rapid population growth it spawned
(C) suspicion of the social and economic changes it initiated
(D) enthusiasm about the way it inspired writers to produce great works
(E) support of the improvement it brought to the lives of workers

35. Which of the following best describes the author's apparent purpose in this passage?

(A) To correct a distorted picture of capitalism's early effects
(B) To help workers understand the history of the labor movement
(C) To demonstrate the impact of modern statistics on historical research
(D) To explain how much capitalism has changed over the years
(E) To create a sense of outrage over the injustices of the early days of capitalism

GO ON TO THE NEXT PAGE

The seventeenth century was the golden age of the amateur. There was not yet a recognition of the fact that there are different categories of knowledge and phenomena. In the desire to solve the great puzzle of the world and to discover relations between groups of phenomena, the love of tracing analogy and the temptation to press an analogy once discerned ever further and further had led many thinkers of the Middle Ages to false conclusions in many matters. The importance of the proper use of analogy and its indispensable service to scientific thought are, of course, not to be questioned. But by the extensive misuse of analogy, and by often reasoning logically from false premises, thinkers had managed to construct a scheme of the universe which was fairly coherent but which, when tested by observation and experiment, was bound to crumble. The seventeenth century inherited such schemes, and much of the ancient and medieval misinformation about natural phenomena remained part of the mental climate of Europe until well on in the century. The important fact, however, that emerges from a study of the scientific thought and opinion of the century is not that such and such persons believed such and such things, but that a good many persons were beginning to question old beliefs, and to discover that much that had been accepted on the authority of the ancients was not true.

Philosophy tended more and more during the century to concern itself with "reason" and with matters amenable to scientific experimentation and mathematical demonstration. The "laws of nature" occupied an increasingly larger share of human thought, and began to take their place by the side of the "revealed truth" of the Bible. To the more devout scientists these studies in natural philosophy seemed to supplement and re-enforce rather than to supersede the truths of the Bible. Sir Thomas Browne, an ardent believer in the Bible, commended those who magnify God by "judicious inquiry into His acts and deliberate researches into His creatures." By the end of the century, thanks to the work of the scientists and philosophers, a state of mind had been induced in which such phenomena as plagues, conflagrations, and death came to be viewed less as evidence of divine displeasure than as natural effects and circumstances, and natural methods were undertaken to deal with them. Before the century was over, both fire insurance and life insurance had arrived in England.

36. The author suggests that philosophers of the Middle Ages were most concerned with

(A) discovering general truths about the universe
(B) proving revealed truths scientifically
(C) examining individual natural phenomena
(D) eliminating misconceptions about phenomena
(E) combining scientific knowledge with philosophy

37. The author mentions the introduction of fire insurance and life insurance in England (lines 50-51) as

(A) an illustration of the effects of the later seventeenth-century view of natural phenomena
(B) a refutation of Sir Thomas Browne's view of scientific study
(C) an example of the influence of economic growth on trends of thought
(D) an example of the seventeenth-century recognition of the errors of medieval thought
(E) an illustration of the seventeenth-century interest in the classification of phenomena

38. The author attributes the misconceptions that seventeenth-century thinkers inherited from the Middle Ages most directly to the medieval

(A) attempts to apply science to religious ideas
(B) failure to recognize different categories of knowledge and phenomena
(C) tendency to carry analogies to extremes
(D) reliance on the incorrect interpretations of their predecessors
(E) failure to use logical reasoning in constructing their theories

39. The author quotes Sir Thomas Browne (lines 41-43) in order to

(A) exemplify the mistaken ideas carried over from the Middle Ages into the seventeenth century
(B) emphasize the increased importance of religious teachings in seventeenth-century thought
(C) illustrate the basic differences between medieval and seventeenth-century ideas
(D) suggest that seventeenth-century studies of natural phenomena were approached cautiously
(E) demonstrate that scientific and revealed truth were not universally regarded as incompatible in the seventeenth century

40. The author is primarily concerned with

(A) making a distinction between scientific thought and scientific opinion in the seventeenth century
(B) describing the decline of religion as an influence on philosophy in the seventeenth century
(C) discussing the mental climate of Europe in the seventeenth century
(D) outlining the religious philosophy of seventeenth-century Europe
(E) discussing medieval misconceptions that influenced seventeenth-century thought

S T O P

IF YOU FINISH BEFORE TIME IS CALLED, YOU MAY CHECK YOUR WORK ON THIS SECTION ONLY. DO NOT WORK ON ANY OTHER SECTION IN THE TEST.

SECTION 5

5

Time—30 minutes
35 QUESTIONS

In this section solve each problem, using any available space on the page for scratchwork. Then decide which is the best of the choices given and blacken the corresponding space on the answer sheet.

The following information is for your reference in solving some of the problems.

Circle of radius r: Area $= \pi r^2$; Circumference $= 2\pi r$
The number of degrees of arc in a circle is 360.
The measure in degrees of a straight angle is 180.

Definitions of symbols:

$=$	is equal to	$\leq$	is less than or equal to
$\neq$	is unequal to	$\geq$	is greater than or equal to
$<$	is less than	$\parallel$	is parallel to
$>$	is greater than	$\perp$	is perpendicular to

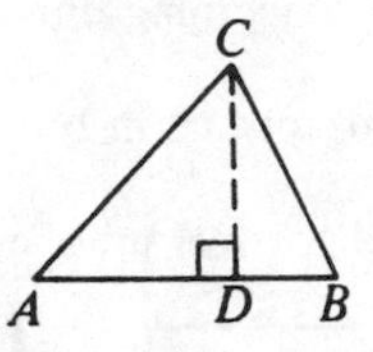

Triangle: The sum of the measures in degrees of the angles of a triangle is 180.
If $\angle CDA$ is a right angle, then

(1) area of $\triangle ABC = \frac{AB \times CD}{2}$

(2) $AC^2 = AD^2 + DC^2$

Note: Figures which accompany problems in this test are intended to provide information useful in solving the problems. They are drawn as accurately as possible EXCEPT when it is stated in a specific problem that its figure is not drawn to scale. All figures lie in a plane unless otherwise indicated. All numbers used are real numbers.

---

1. If $N \times \frac{5}{14} = \frac{5}{14} \times \frac{7}{9}$, then $N =$

(A) $\frac{7}{9}$ (B) $\frac{9}{7}$ (C) 5 (D) 7 (E) 14

2. Which of the following numbers is NOT the product of 11 and an integer?

(A) 11,111 (B) 111,111 (C) 11,111,111
(D) 1,111,111,111 (E) 111,111,111,111

3. If the area of a square is $16y^2$, what is the length of a side in terms of y?

(A) y (B) $2y$ (C) $4y$ (D) y^2 (E) $4y^2$

4. If $12p - 9q = 4$, then $4p - 3q =$

(A) $\frac{1}{4}$ (B) $\frac{1}{3}$ (C) $\frac{3}{4}$ (D) $\frac{4}{3}$ (E) 3

5. The positive difference between the cubes of any two consecutive positive integers is always

(A) an even integer
(B) an odd integer
(C) the product of 3 and an integer
(D) the square of an integer
(E) the cube of an integer

Questions 6-7 refer to the following graphs.

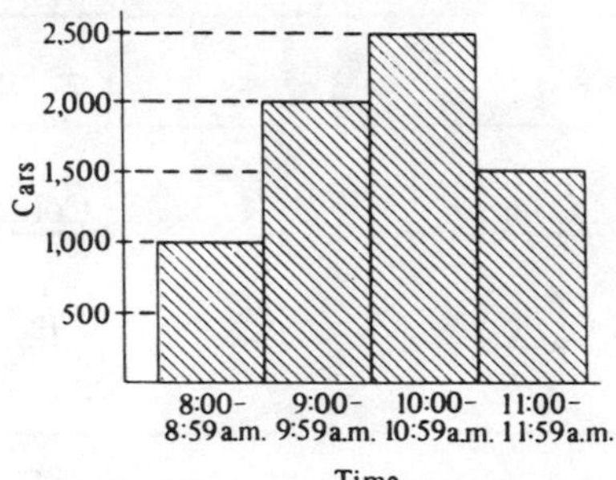

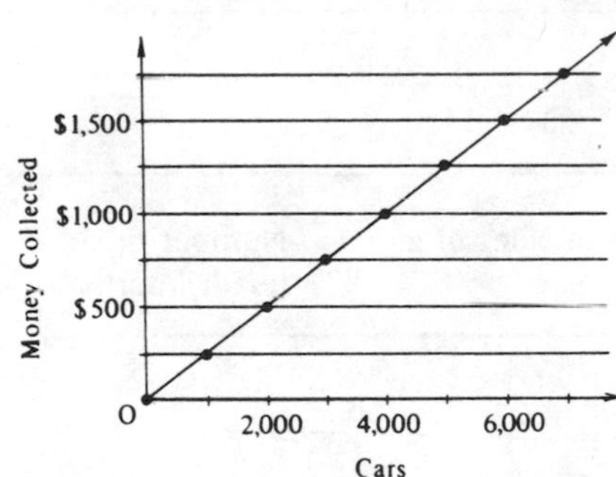

6. The number of cars passing through tollbooth X between 9:00 a.m. and 11:59 a.m., inclusive, is

(A) 3,500 (B) 4,000 (C) 5,500
(D) 6,000 (E) 7,000

7. Of the following, which is the earliest time at which $750 in tolls could have been collected?

(A) 8:00 a.m. (B) 8:59 a.m. (C) 9:59 a.m.
(D) 10:59 a.m. (E) 11:59 a.m.

GO ON TO THE NEXT PAGE

5

Questions 8-27 each consist of two quantities, one in Column A and one in Column B. You are to compare the two quantities and on the answer sheet blacken space

A if the quantity in Column A is greater;
B if the quantity in Column B is greater;
C if the two quantities are equal;
D if the relationship cannot be determined from the information given.

Notes: 1. In certain questions, information concerning one or both of the quantities to be compared is centered above the two columns.
2. In a given question, a symbol that appears in both columns represents the same thing in Column A as it does in Column B.
3. Letters such as x, n, and k stand for real numbers.

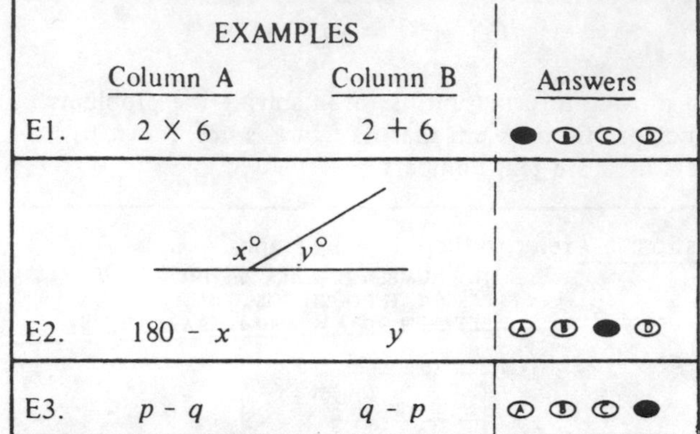

EXAMPLES	Column A	Column B	Answers
E1.	2×6	$2 + 6$	● Ⓑ Ⓒ Ⓓ
E2.	$180 - x$	y	Ⓐ Ⓑ ● Ⓓ
E3.	$p - q$	$q - p$	Ⓐ Ⓑ Ⓒ ●

	Column A	Column B
8.	$\left(\frac{1}{3}\right)^2$	$\left(\frac{1}{2}\right)^2$
9.	The number of hours in a week	150
10.	$\frac{1}{2}+\frac{1}{3}+\frac{1}{11}$	$\frac{1}{11}+\frac{1}{2}+\frac{1}{4}$
11.	Number of sides of a triangle	Number of sides of a quadrilateral

$x > z$
$y < z$

	Column A	Column B
12.	z	0
13.	The average (arithmetic mean) of 1, 2, and k	The average (arithmetic mean) of 2, 3, and k

$T = \{3, 4, 6, 8, 9, 12\}$

A number is selected at random from set T above.

	Column A	Column B
14.	The probability that the number selected will be a multiple of 3	The probability that the number selected will be a multiple of 4

$x + y = 3$
$y < \frac{3}{2}$

	Column A	Column B
15.	x	y

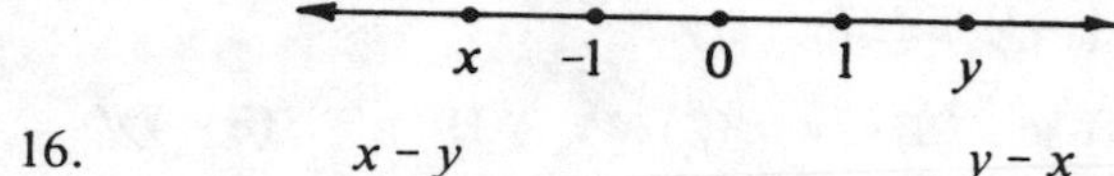

	Column A	Column B
16.	$x - y$	$y - x$

If John had 30 more pencils, he would have twice as many as he actually has. If Carl had 20 fewer pencils, he would have half as many as he actually has.

	Column A	Column B
17.	The number of pencils John actually has	The number of pencils Carl actually has

GO ON TO THE NEXT PAGE

SUMMARY DIRECTIONS FOR COMPARISON QUESTIONS

Answer: A if the quantity in Column A is greater;
B if the quantity in Column B is greater;
C if the two quantities are equal;
D if the relationship cannot be determined from the information given.

	Column A	Column B

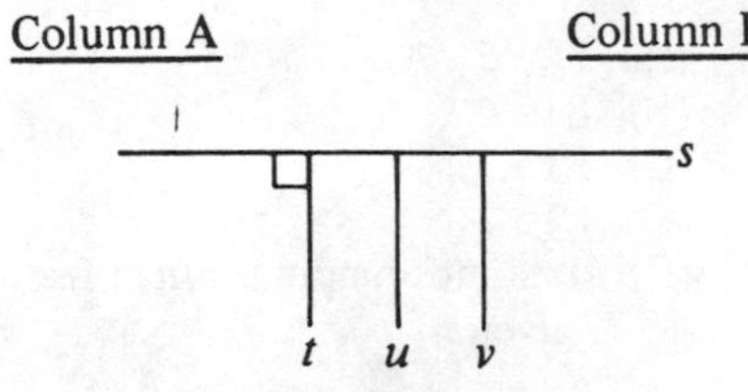

$s, t, u,$ and v are lettered line segments.

$t \parallel u \parallel v$

18. The number of pairs of parallel lettered line segments | The number of pairs of perpendicular lettered line segments

$\frac{1}{N} > 1$

19. N^2 | 1

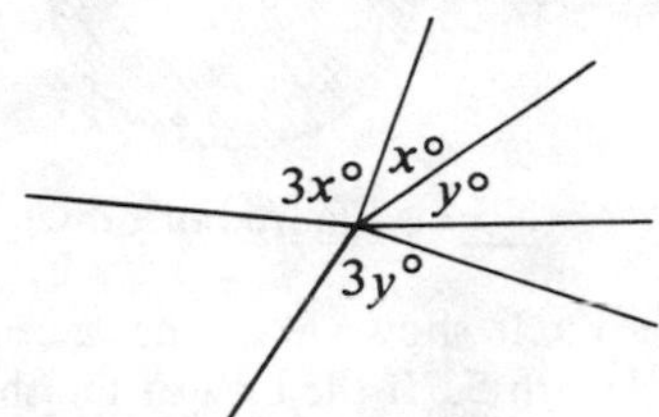

Note: Figure not drawn to scale.

Six line segments meet at a point.

20. x | y

$x + y - z = 10$
$x + y + z = 5$

21. $2x + 2y$ | 14

$xy \neq 0$

22. x^2y | $-xy^2$

	Column A	Column B

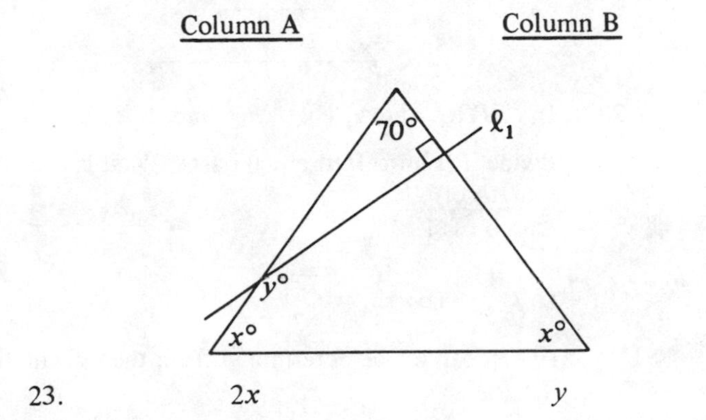

23. $2x$ | y

a is a positive whole number.

24. $a(a^a)$ | $(a+1)^a$

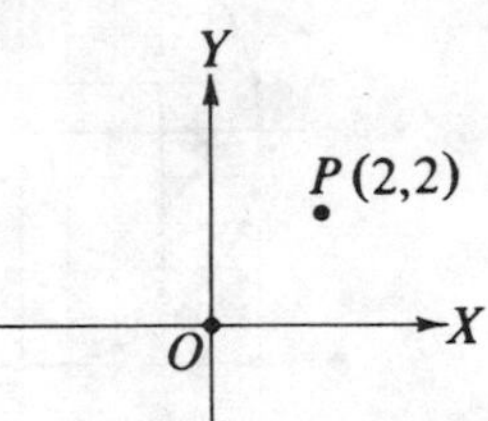

25. Area of a circle with center at point P and circumference passing through O | Area of a circle with circumference passing through points O and P

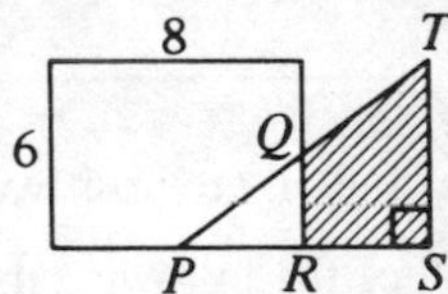

P and Q are midpoints on two sides of the rectangle and Q and R are midpoints on two sides of ΔPST.

26. Perimeter of the shaded region | 18

$5 < xy < 20$ and x and y are integers.

27. xy | $x + y$

GO ON TO THE NEXT PAGE

Solve each of the remaining problems in this section using any available space for scratchwork. Then decide which is the best of the choices given and blacken the corresponding space on the answer sheet.

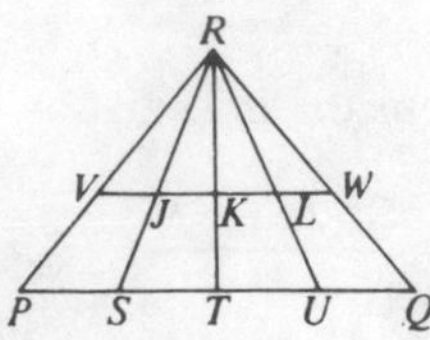

28. In $\triangle PRQ$ above, $VW \parallel PQ$, and S, T, and U divide PQ into four equal parts. What is the ratio $\frac{\text{length of } JL}{\text{length of } VW}$?

(A) $\frac{1}{3}$ (B) $\frac{1}{2}$ (C) $\frac{2}{3}$ (D) $\frac{3}{4}$

(E) It cannot be determined from the information given.

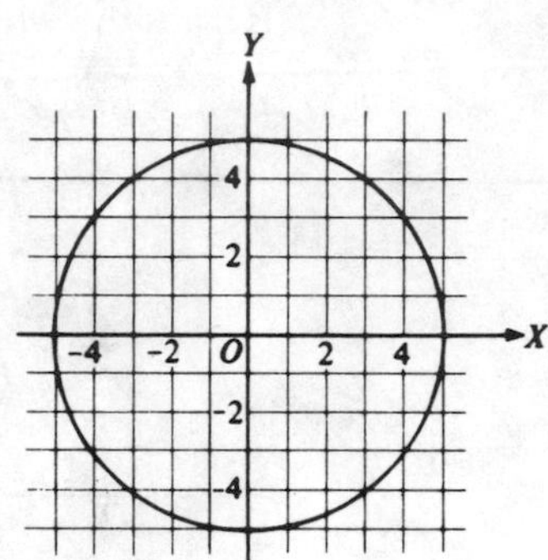

29. What is the circumference of the circle in the figure above?

(A) 5π (B) 10π (C) $\frac{25}{2}\pi$

(D) 20π (E) 25π

---

30. If m and n are positive integers and $m < n$, which of the following must be greater than $\frac{m}{n}$?

I. $\frac{m+1}{n+1}$ II. $\frac{m+1}{n}$ III. $\frac{m}{n+1}$

(A) I only (B) II only (C) III only

(D) I and II only (E) II and III only

31. A machine produces a thingamajig every 0.025 seconds. How many thingamajigs does it produce in an hour?

(A) 2,400 (B) 9,000 (C) 12,000

(D) 14,400 (E) 144,000

32. If $A, B,$ and C are points on a line, in that order, and $AC - AB = 4$, what is the ratio $\frac{AB}{AC}$?

(A) 1 to 5
(B) 1 to 4
(C) 1 to 3
(D) 1 to 2
(E) It cannot be determined from the information given.

33. In a class of 80 seniors, there are 3 boys for every 5 girls. In the junior class there are 3 boys for every 2 girls. If the two classes combined have an equal number of boys and girls, how many students are in the junior class?

(A) 200 (B) 192 (C) 120

(D) 100 (E) 32

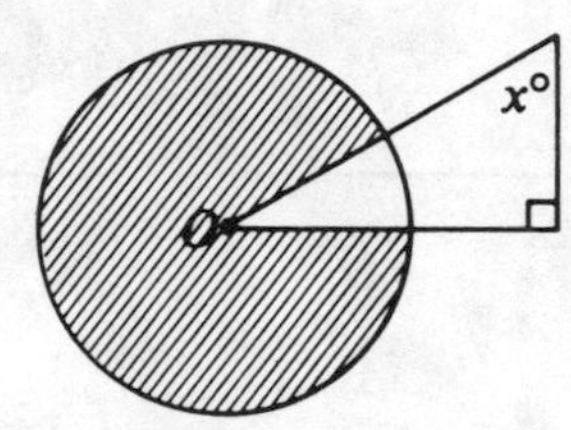

Note: Figure not drawn to scale.

34. The circle shown above has a center O and radius of length 5. If the area of the shaded region is 20π, what is the value of x?

(A) 18 (B) 36 (C) 45 (D) 54 (E) 72

---

35. The price of 10 pounds of apples is d dollars. If the apples weigh an average of 1 pound for every 6 apples, which of the following is the average price, in cents, of a dozen such apples?

(A) $20d$ (B) $\frac{50d}{3}$ (C) $5d$ (D) $\frac{5d}{3}$ (E) $\frac{d}{20}$

S T O P

IF YOU FINISH BEFORE TIME IS CALLED, YOU MAY CHECK YOUR WORK ON THIS SECTION ONLY. DO NOT WORK ON ANY OTHER SECTION IN THE TEST.

Correct Answers for Scholastic Aptitude Test
Form Code 1F

VERBAL		MATHEMATICAL	
Section 1	**Section 3**	**Section 2**	**Section 5**
1. C	1. D	1. B	1. A
2. E	2. E	2. E	2. A
3. A	3. B	3. C	3. C
4. C	4. C	4. D	4. D
5. E	5. B	5. C	5. B
6. B	6. D	6. D	6. D
7. D	7. C	7. A	7. C
8. A	8. D	8. C	*8. B
9. D	9. B	9. E	*9. A
10. D	10. C	10. E	*10. A
11. E	11. B	11. B	*11. B
12. E	12. C	12. C	*12. D
13. C	13. A	13. B	*13. B
14. C	14. E	14. E	*14. A
15. E	15. A	15. C	*15. A
16. D	16. C	16. E	*16. B
17. B	17. D	17. C	*17. B
18. E	18. A	18. C	*18. C
19. D	19. B	19. B	*19. B
20. B	20. A	20. A	*20. D
21. A	21. D	21. E	*21. A
22. D	22. A	22. A	*22. D
23. A	23. D	23. A	*23. B
24. C	24. E	24. C	*24. D
25. C	25. E	25. C	*25. D
26. B	26. C		*26. C
27. C	27. D		*27. D
28. B	28. B		28. B
29. D	29. E		29. B
30. B	30. A		30. D
31. D	31. C		31. E
32. B	32. D		32. E
33. A	33. B		33. D
34. B	34. E		34. A
35. E	35. A		35. A
36. B	36. A		
37. E	37. A		
38. A	38. C		
39. A	39. E		
40. D	40. C		
41. C			
42. A			
43. A			
44. E			
45. C			

*Indicates four-choice questions. (All of the other questions are five-choice.)

The Scoring Process

Machine-scoring is done in three steps:

- *Scanning.* Your answer sheet is "read" by a scanning machine and the oval you filled in for each question is recorded on a computer tape.
- *Scoring.* The computer compares the oval filled in for each question with the correct response. Each correct answer receives one point; omitted questions do not count toward your score. For each wrong answer, a fraction of a point is subtracted to correct for random guessing. For questions with five answer choices, one-fourth of a point is subtracted for each wrong response; for questions with four answer choices, one-third of a point is subtracted for each wrong response. The SAT-verbal test has 85 questions with five answer choices each. If, for example, a student has 44 right, 32 wrong, and 9 omitted, the resulting raw score is determined as follows:

  $$44 \text{ right} - \frac{32 \text{ wrong}}{4} = 44 - 8 = 36 \text{ raw score points}$$

  Obtaining raw scores frequently involves the rounding of fractional numbers to the nearest whole number. For example, a raw score of 36.25 is rounded to 36, the nearest whole number. A raw score of 36.50 is rounded upward to 37.
- *Converting to reported scaled score.* Raw test scores are then placed on the College Board scale of 200 to 800 through a process that adjusts scores to account for minor differences in difficulty among different editions of the test. This process, known as equating, is performed so that a student's reported score is not affected by the edition of the test taken nor by the abilities of the group with whom the student takes the test. As a result of placing SAT scores on the College Board scale, scores earned by students at different times can be compared. For example, an SAT-verbal score of 400 on a test taken at one administration indicates the same level of developed verbal ability as a 400 score obtained on a different edition of the test taken at another time.

How to Score the Test

You can verify the College Board SAT scores reported to you recently by using the information in this booklet along with the copy of your answer sheet. *Before you begin, check that the first two characters (number and letter) of the form code you marked in item 3 on your answer sheet are the same as the form code printed on the front of this booklet.* Compare the responses shown on the copy of your answer sheet with the list of correct answers.

SAT-Verbal Sections 1 and 3

Step A: Count the number of correct answers for *section 1* and record the number in the space provided on the worksheet on the next page. Then do the same for the incorrect answers. (Do not count omitted answers.) To determine subtotal A, use the formula:

$$\text{number correct} - \frac{\text{number incorrect}}{4} = \text{subtotal A}$$

Step B: Count the number of correct answers and the number of incorrect answers for *section 3* and record the numbers in the spaces provided on the worksheet. To determine subtotal B, use the formula:

$$\text{number correct} - \frac{\text{number incorrect}}{4} = \text{subtotal B}$$

Step C: To obtain C, add subtotal A to subtotal B, keeping any decimals. Enter the resulting figure on the worksheet.

Step D: To obtain D, your raw verbal score, round C to the nearest whole number. (For example, any number from 44.50 to 45.49 rounds to 45.) Enter the resulting figure on the worksheet.

Step E: To find your reported SAT-verbal score, look up the total raw verbal score you obtained in step D in the conversion table on page 148. Enter this figure on the worksheet.

SAT-Mathematical Sections 2 and 5

Step A: Count the number of correct answers and the number of incorrect answers for *section 2* and record the numbers in the spaces provided on the worksheet. To determine the subtotal A, use the formula:

$$\text{number correct} - \frac{\text{number incorrect}}{4} = \text{subtotal A}$$

Step B: Count the number of correct answers and the number of incorrect answers for the *five-choice questions (questions 1 through 7 and 28 through 35) in section 5* and record the numbers in the spaces provided on the worksheet. To determine the subtotal B, use the formula:

$$\text{number correct} - \frac{\text{number incorrect}}{4} = \text{subtotal B}$$

Step C: Count the number of correct answers and the number of incorrect answers for the *four-choice questions (questions 8 through 27) in section 5* and record the numbers in the spaces provided on the worksheet. To determine the subtotal C, use the formula:

$$\text{number correct} - \frac{\text{number incorrect}}{3} = \text{subtotal C}$$

Step D: To obtain D, add subtotal A, subtotal B, and subtotal C, keeping any decimals. Enter the resulting figure on the worksheet.

Step E: To obtain E, your raw mathematical score, round D to the nearest whole number. (For example, any number from 44.50 to 45.49 rounds to 45.) Enter the resulting figure on the worksheet.

Step F: To find your reported SAT-mathematical score, look up the total raw mathematical score you obtained in E in the conversion table on page 148. Enter this figure on the worksheet.

SAT SCORING WORKSHEET

FORM CODE 1F

SAT-Verbal Sections

A. Section 1: ________ − ¼ (________) = ________
no. correct no. incorrect subtotal A

B. Section 3: ________ − ¼ (________) = ________
no. correct no. incorrect subtotal B

C. Total unrounded raw score (Total A + B) ________ C

D. Total rounded raw score (Rounded to nearest whole number) ________ D

E. SAT-verbal reported scaled score (See the conversion table on the back cover.) [ ] SAT-verbal score

SAT-Mathematical Sections

A. Section 2: ________ − ¼ (________) = ________
no. correct no. incorrect subtotal A

B. Section 5: Questions 1 through 7 and 28 through 35 (5-choice) ________ − ¼ (________) = ________
no. correct no. incorrect subtotal B

C. Section 5: Questions 8 through 27 (4-choice) ________ − ⅓ (________) = ________
no. correct no. incorrect subtotal C

D. Total unrounded raw score (Total A + B + C) ________ D

E. Total rounded raw score (Rounded to nearest whole number) ________ E

F. SAT-mathematical reported scaled score (See the conversion table on the back cover.) [ ] SAT-math score

Score Conversion Table
Scholastic Aptitude Test
Form Code 1F

Raw Score	College Board Reported Score		Raw Score	College Board Reported Score	
	SAT-Verbal	SAT-Math		SAT-Verbal	SAT-Math
85	800		40	460	630
84	790		39	450	620
83	780		38	440	610
82	770		37	440	600
81	760		36	430	590
80	750		35	420	580
79	740		34	420	570
78	730		33	410	560
77	720		32	400	560
76	710		31	400	550
75	700		30	390	540
74	690		29	380	530
73	680		28	380	520
72	670		27	370	510
71	660		26	360	500
70	660		25	360	490
69	650		24	350	490
68	640		23	350	480
67	640		22	340	470
66	630		21	330	460
65	620		20	330	450
64	620		19	320	440
63	610		18	310	430
62	600		17	310	420
61	600		16	300	420
60	590	800	15	290	410
59	580	790	14	290	400
58	580	780	13	280	390
57	570	780	12	270	380
56	560	770	11	270	370
55	560	760	10	260	360
54	550	750	9	250	350
53	540	740	8	250	350
52	540	730	7	240	340
51	530	720	6	230	330
50	520	710	5	230	320
49	520	710	4	220	310
48	510	700	3	210	300
47	500	690	2	210	290
46	500	680	1	200	280
45	490	670	0	200	270
44	480	660	–1	200	270
43	480	650	–2	200	260
42	470	640	–3	200	250
41	460	640	–4	200	240
			–5	200	230
			–6	200	220
			–7	200	210
			–8 or below	200	200

Test 5
SAT *Form Code 2E*

(Cut here to detach.)

COLLEGE BOARD — SCHOLASTIC APTITUDE TEST and Test of Standard Written English — Side 1

Use a No. 2 pencil only. Be sure each mark is dark and completely fills the intended oval. Completely erase any errors or stray marks.

1. YOUR NAME: (Print) Last / First / M.I.

SIGNATURE: ____ DATE: __ / __ / __

HOME ADDRESS: (Print) Number and Street

City / State / Zip Code

CENTER: (Print) City / State / Center Number

IMPORTANT: Please fill in these boxes exactly as shown on the back cover of your test book.

FOR ETS USE ONLY

2. TEST FORM

3. FORM CODE

4. REGISTRATION NUMBER (Copy from your Admission Ticket.)

5. YOUR NAME — First 4 letters of last name / First Init. / Mid Init.

6. DATE OF BIRTH — Month / Day / Year

Jan. Feb. Mar. Apr. May June July Aug. Sept. Oct. Nov. Dec.

7. SEX — Female / Male

8. TEST BOOK SERIAL NUMBER

Start with number 1 for each new section. If a section has fewer than 50 questions, leave the extra answer spaces blank.

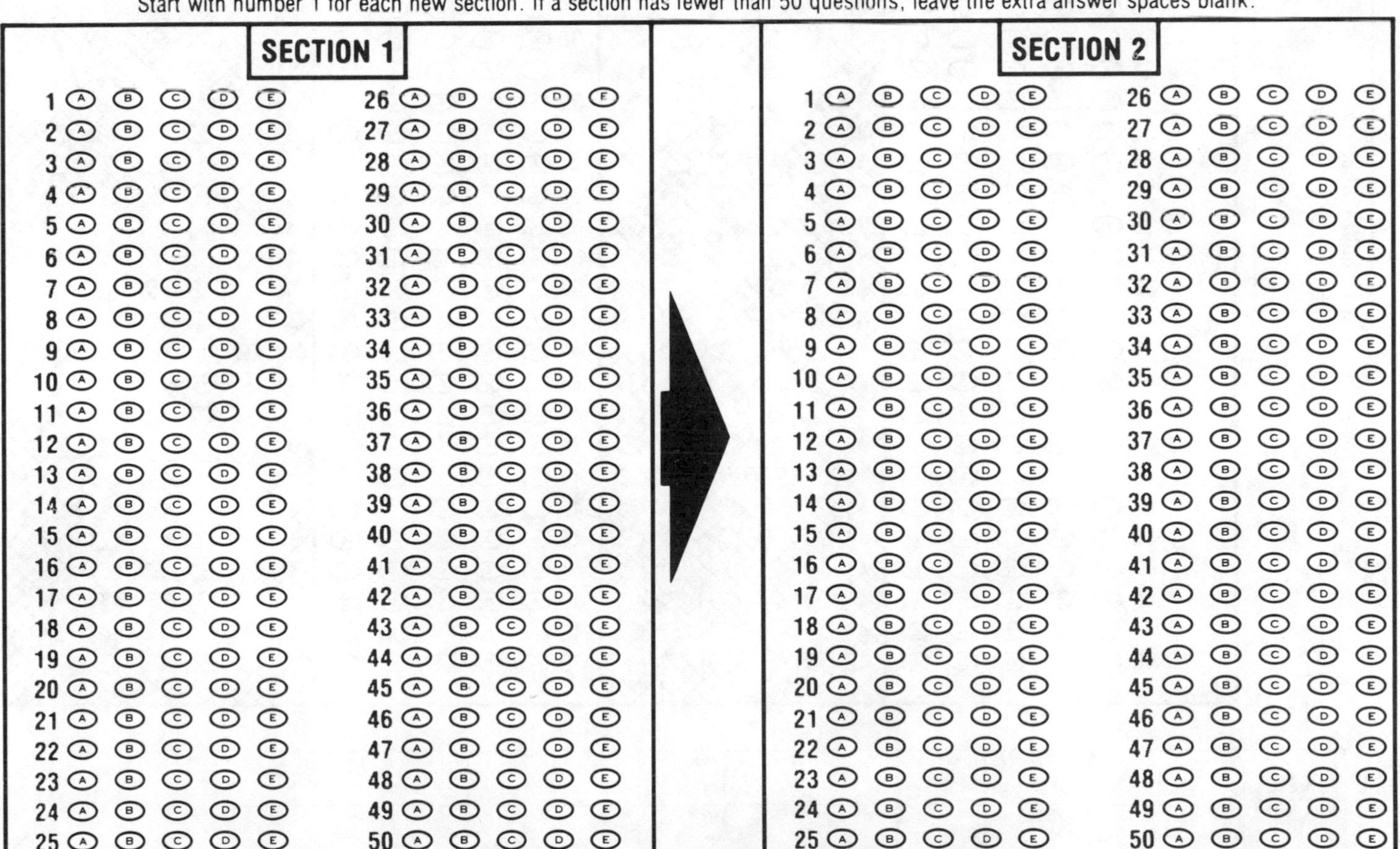

SECTION 1

Questions 1–50: Ⓐ Ⓑ Ⓒ Ⓓ Ⓔ

SECTION 2

Questions 1–50: Ⓐ Ⓑ Ⓒ Ⓓ Ⓔ

Q1362-04

I.N. 574006—110VV25P3015

COLLEGE BOARD — SCHOLASTIC APTITUDE TEST and Test of Standard Written English Side 2

Use a No. 2 pencil only. Be sure each mark is dark and completely fills the intended oval. Completely erase any errors or stray marks.

Start with number 1 for each new section. If a section has fewer than 50 questions, leave the extra answer spaces blank.

	SECTION 3	SECTION 4	SECTION 5	SECTION 6
1	A B C D E	A B C D E	A B C D E	A B C D E
2	A B C D E	A B C D E	A B C D E	A B C D E
3	A B C D E	A B C D E	A B C D E	A B C D E
4	A B C D E	A B C D E	A B C D E	A B C D E
5	A B C D E	A B C D E	A B C D E	A B C D E
6	A B C D E	A B C D E	A B C D E	A B C D E
7	A B C D E	A B C D E	A B C D E	A B C D E
8	A B C D E	A B C D E	A B C D E	A B C D E
9	A B C D E	A B C D E	A B C D E	A B C D E
10	A B C D E	A B C D E	A B C D E	A B C D E
11	A B C D E	A B C D E	A B C D E	A B C D E
12	A B C D E	A B C D E	A B C D E	A B C D E
13	A B C D E	A B C D E	A B C D E	A B C D E
14	A B C D E	A B C D E	A B C D E	A B C D E
15	A B C D E	A B C D E	A B C D E	A B C D E
16	A B C D E	A B C D E	A B C D E	A B C D E
17	A B C D E	A B C D E	A B C D E	A B C D E
18	A B C D E	A B C D E	A B C D E	A B C D E
19	A B C D E	A B C D E	A B C D E	A B C D E
20	A B C D E	A B C D E	A B C D E	A B C D E
21	A B C D E	A B C D E	A B C D E	A B C D E
22	A B C D E	A B C D E	A B C D E	A B C D E
23	A B C D E	A B C D E	A B C D E	A B C D E
24	A B C D E	A B C D E	A B C D E	A B C D E
25	A B C D E	A B C D E	A B C D E	A B C D E
26	A B C D E	A B C D E	A B C D E	A B C D E
27	A B C D E	A B C D E	A B C D E	A B C D E
28	A B C D E	A B C D E	A B C D E	A B C D E
29	A B C D E	A B C D E	A B C D E	A B C D E
30	A B C D E	A B C D E	A B C D E	A B C D E
31	A B C D E	A B C D E	A B C D E	A B C D E
32	A B C D E	A B C D E	A B C D E	A B C D E
33	A B C D E	A B C D E	A B C D E	A B C D E
34	A B C D E	A B C D E	A B C D E	A B C D E
35	A B C D E	A B C D E	A B C D E	A B C D E
36	A B C D E	A B C D E	A B C D E	A B C D E
37	A B C D E	A B C D E	A B C D E	A B C D E
38	A B C D E	A B C D E	A B C D E	A B C D E
39	A B C D E	A B C D E	A B C D E	A B C D E
40	A B C D E	A B C D E	A B C D E	A B C D E
41	A B C D E	A B C D E	A B C D E	A B C D E
42	A B C D E	A B C D E	A B C D E	A B C D E
43	A B C D E	A B C D E	A B C D E	A B C D E
44	A B C D E	A B C D E	A B C D E	A B C D E
45	A B C D E	A B C D E	A B C D E	A B C D E
46	A B C D E	A B C D E	A B C D E	A B C D E
47	A B C D E	A B C D E	A B C D E	A B C D E
48	A B C D E	A B C D E	A B C D E	A B C D E
49	A B C D E	A B C D E	A B C D E	A B C D E
50	A B C D E	A B C D E	A B C D E	A B C D E

9. SIGNATURE:

FOR ETS USE ONLY	VTR	VTFS	VRR	VRFS	VVR	VVFS	WER	WEFS	M4R	M4FS	M5R	M5FS	MTFS
	VTW	VTCS	VRW	VRCS	VVW	VVCS	WEW	WECS	M4W		M5W		MTCS

SECTION 1

Time—30 minutes

45 QUESTIONS

For each question in this section, choose the best answer and blacken the corresponding space on the answer sheet.

Each question below consists of a word in capital letters, followed by five lettered words or phrases. Choose the word or phrase that is most nearly opposite in meaning to the word in capital letters. Since some of the questions require you to distinguish fine shades of meaning, consider all the choices before deciding which is best.

Example:

GOOD: (A) sour (B) bad (C) red (D) hot (E) ugly
Ⓐ ● Ⓒ Ⓓ Ⓔ

1. PRESERVE: (A) disagree (B) destroy (C) hide (D) distinguish (E) withdraw

2. FRUITFUL: (A) barren (B) unique (C) native (D) absorbent (E) extreme

3. COMPLIANCE: (A) sentimentality (B) vitality (C) sorrow (D) inexperience (E) rebellion

4. BYPASS: (A) enlarge (B) advance (C) copy (D) throw away (E) go through

5. DETERMINATE: (A) fundamental (B) luckless (C) inconclusive (D) highly selective (E) producing plentifully

6. ENHANCE: (A) detect (B) misplace (C) conquer (D) impair (E) distribute

7. COHERENT: (A) boring (B) disorganized (C) hostile (D) unrestrained (E) unfaithful

8. JOLLITY: (A) pallor (B) gravity (C) infamy (D) complexity (E) resourcefulness

9. FOIBLE: (A) offhand remark (B) strong point (C) freedom (D) accident (E) responsibility

10. EFFACE: (A) support (B) attack (C) deny (D) restore (E) suffer

11. PONDEROUS: (A) wet (B) shady (C) lightweight (D) mistaken (E) completed

12. DEMISE: (A) union (B) merit (C) birth (D) strain (E) bargain

13. ENIGMATIC: (A) relaxed (B) colorful (C) clear (D) contemptuous of authority (E) excluded from consideration

14. AMELIORATE: (A) agree to (B) make worse (C) disclaim (D) sequester (E) deviate

15. CAPRICIOUS: (A) listless (B) impartial (C) steadfast (D) truthful (E) malicious

Each sentence below has one or two blanks, each blank indicating that something has been omitted. Beneath the sentence are five lettered words or sets of words. Choose the word or set of words that best fits the meaning of the sentence as a whole.

Example:

Although its publicity has been ----, the film itself is intelligent, well-acted, handsomely produced, and altogether ----.

(A) tasteless. .respectable (B) extensive. .moderate (C) sophisticated. .amateur (D) risqué. .crude (E) perfect. .spectacular
● Ⓑ Ⓒ Ⓓ Ⓔ

16. Although the critics agreed that the book was brilliant, so few copies were sold that the work brought the author little ---- reward.

(A) theoretical (B) thoughtful (C) financial (D) abstract (E) informative

17. He is an unbeliever, but he is broad-minded enough to decline the mysteries of religion without ---- them.

(A) denouncing (B) understanding (C) praising (D) doubting (E) studying

18. Wellington, who reacted modestly to his fame, contrasted sharply with Marlborough, who ---- an ostentatious display of his glory.

(A) regretted (B) relished (C) disdained (D) minimized (E) discounted

19. Her ---- media coverage of Hispanic affairs in Los Angeles led Francisca Flores to publish a newsletter aimed at informing the Hispanic community of ---- events.

(A) complacency with. .popular
(B) unhappiness with. .uninteresting
(C) approval of. .unknown
(D) dissatisfaction with. .relevant
(E) confusion about. .imaginative

20. The phenomenon is called viral ---- because the presence of one kind of virus seems to inhibit infection by any other.

(A) proliferation (B) mutation (C) interference (D) epidemic (E) cooperation

GO ON TO THE NEXT PAGE

Each passage below is followed by questions based on its content. Answer all questions following a passage on the basis of what is stated or implied in that passage.

"I always paint what I see," said Turner; yet no painter ever departed further from close imitation or took more liberties with subjects. He elongated steeples, reconstructed buildings, changed the course of rivers, even the course of the sun. Yet one critic says Turner was sincere in thinking that he painted what he saw; that he seemed to be "swept along as by a dream," and the changes he made "came into his head involuntarily."

But the ordinary person's idea of imitation is the setting down with the utmost precision every visible fact in a subject—"making it look like the real thing." Imitation in a painting is, for example, flowers that one can botanize, or fruit that "looks good enough to eat" and has a fly on it one feels the urge to brush off. Such deceptive resemblance gives people the pleasure of surprise rather than an aesthetic pleasure. Carefully realistic pictures may please, but the pictures people enjoy living with leave something to the imagination. "The secret of being a bore," said Voltaire, "is to tell everything."

Actually, few painters try to carry imitation to the point of deceptive resemblance. It cannot be done at all unless the object painted is small enough to be reproduced full size. A true artist never tries to make us believe that his or her medium is anything except a medium. It is paint with which great painters express themselves.

What the ordinary person generally means by imitation of a large subject—say a landscape—is a mirror copy much like a colored photograph: nature with its infinite mass of details crowded into the picture, unsifted, unassimilated, and unarranged. Even if it were possible to put in everything seen, it would not be art any more than copying a poem is creating poetry. The painter uses nature not as a copybook but as a source of inspiration, selects such details as suits his or her purpose, and arranges them in a picture with a discriminating regard for pictorial effect.

If a painting is an unsifted mass of objects, it fails at the very point where art begins, the point that marks the difference between art and imitation. One of the pathetic fallacies of art is that realism of fact creates realism of effect, that increasing the facts of nature in a picture or sculpture increases the "feeling of nature" in it. On the contrary, such techniques decrease the sensation because fullness of fact leaves too little to the imagination. That is the trouble with wax figures and with pictures in which every detail is perfectly defined. What could better give us the facts of nature than a stuffed bird with glass eyes? Yet an artist, employing only one percent of the facts of nature, can give us a rough sketch of a bird that is infinitely better.

21. According to the author, Turner treated nature very

(A) realistically and carefully
(B) crudely and indifferently
(C) dishonestly and carelessly
(D) imaginatively and freely
(E) sketchily and hastily

22. According to the passage, a true work of art can be the product of all the following EXCEPT

(A) an artist's inspiration
(B) the study of nature
(C) careful selection of details
(D) arrangement for a desired effect
(E) photographic realism

23. It can be inferred that the author quotes Voltaire (lines 20-21) to

(A) indicate that Voltaire was a discerning art critic
(B) suggest that people who do not know much about art are boring
(C) identify the source of good imagination
(D) confirm the need for a discriminating choice of details
(E) suggest that artists produce fewer paintings

24. It can be inferred from the passage that a painter who wished "to carry imitation to the point of deceptive resemblance" (lines 22-23) would find which of the following the easiest subject to attempt?

(A) A small vase of flowers
(B) A seascape
(C) A field with distant trees
(D) A street scene
(E) The interior of a small cottage

25. The author believes that an "ordinary" person (lines 10 and 29) would be most likely to agree with which of the following statements about art?

(A) Art and nature are far apart and must not be confused.
(B) A skillful taxidermist practices a craft, not an art.
(C) A photograph "imitates" nature far better than many paintings.
(D) If one recognizes everything in a painting, it is boring art.
(E) A photograph cannot surprise us and therefore cannot be art.

GO ON TO THE NEXT PAGE

Among the things that the Chinese achieved must be counted, of course, the three discoveries that Francis Bacon pointed out as unknown to his Western ancestors but instrumental in changing the face of the world: printing, gunpowder, and the magnet. (It is, of course, because of the early invention of printing in China that we can now know so much more of its antiquity than we do of that of the rest of the world.) Also specifically Chinese are the invention of the kite, with all the knowledge of practical aeronautics that accompanies such a development, and the invention of the seismograph, used to detect and locate earthquakes. There is still some uncertainty, however, as to the actual working mechanism of the latter. Less of a mystery, but just as ingenious, is the "south-pointing carriage," a device that seems to have used differential gearing to keep a figure pointing in a constant direction, no matter where the vehicle was led.

But let it not be thought that one is dealing only with mechanical inventions: the oracle-bones of the Shang period (ca. 1500 to 1000 B.C.) contain omens and astrological texts that match rather well those of the quite separate tradition represented by the clay tablets of the same period found in Mesopotamia, and the Chinese civilization had beautifully drawn maps with accurate coordinate systems far better in detail than those of the West. China also had the mathematics of Pascal's triangle for binomial expansions by A.D. 1303 and Horner's method for solving equations long before Horner. In China, mathematics never became the backbone of astronomical and scientific theory as it did in the West and, though there were transmissions in both directions, the two world cultures remained strikingly different in this important respect. It is, after all, this difference that led the West from Ptolemy to Kepler and Newton, and thence to Einstein. But the nonmathematical theories of chemistry and biology show China as a fair match for the best the West could attain and, in the techniques of industrialization, China scored huge successes in such areas as the production of cast iron and the sensible improvement of carriages and harnesses while Europe was still inventing feudalism and monastic contemplation.

One cannot say all these things, however, without blowing hot and cold with pride of ownership over who did what first and who got which idea from whom. We shall have to find out much more about both the European and the Chinese past before we can make any substantial estimate of the nature and importance of the transmissions between East and West.

26. The chief focus of the passage is on which of the following?

(A) Indicating the many similarities between Chinese and Western cultures
(B) Lamenting the decision of a brilliant culture to relinquish its leadership in the development of various sciences
(C) Showing that, unlike Chinese science, Western science is the result of individual achievements
(D) Proving that Chinese contributions to science were more significant than those of the West
(E) Describing some Chinese scientific achievements and comparing them to those of the West

27. The attitude toward Europe conveyed by the author's use of the words "still inventing" (line 45) is best described as one of

(A) delighted amazement
(B) mild condescension
(C) uncontrolled amusement
(D) grudging admiration
(E) growing anger

28. According to the passage, a divergence in Chinese and Western scientific traditions is most clearly indicated by

(A) Western use of mathematics in the development of scientific theory
(B) the early use of astrology among the Chinese
(C) the completely different mathematical discoveries of each culture
(D) the different mechanical inventions of each culture
(E) Chinese accomplishments with regard to industrial techniques

29. The author's attitude toward the Chinese achievements mentioned in lines 1-45 is best described as one of

(A) disbelief (B) admiration (C) anxiety
(D) ambivalence (E) apathy

30. The final statement in the passage chiefly suggests which of the following?

(A) The history of science is worth study in almost any culture.
(B) Chinese scientific achievement is such that the West would profit greatly from studying it.
(C) More investigation is needed to determine exactly what influence China and the West had on each other.
(D) Two attitudes toward science as divergent as those of China and the West will be hard to reconcile.
(E) Neither China nor the West will ever admit what each has learned from the other.

GO ON TO THE NEXT PAGE

Select the word or set of words that best completes each of the following sentences.

31. This ---- painter was but ---- pianist; yet she seemed more pleased by compliments on her playing than on her painting.
(A) amateur. .a professional
(B) unexceptional. .an untutored
(C) accomplished. .a preeminent
(D) virtuoso. .a mediocre
(E) novice. .a renowned

32. In comparative anatomy, all methods of analysis, save direct observation, are beset with ---- which require great ---- if reliable conclusions are to be drawn.
(A) analogies. .duplication
(B) problems. .supposition
(C) premises. .inducement
(D) pitfalls. .circumspection
(E) judgments. .prerogative

33. The primary quality that a leader must possess is a single-minded dedication to the people's welfare, whereby ---- interests are ---- to the people's interests.
(A) partisan. .subordinated
(B) special. .ascribed
(C) conflicting. .attributed
(D) factional. .preferred
(E) dictatorial. .relegated

34. My heretofore faithful friends, considering their ---- hostile actions against me, must now, ----, be numbered among my enemies.
(A) resentment of. .justifiably
(B) discouragement of. .indiscriminately
(C) revival of. .simultaneously
(D) complicity in. .lamentably
(E) acquiescence in. .auspiciously

35. The candidate's writers showed poor judgment in embroidering the speech with that apocryphal anecdote; it was certainly not an appropriate ----, and thus was as ---- as it was artificial.
(A) development. .pivotal
(B) proposal. .astounding
(C) novelty. .insufficient
(D) digression. .gratuitous
(E) improvisation. .expedient

Each question below consists of a related pair of words or phrases, followed by five lettered pairs of words or phrases. Select the lettered pair that best expresses a relationship similar to that expressed in the original pair.

Example:

YAWN : BOREDOM :: (A) dream : sleep
(B) anger : madness (C) smile : amusement
(D) face : expression (E) impatience : rebellion
Ⓐ Ⓑ ● Ⓓ Ⓔ

36. DANCER : FEET :: (A) surgeon : heart
(B) juggler : hands (C) drummer : drums
(D) conductor : voice (E) musician : eyes

37. RACKET : TENNIS :: (A) puck : hockey
(B) rifle : duck (C) hammer : nail
(D) ball : soccer (E) bat : baseball

38. FERTILIZER : PLANT :: (A) pollen : allergy
(B) bandage : wound (C) flame : fire
(D) nitrogen : atmosphere (E) food : human

39. LIE : DECEIT :: (A) cunning : guilt
(B) wealth : generosity (C) suspicion : distrust
(D) punishment : error (E) loyalty : treason

40. PAPYRUS : PAPER :: (A) canoe : kayak
(B) scroll : book (C) magazine : rack
(D) cave : cavern (E) parchment : bark

41. ISLAND : ARCHIPELAGO :: (A) castle : moat
(B) star : galaxy (C) river : delta
(D) bay : peninsula (E) earth : hemisphere

42. PHOENIX : IMMORTALITY ::
(A) unicorn : cowardice (B) sphinx : mystery
(C) salamander : speed (D) ogre : wisdom
(E) chimera : stability

43. STIPEND : BONUS :: (A) performance : encore
(B) engagement : marriage (C) gift : celebration
(D) reward : superiority (E) battle : victory

44. MATRIARCHY : WOMAN :: (A) legality : lawyer
(B) monarchy : sovereign (C) hierarchy : heir
(D) feudalism : farmer (E) duplicity : thief

45. PERFUNCTORY:ENTHUSIASM ::
(A) hostile:animosity
(B) submissive:defiance
(C) flagrant:criticism
(D) solitary:conviction
(E) honorary:admiration

S T O P

IF YOU FINISH BEFORE TIME IS CALLED, YOU MAY CHECK YOUR WORK ON THIS SECTION ONLY. DO NOT WORK ON ANY OTHER SECTION IN THE TEST.

SECTION 2

Time—30 minutes

25 QUESTIONS

In this section solve each problem, using any available space on the page for scratchwork. Then decide which is the best of the choices given and blacken the corresponding space on the answer sheet.

The following information is for your reference in solving some of the problems.

Circle of radius r: Area $= \pi r^2$; Circumference $= 2\pi r$
The number of degrees of arc in a circle is 360.
The measure in degrees of a straight angle is 180.

Definitions of symbols:

$=$	is equal to	$\leq$	is less than or equal to
$\neq$	is unequal to	$\geq$	is greater than or equal to
$<$	is less than	$\parallel$	is parallel to
$>$	is greater than	$\perp$	is perpendicular to

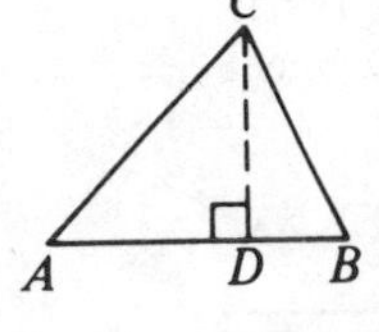

Triangle: The sum of the measures in degrees of the angles of a triangle is 180.

If $\angle CDA$ is a right angle, then

(1) area of $\triangle ABC = \dfrac{AB \times CD}{2}$

(2) $AC^2 = AD^2 + DC^2$

Note: Figures which accompany problems in this test are intended to provide information useful in solving the problems. They are drawn as accurately as possible EXCEPT when it is stated in a specific problem that its figure is not drawn to scale. All figures lie in a plane unless otherwise indicated. All numbers used are real numbers.

---

1. A number 1,010 more than 100,101 is

(A) 100,111 (B) 100,211 (C) 101,101
(D) 101,111 (E) 111,111

2. If $\dfrac{x}{y} = 3$ and $x = 12$, then $x - y =$

(A) 3 (B) 5 (C) 6 (D) 8 (E) 9

3. If $a, b, c, d,$ and e are whole numbers, the expression $a(b(c + d) + e)$ will be an even number whenever which of the following is even?

(A) a (B) b (C) c (D) d (E) e

EMPLOYMENT PATTERN IN COMPANY X

Year	1	2	3	4	5
Number of Workers	23	69	207	621	

4. The number of workers employed by a company has increased by a constant multiple from year to year as shown in the chart above. If this pattern continues, how many workers can the company expect to employ in year 5 ?

(A) 835
(B) 1,035
(C) 1,242
(D) 1,463
(E) 1,863

GO ON TO THE NEXT PAGE

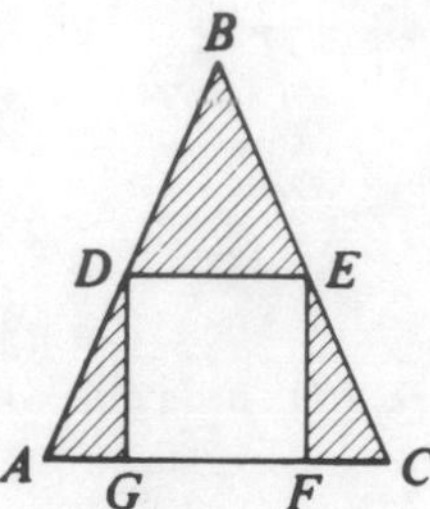

5. In the figure above, the area of triangle ABC is 32 and the total area of the shaded regions is 16. If $DEFG$ is a square, what is the length of segment GF ?

(A) 4 (B) 5 (C) $\sqrt{34}$ (D) 6 (E) $5\sqrt{2}$

Questions 6-7 refer to the information below.

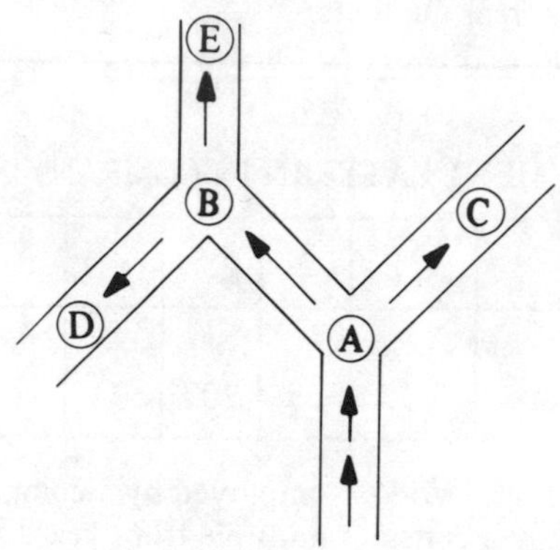

A traffic survey shows that of every 12 cars that arrive at point A, 7 turn toward point B and 5 turn toward point C. Of every 7 cars that arrive at point B, 3 turn toward point D and 4 turn toward point E.

6. Of 48 cars arriving at point A, how many are expected to turn toward point B ?

(A) 15 (B) 20 (C) 28 (D) 30 (E) 36

7. Of 72 cars arriving at point A, how many are expected eventually to turn toward point D ?

(A) 18 (B) 24 (C) 26 (D) 32 (E) 42

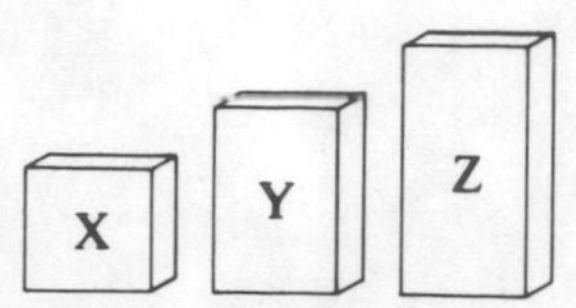

8. In the figure above, the number of grams of cereal in box Y is greater than the number in box X and less than the number in box Z. If box Z contains 500 grams, each of the following could be the total number of grams of cereal in the three boxes EXCEPT

(A) 900 g
(B) 1,000 g
(C) 1,200 g
(D) 1,350 g
(E) 1,500 g

9. The sum of the digits of a three-digit number is 12. If the hundreds' digit is 3 times the tens' digit and the tens' digit is $\frac{1}{2}$ the units' digit, what is the number?

(A) 312
(B) 624
(C) 912
(D) 936
(E) 963

10. The average (arithmetic mean) mass of 4 objects is 50 kilograms. If 3 of the objects each have a mass of 45 kilograms, what is the mass, in kilograms, of the fourth object?

(A) 70 (B) 65 (C) 60 (D) 55 (E) 50

11. If 10 is 5 percent of N, then $N =$

(A) 2
(B) 5
(C) 20
(D) 50
(E) 200

GO ON TO THE NEXT PAGE

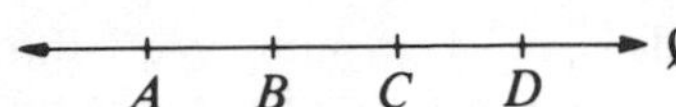

12. Which of the following statements is (are) true of the lengths of the segments on line ℓ above?

I. $AB + CD = AD$
II. $AB + BC = AD - CD$
III. $AC - AB = AD - CD$

(A) I only (B) II only (C) III only
(D) I and II only (E) I, II, and III

13. If $Q = \frac{(x+y)h}{2}$, what is the average (arithmetic mean) of x and y when $Q = 20$ and $h = 5$?

(A) 100
(B) $\frac{25}{2}$
(C) 10
(D) 4
(E) 2

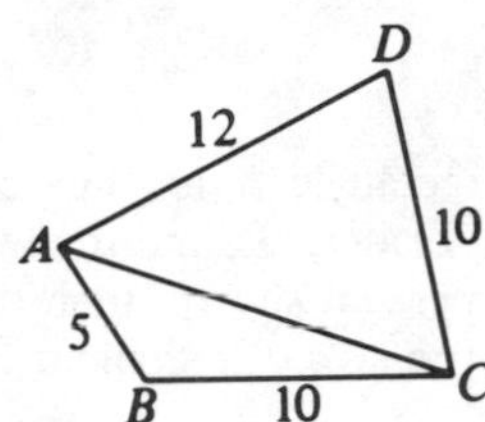

14. In the figure above, the perimeter of ΔACD is how much greater than the perimeter of ΔACB ?

(A) 22 (B) 14 (C) $5\sqrt{5}$ (D) 7 (E) $\sqrt{2}$

15. $\frac{4.5x^6y}{0.3x^2y^2} =$

(A) $\frac{0.15x^4}{y^2}$
(B) $\frac{1.5x^4}{y}$
(C) $\frac{1.5x^3}{y^2}$
(D) $\frac{15x^4}{y}$
(E) $\frac{15x^3}{y}$

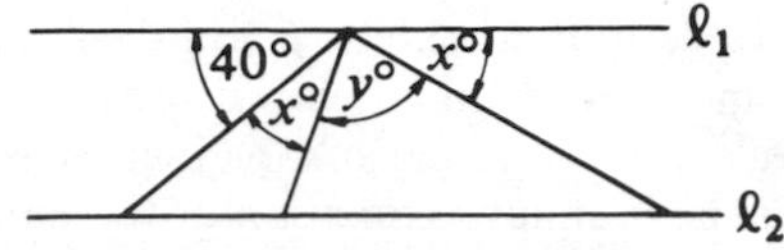

16. In the figure above, if lines ℓ_1 and ℓ_2 are parallel, what is the value of y ?

(A) 30
(B) 40
(C) 70
(D) 80
(E) It cannot be determined from the information given.

17. This question was not counted in computing scores.

18. If half the people in a room leave at the end of every five-minute interval and at the end of twenty minutes the next to the last person leaves, how many people were in the room to start with? (Assume that no one enters the room once the process begins.)

(A) 32
(B) 28
(C) 16
(D) 12
(E) 8

GO ON TO THE NEXT PAGE

19. Susan finds approximately f four-leaf clovers in every square meter of a field. If the field is a rectangle l meters long and w meters wide, what is the best approximation of the number of four-leaf clovers she finds?

(A) flw

(B) fl^2w^2

(C) $\frac{f^2}{lw}$

(D) $\frac{f}{lw}$

(E) $\frac{lw}{f}$

20. What fraction of the number of integer multiples of 2 between 1 and 99 are also integer multiples of 3 ?

(A) $\frac{16}{99}$

(B) $\frac{16}{49}$

(C) $\frac{1}{3}$

(D) $\frac{49}{99}$

(E) $\frac{33}{49}$

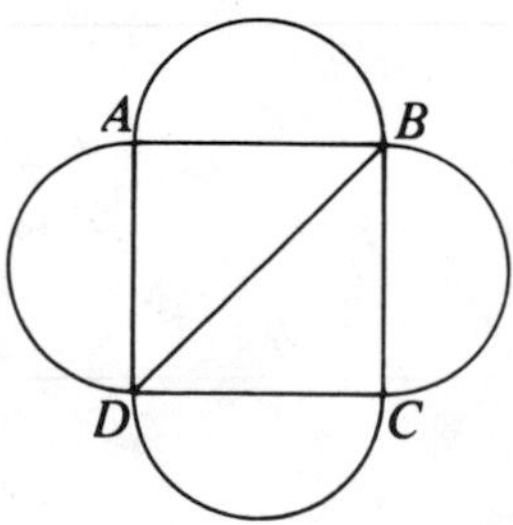

21. In the figure above, $ABCD$ is a square and each arc shown is a semicircle. If diagonal BD is equal to $\sqrt{2}$, what is the sum of the areas of the four semicircles?

(A) $\frac{\pi}{2}$ (B) π (C) $\sqrt{2}\pi$

(D) 2π (E) $2\sqrt{2}\pi$

22. Seven cards in a pile are numbered 1 through 7. One card is drawn. The units' digit of the sum of the numbers on the remaining cards is 7. What is the number on the drawn card?

(A) 1
(B) 3
(C) 5
(D) 7
(E) It cannot be determined from the information given.

23. If for any number x, $\boxed{x}$ is defined as the least integer that is greater than or equal to x, then $\boxed{-2.5} + \boxed{12} =$

(A) 9 (B) 9.5 (C) 10 (D) 11 (E) 14.5

24. A 25-foot ladder is placed against a vertical wall of a building, with the bottom of the ladder standing on concrete 7 feet from the base of the building. If the top of the ladder slips down 4 feet, then the bottom of the ladder will slide out

(A) 4 ft
(B) 5 ft
(C) 6 ft
(D) 7 ft
(E) 8 ft

25. The length of rectangle S is 20 percent longer than the length of rectangle R, and the width of rectangle S is 20 percent shorter than the width of rectangle R. The area of rectangle S is

(A) 20% greater than the area of rectangle R
(B) 4% greater than the area of rectangle R
(C) equal to the area of rectangle R
(D) 4% less than the area of rectangle R
(E) 20% less than the area of rectangle R

S T O P

IF YOU FINISH BEFORE TIME IS CALLED, YOU MAY CHECK YOUR WORK ON THIS SECTION ONLY.
DO NOT WORK ON ANY OTHER SECTION IN THE TEST.

SECTION 3

Time—30 minutes

40 QUESTIONS

For each question in this section, choose the best answer and blacken the corresponding space on the answer sheet.

Each question below consists of a word in capital letters, followed by five lettered words or phrases. Choose the word or phrase that is most nearly opposite in meaning to the word in capital letters. Since some of the questions require you to distinguish fine shades of meaning, consider all the choices before deciding which is best.

Example:

GOOD: (A) sour (B) bad (C) red (D) hot (E) ugly

Ⓐ ● Ⓒ Ⓓ Ⓔ

1. GUSTY: (A) warm (B) calm (C) bright (D) young (E) thin

2. RETREAT: (A) wander (B) budge (C) advance (D) travel (E) stumble

3. PREMEDITATED: (A) unconventional (B) undeliberated (C) unfathomable (D) independent (E) insubordinate

4. IOTA: (A) termination (B) primary cause (C) unmixed solution (D) inconsistency (E) large quantity

5. ABSTRUSE: (A) pure (B) colorless (C) lengthy (D) readily understood (E) cordially welcomed

6. CODDLE: (A) summon (B) clarify (C) abuse (D) separate (E) confess

7. IRREPROACHABLE: (A) isolated (B) essential (C) adjustable (D) recognizable (E) reprehensible

8. RAREFY: (A) obstruct (B) manipulate (C) make denser (D) use carelessly (E) perform faithfully

9. FETTER: (A) interrogate (B) implicate (C) placate (D) decorate (E) liberate

10. NEOLOGISM:
(A) nameless article
(B) foreign object
(C) exaggerated movement
(D) impoverished condition
(E) obsolete expression

Each sentence below has one or two blanks, each blank indicating that something has been omitted. Beneath the sentence are five lettered words or sets of words. Choose the word or set of words that best fits the meaning of the sentence as a whole.

Example:

Although its publicity has been ----, the film itself is intelligent, well-acted, handsomely produced, and altogether ----.

(A) tasteless. .respectable (B) extensive. .moderate (C) sophisticated. .amateur (D) risqué. .crude (E) perfect. .spectacular

● Ⓑ Ⓒ Ⓓ Ⓔ

11. If oil and coal are constantly ----, then someday the natural supply will be ----.

(A) produced. .available
(B) sought. .discovered
(C) supplanted. .reduced
(D) consumed. .exhausted
(E) burned. .useless

12. The 1970's witnessed an unprecedented ---- of the scope of historical studies; the result was that the distinctive experiences of Black Americans, Native Americans, women, and other previously ---- groups moved to the forefront of inquiry.

(A) redefinition. .neglected
(B) recapitulation. .uninvestigated
(C) summarizing. .well-recognized
(D) illumination. .significant
(E) elaboration. .chronicled

13. Although the substance is normally quite ----, scientists found that when tempered with other elements it could be stored safely in metal containers.

(A) voluminous (B) caustic (C) insoluble (D) vapid (E) heterogeneous

14. Norton is a drama critic who is evidently never ----; he writes a ---- review of every play he sees.

(A) astonished. .dazed (B) impressed. .rave (C) disgruntled. .peevish (D) pleased. .carping (E) satisfied. .reverential

15. Games and athletic contests are so intimately a part of life that they are valuable ---- the intensity and vitality of a given culture at any one time.

(A) modifiers of (B) antidotes to (C) exceptions to (D) obstacles to (E) indices of

GO ON TO THE NEXT PAGE

3

Each question below consists of a related pair of words or phrases, followed by five lettered pairs of words or phrases. Select the lettered pair that best expresses a relationship similar to that expressed in the original pair.

Example:

YAWN : BOREDOM :: (A) dream : sleep
(B) anger : madness (C) smile : amusement
(D) face : expression (E) impatience : rebellion

Ⓐ Ⓑ ● Ⓓ Ⓔ

16. STABLE : HORSE :: (A) kennel : dog
(B) trap : fox (C) flower : bee
(D) hutch : cat (E) forest : bird

17. DEGREE : TEMPERATURE :: (A) heat : cold
(B) activity : pace (C) bank : currency
(D) minute : time (E) acre : volume

18. BOW : CELLO :: (A) mute : trumpet
(B) pedal : piano (C) string : violin
(D) skin : drum (E) pick : banjo

19. COWER : FEAR :: (A) pursue : despair
(B) wobble : power (C) plod : energy
(D) rove : speed (E) strut : pride

20. CROWD : NUMBER :: (A) room : wall
(B) table : leg (C) street : sidewalk
(D) treasure : worth (E) painting : variety

21. BUNGLER : SKILL :: (A) fool : amusement
(B) critic : error (C) daredevil : caution
(D) braggart : confidence (E) genius : intelligence

22. CONVOKE : ASSEMBLY :: (A) muster : troops
(B) challenge : opponents (C) veto : legislation
(D) canvass : membership (E) disband : army

23. ANECDOTE : NARRATIVE :: (A) dogma : belief
(B) vendetta : revenge (C) code : signal
(D) snack : meal (E) jester : comedy

24. ASSUAGE : ANGUISH ::
(A) investigate : annoyance (B) discuss : torment
(C) alleviate : affliction (D) assert : hatred
(E) inflame : pain

25. ALCHEMIST : TRANSMUTATION ::
(A) traitor : loyalty
(B) proselytizer : conversion
(C) scientist : equivocation
(D) anarchist : tranquillity
(E) astronomer : consternation

GO ON TO THE NEXT PAGE

Each passage below is followed by questions based on its content. Answer all questions following a passage on the basis of what is stated or implied in that passage.

The warden slowly turned his glass. Then he said, "I will now present you with proof of a total inner security. I could answer, 'I was director of a theater' or 'the leading actor in a repertory company.' In actual fact, I was the reviewer on a pretentious literary weekly. In other words, an intellectual dilettante." The warden sipped his whisky. "You see? I no longer feel the need to gild the dandelion. I have reached the degree of detachment and security where I can be ruthless without rancor, even toward myself." He pierced the yolk of a fried egg with his fork. "And you, Doctor? Of which illustrious medical college were you the youthful Chief Internist?"

The doctor hesitated; then the whisky seduced him. "I worked for a rural general practitioner just before I came here."

"Must have been fascinating."

"Disgusting. I spent most of my time being ashamed of myself."

"It is the privilege of youth to spend most of its time being ashamed of itself. You have progressed since then, I trust?"

"Somewhat."

The warden gave him a searching look. "Don't tell me you still indulge in attacks of conscience? That's a luxury you can ill afford in a place like this." He poured more whisky for them. "Well, here's to us: two forlorn nonentities on the pinnacle of power in a forgotten place. Cheers."

They drank.

The doctor looked at him uneasily. This line of conversation held a hidden menace, something he could not define but sensed quite clearly.

26. It can be inferred from the passage that the warden considers himself well qualified for his present job because of his ability to

(A) feign servility to his superiors
(B) remain emotionally aloof
(C) devote unusually long hours to his work
(D) require little in the way of physical comforts
(E) supplement his career with active participation in the arts

27. The warden's toast in lines 28-30 LEAST expresses which of the following?

(A) Sarcasm (B) Self-pity (C) Bitterness (D) Mistrust (E) Resignation

28. It can be inferred that the doctor's uneasiness at the end of the passage (lines 32-34) serves to forecast

(A) a sudden increase in the number of prisoners
(B) an abrupt shift in command at the prison
(C) the possibility of conflict between himself and the warden
(D) the warden's increasing inability to remain objective about his work
(E) the imminent arrival of another doctor in the prison

Our Sun was born, leading astronomers now believe, about five billion years ago, the spawn of a gigantic swirling nebula of gas and dust. As the particles coalesced, gravitation pulled them swiftly together and they heated up. Within a few million years the new body developed an interior temperature of millions of degrees, enough to ignite the processes of nuclear fusion. Hydrogen atoms fused to form helium atoms, giving off energy in the process, and the Sun began to shine.

The Sun has changed little since then, and likely will change little until the hydrogen at its center nears exhaustion, in perhaps another five billion years. Then, according to well-developed theories of stellar evolution, the outer layers will begin to expand and the Sun will swell and redden. Eventually it will loom across 25 percent of the Earth's sky, having increased a hundred times in diameter and a thousand times in brightness. Its hot breath may melt Mercury and Venus. The Earth may be reduced to a desolate, baking rock, its oceans completely boiled away. And earthlings, if they have survived, will have fled to some more hospitable part of the galaxy.

For a hundred million more years the swollen Sun will continue to deplete its nuclear fuel until finally only a tiny core will remain, and a frozen, presumably lifeless Earth will swing bleakly around a faint Sun no larger in the sky than the tiny planet Mars.

29. The primary purpose of the passage is to

(A) describe the relation between the Sun and the rest of the galaxy
(B) discuss a theory about the formation of the solar system
(C) give one example of the importance of the Sun to our universe
(D) sketch out the theoretical life cycle of the Sun
(E) explain the processes of nuclear fusion

30. Which of the following does the author most clearly imply about the sequence of events outlined in the passage?

(A) It is completely certain.
(B) It is possible, but rather unlikely.
(C) It is highly improbable.
(D) It represents one of many theories on the subject.
(E) It represents the best current thinking on the subject.

GO ON TO THE NEXT PAGE

31. It can be inferred from the passage that all of the following might explain why the author describes the Earth as "presumably lifeless" (line 28) EXCEPT:

(A) Surviving earthlings will probably have fled to a more hospitable climate.
(B) If the Earth is frozen, it will probably also be lifeless.
(C) Although the Earth will probably be frozen, the climate might become warmer again.
(D) Although human life will no doubt vanish from Earth, some other forms might still exist.
(E) The heat of the Sun will probably be insufficient to allow much life as we know it.

Virginia Woolf, writing from the vantage point of twentieth-century England, once speculated on the fate of a woman born in Shakespeare's day with a touch of Shakespeare's genius: she imagined a life marred by family tyranny, social hostility, thwarted ambition, and, finally, suicide. But had Woolf ever heard of Anne Bradstreet (who was born in Shakespeare's forty-eighth year), she would have had to draw up an entirely different scenario that would involve emigration to the New World. For Bradstreet had an excellent education and received from her society, the middle-class Puritan elite, every encouragement to write and publish. Although she was married at sixteen and raised eight children—conditions that Virginia Woolf thought inimical to literary composition—Bradstreet became the first professional woman poet writing in the English language after—and surely because—she left England at eighteen and came to America.

Yet if Anne Bradstreet is remembered today in America, it is not, correctly, as the American colonies' first poet, but as a "Puritan poet," even though her 1650 edition is an essentially secular volume—not only not "Puritan," but not particularly Christian. She did write important religious verse, but at a later time. However, we have no warrant for describing her as unrepresentative, for it was the New England Puritans who insisted that she be published, and who gave Bradstreet's first book the memorable title, with its boasting reference to both the sexual and national identity of the poet, *The Tenth Muse Lately Sprung Up in America*.

32. According to the passage, Virginia Woolf's scenario did not take into account Anne Bradstreet's success because

(A) Anne Bradstreet was not a contemporary of Shakespeare
(B) Anne Bradstreet was not primarily known as a poet
(C) Virginia Woolf did not know about Anne Bradstreet
(D) Virginia Woolf did not like Anne Bradstreet's poetry
(E) Virginia Woolf had limited her consideration to women born in England

33. The author apparently believes that Anne Bradstreet can be correctly described as a "Puritan poet" (line 22) because Anne Bradstreet

(A) lived in a Puritan society that encouraged her career
(B) acted as an apologist for the Puritans, explaining their views
(C) received most of her education and training from the American Puritans
(D) chose only religious subjects of interest to New England Puritans
(E) wrote poetry that could have appeared only in Puritan New England

34. The author suggests that the title of Anne Bradstreet's first book is significant primarily because it

(A) emphasized the Puritans' control over publications in their colony
(B) omitted her name and the content of the work
(C) acknowledged her as America's first English-speaking poet
(D) defied the existing traditions associated with Puritan poetry
(E) reflected her society's esteem for her as a poet, a woman, and an American

35. The author apparently believes that the most significant factor leading to Anne Bradstreet's success as a poet was her

(A) piety
(B) education
(C) early marriage
(D) emigration to America
(E) association with other writers

GO ON TO THE NEXT PAGE

In the medical sciences the word "normal" is in constant use but, as a rule, without proper clarification of its meaning. It is commonly held to be synonymous with "healthy," but health too awaits a better definition and a closer study. It is an old and, to a large extent, just criticism of physicians that they have considered the symptoms, causes, and measurements of disease without sufficient reference to the symptoms, causes, and measurements of health; that they have refined their methods of detecting departures from the normal without first reviewing the idea of normal or discussing its limitations. That "normal," in biological usage, means something other than "not deviating from a fixed standard" can scarcely be disputed: in all animals, variation is so constantly at work that no rigid pattern–whether anatomical, physiological, psychological, or immunological–is possible. Yet, due to the neglect of the study of "healthy" populations and of what may best be described as "normal variability," many findings have been judged abnormal (in the sense of pathological) with quite inadequate justification.

When we speak of normal variability, we must distinguish between two types: individual variability across time and under differing conditions of activity; and variability under set conditions of age, sex, and activity in a particular population or species. In the individual (apart from the slower changes of growth, maturity, and senescence) functional fluctuations–for instance, of pulse rate, blood pressure, body temperature, and tissue chemistry–occur from minute to minute. Within a particular population or species, we find those variations that account for differences among individuals, even under standard conditions, in their healthiest moods and most favored communities–variations that help to explain the differing resistances and susceptibilities of individuals to stress and other harmful agencies.

A moment's thought will suggest that both types of variability are essential to survival. Without continuous and swift physiochemical variations in the individual, there could be no adaptation to constantly changing environmental conditions, or to the impositions of action and inaction or fasting and repletion, or to the ebb and flow of emotional stimuli. Without species variations, there could be no communal equilibrium or adaptability, no maintenance of a stock by the emergence of types better fitted for survival in a changing and exacting world, no natural distribution of functions within the group, no slow adaptations to changes in the external environment and, in the case of humans, no scope for adjustment to changing occupations and social systems. In brief–in both the individual and the community–there could be no adaptability without variability. Complete standardization is incompatible with life.

36. Which of the following best restates the criticism of physicians mentioned in lines 5-13?

(A) Physicians sometimes fail to consider adequately the symptoms, causes, and measurements of disease.
(B) Physicians may decide to bring up to date the old definitions of "normality" and "health."
(C) Physicians do not regularly diagnose a departure from the normal as a pathological abnormality.
(D) Physicians have devoted more time and effort to the treatment of ill health than they have to the study of what is meant by "healthy."
(E) Physicians do not define illness in sufficient detail to be able always to recognize and study deviations from the normal.

37. In the second paragraph, the author's chief distinction is between which of the following?

(A) Slow changes and reversible changes
(B) Normal variability and abnormal variability
(C) Temporal variability and variations in heredity
(D) Changes within a single person and differences within a group
(E) Functional fluctuations and standard biological conditions

38. According to the passage, individual variability is directly responsible for all of the following EXCEPT

(A) dealing with human emotions
(B) adjusting to nutritional fluctuations
(C) contending with impermanent surroundings
(D) coping with changing levels of activity
(E) maintaining communal equilibrium

GO ON TO THE NEXT PAGE

39. The author concludes that "complete standardization is incompatible with life" (lines 58-59) primarily because
(A) the great number of individuals prevents the establishment of patterns of normality
(B) there has been a neglect of the study of healthy populations and of normal variability
(C) a significant level of variation must be in operation to ensure survival
(D) functional fluctuations are directly responsible for the ability of a species to adapt over time
(E) humans would take longer to adjust to changing social conditions without variation

40. The primary purpose of the passage is to
(A) criticize physicians for their apparent disregard of the symptoms, causes, and measurements of normal variability
(B) describe the differences between "normal" and "abnormal" in the biological sense of the words
(C) elaborate the idea of a fixed standard of health and normality
(D) advocate the concept and clarify the meaning of "normal variability"
(E) differentiate among various types of conditions usually labeled "normal"

S T O P

IF YOU FINISH BEFORE TIME IS CALLED, YOU MAY CHECK YOUR WORK ON THIS SECTION ONLY. DO NOT WORK ON ANY OTHER SECTION IN THE TEST.

SECTION 5

Time—30 minutes

35 QUESTIONS

In this section solve each problem, using any available space on the page for scratchwork. Then decide which is the best of the choices given and blacken the corresponding space on the answer sheet.

The following information is for your reference in solving some of the problems.

Circle of radius r: Area $= \pi r^2$; Circumference $= 2\pi r$
The number of degrees of arc in a circle is 360.
The measure in degrees of a straight angle is 180.

Definitions of symbols:

$=$	is equal to	$\leq$	is less than or equal to
$\neq$	is unequal to	$\geq$	is greater than or equal to
$<$	is less than	$\parallel$	is parallel to
$>$	is greater than	$\perp$	is perpendicular to

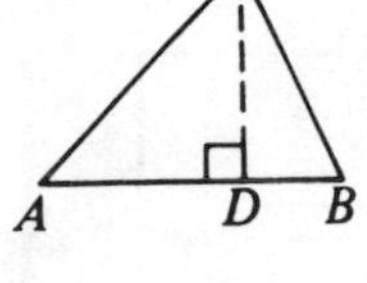

Triangle: The sum of the measures in degrees of the angles of a triangle is 180.

If $\angle CDA$ is a right angle, then

(1) area of $\triangle ABC = \dfrac{AB \times CD}{2}$

(2) $AC^2 = AD^2 + DC^2$

Note: Figures which accompany problems in this test are intended to provide information useful in solving the problems. They are drawn as accurately as possible EXCEPT when it is stated in a specific problem that its figure is not drawn to scale. All figures lie in a plane unless otherwise indicated. All numbers used are real numbers.

---

1. If $2x + 1 = 5$, then $4x =$

(A) 8 (B) 10 (C) 12 (D) 16 (E) 24

2. A florist buys roses at \$0.50 apiece and sells them for \$1.00 apiece. If there are no other expenses, how many roses must be sold in order to make a profit of \$300 ?

(A) 100
(B) 150
(C) 200
(D) 300
(E) 600

3. If $x \div 7 = 392 \div 8$, then $x =$

(A) 343
(B) 336
(C) 329
(D) 322
(E) 315

4. The fraction $\frac{4}{3}$ is NOT between

(A) $\frac{1}{2}$ and $\frac{3}{2}$

(B) $\frac{2}{3}$ and 1

(C) 1 and 2

(D) $\frac{5}{4}$ and $\frac{6}{4}$

(E) $\frac{6}{5}$ and $\frac{7}{5}$

5. If the average (arithmetic mean) of -5 and x is -5, then $x =$

(A) 10
(B) 5
(C) 0
(D) -5
(E) -10

6. The perimeter of a 7-sided figure is 15. If the length of each side of the figure is increased by 2 units, what is the perimeter of the new figure?

(A) 22 (B) 24 (C) 29 (D) 30 (E) 119

7. What is the sum of all the positive integer factors of 20 ?

(A) 12
(B) 21
(C) 30
(D) 33
(E) 42

GO ON TO THE NEXT PAGE

5

Questions 8-27 each consist of two quantities, one in Column A and one in Column B. You are to compare the two quantities and on the answer sheet blacken space

A if the quantity in Column A is greater;
B if the quantity in Column B is greater;
C if the two quantities are equal;
D if the relationship cannot be determined from the information given.

Notes: 1. In certain questions, information concerning one or both of the quantities to be compared is centered above the two columns.
2. In a given question, a symbol that appears in both columns represents the same thing in Column A as it does in Column B.
3. Letters such as x, n, and k stand for real numbers.

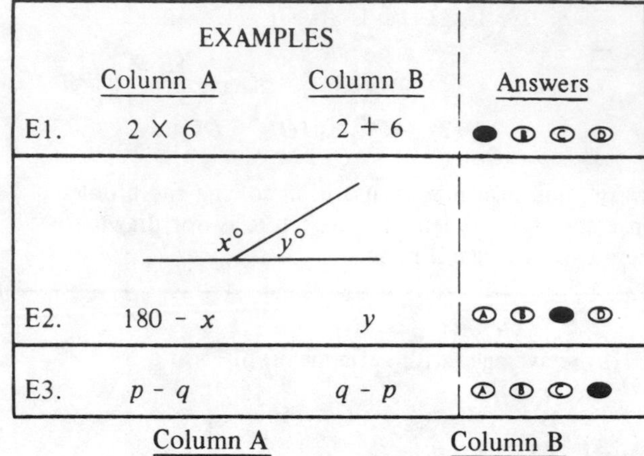

EXAMPLES

	Column A	Column B	Answers
E1.	2×6	$2 + 6$	● Ⓑ Ⓒ Ⓓ
E2.	$180 - x$	y	Ⓐ Ⓑ ● Ⓓ
E3.	$p - q$	$q - p$	Ⓐ Ⓑ Ⓒ ●

	Column A	Column B
8.	The number of tens in 48	The number of hundreds in 348

$x \neq 0$

9.	$\frac{1}{x^2}$	0
10.	$4(2x - 2)$	$2(4x - 4)$
11.	The length of the hypotenuse of a right triangle with legs of lengths 8 and 6	The length of the hypotenuse of a right triangle with legs of lengths 12 and 5

The sum of two positive numbers is 24.
The difference of the numbers is 10.

12.	The larger of these two numbers	18

	Column A	Column B
13.	$8 - (7 - 6 - 5)$	$8 - 7 - (6 - 5)$
14.	Volume of a rectangular block with dimensions 1 meter by 2 meters by 3 meters	Volume of a rectangular block with dimensions 1 meter by 12 meters by 0.5 meters

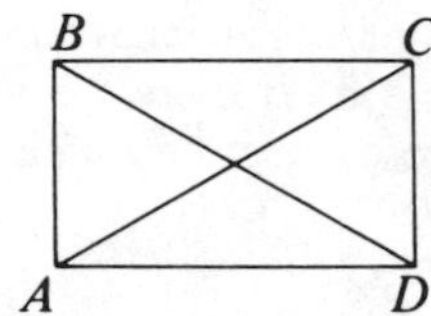

Note: Figure not drawn to scale.

In parallelogram $ABCD$, $\angle ABC \neq \angle BAD$.

15.	Length of AC	Length of BD

$2x + 2 < 1$

16.	x	0

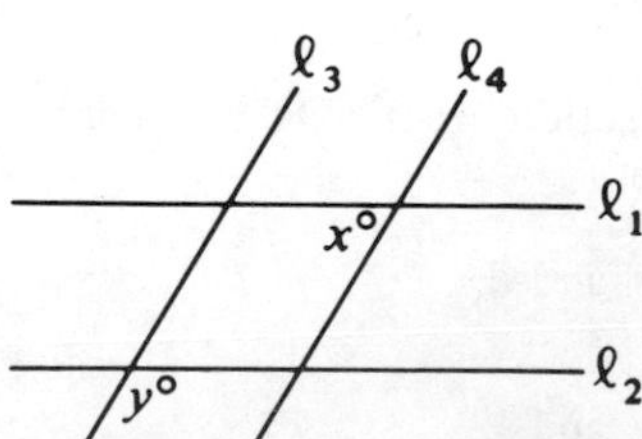

Lines ℓ_1 and ℓ_2 are parallel.
Lines ℓ_3 and ℓ_4 are parallel.

17.	x	$180 - y$

GO ON TO THE NEXT PAGE

SUMMARY DIRECTIONS FOR COMPARISON QUESTIONS

Answer: A if the quantity in Column A is greater;
B if the quantity in Column B is greater;
C if the two quantities are equal;
D if the relationship cannot be determined from the information given.

	Column A	Column B
	$x + y = 5$ $x - 2y = 7$	
18.	x	y
19.	Area of a circle with radius r	Area of a circle with diameter $2r$
	$x + y = y$	
20.	x	y

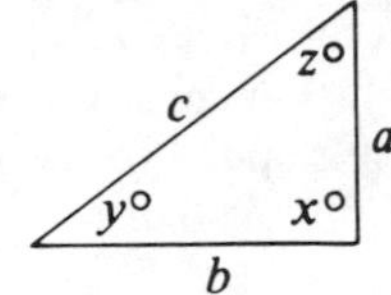

Note: Figure not drawn to scale.

$180 > x > y + z$

	Column A	Column B
21.	c^2	$a^2 + b^2$
	The average (arithmetic mean) of 18, 30, x, and y equals 12. $x > 0$	
22.	y	0
	Juan is h years old and Lisa is k years older than Juan.	
23.	$k - h$	$h - k$
24.	Remainder when 731^{500} is divided by 10	1

	Column A	Column B
	x is a 2-digit number divisible by 2, 3, and 7.	
25.	x	84
	$m > 0$	
26.	$\frac{m}{0.25}$	$3m$
	$a^2 = b^2$	
27.	ab	a^2

GO ON TO THE NEXT PAGE

Solve each of the remaining problems in this section using any available space for scratchwork. Then decide which is the best of the choices given and blacken the corresponding space on the answer sheet.

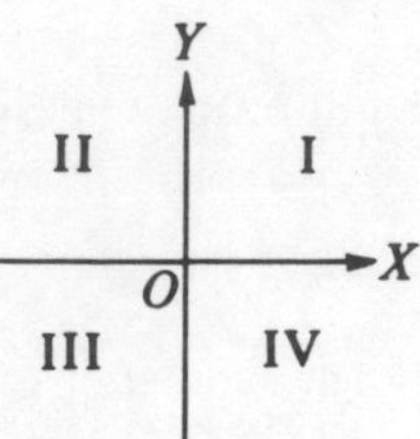

28. In the figure above, which quadrants contain pairs (x, y) that satisfy the condition $\frac{x}{y} = 1$?

(A) I only
(B) I and II only
(C) I and III only
(D) II and IV only
(E) I, II, III, and IV

29. If it is now 4:00 p.m. Saturday, in 253 hours from now, what time and day will it be? (Assume no daylight saving time changes in the period.)

(A) 5:00 a.m. Saturday
(B) 1:00 a.m. Sunday
(C) 5:00 p.m. Tuesday
(D) 1:00 a.m. Wednesday
(E) 5:00 a.m. Wednesday

30. If $\boxed{\begin{matrix} a & b \\ c & d \end{matrix}}$ is defined to equal $ab - cd$

and $\boxed{\begin{matrix} a & b \\ c & d \end{matrix}} + y = 0$, then $y =$

(A) $ab - cd$
(B) $ac - bd$
(C) $ad - bc$
(D) $bc - ad$
(E) $cd - ab$

31. Milk costs x cents per half-gallon and y cents per gallon. If a gallon of milk costs z cents less than 2 half-gallons, which of the following equations must be true?

(A) $x - 2y + z = 0$
(B) $2x - y + z = 0$
(C) $x - y - z = 0$
(D) $2x - y - z = 0$
(E) $x + 2y - z = 0$

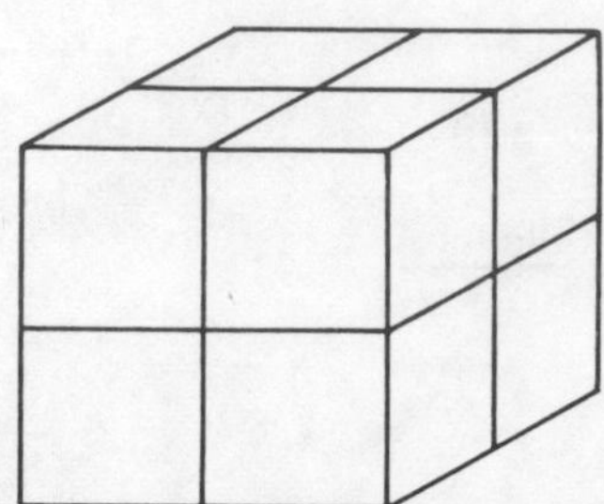

32. The large solid wooden cube above is composed of 8 smaller cubes of equal size and the total surface of the large cube is painted purple. If each of the smaller cubes is then cut into 8 cubes of equal size, how many of the smallest cubes will have exactly 3 purple faces?

(A) 4 (B) 8 (C) 16 (D) 24 (E) 32

33. In a 10-kilogram solution of water and alcohol, the ratio by mass of water to alcohol is 3:2. If 6 kilograms of a solution consisting of 2 parts water to 1 part alcohol is added to the 10-kilogram solution, what fraction by mass of the new solution is alcohol?

(A) $\frac{5}{8}$ (B) $\frac{3}{8}$ (C) $\frac{1}{3}$ (D) $\frac{5}{16}$ (E) $\frac{3}{16}$

34. If it takes 10 people 12 hours to do a certain job, how many hours would it take 6 people, working at the same rate, to do $\frac{1}{4}$ of the same job?

(A) 6 (B) 5 (C) $4\frac{1}{2}$ (D) 4 (E) $3\frac{3}{4}$

35. The twelve-hour digital clock above shows one example of a time at which the number representing the hour is equal to the number representing the minutes. What is the LEAST possible number of minutes from the instant one such "double" reading appears to the instant the next appears?

(A) 11 (B) 30 (C) 49 (D) 60 (E) 61

S T O P

IF YOU FINISH BEFORE TIME IS CALLED, YOU MAY CHECK YOUR WORK ON THIS SECTION ONLY. DO NOT WORK ON ANY OTHER SECTION IN THE TEST.

Correct Answers for Scholastic Aptitude Test
Form Code 2E

VERBAL		MATHEMATICAL	
Section 1	Section 3	Section 2	Section 5
1. B	1. B	1. D	1. A
2. A	2. C	2. D	2. E
3. E	3. B	3. A	3. A
4. E	4. E	4. E	4. B
5. C	5. D	5. A	5. D
6. D	6. C	6. C	6. C
7. B	7. E	7. A	7. E
8. B	8. C	8. E	*8. A
9. B	9. E	9. B	*9. A
10. D	10. E	10. B	*10. C
11. C	11. D	11. E	*11. B
12. C	12. A	12. B	*12. B
13. C	13. B	13. D	*13. A
14. B	14. D	14. D	*14. C
15. C	15. E	15. D	*15. D
16. C	16. A	16. E	*16. B
17. A	17. D	17. †	*17. C
18. B	18. E	18. C	*18. A
19. D	19. E	19. A	*19. C
20. C	20. D	20. B	*20. D
21. D	21. C	21. A	*21. A
22. E	22. A	22. A	*22. B
23. D	23. D	23. C	*23. D
24. A	24. C	24. E	*24. C
25. C	25. B	25. D	*25. D
26. E	26. B		*26. A
27. B	27. D		*27. D
28. A	28. C		28. C
29. B	29. D		29. E
30. C	30. E		30. E
31. D	31. C		31. D
32. D	32. C		32. B
33. A	33. A		33. B
34. D	34. E		34. B
35. D	35. D		35. C
36. B	36. D		
37. E	37. D		
38. E	38. E		
39. C	39. C		
40. B	40. D		
41. B			
42. B			
43. A			
44. B			
45. B			

*Indicates four-choice questions. (All of the other questions are five-choice.)

†Not scored

The Scoring Process

Machine-scoring is done in three steps:

- *Scanning.* Your answer sheet is "read" by a scanning machine and the oval you filled in for each question is recorded on a computer tape.
- *Scoring.* The computer compares the oval filled in for each question with the correct response. Each correct answer receives one point; omitted questions do not count toward your score. For each wrong answer, a fraction of a point is subtracted to correct for random guessing. For questions with five answer choices, one-fourth of a point is subtracted for each wrong response; for questions with four answer choices, one-third of a point is subtracted for each wrong response. The SAT-verbal test has 85 questions with five answer choices each. If, for example, a student has 44 right, 32 wrong, and 9 omitted, the resulting raw score is determined as follows:

  $$44 \text{ right} - \frac{32 \text{ wrong}}{4} = 44 - 8 = 36 \text{ raw score points}$$

  Obtaining raw scores frequently involves the rounding of fractional numbers to the nearest whole number. For example, a raw score of 36.25 is rounded to 36, the nearest whole number. A raw score of 36.50 is rounded upward to 37.
- *Converting to reported scaled score.* Raw test scores are then placed on the College Board scale of 200 to 800 through a process that adjusts scores to account for minor differences in difficulty among different editions of the test. This process, known as equating, is performed so that a student's reported score is not affected by the edition of the test taken nor by the abilities of the group with whom the student takes the test. As a result of placing SAT scores on the College Board scale, scores earned by students at different times can be compared. For example, an SAT-verbal score of 400 on a test taken at one administration indicates the same level of developed verbal ability as a 400 score obtained on a different edition of the test taken at another time.

How to Score the Test

You can verify the College Board SAT scores reported to you recently by using the information in this booklet along with the copy of your answer sheet. *Before you begin, check that the first two characters (number and letter) of the form code you marked in item 3 on your answer sheet are the same as the form code printed on the front of this booklet.* Compare the responses shown on the copy of your answer sheet with the list of correct answers.

SAT-Verbal Sections 1 and 3

Step A: Count the number of correct answers for *section 1* and record the number in the space provided on the worksheet on the next page. Then do the same for the incorrect answers. (Do not count omitted answers.) To determine subtotal A, use the formula:

$$\text{number correct} - \frac{\text{number incorrect}}{4} = \text{subtotal A}$$

Step B: Count the number of correct answers and the number of incorrect answers for *section 3* and record the numbers in the spaces provided on the worksheet. To determine subtotal B, use the formula:

$$\text{number correct} - \frac{\text{number incorrect}}{4} = \text{subtotal B}$$

Step C: To obtain C, add subtotal A to subtotal B, keeping any decimals. Enter the resulting figure on the worksheet.

Step D: To obtain D, your raw verbal score, round C to the nearest whole number. (For example, any number from 44.50 to 45.49 rounds to 45.) Enter the resulting figure on the worksheet.

Step E: To find your reported SAT-verbal score, look up the total raw verbal score you obtained in step D in the conversion table on page 174. Enter this figure on the worksheet.

SAT-Mathematical Sections 2 and 5

Step A: Count the number of correct answers and the number of incorrect answers for *section 2* and record the numbers in the spaces provided on the worksheet. To determine the subtotal A, use the formula:

$$\text{number correct} - \frac{\text{number incorrect}}{4} = \text{subtotal A}$$

Step B: Count the number of correct answers and the number of incorrect answers for the *five-choice questions (questions 1 through 7 and 28 through 35) in section 5* and record the numbers in the spaces provided on the worksheet. To determine the subtotal B, use the formula:

$$\text{number correct} - \frac{\text{number incorrect}}{4} = \text{subtotal B}$$

Step C: Count the number of correct answers and the number of incorrect answers for the *four-choice questions (questions 8 through 27) in section 5* and record the numbers in the spaces provided on the worksheet. To determine the subtotal C, use the formula:

$$\text{number correct} - \frac{\text{number incorrect}}{3} = \text{subtotal C}$$

Step D: To obtain D, add subtotal A, subtotal B, and subtotal C, keeping any decimals. Enter the resulting figure on the worksheet.

Step E: To obtain E, your raw mathematical score, round D to the nearest whole number. (For example, any number from 44.50 to 45.49 rounds to 45.) Enter the resulting figure on the worksheet.

Step F: To find your reported SAT-mathematical score, look up the total raw mathematical score you obtained in E in the conversion table on page 174. Enter this figure on the worksheet.

SAT SCORING WORKSHEET

FORM CODE 2E

SAT-Verbal Sections

A. Section 1:	______ no. correct	− ¼	(______) no. incorrect	=	______ subtotal A
B. Section 3:	______ no. correct	− ¼	(______) no. incorrect	=	______ subtotal B
C. Total unrounded raw score (Total A + B)					______ C
D. Total rounded raw score (Rounded to nearest whole number)					______ D
E. SAT-verbal reported scaled score (See the conversion table on the back cover.)					[ ] SAT-verbal score

SAT-Mathematical Sections

A. Section 2:	______ no. correct	− ¼	(______) no. incorrect	=	______ subtotal A
B. Section 5: Questions 1 through 7 and 28 through 35 (5-choice)	______ no. correct	− ¼	(______) no. incorrect	=	______ subtotal B
C. Section 5: Questions 8 through 27 (4-choice)	______ no. correct	− ⅓	(______) no. incorrect	=	______ subtotal C
D. Total unrounded raw score (Total A + B + C)					______ D
E. Total rounded raw score (Rounded to nearest whole number)					______ E
F. SAT-mathematical reported scaled score (See the conversion table on the back cover.)					[ ] SAT-math score

Score Conversion Table
Scholastic Aptitude Test
Form Code 2E

Raw Score	College Board Reported Score		Raw Score	College Board Reported Score	
	SAT-Verbal	SAT-Math		SAT-Verbal	SAT-Math
85	800		40	460	620
84	790		39	450	610
83	780		38	450	600
82	770		37	440	590
81	760		36	430	580
80	750		35	430	570
79	740		34	420	560
78	730		33	410	550
77	720		32	410	540
76	710		31	400	540
75	700		30	390	530
74	690		29	390	520
73	680		28	380	510
72	670		27	380	500
71	670		26	370	490
70	660		25	360	480
69	650		24	360	470
68	640		23	350	460
67	630		22	340	460
66	630		21	330	450
65	620		20	330	440
64	610		19	320	430
63	610		18	310	420
62	600		17	310	410
61	590		16	300	400
60	580		15	290	390
59	580	800	14	290	390
58	570	790	13	280	380
57	560	780	12	270	370
56	560	770	11	260	360
55	550	760	10	260	350
54	550	750	9	250	340
53	540	740	8	240	330
52	530	730	7	230	320
51	530	720	6	230	310
50	520	710	5	220	300
49	510	700	4	210	300
48	510	690	3	200	290
47	500	690	2	200	280
46	500	680	1	200	270
45	490	670	0	200	260
44	480	660	−1	200	250
43	480	650	−2	200	240
42	470	640	−3	200	230
41	470	630	−4	200	220
			−5	200	210
			−6	200	210
			−7 or below	200	200

Test 6
SAT *Form Code 2F*

(Cut here to detach.)

COLLEGE BOARD — SCHOLASTIC APTITUDE TEST and Test of Standard Written English

Side 1

Use a No. 2 pencil only. Be sure each mark is dark and completely fills the intended oval. Completely erase any errors or stray marks.

1.

YOUR NAME: (Print) ____ Last ____ First ____ M.I.

SIGNATURE: ____ **DATE:** ___/___/___

HOME ADDRESS: (Print) ____ Number and Street

____ City ____ State ____ Zip Code

CENTER: (Print) ____ City ____ State ____ Center Number

IMPORTANT: Please fill in these boxes exactly as shown on the back cover of your test book.

FOR ETS USE ONLY

3. FORM CODE

0	A	J	S	0	0	0
1	B	K	T	1	1	1
2	C	L	U	2	2	2
3	D	M	V	3	3	3
4	E	N	W	4	4	4
5	F	O	X	5	5	5
6	G	P	Y	6	6	6
7	H	Q	Z	7	7	7
8	I	R		8	8	8
9				9	9	9

4. REGISTRATION NUMBER
(Copy from your Admission Ticket.)

0	0	0	0	0	0	0
1	1	1	1	1	1	1
2	2	2	2	2	2	2
3	3	3	3	3	3	3
4	4	4	4	4	4	4
5	5	5	5	5	5	5
6	6	6	6	6	6	6
7	7	7	7	7	7	7
8	8	8	8	8	8	8
9	9	9	9	9	9	9

5. YOUR NAME

First 4 letters of last name				First Init.	Mid. Init.
A	A	A	A	A	A
B	B	B	B	B	B
C	C	C	C	C	C
D	D	D	D	D	D
E	E	E	E	E	E
F	F	F	F	F	F
G	G	G	G	G	G
H	H	H	H	H	H
I	I	I	I	I	I
J	J	J	J	J	J
K	K	K	K	K	K
L	L	L	L	L	L
M	M	M	M	M	M
N	N	N	N	N	N
O	O	O	O	O	O
P	P	P	P	P	P
Q	Q	Q	Q	Q	Q
R	R	R	R	R	R
S	S	S	S	S	S
T	T	T	T	T	T
U	U	U	U	U	U
V	V	V	V	V	V
W	W	W	W	W	W
X	X	X	X	X	X
Y	Y	Y	Y	Y	Y
Z	Z	Z	Z	Z	Z

6. DATE OF BIRTH

Month	Day		Year	
Jan.				
Feb.				
Mar.	0	0	0	0
Apr.	1	1	1	1
May	2	2	2	2
June	3	3	3	3
July		4	4	4
Aug.		5	5	5
Sept.		6	6	6
Oct.		7	7	7
Nov.		8		8
Dec.		9		9

7. SEX

Female

Male

8. TEST BOOK SERIAL NUMBER

Start with number 1 for each new section. If a section has fewer than 50 questions, leave the extra answer spaces blank.

SECTION 1

1	A	B	C	D	E	26	A	B	C	D	E
2	A	B	C	D	E	27	A	B	C	D	E
3	A	B	C	D	E	28	A	B	C	D	E
4	A	B	C	D	E	29	A	B	C	D	E
5	A	B	C	D	E	30	A	B	C	D	E
6	A	B	C	D	E	31	A	B	C	D	E
7	A	B	C	D	E	32	A	B	C	D	E
8	A	B	C	D	E	33	A	B	C	D	E
9	A	B	C	D	E	34	A	B	C	D	E
10	A	B	C	D	E	35	A	B	C	D	E
11	A	B	C	D	E	36	A	B	C	D	E
12	A	B	C	D	E	37	A	B	C	D	E
13	A	B	C	D	E	38	A	B	C	D	E
14	A	B	C	D	E	39	A	B	C	D	E
15	A	B	C	D	E	40	A	B	C	D	E
16	A	B	C	D	E	41	A	B	C	D	E
17	A	B	C	D	E	42	A	B	C	D	E
18	A	B	C	D	E	43	A	B	C	D	E
19	A	B	C	D	E	44	A	B	C	D	E
20	A	B	C	D	E	45	A	B	C	D	E
21	A	B	C	D	E	46	A	B	C	D	E
22	A	B	C	D	E	47	A	B	C	D	E
23	A	B	C	D	E	48	A	B	C	D	E
24	A	B	C	D	E	49	A	B	C	D	E
25	A	B	C	D	E	50	A	B	C	D	E

SECTION 2

1	A	B	C	D	E	26	A	B	C	D	E
2	A	B	C	D	E	27	A	B	C	D	E
3	A	B	C	D	E	28	A	B	C	D	E
4	A	B	C	D	E	29	A	B	C	D	E
5	A	B	C	D	E	30	A	B	C	D	E
6	A	B	C	D	E	31	A	B	C	D	E
7	A	B	C	D	E	32	A	B	C	D	E
8	A	B	C	D	E	33	A	B	C	D	E
9	A	B	C	D	E	34	A	B	C	D	E
10	A	B	C	D	E	35	A	B	C	D	E
11	A	B	C	D	E	36	A	B	C	D	E
12	A	B	C	D	E	37	A	B	C	D	E
13	A	B	C	D	E	38	A	B	C	D	E
14	A	B	C	D	E	39	A	B	C	D	E
15	A	B	C	D	E	40	A	B	C	D	E
16	A	B	C	D	E	41	A	B	C	D	E
17	A	B	C	D	E	42	A	B	C	D	E
18	A	B	C	D	E	43	A	B	C	D	E
19	A	B	C	D	E	44	A	B	C	D	E
20	A	B	C	D	E	45	A	B	C	D	E
21	A	B	C	D	E	46	A	B	C	D	E
22	A	B	C	D	E	47	A	B	C	D	E
23	A	B	C	D	E	48	A	B	C	D	E
24	A	B	C	D	E	49	A	B	C	D	E
25	A	B	C	D	E	50	A	B	C	D	E

COLLEGE BOARD — SCHOLASTIC APTITUDE TEST and Test of Standard Written English

Side 2

Use a No. 2 pencil only. Be sure each mark is dark and completely fills the intended oval. Completely erase any errors or stray marks.

Start with number 1 for each new section. If a section has fewer than 50 questions, leave the extra answer spaces blank.

SECTION 3	SECTION 4	SECTION 5	SECTION 6
1 A B C D E	1 A B C D E	1 A B C D E	1 A B C D E
2 A B C D E	2 A B C D E	2 A B C D E	2 A B C D E
3 A B C D E	3 A B C D E	3 A B C D E	3 A B C D E
4 A B C D E	4 A B C D E	4 A B C D E	4 A B C D E
5 A B C D E	5 A B C D E	5 A B C D E	5 A B C D E
6 A B C D E	6 A B C D E	6 A B C D E	6 A B C D E
7 A B C D E	7 A B C D E	7 A B C D E	7 A B C D E
8 A B C D E	8 A B C D E	8 A B C D E	8 A B C D E
9 A B C D E	9 A B C D E	9 A B C D E	9 A B C D E
10 A B C D E	10 A B C D E	10 A B C D E	10 A B C D E
11 A B C D E	11 A B C D E	11 A B C D E	11 A B C D E
12 A B C D E	12 A B C D E	12 A B C D E	12 A B C D E
13 A B C D E	13 A B C D E	13 A B C D E	13 A B C D E
14 A B C D E	14 A B C D E	14 A B C D E	14 A B C D E
15 A B C D E	15 A B C D E	15 A B C D E	15 A B C D E
16 A B C D E	16 A B C D E	16 A B C D E	16 A B C D E
17 A B C D E	17 A B C D E	17 A B C D E	17 A B C D E
18 A B C D E	18 A B C D E	18 A B C D E	18 A B C D E
19 A B C D E	19 A B C D E	19 A B C D E	19 A B C D E
20 A B C D E	20 A B C D E	20 A B C D E	20 A B C D E
21 A B C D E	21 A B C D E	21 A B C D E	21 A B C D E
22 A B C D E	22 A B C D E	22 A B C D C	22 A B C D E
23 A B C D E	23 A B C D E	23 A B C D E	23 A B C D E
24 A B C D E	24 A B C D E	24 A B C D E	24 A B C D E
25 A B C D E	25 A B C D E	25 A B C D E	25 A B C D E
26 A B C D E	26 A B C D E	26 A B C D E	26 A B C D E
27 A B C D E	27 A B C D E	27 A B C D E	27 A B C D E
28 A B C D E	28 A B C D E	28 A B C D E	28 A B C D E
29 A B C D E	29 A B C D E	29 A B C D E	29 A B C D E
30 A B C D E	30 A B C D E	30 A B C D E	30 A B C D E
31 A B C D E	31 A B C D E	31 A B C D E	31 A B C D E
32 A B C D E	32 A B C D E	32 A B C D E	32 A B C D E
33 A B C D E	33 A B C D E	33 A B C D E	33 A B C D E
34 A B C D E	34 A B C D E	34 A B C D E	34 A B C D E
35 A B C D E	35 A B C D E	35 A B C D E	35 A B C D E
36 A B C D E	36 A B C D E	36 A B C D E	36 A B C D E
37 A B C D E	37 A B C D E	37 A B C D E	37 A B C D E
38 A B C D E	38 A B C D E	38 A B C D E	38 A B C D E
39 A B C D E	39 A B C D E	39 A B C D E	39 A B C D E
40 A B C D E	40 A B C D E	40 A B C D E	40 A B C D E
41 A B C D E	41 A B C D E	41 A B C D E	41 A B C D E
42 A B C D E	42 A B C D E	42 A B C D E	42 A B C D E
43 A B C D E	43 A B C D E	43 A B C D E	43 A B C D E
44 A B C D E	44 A B C D E	44 A B C D E	44 A B C D E
45 A B C D E	45 A B C D E	45 A B C D E	45 A B C D E
46 A B C D E	46 A B C D E	46 A B C D E	46 A B C D E
47 A B C D E	47 A B C D E	47 A B C D E	47 A B C D E
48 A B C D E	48 A B C D E	48 A B C D E	48 A B C D E
49 A B C D E	49 A B C D E	49 A B C D E	49 A B C D E
50 A B C D E	50 A B C D E	50 A B C D E	50 A B C D E

9. SIGNATURE: ______________________

FOR ETS USE ONLY	VTR	VTFS	VRR	VRFS	VVR	VVFS	WER	WEFS	M4R	M4FS	M5R	M5FS	MTFS
	VTW	VTCS	VRW	VRCS	VVW	VVCS	WEW	WECS	M4W		M5W		MTCS

FORM CODE 2F

SECTION 1

Time—30 minutes

40 QUESTIONS

For each question in this section, choose the best answer and blacken the corresponding space on the answer sheet.

Each question below consists of a word in capital letters, followed by five lettered words or phrases. Choose the word or phrase that is most nearly opposite in meaning to the word in capital letters. Since some of the questions require you to distinguish fine shades of meaning, consider all the choices before deciding which is best.

Example:

GOOD: (A) sour (B) bad (C) red (D) hot (E) ugly

Ⓐ ● Ⓒ Ⓓ Ⓔ

1. AGITATION: (A) originality (B) curiosity (C) serenity (D) intelligence (E) significance

2. MOBILE: (A) fixed (B) perceptive (C) excluded (D) simplified (E) basic

3. JUNCTURE: (A) separation (B) complexity (C) assumption (D) offensive comment (E) valuable merchandise

4. DETAIN: (A) amuse (B) flatter (C) expedite (D) display clearly (E) invest money

5. STATELY: (A) remote (B) final (C) unusual (D) impractical (E) humble

6. SPURN: (A) react (B) inform (C) embrace (D) bring order to (E) remain firm

7. CONSEQUENTIAL: (A) repellent (B) trivial (C) unauthorized (D) bringing bad luck (E) not easily attained

8. INSULARITY: (A) broadmindedness (B) bluntness (C) courage (D) loss of freedom (E) complexity of design

9. REND: (A) thicken (B) display (C) unify (D) moisten repeatedly (E) contaminate accidentally

10. EXIGENT: (A) lacking urgency (B) without permission (C) inviting interest (D) unfashionable (E) unceremonious

Each sentence below has one or two blanks, each blank indicating that something has been omitted. Beneath the sentence are five lettered words or sets of words. Choose the word or set of words that best fits the meaning of the sentence as a whole.

Example:

Although its publicity has been ----, the film itself is intelligent, well-acted, handsomely produced, and altogether ----.

(A) tasteless. .respectable (B) extensive. .moderate (C) sophisticated. .amateur (D) risqué. .crude (E) perfect. .spectacular

11. Although we often use the terms porpoise and dolphin ----, careful marine biologists observe the ---- the two.

(A) carelessly. .behavior of
(B) consciously. .similarity between
(C) definitively. .habitats of
(D) interchangeably. .distinctions between
(E) accurately. .history of

12. Either the sunsets at Nome are ----, or the one I saw was a poor example.

(A) gorgeous (B) overrated (C) unobserved (D) exemplary (E) unappreciated

13. He had a delightfully indulgent way of showing his ---- for his friends; these actions in themselves ---- a kind heart.

(A) respect. .contradicted
(B) concern. .deprecated
(C) disdain. .established
(D) intolerance. .denoted
(E) fondness. .betokened

GO ON TO THE NEXT PAGE

14. Ridges on the fingertips are thought to increase ---- in gripping by ---- friction at the surface of contact.

(A) leverage. .converting
(B) efficiency. .creating
(C) strength. .soothing
(D) endurance. .demonstrating
(E) independence. .spreading

15. Fortunately, ---- is one of the bad habits in writing that has gradually gone out of fashion since the daily newspaper first set a standard of ---- reporting of events.

(A) imprecision. .swift
(B) superficiality. .routine
(C) irreverence. .detailed
(D) redundancy. .documented
(E) circumlocution. .concise

Each question below consists of a related pair of words or phrases, followed by five lettered pairs of words or phrases. Select the lettered pair that best expresses a relationship similar to that expressed in the original pair.

Example:

YAWN : BOREDOM :: (A) dream : sleep
(B) anger : madness (C) smile : amusement
(D) face : expression (E) impatience : rebellion

16. CONCERT : AUDIENCE :: (A) restaurant : waiters
(B) orchestra : musicians (C) game : spectators
(D) school : cheerleaders (E) zoo : keepers

17. WATER : RESERVOIR :: (A) oil : fuel
(B) money : bank (C) lake : ocean
(D) parent : family (E) beach : inlet

18. WALK : PROWL ::
(A) cheat : pretend
(B) speak : shout
(C) applaud : disapprove
(D) listen : eavesdrop
(E) smile : grin

19. STAGNANT : MOTION :: (A) arid : moisture
(B) morbid : dread (C) neutral : balance
(D) marred : fault (E) tilled : irrigation

20. RETOUCH : PICTURE :: (A) design : dress
(B) orchestrate : song (C) publish : magazine
(D) emend : text (E) concoct : pastry

21. CAMOUFLAGE : APPEARANCE ::
(A) compensate : payment
(B) decipher : code
(C) experiment : hypothesis
(D) bluff : intention
(E) invest : chance

22. BIRD : MOLT :: (A) bear : hibernate
(B) snake : slough (C) fish : catch
(D) hawk : prey (E) rabbit : trap

23. INTROSPECTIVE : SELF ::
(A) pompous : thoughts
(B) conceited : others
(C) miserly : accomplishments
(D) impetuous : decisions
(E) scrupulous : principles

24. INCITE : SEDITIONIST :: (A) parade : heckler
(B) assault : victor (C) abdicate : autocrat
(D) arbitrate : mediator (E) donate : financier

25. NOISE : DIN :: (A) injury : pride
(B) voice : speech (C) sincerity : homage
(D) emotion : fervor (E) signal : message

GO ON TO THE NEXT PAGE

Each passage below is followed by questions based on its content. Answer all questions following a passage on the basis of what is stated or implied in that passage.

April 23rd to July 5th, 1832: The climate, during the months of May and June, the beginning of winter, was delightful. The mean temperature, from observations taken at nine o'clock, both morning and evening, was only 72°. It often rained heavily, but the drying southerly winds soon again rendered the walks pleasant. One morning, in the course of six hours, 1.6 inches of rain fell. As this storm passed over the forests which surround the mountain, the sound produced by the drops pattering on the countless multitude of leaves was very remarkable; it could be heard at the distance of a quarter of a mile, and was like the rushing of a great body of water. After the hotter days, it was delicious to sit quietly in the garden and watch the evening pass into night. Nature, in these climes, chooses vocalists from more humble performers than in Europe. A small frog, of the genus *Hyla*, sits on a blade of grass about an inch above the surface of the water, and sends forth a pleasing chirp: when several are together they sing in harmony on different notes. I had some difficulty in catching a specimen of this frog. The genus *Hyla* has its toes terminated by small suckers; and I found this animal could crawl up a pane of glass, when placed absolutely perpendicular. Various cicadae and crickets, at the same time, keep up a ceaseless shrill cry, but which, softened by the distance, is not unpleasant. Every evening after dark this great concert commenced; and often have I sat listening to it, until my attention has been drawn away by some curious passing insect.

26. According to the passage, the sound of the rain was "very remarkable" (lines 11-12) because of its

(A) duration
(B) dissonance and shrillness
(C) loudness and power
(D) fresh, rejuvenating associations
(E) eerie, mysterious quality

27. For a human being to perform a feat comparable to that performed by the frog (lines 25-26), that human being would have to

(A) climb to the top of an icy trail on skis
(B) walk up the side of a building
(C) slide across thin ice without cracking it
(D) climb to the top of a tall shade tree
(E) walk barefoot across a thin wire

28. In the passage, the author exhibits all of the following attitudes toward the surroundings EXCEPT

(A) curiosity
(B) wonder
(C) pleasure
(D) anxiety
(E) objectivity

Ann Beattie has done more than write short stories and two novels; within six short years she has become the voice of the contemporary United States. Of course, in a nation that touts the writing of the Great American Novel as one of its most chimerical achievements, it is preposterous to suppose that one author could mean all things to all people at all times. Instead, it seems that American fiction moves by decades; every ten years there emerges a new writer who is not only perfectly attuned to his or her times, but who can precisely transmit the essence of that era onto the page—not just documentation, but illumination as well. The work of F. Scott Fitzgerald illuminates the 1920's; the 1950's belong to J. D. Salinger.

With great wit and a hawk's eye for detail, Beattie writes about the generation that survived the Vietnam era, the drug and sexual revolutions, and came to rest, burned out, in the seventies. Her people are rootless. They have severed their ties with the old traditions, yet, to their bewilderment, they find themselves dissatisfied with the new "traditions" as well: communal living, unstructured child-rearing, absence of career goals. Their thoughts are as disjointed as their lives. These are not men and women grappling with great moral issues; these are people simply waiting, looking for some measure of satisfaction, some happiness. The problem is, more often than not, that they do not know where to begin to look, and, as is typical of the "me generation," their search frequently entails hurting others.

29. The word "chimerical" as used in line 6 means

(A) elusive (B) contemptible (C) innovative (D) significant (E) original

30. According to information presented in the passage, which of the following best describes a typical Beattie character?

(A) Experimental and relentlessly revolutionary
(B) Creative and refreshingly open-minded
(C) Discontented and often insensitive to others
(D) Goal-oriented, but not dependent on old traditions
(E) Uncertain, but optimistic and unselfish

31. The style and content of this passage indicate that it is most likely an excerpt from

(A) a plot summary on a book jacket
(B) a study of great American novels
(C) a brief biographical sketch of Beattie
(D) a paper on life-styles in the seventies
(E) an article on Beattie and her works

GO ON TO THE NEXT PAGE

In the early years of the Third French Republic (1870-1940), an urgent need was felt for an adequate patron, preferably drawn from the great leaders of the First Republic. Danton seemed promising material and, after a band of official historians had gotten to work on him, his statue glared forth with audacity from its pedestal. Respected historian Albert Mathiez, however, set to work to attack this new idol and, after twenty-four years of research, made it pretty clear that Danton was unprincipled, venal, implicated in treasonable negotiations, by no means an ardent republican, and, with all this, not a very influential politician after all.

Needless to say, in spite of Mathiez' work, Danton's statue is still firm on its pedestal, his reputation spotless in the school books of France today. The Third Republic properly made Danton great: in its amoral complacency, he would have been quite at home. Danton always believed that a popular system of government for his country was absurd; that the people were too ignorant, too inconsistent, and too corrupt to support a legal administration; that, habituated to obey, they required a master. His conduct was in perfect unison with those beliefs when he acted, but he was too voluptuous for his ambition, too indolent to acquire supreme power. Moreover, his objective seems to have been great wealth rather than great fame.

32. The author's primary purpose in this passage is to

(A) describe and assess the reputation and character of Danton
(B) denounce Danton as one chiefly concerned with enhancing his own notoriety
(C) show the impossibility of drawing an accurate historical picture of a figure like Danton
(D) expose the government leaders' exploitation of Danton's reputation for personal gain
(E) explore the influence of the First French Republic on the Third

33. The tone of the first two sentences of the second paragraph (lines 14-19) can best be described as

(A) honest and straightforward
(B) scholarly
(C) indifferent
(D) ironic
(E) sensational and melodramatic

34. It can be inferred from the passage that Mathiez' findings about Danton were

(A) accepted by the public as accurate
(B) refuted by later writers
(C) largely ignored
(D) attacked as an attempt to embarrass the government
(E) the cause of continuing controversy and debate

35. The author suggests that one of the reasons Danton was a particularly appropriate patron for the Third French Republic was that its people

(A) admired his efforts to structure the government during the First French Republic
(B) shared his distaste for fame and hero worship
(C) bore out his cynical beliefs about the nation
(D) shared his ambition for political power
(E) were driven like him to acquire wealth

GO ON TO THE NEXT PAGE

In connection with the appraisal of mineral resources, the need to differentiate the known and the recoverable from the undiscovered and the uneconomic requires that a resource classification system convey two prime elements of information: one, the degree of certainty about the existence of the materials, and two, the economic feasibility of recovering them. These two elements have generally been recognized in existing terminology, but inconsistently and incompletely. Thus, as used by both the mining and the petroleum industries, the term "reserves" generally refers to economically recoverable material in identified deposits, and the term "resources" includes, in addition, both identified deposits that cannot be profitably recovered now and deposits not yet discovered.

The degree of certainty about the existence of the materials is described by terms such as "proved," "probable," and "possible," the terms traditionally used by industry, and "measured," "indicated," and "inferred," the terms devised during the Second World War by the Geological Survey and the Bureau of Mines to serve the broader purpose of national resource appraisal. Use of these degree-of-certainty terms is by no means standard, but all of their definitions show that they refer only to deposits or structures known or surmised to exist. Moreover, these terms are usually linked to deposits minable at a profit; the classification system comprising these terms thus neglects deposits that might become minable as the result of economic or technological developments.

To remedy these defects, I have suggested that existing terminology be expanded into a broader framework involving both degree of certainty and feasibility of recovery. Either of the series of terms already used to describe degree of certainty may be used with reference to identified deposits and applied not only to presently minable deposits but to others that have been identified with the same degree of certainty. Feasibility-of-recovery categories can be designated by the terms "recoverable," "paramarginal," and "submarginal. . . ." Paramarginal resources are defined here as those that are recoverable if the price of the resource increases to as much as one and one-half times that prevailing now. Over the longer period, we can also expect that technological advances will make it profitable to mine resources that would be even more costly to exploit now. That, of course, is the reason for trying to take account of submarginal resources. It is reasonable to believe that continued technological progress will create recoverable reserves from this category.

36. According to the passage, industry commonly defines "reserves" (line 12) as which of the following?

I. Currently unidentified or economically unrecoverable
II. Existing in known deposits
III. Profitable to develop

(A) I only (B) II only (C) III only
(D) II and III only (E) I, II, and III

37. It can be inferred that the author's "broader framework" (lines 34-35) is most innovative in its treatment of which of the following?

(A) Degree of certainty
(B) Feasibility of recovery
(C) Magnitude of supply
(D) Probability of existence
(E) Margin of error

GO ON TO THE NEXT PAGE

38. The price factor referred to in lines 45-47 reflects the assumption that

(A) technological progress will facilitate differentiation of paramarginal and submarginal resources
(B) increases in the value of a resource may make the mining of its paramarginal deposits economically worthwhile
(C) prices higher than one and one-half times those prevailing will never be acceptable
(D) inflationary price increases of minerals will probably not affect their recoverability
(E) costs of mining submarginal resources vary from place to place

39. Based on the information in the passage, it would be contradictory to use which of the following pairs of terms to label a certain mineral deposit?

(A) Submarginal and proved
(B) Inferred and paramarginal
(C) Indicated and submarginal
(D) Probable and recoverable
(E) Measured and possible

40. The author apparently feels that the terminology traditionally used in connection with resource appraisal is

(A) totally unsuitable
(B) inaccurate and excessively full of jargon
(C) in need of elaboration and standardization
(D) complex to use but appropriate
(E) useful and precise

S T O P

IF YOU FINISH BEFORE TIME IS CALLED, YOU MAY CHECK YOUR WORK ON THIS SECTION ONLY. DO NOT WORK ON ANY OTHER SECTION IN THE TEST.

3

SECTION 3

Time—30 minutes

25 QUESTIONS

In this section solve each problem, using any available space on the page for scratchwork. Then decide which is the best of the choices given and blacken the corresponding space on the answer sheet.

The following information is for your reference in solving some of the problems.

Circle of radius r: Area $= \pi r^2$; Circumference $= 2\pi r$
The number of degrees of arc in a circle is 360.
The measure in degrees of a straight angle is 180.

Definitions of symbols:

$=$	is equal to	$\leq$	is less than or equal to
$\neq$	is unequal to	$\geq$	is greater than or equal to
$<$	is less than	$\parallel$	is parallel to
$>$	is greater than	$\perp$	is perpendicular to

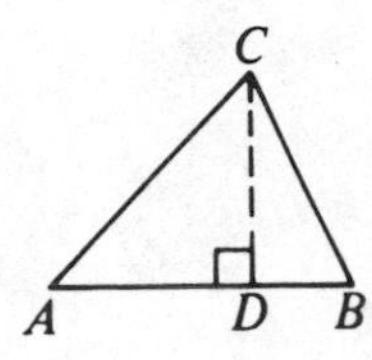

Triangle: The sum of the measures in degrees of the angles of a triangle is 180.

If $\angle CDA$ is a right angle, then

(1) area of $\triangle ABC = \dfrac{AB \times CD}{2}$

(2) $AC^2 = AD^2 + DC^2$

Note: Figures which accompany problems in this test are intended to provide information useful in solving the problems. They are drawn as accurately as possible EXCEPT when it is stated in a specific problem that its figure is not drawn to scale. All figures lie in a plane unless otherwise indicated. All numbers used are real numbers.

---

1. If $\dfrac{24 \times 3}{y} = 9$, then $y =$

(A) $\frac{1}{8}$

(B) 3

(C) 8

(D) 16

(E) 24

2. Of the following computations for the volume of a box, which represents the greatest value less than 100 ?

(A) $2 \times 4 \times 7$
(B) $2 \times 4 \times 8$
(C) $3 \times 3 \times 9$
(D) $3 \times 4 \times 6$
(E) $3 \times 5 \times 7$

3. The weights of four packages, A, B, C, and D, are in the order $A < B < C < D$. Which of the following could be true about the combined weights of certain of these packages?

(A) $A + C = B$

(B) $B + C = A$

(C) $A + B = C + D$

(D) $A + D = B + C$

(E) $A + B + D = C$

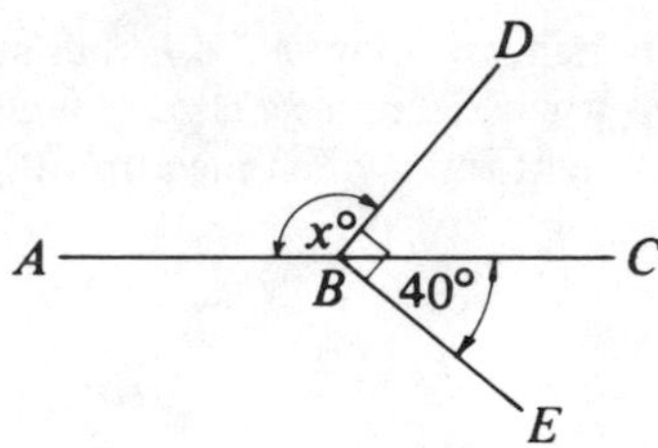

4. In the figure above, $DB \perp BE$ and AC is a line segment. What is the value of x ?

(A) 40 (B) 70 (C) 130 (D) 150 (E) 160

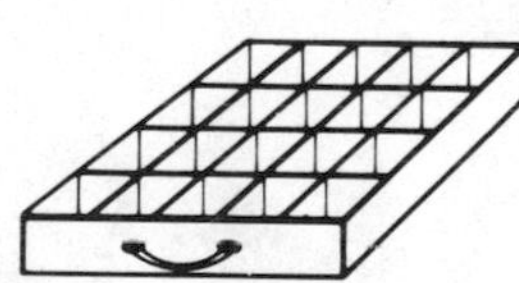

5. The figure above represents one compartmented drawer of a chest of identical drawers. If each compartment in each drawer contains 25 nails and if the chest contains 3,000 nails, exactly how many drawers are in the chest?

(A) 5 (B) 6 (C) 10 (D) 12 (E) 20

GO ON TO THE NEXT PAGE

6. If x, y, and z are odd numbers, which of the following is an odd number?

(A) $(x + y) + (y + z)$
(B) $x - y$
(C) $x + y + z$
(D) $xy + z$
(E) $(x - y) + (y - z)$

□4
3□
□3
5□
□1
15□

7. In the addition problem shown above, □ represents the same digit in each number. What must □ represent in order to make the answer correct?

(A) 8 (B) 6 (C) 5 (D) 4 (E) 2

---

8. On a certain map, two points 2.4 inches apart indicate two towns 12 miles apart. How long, in miles, is a straight road which measures 0.2 inch on the map?

(A) 1.0
(B) 2.5
(C) 5.0
(D) 10.0
(E) 12.0

9. If $y = 6x$ and $x = 2z$, what is y in terms of z ?

(A) $\frac{1}{3}z$

(B) $3z$

(C) $4z$

(D) $8z$

(E) $12z$

10. Let m equal the greatest possible 3-digit number in which no digit is repeated. Let n equal the least positive 3-digit number that can be made using all of the digits of m. What is the value of $m - n$?

(A) 198
(B) 222
(C) 864
(D) 885
(E) 888

11. If $y = \frac{1}{2}$, then $y^2 - y + \frac{1}{4} =$

(A) 0 (B) $\frac{1}{4}$ (C) $\frac{1}{2}$ (D) $\frac{3}{4}$ (E) 1

12. If $\frac{3}{4}x = \frac{6}{8}x$, what is the value of x ?

(A) 0 (B) 1 (C) 4 (D) 8
(E) It cannot be determined from the information given.

13. Which of the following rectangles, not necessarily drawn to scale, has an area equal to that of a circle of radius r ?

(A) (B) (C)

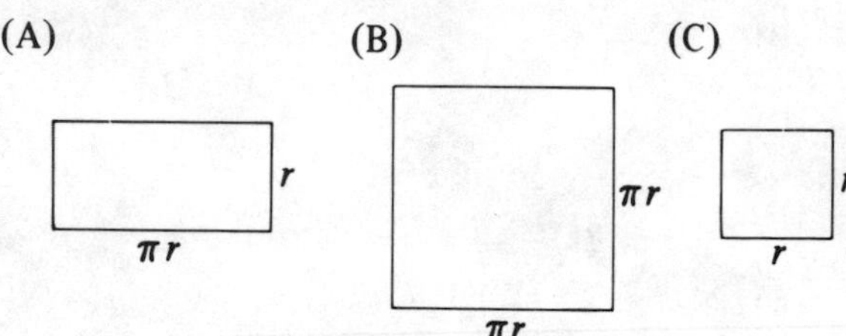

(D) (E)

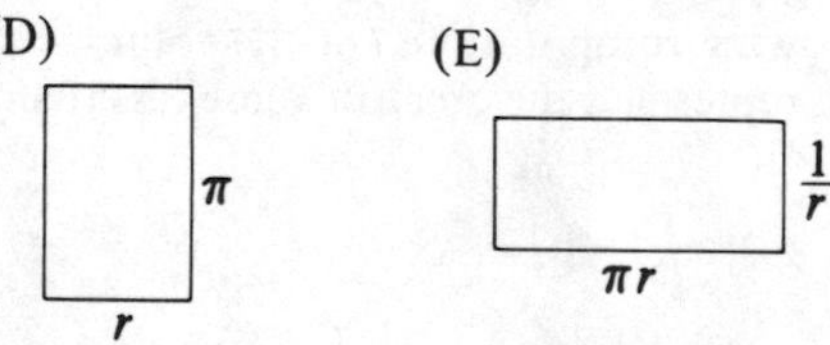

GO ON TO THE NEXT PAGE

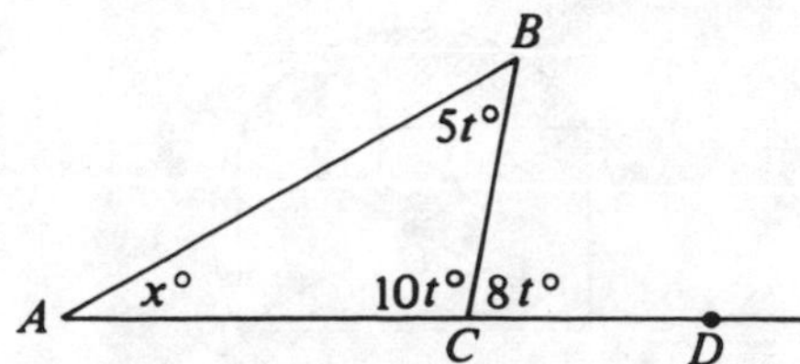

14. In the figure above, ACD is a line segment. What is the value of x ?

(A) 30 (B) 33 (C) 36 (D) 40 (E) 45

Questions 15-16 refer to the operation represented by ∇ and defined by the equation $x \nabla y = x + y + xy$ for all numbers x and y; for example, $(-6) \nabla (2) = (-6) + (2) + (-12) = -16$.

15. $\left(-\frac{1}{2}\right) \nabla\ 3 =$

(A) -5

(B) $-\frac{3}{2}$

(C) 1

(D) 4

(E) 5

16. If $8 \nabla k = 3$, then $k =$

(A) -5

(B) $-\frac{5}{9}$

(C) $\frac{3}{8}$

(D) $\frac{5}{9}$

(E) 5

17. If the first question in Part B of a test is number 45, the last question in Part B is number 95, and, in general, the nth question in Part B is number $(44 + n)$, how many questions are there altogether in Part B of the test?

(A) 59
(B) 51
(C) 50
(D) 49
(E) 40

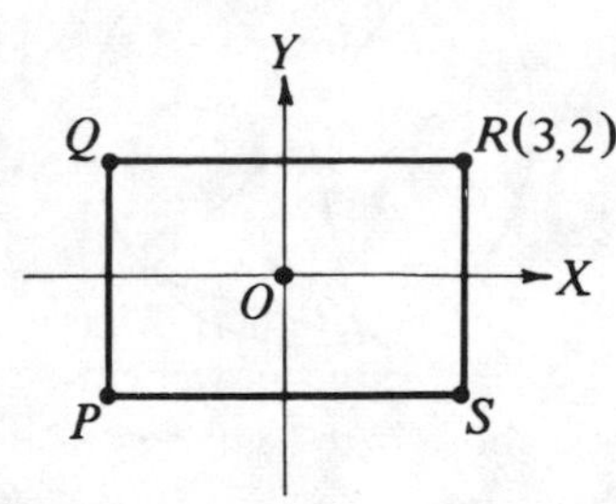

18. In the figure above, the sides of rectangle $PQRS$ are parallel to the X- and Y-axes as shown. If the rectangle is rotated clockwise about the origin until vertex R is on the positive X-axis, what will be the new coordinates of R ?

(A) (2, 0) (B) $(\sqrt{5}, 0)$ (C) (3, 0)
(D) $(\sqrt{13}, 0)$ (E) (5, 0)

19. After the 1st bounce, a certain ball always bounces $\frac{2}{3}$ of the height of its previous bounce. If the height of its 5th bounce is 1 meter, the height of its 3rd bounce in meters was

(A) $\frac{4}{9}$

(B) $1\frac{1}{2}$

(C) 2

(D) $2\frac{1}{4}$

(E) $2\frac{1}{2}$

GO ON TO THE NEXT PAGE

20. After Jane gave Bill \$4, she then had \$12 more than Bill. How much more money than Bill did Jane have originally?

(A) \$4
(B) \$8
(C) \$12
(D) \$16
(E) \$20

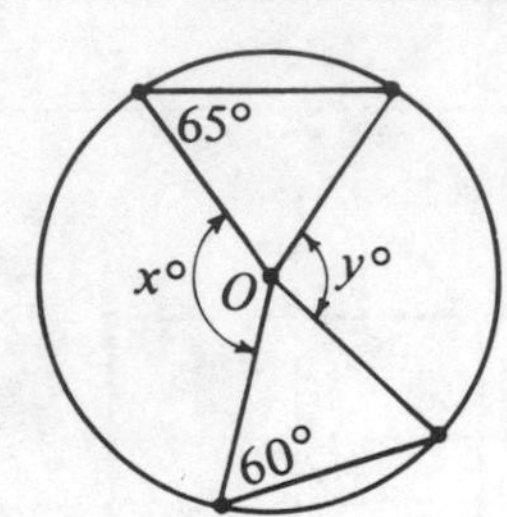

21. In the circle above with center O, $x + y =$

(A) 110 (B) 125 (C) 180
(D) 240 (E) 250

22. On a certain test, a class with 10 students had an average (arithmetic mean) score of 60 and a class with 15 students had an average score of 80. What was the average score on that test for the 25 students?

(A) 70 (B) 71 (C) 72 (D) 75
(E) It cannot be determined from the information given.

23. If $x^3y^2z < 0$, which of the following must be true?

I. $xz < 0$
II. $yz < 0$
III. $xyz < 0$

(A) None
(B) I only
(C) III only
(D) I and II
(E) II and III

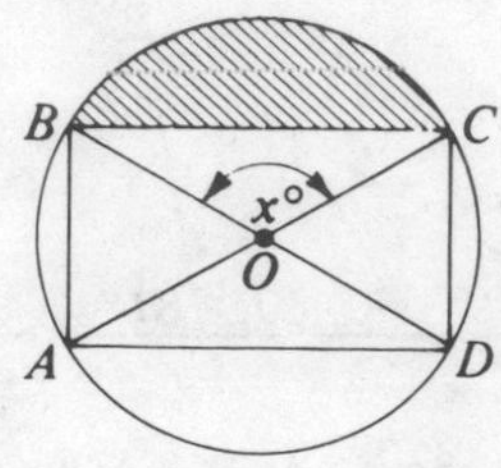

24. In the figure above, the vertices of rectangle $ABCD$ lie on a circle with center O. If $BD = 8$, $CD = 4$, and $x = 120$, what is the perimeter of the shaded region?

(A) $\frac{8}{3}\pi + 2\sqrt{3}$

(B) $\frac{8}{3}\pi + 4\sqrt{2}$

(C) $\frac{8}{3}\pi + 4\sqrt{3}$

(D) $8\pi + 2\sqrt{3}$

(E) $8\pi + 4\sqrt{3}$

25. In $2n$ years, Lisa will be $(6m + 1)$ times her current age. In terms of m and n, what is Lisa's current age?

(A) $\frac{n}{3m}$

(B) $\frac{2n}{6m + 1}$

(C) $\frac{2n - 1}{6m - 1}$

(D) $6m - 2n + 1$

(E) It cannot be determined from the information given.

S T O P

IF YOU FINISH BEFORE TIME IS CALLED, YOU MAY CHECK YOUR WORK ON THIS SECTION ONLY. DO NOT WORK ON ANY OTHER SECTION IN THE TEST.

SECTION 5

Time—30 minutes

35 QUESTIONS

5

In this section solve each problem, using any available space on the page for scratchwork. Then decide which is the best of the choices given and blacken the corresponding space on the answer sheet.

The following information is for your reference in solving some of the problems.

Circle of radius r: Area $= \pi r^2$; Circumference $= 2\pi r$
The number of degrees of arc in a circle is 360.
The measure in degrees of a straight angle is 180.

Definitions of symbols:

$=$	is equal to	$\leq$	is less than or equal to
$\neq$	is unequal to	$\geq$	is greater than or equal to
$<$	is less than	$\parallel$	is parallel to
$>$	is greater than	$\perp$	is perpendicular to

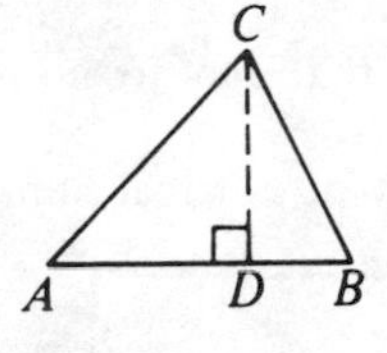

Triangle: The sum of the measures in degrees of the angles of a triangle is 180.

If $\angle CDA$ is a right angle, then

(1) area of $\triangle ABC = \frac{AB \times CD}{2}$

(2) $AC^2 = AD^2 + DC^2$

Note: Figures which accompany problems in this test are intended to provide information useful in solving the problems. They are drawn as accurately as possible EXCEPT when it is stated in a specific problem that its figure is not drawn to scale. All figures lie in a plane unless otherwise indicated. All numbers used are real numbers.

---

1. If $0.25 + 0.25 + x = 1$, then $x =$

(A) 50 (B) 25 (C) $\frac{1}{2}$ (D) $\frac{1}{4}$ (E) $\frac{1}{8}$

2. Which of the following is (are) true?

I. $12^2 = 144$
II. $12^3 = 3^{12}$
III. $12^6 = 72$

(A) I only (B) II only (C) III only
(D) I and III only (E) I, II, and III

3. If 2 out of 30 students in a class are athletes, what fraction of the students in this class are athletes?

(A) $\frac{1}{60}$ (B) $\frac{1}{28}$ (C) $\frac{1}{16}$ (D) $\frac{1}{15}$ (E) $\frac{1}{14}$

4. Which of the following numbers can be used to show that not all odd numbers are primes?

(A) 3 (B) 5 (C) 7 (D) 11 (E) 15

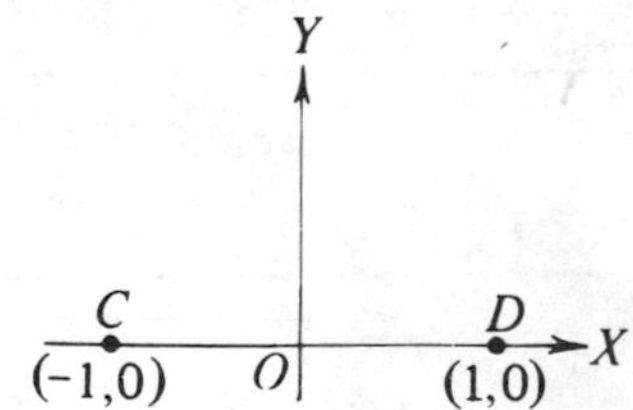

5. Points C and D lie in the XY-plane with coordinates as shown in the figure above. If Q is a point, not shown, equidistant from C and D, then Q can be any point on

(A) the Y-axis
(B) the X-axis
(C) line segment CD
(D) the line with equation $x = y$
(E) the line with equation $x = -y$

6. Three persons line up at a ticket window. In how many different orders can they arrange themselves in line?

(A) 3
(B) 4
(C) 6
(D) 9
(E) 12

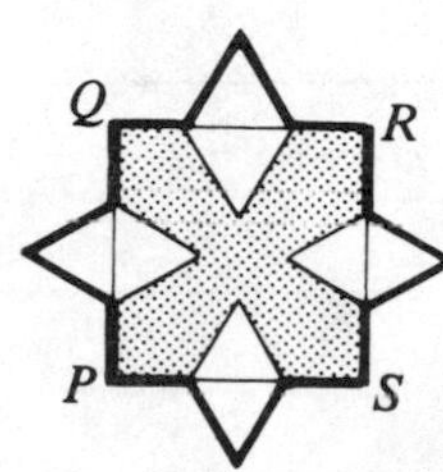

7. In the figure above, all triangles have the same area. If the area of the shaded region is 84 and the area of square $PQRS$ is 100, what is the total area of the regions outlined by the heavy line?

(A) 16 (B) 92 (C) 108 (D) 116 (E) 132

GO ON TO THE NEXT PAGE

5

Questions 8-27 each consist of two quantities, one in Column A and one in Column B. You are to compare the two quantities and on the answer sheet blacken space

A if the quantity in Column A is greater;
B if the quantity in Column B is greater;
C if the two quantities are equal;
D if the relationship cannot be determined from the information given.

Notes: 1. In certain questions, information concerning one or both of the quantities to be compared is centered above the two columns.
2. In a given question, a symbol that appears in both columns represents the same thing in Column A as it does in Column B.
3. Letters such as x, n, and k stand for real numbers.

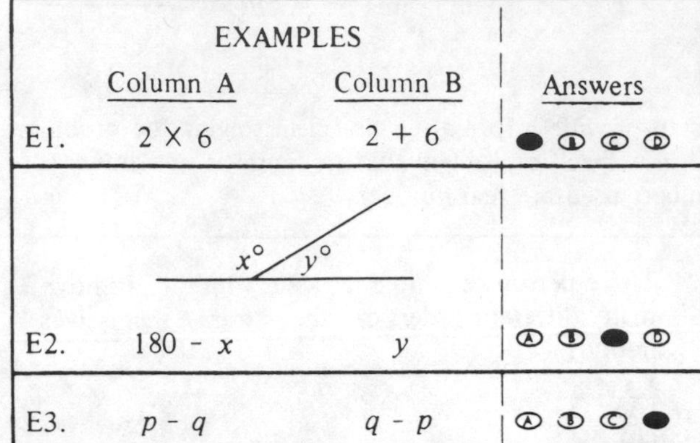

EXAMPLES

	Column A	Column B	Answers
E1.	2×6	$2 + 6$	● Ⓑ Ⓒ Ⓓ
E2.	$180 - x$	y	Ⓐ Ⓑ ● Ⓓ
E3.	$p - q$	$q - p$	Ⓐ Ⓑ Ⓒ ●

	Column A	Column B
8.	$59{,}000 \div 10$	590×10
9.	$\frac{10x - 60}{2}$	$5x - 30$

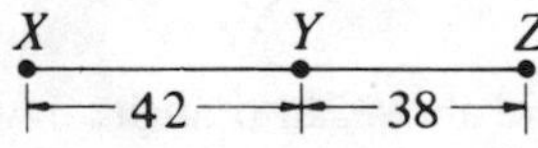

Points X, Y, and Z are on the same line segment.

	Column A	Column B
10.	The distance from X to the midpoint of YZ	60
11.	$(-1)^{87}$	$(-1)^{78}$

$-3 < x < 3$

	Column A	Column B
12.	$-x$	-4

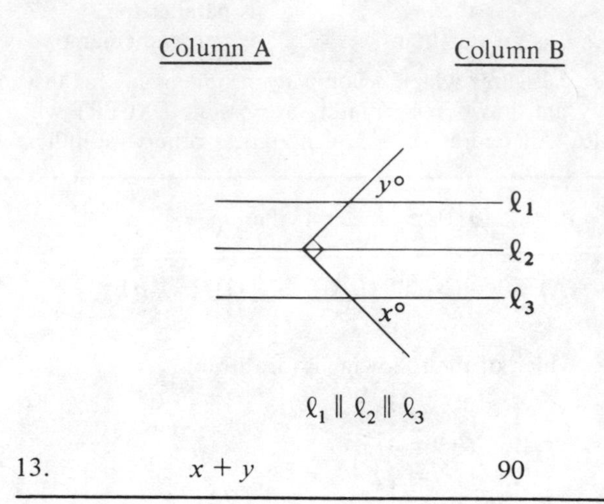

$\ell_1 \parallel \ell_2 \parallel \ell_3$

	Column A	Column B
13.	$x + y$	90
14.	$\left(\frac{1}{2}\right)^4$	$\left(\frac{1}{3}\right)^2$

In a school with 6 classrooms, there are more than 1 and less than 20 students in 1 classroom and exactly 20 students in each of the other 5 classrooms.

	Column A	Column B
15.	Average (arithmetic mean) number of students per classroom	20

$a = -b$

	Column A	Column B
16.	$a + b$	0

$88 < 8x < 100$

	Column A	Column B
17.	x	11.5
18.	$p(r + s) + q(r + s)$	$(p + q)(r + s)$

GO ON TO THE NEXT PAGE

SUMMARY DIRECTIONS FOR COMPARISON QUESTIONS

Answer: A if the quantity in Column A is greater;
B if the quantity in Column B is greater;
C if the two quantities are equal;
D if the relationship cannot be determined from the information given.

	Column A	Column B
	$4k = 5m$ $k > 0$	
19.	k	m
	A scale drawing is made of the floor of a room.	
20.	The perimeter of the drawing when a scale of 1 centimeter to 1 meter is used	The perimeter of the drawing when a scale of 1 centimeter to 0.5 meter is used
	$(x - p)(x + q) = 15$ $x > p$	
21.	x	q

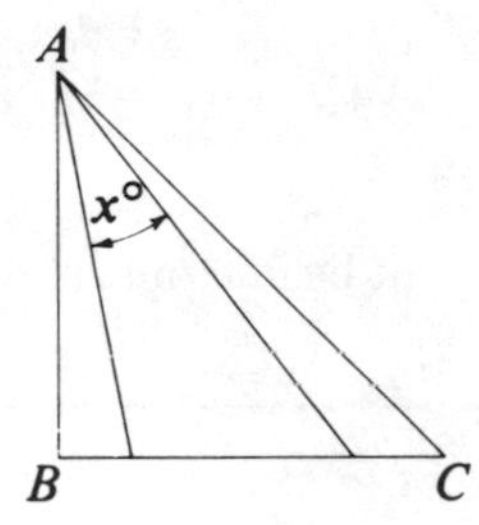

$AB = 3$, $BC = 3$, and $AC = 3\sqrt{2}$

	Column A	Column B
22.	x	45

	Column A	Column B
	In a sequence S of numbers, the first term is 3, the second term is -3, the third term is 3, and so on, with all odd numbered terms equal and all even numbered terms equal. x and y are consecutive terms of S.	
23.	$x + y$	xy
	The volume of a cylinder is equal to the area of its base times its height.	
24.	The volume of a cylinder with base of radius r and height h	The volume of a cylinder with base of radius $2h$ and height r
	$n > 0$	
25.	16% of n	$\frac{4n}{25}$

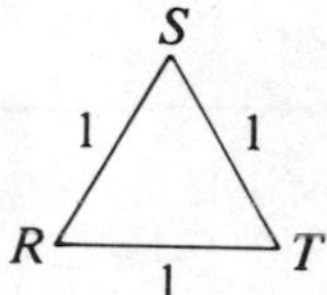

	Column A	Column B
26.	The area of ΔRST	0.5

r is an integer greater than 1 and  $\boxed{r}$ is defined as the least integer factor of r that is greater than 1.

	Column A	Column B
27.	$\boxed{r}$	$\boxed{r+1}$

GO ON TO THE NEXT PAGE

5

Solve each of the remaining problems in this section using any available space for scratchwork. Then decide which is the best of the choices given and blacken the corresponding space on the answer sheet.

28. One-eighth of an hour is what fraction of the time between noon on Monday and noon on Wednesday of the same week?

(A) $\frac{1}{16}$ (B) $\frac{1}{192}$ (C) $\frac{1}{384}$

(D) $\frac{1}{392}$ (E) $\frac{1}{476}$

	Event I	Event II	Event III
First Place (5 points)	School A	School B	
Second Place (3 points)		School C	
Third Place (1 point)			

29. Shown above is a partially completed score card for an athletic contest among schools A, B, and C. If each school entered one contestant in each of three events and there were no ties, what is the least possible total score that any one of these schools could achieve for all three events?

(A) 3 (B) 4 (C) 5 (D) 6 (E) 7

30. If x is the average (arithmetic mean) of k and 10, and y is the average of k and 4, what is the average of x and y ?

(A) 14 (B) 7 (C) $\frac{k+14}{4}$

(D) $\frac{k+14}{2}$ (E) $\frac{k+7}{2}$

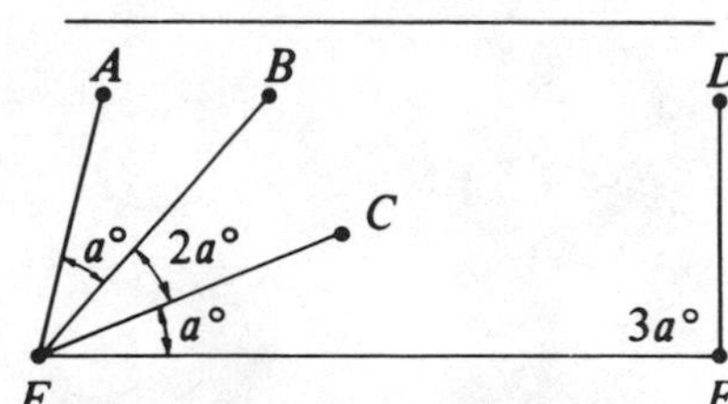

Note: Figure not drawn to scale.

31. If the figure above were redrawn to scale so that $a = 30$, and if segments FA, FB, FC, and ED were extended indefinitely upward, how many points of intersection would there be in addition to E and F?

(A) 0 (B) 1 (C) 2 (D) 3 (E) 4

32. Two runners, A and B, pass a post that is 100 meters from the finish line at the same time and then run the final 100 meters of a race at different constant speeds. After the runners pass the post, A runs 80 meters in the same time that B runs 60 meters. How many meters will B have left to run in the race when A reaches the finish line?

(A) 15
(B) 20
(C) 25
(D) 35
(E) 40

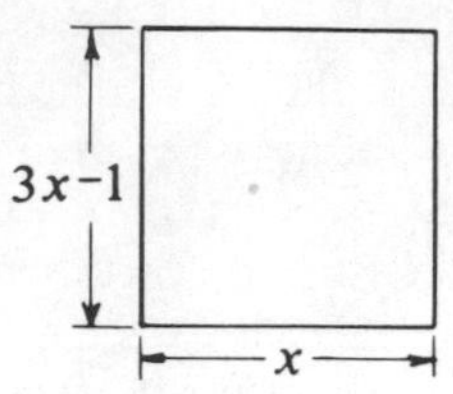

33. The figure above is a square. What is its area?

(A) 9

(B) 4

(C) 1

(D) $\frac{1}{4}$

(E) It cannot be determined from the information given.

34. If the cost of p pencils is c cents, what is the cost, in cents, of n pencils at the same rate?

(A) nc (B) $\frac{nc}{p}$ (C) $\frac{pc}{n}$ (D) pn (E) $\frac{pn}{c}$

35. If m is 10 percent greater than y and n is 20 percent greater than x, then mn is what percent greater than xy ?

(A) 20%
(B) 30%
(C) 32%
(D) 100%
(E) 200%

S T O P

IF YOU FINISH BEFORE TIME IS CALLED, YOU MAY CHECK YOUR WORK ON THIS SECTION ONLY. DO NOT WORK ON ANY OTHER SECTION IN THE TEST.

SECTION 6
Time—30 minutes
45 QUESTIONS

For each question in this section, choose the best answer and blacken the corresponding space on the answer sheet.

Each question below consists of a word in capital letters, followed by five lettered words or phrases. Choose the word or phrase that is most nearly opposite in meaning to the word in capital letters. Since some of the questions require you to distinguish fine shades of meaning, consider all the choices before deciding which is best.

Example:

GOOD: (A) sour (B) bad (C) red (D) hot (E) ugly
Ⓐ ● Ⓒ Ⓓ Ⓔ

1. PRECISE: (A) original (B) inexact (C) obsolete (D) unproductive (E) eventual

2. FATIGUE: (A) pursue (B) revise (C) diet (D) refresh (E) discard

3. INQUISITIVE: (A) undecided (B) incurious (C) defective (D) misinformed (E) distraught

4. FLOURISH: (A) wither (B) relax (C) enact (D) recklessly indulge (E) quietly forego

5. ECSTASY: (A) trickery (B) incompetence (C) uncertainty (D) misconduct (E) wretchedness

6. LISTLESS: (A) energetic (B) unconcerned (C) pathetic (D) hopeful (E) regulated

7. CRASS: (A) free (B) large (C) legal (D) actual (E) delicate

8. REPROOF: (A) guidance (B) praise (C) understanding (D) relief (E) ambition

9. INTREPID: (A) extroverted (B) exclusive (C) fearful (D) baffling (E) adroit

10. DESIST: (A) beg (B) satisfy (C) go on (D) push together (E) look up to

11. PARODY: (A) singularity (B) abstinence (C) monotony (D) reverent imitation (E) unforgivable insult

12. REPLETE: (A) devoid (B) tasteful (C) straight (D) dissimilar (E) untouched

13. BANEFUL: (A) brilliant (B) beneficial (C) mysterious (D) rough (E) careful

14. RHAPSODIZE: (A) paralyze (B) drone (C) perfect (D) ingratiate (E) render

15. RETICENCE: (A) prediction (B) nonsense (C) boredom (D) popularity (E) candor

Each sentence below has one or two blanks, each blank indicating that something has been omitted. Beneath the sentence are five lettered words or sets of words. Choose the word or set of words that best fits the meaning of the sentence as a whole.

Example:

Although its publicity has been ----, the film itself is intelligent, well-acted, handsomely produced, and altogether ----.
(A) tasteless. .respectable (B) extensive. .moderate (C) sophisticated. .amateur (D) risqué. .crude (E) perfect. .spectacular
● Ⓑ Ⓒ Ⓓ Ⓔ

16. Prolonged secrecy ---- suspicion and allows rumor or false report to harden into accepted fact.
(A) imitates (B) impounds (C) nourishes (D) exorcises (E) invalidates

17. The prime minister presented a ---- program that called for radical revision of the constitution without specifying the nature of the ----.
(A) limited. .reaction (B) vague. .changes (C) viable. .sanctions (D) unique. .traditions (E) logical. .connections

18. This interest in the past as a repository of the unfamiliar was parallel to that which prompted the naturalists to collect and exhibit ---- forms of life in the newly established museums.
(A) exotic (B) native (C) modern (D) typical (E) higher

19. Direct and provocative, this volume will be no ---- for those who take books as their opiate, finding passive reading easier than thinking.
(A) goad (B) enigma (C) catalyst (D) sedative (E) challenge

20. Although William the Conqueror preserved whatever institutions of the Anglo-Saxon regime suited his purpose, innovation was more evident than the maintenance of ---- during his reign.
(A) creativity (B) revolt (C) continuity (D) suppression (E) invasion

GO ON TO THE NEXT PAGE

Each passage below is followed by questions based on its content. Answer all questions following a passage on the basis of what is stated or implied in that passage.

Despite popular belief, there is nothing especially attractive about a red flag for a bull. Anything waving excites the animal. Apparently, however, a white flag or cape seems brighter to him, and hence is more effective, for the bull is color-blind. Of all the mammals, only humans and some primates enjoy the luxury of color vision. In addition to hundreds of shades of gray, humans can distinguish numerous shades of color. Most mammals see objects only in various shades of gray.

The day-active birds and most reptiles and insects see color, as do a number of fish and crustaceans. But this does not necessarily mean that they see colors as we do. Part of the difference in the colors an animal can see lies in the extent of the spectrum it can perceive. One of the most convincing demonstrations on insects was performed by the British entomologist, H. Eltringham. He caught several of the common butterflies known as tortoise shells, in the pattern of whose wings red is conspicuous. He painted over their compound eyes with a clear red lacquer, fitting them in this way with harmless red glasses. Letting them free, he noted that they flew as well as usual. Apparently the tortoise shell could see with red light, which alone could pass through the red lacquer. When the same test was tried on the white butterfly known as the large cabbage, the insect flew about aimlessly. These observations reflect a logical extrapolation from the normal behavior of the two butterflies, since the tortoise shell commonly visits red flowers, whereas the large cabbage rarely does so. Apparently, the large cabbage sees red flowers as black.

For many insects, the solar spectrum they can perceive includes a very bright band beyond the blue and violet, in the ultraviolet. To a honeybee or housefly, this is the most stimulating part of sunlight. Objects that reflect ultraviolet are far brighter to most insects than objects that do not. Human beings fail to see these differences, since the slightly yellowish lens of our eye absorbs light energy at such short wavelengths.

We can, however, use photographic film sensitive to ultraviolet and learn what an insect sees by means of this component of sunlight. Most things that reflect light visible to us also reflect some ultraviolet. A few provide surprises. The common yellow daisy, for example, absorbs ultraviolet light except at the tips of the petals which are intensely reflecting. In consequence, this flower is visible to insects as a halo of bright ultraviolet spots surrounding the central core where the nectar and pollen wait.

21. Which of the following best expresses the main idea of the passage?

(A) Most animals are color-blind.
(B) Not all animals see color the same way.
(C) Insects can perceive a wider spectrum of colors than can other animals.
(D) Color vision is found only in highly developed animals.
(E) Humans are unable to see what other animals see.

22. It can be inferred from the passage that by daylight a color-blind animal would be able to see which of the following?

(A) Only white objects
(B) Only vague outlines of objects
(C) Only objects that reflect ultraviolet light
(D) Any object, but only if it moved
(E) Any object, but only in shades of gray

23. It can be inferred from the passage that which of the following animals would most likely be able to distinguish colors?

(A) Owl (B) Goat (C) Robin (D) Mouse (E) Rabbit

24. From which of the following observations could one infer most strongly that an animal can see in red light?

(A) Its body has red markings.
(B) Its only predator is a red-colored bird.
(C) It rarely visits red flowers.
(D) It eats only red-colored grubs.
(E) It lives in a house made of red mud.

25. According to the passage, ultraviolet is very stimulating to most insects because it

(A) appears very bright to them
(B) is reflected only by flowers
(C) has the power to block out other colors
(D) creates a halo of light around an object
(E) is of such rare occurrence

GO ON TO THE NEXT PAGE

Does the totality of a language tell anything about the people who speak it? Consider the English verb "grab." An English speaker says, "I grab it," "I grabbed it," "I will grab it," and so on. Only context tells the listener what it is that is being grabbed and how it is being done. "I grabbed it" is a vague sentence—except in one way. English is remarkably concerned about tense. It insists on knowing whether I grab it now, or grabbed it sometime in the past, or will grab it at a future time. The English language is preoccupied with time; so is the culture of its speakers, who take considerable interest in calendars, record-keeping, history, stock-market forecasts, and the precise time throughout the waking day.

No such statement as "I grabbed it" would be possible in Navajo. In Navajo, tense is of little importance, but the language is considerably more discriminating in other ways. The Navajo language would describe much more about the pronoun "I" of this sentence. The Navajo would not be content merely with "grabbed" either; the verb would have to state more about why and how the act is being done, and whether the thing being grabbed is big or little, animate or inanimate. Further, a Navajo could not simply say "it": the thing being grabbed would have to be described much more precisely and put in a category.

Linguistic studies of the Navajo indicate that the elements that make up their universe are very precisely described. The Navajo language seems to require a perception of the universe that is more exacting than that of English speakers. But is this a true picture of the Navajo? Do they perceive the world any differently from speakers of English? Anthropological and psychological studies of the Navajo show that they visualize themselves as living in an eternal and unchanging universe made up of physical, social, and supernatural forces, among which they try to maintain a balance. To the Navajo, the good life consists of maintaining intact all the complex relationships of the universe. It is obvious that to do so demands a language that makes the most exacting discriminations.

This is not to say that the Navajo hold such a world view because of the structure of their language. It merely suggests that there is an interaction between the language and their culture. Language is more than a way of communicating. It is a living system that is a part of the cultural equipment of a group, and it reveals a culture at least as much as do pottery, kinship groups, and political institutions.

26. The passage as a whole suggests that language provides information about its users by revealing

(A) chiefly their world view
(B) chiefly their concept of time
(C) only the culture of English-speaking peoples
(D) only their environment
(E) only their past experience

27. The author refers to "stock-market forecasts" (lines 13-14) as an example of

(A) a time-oriented concern
(B) a questionable faith in the future
(C) the ambiguities in language
(D) concepts common to all languages
(E) English speakers' avoidance of abstract ideas

28. The author bases the answer to the question "But is this a true picture of the Navajo?" (lines 33-34) primarily on

(A) linguists' analyses of the Navajo language
(B) personal experiences in present-day Navajo societies
(C) comparisons between the English language and the Navajo language
(D) the research of anthropologists and psychologists
(E) depictions of the Navajo in the literature of various cultures

29. The passage implies that the relative unimportance of tense in the Navajo language mirrors the Navajo's

(A) emphasis on abstract ideas
(B) desire for exact description
(C) vision of the universe as eternal and unchanging
(D) complex relationships among kinship groups
(E) preoccupation with keeping records

30. According to the passage, the Navajo regard the complex relationships among the various forces in the universe with

(A) insatiable curiosity
(B) bewildered despair
(C) respectful appreciation
(D) deliberate indifference
(E) aloof skepticism

GO ON TO THE NEXT PAGE

Select the word or set of words that best completes each of the following sentences.

31. To the extent that economic change opens new horizons and creates new aspirations and desires without immediate possibilities of fulfillment, it ---- the ---- within a social structure.

(A) alleviates. .problems
(B) increases. .tensions
(C) simplifies. .bureaucracy
(D) reduces. .pressures
(E) emphasizes. .improvement

32. Matisse was unusually ---- about his painting; to read his statements is to see more clearly through his eyes his intents and his technical procedures.

(A) modest (B) evasive (C) superficial (D) articulate (E) intemperate

33. Some collect rare objects for ---- reasons whereas others ---- their own taste in the pursuit of profitable investment.

(A) aesthetic. .ignore
(B) sentimental. .misconstrue
(C) various. .expand
(D) personal. .trust
(E) valid. .refine

34. It has been ---- that the intelligence of various species of animals differs only in degree, but new experiments show that the differences are ----.

(A) argued. .irrefutable
(B) advanced. .objective
(C) observed. .recognizable
(D) doubted. .questionable
(E) assumed. .qualitative

35. The nostalgic associations we bring to this revived musical can give it an ----, though still affecting, poignancy; however, they cannot quite cover up its flaws.

(A) unsettling (B) incisive (C) unflinching (D) internal (E) unearned

Each question below consists of a related pair of words or phrases, followed by five lettered pairs of words or phrases. Select the lettered pair that best expresses a relationship similar to that expressed in the original pair.

Example:

YAWN : BOREDOM :: (A) dream : sleep (B) anger : madness (C) smile : amusement (D) face : expression (E) impatience : rebellion

Ⓐ Ⓑ ● Ⓓ Ⓔ

36. PLUG : SOCKET :: (A) key : lock (B) chair : desk (C) wire : electricity (D) current : switch (E) fan : wind

37. RAGE : ANGER :: (A) bliss : apathy (B) fear : shame (C) delight : pleasure (D) frustration : patience (E) approval : censure

38. VERTEX : PYRAMID :: (A) strand : hair (B) rectangle : box (C) rung : ladder (D) frame : picture (E) summit : mountain

39. MOVIE : DIRECTOR :: (A) store : salesperson (B) business : manager (C) book : critic (D) competition : athlete (E) product : advertiser

40. CUTLERY : KNIFE :: (A) machinery : fuel (B) lumber : saw (C) suitcase : handle (D) bookcase : volume (E) furniture : chair

41. ASPIRANT : AMBITION :: (A) mentor : malice (B) renegade : faith (C) virtuoso : innocence (D) rebel : defiance (E) antagonist : maturity

42. ANARCHISM : GOVERNMENT :: (A) paternalism : ancestors (B) pacifism : war (C) realism : progress (D) capitalism : commerce (E) socialism : society

43. STUPIDITY : DUNCE :: (A) obstinacy : introvert (B) flattery : sycophant (C) fear : clown (D) acuity : hypocrite (E) deceit : vagrant

44. REMISSION : DISEASE ::
(A) recollection : imagination
(B) resurgence : determination
(C) prescription : diagnosis
(D) quiescence : storm
(E) regression : violence

45. DISCUSSION : ALTERCATION ::
(A) planning : action
(B) speech : tirade
(C) uncertainty : change
(D) dialogue : conversation
(E) group : convention

S T O P

IF YOU FINISH BEFORE TIME IS CALLED, YOU MAY CHECK YOUR WORK ON THIS SECTION ONLY. DO NOT WORK ON ANY OTHER SECTION IN THE TEST.

Correct Answers for Scholastic Aptitude Test
Form Code 2F

VERBAL		MATHEMATICAL	
Section 1	Section 6	Section 3	Section 5
1. C	1. B	1. C	1. C
2. A	2. D	2. C	2. A
3. A	3. B	3. D	3. D
4. C	4. A	4. C	4. E
5. E	5. E	5. B	5. A
6. C	6. A	6. C	6. C
7. B	7. E	7. E	7. D
8. A	8. B	8. A	*8. C
9. C	9. C	9. E	*9. C
10. A	10. C	10. A	*10. A
11. D	11. D	11. A	*11. B
12. B	12. A	12. E	*12. A
13. E	13. B	13. A	*13. C
14. B	14. B	14. A	*14. B
15. E	15. E	15. C	*15. B
16. C	16. C	16. B	*16. C
17. B	17. B	17. B	*17. D
18. D	18. A	18. D	*18. C
19. A	19. D	19. D	*19. A
20. D	20. C	20. E	*20. B
21. D	21. B	21. E	*21. D
22. B	22. E	22. C	*22. B
23. E	23. C	23. B	*23. A
24. D	24. D	24. C	*24. D
25. D	25. A	25. A	*25. C
26. C	26. A		*26. B
27. B	27. A		*27. D
28. D	28. D		28. C
29. A	29. C		29. C
30. C	30. C		30. E
31. E	31. B		31. B
32. A	32. D		32. C
33. D	33. A		33. D
34. C	34. E		34. B
35. C	35. E		35. C
36. D	36. A		
37. B	37. C		
38. B	38. E		
39. E	39. B		
40. C	40. E		
	41. D		
	42. B		
	43. B		
	44. D		
	45. B		

*Indicates four-choice questions. (All of the other questions are five-choice.)

The Scoring Process

Machine-scoring is done in three steps:

- *Scanning.* Your answer sheet is "read" by a scanning machine and the oval you filled in for each question is recorded on a computer tape.
- *Scoring.* The computer compares the oval filled in for each question with the correct response. Each correct answer receives one point; omitted questions do not count toward your score. For each wrong answer, a fraction of a point is subtracted to correct for random guessing. For questions with five answer choices, one-fourth of a point is subtracted for each wrong response; for questions with four answer choices, one-third of a point is subtracted for each wrong response. The SAT-verbal test has 85 questions with five answer choices each. If, for example, a student has 44 right, 32 wrong, and 9 omitted, the resulting raw score is determined as follows:

  $$44 \text{ right} - \frac{32 \text{ wrong}}{4} = 44 - 8 = 36 \text{ raw score points}$$

  Obtaining raw scores frequently involves the rounding of fractional numbers to the nearest whole number. For example, a raw score of 36.25 is rounded to 36, the nearest whole number. A raw score of 36.50 is rounded upward to 37.
- *Converting to reported scaled score.* Raw test scores are then placed on the College Board scale of 200 to 800 through a process that adjusts scores to account for minor differences in difficulty among different editions of the test. This process, known as equating, is performed so that a student's reported score is not affected by the edition of the test taken nor by the abilities of the group with whom the student takes the test. As a result of placing SAT scores on the College Board scale, scores earned by students at different times can be compared. For example, an SAT-verbal score of 400 on a test taken at one administration indicates the same level of developed verbal ability as a 400 score obtained on a different edition of the test taken at another time.

How to Score the Test

You can verify the College Board SAT scores reported to you recently by using the information in this booklet along with the copy of your answer sheet. *Before you begin, check that the first two characters (number and letter) of the form code you marked in item 3 on your answer sheet are the same as the form code printed on the front of this booklet.* Compare the responses shown on the copy of your answer sheet with the list of correct answers.

SAT-Verbal Sections 1 and 6

Step A: Count the number of correct answers for *section 1* and record the number in the space provided on the worksheet on the next page. Then do the same for the incorrect answers. (Do not count omitted answers.) To determine subtotal A, use the formula:

$$\text{number correct} - \frac{\text{number incorrect}}{4} = \text{subtotal A}$$

Step B: Count the number of correct answers and the number of incorrect answers for *section 6* and record the numbers in the spaces provided on the worksheet. To determine subtotal B, use the formula:

$$\text{number correct} - \frac{\text{number incorrect}}{4} = \text{subtotal B}$$

Step C: To obtain C, add subtotal A to subtotal B, keeping any decimals. Enter the resulting figure on the worksheet.

Step D: To obtain D, your raw verbal score, round C to the nearest whole number. (For example, any number from 44.50 to 45.49 rounds to 45.) Enter the resulting figure on the worksheet.

Step E: To find your reported SAT-verbal score, look up the total raw verbal score you obtained in step D in the conversion table on page 200. Enter this figure on the worksheet.

SAT-Mathematical Sections 3 and 5

Step A: Count the number of correct answers and the number of incorrect answers for *section 3* and record the numbers in the spaces provided on the worksheet. To determine the subtotal A, use the formula:

$$\text{number correct} - \frac{\text{number incorrect}}{4} = \text{subtotal A}$$

Step B: Count the number of correct answers and the number of incorrect answers for the *five-choice questions (questions 1 through 7 and 28 through 35) in section 5* and record the numbers in the spaces provided on the worksheet. To determine the subtotal B, use the formula:

$$\text{number correct} - \frac{\text{number incorrect}}{4} = \text{subtotal B}$$

Step C: Count the number of correct answers and the number of incorrect answers for the *four-choice questions (questions 8 through 27) in section 5* and record the numbers in the spaces provided on the worksheet. To determine the subtotal C, use the formula:

$$\text{number correct} - \frac{\text{number incorrect}}{3} = \text{subtotal C}$$

Step D: To obtain D, add subtotal A, subtotal B, and subtotal C, keeping any decimals. Enter the resulting figure on the worksheet.

Step E: To obtain E, your raw mathematical score, round D to the nearest whole number. (For example, any number from 44.50 to 45.49 rounds to 45.) Enter the resulting figure on the worksheet.

Step F: To find your reported SAT-mathematical score, look up the total raw mathematical score you obtained in E in the conversion table on page 200. Enter this figure on the worksheet.

SAT SCORING WORKSHEET

FORM CODE 2F

SAT-Verbal Sections

A. Section 1: ____________ − ¼ (____________) = ____________
no. correct no. incorrect subtotal A

B. Section 6: ____________ − ¼ (____________) = ____________
no. correct no. incorrect subtotal B

C. Total unrounded raw score
(Total A + B) ____________ C

D. Total rounded raw score
(Rounded to nearest whole number) ____________ D

E. SAT-verbal reported scaled score
(See the conversion table on the back cover.) [ ] SAT-verbal score

SAT-Mathematical Sections

A. Section 3: ____________ − ¼ (____________) = ____________
no. correct no. incorrect subtotal A

B. Section 5:
Questions <u>1 through 7</u> and <u>28 through 35</u> (5-choice) ____________ − ¼ (____________) = ____________
no. correct no. incorrect subtotal B

C. Section 5:
Questions <u>8 through 27</u> (4-choice) ____________ − ⅓ (____________) = ____________
no. correct no. incorrect subtotal C

D. Total unrounded raw score
(Total A + B + C) ____________ D

E. Total rounded raw score
(Rounded to nearest whole number) ____________ E

F. SAT-mathematical reported scaled score
(See the conversion table on the back cover.) [ ] SAT-math score

Score Conversion Table
Scholastic Aptitude Test
Form Code 2F

Raw Score	College Board Reported Score		Raw Score	College Board Reported Score	
	SAT-Verbal	SAT-Math		SAT-Verbal	SAT-Math
85	800		40	460	620
84	790		39	450	610
83	780		38	440	600
82	770		37	440	590
81	760		36	430	580
80	750		35	430	570
79	740		34	420	570
78	730		33	410	560
77	720		32	410	550
76	710		31	400	540
75	700		30	390	530
74	690		29	390	520
73	680		28	380	520
72	670		27	380	510
71	670		26	370	500
70	660		25	360	490
69	650		24	360	480
68	650		23	350	470
67	640		22	340	460
66	630		21	340	460
65	620		20	330	450
64	610		19	320	440
63	610		18	320	430
62	600		17	310	420
61	590		16	300	410
60	590	800	15	300	400
59	580	790	14	290	390
58	570	780	13	280	390
57	560	770	12	270	380
56	560	760	11	270	370
55	550	750	10	260	360
54	550	740	9	250	350
53	540	730	8	250	340
52	530	720	7	240	330
51	530	710	6	230	320
50	520	700	5	220	310
49	510	700	4	220	300
48	510	690	3	210	290
47	500	680	2	200	280
46	490	670	1	200	270
45	490	660	0	200	260
44	480	650	−1	200	250
43	480	640	−2	200	240
42	470	630	−3	200	230
41	460	630	−4	200	220
			−5	200	210
			−6 or below	200	200

Test 7
SAT *Form Code 2Y*

(Cut here to detach.)

COLLEGE BOARD — SCHOLASTIC APTITUDE TEST and Test of Standard Written English

Side 1

Use a No. 2 pencil only. Be sure each mark is dark and completely fills the intended oval. Completely erase any errors or stray marks.

1.

YOUR NAME: (Print) ______ Last ______ First ______ M.I.

SIGNATURE: ______ **DATE:** ___ / ___ / ___

HOME ADDRESS: (Print) ______ Number and Street

______ City ______ State ______ Zip Code

CENTER: (Print) ______ City ______ State ______ Center Number

5. YOUR NAME

First 4 letters of last name | First Init. | Mid. Init.

IMPORTANT: Please fill in these boxes exactly as shown on the back cover of your test book.

FOR ETS USE ONLY

2. TEST FORM

3. FORM CODE

4. REGISTRATION NUMBER

(Copy from your Admission Ticket.)

6. DATE OF BIRTH

Month	Day	Year
Jan.		
Feb.		
Mar.		
Apr.		
May		
June		
July		
Aug.		
Sept.		
Oct.		
Nov.		
Dec.		

7. SEX

Female

Male

8. TEST BOOK SERIAL NUMBER

Start with number 1 for each new section. If a section has fewer than 50 questions, leave the extra answer spaces blank.

SECTION 1

1–50 Ⓐ Ⓑ Ⓒ Ⓓ Ⓔ

SECTION 2

1–50 Ⓐ Ⓑ Ⓒ Ⓓ Ⓔ

Q1362-04

I.N. 574006—110VV25P3015

COLLEGE BOARD — SCHOLASTIC APTITUDE TEST and Test of Standard Written English **Side 2**

Use a No. 2 pencil only. Be sure each mark is dark and completely fills the intended oval. Completely erase any errors or stray marks.

Start with number 1 for each new section. If a section has fewer than 50 questions, leave the extra answer spaces blank.

	SECTION 3	SECTION 4	SECTION 5	SECTION 6
1	A B C D E	A B C D E	A B C D E	A B C D E
2	A B C D E	A B C D E	A B C D E	A B C D E
3	A B C D E	A B C D E	A B C D E	A B C D E
4	A B C D E	A B C D E	A B C D E	A B C D E
5	A B C D E	A B C D E	A B C D E	A B C D E
6	A B C D E	A B C D E	A B C D E	A B C D E
7	A B C D E	A B C D E	A B C D E	A B C D E
8	A B C D E	A B C D E	A B C D E	A B C D E
9	A B C D E	A B C D E	A B C D E	A B C D E
10	A B C D E	A B C D E	A B C D E	A B C D E
11	A B C D E	A B C D E	A B C D E	A B C D E
12	A B C D E	A B C D E	A B C D E	A B C D E
13	A B C D E	A B C D E	A B C D E	A B C D E
14	A B C D E	A B C D E	A B C D E	A B C D E
15	A B C D E	A B C D E	A B C D E	A B C D E
16	A B C D E	A B C D E	A B C D E	A B C D E
17	A B C D E	A B C D E	A B C D E	A B C D E
18	A B C D E	A B C D E	A B C D F	A B C D E
19	A B C D E	A B C D E	A B C D E	A B C D E
20	A B C D E	A B C D E	A B C D E	A B C D E
21	A B C D E	A B C D E	A B C D E	A B C D E
22	A B C D E	A B C D E	A B C D E	A B C D E
23	A B C D E	A B C D E	A B C D E	A B C D E
24	A B C D E	A B C D E	A B C D E	A B C D E
25	A B C D E	A B C D E	A B C D E	A B C D E
26	A B C D E	A B C D E	A B C D E	A B C D E
27	A B C D E	A B C D E	A B C D E	A B C D E
28	A B C D E	A B C D E	A B C D E	A B C D E
29	A B C D E	A B C D E	A B C D E	A B C D E
30	A B C D E	A B C D E	A B C D E	A B C D E
31	A B C D E	A B C D E	A B C D E	A B C D E
32	A B C D E	A B C D E	A B C D E	A B C D E
33	A B C D E	A B C D E	A B C D E	A B C D E
34	A B C D E	A B C D E	A B C D E	A B C D E
35	A B C D E	A B C D E	A B C D E	A B C D E
36	A B C D E	A B C D E	A B C D E	A B C D E
37	A B C D E	A B C D E	A B C D E	A B C D E
38	A B C D E	A B C D E	A B C D E	A B C D E
39	A B C D E	A B C D E	A B C D E	A B C D E
40	A B C D E	A B C D E	A B C D E	A B C D E
41	A B C D E	A B C D E	A B C D E	A B C D E
42	A B C D E	A B C D E	A B C D E	A B C D E
43	A B C D E	A B C D E	A B C D E	A B C D E
44	A B C D E	A B C D E	A B C D E	A B C D E
45	A B C D E	A B C D E	A B C D E	A B C D E
46	A B C D E	A B C D E	A B C D E	A B C D E
47	A B C D E	A B C D E	A B C D E	A B C D E
48	A B C D E	A B C D E	A B C D E	A B C D E
49	A B C D E	A B C D E	A B C D E	A B C D E
50	A B C D E	A B C D E	A B C D E	A B C D E

9. SIGNATURE: ____________________

FOR ETS USE ONLY	VTR	VTFS	VRR	VRFS	VVR	VVFS	WER	WEFS	M4R	M4FS	M5R	M5FS	MTFS
	VTW	VTCS	VRW	VRCS	VVW	VVCS	WEW	WECS	M4W		M5W		MTCS

FORM CODE 2Y

SECTION 1

Time—30 minutes

45 QUESTIONS

For each question in this section, choose the best answer and blacken the corresponding space on the answer sheet.

Each question below consists of a word in capital letters, followed by five lettered words or phrases. Choose the word or phrase that is most nearly opposite in meaning to the word in capital letters. Since some of the questions require you to distinguish fine shades of meaning, consider all the choices before deciding which is best.

Example:

GOOD: (A) sour (B) bad (C) red (D) hot (E) ugly

Ⓐ ● Ⓒ Ⓓ Ⓔ

1. PROHIBIT: (A) recognize (B) conflict (C) permit (D) comply with (E) shrink from

2. EXTEND: (A) begin (B) advance (C) retract (D) ordain (E) dispose

3. SYNTHETIC: (A) dynamic (B) authentic (C) fruitful (D) open-minded (E) pathetic

4. INGRATITUDE: (A) initiative (B) propensity (C) sincerity (D) appreciation (E) self-denial

5. SPECIFY: (A) anticipate (B) discuss fully (C) return (D) cast doubt upon (E) generalize

6. PROFUSE: (A) ugly (B) tardy (C) meager (D) unlikely (E) disorganized

7. CRAVE: (A) demand silence (B) cheer up (C) disdain (D) cause (E) mar

8. COAGULATE: (A) flow freely (B) disperse quietly (C) complete (D) protect (E) sterilize

9. SLEEPER: (A) obstacle (B) miniature (C) bitter dispute (D) concealed evidence (E) predicted winner

10. INCISIVE: (A) habitual (B) disturbing (C) overbearing (D) obtuse (E) unworthy

11. RESCIND: (A) summarize (B) oppose (C) maximize (D) restore (E) disturb

12. PRODIGIOUS: (A) puny (B) swift (C) distant (D) restless (E) irregular

13. QUALIFIED: (A) underlying (B) disregarded (C) unrestricted (D) predetermined (E) rehabilitated

14. PIQUE: (A) stability (B) servility (C) lethargy (D) delight (E) mercy

15. PULCHRITUDE: (A) dispassion (B) innocence (C) unkindness (D) monotony (E) ugliness

Each sentence below has one or two blanks, each blank indicating that something has been omitted. Beneath the sentence are five lettered words or sets of words. Choose the word or set of words that best fits the meaning of the sentence as a whole.

Example:

Although its publicity has been ----, the film itself is intelligent, well-acted, handsomely produced, and altogether ----.

(A) tasteless. .respectable (B) extensive. .moderate (C) sophisticated. .amateur (D) risqué. .crude (E) perfect. .spectacular

● Ⓑ Ⓒ Ⓓ Ⓔ

16. The author includes very little ---- of the dragon: monsters are more fearful if pictured in the imagination.

(A) protection (B) description (C) suspicion (D) defense (E) criticism

17. Human beings are much less creatures of instinct than other animals are; nearly all our behavior patterns are ---- rather than ----.

(A) learned. .inherited (B) predictable. .erratic (C) routine. .diversified (D) innate. .acquired (E) conventional. .arbitrary

18. He angrily ---- Plato as more consistently ---- than any other philosopher on all questions involving physical science, politics, ethics, or education.

(A) approved. .debatable (B) defended. .refuted (C) condemned. .wrong (D) quoted. .brilliant (E) derided. .acceptable

19. The business community needs to ---- the role of profits so that their importance will be better understood by all the people who benefit from them.

(A) minimize (B) disclaim (C) elucidate (D) diversify (E) equivocate

20. State ownership of the country's productive resources may unfortunately ---- rather than ameliorate environmental problems.

(A) counteract
(B) expedite
(C) exacerbate
(D) diminish
(E) stigmatize

1

Each passage below is followed by questions based on its content. Answer all questions following a passage on the basis of what is stated or implied in that passage.

Only during the nineteen-thirties did Puerto Rico begin to deviate from colonial patterns and develop her own industry. Though this study investigates mainland cultural influences in the Island's economic development since 1930, attention is not focused on enterprises operated from the mainland. These enterprises have flourished since the beginning of tax exemption, but their operations are not characteristic of Puerto Rican entrepreneurship. The influence of mainland entrepreneurs on the Island and of government programs, however, has not been ignored.

I eschewed any attempt to determine what changes were good or bad for Puerto Rican life. Economic efficiency often comes at the expense of social efficiency or the good life, but I withheld judgment as far as possible.

The two most important forces operating in business are physical and cultural. Geography, climate, cost of transportation, and location of population are all measurable. Culture, however, involves psychological elements. No effort has yet been made to relate these problematic cultural factors to economic development, but by placing them within the economic process, I hope at least to define the problem.

Data was drawn from interviews with established businessmen knowledgeable about the history of business in the Island, interviews with younger entrepreneurs involved in important manufacturing, prior statistics, government documents, and journalists' analyses covering the period of mainland control. The older businessmen were employers of over a hundred workers, though several managed family businesses of five hundred or more. The younger group headed firms employing less than fifty workers.

For comparative purposes, data on entrepreneurial activity in the mainland came from interviews with urban manufacturers and with a panel whose members were selected for diversity in business activity in rural areas.

Questionnaires covered origins of the firm, character of mainland contacts, employee relations, and government relations. Cultural influences were deduced rather than inquired about directly. Mainland business practices were used as an inexact basis for comparison. The inexactness arises from the fact that comparable business activities are larger than those in the Island and operate at a later stage of economic development. Furthermore, the influence of culture on business in the United States has not been thoroughly analyzed. Surprisingly, intensive research in the smaller test area supplied better information than exists for the larger area. This is generally true of investigations into business-culture relationships in larger Western countries.

In spite of these problems, it is possible to formulate hypotheses regarding the comparative character of mainland and Puerto Rican entrepreneurship and the relation of general cultural factors to business. It is first necessary, however, to sketch some aspects of Puerto Rican history that determined the environment for entrepreneurship.

21. The primary purpose of the passage is to
(A) paraphrase a document
(B) provide an introduction
(C) explain the implications of a proposal
(D) refute previously accepted theories
(E) justify a choice of subject matter

22. The author's analysis is based on all of the following EXCEPT
(A) personal interviews
(B) previous studies
(C) newspaper accounts
(D) psychology textbooks
(E) questionnaires

23. The author suggests that cultural factors withstand systematization because they
(A) occur infrequently
(B) change constantly
(C) are unrecognizable
(D) are intangible
(E) are illogical

24. The passage implies that the author wishes to describe the economic changes in Puerto Rico in a tone that is
(A) patriotic (B) humble (C) reflective
(D) inspirational (E) objective

25. The author states that the discussion will include the period since 1930 because during that period
(A) mainland influences were completely eliminated
(B) Puerto Rico began to develop locally owned businesses
(C) government programs were created to aid private businessmen
(D) Puerto Rican businesses began to sell more products on the mainland
(E) the Island's international economic relations became more secure

The zoological units (technically, polyps) of every coral mass are of basic coelenterate design, each a simple and usually tiny thimble of translucent tissue fringed, flowerlike, with a corona of waving tentacles, and each loaded with symbiotic algae. The coral polyp surrenders some of its autonomy, affixing its limestone hut snugly to those of its neighbors. What factors or benefits support this type of social cohesion are unknown. In any case, the resulting limestone structure is architecturally distinct for each coral species, of which there are some twenty-five hundred throughout the marine world. A cursory glance into a pool reveals platters, tiers, cerebrally convoluted lumps, fans, a forest of antlerlike branchings–each representing a discrete species. Frustrating, however, to any attempt at quick identification is the fact that a coral colony growing in a quiet tide pool may vary considerably in configuration from that of the identical species located on the buffeted outer reef. Clearly, the form into which the individual stone chambers are welded is affected by the physical character of the environment.

After the normal demise of coral polyps, their calcareous remains persist, and on these grow new polyps, with new limestone thus ever being added to the sun-exposed outer surface of the ancestral structure. In the course of geological time, this amassment of coral gravestones–along with a miscellaneous accumulation of mollusk shells, arthropod and echinoderm husks, foraminifera shells, and the leavings of such calcareous sea plants as Lithothamnion and Porolithon–builds shores, atolls, and islands of staggering bulk. Some reefs grow with only moderate speed, others so rapidly as to render obsolete any navigation charts older than twenty years.

The vast tonnage of limestone underlying every reef's viable upper crust may extend downward even thousands of feet, and this seems puzzling in view of calcareous deposition having occurred only in the sun-illumined shallows of the surface zone. A generally accepted explanation holds that atolls and other coral structures thicken vertically in response to the sea floor's slow subsidence, provided, of course, that reef growth at the surface is fast enough to keep pace with bottom sinkage.

Among destructive elements continually at work on the reef are, paradoxically, those hosts of creatures that themselves find the limestone labyrinth a refuge–the bacteria and protozoa; the sponges, echinoderms, and worms; the mollusks, shrimps, and crabs; the legions of glittery reef fishes–all rubbing, boring, burrowing, and tearing at what the coral masons and their algal collaborators have hewn from sunlight, water, and mineral. And finally, the sea itself, with its eroding tides, violent storms, and crushing surf, contributes to the reef's destruction.

26. This passage is primarily concerned with discussing the

(A) identification of coral
(B) life cycle of coral
(C) nature of coral deposits
(D) origin of islands, atolls, and reefs
(E) organisms that hinder the growth of coral reefs

27. According to the passage, what happens to the remains of dead coral polyps?

(A) They dissolve into the water.
(B) They become a base for new deposits.
(C) They are inhabited by algae.
(D) They are quickly destroyed by erosion.
(E) They sink to the ocean floor.

28. According to the passage, the relationship between coral polyps and algae is one of

(A) parasitism (B) enmity (C) predation
(D) emulation (E) cooperation

29. Which of the following can be inferred about the ocean floor under a very thick coral reef?

I. It has been slowly sinking over a long period of time.
II. It is composed of limestone.
III. It used to be near the surface of the ocean.

(A) I only (B) II only (C) I and II only
(D) I and III only (E) I, II, and III

30. The style of the passage can best be described as

(A) argumentative (B) rhetorical
(C) contemplative (D) expository
(E) derogatory

GO ON TO THE NEXT PAGE

Select the word or set of words that best completes each of the following sentences.

31. Susan did not resent the arduous work, for she believed that every ---- that demands thought, attention, and independent judgment ---- the quality of daily life.

(A) task. .heightens (B) profession. .belittles (C) hobby. .undercuts (D) folly. .exalts (E) diversion. .disrupts

32. The Sybarites of ancient times were not only physically ---- but also intellectually ----; they had others do everything for them, even their thinking.

(A) active. .independent (B) slothful. .energetic (C) spent. .brilliant (D) aggressive. .aloof (E) indolent. .lazy

33. Modern physicists are inclined to believe in the validity of general relativity for ---- reasons, because it is mathematically so elegant and philosophically so ----.

(A) practical. .intricate
(B) technical. .problematical
(C) aesthetic. .satisfying
(D) misguided. .useful
(E) irrational. .verifiable

34. The study of history leads one away from the extremes of belief, thus allowing one to develop conviction without dogmatism, devotion without ----.

(A) comprehension
(B) realism
(C) moderation
(D) fanaticism
(E) skepticism

35. What makes the modern period in art ---- is that this time, in most categories, the older ---- has not been replaced by something equally substantial, accessible, and satisfying.

(A) exacting. .efficiency
(B) ideal. .illusiveness
(C) unique. .ignorance
(D) unprecedented. .reality
(E) worthless. .depravity

Each question below consists of a related pair of words or phrases, followed by five lettered pairs of words or phrases. Select the lettered pair that best expresses a relationship similar to that expressed in the original pair.

Example:

YAWN : BOREDOM :: (A) dream : sleep (B) anger : madness (C) smile : amusement (D) face : expression (E) impatience : rebellion

Ⓐ Ⓑ ● Ⓓ Ⓔ

36. CAPTAIN : CREW :: (A) student : faculty (B) mascot : team (C) defendant : jury (D) chairperson : committee (E) representative : senate

37. HOMESTRETCH : RACE :: (A) source : essay (B) gallery : play (C) finale : opera (D) applause : oration (E) prelude : concerto

38. ROBBERY : THIEF :: (A) jewelry : burglar (B) forgery : counterfeiter (C) hostage : kidnaper (D) sabotage : plunderer (E) capture : fugitive

39. MENAGERIE : ANIMALS :: (A) circus : acrobats (B) gallery : paintings (C) sachet : powders (D) archives : events (E) factory : furniture

40. PILGRIM : PIETY :: (A) explorer : curiosity (B) miser : poverty (C) gambler : winner (D) knight : beauty (E) monk : loneliness

41. DIPLOMA : GRADUATION :: (A) title : land (B) supplement : will (C) license : hunter (D) deed : purchase (E) summons : court

42. FURROW : PLOW :: (A) field : grain (B) wake : vessel (C) arrow : bow (D) bale : twine (E) promontory : shore

43. MICROBE : ORGANISM :: (A) microcosm : world (B) microscope : cell (C) microfilm : camera (D) animal : vegetable (E) vitamin : protein

44. INCESSANT : RESPITE ::
(A) static : progress
(B) strategic : crisis
(C) inaudible : silence
(D) eventual : possibility
(E) catastrophic : accident

45. LAMPOON : RIDICULE :: (A) dirge : frivolity (B) treatise : diligence (C) diatribe : mediocrity (D) panegyric : praise (E) encore : entertainment

S T O P

IF YOU FINISH BEFORE TIME IS CALLED, YOU MAY CHECK YOUR WORK ON THIS SECTION ONLY.
DO NOT WORK ON ANY OTHER SECTION IN THE TEST.

SECTION 2

Time—30 minutes

25 QUESTIONS

In this section solve each problem, using any available space on the page for scratchwork. Then decide which is the best of the choices given and blacken the corresponding space on the answer sheet.

The following information is for your reference in solving some of the problems.

Circle of radius r: Area $= \pi r^2$; Circumference $= 2\pi r$
The number of degrees of arc in a circle is 360.
The measure in degrees of a straight angle is 180.

Definitions of symbols:

$=$	is equal to	$\leq$	is less than or equal to
$\neq$	is unequal to	$\geq$	is greater than or equal to
$<$	is less than	$\parallel$	is parallel to
$>$	is greater than	$\perp$	is perpendicular to

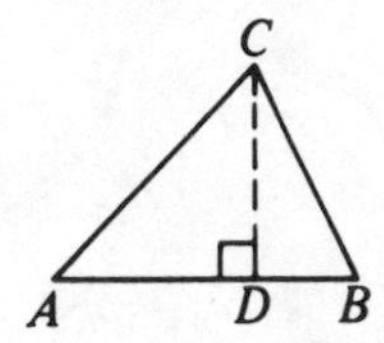

Triangle: The sum of the measures in degrees of the angles of a triangle is 180.

If $\angle CDA$ is a right angle, then

(1) area of $\triangle ABC = \dfrac{AB \times CD}{2}$

(2) $AC^2 = AD^2 + DC^2$

Note: Figures which accompany problems in this test are intended to provide information useful in solving the problems. They are drawn as accurately as possible EXCEPT when it is stated in a specific problem that its figure is not drawn to scale. All figures lie in a plane unless otherwise indicated. All numbers used are real numbers.

---

1. Three dogs weigh 6, 10, and 12 kilograms, respectively. The weight of the lightest dog is how much less than the average (arithmetic mean) weight of the three dogs?

(A) 6 kg (B) 4 kg (C) $3\frac{2}{3}$ kg

(D) $3\frac{1}{3}$ kg (E) $2\frac{2}{3}$ kg

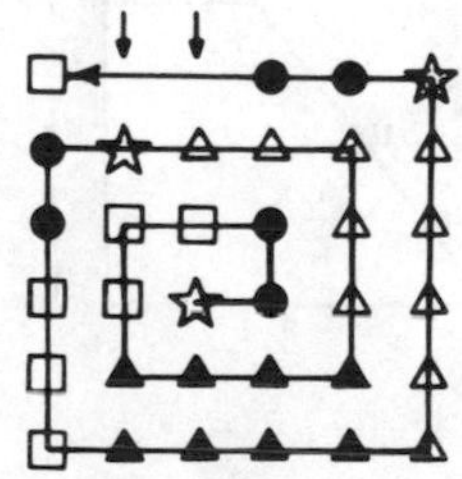

2. In the figure above, the pattern is repeated every 15 symbols. Which of the following, when placed below the arrows in the design above, will continue the pattern of the design?

(A) □ □ (B) ● ● (C) ▲ ▲

(D) ☆ △ (E) △ ☆

3. 50 per cent of 50 per cent of 1 is

(A) $\frac{1}{8}$ (B) $\frac{1}{4}$ (C) $\frac{1}{2}$ (D) 1 (E) 2

4. From which of the following statements taken separately or together can it be determined that x is greater than y ?

I. $x > 17$
II. $y < 10$

(A) I alone but not II
(B) II alone but not I
(C) I and II taken together but neither taken alone
(D) Both I alone and II alone
(E) Neither I nor II nor both

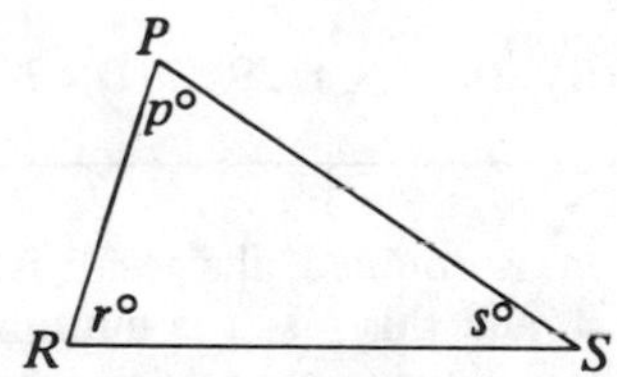

Note: Figure not drawn to scale.

5. In $\triangle RPS$ above, if $RP < PS$, which of the following is true?

(A) $s > p$ (B) $r > p$ (C) $r < s$
(D) $r = s$ (E) $r > s$

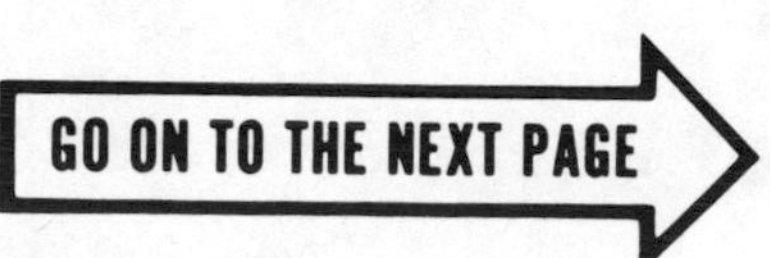

6. If $y = \frac{1}{xz}$, what is the value of x when $y = \frac{1}{6}$ and $z = 2$?

(A) $\frac{1}{12}$

(B) $\frac{1}{8}$

(C) $\frac{1}{3}$

(D) 3

(E) 12

7. If xy is positive, which of the following CANNOT be true about x and y ?

(A) $x < y < 0$
(B) $y < x < 0$
(C) $x < 0 < y$
(D) $0 < x < y$
(E) $0 < y < x$

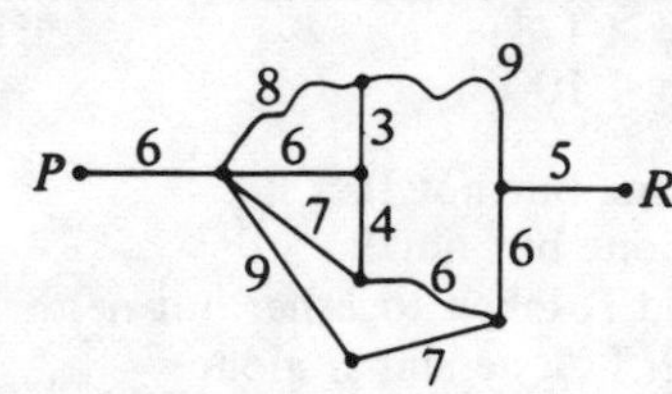

8. If the road distances between any two points are as indicated on the map above, what is the shortest road distance from P to R ?

(A) 27 (B) 28 (C) 29 (D) 30 (E) 33

9. A number m is doubled, the result is then increased by 3, and this result is multiplied by 5. Which of the following expressions corresponds to the statement above concerning m ?

(A) $5(2m + 3)$
(B) $2m + 3(5)$
(C) $15(m + 2)$
(D) $5[3(m + 2)]$
(E) $5[(m + 2) + 3]$

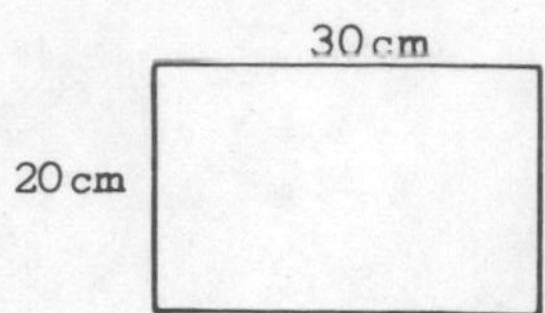

10. In the scale drawing of the rectangular dining room shown above, the scale used was 5 cm = 1 meter. What is the actual area, in square meters, of the room?

(A) 10 (B) 12 (C) 24 (D) 120 (E) 250

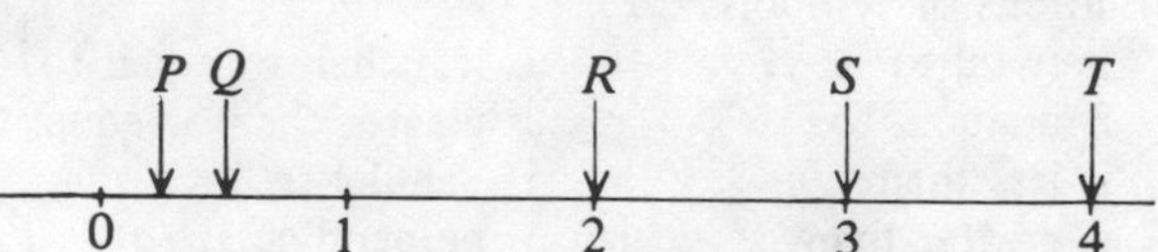

11. Of the following, the closest approximation to the product of the five numbers indicated by arrows on the number line above is

(A) $\frac{1}{2}$ (B) $\frac{3}{4}$ (C) 2 (D) 3 (E) 6

12. For how many integers x is $3 < 2x < 5$?

(A) None (B) One (C) Two
(D) Three (E) Infinitely many

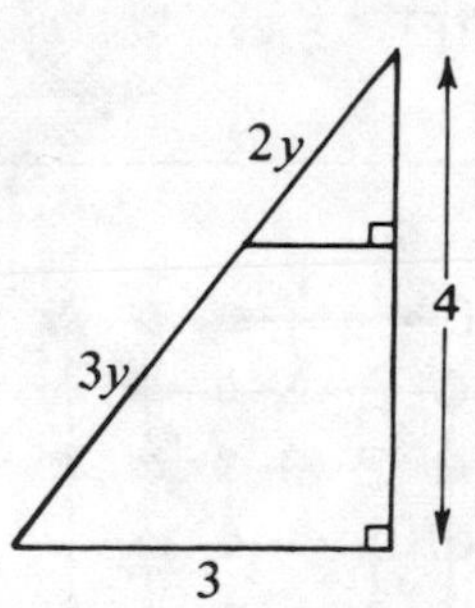

13. In the figure above, $y =$

(A) 1 (B) 2 (C) 3 (D) 4 (E) 5

GO ON TO THE NEXT PAGE

14. The sum of the first n positive integers $1 + 2 + 3 + \ldots + n$ is $\frac{n(n+1)}{2}$. The sum of the first 25 positive integers is

(A) 150
(B) 300
(C) 325
(D) 351
(E) 650

15. What is the sum of the areas of two squares with sides of 1 and 3, respectively?

(A) 3
(B) 4
(C) 9
(D) 10
(E) 16

16. $\sqrt{1 - \left(\frac{1}{2} + \frac{1}{4} + \frac{1}{8} + \frac{1}{16}\right)} =$

(A) $\frac{1}{2\sqrt{2}}$

(B) $\frac{1}{4}$

(C) $\frac{1}{4\sqrt{2}}$

(D) $\frac{1}{8}$

(E) $\frac{1}{16}$

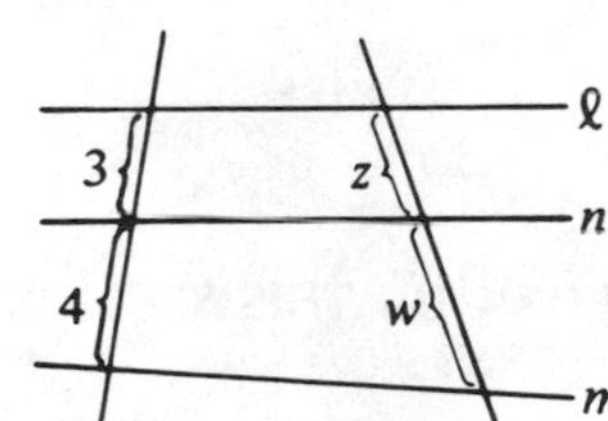

Note: Figure not drawn to scale.

17. In the figure above line ℓ is parallel to line n, but line n is not parallel to line m. If $z + w = 5$, what is the ratio of z to w?

(A) 1 : 3 (B) 2 : 3 (C) 3 : 4 (D) 4 : 3
(E) It cannot be determined from the information given.

18. In one month, a fleet of trucks used 2,000 liters of gasoline at $0.25 per liter. If the total distance traveled by the fleet during that time was 4,000 kilometers, the gasoline cost per kilometer was approximately

(A) $0.050
(B) $0.0625
(C) $0.0833
(D) $0.125
(E) $0.222

19. In a certain cave with a ceiling 5 meters high, a stalactite begins to grow downward from the ceiling at the rate of 0.004 centimeters per year. At the same instant a stalagmite begins to grow upward directly beneath the stalactite at the rate of 0.006 centimeters per year. At these rates how many years would it take for this stalactite and this stalagmite to touch? (1 meter = 100 centimeters)

(A) 500
(B) 2,000
(C) 20,000
(D) 25,000
(E) 50,000

20. The sum of three consecutive odd integers is N. In terms of N, what is the sum of the next three consecutive <u>even</u> integers that follow the greatest of the three <u>odd</u> integers?

(A) $N + 6$
(B) $N + 12$
(C) $N + 15$
(D) $N + 18$
(E) It cannot be determined from the information given.

GO ON TO THE NEXT PAGE

21. A cube has a volume of 72. If it is divided into 8 equal cubes, the ratio of an edge of a smaller cube to an edge of the original cube is

(A) 1:2
(B) 1:3
(C) $1:3\sqrt{2}$
(D) 2:9
(E) 1:9

22. If $m^2 = 16$ and $n^2 = 36$, then the difference between the greatest possible value of $m - n$ and the least possible value of $m - n$ is

(A) 20 (B) 10 (C) 4 (D) 2 (E) -2

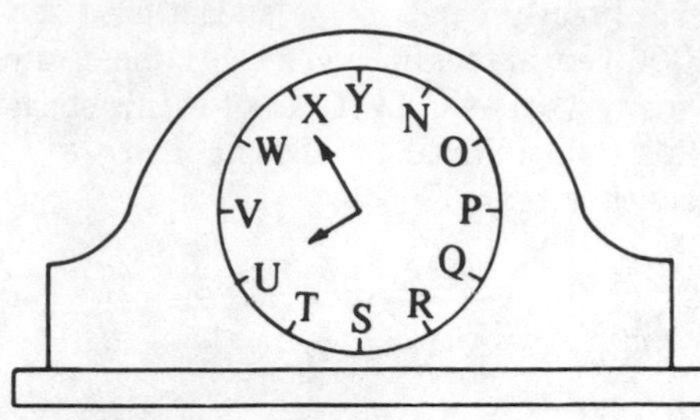

23. The figure above shows a twelve-hour clock marked with letters representing the numbers 1 through 12 in their customary arrangement on its face. Which of the following is a correct representation in these letters of the time indicated by the hands?

(A) X minutes of U
(B) X minutes after T
(C) N minutes of U
(D) R minutes of U
(E) 5X minutes after U

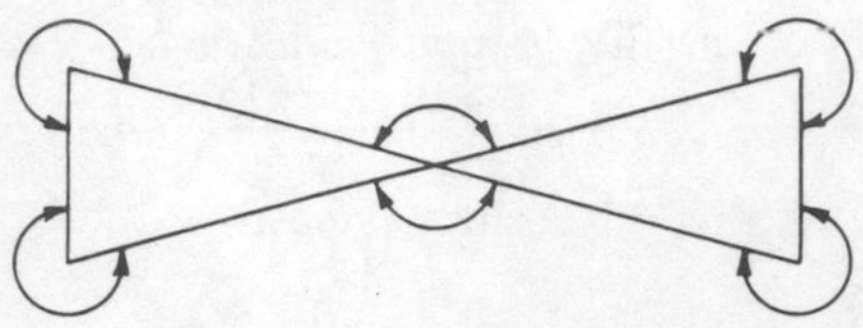

24. What is the sum of the degree measures of all the exterior angles indicated by arrows in the figure above?

(A) 360 (B) 720 (C) 1,080
(D) 1,440 (E) 1,800

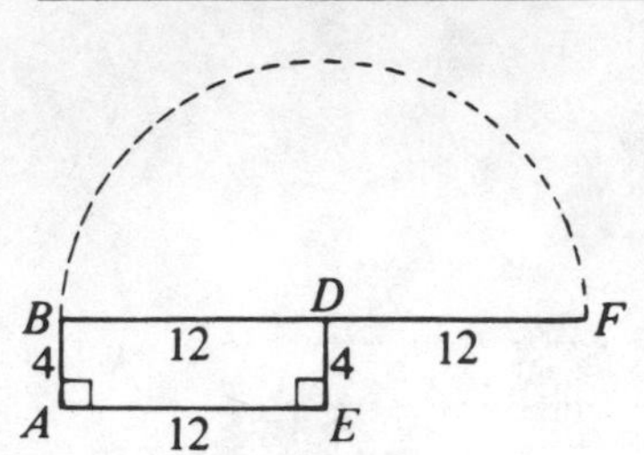

25. If, in the figure above, arc BF is a semicircle having radius 12 and C is a point, not shown, on arc BF, which of the following gives all possible values of the perimeter P of pentagon $ABCDE$?

(A) $32 < P < 56$
(B) $32 < P < 44$
(C) $32 < P < 32 + 12\sqrt{2}$
(D) $P = 44$
(E) $P = 32$

S T O P

IF YOU FINISH BEFORE TIME IS CALLED, YOU MAY CHECK YOUR WORK ON THIS SECTION ONLY. DO NOT WORK ON ANY OTHER SECTION IN THE TEST.

SECTION 3

Time—30 minutes

40 QUESTIONS

For each question in this section, choose the best answer and blacken the corresponding space on the answer sheet.

Each question below consists of a word in capital letters, followed by five lettered words or phrases. Choose the word or phrase that is most nearly opposite in meaning to the word in capital letters. Since some of the questions require you to distinguish fine shades of meaning, consider all the choices before deciding which is best.

Example:

GOOD: (A) sour (B) bad (C) red (D) hot (E) ugly

Ⓐ ● Ⓒ Ⓓ Ⓔ

1. BLUNDER: (A) reveal (B) dash (C) move gracefully (D) change radically (E) accept unquestioningly

2. DISTINGUISHED: (A) temperamental (B) inaccurate (C) commonplace (D) impulsive (E) uncomfortable

3. SUMMARY: (A) difficult question (B) extended account (C) important statement (D) elegant style (E) novel thought

4. CORRUPTION: (A) understanding (B) intervention (C) abstention (D) flexibility (E) purity

5. TEMPERATE: (A) extreme (B) suspect (C) distant (D) independent (E) distasteful

6. UTTER: (A) leave unspoken (B) deny angrily (C) remain unmoved (D) let alone (E) give generously

7. PROVINCIAL: (A) unlucky (B) minor (C) sophisticated (D) average (E) permanent

8. VIRULENCE: (A) fragrance (B) corpulence (C) cleanliness (D) innocuousness (E) ignorance

9. GAMELY: (A) awkwardly (B) seriously (C) without caution (D) without courage (E) without skill

10. PEJORATIVE: (A) approbatory (B) hypothetical (C) vicarious (D) ambiguous (E) tentative

Each sentence below has one or two blanks, each blank indicating that something has been omitted. Beneath the sentence are five lettered words or sets of words. Choose the word or set of words that best fits the meaning of the sentence as a whole.

Example:

Although its publicity has been ----, the film itself is intelligent, well-acted, handsomely produced, and altogether ----.

(A) tasteless. .respectable (B) extensive. .moderate (C) sophisticated. .amateur (D) risqué. .crude (E) perfect. .spectacular

● Ⓑ Ⓒ Ⓓ Ⓔ

11. Nutritionists declare that the mineral selenium, despite its toxic aspects, is ---- to life, even though it is needed in extremely small quantities.

(A) destructive (B) insignificant (C) essential (D) extraneous (E) vulnerable

12. Although much work has gone into the book, it lacks sufficient balance and depth to qualify as a ---- explanation of Cuban economic development.

(A) partisan (B) comprehensive (C) fictitious (D) fragmentary (E) gratuitous

13. It would be ---- for any serious candidate to ---- such an influential constituency.

(A) profitable. .snub (B) illogical. .appease (C) foolish. .offend (D) selfish. .overrate (E) immaterial. .recognize

14. In spite of the ---- of the speech, most of the audience was ---- well before the speaker had finished.

(A) importance. .interested (B) pedantry. .bored (C) excellence. .stirred (D) brevity. .asleep (E) reliability. .convinced

15. Because disuse ---- the intelligence as surely as it withers muscles, grave consequences await humanity if the stimuli for a full utilization of mental powers are diminished further.

(A) whets (B) deters (C) augments (D) distends (E) atrophies

GO ON TO THE NEXT PAGE

3

Each question below consists of a related pair of words or phrases, followed by five lettered pairs of words or phrases. Select the lettered pair that best expresses a relationship similar to that expressed in the original pair.

Example:

YAWN : BOREDOM :: (A) dream : sleep
(B) anger : madness (C) smile : amusement
(D) face : expression (E) impatience : rebellion

Ⓐ Ⓑ ● Ⓓ Ⓔ

16. BOOK : PAGES :: (A) question : answers
(B) lighthouse : ships (C) sentence : words
(D) ring : fingers (E) ocean : tides

17. FADE : DISAPPEAR :: (A) sink : swim
(B) wink : smile (C) decelerate : stop
(D) scrub : stain (E) destroy : dismantle

18. IMMEDIATELY : DELAY ::
(A) voluntarily : motive (B) urgently : aid
(C) continuously : effort (D) flawlessly : error
(E) accidentally : injury

19. HORTICULTURE : PLANTS :: (A) printing : ink
(B) geography : planets (C) biology : texts
(D) geology : ruins (E) forestry : trees

20. WINCE : PAIN :: (A) forget : confidence
(B) tremble : fright (C) grovel : embarrassment
(D) glower : anguish (E) growl : delight

21. UPSTREAM : SOURCE :: (A) upwind : vane
(B) uphill : peak (C) upright : foot
(D) upward : angle (E) upstage : theater

22. ARABLE : FARMERS :: (A) habitable : occupants
(B) curable : patients (C) abominable : consumers
(D) legible : writers (E) inaccessible : travelers

23. HACKNEYED : PHRASE ::
(A) obscure : text
(B) unpublished : manuscript
(C) amateurish : profession
(D) frequent : punctuality
(E) threadbare : clothing

24.

This question was not counted in computing scores.

25. DICTUM : DOGMATIC :: (A) mandate : idealistic
(B) jargon : explicit (C) epigram : candid
(D) riddle : cryptic (E) retort : symbolic

GO ON TO THE NEXT PAGE

Each passage below is followed by questions based on its content. Answer all questions following a passage on the basis of what is stated or implied in that passage.

The last time Ivan had tried to do it, his method had been, in the doctor's words, a masterpiece of gruesome inventiveness; he would have succeeded, had not an envious fellow patient thought he was learning to fly—and stopped him. What he really wanted to do was to tear a hole in his world and escape.

The system of his delusions had been the subject of an elaborate paper in a scientific monthly; "referential mania," Herman Brink had called it. In these very special cases the patient imagines that everything happening around him is a veiled reference to his personality and existence. Phenomenal nature shadows him wherever he goes. Clouds in the staring sky transmit to one another, by means of slow signs, incredibly detailed information regarding him. His inmost thoughts are discussed at night by darkly gesticulating trees. He must be always on his guard and devote every minute and module of life to the decoding of the undulation of things. The very air he exhales is indexed and filed away.

26. In the first paragraph Ivan is described as having unsuccessfully attempted to

(A) destroy the prison cell
(B) describe his affliction
(C) establish dominance over the other patients
(D) escape the asylum by airlift
(E) take his own life

27. According to the passage, Ivan's mental representation of the world is a

(A) naïve, harmless illusion
(B) construct without rational organization
(C) system making no allowance for individual worth
(D) structure of integrated, terrifying delusions
(E) complex of notions resembling those of primitive men

John Philip Sousa was no Beethoven. Nevertheless, he was Sousa. When you say "a Sousa march," the phrase means something pretty definite to almost anyone who hears you. Nobody asks, "Which Sousa march?" It does not matter. Any one of them bears the imprint of a vigorous, clear-cut, decidedly original musical personality. They are not "festival" marches, or any other concert variant of the original form. They are intensely practical. Sousa started as a navy bandmaster and did most of his work in the open air and in motion. The marches he wrote, first for the Marine Band and later for his own, were intended to set the pace for marching men.

They have a deceptive simplicity, those Sousa marches. Their tunes are so uncomplicated, so easy to catch, so essentially spontaneous and melodic, that one can easily underrate them. Simple as they may be, they are Sousa's tunes and no one else's. It took only a minor grade of inspiration to write them, perhaps. It was, nonetheless, genuine inspiration.

We do rightly, of course, to judge people by their reach as well as their grasp. It is only fitting to admire Beethoven and Wagner for their pretensions as well as for their achievements. They dared more than others. If they won greater glory, they also risked a more disastrous failure. Yet I think it is not always necessary to be technically "great" in order to be immortal. The giants of art stir our hearts and souls and imaginations. Sousa stirs only our feet. Nevertheless, he does stir them.

28. The primary purpose of the passage appears to be to

(A) set forth a new definition of artistic greatness
(B) defend the worth of the music of John Philip Sousa
(C) emphasize the practical importance of music
(D) explain the relationship between inspiration and immortality
(E) compare the music of Sousa with that of Beethoven

29. The author would be most likely to use which of the following terms in describing the music of John Philip Sousa?

(A) Memorable (B) Intricate (C) Overrated (D) Soul-stirring (E) Pretentious

30. Sousa's work is "practical" (line 10) in the sense that it is

(A) often imitated
(B) easily remembered
(C) readily learned
(D) used for actual military marching
(E) the high point of military concerts

31. Which of the following is the best interpretation of lines 23-24 ?

(A) A person's past generally determines the success that the person will have in the future.
(B) A person who is sincere is as worthy as a person who is successful.
(C) It is wise to consider people's goals as well as their deeds.
(D) It is necessary to applaud the humble as well as the proud.
(E) It is better to praise talent than ambition.

GO ON TO THE NEXT PAGE

In published works, drawings and photographs of hailstones are often accompanied by measurements of size and sometimes by data on weight, but not by data on density. The earliest more or less reliable values for density were those obtained by List. These measurements, however, were not made on freshly fallen hailstones but on ones that had been kept before and during measurement at a temperature below 0° C. This fact is of decisive importance, as was established only later, because the hailstones normally contain liquid water and thus exhibit a density greater than that of ice.

It is also important to indicate and classify the forms of hailstones, because their forms are responsible for their aerodynamic behavior when falling and because their forms should permit conclusions to be drawn retrospectively about the conditions in which the hailstones originated. But because different growth phases can succeed one another in the development of these ice particles, it is necessary to learn all the different forms through which a hailstone passes during its growth. For this purpose, cross sections must be prepared in order to gain a picture of the inner structure.

Here the methods devised by M. de Quevrain for research on snow proved to be invaluable. By means of a special circular saw, ice sections 0.2 millimeter or more thick are cut out of the hailstones. A variety of such thin sections can be prepared from any given hailstone. When light penetrates these sections, the arrangement of the air pockets becomes visible, and the forms at different stages of growth may be inferred wherever the air bubbles are arranged in onionskin-like layers. From the symmetry of the sections, it is also possible to recognize the oldest part of the hailstone.

32. The author implies that List's data on the density of hailstones do not describe the density of freshly fallen hailstones because
(A) the evaporation of hailstones during storage will inevitably alter their density
(B) normally a hailstone has a temperature many degrees above 0° C
(C) the hailstones used in his research consisted entirely of ice
(D) his research was a pioneering effort and therefore his data were only "more or less" reliable
(E) it was learned only later that he was dealing with liquid water

33. The author indicates that the value of cross-sectioning techniques lies in the experimenter's ability to use them to
(A) determine the liquid water content of the hailstones he is observing
(B) reconstruct the aerodynamic properties exhibited by the hailstone in falling
(C) determine the characteristics of the most recent layer which was formed
(D) calculate the density of the hailstone
(E) infer the characteristics of the environment in which formation took place

34. Which of the following facts provides the best evidence for the author's statement about the comparative density of ice and liquid water?
(A) Glaciers move very slowly even on quite steep slopes where liquid water runs rapidly.
(B) Icebergs may be seen drifting quite far south in the Atlantic.
(C) Ice on the wings of an aircraft may make flight impossible, but rainstorms seldom interfere.
(D) It is possible to walk across a frozen stream in winter, but it is not possible when the stream has thawed.
(E) Water appears on the surface of a skating rink on a spring day.

35. On the basis of the passage, which of the following substances seem(s) to be present in the average freshly fallen hailstone?
I. Ice
II. Air
III. Liquid water
(A) I only
(B) III only
(C) I and II only
(D) I and III only
(E) I, II, and III

GO ON TO THE NEXT PAGE

Alice, as you will recall, was a level-headed sensible girl, with the role of straight man for the remarkable characters in whose company she found herself. She asked the honest questions. They gave the brilliant replies. You will also recall that in her brief visits she was never quite integrated into Wonderland and the Looking-Glass world—in that universe but not of it. If she had been destined to stay permanently with her new playmates, something would have been necessary to correct this state of social maladjustment. Alice had a certain lack of insight, and all hands might have done with some psychotherapy.

I suppose it is because of its history, the course of its earlier development and its origins, that psychology is not yet fully integrated with the realm of biology though, inescapably and permanently, it is now in that realm. We do not communicate well enough: not as geneticist communicates with botanist, or physiologist with biochemist. A psychologist, even a comparative psychologist, could not step into a job in zoology as a physiologist might into pharmacology or neuroanatomy. The clinical neurologist complains that psychologists are complicating the problem of aphasia; the neurosurgeon does not understand what the objections are to localizing a stuff called consciousness or memory or something else in this part of the brain or that. For their part, psychologists too often fail to keep themselves informed about what goes on in the neurological field and, in defense of such ignorance, too often deny that it has any relevance for their work—a position so preposterous and indefensible that it is hard to attack.

There are no tougher problems than ours, nor more urgent ones. If it were possible to communicate better, we might increase the rate of progress in solving them. I do not hold much with team research, except in the applied field ("team research" here means unified control of what the individual investigator does, either by a director of research or by committee). I am not talking about this, but about the stimulation to new ideas, the criticism and guidance that is possible when workers with different backgrounds and skills effectively understand each other's language and modes of thought.

It may not be bias for me to argue that for such collaboration the electrophysiologist and neurochemist must do more homework in psychology. The converse holds as well, and I have put in a fair amount of effort persuading psychologists to do more boning up on the biological bases of psychology.

I do not think it fair to say that a camel will go through the eye of a needle sooner than one could make a psychologist out of an electrophysiologist or an anatomist. That would be inaccurate as well as unfair. I know workers in other biological disciplines who really understand modern psychology, its whys and wherefores. But such understanding demands as much effort as for a psychologist learning the anatomy of the reticular formation or the functioning of the pituitary. My own estimate frankly is that it demands more.

36. The author's attitude toward his subject matter is that of a

(A) psychologist applauding biologists
(B) biologist criticizing psychologists
(C) biologist persuading psychologists to study biology
(D) biologist describing psychology's dependence on biology
(E) psychologist urging greater contact between psychology and biology

37. The author implies that when psychology was first developed it was

(A) more respected than it is now
(B) closely allied with genetics
(C) less involved with team research
(D) not a unique and independent science
(E) not included among the biological sciences

38. With which of the following statements would the author be LEAST likely to agree?

(A) Psychologists should become more familiar with zoology.
(B) There should be greater control over the individual research done in the biological sciences.
(C) Physiologists are generally well acquainted with pharmacology and neuroanatomy.
(D) It is possible for an electrophysiologist to comprehend psychology well.
(E) There is an effective interchange of ideas between geneticists and botanists.

39. In the last sentence of the passage, the word "it" refers to the

(A) comprehension of psychology by workers in other biological disciplines
(B) ability of a psychologist to learn the anatomy of the reticular formation
(C) realization that a camel will not go through the eye of a needle
(D) effort required to make a psychologist out of an anatomist
(E) communication between psychologists and scientists in other fields

40. It can be inferred that the clinical neurologist regards aphasia as a

(A) psychological phenomenon to be treated by psychologists
(B) physiological phenomenon to be treated by neurologists
(C) psychological-physiological phenomenon to be treated by a team of psychologists and neurologists
(D) disorder of the memory aspects of the consciousness
(E) neurological problem that has been neglected by psychologists

S T O P

IF YOU FINISH BEFORE TIME IS CALLED, YOU MAY CHECK YOUR WORK ON THIS SECTION ONLY. DO NOT WORK ON ANY OTHER SECTION IN THE TEST.

SECTION 5

Time—30 minutes

35 QUESTIONS

In this section solve each problem, using any available space on the page for scratchwork. Then decide which is the best of the choices given and blacken the corresponding space on the answer sheet.

The following information is for your reference in solving some of the problems.

Circle of radius r: Area $= \pi r^2$; Circumference $= 2\pi r$
The number of degrees of arc in a circle is 360.
The measure in degrees of a straight angle is 180.

Definitions of symbols:

$=$	is equal to	$\leq$	is less than or equal to
$\neq$	is unequal to	$\geq$	is greater than or equal to
$<$	is less than	$\parallel$	is parallel to
$>$	is greater than	$\perp$	is perpendicular to

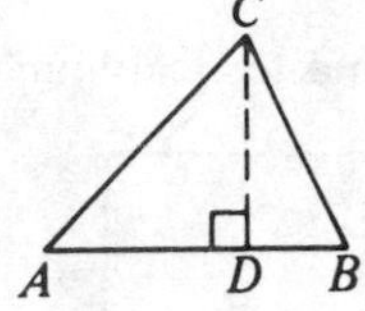

Triangle: The sum of the measures in degrees of the angles of a triangle is 180.

If $\angle CDA$ is a right angle, then

(1) area of $\triangle ABC = \frac{AB \times CD}{2}$

(2) $AC^2 = AD^2 + DC^2$

Note: Figures which accompany problems in this test are intended to provide information useful in solving the problems. They are drawn as accurately as possible EXCEPT when it is stated in a specific problem that its figure is not drawn to scale. All figures lie in a plane unless otherwise indicated. All numbers used are real numbers.

---

1. If $0 < a < b < c$, which of the following products is greatest?

(A) $a \times a$ (B) $a \times c$ (C) $b \times b$
(D) $b \times c$ (E) $c \times c$

2. If $\frac{2}{3}x = 1$, then $\frac{1}{3}x =$

(A) $\frac{1}{3}$ (B) $\frac{1}{2}$ (C) $\frac{2}{3}$ (D) $\frac{3}{2}$ (E) 2

3. In the mid-Atlantic, a ship is traveling in a direction 10° east of north. The captain swings the ship 15° to the left. In what new direction is the ship traveling?

(A) 25° east of north
(B) 25° west of north
(C) 10° west of north
(D) 5° west of north
(E) 5° east of north

4. If the "center" of a number is defined to be $\frac{1}{2}$ of the number, then what number is the "center" of itself?

(A) −1 (B) 0 (C) 1 (D) 2 (E) 10

5. How many bottles of soda at 35 cents each can be purchased with an amount equal to the cost of 14 bottles at 90 cents each?

(A) 18
(B) 24
(C) 30
(D) 36
(E) 42

6. If $5x = 3$ and $3y - 5x = 9$, what is the value of y ?

(A) 2
(B) 3
(C) 4
(D) 5
(E) It cannot be determined from the information given.

7. The 1st term of a sequence is 1. Each term after the 1st is found by adding 3 to the previous term and then multiplying this sum by 3. Thus 12 is the 2nd term. Which of the following describes the terms of this sequence?

(A) All the terms are odd.
(B) All the terms are even.
(C) The terms follow the pattern: odd, even, odd, even, etc.
(D) The terms follow the pattern: odd, odd, even, even, odd, odd, even, even, etc.
(E) The terms follow the pattern: odd, even, even, odd, even, even, etc.

5

Questions 8-27 each consist of two quantities, one in Column A and one in Column B. You are to compare the two quantities and on the answer sheet blacken space

- A if the quantity in Column A is greater;
- B if the quantity in Column B is greater;
- C if the two quantities are equal;
- D if the relationship cannot be determined from the information given.

Notes:
1. In certain questions, information concerning one or both of the quantities to be compared is centered above the two columns.
2. In a given question, a symbol that appears in both columns represents the same thing in Column A as it does in Column B.
3. Letters such as x, n, and k stand for real numbers.

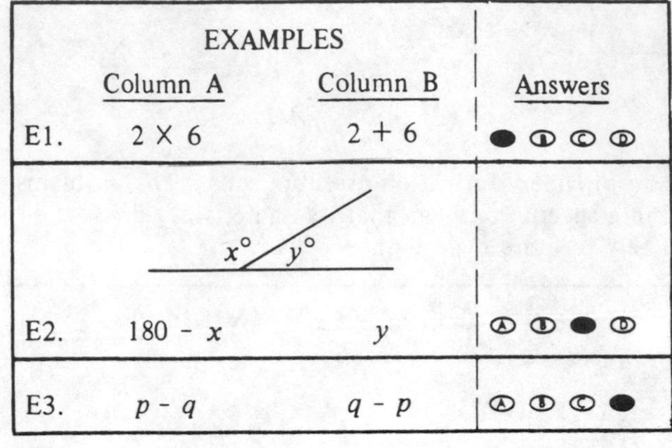

EXAMPLES

	Column A	Column B	Answers
E1.	2×6	$2 + 6$	● Ⓑ Ⓒ Ⓓ
E2.	$180 - x$	y	Ⓐ Ⓑ ● Ⓓ
E3.	$p - q$	$q - p$	Ⓐ Ⓑ Ⓒ ●

	Column A	Column B
8.	$\frac{1}{4}$ dozen	4

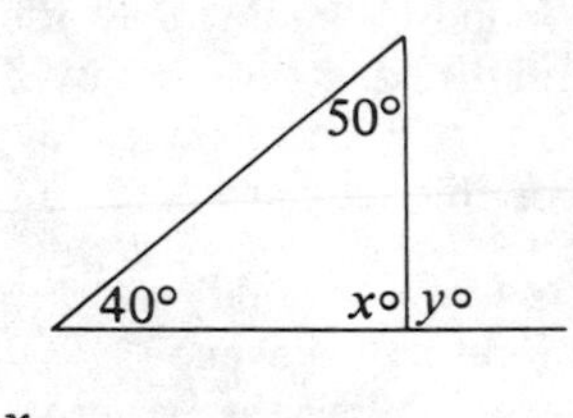

9.	x	y

There are 51 books on a shelf. Two-thirds of the books have hard covers and the rest are paperbacks.

10.	Number of paperbacks	18

$w + x > y + z$

11.	w	z

	Column A	Column B
	$a > 0$	
12.	$2a \times \frac{a}{4} \times 8a$	$\frac{a}{2} \times 4a \times \frac{a}{8}$
13.	$\frac{4}{7}$ of 7	$\frac{7}{4}$ of 4
14.	$27 \times (54 + 39)$	$(27 \times 54) + 39$
15.	z	$\frac{2z + 1}{2}$
	$x > 1$	
16.	$\frac{x + x + x}{x \cdot x}$	$\frac{3}{x^2}$

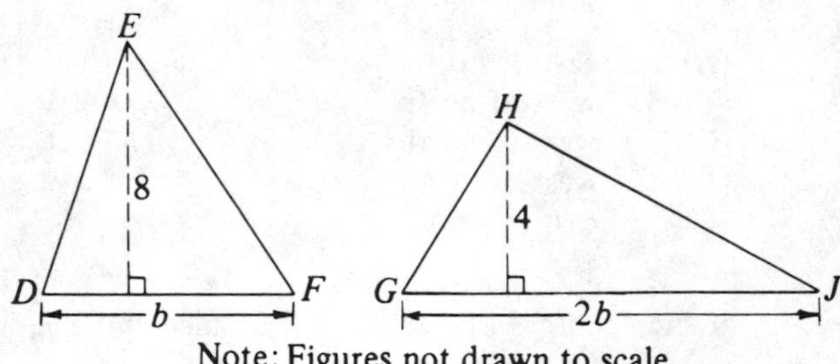

Note: Figures not drawn to scale.

17.	Area of ΔDEF	Area of ΔGHJ

GO ON TO THE NEXT PAGE

SUMMARY DIRECTIONS FOR COMPARISON QUESTIONS

Answer: A if the quantity in Column A is greater;
B if the quantity in Column B is greater;
C if the two quantities are equal;
D if the relationship cannot be determined from the information given.

	Column A	Column B
18.	$0.5 + 0.4 + 0.3$	0.3×0.4

$x \neq \pm 2$

	Column A	Column B
19.	$\frac{x^2 + 4x + 4}{x + 2}$	$\frac{x^2 - 4}{x - 2}$

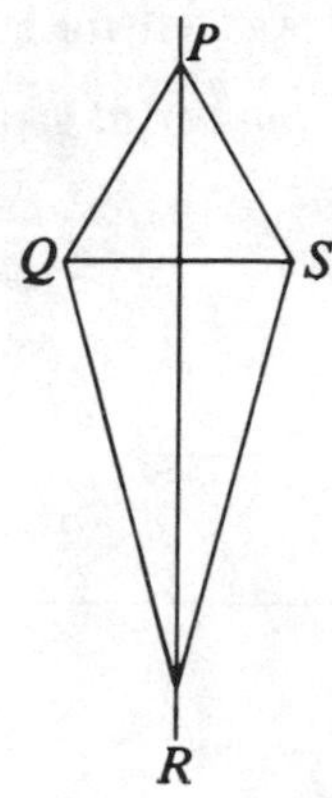

Area $\triangle PQR <$ area $\triangle PSR$ and $QS \perp PR$.

	Column A	Column B
20.	$PQ + QR$	$PS + SR$

$*$ represents one of the operations $+$, $-$, $\times$, or $\div$ and $x * x = 0$ for all numbers x.

	Column A	Column B
21.	$x * y$	$y * x$

$\frac{p}{q} = 1$ and $\frac{q}{p} = 1$

	Column A	Column B
22.	p	1

	Column A	Column B
23.	Ratio of $\frac{1}{2}$ to $\frac{1}{3}$	Ratio of $\frac{2}{3}$ to $\frac{1}{2}$

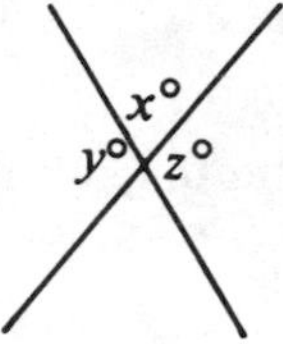

$x + y + z = 4x$

	Column A	Column B
24.	$\frac{3}{2}x$	y

x is a positive number.

	Column A	Column B
25.	x	$\frac{1}{x}$

Ann has 6 more marbles than Nancy, Nancy has 3 more marbles than Joe, and Joe has 4 more marbles than Pete.

	Column A	Column B
26.	The least number of marbles that must change hands if each is to have an equal number of marbles	8

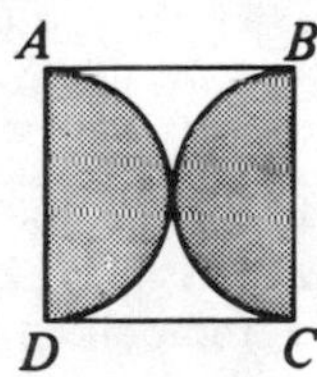

$ABCD$ is a square and the two shaded regions are semicircles.

	Column A	Column B
27.	The ratio of the total shaded area to the area of the square	$\frac{\pi}{4}$

GO ON TO THE NEXT PAGE

5

Solve each of the remaining problems in this section using any available space for scratchwork. Then decide which is the best of the choices given and blacken the corresponding space on the answer sheet.

28. At some point in the season, five teams have the following records:

	Games Won	Games Lost
Team 1	3	1
Team 2	4	2
Team 3	6	3
Team 4	5	2
Team 5	3	2

If there were no ties, which team has won the greatest per cent of its games?

(A) Team 1
(B) Team 2
(C) Team 3
(D) Team 4
(E) Team 5

29. $5 \times 10^{-3} \times 6 \times 10^{2} \times 2 \times 10^{-1} =$

(A) 0.000060 (B) 0.060 (C) 0.60
(D) 6.0 (E) 6,000,000

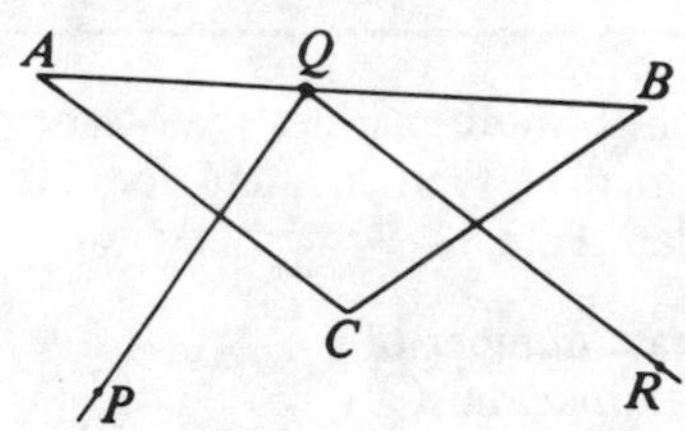

30. In the figure above, if $\angle AQR = 145°$ and $\angle BQP = 122°$, then the degree measure of $\angle PQR =$

(A) 87 (B) 88 (C) 89 (D) 90 (E) 91

31. If the odometer of an automobile registers 62,222 miles, what is the LEAST number of miles that the automobile must travel before the odometer again shows four of the five digits the same?

(A) 99
(B) 444
(C) 555
(D) 999
(E) 1,111

A B 36° D C

32. In the circle above, AC and BD are diameters of length 10. The sum of the lengths of the darkened arcs is

(A) 4π (B) 8π (C) 9π (D) 10π (E) 16π

33. A carpenter used $\frac{1}{3}$ of his lumber for one project and $\frac{3}{5}$ of what was left for another project. If he had 30 units of lumber to start with, how many units did he have left after the two projects?

(A) 8
(B) 6
(C) 4
(D) 3
(E) 2

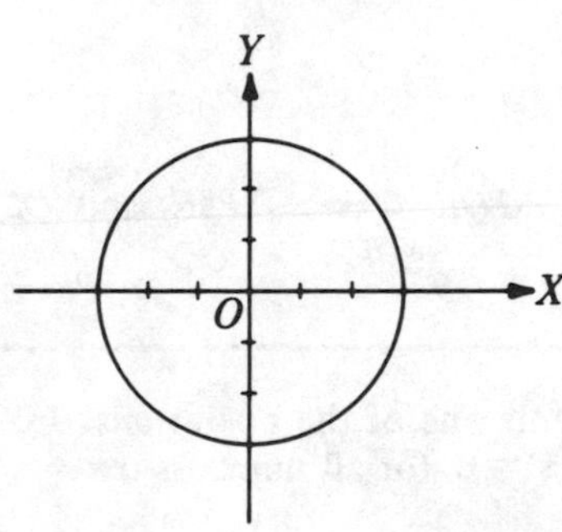

34. The circle above has center at the origin and radius 3. How many ordered pairs (x, y) satisfy the conditions that x and y are integers and (x, y) is <u>inside</u> the circle shown?

(A) 9 (B) 13 (C) 16 (D) 20 (E) 25

35. For all numbers x and y, let $x \Phi y$ be defined by the equation $x \Phi y = (x - y)^2 + (x + y)^2$. What is the value of $\sqrt{28} \Phi \sqrt{23}$?

(A) 56 (B) 100 (C) 100.1
(D) 102 (E) 105.25

S T O P

IF YOU FINISH BEFORE TIME IS CALLED, YOU MAY CHECK YOUR WORK ON THIS SECTION ONLY. DO NOT WORK ON ANY OTHER SECTION IN THE TEST.

Correct Answers for Scholastic Aptitude Test Form Code 2Y

VERBAL		MATHEMATICAL	
Section 1	Section 3	Section 2	Section 5
1. C	1. C	1. D	1. E
2. C	2. C	2. A	2. B
3. B	3. B	3. B	3. D
4. D	4. E	4. C	4. B
5. E	5. A	5. E	5. D
6. C	6. A	6. D	6. C
7. C	7. C	7. C	7. C
8. A	8. D	8. B	*8. B
9. E	9. D	9. A	*9. C
10. D	10. A	10. C	*10. B
11. D	11. C	11. D	*11. D
12. A	12. B	12. B	*12. A
13. C	13. C	13. A	*13. B
14. D	14. D	14. C	*14. A
15. E	15. E	15. D	*15. B
16. B	16. C	16. B	*16. A
17. A	17. C	17. E	*17. C
18. C	18. D	18. D	*18. A
19. C	19. E	19. E	*19. C
20. C	20. B	20. C	*20. B
21. B	21. B	21. A	*21. D
22. D	22. A	22. A	*22. D
23. D	23. E	23. D	*23. A
24. E	24. †	24. D	*24. C
25. B	25. D	25. A	*25. D
26. C	26. E		*26. C
27. B	27. D		*27. C
28. E	28. B		28. A
29. D	29. A		29. C
30. D	30. D		30. A
31. A	31. C		31. B
32. E	32. C		32. B
33. C	33. E		33. A
34. D	34. B		34. E
35. D	35. E		35. D
36. D	36. E		
37. C	37. E		
38. B	38. B		
39. B	39. A		
40. A	40. B		
41. D			
42. B			
43. A			
44. A			
45. D			

*Indicates four-choice questions. (All of the other questions are five-choice.)
†Not scored

The Scoring Process

Machine-scoring is done in three steps:

- *Scanning.* Your answer sheet is "read" by a scanning machine and the oval you filled in for each question is recorded on a computer tape.
- *Scoring.* The computer compares the oval filled in for each question with the correct response. Each correct answer receives one point; omitted questions do not count toward your score. For each wrong answer, a fraction of a point is subtracted to correct for random guessing. For questions with five answer choices, one-fourth of a point is subtracted for each wrong response; for questions with four answer choices, one-third of a point is subtracted for each wrong response. The SAT-verbal test has 85 questions with five answer choices each. If, for example, a student has 44 right, 32 wrong, and 9 omitted, the resulting raw score is determined as follows:

  $$44 \text{ right} - \frac{32 \text{ wrong}}{4} = 44 - 8 = 36 \text{ raw score points}$$

  Obtaining raw scores frequently involves the rounding of fractional numbers to the nearest whole number. For example, a raw score of 36.25 is rounded to 36, the nearest whole number. A raw score of 36.50 is rounded upward to 37.
- *Converting to reported scaled score.* Raw test scores are then placed on the College Board scale of 200 to 800 through a process that adjusts scores to account for minor differences in difficulty among different editions of the test. This process, known as equating, is performed so that a student's reported score is not affected by the edition of the test taken nor by the abilities of the group with whom the student takes the test. As a result of placing SAT scores on the College Board scale, scores earned by students at different times can be compared. For example, an SAT-verbal score of 400 on a test taken at one administration indicates the same level of developed verbal ability as a 400 score obtained on a different edition of the test taken at another time.

How to Score the Test

You can verify the College Board SAT scores reported to you recently by using the information in this booklet along with the copy of your answer sheet. *Before you begin, check that the first two characters (number and letter) of the form code you marked in item 3 on your answer sheet are the same as the form code printed on the front of this booklet.* Compare the responses shown on the copy of your answer sheet with the list of correct answers.

SAT-Verbal Sections 1 and 3

Step A: Count the number of correct answers for *section 1* and record the number in the space provided on the worksheet on the next page. Then do the same for the incorrect answers. (Do not count omitted answers.) To determine subtotal A, use the formula:

$$\text{number correct} - \frac{\text{number incorrect}}{4} = \text{subtotal A}$$

Step B: Count the number of correct answers and the number of incorrect answers for *section 3* and record the numbers in the spaces provided on the worksheet. To determine subtotal B, use the formula:

$$\text{number correct} - \frac{\text{number incorrect}}{4} = \text{subtotal B}$$

Step C: To obtain C, add subtotal A to subtotal B, keeping any decimals. Enter the resulting figure on the worksheet.

Step D: To obtain D, your raw verbal score, round C to the nearest whole number. (For example, any number from 44.50 to 45.49 rounds to 45.) Enter the resulting figure on the worksheet.

Step E: To find your reported SAT-verbal score, look up the total raw verbal score you obtained in step D in the conversion table on page 226. Enter this figure on the worksheet.

SAT-Mathematical Sections 2 and 5

Step A: Count the number of correct answers and the number of incorrect answers for *section 2* and record the numbers in the spaces provided on the worksheet. To determine the subtotal A, use the formula:

$$\text{number correct} - \frac{\text{number incorrect}}{4} = \text{subtotal A}$$

Step B: Count the number of correct answers and the number of incorrect answers for the *five-choice questions (questions 1 through 7 and 28 through 35) in section 5* and record the numbers in the spaces provided on the worksheet. To determine the subtotal B, use the formula:

$$\text{number correct} - \frac{\text{number incorrect}}{4} = \text{subtotal B}$$

Step C: Count the number of correct answers and the number of incorrect answers for the *four-choice questions (questions 8 through 27) in section 5* and record the numbers in the spaces provided on the worksheet. To determine the subtotal C, use the formula:

$$\text{number correct} - \frac{\text{number incorrect}}{3} = \text{subtotal C}$$

Step D: To obtain D, add subtotal A, subtotal B, and subtotal C, keeping any decimals. Enter the resulting figure on the worksheet.

Step E: To obtain E, your raw mathematical score, round D to the nearest whole number. (For example, any number from 44.50 to 45.49 rounds to 45.) Enter the resulting figure on the worksheet.

Step F: To find your reported SAT-mathematical score, look up the total raw mathematical score you obtained in E in the conversion table on page 226. Enter this figure on the worksheet.

SAT SCORING WORKSHEET

FORM CODE 2Y

SAT-Verbal Sections

A. Section 1:	______ no. correct	$- \frac{1}{4}$	(______) no. incorrect	=	______ subtotal A
B. Section 3:	______ no. correct	$- \frac{1}{4}$	(______) no. incorrect	=	______ subtotal B
C. Total unrounded raw score (Total A + B)					______ C
D. Total rounded raw score (Rounded to nearest whole number)					______ D
E. SAT-verbal reported scaled score (See the conversion table on the back cover.)					[ ] SAT-verbal score

SAT-Mathematical Sections

A. Section 2:	______ no. correct	$- \frac{1}{4}$	(______) no. incorrect	=	______ subtotal A
B. Section 5: Questions 1 through 7 and 28 through 35 (5-choice)	______ no. correct	$- \frac{1}{4}$	(______) no. incorrect	=	______ subtotal B
C. Section 5: Questions 8 through 27 (4-choice)	______ no. correct	$- \frac{1}{3}$	(______) no. incorrect	=	______ subtotal C
D. Total unrounded raw score (Total A + B + C)					______ D
E. Total rounded raw score (Rounded to nearest whole number)					______ E
F. SAT-mathematical reported scaled score (See the conversion table on the back cover.)					[ ] SAT-math score

Score Conversion Table
Scholastic Aptitude Test
Form Code 2Y

Raw Score	College Board Reported Score		Raw Score	College Board Reported Score	
	SAT-Verbal	SAT-Math		SAT-Verbal	SAT-Math
			40	470	600
84	800		39	460	600
83	790		38	450	590
82	780		37	450	580
81	770		36	440	570
80	760		35	430	560
79	750		34	430	550
78	750		33	420	540
77	740		32	410	530
76	730		31	400	520
75	730		30	400	520
74	720		29	390	510
73	710		28	380	500
72	700		27	370	490
71	700		26	370	480
70	690		25	360	470
69	680		24	350	460
68	670		23	350	450
67	670		22	340	450
66	660		21	330	440
65	650		20	320	430
64	650		19	320	420
63	640		18	310	410
62	630		17	300	400
61	620		16	290	390
60	620	800	15	290	380
59	610	790	14	280	370
58	600	780	13	270	370
57	590	770	12	260	360
56	590	760	11	260	350
55	580	750	10	250	340
54	570	740	9	240	330
53	560	730	8	240	320
52	560	720	7	230	310
51	550	710	6	220	300
50	540	700	5	210	300
49	540	690	4	210	290
48	530	680	3	200	280
47	520	670	2	200	270
46	510	660	1	200	260
45	510	650	0	200	250
44	500	640	– 1	200	240
43	490	630	– 2	200	230
42	480	620	– 3	200	220
41	480	610	– 4	200	220
			– 5	200	210
			– 6 or below	200	200

Test 8
SAT *Form Code 3H*

(Cut here to detach.)

COLLEGE BOARD — SCHOLASTIC APTITUDE TEST and Test of Standard Written English — Side 1

Use a No. 2 pencil only. Be sure each mark is dark and completely fills the intended oval. Completely erase any errors or stray marks.

1\.
YOUR NAME: (Print) ______ Last ______ First ______ M.I.

SIGNATURE: ______ DATE: ___/___/___

HOME ADDRESS: (Print) ______ Number and Street

______ City ______ State ______ Zip Code

CENTER: (Print) ______ City ______ State ______ Center Number

IMPORTANT: Please fill in these boxes exactly as shown on the back cover of your test book.

FOR ETS USE ONLY

2\. TEST FORM

3\. FORM CODE

0	A	J	S	0	0	0
1	B	K	T	1	1	1
2	C	L	U	2	2	2
3	D	M	V	3	3	3
4	E	N	W	4	4	4
5	F	O	X	5	5	5
6	G	P	Y	6	6	6
7	H	Q	Z	7	7	7
8	I	R		8	8	8
9				9	9	9

4\. REGISTRATION NUMBER (Copy from your Admission Ticket.)

0	0	0	0	0	0	0
1	1	1	1	1	1	1
2	2	2	2	2	2	2
3	3	3	3	3	3	3
4	4	4	4	4	4	4
5	5	5	5	5	5	5
6	6	6	6	6	6	6
7	7	7	7	7	7	7
8	8	8	8	8	8	8
9	9	9	9	9	9	9

5\. YOUR NAME

First 4 letters of last name				First Init.	Mid Init.
A	A	A	A	A	A
B	B	B	B	B	B
C	C	C	C	C	C
D	D	D	D	D	D
E	E	E	E	E	E
F	F	F	F	F	F
G	G	G	G	G	G
H	H	H	H	H	H
I	I	I	I	I	I
J	J	J	J	J	J
K	K	K	K	K	K
L	L	L	L	L	L
M	M	M	M	M	M
N	N	N	N	N	N
O	O	O	O	O	O
P	P	P	P	P	P
Q	Q	Q	Q	Q	Q
R	R	R	R	R	R
S	S	S	S	S	S
T	T	T	T	T	T
U	U	U	U	U	U
V	V	V	V	V	V
W	W	W	W	W	W
X	X	X	X	X	X
Y	Y	Y	Y	Y	Y
Z	Z	Z	Z	Z	Z

6\. DATE OF BIRTH

Month	Day		Year	
Jan.				
Feb.				
Mar.	0	0	0	0
Apr.	1	1	1	1
May	2	2	2	2
June	3	3	3	3
July		4	4	4
Aug.		5	5	5
Sept.		6	6	6
Oct.		7	7	7
Nov.		8		8
Dec.		9		9

7\. SEX
Female
Male

8\. TEST BOOK SERIAL NUMBER

Start with number 1 for each new section. If a section has fewer than 50 questions, leave the extra answer spaces blank.

SECTION 1

1	A	B	C	D	E	26	A	B	C	D	E
2	A	B	C	D	E	27	A	B	C	D	E
3	A	B	C	D	E	28	A	B	C	D	E
4	A	B	C	D	E	29	A	B	C	D	E
5	A	B	C	D	E	30	A	B	C	D	E
6	A	B	C	D	E	31	A	B	C	D	E
7	A	B	C	D	E	32	A	B	C	D	E
8	A	B	C	D	E	33	A	B	C	D	E
9	A	B	C	D	E	34	A	B	C	D	E
10	A	B	C	D	E	35	A	B	C	D	E
11	A	B	C	D	E	36	A	B	C	D	E
12	A	B	C	D	E	37	A	B	C	D	E
13	A	B	C	D	E	38	A	B	C	D	E
14	A	B	C	D	E	39	A	B	C	D	E
15	A	B	C	D	E	40	A	B	C	D	E
16	A	B	C	D	E	41	A	B	C	D	E
17	A	B	C	D	E	42	A	B	C	D	E
18	A	B	C	D	E	43	A	B	C	D	E
19	A	B	C	D	E	44	A	B	C	D	E
20	A	B	C	D	E	45	A	B	C	D	E
21	A	B	C	D	E	46	A	B	C	D	E
22	A	B	C	D	E	47	A	B	C	D	E
23	A	B	C	D	E	48	A	B	C	D	E
24	A	B	C	D	E	49	A	B	C	D	E
25	A	B	C	D	E	50	A	B	C	D	E

SECTION 2

1	A	B	C	D	E	26	A	B	C	D	E
2	A	B	C	D	E	27	A	B	C	D	E
3	A	B	C	D	E	28	A	B	C	D	E
4	A	B	C	D	E	29	A	B	C	D	E
5	A	B	C	D	E	30	A	B	C	D	E
6	A	B	C	D	E	31	A	B	C	D	E
7	A	B	C	D	E	32	A	B	C	D	E
8	A	B	C	D	E	33	A	B	C	D	E
9	A	B	C	D	E	34	A	B	C	D	E
10	A	B	C	D	E	35	A	B	C	D	E
11	A	B	C	D	E	36	A	B	C	D	E
12	A	B	C	D	E	37	A	B	C	D	E
13	A	B	C	D	E	38	A	B	C	D	E
14	A	B	C	D	E	39	A	B	C	D	E
15	A	B	C	D	E	40	A	B	C	D	E
16	A	B	C	D	E	41	A	B	C	D	E
17	A	B	C	D	E	42	A	B	C	D	E
18	A	B	C	D	E	43	A	B	C	D	E
19	A	B	C	D	E	44	A	B	C	D	E
20	A	B	C	D	E	45	A	B	C	D	E
21	A	B	C	D	E	46	A	B	C	D	E
22	A	B	C	D	E	47	A	B	C	D	E
23	A	B	C	D	E	48	A	B	C	D	E
24	A	B	C	D	E	49	A	B	C	D	E
25	A	B	C	D	E	50	A	B	C	D	E

Q1362-04

I.N. 574006—110VV25P3015

COLLEGE BOARD — SCHOLASTIC APTITUDE TEST and Test of Standard Written English Side 2

Use a No. 2 pencil only. Be sure each mark is dark and completely fills the intended oval. Completely erase any errors or stray marks.

Start with number 1 for each new section. If a section has fewer than 50 questions, leave the extra answer spaces blank.

SECTION 3	SECTION 4	SECTION 5	SECTION 6
1 A B C D E	1 A B C D E	1 A B C D E	1 A B C D E
2 A B C D E	2 A B C D E	2 A B C D E	2 A B C D E
3 A B C D E	3 A B C D E	3 A B C D E	3 A B C D E
4 A B C D E	4 A B C D E	4 A B C D E	4 A B C D E
5 A B C D E	5 A B C D E	5 A B C D E	5 A B C D E
6 A B C D E	6 A B C D E	6 A B C D E	6 A B C D E
7 A B C D E	7 A B C D E	7 A B C D E	7 A B C D E
8 A B C D E	8 A B C D E	8 A B C D E	8 A B C D E
9 A B C D E	9 A B C D E	9 A B C D E	9 A B C D E
10 A B C D E	10 A B C D E	10 A B C D E	10 A B C D E
11 A B C D E	11 A B C D E	11 A B C D E	11 A B C D E
12 A B C D E	12 A B C D E	12 A B C D E	12 A B C D E
13 A B C D E	13 A B C D E	13 A B C D E	13 A B C D E
14 A B C D E	14 A B C D E	14 A B C D E	14 A B C D E
15 A B C D E	15 A B C D E	15 A B C D E	15 A B C D E
16 A B C D E	16 A B C D E	16 A B C D E	16 A B C D E
17 A B C D E	17 A B C D E	17 A B C D E	17 A B C D E
18 A B C D E	18 A B C D E	18 A B C D E	18 A B C D E
19 A B C D E	19 A B C D E	19 A B C D E	19 A B C D E
20 A B C D E	20 A B C D E	20 A B C D E	20 A B C D E
21 A B C D E	21 A B C D E	21 A B C D E	21 A B C D E
22 A B C D E	22 A B C D E	22 A B C D E	22 A B C D E
23 A B C D E	23 A B C D E	23 A B C D E	23 A B C D E
24 A B C D E	24 A B C D E	24 A B C D E	24 A B C D E
25 A B C D E	25 A B C D E	25 A B C D E	25 A B C D E
26 A B C D E	26 A B C D E	26 A B C D E	26 A B C D E
27 A B C D E	27 A B C D E	27 A B C D E	27 A B C D E
28 A B C D E	28 A B C D E	28 A B C D E	28 A B C D E
29 A B C D E	29 A B C D E	29 A B C D E	29 A B C D E
30 A B C D E	30 A B C D E	30 A B C D E	30 A B C D E
31 A B C D E	31 A B C D E	31 A B C D E	31 A B C D E
32 A B C D E	32 A B C D E	32 A B C D E	32 A B C D E
33 A B C D E	33 A B C D E	33 A B C D E	33 A B C D E
34 A B C D E	34 A B C D E	34 A B C D E	34 A B C D E
35 A B C D E	35 A B C D E	35 A B C D E	35 A B C D E
36 A B C D E	36 A B C D E	36 A B C D E	36 A B C D E
37 A B C D E	37 A B C D E	37 A B C D E	37 A B C D E
38 A B C D E	38 A B C D E	38 A B C D E	38 A B C D E
39 A B C D E	39 A B C D E	39 A B C D E	39 A B C D E
40 A B C D E	40 A B C D E	40 A B C D E	40 A B C D E
41 A B C D E	41 A B C D E	41 A B C D E	41 A B C D E
42 A B C D E	42 A B C D E	42 A B C D E	42 A B C D E
43 A B C D E	43 A B C D E	43 A B C D E	43 A B C D E
44 A B C D E	44 A B C D E	44 A B C D E	44 A B C D E
45 A B C D E	45 A B C D E	45 A B C D E	45 A B C D E
46 A B C D E	46 A B C D E	46 A B C D E	46 A B C D E
47 A B C D E	47 A B C D E	47 A B C D E	47 A B C D E
48 A B C D E	48 A B C D E	48 A B C D E	48 A B C D E
49 A B C D E	49 A B C D E	49 A B C D E	49 A B C D E
50 A B C D E	50 A B C D E	50 A B C D E	50 A B C D E

9. SIGNATURE: ____________________

FOR ETS USE ONLY	VTR	VTFS	VRR	VRFS	VVR	VVFS	WER	WEFS	M4R	M4FS	M5R	M5FS	MTFS	
	VTW	VTCS	VRW	VRCS	VVW	VVCS	WEW	WECS	M4W		M5W		MTCS	

FORM CODE 3H

SECTION 1

Time—30 minutes

45 QUESTIONS

For each question in this section, choose the best answer and blacken the corresponding space on the answer sheet.

Each question below consists of a word in capital letters, followed by five lettered words or phrases. Choose the word or phrase that is most nearly opposite in meaning to the word in capital letters. Since some of the questions require you to distinguish fine shades of meaning, consider all the choices before deciding which is best.

Example:

GOOD: (A) sour (B) bad (C) red (D) hot (E) ugly

Ⓐ ● Ⓒ Ⓓ Ⓔ

1. MASSIVE: (A) simple (B) quiet (C) small (D) shallow (E) reliable

2. UNSTABLE: (A) inflatable (B) remarkable (C) technical (D) relieved (E) fixed

3. IMPROVE: (A) denounce (B) ruin (C) assess (D) reject (E) despise

4. LOITER: (A) crowd (B) reveal (C) disdain (D) hasten (E) straighten

5. CONFOUND: (A) enlighten (B) excavate (C) agitate (D) enclose (E) pierce

6. APATHY: (A) vagrancy (B) depravity (C) security (D) enthusiastic devotion (E) sudden reluctance

7. EXPENDITURES: (A) actions (B) receipts (C) complaints (D) associations (E) acknowledgments

8. THEATRICAL: (A) unaffected (B) disquieting (C) auditory (D) imprecise (E) satisfying

9. INEXTRICABLE: (A) reasonable (B) durable (C) separable (D) finite (E) appropriate

10. CLEMENCY: (A) foolishness (B) sadness (C) loudness (D) restlessness (E) harshness

11. ADVERSITY: (A) prosperity (B) independence (C) availability (D) sanity (E) versatility

12. TABLE: (A) illustrate clearly (B) consider immediately (C) travel separately (D) trespass (E) guess

13. CAPRICIOUS: (A) feeble (B) scant (C) constant (D) heavy (E) ungainly

14. TRUNCATE: (A) infer (B) vibrate (C) outline (D) lengthen (E) liquefy

15. ACERBIC: (A) dense (B) nearby (C) kindly (D) slow (E) flawed

Each sentence below has one or two blanks, each blank indicating that something has been omitted. Beneath the sentence are five lettered words or sets of words. Choose the word or set of words that best fits the meaning of the sentence as a whole.

Example:

Although its publicity has been ----, the film itself is intelligent, well-acted, handsomely produced, and altogether ----.

(A) tasteless. .respectable (B) extensive. .moderate (C) sophisticated. .amateur (D) risqué. .crude (E) perfect. .spectacular

● Ⓑ Ⓒ Ⓓ Ⓔ

16. Few people appreciate the irony of a situation in which a flour company removes approximately twenty vitamins from the flour, puts four back, and then touts its product as ----.

(A) inexpensive (B) processed (C) enriched (D) edible (E) novel

17. Because of the dramatic qualities of her voice, a voice too rich for humorous roles, she ---- comedy.

(A) avoided (B) interpreted (C) preferred (D) inspired (E) analyzed

18. Newton gave due credit to his ---- when he said, "If I have seen a little farther than others, it is because I have stood on the shoulders of giants."

(A) disciples (B) opposition (C) progeny (D) predecessors (E) imitators

19. By nature a scholar, this candidate ---- all the rules of the game of politics, disdaining to solicit votes or to cater to powerful groups.

(A) restored (B) evaluated (C) obscured (D) flouted (E) invented

20. Business is not ---- in this economist's view; in fact, he describes it as an intricate ----.

(A) variegated. .collage
(B) moribund. .fiasco
(C) hierarchical. .bureaucracy
(D) prodigious. .achievement
(E) monolithic. .mosaic

GO ON TO THE NEXT PAGE

Each passage below is followed by questions based on its content. Answer all questions following a passage on the basis of what is stated or implied in that passage.

The Circumlocution Office was (as everybody knew without being told) the most important department of the government. No public business of any kind could possibly be done at any time without the acquiescence of the Circumlocution Office. It was equally impossible to do the plainest right and to undo the plainest wrong without the express authority of the Circumlocution Office.

This glorious establishment had been early in the field, when the one sublime principle involving the difficult art of governing a country was first distinctly revealed to the modern mind. It had been foremost to study that bright revelation and to carry its shining influence through the whole of the official proceedings. Whatever was required to be done, the Circumlocution Office was beforehand with all the public departments in the art of perceiving—How Not To Do It.

It is true that How Not To Do It was the great study and object of all public departments and professional politicians all round the Circumlocution Office. It is true that every victorious political party, elected because it had upheld a certain thing as necessary to be done, was no sooner come into office than it applied its utmost faculties to discovering How Not To Do It. All this is true, but the Circumlocution Office went further.

The Circumlocution Office went on mechanically, every day, keeping this wonderful, all-sufficient wheel of statesmanship, How Not To Do It, in motion. The Circumlocution Office was down upon any ill-advised public servants who were going to do it (or who appeared to be, by any surprising accident, in remote danger of doing it) with a memorandum, and a letter of instructions that extinguished them.

This spirit of national efficiency in the Circumlocution Office had gradually led to its having something to do with everything. Mechanics, philosophers, petitioners, people with grievances, people who wanted to prevent grievances, people who couldn't get rewarded for merit, and people who couldn't get punished for demerit—all were indiscriminately tucked up under the Circumlocution Office's mountain of loose papers. Indeed, numbers of people were lost in the Circumlocution Office. Unfortunates who had been wronged, who in slow lapse of time had passed safely through other public departments, got referred at last to the Circumlocution Office and never reappeared in the light of day. Committees met upon them, secretaries minuted upon them, commissioners gabbled about them, clerks registered, checked, and ticked them off, and they melted away. In short, all the business of the country went through the Circumlocution Office, except the business that never came out of it; and that was prodigious.

21. Which of the following titles best describes the passage?
    (A) An Objective Record of the Circumlocution Office
    (B) How to Use the Circumlocution Office
    (C) An Ironic View of a Government Institution
    (D) Crimes and Abuses of the New Government
    (E) The Development of Modern Political Institutions

22. The style and point of view suggest that the passage is most likely drawn from which of the following sources?
    (A) The report of an official of the Circumlocution Office
    (B) A carefully researched account by a historian
    (C) The diary of a successful politician
    (D) A description of a problem by a satiric observer
    (E) The formal complaint of an innocent person against the office

23. Which of the following best describes the author's style in the second paragraph?
    (A) Comically inflated with superlatives
    (B) Highly specific in its examples
    (C) Alternately formal and informal
    (D) Heavily dependent on personal memories
    (E) Direct and immediate in stating an idea

24. The author would most likely view the Circumlocution Office as which of the following?
    (A) A brutal monster
    (B) A beneficent dictator
    (C) A gigantic roadblock
    (D) An admirable masterpiece
    (E) A ruthless politician

25. The author uses all of the following to support the main point of the passage EXCEPT
    (A) repetition of a motto
    (B) grandiose language
    (C) listing of examples
    (D) extensive quotation
    (E) exaggeration of fact

The scene has changed from Florence to Rome, from the city of sharp wits, light feet, graceful movement, to a city of weight, a city that is like a huge compost-heap of human hopes and ambitions, despoiled of its ornament, almost unintelligible, a wilderness of imperial splendor, with the statue of only one ancient emperor, Marcus Aurelius, surviving aboveground in the sunshine through the centuries. The scale has changed. I am standing in the courtyard of the Vatican, at the end of which the architect Bramante has built a sun-trap, known as the Belvedere, from which the pope could enjoy the view of the ancient city. It is in the form of a niche, but instead of being designed to hold a life-size statue it is enormous—in fact it has always been known as *il nicchione*, the monster niche. It is the outward and visible sign of the great change that overcame the civilization of the Renaissance in about the year 1500. This is no longer a world of free and active individuals, but a world of giants and heroes.

In the niche is a bronze pinecone big enough to contain a person. It came from that earlier world of giants, antiquity, and was probably the finial of Hadrian's tomb. But in the Middle Ages it was thought to have marked the point at which the chariots turned in their races round the hippodrome, and since in that hippodrome many Christian martyrs were put to death, it was here that the Christian Church elected to make its headquarters. Huge, cloudy concepts, compared to the sharp focus of Florence. But in Rome they were not so cloudy after all, because the huge buildings of antiquity were there. Even after three centuries in which they were used as quarries, and in which our sense of scale has expanded, they still are surprisingly big. In the Middle Ages people had been crushed by this gigantic scale. They said that these buildings must be the work of demons, or at best they treated them simply as natural phenomena—like mountains—and built their huts in them, as people take advantage of a ravine or sheltering escarpment. Rome was a city of cowherds and stray goats in which nothing was built except a few fortified towers.

But by 1500 the Romans had begun to realize that these ancient buildings had been built by people. The lively and intelligent individuals who created the Renaissance, bursting with vitality and confidence, were not in a mood to be crushed by antiquity. They meant to absorb it, to equal it, to master it. They were going to produce their own race of giants and heroes.

26. The author's main purpose in this passage is best defined as an attempt to show how

(A) the Renaissance languished as it moved from Florence to Rome
(B) those who created the spirit of Renaissance Rome responded to the legacy of ancient Rome
(C) the styles of Renaissance Florence and Renaissance Rome contrasted with each other
(D) historical continuity was maintained between the Middle Ages and the Renaissance
(E) Rome developed from ancient times to the Renaissance

27. The author views the architecture of ancient Rome and of Renaissance Rome primarily as

(A) a record of human thought
(B) a kind of dangerous obsession
(C) a monument to spiritual decadence
(D) a statement of religious faith
(E) an expression of human grandeur

28. The difference between Florence and Rome is seen by the author as most fundamentally one of

(A) cleverness (B) power (C) luxury
(D) proportion (E) freedom

29. From the passage as a whole, it can be inferred that the author regards the statue of the Emperor Marcus Aurelius primarily as

(A) a tribute to the final victor in the long and confused struggles of the Roman Empire
(B) an artistic expression of life's perpetual renewal in the sunlight
(C) a happy exception to the decay that befell ancient Rome's symbols of imperial power
(D) the single clue to the otherwise inexplicable history of the Roman Empire
(E) the sole surviving example of ancient Roman greatness in the wasteland of time

30. The author thinks of "*il nicchione*" (line 16) as an outward and visible sign of the change that overcame the civilization of the Renaissance because

(A) its size reflects the tremendous confidence and aspirations of the Romans who lived at that time
(B) its function as a vantage point for the pope symbolized the pope's authority over Romans at that time
(C) it glorified Rome by dramatizing the past history of the city
(D) it reduced other relics of Rome's ancient glory to mere ornaments
(E) its use as a private retreat for the pope showed that life was being lived on a simpler and more personal scale than in ancient Rome

GO ON TO THE NEXT PAGE

Select the word or set of words that best completes each of the following sentences.

31. Although it was once ----, the small piglike animal known as a peccary is found today only in the Western Hemisphere.

(A) domesticated (B) widespread (C) dwindling (D) primordial (E) eradicable

32. Researchers are looking for a harmless preservative for cured-meat products to replace nitrites should nitrites be ----.

(A) supplemented (B) studied (C) conserved (D) publicized (E) banned

33. The passage of the fair housing bill, an important political victory for its supporters, received scant attention from the press even though it was ---- setback for the opposition and, therefore, highly ----.

(A) a minor. .boring
(B) a devastating. .newsworthy
(C) an unusual. .uninteresting
(D) a famous. .discreet
(E) an inconsequential. .readable

34. Interestingly, few of the statues of Queen Victoria that were erected displayed attributes so ---- as feet.

(A) utopian (B) mundane (C) esoteric (D) chimerical (E) resplendent

35. His habitual ---- had seemingly left its imprint on both his physique and speech, the one lean, the other ----.

(A) puritanism. .indecent
(B) duplicity. .guileless
(C) frugality. .laconic
(D) debauchery. .bombastic
(E) loquacity. .refined

Each question below consists of a related pair of words or phrases, followed by five lettered pairs of words or phrases. Select the lettered pair that best expresses a relationship similar to that expressed in the original pair.

Example:

YAWN : BOREDOM :: (A) dream : sleep (B) anger : madness (C) smile : amusement (D) face : expression (E) impatience : rebellion

Ⓐ Ⓑ ● Ⓓ Ⓔ

36. AUTOBIOGRAPHY : AUTHOR ::
(A) autograph : signature
(B) self-sufficiency : provision
(C) automation : worker
(D) self-portrait : artist
(E) autopsy : doctor

37. CUMULUS : CLOUD :: (A) lake : ocean (B) carnivore : meat (C) glacier : blizzard (D) evergreen : tree (E) evening : daylight

38. PATTER : RAIN :: (A) rainbow : storm (B) call : telephone (C) clank : chain (D) volume : radio (E) eruption: volcano

39. SOLITUDE : RECLUSE ::
(A) attention : exhibitionist
(B) courtesy : braggart
(C) poverty : donor
(D) abuse : official
(E) persecution : director

40. METICULOUS : DETAIL :: (A) tidy : order (B) wicked : morality (C) memorable : facts (D) uninformed : events (E) jovial : smile

41. FETTER : MOBILITY ::
(A) nourish : appetite (B) enfeeble : strength (C) soothe : composure (D) distract : ignorance (E) fortify : reconnaissance

42. INDECIPHERABLE : DECODED ::
(A) enfranchised : voted
(B) anarchical : reprimanded
(C) irrefutable : disproved
(D) prodigal : returned
(E) infamous : known

43. AUTHORITARIAN : DISCIPLINE ::
(A) heckler : sincerity
(B) pragmatist : utility
(C) glutton : abstinence
(D) polemicist : conciliation
(E) infiltrator : purity

44. EXHORTATION : ENCOURAGE ::
(A) eulogy : condemn (B) tirade : reproach (C) conversation : debate (D) lecture : ramble (E) sermon : praise

45. DISCERNING : NUANCES ::
(A) hypocritical : motives (B) brave : decisions (C) artless : possessions (D) slothful : results (E) sensitive : slights

S T O P

IF YOU FINISH BEFORE TIME IS CALLED, YOU MAY CHECK YOUR WORK ON THIS SECTION ONLY. DO NOT WORK ON ANY OTHER SECTION IN THE TEST.

SECTION 2

Time—30 minutes

25 QUESTIONS

In this section solve each problem, using any available space on the page for scratchwork. Then decide which is the best of the choices given and blacken the corresponding space on the answer sheet.

The following information is for your reference in solving some of the problems.

Circle of radius r: Area $= \pi r^2$; Circumference $= 2\pi r$
The number of degrees of arc in a circle is 360.
The measure in degrees of a straight angle is 180.

Definitions of symbols:

$=$	is equal to	$\leq$	is less than or equal to
$\neq$	is unequal to	$\geq$	is greater than or equal to
$<$	is less than	$\parallel$	is parallel to
$>$	is greater than	$\perp$	is perpendicular to

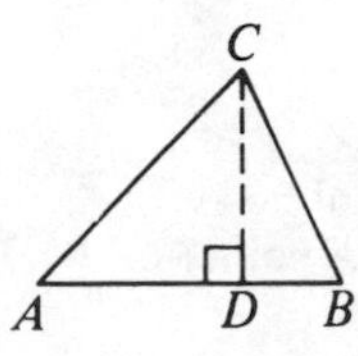

Triangle: The sum of the measures in degrees of the angles of a triangle is 180.

If $\angle CDA$ is a right angle, then

(1) area of $\triangle ABC = \frac{AB \times CD}{2}$

(2) $AC^2 = AD^2 + DC^2$

Note: Figures which accompany problems in this test are intended to provide information useful in solving the problems. They are drawn as accurately as possible EXCEPT when it is stated in a specific problem that its figure is not drawn to scale. All figures lie in a plane unless otherwise indicated. All numbers used are real numbers.

---

1. If $x + y = 9$, then $2x + 2y =$

(A) 3 (B) $\frac{9}{2}$ (C) 18 (D) 36 (E) 81

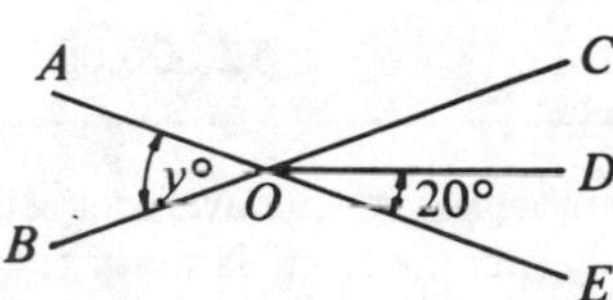

2. In the figure above, if segments BC and AE intersect at O and segment OD bisects $\angle COE$, then $y =$

(A) 10 (B) 20 (C) 30 (D) 40 (E) 60

3. If the cost of a pound of peanuts is $\frac{1}{2}$ the cost of a pound of walnuts, and walnuts cost $2.40 per pound, what is the total cost of 1 pound of peanuts and $\frac{1}{2}$ pound of walnuts?

(A) $1.20
(B) $1.80
(C) $2.40
(D) $3.60
(E) $4.80

4. For all $n \neq 0$, $n \times \frac{1}{n} =$

(A) 0 (B) 1 (C) n (D) $\frac{n^2+1}{n}$ (E) $\frac{1}{n^2}$

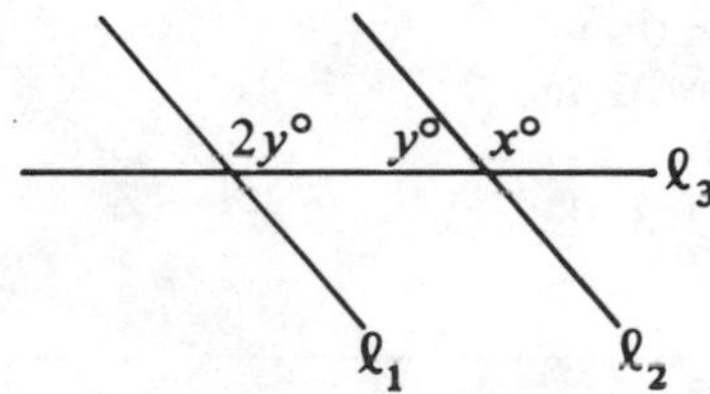

Note: Figure not drawn to scale.

5. If $\ell_1 \parallel \ell_2$ in the figure above, what is the value of x?

(A) 60 (B) 90 (C) 100 (D) 120 (E) 150

GO ON TO THE NEXT PAGE

6. The set T consists of all multiples of 3, that is, $T = \{\ldots, -9, -6, -3, 0, 3, 6, 9, \ldots\}$. If the integers a and b are in T, all of the following must be in T EXCEPT

(A) ab

(B) $a + b$

(C) $a - b$

(D) $-a - b$

(E) $\frac{a}{b}$

7. If a team received 45 points out of a total of 60 points, what percent of the total number of points did it receive?

(A) 65%
(B) 70%
(C) 75%
(D) 80%
(E) 85%

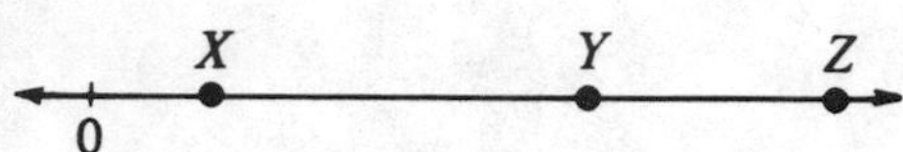

8. If X, Y, and Z indicate numbers on the number line as shown in the figure above, then the average (arithmetic mean) of X, Y, and Z is

(A) between 0 and X
(B) between X and Y
(C) equal to Y
(D) between Y and Z
(E) greater than Z

9. Bob bought a total of 40 feet of tubing, some of which was copper and some of which was brass. If both types of tubing sell for $1.50 per foot and Bob spent a total of $60 for his purchase, how many feet of copper tubing did he buy?

(A) 10
(B) 15
(C) 20
(D) 30
(E) It cannot be determined from the information given.

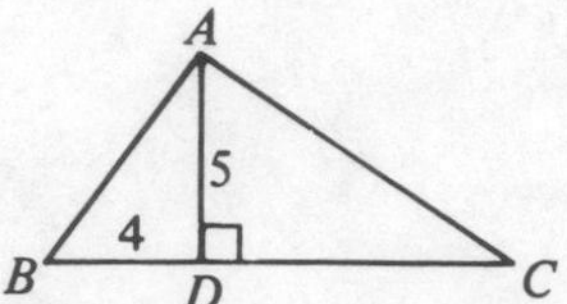

10. If the area of ΔABC in the figure above is 30, then the length of DC is

(A) 2 (B) 4 (C) 6 (D) 8 (E) 12

11. If $40 \cdot 20{,}000 = 8 \cdot 10^x$, then $x =$

(A) 4
(B) 5
(C) 6
(D) 7
(E) 8

INCOME FOR THE EXCEL COMPANY

January to April, 1980

January	+ $4,700,000
February	- $4,000,000
March	+ $5,300,000
April	+ $2,000,000

12. Based on the table above, the average (arithmetic mean) monthly income from January to April, inclusive, for the Excel Company was

(A) $2,000,000
(B) $3,000,000
(C) $3,500,000
(D) $4,000,000
(E) $4,100,000

GO ON TO THE NEXT PAGE

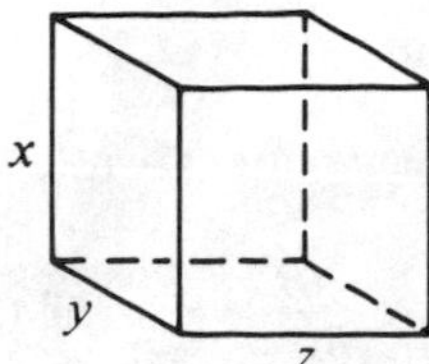

Note: Figure not drawn to scale.

13. In the figure above, x, y, and z are the dimensions of the rectangular solid and each of these dimensions is an integer greater than 1. Each of the the following could be the volume of the rectangular solid EXCEPT

(A) 8 (B) 12 (C) 24 (D) 27 (E) 69

---

14. If 2 more than x is 3 more than y, what is x in terms of y?

(A) $y+1$
(B) $y+2$
(C) $y+3$
(D) $y+4$
(E) $y+5$

15. If $p, q, r, s,$ and t are consecutive integers such that $p<q<r<s<t$ and $p+t=0$, what is the value of r?

(A) 3
(B) 2
(C) 1
(D) 0
(E) It cannot be determined from the information given.

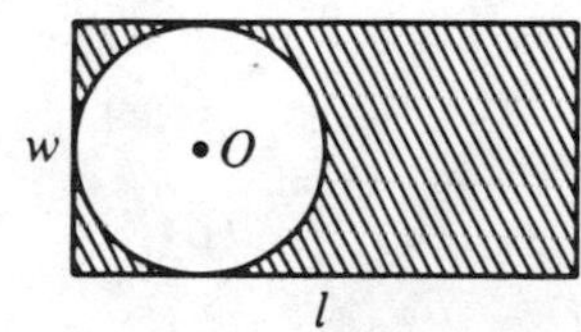

16. In the figure above, a circle with center O touches three sides of a rectangle of length l and width w. Which of the following gives the area of the shaded region?

(A) $\frac{\pi w^2}{4}$ (B) $lw - 2\pi w$ (C) $lw - \pi w^2$

(D) $lw - \frac{\pi w^2}{2}$ (E) $lw - \frac{\pi w^2}{4}$

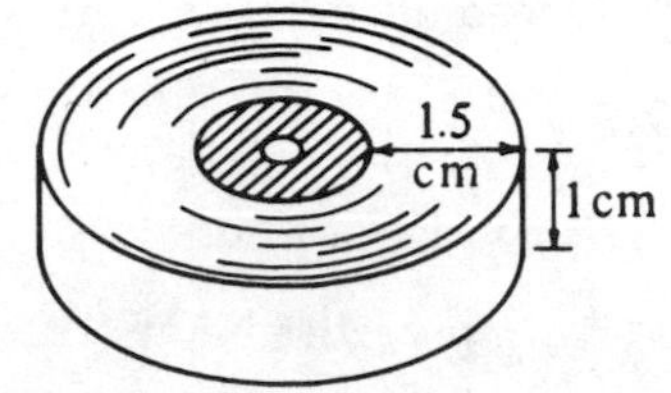

17. In the figure above, tape 1.0 centimeter wide and 0.005 centimeter thick is tightly wrapped around a spool until 1.5 centimeters has been added to the radius of the spool. Approximately how many times is the tape wrapped around the spool?

(A) 33 (B) 150 (C) 300
(D) 333 (E) 3,000

---

18. Of the 45 students in a room, the ratio of girls to boys is 2 to 3. How many girls are in the room?

(A) 18
(B) 20
(C) 27
(D) 30
(E) 33

GO ON TO THE NEXT PAGE

Questions 19-20 refer to the following definition.

For all integers x,

$\textcircled{x} = x$ if x is positive or zero and

$\textcircled{x} = x + 1$ if x is negative.

19. $\textcircled{18} + \textcircled{-18} =$

(A) -1
(B) 0
(C) 1
(D) 2
(E) 36

20. The solution set for $\textcircled{x} + 2 = \textcircled{x+2}$ is the set of all integers x such that

(A) $x = 0$
(B) $x \geqq 0$
(C) $x \leqq -2$
(D) $x \leqq -3$ or $x \geqq 0$
(E) $x \neq 0$

---

21. If $x < -1$, then

(A) $x < x^2 < x^3$
(B) $x < x^3 < x^2$
(C) $x^2 < x^3 < x$
(D) $x^3 < x < x^2$
(E) $x^3 < x^2 < x$

22. Bill has savings of s dollars that earn no interest. If he earns k dollars per week, spends p dollars per week where $p > k$, and makes up the shortage from s, how many weeks will his savings last?

(A) $\frac{s}{p-k}$ (B) $\frac{p-k}{s}$ (C) $\frac{p-s}{k}$

(D) $\frac{s}{k-p}$ (E) $\frac{s-k}{p}$

Note: Figure not drawn to scale.

23. In the figure above, $\frac{AB}{BC} = \frac{3}{4}$ and $\frac{BC}{CD} = \frac{3}{5}$.
If $AD = 82$, then $AB =$

(A) $\frac{41}{6}$

(B) 12

(C) 18

(D) 24

(E) 40

---

24. If $a = x + \frac{1}{3} = \frac{x+2}{3}$, then $a =$

(A) $\frac{1}{2}$

(B) $\frac{2}{3}$

(C) $\frac{3}{4}$

(D) $\frac{4}{5}$

(E) $\frac{5}{6}$

25. If the circumference of circle R is 2π inches longer than the circumference of circle Q, the radius of R is how many inches longer than the radius of Q?

(A) $\frac{1}{2\pi}$ (B) 1 (C) $\frac{4}{\pi}$ (D) 2 (E) 2π

S T O P

IF YOU FINISH BEFORE TIME IS CALLED, YOU MAY CHECK YOUR WORK ON THIS SECTION ONLY. DO NOT WORK ON ANY OTHER SECTION IN THE TEST.

SECTION 4

Time—30 minutes

40 QUESTIONS

For each question in this section, choose the best answer and blacken the corresponding space on the answer sheet.

Each question below consists of a word in capital letters, followed by five lettered words or phrases. Choose the word or phrase that is most nearly opposite in meaning to the word in capital letters. Since some of the questions require you to distinguish fine shades of meaning, consider all the choices before deciding which is best.

Example:

GOOD: (A) sour (B) bad (C) red (D) hot (E) ugly
Ⓐ ● Ⓒ Ⓓ Ⓔ

1. SECONDHAND: (A) essential (B) plain (C) public (D) busy (E) new

2. FLOURISH: (A) repeat (B) decay (C) creep (D) hurl suddenly (E) sail gracefully

3. IMMUNITY:
(A) allowance for error
(B) need for supervision
(C) change of direction
(D) lack of resistance
(E) desire for improvement

4. RESOURCEFUL: (A) grateful (B) hopeful (C) impressionable (D) unlikely to occur (E) unable to cope

5. FACILITATE: (A) intensify (B) mobilize (C) decline (D) complicate (E) meditate

6. FITFUL: (A) brittle (B) original (C) awkward (D) constant (E) recognizable

7. VIABLE: (A) affiliated (B) prevalent (C) easy to annoy (D) incapable of development (E) difficult to express

8. STRIDENCY: (A) accuracy (B) misfortune (C) urgency (D) kindness to strangers (E) soothing tone

9. VILIFICATION: (A) reliable performance (B) need for assistance (C) high praise (D) rapid recovery (E) lack of variety

10. ENDEMIC: (A) alien (B) bloated (C) energetic (D) virulent (E) angelic

Each sentence below has one or two blanks, each blank indicating that something has been omitted. Beneath the sentence are five lettered words or sets of words. Choose the word or set of words that best fits the meaning of the sentence as a whole.

Example:

Although its publicity has been ----, the film itself is intelligent, well-acted, handsomely produced, and altogether ----.

(A) tasteless. .respectable (B) extensive. .moderate (C) sophisticated. .amateur (D) risqué. .crude (E) perfect. .spectacular
● Ⓑ Ⓒ Ⓓ Ⓔ

11. Far from being mere replicas of seventeenth-century African culture, Maroon societies have continually developed as their members have ---- the artistic heritage bequeathed by their ancestors, adapting it creatively to their changing lives.
(A) confused (B) invented (C) repressed (D) denied (E) modified

12. Political experts believe that the prime minister's defeat in the election is ---- because even his own party finds his stance ----.
(A) plausible. .justified
(B) inevitable. .insupportable
(C) avoidable. .objectionable
(D) uncertain. .trivial
(E) sure. .popular

GO ON TO THE NEXT PAGE

13. Specialization has been emphasized to such a degree that some students ---- nothing that is ---- to their primary area of interest.

(A) ignore. .contradictory
(B) incorporate. .necessary
(C) recognize. .fundamental
(D) appreciate. .relevant
(E) value. .extraneous

14. In order to be sold to worldwide television, a movie should be ----; that is, it should neither use strong language nor tackle a controversial theme.

(A) didactic (B) innocuous (C) illustrative (D) derivative (E) spurious

15. The composer's works were never original; they were merely ---- of other composers' music.

(A) a pastiche
(B) a privation
(C) a determinant
(D) an insurgence
(E) a repudiation

Each question below consists of a related pair of words or phrases, followed by five lettered pairs of words or phrases. Select the lettered pair that best expresses a relationship similar to that expressed in the original pair.

Example:

YAWN : BOREDOM :: (A) dream : sleep
(B) anger : madness (C) smile : amusement
(D) face : expression (E) impatience : rebellion

Ⓐ Ⓑ ● Ⓓ Ⓔ

16. BARK : TREE :: (A) skin : fruit (B) dew : grass (C) seed : flower (D) peak : hill (E) wake : boat

17. EXCERPT : BOOK :: (A) type : page (B) script : play (C) solo : routine (D) clip : film (E) drama : musical

18. PIROUETTE : DANCER :: (A) touchdown : referee (B) motivation : coach (C) somersault : acrobat (D) model : sculptor (E) rink : skater

19. HARBOR : SAFETY :: (A) quicksand : security (B) music : disturbance (C) prison : confinement (D) restaurant : starvation (E) oasis : thirst

20. BLUEPRINT : BUILDING :: (A) receipt : money (B) symphony : concert (C) map : automobile (D) briefcase : lawyer (E) agenda : meeting

21. GULLY : EROSION :: (A) drought : precipitation (B) mine : excavation (C) clot : dispersion (D) forest : cultivation (E) water : inundation

22. REPREHENSIBLE : BLAME ::
(A) virtuous : isolation
(B) enviable : restriction
(C) disrespectful : honor
(D) trustworthy : confidence
(E) questionable : ignorance

23. MORTIFY : EMBARRASS :: (A) unleash : abandon (B) overlook : recognize (C) tease : compliment (D) laugh : amuse (E) rout : defeat

24. BLUNTNESS : HONING ::
(A) leakiness : caulking
(B) sloppiness : skipping
(C) monotony : rehearsing
(D) maturity : developing
(E) brightness : polishing

25. APOCRYPHAL : AUTHENTICATION ::
(A) ridiculous : familiarity
(B) detrimental : intention
(C) mystical : intolerance
(D) dogmatic : impatience
(E) profane : sanctity

GO ON TO THE NEXT PAGE

Each passage below is followed by questions based on its content. Answer all questions following a passage on the basis of what is stated or implied in that passage.

When lung disease frustrates the intake of oxygen, the bone marrow makes up for the shortage by increasing the production of new red blood cells and releasing them into the circulatory system to transport whatever oxygen is available to the various areas of the body. Patients with chronic bronchitis and emphysema, for example, often have as many as eight million red blood cells per cubic millimeter of blood, as opposed to the five million found in normal blood.

A shortage of atmospheric oxygen produces the same biological effect. At high altitudes, respiration automatically deepens in the attempt to compensate for the smaller amount of oxygen contained in each normal breath. This adaptation, however, is relatively inefficient: the extra muscular effort consumes so much oxygen that it tends to defeat its own purpose. The body, therefore, must undertake a more rewarding form of acclimatization and, after a few weeks, the blood begins to show a recognizable increase in the number of circulating red blood cells. Thus, it is not unusual to see a new arrival in the Andes who has formerly lived at a low altitude prostrated by breathlessness, while local inhabitants are able to do heavy work without any sign of respiratory distress. The high blood count of the inhabitants is an expression of furiously energetic activity on the part of the bone marrow.

26. According to the passage, the first response of an individual to a shortage of atmospheric oxygen is

(A) a surge of activity in the bone marrow
(B) an increase in respiratory intake
(C) an increase in the number of respiratory passages
(D) an increase in the growth rate of muscle cells
(E) an increase in the blood cell count

27. Which of the following statements about deeper-than-normal breathing is supported by the passage?

(A) It enables the lungs to acclimatize to high altitudes.
(B) It satisfactorily compensates for oxygen deficiency.
(C) It is a largely self-defeating response to oxygen deficiency.
(D) It is a characteristic of inhabitants of mountainous regions.
(E) It stimulates bone marrow activity.

28. It can be inferred from the passage that bronchitis patients suffer from a lack of oxygen because

(A) they cannot adapt their breathing to their environment
(B) they have poor blood circulation
(C) their blood cell count is below normal
(D) their lungs do not function properly
(E) their bone marrow is inactive

GO ON TO THE NEXT PAGE

A supernova, the catastrophic explosion of a massive star, is believed to occur in a galaxy about twice a century. The last supernova visible from the Earth in our own galaxy was seen in 1604, five years before the telescope was used for celestial observation. Since thousands of galaxies are visible from the Earth with large telescopes, however, on the average one may expect to see a supernova in one galaxy or another once every few months. Indeed, in observatories around the world there are astronomers monitoring the sky for the appearance of such stellar explosions in distant galaxies—explosions that for a few weeks may outshine all the rest of a galaxy's billions of stars combined.

Nearly 400 extragalactic supernovas have been observed over the past 90 years. Such observations have helped to make it possible to develop a complete picture of the life cycle of stars. It is believed by most astrophysicists that a supernova is a violent explosion that disrupts a star and ends its life as a normal star. Some supernovas may leave behind cosmic ashes in the form of a neutron star or a black hole. It has also been suggested that the tremendous heat and pressure generated in the explosion synthesize new elements and then expel them into the interstellar gas of a galaxy and that perhaps supernovas are the origin of the cosmic rays that steadily bombard the Earth. It has been imagined further that the energy released by the supernovas is somehow related to such exotic and powerful extragalactic energy emitters as the Seyfert galaxies and the quasars.

29. According to the passage, all of the following are true of supernovas EXCEPT that they

(A) are sometimes visible without a telescope
(B) have only recently begun to occur
(C) are extraordinarily bright
(D) represent an explosion of some type
(E) produce great amounts of heat

30. According to the passage, we could expect a supernova to occur within our galaxy

(A) once every month or two
(B) hundreds of times a century
(C) at least twice every decade
(D) about once every fifty years
(E) once every other century

31. Which of the following questions does the passage answer?

(A) When did the first supernova occur?
(B) What is the normal life cycle of a star?
(C) What characteristics do scientists associate with supernovas?
(D) What causes a supernova to develop into a neutron star?
(E) How do scientists determine the next star that will become a supernova?

32. Which of the following assessments of the state of scientific knowledge about supernovas and their effects can be inferred from the passage?

(A) The crucial facts about the effects have been clearly established.
(B) Further study of supernovas will yield little additional information.
(C) Recent studies have employed questionable methodology.
(D) Today's scientists know little more about supernovas than did their predecessors.
(E) Many theories are still of speculative nature.

GO ON TO THE NEXT PAGE

The subject of my study is women who are initiating social change in a small region in Texas. The women are Mexican Americans who are, or were, migrant agricultural workers. There is more than one kind of innovation at work in the region, of course, but I have chosen to focus on three related patterns of family behavior.

The pattern I life-style represents how migrant farm workers of all nationalities lived in the past and how many continue to live. I treat this pattern as a baseline with which to compare the changes represented by patterns II and III. Families in pattern I work on farms year round, migrating for as many as ten months each year. They work and travel in extended kin units, with the eldest male occupying the position of authority. Families are large—eight or nine children are not unusual—and all members are economic contributors in this strategy of family migration.

Families in pattern II manifest some differences in behavior while still maintaining aspects of pattern I. They continue to migrate but on a reduced scale, often modifying their schedules of migration to allow children to finish the school year. Parents in this pattern often find temporary local jobs as checkers or clerks to offset lost farming income. Pattern II families usually have fewer children than do pattern I families.

The greatest amount of change from pattern I, however, is found in pattern III families, who no longer migrate at all. Both parents work full time in the area and have an average of three children. Children attend school for the entire school year. In pattern III, the women in particular create new roles for themselves for which no local models exist. They not only work full time but may, in addition, return to school. They also assume a greater responsibility in family decisions than do women in the other patterns. Although these women are in the minority among residents of the region, they serve as role models for others, causing ripples of change to spread in their communities.

New opportunities have continued to be determined by preexisting values. When federal jobs became available in the region, most involved working under the direction of female professionals such as teachers or nurses. Such positions were unacceptable to many men in the area because they were not accustomed to being subordinate to women. Women therefore took the jobs, at first, because the income was desperately needed. But some of the women decided to stay at their jobs after the family's financial distress was over. These women enjoyed their work, its responsibility, and the companionship of fellow women workers. The steady, relatively high income allowed their families to stop migrating. And, as the efficaciousness of these women became increasingly apparent, they and their families became even more willing to consider changes in their lives that they would not have considered before.

33. Which of the following titles best reflects the main focus of the passage?

(A) A Study of Three Mexican-American Families at Work in Texas
(B) Innovative Career Women: Effects on Family Unity
(C) Changes in the Life-styles of Migrant Mexican-American Families
(D) Farming or Family: The Unavoidable Choice for Migrant Farm Workers
(E) Recent Changes in Methods of Farming in Texas

34. According to the passage, pattern I families are characterized by which of the following?

(A) Small numbers of children
(B) Brief periods of migrant labor
(C) Female figures of family authority
(D) Commercial as well as agricultural sources of income
(E) Parents and children working and traveling together

35. All of the following statements about pattern II children express differences between them and pattern I children EXCEPT:

(A) They migrate for part of each year.
(B) They have fewer siblings.
(C) They spend less time contributing to family income.
(D) They spend more months in school.
(E) Their parents sometimes work at jobs other than farming.

36. According to the passage, which of the following is NOT true of women in pattern III families?

(A) They earn a reliable and comparatively high income.
(B) They continue to work solely to meet the urgent needs of their families.
(C) They are more involved in the deciding of family issues than they once were.
(D) They enjoy the fellowship involved in working with other women.
(E) They serve as models of behavior for others in the region.

37. The author's attitude toward the three patterns of behavior mentioned in the passage is best described as one of

(A) great admiration
(B) grudging respect
(C) unbiased objectivity
(D) dissatisfaction
(E) indifference

GO ON TO THE NEXT PAGE

Human beings are consistent in their codes of honor but endlessly fickle in deciding to whom these codes apply. The genius of human sociability is in fact the ease with which alliances are formed, broken, and reconstituted, always with strong emotional appeals to rules believed to be absolute. The important distinction today, as it appears to have been since the Ice Age, is between the in-group and the out-group, but the precise location of the dividing line is shifted back and forth with ease. Professional sports thrive on the durability of this basic phenomenon. For a few hours the spectators can resolve their world into an elemental physical struggle between tribal surrogates. The athletes come from everywhere and are sold and traded on an almost yearly basis. The teams themselves are sold from city to city. But it does not matter; the fan identifies with an aggressive in-group, admires teamwork, bravery, and sacrifice, and shares the exultation of the victors.

Nations play by the same rules. During the past thirty years geopolitical alignments have changed from a confrontation between the Axis and the Allies to one between the communist world and the free world, then to oppositions between largely economic blocs. The substance matters little, the form is all.

38. A main point of the passage is that

(A) the adversarial relations between groups are artificial and changeable
(B) the practice of trading and selling players belies the sporting spirit
(C) people no longer find it possible to believe in codes of honor
(D) nations are able to resolve their differences through surrogates
(E) people no longer need to distinguish between opposing social forces

39. According to the author, human alliances are most notable for their

(A) durability (B) destructiveness (C) uselessness (D) fluidity (E) hypocrisy

40. It can be inferred that the author considers the kind of human fickleness described in the passage to be a sign of

(A) immorality (B) benevolence (C) indecisiveness (D) apathy (E) adaptability

S T O P

IF YOU FINISH BEFORE TIME IS CALLED, YOU MAY CHECK YOUR WORK ON THIS SECTION ONLY. DO NOT WORK ON ANY OTHER SECTION IN THE TEST.

SECTION 5

Time—30 minutes

35 QUESTIONS

In this section solve each problem, using any available space on the page for scratchwork. Then decide which is the best of the choices given and blacken the corresponding space on the answer sheet.

The following information is for your reference in solving some of the problems.

Circle of radius r: Area $= \pi r^2$; Circumference $= 2\pi r$
The number of degrees of arc in a circle is 360.
The measure in degrees of a straight angle is 180.

Definitions of symbols:

$=$	is equal to	$\leq$	is less than or equal to
$\neq$	is unequal to	$\geq$	is greater than or equal to
$<$	is less than	$\parallel$	is parallel to
$>$	is greater than	$\perp$	is perpendicular to

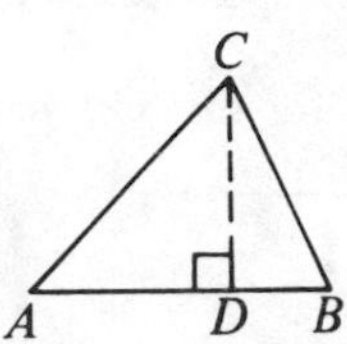

Triangle: The sum of the measures in degrees of the angles of a triangle is 180.

If $\angle CDA$ is a right angle, then

(1) area of $\triangle ABC = \frac{AB \times CD}{2}$

(2) $AC^2 = AD^2 + DC^2$

Note: Figures which accompany problems in this test are intended to provide information useful in solving the problems. They are drawn as accurately as possible EXCEPT when it is stated in a specific problem that its figure is not drawn to scale. All figures lie in a plane unless otherwise indicated. All numbers used are real numbers.

---

1. $\left(\frac{7}{15} \cdot \frac{9}{14}\right) \div \frac{9}{10} =$

(A) $\frac{1}{6}$ (B) $\frac{1}{3}$ (C) $\frac{1}{2}$ (D) $\frac{3}{5}$ (E) $\frac{2}{3}$

2. If a man's age now is n years, then in terms of n, how many years old will he be 5 years from now?

(A) $5 - n$ (B) $n + 5$ (C) $\frac{5}{n}$

(D) $n - 5$ (E) $5n$

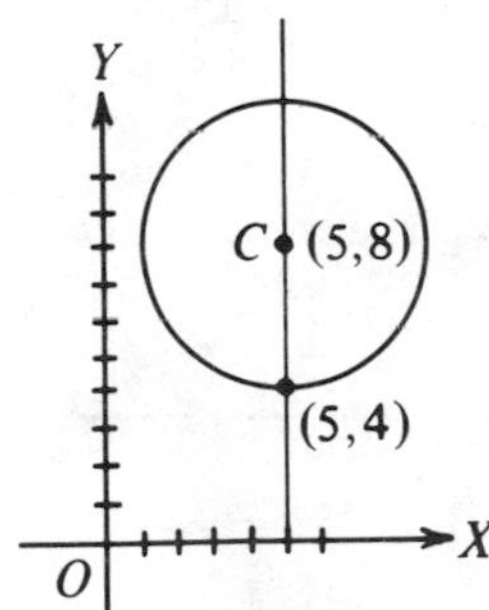

3. In the figure above, what is the circumference of the circle with center C?

(A) 2π (B) 4π (C) 5π (D) 8π (E) 10π

4. What are all values of x for which $x(x-3)=0$?

(A) 0 (B) 3 (C) 0, −3
(D) 0, 3 (E) 0, 3, −3

5. Seven children start to count off "one, two, three, four" in a game. Each child who calls "four" drops out and the next child starts over at "one." Rosa starts the counting. At which of her calls will Rosa drop out?

(A) Second (B) Third (C) Fourth
(D) Fifth (E) Sixth

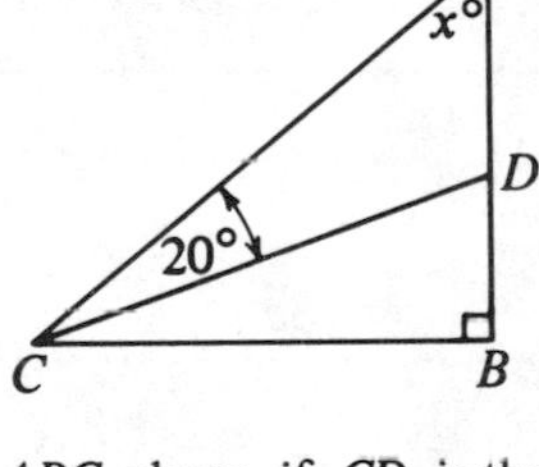

6. In right $\triangle ABC$ above, if CD is the bisector of $\angle ACB$, then $x =$

(A) 15 (B) 20 (C) 25 (D) 40 (E) 50

A B C D E

$x-\frac{3}{2}$ $x-1$ $x-\frac{1}{2}$ x $x+\frac{1}{2}$ $x+1$

7. The fraction $\frac{3x-1}{3}$ falls in which lettered region on the number line above?

(A) A (B) B (C) C (D) D (E) E

GO ON TO THE NEXT PAGE

5

Questions 8-27 each consist of two quantities, one in Column A and one in Column B. You are to compare the two quantities and on the answer sheet blacken space

- A if the quantity in Column A is greater;
- B if the quantity in Column B is greater;
- C if the two quantities are equal;
- D if the relationship cannot be determined from the information given.

Notes:
1. In certain questions, information concerning one or both of the quantities to be compared is centered above the two columns.
2. In a given question, a symbol that appears in both columns represents the same thing in Column A as it does in Column B.
3. Letters such as x, n, and k stand for real numbers.

EXAMPLES

	Column A	Column B	Answers
E1.	2×6	$2 + 6$	● Ⓑ Ⓒ Ⓓ
	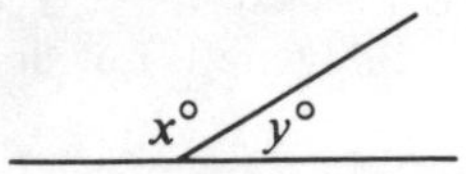		
E2.	$180 - x$	y	Ⓐ Ⓑ ● Ⓓ
E3.	$p - q$	$q - p$	Ⓐ Ⓑ Ⓒ ●

	Column A	Column B
8.	$10^6 - 2^6$	$10^6 - 3^6$
9.	The number of seconds in a half hour	1,800

$y = 2x$ and $x \neq 0$

10.	$2x - y$	$2xy$

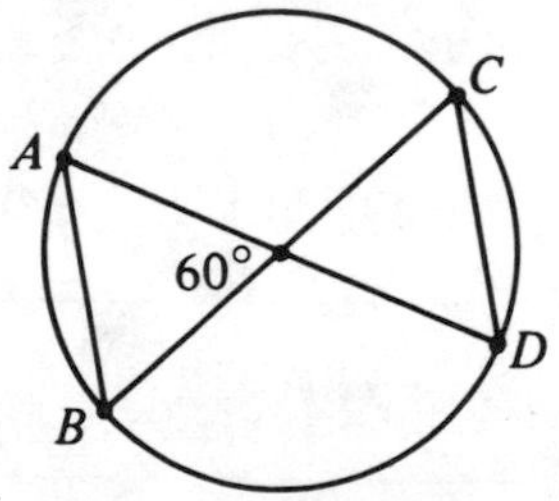

AD and BC intersect at the center of the circle.

11.	Length of chord AB	Length of chord CD

	Column A	Column B

$x < 0$

12.	$\sqrt{x^2 + 1}$	$\sqrt{x^2}$
13.	Twice an even integer greater than 5	Three times an even integer greater than 2

x and y are positive integers less than 10.

14.	$x - y$	9

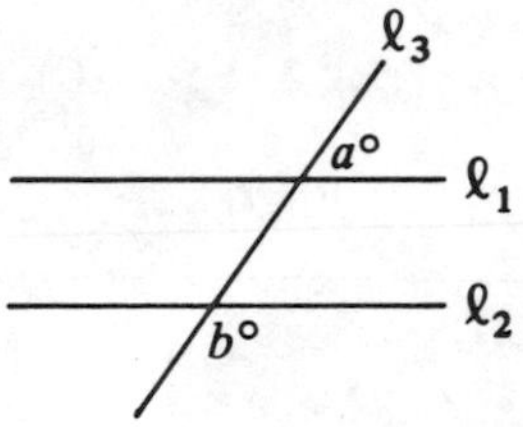

Parallel lines ℓ_1 and ℓ_2 are intersected by line ℓ_3.

15.	a	$180 - b$

$2x - 7 = 13$

16.	$2x + 7$	21

A film cartoon is shown at the rate of 24 frames per second.

17.	The number of frames used for a 6-minute cartoon shown at this rate	8,640

GO ON TO THE NEXT PAGE

SUMMARY DIRECTIONS FOR COMPARISON QUESTIONS

Answer: A if the quantity in Column A is greater;
B if the quantity in Column B is greater;
C if the two quantities are equal;
D if the relationship cannot be determined from the information given.

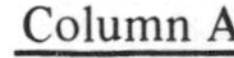

	Column A	Column B

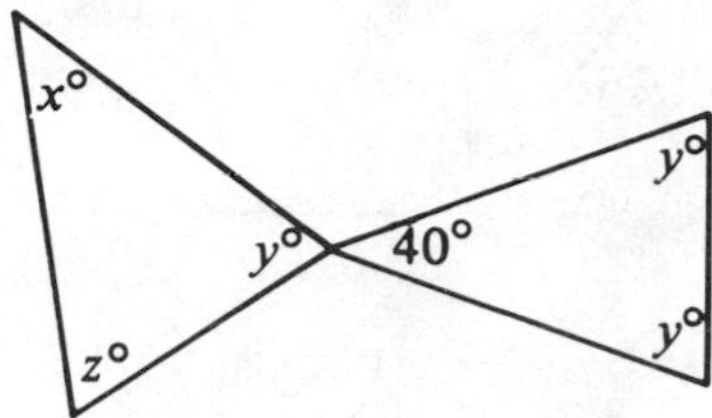

Note: Figure not drawn to scale.

	Column A	Column B
18.	x	65

Questions 19-20 refer to the following definitions.

For all nonzero numbers x and y, let $x \circ y = \frac{x}{y}$ and $x \Delta y = \frac{y}{x}$.

	Column A	Column B
19.	$3 \circ 2$	$3 \Delta 2$

$z \neq 0$

	Column A	Column B
20.	$1 \circ z$	$1 \Delta z$

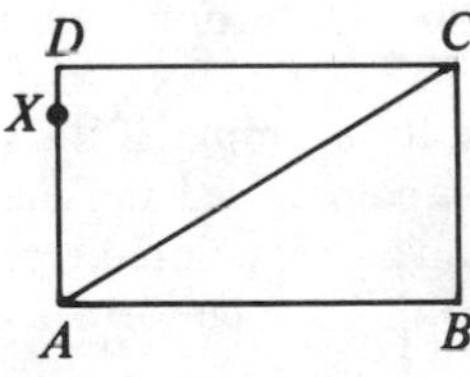

Rectangle $ABCD$

	Column A	Column B
21.	Length of diagonal AC	Length of a line segment from X to a point Y (not shown) on segment BC.

	Column A	Column B
22.	$\frac{1}{\frac{3}{2} - 1}$	$\frac{3}{2} - 1$

	Column A	Column B

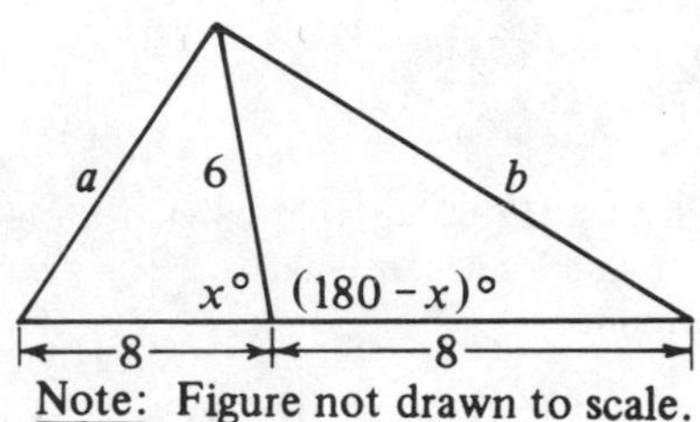

Note: Figure not drawn to scale.

	Column A	Column B
23.	a	b

$x = \frac{2}{3}r,\ r = \frac{12}{5}y,\ y = \frac{5}{2}z$

	Column A	Column B
24.	x	$4z$

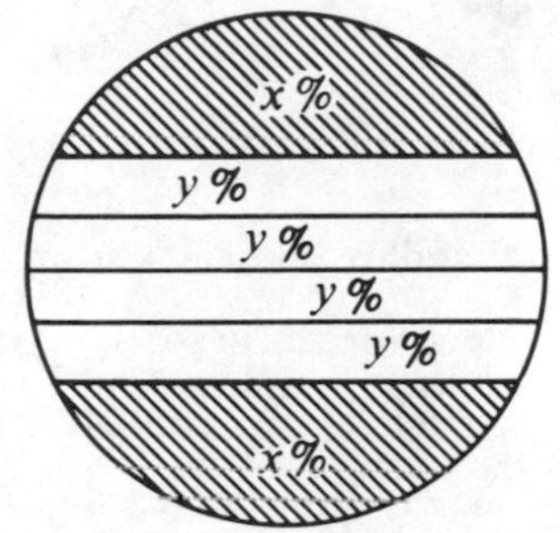

$2x\%$ of the circle is shaded and $4y\%$ is unshaded.

$x > 30$

	Column A	Column B
25.	y	10

x and y are positive integers.

	Column A	Column B
26.	$(3^x)^y$	$3^x \cdot 3^y$

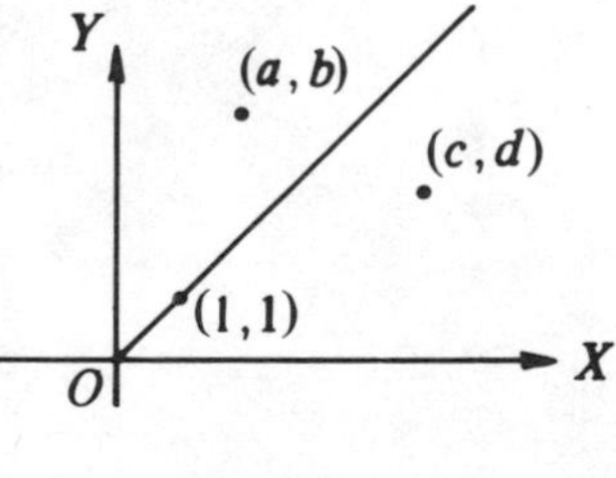

	Column A	Column B
27.	$\frac{b}{a}$	$\frac{d}{c}$

GO ON TO THE NEXT PAGE

5

Solve each of the remaining problems in this section using any available space for scratchwork. Then decide which is the best of the choices given and blacken the corresponding space on the answer sheet.

28. If $3x + 2y = 17$ and x and y are positive integers, then y could equal which of the following?

(A) 2
(B) 3
(C) 4
(D) 5
(E) 6

29. If a six-sided polygon has 3 sides of length $x + y$ each and 3 sides of length $x - y$ each, what is its perimeter?

(A) $3x$ (B) $3y$ (C) $6x$
(D) $6y$ (E) $6x - 6y$

30. If $\frac{11k}{4}$ is an integer, then k could be any of the following EXCEPT

(A) −96
(B) −28
(C) 0
(D) 4
(E) 6

31. On the first day of a sale, a store owner sold $\frac{1}{2}$ of the television sets in stock. After 3 sets were sold on the second day, $\frac{2}{5}$ of the original number of sets remained. How many sets were in stock before the sale?

(A) 10
(B) 20
(C) 30
(D) 40
(E) 50

32. If $\frac{y+x}{y} = 2$ and $\frac{z+x}{z} = 3$, what is the value of $\frac{y}{z}$?

(A) $\frac{5}{2}$

(B) 2

(C) $\frac{3}{2}$

(D) 1

(E) $\frac{2}{3}$

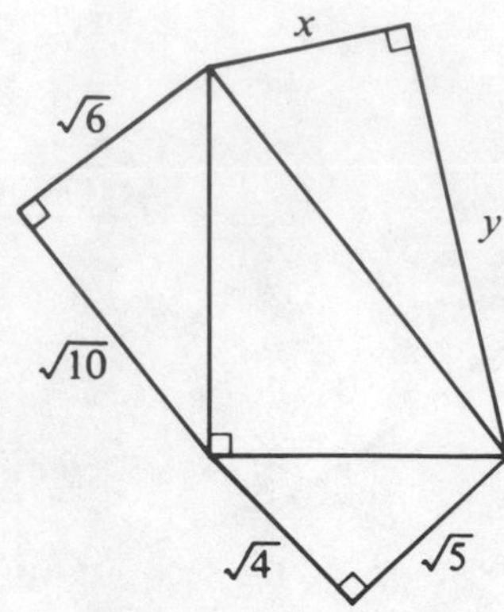

33. In the figure above, $x^2 + y^2 =$

(A) 5 (B) 7 (C) 25 (D) 80 (E) 625

34. The longest of 4 rods of unequal lengths is 70 centimeters and the shortest is 50 centimeters. If x centimeters is the average (arithmetic mean) length of the 4 rods, which of the following indicates all possible values of x and only those possible values?

(A) $50 < x < 70$
(B) $51 < x < 69$
(C) $54 < x < 64$
(D) $55 < x < 65$
(E) $59 < x < 61$

35. A "word" is defined as a sequence of three dots arranged in a row. Each dot is colored either red or green. Two such "words" are said to be different if at least one pair of corresponding dots has different colors, for example, if the second dot of one sequence is colored red and the second dot of the second sequence is colored green. How many different "words" can be formed?

(A) 3
(B) 5
(C) 6
(D) 8
(E) 9

S T O P

IF YOU FINISH BEFORE TIME IS CALLED, YOU MAY CHECK YOUR WORK ON THIS SECTION ONLY. DO NOT WORK ON ANY OTHER SECTION IN THE TEST.

Correct Answers for Scholastic Aptitude Test
Form Code 3H

VERBAL		MATHEMATICAL	
Section 1	Section 4	Section 2	Section 5
1. C	1. E	1. C	1. B
2. E	2. B	2. D	2. B
3. B	3. D	3. C	3. D
4. D	4. E	4. B	4. D
5. A	5. D	5. D	5. A
6. D	6. D	6. E	6. E
7. B	7. D	7. C	7. C
8. A	8. E	8. B	*8. A
9. C	9. C	9. E	*9. C
10. E	10. A	10. D	*10. B
11. A	11. E	11. B	*11. C
12. B	12. B	12. A	*12. A
13. C	13. E	13. E	*13. D
14. D	14. B	14. A	*14. B
15. C	15. A	15. D	*15. C
16. C	16. A	16. E	*16. A
17. A	17. D	17. C	*17. C
18. D	18. C	18. A	*18. D
19. D	19. C	19. C	*19. A
20. E	20. E	20. D	*20. D
21. C	21. B	21. D	*21. A
22. D	22. D	22. A	*22. A
23. A	23. E	23. C	*23. D
24. C	24. A	24. E	*24. C
25. D	25. E	25. B	*25. B
26. B	26. B		*26. D
27. E	27. C		*27. A
28. D	28. D		28. C
29. C	29. B		29. C
30. A	30. D		30. E
31. B	31. C		31. C
32. E	32. E		32. B
33. B	33. C		33. C
34. B	34. E		34. D
35. C	35. A		35. D
36. D	36. B		
37. D	37. C		
38. C	38. A		
39. A	39. D		
40. A	40. E		
41. B			
42. C			
43. B			
44. B			
45. E			

*Indicates four-choice questions. (All of the other questions are five-choice.)

The Scoring Process

Machine-scoring is done in three steps:

- *Scanning.* Your answer sheet is "read" by a scanning machine and the oval you filled in for each question is recorded on a computer tape.
- *Scoring.* The computer compares the oval filled in for each question with the correct response. Each correct answer receives one point; omitted questions do not count toward your score. For each wrong answer, a fraction of a point is subtracted to correct for random guessing. For questions with five answer choices, one-fourth of a point is subtracted for each wrong response; for questions with four answer choices, one-third of a point is subtracted for each wrong response. The SAT-verbal test has 85 questions with five answer choices each. If, for example, a student has 44 right, 32 wrong, and 9 omitted, the resulting raw score is determined as follows:

  $$44 \text{ right} - \frac{32 \text{ wrong}}{4} = 44 - 8 = 36 \text{ raw score points}$$

  Obtaining raw scores frequently involves the rounding of fractional numbers to the nearest whole number. For example, a raw score of 36.25 is rounded to 36, the nearest whole number. A raw score of 36.50 is rounded upward to 37.
- *Converting to reported scaled score.* Raw test scores are then placed on the College Board scale of 200 to 800 through a process that adjusts scores to account for minor differences in difficulty among different editions of the test. This process, known as equating, is performed so that a student's reported score is not affected by the edition of the test taken nor by the abilities of the group with whom the student takes the test. As a result of placing SAT scores on the College Board scale, scores earned by students at different times can be compared. For example, an SAT-verbal score of 400 on a test taken at one administration indicates the same level of developed verbal ability as a 400 score obtained on a different edition of the test taken at another time.

How to Score the Test

You can verify the College Board SAT scores reported to you recently by using the information in this booklet along with the copy of your answer sheet. *Before you begin, check that the first two characters (number and letter) of the form code you marked in item 3 on your answer sheet are the same as the form code printed on the front of this booklet.* Compare the responses shown on the copy of your answer sheet with the list of correct answers.

SAT-Verbal Sections 1 and 4

Step A: Count the number of correct answers for *section 1* and record the number in the space provided on the worksheet on the next page. Then do the same for the incorrect answers. (Do not count omitted answers.) To determine subtotal A, use the formula:

$$\text{number correct} - \frac{\text{number incorrect}}{4} = \text{subtotal A}$$

Step B: Count the number of correct answers and the number of incorrect answers for *section 4* and record the numbers in the spaces provided on the worksheet. To determine subtotal B, use the formula:

$$\text{number correct} - \frac{\text{number incorrect}}{4} = \text{subtotal B}$$

Step C: To obtain C, add subtotal A to subtotal B, keeping any decimals. Enter the resulting figure on the worksheet.

Step D: To obtain D, your raw verbal score, round C to the nearest whole number. (For example, any number from 44.50 to 45.49 rounds to 45.) Enter the resulting figure on the worksheet.

Step E: To find your reported SAT-verbal score, look up the total raw verbal score you obtained in step D in the conversion table on page 252. Enter this figure on the worksheet.

SAT-Mathematical Sections 2 and 5

Step A: Count the number of correct answers and the number of incorrect answers for *section 2* and record the numbers in the spaces provided on the worksheet. To determine the subtotal A, use the formula:

$$\text{number correct} - \frac{\text{number incorrect}}{4} = \text{subtotal A}$$

Step B: Count the number of correct answers and the number of incorrect answers for the *five-choice questions (questions 1 through 7 and 28 through 35) in section 5* and record the numbers in the spaces provided on the worksheet. To determine the subtotal B, use the formula:

$$\text{number correct} - \frac{\text{number incorrect}}{4} = \text{subtotal B}$$

Step C: Count the number of correct answers and the number of incorrect answers for the *four-choice questions (questions 8 through 27) in section 5* and record the numbers in the spaces provided on the worksheet. To determine the subtotal C, use the formula:

$$\text{number correct} - \frac{\text{number incorrect}}{3} = \text{subtotal C}$$

Step D: To obtain D, add subtotal A, subtotal B, and subtotal C, keeping any decimals. Enter the resulting figure on the worksheet.

Step E: To obtain E, your raw mathematical score, round D to the nearest whole number. (For example, any number from 44.50 to 45.49 rounds to 45.) Enter the resulting figure on the worksheet.

Step F: To find your reported SAT-mathematical score, look up the total raw mathematical score you obtained in E in the conversion table on page 252. Enter this figure on the worksheet.

SAT-SCORING WORKSHEET

FORM CODE 3H

SAT-Verbal Sections

A. Section 1: ______ no. correct − ¼ (______ no. incorrect) = ______ subtotal A

B. Section 4: ______ no. correct − ¼ (______ no. incorrect) = ______ subtotal B

C. Total unrounded raw score (Total A + B) ______ C

D. Total rounded raw score (Rounded to nearest whole number) ______ D

E. SAT-verbal reported scaled score (See the conversion table on the back cover.) [ ] SAT-verbal score

SAT-Mathematical Sections

A. Section 2: ______ no. correct − ¼ (______ no. incorrect) = ______ subtotal A

B. Section 5: Questions 1 through 7 and 28 through 35 (5-choice) ______ no. correct − ¼ (______ no. incorrect) = ______ subtotal B

C. Section 5: Questions 8 through 27 (4-choice) ______ no. correct − ⅓ (______ no. incorrect) = ______ subtotal C

D. Total unrounded raw score (Total A + B + C) ______ D

E. Total rounded raw score (Rounded to nearest whole number) ______ E

F. SAT-mathematical reported scaled score (See the conversion table on the back cover.) [ ] SAT-math score

Score Conversion Table
Scholastic Aptitude Test
Form Code 3H

Raw Score	College Board Reported Score		Raw Score	College Board Reported Score	
	SAT-Verbal	SAT-Math		SAT-Verbal	SAT-Math
85	800		40	460	590
84	780		39	460	580
83	760		38	450	570
82	750		37	450	560
81	740		36	440	550
80	730		35	430	540
79	720		34	430	530
78	710		33	420	530
77	700		32	410	520
76	700		31	410	510
75	690		30	400	500
74	680		29	400	490
73	680		28	390	480
72	670		27	380	470
71	660		26	380	460
70	660		25	370	450
69	650		24	360	450
68	640		23	360	440
67	640		22	350	430
66	630		21	340	420
65	620		20	340	410
64	620		19	330	410
63	610		18	320	400
62	610		17	310	390
61	600		16	310	380
60	590	800	15	300	370
59	590	780	14	290	370
58	580	760	13	280	360
57	570	750	12	280	350
56	570	740	11	270	340
55	560	730	10	260	330
54	550	720	9	250	320
53	550	710	8	250	310
52	540	700	7	240	310
51	530	690	6	230	300
50	530	680	5	220	290
49	520	670	4	220	280
48	510	660	3	210	270
47	510	660	2	200	260
46	500	650	1	200	250
45	500	640	0	200	250
44	490	630	−1	200	240
43	480	620	−2	200	230
42	480	610	−3	200	220
41	470	600	−4	200	210
			−5	200	210
			−6 or below	200	200

Test 9
SAT *Form Code 4E & 4V*

COLLEGE BOARD — SCHOLASTIC APTITUDE TEST and Test of Standard Written English Side 1

Use a No. 2 pencil only. Be sure each mark is dark and completely fills the intended oval. Completely erase any errors or stray marks.

1. YOUR NAME: (Print) ______ Last ______ First ______ M.I.

SIGNATURE: ______ DATE: ___ / ___ / ___

HOME ADDRESS: (Print) ______ Number and Street

______ City ______ State ______ Zip Code

CENTER: (Print) ______ City ______ State ______ Center Number

IMPORTANT: Please fill in these boxes exactly as shown on the back cover of your test book.

FOR ETS USE ONLY

2. TEST FORM

3. FORM CODE

0	A	J	S	0	0	0
1	B	K	T	1	1	1
2	C	L	U	2	2	2
3	D	M	V	3	3	3
4	E	N	W	4	4	4
5	F	O	X	5	5	5
6	G	P	Y	6	6	6
7	H	Q	Z	7	7	7
8	I	R		8	8	8
9				9	9	9

4. REGISTRATION NUMBER (Copy from your Admission Ticket.)

0	0	0	0	0	0	0
1	1	1	1	1	1	1
2	2	2	2	2	2	2
3	3	3	3	3	3	3
4	4	4	4	4	4	4
5	5	5	5	5	5	5
6	6	6	6	6	6	6
7	7	7	7	7	7	7
8	8	8	8	8	8	8
9	9	9	9	9	9	9

5. YOUR NAME

First 4 letters of last name				First Init.	Mid. Init.
A	A	A	A	A	A
B	B	B	B	B	B
C	C	C	C	C	C
D	D	D	D	D	D
E	E	E	E	E	E
F	F	F	F	F	F
G	G	G	G	G	G
H	H	H	H	H	H
I	I	I	I	I	I
J	J	J	J	J	J
K	K	K	K	K	K
L	L	L	L	L	L
M	M	M	M	M	M
N	N	N	N	N	N
O	O	O	O	O	O
P	P	P	P	P	P
Q	Q	Q	Q	Q	Q
R	R	R	R	R	R
S	S	S	S	S	S
T	T	T	T	T	T
U	U	U	U	U	U
V	V	V	V	V	V
W	W	W	W	W	W
X	X	X	X	X	X
Y	Y	Y	Y	Y	Y
Z	Z	Z	Z	Z	Z

6. DATE OF BIRTH

Month	Day		Year	
Jan.				
Feb.				
Mar.	0	0	0	0
Apr.	1	1	1	1
May	2	2	2	2
June	3	3	3	3
July		4	4	4
Aug.		5	5	5
Sept.		6	6	6
Oct.		7	7	7
Nov.		8		8
Dec.		9		9

7. SEX

Female

Male

8. TEST BOOK SERIAL NUMBER

(Cut here to detach.)

Start with number 1 for each new section. If a section has fewer than 50 questions, leave the extra answer spaces blank.

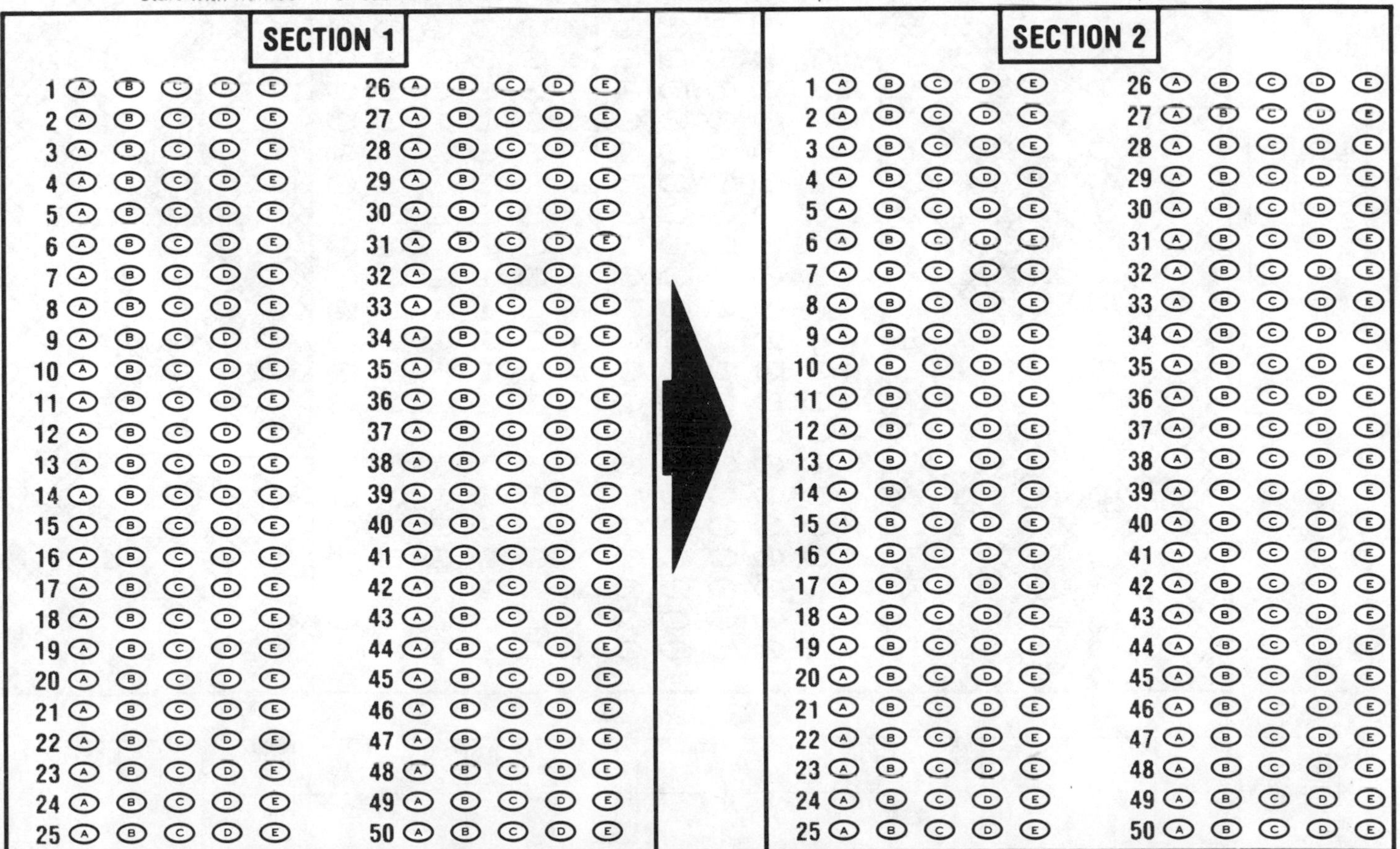

Q1362-04

I.N. 574006—110VV25P3015

COLLEGE BOARD — SCHOLASTIC APTITUDE TEST and Test of Standard Written English Side 2

Use a No. 2 pencil only. Be sure each mark is dark and completely fills the intended oval. Completely erase any errors or stray marks.

Start with number 1 for each new section. If a section has fewer than 50 questions, leave the extra answer spaces blank.

	SECTION 3	SECTION 4	SECTION 5	SECTION 6
1	A B C D E	A B C D E	A B C D E	A B C D E
2	A B C D E	A B C D E	A B C D E	A B C D E
3	A B C D E	A B C D E	A B C D E	A B C D E
4	A B C D E	A B C D E	A B C D E	A B C D E
5	A B C D E	A B C D E	A B C D E	A B C D E
6	A B C D E	A B C D E	A B C D E	A B C D E
7	A B C D E	A B C D E	A B C D E	A B C D E
8	A B C D E	A B C D E	A B C D E	A B C D E
9	A B C D E	A B C D E	A B C D E	A B C D E
10	A B C D E	A B C D E	A B C D E	A B C D E
11	A B C D E	A B C D E	A B C D E	A B C D E
12	A B C D E	A B C D E	A B C D E	A B C D E
13	A B C D E	A B C D E	A B C D E	A B C D E
14	A B C D E	A B C D E	A B C D E	A B C D E
15	A B C D E	A B C D E	A B C D E	A B C D E
16	A B C D E	A B C D E	A B C D E	A B C D E
17	A B C D E	A B C D E	A B C D E	A B C D E
18	A B C D E	A B C D E	A B C D E	A B C D E
19	A B C D E	A B C D E	A B C D E	A B C D E
20	A B C D E	A B C D E	A B C D E	A B C D E
21	A B C D E	A B C D E	A B C D E	A B C D E
22	A B C D E	A B C D E	A B C D E	A B C D E
23	A B C D E	A B C D E	A B C D E	A B C D E
24	A B C D E	A B C D E	A B C D E	A B C D E
25	A B C D E	A B C D E	A B C D E	A B C D E
26	A B C D E	A B C D E	A B C D E	A B C D E
27	A B C D E	A B C D E	A B C D E	A B C D E
28	A B C D E	A B C D E	A B C D E	A B C D E
29	A B C D E	A B C D E	A B C D E	A B C D E
30	A B C D E	A B C D E	A B C D E	A B C D E
31	A B C D E	A B C D E	A B C D E	A B C D E
32	A B C D E	A B C D E	A B C D E	A B C D E
33	A B C D E	A B C D E	A B C D E	A B C D E
34	A B C D E	A B C D E	A B C D E	A B C D E
35	A B C D E	A B C D E	A B C D E	A B C D E
36	A B C D E	A B C D E	A B C D E	A B C D E
37	A B C D E	A B C D E	A B C D E	A B C D E
38	A B C D E	A B C D E	A B C D E	A B C D E
39	A B C D E	A B C D E	A B C D E	A B C D E
40	A B C D E	A B C D E	A B C D E	A B C D E
41	A B C D E	A B C D E	A B C D E	A B C D E
42	A B C D E	A B C D E	A B C D E	A B C D E
43	A B C D E	A B C D E	A B C D E	A B C D E
44	A B C D E	A B C D E	A B C D E	A B C D E
45	A B C D E	A B C D E	A B C D E	A B C D E
46	A B C D E	A B C D E	A B C D E	A B C D E
47	A B C D E	A B C D E	A B C D E	A B C D E
48	A B C D E	A B C D E	A B C D E	A B C D E
49	A B C D E	A B C D E	A B C D E	A B C D E
50	A B C D E	A B C D E	A B C D E	A B C D E

9. SIGNATURE:

FOR ETS USE ONLY	VTR	VTFS	VRR	VRFS	VVR	VVFS	WER	WEFS	M4R	M4FS	M5R	M5FS	MTFS
	VTW	VTCS	VRW	VRCS	VVW	VVCS	WEW	WECS	M4W		M5W		MTCS

SECTION 1

Time—30 minutes

45 QUESTIONS

For each question in this section, choose the best answer and blacken the corresponding space on the answer sheet.

Each question below consists of a word in capital letters, followed by five lettered words or phrases. Choose the word or phrase that is most nearly opposite in meaning to the word in capital letters. Since some of the questions require you to distinguish fine shades of meaning, consider all the choices before deciding which is best.

Example:

GOOD: (A) sour (B) bad (C) red (D) hot (E) ugly

Ⓐ ● Ⓒ Ⓓ Ⓔ

1. HEFTY: (A) arid (B) smooth (C) shapely (D) horizontal (E) lightweight

2. CRUCIAL: (A) inaccurate (B) unessential (C) uninspiring (D) preferential (E) reputable

3. RUFFLE: (A) enlarge (B) censor (C) avoid (D) calm (E) eject

4. CONGLOMERATE: (A) retract (B) darken (C) separate (D) reveal (E) stir

5. MONUMENTAL: (A) biased (B) vacant (C) trivial (D) ambiguous (E) ingenious

6. BRAWN: (A) frailness (B) silence (C) innocence (D) foolishness (E) sluggishness

7. DISLODGE: (A) amass (B) befriend (C) validate (D) solicit (E) entrench

8. ADVOCACY: (A) disrepute (B) opposition (C) ascendancy (D) justice (E) unconsciousness

9. COGNATE: (A) impartial (B) unrelated (C) unlikely (D) inconvenient (E) expendable

10. QUIXOTIC: (A) fortunate (B) practical (C) devoted (D) proud (E) kindly

11. WORKADAY: (A) superficial (B) competitive (C) extraordinary (D) confidential (E) deceptive

12. DISTENSION: (A) proximity (B) regularity (C) pleasure (D) contraction (E) repulsion

13. BEMUSE: (A) enlighten (B) pervade (C) savor (D) return promptly (E) make responsible

14. PROCLIVITY: (A) emptiness (B) recklessness (C) inactivity (D) negligence (E) disinclination

15. IMPECUNIOUS: (A) rich (B) strong (C) guilty (D) rude (E) hazardous

Each sentence below has one or two blanks, each blank indicating that something has been omitted. Beneath the sentence are five lettered words or sets of words. Choose the word or set of words that best fits the meaning of the sentence as a whole.

Example:

Although its publicity has been ----, the film itself is intelligent, well-acted, handsomely produced, and altogether ----.

(A) tasteless. .respectable (B) extensive. .moderate (C) sophisticated. .amateur (D) risqué. .crude (E) perfect. .spectacular

● Ⓑ Ⓒ Ⓓ Ⓔ

16. Although it seems to have been a fixture of the square since the city's origin, the produce market actually opened only ----.
(A) enthusiastically (B) recently (C) frequently (D) illegally (E) graciously

17. The grave problems that afflicted him were the purely ---- ones of hunger, pain, and fatigue.
(A) physical (B) imaginary (C) irrelevant (D) hereditary (E) coincidental

18. Her ability to analyze issues fairly and competently has earned her the ---- of even her most ---- peers.
(A) solicitation. .unbiased
(B) attention. .sympathetic
(C) suspicion. .discerning
(D) reputation. .knowledgeable
(E) respect. .exacting

19. Until the mid-1800's, the occasional reports by European explorers of the existence of gorillas were generally disbelieved and swiftly ---- the realm of tall tales.
(A) extracted from (B) confused with (C) relegated to (D) compared to (E) exalted to

20. The historian's assertion that there is a ---- of verifiable information about nineteenth-century Native Americans is ----, for there exist many transcripts of authentic oral accounts of their activities.
(A) wealth. .fallacious
(B) shortage. .legitimate
(C) depletion. .irrefutable
(D) paucity. .erroneous
(E) surfeit. .implausible

GO ON TO THE NEXT PAGE

Each passage below is followed by questions based on its content. Answer all questions following a passage on the basis of what is stated or implied in that passage.

Public officials are now considering both the separate and additive effects on humans of lead, mercury, and cadmium, along with a variety of other chemicals in our atmosphere. Each of these materials, regarded separately or together, is known to interfere with several systems of the human body. The first of these, lead, poses a particular threat to large numbers of people. The quantity of lead that the average American absorbs suggests the probable emergence of as yet undiscovered disorders.

Even before 650 B.C., lead ore was mined on a small scale in order to extract the silver from it. With the invention of coinage, the demand for silver led to an enormous increase in the amount of available lead ore. At the time of the Roman Empire, the wealthy used elegant metal containers for food and drink. Since acidic wine leached copper from bronze or copper vessels, producing obvious toxic effects, containers came to be lined with lead, which did not cause vomiting and actually tasted good. In fact, however, lead is more toxic than copper, and yet the members of the Roman aristocracy added lead to their diets in more than a dozen ways.

During the second century A. D., the Roman aristocracy began to show signs of an inability to reproduce; it was gradually replaced by a new leadership, which adopted a similar way of life. This new aristocracy also failed to reproduce, and today we surmise that lead may have contributed to this failure. We know that lead causes miscarriages and sterility, and that human bones store ninety percent of the body's total burden of lead. The fact that poisonous levels of lead have been measured in the exhumed bones of Roman aristocrats should give us pause, for per capita use of lead by the Romans apparently reached only fifty percent of what it is in the United States today.

Our bodies absorb up to ten percent of the lead we eat, but up to fifty percent of the lead we breathe. In contrast to the atmosphere surrounding those Roman aristocrats, the atmosphere of our metropolitan areas is filled with lead, mostly from the exhaust of automobiles. This cloud of pollution seems to be increasing in area rather than density.

Much of the lead we take in is usually excreted in the urine, but a portion accumulates in the bones, replacing some of the calcium there. Under certain conditions, that lead may be released into the blood at toxic levels. Lead poisoning symptoms can appear in different parts of the body: the gastrointestinal tract, the central nervous system, the heart, the kidneys, and the liver. Apparently any amount of lead in the human body does some damage, but the effects of subclinical toxicity are difficult to identify. Uncertainty about the nature of low-level lead poisoning makes action to combat the problem frustratingly difficult to generate.

The reading passages in this test are brief excerpts or adaptations of excerpts from published material. The ideas contained in them do not necessarily represent the opinions of the College Board or Educational Testing Service. To make the text suitable for testing purposes, we may in some cases have altered the style, contents, or point of view of the original.

21. The passage is chiefly concerned with

(A) comparing the effect of lead with that of other atmospheric pollutants
(B) discussing the harm that can result from the absorption of lead
(C) suggesting how society can protect itself from chemical poisoning
(D) presenting a new theory to explain the fall of the Roman Empire
(E) showing the additive toxicity of lead with other environmental poisons

22. The passage suggests that by Roman times lead containers were widely used for which of the following reasons?

I. Lead was in abundant supply.
II. Lead imparted a pleasant taste to food and drink.
III. Lead was considered an antidote to copper poisoning.

(A) I only
(B) II only
(C) I and II only
(D) II and III only
(E) I, II, and III

23. The author's primary point in discussing the Roman aristocracy is best summarized by which of the following axioms?

(A) When in Rome, do as the Romans do.
(B) Power corrupts; absolute power corrupts absolutely.
(C) Every cloud has a silver lining.
(D) The past is prologue.
(E) No news is good news.

24. On the basis of the information in the passage, which of the following would do most to reduce the hazards currently associated with exposure to lead?

(A) Banning the use of metal containers for food and beverages
(B) Increasing the amount of calcium in daily diets
(C) Drinking large amounts of water
(D) Reducing the number of lead smelting plants
(E) Reducing the amount of lead in gasoline

25. The tone of the passage is best described as

(A) cautionary
(B) defensive
(C) cynical
(D) conspiratorial
(E) inspirational

GO ON TO THE NEXT PAGE

The decision to use the Black man as a soldier against the Confederacy did not really grow out of any broad humanitarian resolve. General Halleck put the thing quite bluntly in a message to General Grant in March 1863. It was good policy, he said, to withdraw as many slaves from the South as possible; and an equally good policy, having withdrawn them, to use them to help win the war. If Grant found—as he undoubtedly would—that many of the people in his army objected, he must ride down their objections and see that this new policy was carried out.

This new policy was a good deal more far-reaching than Halleck dreamed. To accept the Black man as a soldier in the Union army was to state, in a backhanded but decisive way, that the base of membership in the American community had been immeasurably widened. Once widened, it could not again be narrowed. The war henceforth would be fought for this expanded base, even though some of the men who were most effectively fighting it had no idea that the base needed to be expanded.

Grant dutifully went to work, ordering his staff not only to organize Black regiments and render them effective, but also to remove prejudice against them. Removing that prejudice would not be easy, for some officers and enlisted men had vowed that they would throw down their arms and go home if Black men became soldiers. This anarchic opposition was quickly put down, partly because of Grant's orders and partly because of the unexpected intervention of a rather unlikely hero—lanky, dry-as-dust Lorenzo Thomas, adjutant general of the army, the paper shuffler from Washington. Part of Thomas' job was to speed the raising of Black regiments, and he took to this with crusty enthusiasm. He called troops together and warned them that Blacks fleeing from slavery were to be made welcome: "They are to be received with open arms; they are to be fed and clothed; they are to be armed." He was empowered, he added, to dismiss from the army "any man, be his rank what it may, whom I find maltreating the freedmen. This part of my duty I will most assuredly perform if any case comes before me."

One discontented army division was specially addressed by Thomas. Men who left the army because of the recruiting of Blacks, he warned, would be considered guilty of treason and would be shot, and there would be courts-martial for all who interfered with the program. The men talked it over around campfires afterward and decided to cooperate.

26. According to the passage, Halleck's order to Grant was motivated by considerations best described as

(A) capricious (B) ideological (C) compassionate (D) vengeful (E) pragmatic

27. According to the passage, in his message to Grant, Halleck anticipated which of the following difficulties?

(A) Reluctance of Black men to enlist
(B) Grant's objections to the proposal
(C) Strong disapproval from White soldiers
(D) Inadequate time to ready the new recruits for battle
(E) The public outcry against the policy

28. The author probably considers Lorenzo Thomas "a rather unlikely hero" (line 32) because Thomas

(A) was known to lack courage
(B) seemed a dull bureaucrat
(C) wielded no political clout
(D) was opposed to Halleck and Grant
(E) had little regard for army procedure

29. All of the following can be inferred from the passage to be measures taken by the Union army to accommodate Black soldiers EXCEPT

(A) providing the necessities of life
(B) training them for combat missions
(C) supplying them with needed weaponry
(D) granting them a voice in setting strategy
(E) punishing those who mistreated them

30. The author attributes such success as Halleck's policy had to

(A) military ingenuity
(B) urgency of need
(C) strong high-level support
(D) good fortune
(E) general good will

GO ON TO THE NEXT PAGE

Select the word or set of words that best completes each of the following sentences.

31. This book has neither merit nor distinction, and it all but ---- whatever prestige the author may once have had.

(A) challenges (B) maximizes (C) epitomizes (D) nullifies (E) encompasses

32. Far from exercising a counterinfluence to intellectual orthodoxy, the movement itself has become a center of ----.

(A) conformity (B) notoriety (C) enmity (D) theology (E) idealism

33. People, being prisoners of ----, have made falling a basic metaphor for failure, from the fall of the stock market to the fall of a government.

(A) politics (B) gravity (C) greed (D) turbulence (E) emotion

34. The movie avoids many of the ---- of the novel, bringing into sharper focus characters who originally were amiable or disagreeable ----.

(A) subtleties. .monsters
(B) excellences. .stereotypes
(C) allusions. .individuals
(D) particulars. .nonentities
(E) shortcomings. .blurs

35. Even the most insulated and ---- government has to be concerned today about the popular mind; some systems may be less ---- than others, but at some point all must pay attention.

(A) parochial. .vociferous
(B) corrupt. .theoretical
(C) arbitrary. .sensitive
(D) obscure. .refined
(E) vibrant. .responsive

Each question below consists of a related pair of words or phrases, followed by five lettered pairs of words or phrases. Select the lettered pair that best expresses a relationship similar to that expressed in the original pair.

Example:

YAWN : BOREDOM :: (A) dream : sleep (B) anger : madness (C) smile : amusement (D) face : expression (E) impatience : rebellion

Ⓐ Ⓑ ● Ⓓ Ⓔ

36. GRAPE : VINE :: (A) wire : pole (B) snail : shell (C) cherry : pie (D) pumpkin : seed (E) apple : tree

37. SUIT : OVERCOAT :: (A) wig : hairdo (B) finger : glove (C) parasol : sun (D) shoes : galoshes (E) uniform : costume

38. BAT : MAMMAL :: (A) pine : tree (B) pup : seal (C) butterfly : insect (D) starfish : clam (E) ram : sheep

39. PLAGIARIZE : WORDS :: (A) embezzle : funds (B) imagine : visions (C) renovate : repairs (D) paint : colors (E) edit : publications

40. ENDURE : SURVIVOR :: (A) condemn : culprit (B) applaud : performer (C) evade : guardian (D) excel : imitator (E) compete : rival

41. PROGRAM : DRAMA :: (A) scale : map (B) agenda : meeting (C) footnote : article (D) amendment : bill (E) ticket : performance

42. VENDETTA : REVENGE ::
(A) exploration : discovery
(B) excitement : frenzy
(C) investment : deficit
(D) mistake : correction
(E) insomnia : nightmare

43. PREMISE : ARGUMENT ::
(A) location : filming
(B) profit : contract
(C) foundation : edifice
(D) presentation : package
(E) referee : dispute

44. SUBJUGATE : OBEDIENCE ::
(A) think : intelligence (B) arrest : illegality (C) frighten : apprehension (D) annoy : mistake (E) describe : event

45. TEMPER : ACTION :: (A) breathe : air (B) soothe : pleasure (C) soften : blow (D) operate : machine (E) shock : audience

S T O P

IF YOU FINISH BEFORE TIME IS CALLED, YOU MAY CHECK YOUR WORK ON THIS SECTION ONLY. DO NOT WORK ON ANY OTHER SECTION IN THE TEST.

SECTION 2

Time—30 minutes

25 QUESTIONS

In this section solve each problem, using any available space on the page for scratchwork. Then decide which is the best of the choices given and blacken the corresponding space on the answer sheet.

The following information is for your reference in solving some of the problems.

Circle of radius r: Area $= \pi r^2$; Circumference $= 2\pi r$
The number of degrees of arc in a circle is 360.
The measure in degrees of a straight angle is 180.

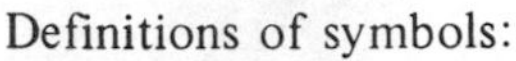

Definitions of symbols:

$=$	is equal to	$\leq$	is less than or equal to
$\neq$	is unequal to	$\geq$	is greater than or equal to
$<$	is less than	$\parallel$	is parallel to
$>$	is greater than	$\perp$	is perpendicular to

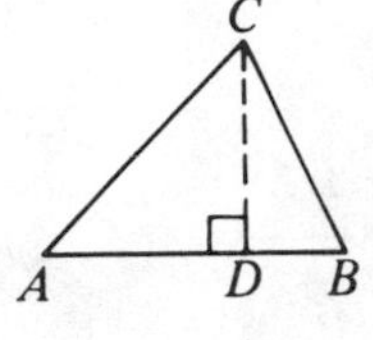

Triangle: The sum of the measures in degrees of the angles of a triangle is 180.

If $\angle CDA$ is a right angle, then

(1) area of $\triangle ABC = \dfrac{AB \times CD}{2}$

(2) $AC^2 = AD^2 + DC^2$

Note: Figures which accompany problems in this test are intended to provide information useful in solving the problems. They are drawn as accurately as possible EXCEPT when it is stated in a specific problem that its figure is not drawn to scale. All figures lie in a plane unless otherwise indicated. All numbers used are real numbers.

---

1. If $(2+3)(n+5)=30$, then $n =$

(A) 0 (B) 1 (C) 2 (D) 5 (E) 6

	Arthur	Bob
Round 1	15	47
Round 2	11	15
Round 3	47	49
Round 4	60	3
Round 5	17	34
Total	150	148

2. Arthur and Bob played five rounds of a card game. The table above shows their scores in the individual rounds. By how many points was Bob leading Arthur at the end of the first three rounds?

(A) 2 (B) 4 (C) 32 (D) 38 (E) 48

3. If $\dfrac{3^2+3^2+3^2}{3^x} = 3$, then $x =$

(A) 2
(B) 3
(C) 9
(D) 27
(E) 81

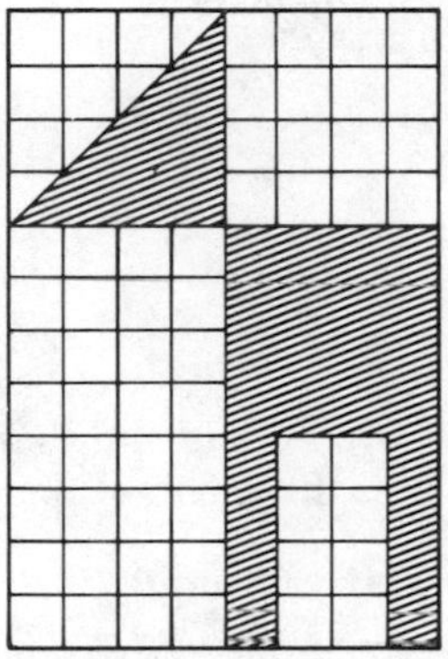

4. In the grid of squares above, each small square has side of length 1. What is the sum of the areas of the shaded regions?

(A) 48 (B) 40 (C) 32 (D) 24 (E) 16

5. If the first and last digits are interchanged in each of the following numbers, which will yield the number with the least value?

(A) 4,321 (B) 3,241 (C) 2,431
(D) 4,231 (E) 3,421

GO ON TO THE NEXT PAGE

6. If $\frac{2x}{3} = 8$, then $4x =$

(A) 12 (B) 16 (C) 24 (D) 32 (E) 48

Card	Entry
A	N
B	$N \times 2$
C	$(N \times 2) \div 3$
D	$[(N \times 2) \div 3] + 15$
E	$[(N \times 2) \div 3] + 15 - 1$

7. According to the table above, which card has the entry with the greatest value when $N = 15$?

(A) *A* (B) *B* (C) *C* (D) *D* (E) *E*

8. If x and y are positive numbers, $xy = 24$, and $\frac{x}{y} = \frac{3}{2}$, what is the value of x ?

(A) 3
(B) 4
(C) 6
(D) 8
(E) 12

9. If the lengths of two sides of an isosceles triangle are 5 and 9, what is the length of the third side?

(A) 4 (B) 5 (C) 7 (D) 9
(E) It cannot be determined from the information given.

10. If $x = 9.000001$, then $\frac{x^2 - 7x + 6}{x - 1}$ rounded to the nearest whole number is

(A) 3
(B) 6
(C) 8
(D) 15
(E) 24

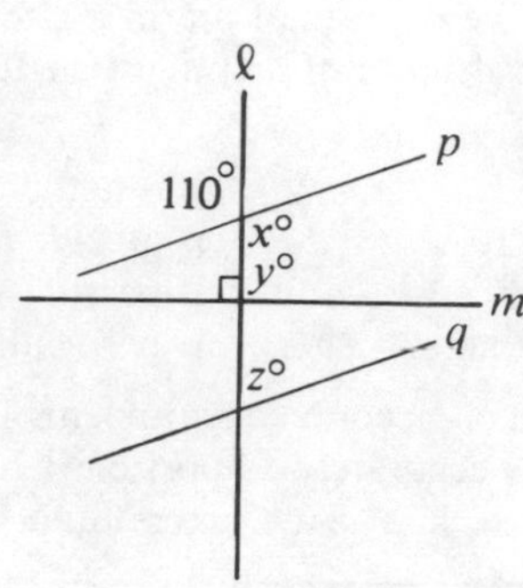

11. In the figure above, ℓ is perpendicular to m and p is parallel to q. What is the value of $x + y + z$?

(A) 180 (B) 220 (C) 230
(D) 270 (E) 310

12. Jean worked x hours and earned \$20. Pam worked y hours and earned \$40. If they both earn the same hourly wage and $x + y = 15$, how many hours did Jean work?

(A) 2
(B) 4
(C) 5
(D) 8
(E) 10

GO ON TO THE NEXT PAGE

13. The average (arithmetic mean) of Pat's scores for 3 rounds of golf was 75. If the average of her scores of the first 2 rounds was also 75, what was her score for the third round?

(A) 70
(B) 75
(C) 80
(D) 85
(E) It cannot be determined from the information given.

14. If $5m + 4n = 14$ and $4m + 3n = 11$, then $7(m + n) =$

(A) 7
(B) 14
(C) 21
(D) 28
(E) 35

15. If 5 people share a cash prize equally, what percent of the prize do 2 of them together receive?

(A) 5% (B) 10% (C) 20%
(D) 25% (E) 40%

16. Two circles with radii r and $r + 2$ have areas that differ by 8π. What is the radius of the <u>larger</u> circle?

(A) 1
(B) 2
(C) 3
(D) 8
(E) 9

17. For how many two-digit positive numbers will doubling the tens' digit yield a two-digit number that is double the original number?

(A) None (B) One (C) Two
(D) Three (E) Four

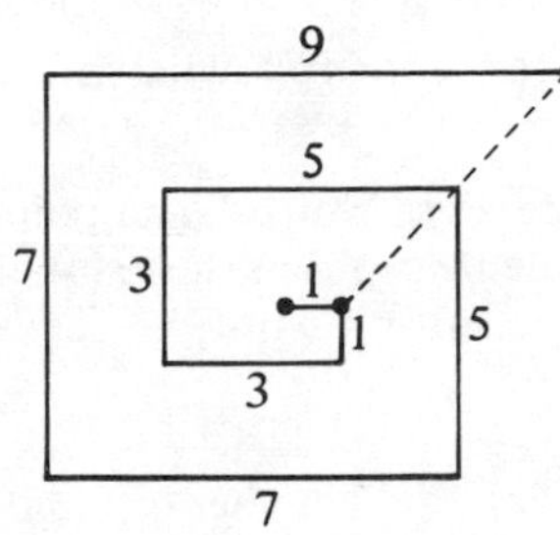

18. The figure above is formed by connecting perpendicular line segments that have lengths as shown. What is the length of the dashed line segment?

(A) 5 (B) $2\sqrt{7}$ (C) $4\sqrt{2}$
(D) $\sqrt{34}$ (E) $\sqrt{41}$

19. The operation $\odot$ is defined for all numbers s and t by the equation $s \odot t = st + 1$. For example, $4 \odot 5 = 4 \cdot 5 + 1 = 21$. If $s \neq 0$ and r is a number such that $s \odot r = 1$, then $r =$

(A) $-\frac{1}{s}$

(B) 0

(C) $-s + 1$

(D) $\frac{1}{s}$

(E) $s + 1$

GO ON TO THE NEXT PAGE

Questions 20-21 refer to the following game.

A computer generates "words," and points are assigned as shown in the table below each time any of the four letter pairs given appears in a word.

Letter Pair	Number of Points
"AA"	10
"AB"	4
"BA"	3
"BB"	5

For example, the word BABT is assigned 3 points for "BA" and 4 more for "AB," making a total of 7 points.

20. Which of the following words would be assigned the most points?

(A) SABBAQ
(B) BUBBLZ
(C) TABBYL
(D) BARNAB
(E) AARDVA

21. If 12 points are assigned to a certain word, which of the following statements must be true?

I. AA is not in the word.
II. AB and BA are both in the word.
III. If BB is in the word, then AB is in the word.

(A) I only (B) II only (C) III only
(D) I and III only (E) I, II, and III

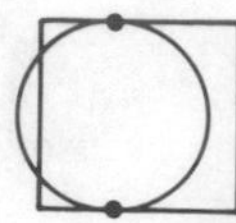

22. In the figure above, the area of the square with two sides tangent to the circle is $4a^2\pi$. What is the area of the circle?

(A) $a\pi^2$ (B) $a^2\pi^2$ (C) $a^2\pi$ (D) $2a^2\pi$
(E) It cannot be determined from the information given.

---

23. The sum of n consecutive positive integers is always an even integer if n is a multiple of

(A) 2
(B) 3
(C) 4
(D) 5
(E) 6

24. The ratio of John's allowance to Mary's is 2 to 5. The ratio of John's allowance to Bill's is 3 to 7. What is the ratio of Mary's allowance to Bill's ?

(A) 15 to 14
(B) 14 to 15
(C) 10 to 21
(D) 35 to 6
(E) 6 to 35

25. If the volume of a cube is 1 cubic centimeter, then the distance from any vertex to the center point inside the cube is

(A) $\frac{1}{2}$ cm

(B) $\frac{\sqrt{2}}{2}$ cm

(C) $\sqrt{2}$ cm

(D) $\frac{\sqrt{3}}{2}$ cm

(E) $\sqrt{3}$ cm

S T O P

IF YOU FINISH BEFORE TIME IS CALLED, YOU MAY CHECK YOUR WORK ON THIS SECTION ONLY. DO NOT WORK ON ANY OTHER SECTION IN THE TEST.

SECTION 4

Time—30 minutes

40 QUESTIONS

For each question in this section, choose the best answer and blacken the corresponding space on the answer sheet.

Each question below consists of a word in capital letters, followed by five lettered words or phrases. Choose the word or phrase that is most nearly opposite in meaning to the word in capital letters. Since some of the questions require you to distinguish fine shades of meaning, consider all the choices before deciding which is best.

Example:

GOOD: (A) sour (B) bad (C) red (D) hot (E) ugly

Ⓐ ● Ⓒ Ⓓ Ⓔ

1. SINCERE: (A) puzzled (B) depressed (C) repetitive (D) dishonest (E) unimaginative

2. ANCHOR: (A) release from restraint (B) ease anxiety (C) gauge accurately (D) board carefully (E) prevent spoilage

3. QUACK:
(A) wealthy inventor
(B) popular politician
(C) qualified physician
(D) well-known writer
(E) entertaining actor

4. IRREPARABLE: (A) amiable (B) mendable (C) grateful (D) confusing (E) divisible

5. BARBARISM: (A) acceptable diction (B) pious excuse (C) liberating action (D) vague definition (E) antagonistic gesture

6. DITHER: (A) repeat (B) blame (C) act with assurance (D) respond as expected (E) record with accuracy

7. COPIOUS: (A) selfish (B) unholy (C) spoiled (D) outrageous (E) sparse

8. SUBTLE: (A) gross (B) brave (C) convincing (D) determined (E) overcautious

9. ACCOLADE: (A) sobriety (B) debate (C) reproach (D) disorder (E) refreshment

10. INVETERATE: (A) nervous (B) unthinking (C) ambiguous (D) naturally skeptical (E) readily changeable

Each sentence below has one or two blanks, each blank indicating that something has been omitted. Beneath the sentence are five lettered words or sets of words. Choose the word or set of words that best fits the meaning of the sentence as a whole.

Example:

Although its publicity has been ----, the film itself is intelligent, well-acted, handsomely produced, and altogether ----.

(A) tasteless. .respectable (B) extensive. .moderate (C) sophisticated. .amateur (D) risqué. .crude (E) perfect. .spectacular

● Ⓑ Ⓒ Ⓓ Ⓔ

11. Explanations given to the patient by the anesthetist prior to surgery often ---- anxiety and ---- the need for analgesics.

(A) intensify. .counteract
(B) parallel. .assume
(C) explore. .prepare
(D) relieve. .reduce
(E) ignore. .preclude

12. The jellyfish's slow pulsing action propels it in a graceful, seemingly ---- drift, but its tentacles contain a poison potent enough to stun a swimming human.

(A) sinister (B) rhythmic (C) murky (D) harmless (E) patient

13. The production's slight romantic appeal depends on its two stars, who are ---- to watch even when they are delivering ---- speeches.

(A) overbearing. .innocent
(B) farcical. .complex
(C) attractive. .creative
(D) impossible. .dull
(E) pleasant. .empty

GO ON TO THE NEXT PAGE

14. The murderous capriciousness of Nero infused the Roman Empire with such pervasive ---- that not even the most ---- citizens felt safe.

(A) distaste. .vulgar
(B) paranoia. .suspicious
(C) enthusiasm. .apathetic
(D) unease. .oppressed
(E) panic. .distinguished

15. His inclination to succumb to flattery made him ---- to the ---- of people who wished to take advantage of him.

(A) immune. .predilection
(B) prejudicial. .intentions
(C) susceptible. .cajolery
(D) resistant. .blandishments
(E) amenable. .rejection

Each question below consists of a related pair of words or phrases, followed by five lettered pairs of words or phrases. Select the lettered pair that best expresses a relationship similar to that expressed in the original pair.

Example:

YAWN : BOREDOM :: (A) dream : sleep
(B) anger : madness (C) smile : amusement
(D) face : expression (E) impatience : rebellion

16. SPILL : POUR :: (A) lose : find
(B) stutter : hear (C) neglect : care
(D) stumble : walk (E) ponder : forget

17. INTRUDER : PRIVACY :: (A) blot : ink
(B) ripple : calm (C) noise : clamor
(D) animal : forest (E) hermit : solitude

18. FADED : COLOR :: (A) humid : moisture
(B) livid : anger (C) pungent : smell
(D) muted : sound (E) cloying : taste

19. PSEUDONYM : NAME :: (A) disguise : identity
(B) motive : purpose (C) talent : stardom
(D) mission : dedication (E) prestige : fame

20. EXCLAIM : UTTER :: (A) suppose : describe
(B) conceal : destroy (C) hurl : throw
(D) blink : stare (E) adore : spoil

21. FLEDGLING : BIRD :: (A) sty : pig
(B) kitten : cat (C) fodder : cow
(D) school : fish (E) stallion : horse

22. OSTENTATIOUS : APPAREL ::
(A) proud : character
(B) palatable : food
(C) bombastic : language
(D) voluminous : correspondence
(E) bedecked : flowers

23. INDOLENT : WORK :: (A) inquisitive : learn
(B) judgmental : accuse (C) blithe : laugh
(D) confident : win (E) modest : boast

24. REPAST : NOURISHES ::
(A) theory : verifies
(B) severance : attaches
(C) remedy : diagnoses
(D) inoculation : immunizes
(E) exhaustion : refreshes

25. NEFARIOUS : VIRTUE ::
(A) remorseless : pity
(B) ingenuous : youth
(C) altruistic : money
(D) melancholy : sympathy
(E) seductive : motivation

GO ON TO THE NEXT PAGE

Each passage below is followed by questions based on its content. Answer all questions following a passage on the basis of what is stated or implied in that passage.

Science fiction gives expression to thoughts and emotions that I think it valuable to entertain. It is sobering and cathartic to remember, now and then, our collective smallness, our apparent isolation, the seeming indifference of nature, the slow biological, geological, and astronomical processes that may, in the long run, make many of our hopes (and some of our fears) ridiculous.

Science fiction stories of this type may explain the hardly disguised political rancor I detected in one article on science fiction. The insinuation was that those who read or wrote it were probably hostile to the state. What lurks behind such a hint is probably something like this. If we were all on board ship and there were trouble among the stewards, I can just conceive the chief steward looking with disfavor on anyone who stole away from the fierce debates in the pantry to take a breather on deck. For up there one would taste the salt, would see the vastness of the water, would remember that the ship had a whither and a whence. What had seemed, in the hot, lighted rooms down below, to be the scene for a political crisis would appear once more as a tiny eggshell moving rapidly through an element in which humanity cannot survive. It would not necessarily change the steward's convictions about the rights and wrongs of the dispute down below, but it would probably show them in a new light.

26. The author asserts that readers and writers of science fiction can most accurately be described as

(A) seekers after an implausible dream
(B) those who view humanity in the largest perspective
(C) refugees from a harsh reality
(D) those who are best qualified to make moral judgments
(E) enemies of the established order

27. The author uses the story of the ship to do which of the following?

(A) Introduce an unpopular idea
(B) Revoke a belief formerly held by the author
(C) Provide an example of a confusing problem
(D) Dramatize a typical science fiction episode
(E) Illustrate a belief held by the author

28. Part of what the author means in saying that the ship has "a whither and a whence" (line 21) is that

(A) individuals in a state should not argue
(B) politicians have sought and will seek office because they desire power
(C) we lack a clear conception of our own reason for existence
(D) we should not forget that the world has a past and a future
(E) what has occurred and what will occur in society is inevitable

There is such an incalculable amount of sand—wet and dry—in the world that geologists have had a hard time accounting for it. Sandstone is a minor source; most sand starts as tiny crystals of quartz which break off granite and other hard igneous rocks. Gypsum is still another source; some of the dunes at White Sands National Monument in New Mexico are almost pure gypsum from a dried-up lake bed.

Wind-borne sand particles scud along the ground, colliding with each other, bouncing off obstructions and wearing off their rough irregularities. Eventually, smoothed and rounded, they approach a perfectly spherical shape—and may keep it, without further wearing, for millions of years. It was once believed that sand grains were rounded while washing down river beds, but laboratory experiments showed that they are too lightweight to abrade each other in water. A cube of quartz a fiftieth of an inch across, it was estimated, would have to be transported by water a distance equivalent to 50 times around the world before it became fully rounded, but wind abrasion would round it off 100 to 1,000 times more rapidly. Thus it is evident that most of the rounded sand grains in the world have been exposed to wind abrasion at one time or another.

29. The author's reference to White Sands National Monument does which of the following?

(A) Illustrates a general statement
(B) Resolves an apparent paradox
(C) Raises a new question
(D) Emphasizes a contrast
(E) Proves a theory

30. The results of the laboratory experiments were significant because they

(A) proved that moving water is the sole agent in the creation of sand
(B) revised current beliefs that scientists held about the size of sand grains
(C) enabled elaborate calculations to take place
(D) called into question a previously accepted model
(E) provided controversial evidence of the makeup of sand

31. The passage indicates that grains of sand assume their final shape primarily through which of the following?

(A) Debilitation (B) Sedimentation
(C) Fragmentation (D) Compounding
(E) Weathering

32. The passage is most probably an excerpt from which of the following?

(A) An informal article written for a general audience
(B) A proposal for a complex research project
(C) A college textbook that explains the laws of physics
(D) A report by a scientist who made a dramatic discovery
(E) An impressionistic memoir by a distinguished geologist

GO ON TO THE NEXT PAGE

(This passage was written in 1855.)

It would seem to us that the late edition of Margaret Fuller's *Woman in the Nineteenth Century* has been unduly thrust into the background by less comprehensive and candid productions on the same subject. Notwithstanding certain defects of taste and a sort of vague spiritualism and grandiloquence that belong to all but the very best American writers, the book is a valuable one. There is no exaggeration of woman's moral excellence or intellectual capabilities; no injudicious insistence on her fitness for this or that function hitherto engrossed by men; but a calm plea for the removal of unjust laws and artificial restrictions, so that the possibilities of her nature may have room for development.

So far as the difference in date allows, there is a striking similarity in the trains of thought of Margaret Fuller and of Mary Wollstonecraft, who wrote *The Rights of Women* sixty years before *Woman in the Nineteenth Century* was written. Both writers communicate a strong understanding of the subject; but Margaret Fuller's mind is like some regions of her own American continent, where you are constantly stepping from the sunny clearings into the mysterious twilight of the tangled forest—she often passes in one breath from forcible reasoning to dreamy vagueness. Mary Wollstonecraft, on the other hand, is nothing if not rational; her grave pages are lit up by no ray of fancy. Margaret Fuller is more of the literary woman, who would not have been satisfied without intellectual production; Mary Wollstonecraft, we imagine, wrote not at all for writing's sake, but from the pressure of other motives.

33. It can be inferred from the passage that which of the following can be found in *Woman in the Nineteenth Century*?

I. Reasoned arguments
II. Lucid assessments
III. Hazy discourses

(A) I only
(B) II only
(C) I and II only
(D) I and III only
(E) I, II, and III

34. In context, the word "engrossed" (line 11) is best interpreted to mean

(A) avoided
(B) pondered
(C) monopolized
(D) collected
(E) mismanaged

35. According to the author, Margaret Fuller and Mary Wollstonecraft are alike in that they

(A) have similar literary styles
(B) belonged to the same generation
(C) became writers for similar reasons
(D) have both been unduly overlooked
(E) express many of the same ideas

GO ON TO THE NEXT PAGE

At midnight it was so dark that the most practiced eye could barely pierce the gloom. But a faint drip of oars struck the ears of the Spaniards as they watched from the decks. A few moments afterward, the sea became suddenly luminous, and six flaming galleons appeared at a slight distance, bearing steadily down upon them before the wind and tide.

The Spanish captain, Medina-Sidonia, and most of his sailors had engaged in King Philip's siege of Antwerp three years before. They realized with horror that the flaming devil-ships designed by Gianibelli on that earlier occasion were now turned against them, rending sky and ocean in their wake. The Spaniards knew that the famous engineer was at that moment in the employ of Queen Elizabeth and the English navy.

In a moment, panic spread with contagious rapidity among Medina-Sidonia's men. There were shouts throughout the fleet, "The fire ships of Antwerp, the fire ships of Antwerp!" In an instant, every cable was cut and every galleon made frantic attempts to escape imminent destruction. The confusion was beyond description. Four of the clumsiest ships became entangled with each other. Two others were consumed by the flaming vessels. Medina-Sidonia, who had been warned by King Philip's spies that some such artifice might be attempted, and who had, early that morning, sent out a party of sailors to search for indications of the scheme, was not dismayed. He commanded every ship to return to its post and await further orders when the danger was past. But it was useless in that moment of unreasonable panic to issue commands.

The despised Mantuan had met with many rebuffs from the Spaniards at King Philip's court. Owing to official incredulity, he had been but partially successful in engineering the Spanish offensive at Antwerp. But now he had his revenge, for by the mere terror of his reputation, he inflicted more damage on Philip's fleet than had been accomplished by all of Queen Elizabeth's seadogs: Howard, Drake, Hawkins, and Frobisher.

While darkness lasted, the uproar continued. When Monday morning dawned, several of the huge Spanish vessels lay disabled, while the rest of the once-mighty fleet drove on toward the Flemish coast. The threatened gale had begun to blow, and those awkward riders of the storm floundered in the heavy seas. Meanwhile, the small but mobile English fleet was all astir to pursue the Spaniards, now drifting into the North Sea.

36. In describing the assault of the English fire ships, the author does NOT explain why

(A) Medina-Sidonia was not surprised by the English tactics
(B) the Spanish sailors were terrified
(C) it was useless for Medina-Sidonia to issue commands
(D) a search party had been sent out that morning
(E) Medina-Sidonia had failed to forewarn his men

37. It can be inferred from the passage that the "despised Mantuan" (line 34) is

(A) the English admiral
(B) Medina-Sidonia
(C) Gianibelli
(D) the captain of one of the "devil-ships"
(E) the king of Spain

38. The phrase "riders of the storm" (line 48) refers to

(A) the English sailors
(B) the Spanish sailors
(C) the English ships
(D) the Spanish ships
(E) Gianibelli's sailors

39. All of the following can be inferred about Medina-Sidonia EXCEPT that he

(A) suspected an assault by the English fire ships
(B) ordered his fleet to surrender
(C) remained calm in the face of attack
(D) was in the employ of King Philip
(E) had been present at the siege of Antwerp

40. According to the passage, the primary cause of the rout of the Spanish fleet was the

(A) Spanish sailors' lack of experience
(B) bravery of the English seadogs
(C) fear inspired by Gianibelli's reputation
(D) rigors of a storm at sea
(E) unreasonable orders of Medina-Sidonia

S T O P

IF YOU FINISH BEFORE TIME IS CALLED, YOU MAY CHECK YOUR WORK ON THIS SECTION ONLY. DO NOT WORK ON ANY OTHER SECTION IN THE TEST.

SECTION 5

Time—30 minutes

35 QUESTIONS

In this section solve each problem, using any available space on the page for scratchwork. Then decide which is the best of the choices given and blacken the corresponding space on the answer sheet.

The following information is for your reference in solving some of the problems.

Circle of radius r: Area $= \pi r^2$; Circumference $= 2\pi r$
The number of degrees of arc in a circle is 360.
The measure in degrees of a straight angle is 180.

Definitions of symbols:

$=$	is equal to	$\leq$	is less than or equal to
$\neq$	is unequal to	$\geq$	is greater than or equal to
$<$	is less than	$\parallel$	is parallel to
$>$	is greater than	$\perp$	is perpendicular to

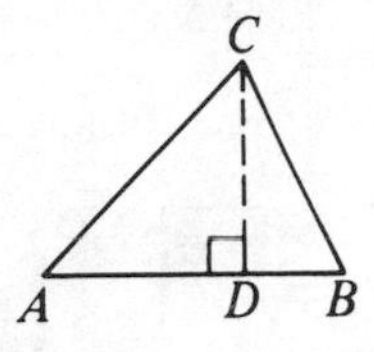

Triangle: The sum of the measures in degrees of the angles of a triangle is 180.

If $\angle CDA$ is a right angle, then

(1) area of $\triangle ABC = \dfrac{AB \times CD}{2}$

(2) $AC^2 = AD^2 + DC^2$

Note: Figures which accompany problems in this test are intended to provide information useful in solving the problems. They are drawn as accurately as possible EXCEPT when it is stated in a specific problem that its figure is not drawn to scale. All figures lie in a plane unless otherwise indicated. All numbers used are real numbers.

---

1. What number increased by 8 equals 3 times the number?

(A) 2 (B) 3 (C) 4 (D) 5 (E) 6

2. If it was 3:15 four hours ago, what time will it be $\frac{1}{2}$ hour from now?

(A) 3:45 (B) 6:45 (C) 7:15
(D) 7:45 (E) 11:45

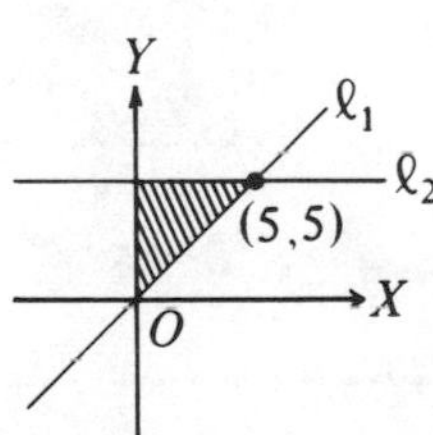

3. In the figure above, if ℓ_2 is parallel to the X-axis, which of the following points lies in the shaded region?

(A) (2, 4) (B) (−2, 4) (C) (2, 6)
(D) (4, 2) (E) (6, 2)

4. Of the following, the closest approximation to $\dfrac{0.512(198.7)}{2.01}$ is

(A) 5 (B) 25 (C) 50 (D) 100 (E) 2,500

5. Jeff is taller than Kim, but he is shorter than Mary. If j, k, and m are the heights in inches of Jeff, Kim, and Mary, respectively, which of the following is true?

(A) $j < k < m$
(B) $k < j < m$
(C) $k < m < j$
(D) $m < j < k$
(E) $m < k < j$

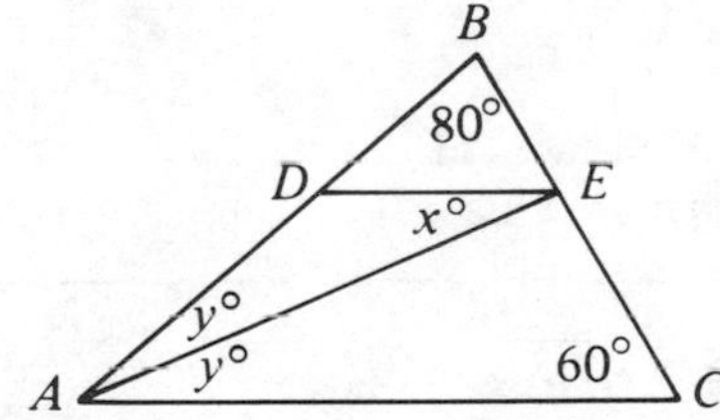

Note: Figure not drawn to scale.

6. In $\triangle ABC$ above, if $DE \parallel AC$, then $x =$

(A) 70 (B) 50 (C) 40 (D) 30 (E) 20

7. On a pool table there are 15 balls, each labeled with a different integer from 1 to 15 inclusive. If 3 even-numbered balls are removed, what fraction of the remaining balls are even numbered?

(A) $\frac{4}{7}$ (B) $\frac{1}{2}$ (C) $\frac{5}{12}$ (D) $\frac{1}{3}$ (E) $\frac{1}{4}$

GO ON TO THE NEXT PAGE

5

Questions 8-27 each consist of two quantities, one in Column A and one in Column B. You are to compare the two quantities and on the answer sheet blacken space

- A if the quantity in Column A is greater;
- B if the quantity in Column B is greater;
- C if the two quantities are equal;
- D if the relationship cannot be determined from the information given.

Notes:
1. In certain questions, information concerning one or both of the quantities to be compared is centered above the two columns.
2. In a given question, a symbol that appears in both columns represents the same thing in Column A as it does in Column B.
3. Letters such as x, n, and k stand for real numbers.

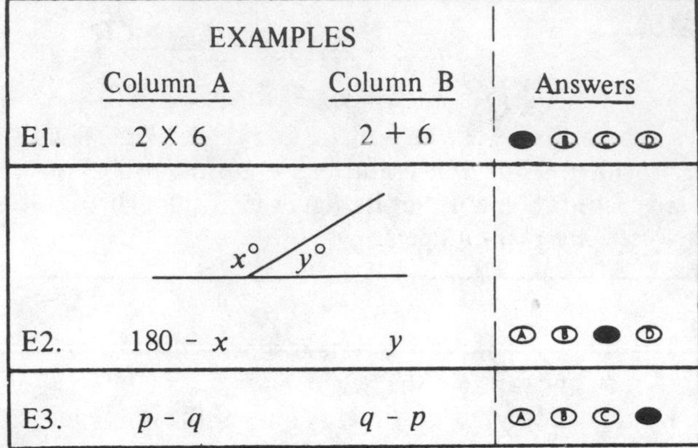

EXAMPLES

	Column A	Column B	Answers
E1.	2×6	$2 + 6$	● Ⓑ Ⓒ Ⓓ
E2.	$180 - x$	y	Ⓐ Ⓑ ● Ⓓ
E3.	$p - q$	$q - p$	Ⓐ Ⓑ Ⓒ ●

	Column A	Column B
	$34 - 2n = 6$	
8.	n	20
	One face of a solid cube is white and the remaining faces are blue.	
9.	The number of faces of the cube that are blue	4
10.	$\sqrt{35} + \sqrt{63}$	$6 + 8$
11.	The number of days in x years	y days
	x is an odd integer and $6 < x < 9$.	
12.	$x + 1$	8

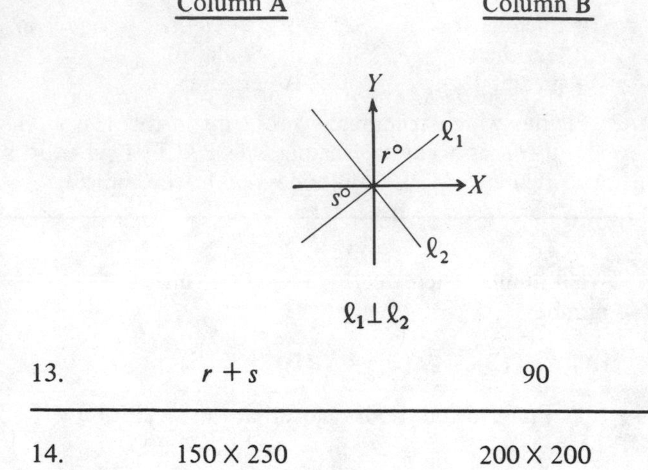

	Column A	Column B
	$\ell_1 \perp \ell_2$	
13.	$r + s$	90
14.	150×250	200×200

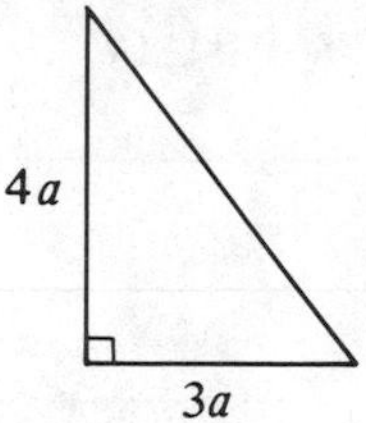

	Column A	Column B
15.	$(3a)^2 + (4a)^2$	$(5a)^2$
	$n > 0$	
16.	$\frac{n+2}{3}$	$\frac{n+4}{6}$
	$x > 1$	
17.	The average speed when x kilometers is traveled in 1 hour	The average speed when 1 kilometer is traveled in x hours

GO ON TO THE NEXT PAGE

SUMMARY DIRECTIONS FOR COMPARISON QUESTIONS

Answer: A if the quantity in Column A is greater;
B if the quantity in Column B is greater;
C if the two quantities are equal;
D if the relationship cannot be determined from the information given.

	Column A	Column B

In $\triangle ABC$, AC is 5 and CB is 8.

18. Area $\triangle ABC$ — 20

For all positive x, $\triangle x = \frac{x}{2}$.

For all negative x, $\triangle x = x^2$.

19.  

$$-\frac{1}{2} = \frac{1}{2}x$$

20. $-x$ — $-\frac{1}{4}$

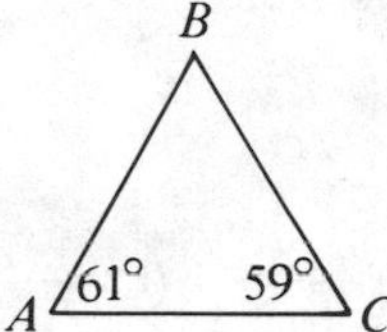

21. Length of AC — Length of BC

---

n is a positive integer and $0 < x < 1$.

22. $\frac{n}{x}$ — n

The average (arithmetic mean) of x and y is 4 and $x - y + 2 = 0$.

23. x — 3

	Column A	Column B

p, q, r, s, and t are all positive integers.

$$p < q < r < s < t$$

$$p \times q = 3 \quad \text{and} \quad s \times t = 50$$

24. r — 4

Of 100 workers, exactly 90 percent pick pears, exactly 80 percent pick apples, and exactly 60 percent pick peaches.

25. The number of workers who pick both apples and peaches — 40

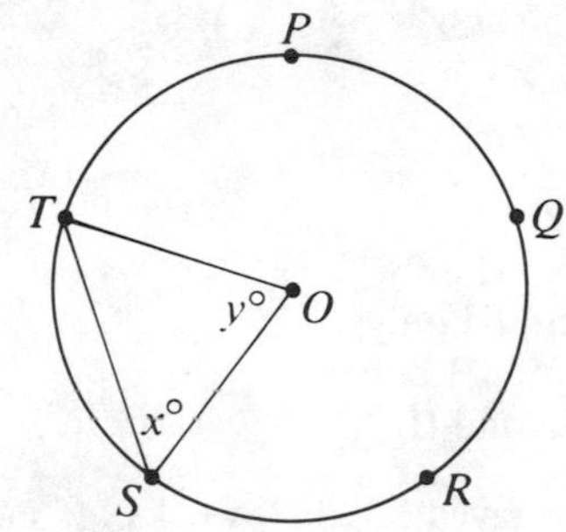

Points P, Q, R, S, and T are equally spaced on the circumference of the circle with center O.

26. x — y

---

a, b, and c are positive.

27. $a + b + c$ — $\frac{1}{a + b + c}$

GO ON TO THE NEXT PAGE

Solve each of the remaining problems in this section using any available space for scratchwork. Then decide which is the best of the choices given and blacken the corresponding space on the answer sheet.

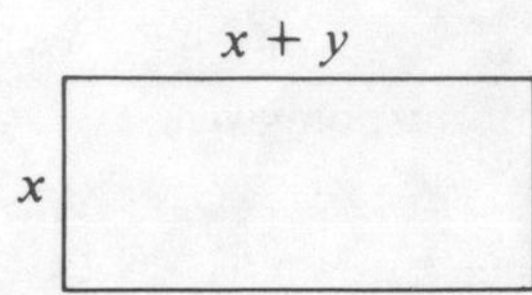

28. The rectangle above has width x and length $x + y$. What is its perimeter in terms of x and y?

(A) $x^2 + xy$
(B) $4x + 2y$
(C) $4x + y$
(D) $2x + 2y$
(E) $2x + y$

---

29. If x and y are positive integers and $x + 2y = 9$, then the greatest possible value of x is

(A) 3 (B) 4 (C) 6 (D) 7 (E) 9

30. If x and y are negative numbers, which of the following must always be negative?

I. $x + y$
II. $x \cdot y$
III. $x - y$

(A) I only
(B) I and II only
(C) I and III only
(D) II and III only
(E) I, II, and III

31. Alice has saved $39 in 6 weeks. If she continues to save at the same weekly rate, in how many <u>more</u> weeks will her total savings be $104 ?

(A) 22
(B) 16
(C) 14
(D) 12
(E) 10

$N \quad O \quad P \quad Q \quad R \quad S$

32. In the figure above, NS is divided into five equal segments as shown. A circle, not shown, with center O and radius $\frac{1}{4}$ the length of NS will intersect NS between

(A) N and O
(B) O and P
(C) P and Q
(D) Q and R
(E) R and S

$$\begin{array}{r} PQ \\ +\,QP \\ \hline TPT \end{array}$$

33. Each of the three letters in the sum above represents a different digit. What is the value of P?

(A) 5 (B) 4 (C) 3 (D) 2 (E) 1

---

34. $\dfrac{1}{10^{19}} - \dfrac{1}{10^{20}} =$

(A) $\dfrac{1}{10}$ (B) $\dfrac{9}{10^{20}}$ (C) $\dfrac{1}{10^{20}}$

(D) $-\dfrac{9}{10^{20}}$ (E) $-\dfrac{1}{10}$

35. The average (arithmetic mean) of three integers p, r, and 6 is 8. Which of the following could NOT be the value of the product pr ?

(A) 17 (B) 18 (C) 77 (D) 80 (E) 81

S T O P

IF YOU FINISH BEFORE TIME IS CALLED, YOU MAY CHECK YOUR WORK ON THIS SECTION ONLY. DO NOT WORK ON ANY OTHER SECTION IN THE TEST.

Correct Answers for Scholastic Aptitude Test Form Codes 4E and 4V

VERBAL		MATHEMATICAL	
Section 1	Section 4	Section 2	Section 5
1. E	1. D	1. B	1. C
2. B	2. A	2. D	2. D
3. D	3. C	3. A	3. A
4. C	4. B	4. C	4. C
5. C	5. A	5. D	5. B
6. A	6. C	6. E	6. E
7. E	7. E	7. B	7. D
8. B	8. A	8. C	*8. B
9. B	9. C	9. E	*9. A
10. B	10. E	10. A	*10. B
11. C	11. D	11. D	*11. D
12. D	12. D	12. C	*12. C
13. A	13. E	13. B	*13. C
14. E	14. E	14. C	*14. B
15. A	15. C	15. E	*15. C
16. B	16. D	16. C	*16. A
17. A	17. B	17. E	*17. A
18. E	18. D	18. C	*18. D
19. C	19. A	19. B	*19. C
20. D	20. C	20. A	*20. A
21. B	21. B	21. D	*21. B
22. C	22. C	22. B	*22. A
23. D	23. E	23. C	*23. C
24. E	24. D	24. A	*24. C
25. A	25. A	25. D	*25. D
26. E	26. B		*26. B
27. C	27. E		*27. D
28. B	28. D		28. B
29. D	29. A		29. D
30. C	30. D		30. A
31. D	31. E		31. E
32. A	32. A		32. C
33. B	33. E		33. D
34. E	34. C		34. B
35. C	35. E		35. B
36. E	36. E		
37. D	37. C		
38. C	38. D		
39. A	39. B		
40. E	40. C		
41. B			
42. A			
43. C			
44. C			
45. C			

*Indicates four-choice questions. (All of the other questions are five-choice.)

The Scoring Process

Machine-scoring is done in three steps:

- *Scanning.* Your answer sheet is "read" by a scanning machine and the oval you filled in for each question is recorded on a computer tape.
- *Scoring.* The computer compares the oval filled in for each question with the correct response. Each correct answer receives one point; omitted questions do not count toward your score. For each wrong answer, a fraction of a point is subtracted to correct for random guessing. For questions with five answer choices, one-fourth of a point is subtracted for each wrong response; for questions with four answer choices, one-third of a point is subtracted for each wrong response. The SAT-verbal test has 85 questions with five answer choices each. If, for example, a student has 44 right, 32 wrong, and 9 omitted, the resulting raw score is determined as follows:

  $$44 \text{ right} - \frac{32 \text{ wrong}}{4} = 44 - 8 = 36 \text{ raw score points}$$

  Obtaining raw scores frequently involves the rounding of fractional numbers to the nearest whole number. For example, a raw score of 36.25 is rounded to 36, the nearest whole number. A raw score of 36.50 is rounded upward to 37.
- *Converting to reported scaled score.* Raw test scores are then placed on the College Board scale of 200 to 800 through a process that adjusts scores to account for minor differences in difficulty among different editions of the test. This process, known as equating, is performed so that a student's reported score is not affected by the edition of the test taken nor by the abilities of the group with whom the student takes the test. As a result of placing SAT scores on the College Board scale, scores earned by students at different times can be compared. For example, an SAT-verbal score of 400 on a test taken at one administration indicates the same level of developed verbal ability as a 400 score obtained on a different edition of the test taken at another time.

How to Score the Test

You can verify the College Board SAT scores reported to you recently by using the information in this booklet along with the copy of your answer sheet. *Before you begin, check that the first two characters (number and letter) of the form code you marked in item 3 on your answer sheet are the same as the form code printed on the front of this booklet.* Compare the responses shown on the copy of your answer sheet with the list of correct answers.

SAT-Verbal Sections 1 and 4

Step A: Count the number of correct answers for *section 1* and record the number in the space provided on the worksheet on the next page. Then do the same for the incorrect answers. (Do not count omitted answers.) To determine subtotal A, use the formula:

$$\text{number correct} - \frac{\text{number incorrect}}{4} = \text{subtotal A}$$

Step B: Count the number of correct answers and the number of incorrect answers for *section 4* and record the numbers in the spaces provided on the worksheet. To determine subtotal B, use the formula:

$$\text{number correct} - \frac{\text{number incorrect}}{4} = \text{subtotal B}$$

Step C: To obtain C, add subtotal A to subtotal B, keeping any decimals. Enter the resulting figure on the worksheet.

Step D: To obtain D, your raw verbal score, round C to the nearest whole number. (For example, any number from 44.50 to 45.49 rounds to 45.) Enter the resulting figure on the worksheet.

Step E: To find your reported SAT-verbal score, look up the total raw verbal score you obtained in step D in the conversion table on page 278. Enter this figure on the worksheet.

SAT-Mathematical Sections 2 and 5

Step A: Count the number of correct answers and the number of incorrect answers for *section 2* and record the numbers in the spaces provided on the worksheet. To determine the subtotal A, use the formula:

$$\text{number correct} - \frac{\text{number incorrect}}{4} = \text{subtotal A}$$

Step B: Count the number of correct answers and the number of incorrect answers for the *five-choice questions (questions 1 through 7 and 28 through 35) in section 5* and record the numbers in the spaces provided on the worksheet. To determine the subtotal B, use the formula:

$$\text{number correct} - \frac{\text{number incorrect}}{4} = \text{subtotal B}$$

Step C: Count the number of correct answers and the number of incorrect answers for the *four-choice questions (questions 8 through 27) in section 5* and record the numbers in the spaces provided on the worksheet. To determine the subtotal C, use the formula:

$$\text{number correct} - \frac{\text{number incorrect}}{3} = \text{subtotal C}$$

Step D: To obtain D, add subtotal A, subtotal B, and subtotal C, keeping any decimals. Enter the resulting figure on the worksheet.

Step E: To obtain E, your raw mathematical score, round D to the nearest whole number. (For example, any number from 44.50 to 45.49 rounds to 45.) Enter the resulting figure on the worksheet.

Step F: To find your reported SAT-mathematical score, look up the total raw mathematical score you obtained in E in the conversion table on page 278. Enter this figure on the worksheet.

SAT-SCORING WORKSHEET

FORM CODES 4E and 4V

SAT-Verbal Sections

A. Section 1:	______ no. correct	− 1/4	(______) no. incorrect	=	______ subtotal A
B. Section 4:	______ no. correct	− 1/4	(______) no. incorrect	=	______ subtotal B
C. Total unrounded raw score (Total A + B)					______ C
D. Total rounded raw score (Rounded to nearest whole number)					______ D
E. SAT-verbal reported scaled score (See the conversion table on the back cover.)					[ ] SAT-verbal score

SAT-Mathematical Sections

A. Section 2:	______ no. correct	− 1/4	(______) no. incorrect	=	______ subtotal A
B. Section 5: Questions 1 through 7 and 28 through 35 (5-choice)	______ no. correct	− 1/4	(______) no. incorrect	=	______ subtotal B
C. Section 5: Questions 8 through 27 (4-choice)	______ no. correct	− 1/3	(______) no. incorrect	=	______ subtotal C
D. Total unrounded raw score (Total A + B + C)					______ D
E. Total rounded raw score (Rounded to nearest whole number)					______ E
F. SAT-mathematical reported scaled score (See the conversion table on the back cover.)					[ ] SAT-math score

Score Conversion Table
Scholastic Aptitude Test
Form Codes 4E and 4V

Raw Score	College Board Reported Score		Raw Score	College Board Reported Score	
	SAT-Verbal	SAT-Math		SAT-Verbal	SAT-Math
85	800		40	450	590
84	780		39	440	580
83	770		38	440	570
82	760		37	430	560
81	750		36	420	550
80	740		35	420	540
79	730		34	410	530
78	720		33	410	530
77	710		32	400	520
76	700		31	390	510
75	690		30	390	500
74	680		29	380	490
73	680		28	370	480
72	670		27	370	470
71	660		26	360	460
70	650		25	350	450
69	650		24	350	440
68	640		23	340	430
67	630		22	330	420
66	620		21	330	410
65	610		20	320	410
64	610		19	310	400
63	600		18	310	390
62	590		17	300	380
61	580		16	290	370
60	580	800	15	280	360
59	570	780	14	280	350
58	560	760	13	270	340
57	560	750	12	260	340
56	550	740	11	260	330
55	540	730	10	250	320
54	540	720	9	240	310
53	530	710	8	230	310
52	520	700	7	230	300
51	520	690	6	220	290
50	510	680	5	210	280
49	500	670	4	210	280
48	500	660	3	200	270
47	490	650	2	200	260
46	490	640	1	200	250
45	480	640	0	200	250
44	470	630	–1	200	240
43	470	620	–2	200	230
42	460	610	–3	200	230
41	450	600	–4	200	220
			–5	200	210
			–6 or below	200	200

Test 10
SAT *Form Code 4X*

(Cut here to detach.)

COLLEGE BOARD — SCHOLASTIC APTITUDE TEST and Test of Standard Written English

Side 1

Use a No. 2 pencil only. Be sure each mark is dark and completely fills the intended oval. Completely erase any errors or stray marks.

1. YOUR NAME: (Print) ______ Last ______ First ______ M.I.

SIGNATURE: ______ **DATE:** ___ / ___ / ___

HOME ADDRESS: (Print) ______ Number and Street

______ City ______ State ______ Zip Code

CENTER: (Print) ______ City ______ State ______ Center Number

IMPORTANT: Please fill in these boxes exactly as shown on the back cover of your test book.

FOR ETS USE ONLY

2. TEST FORM

3. FORM CODE

0	A	J	S	0	0	0
1	B	K	T	1	1	1
2	C	L	U	2	2	2
3	D	M	V	3	3	3
4	E	N	W	4	4	4
5	F	O	X	5	5	5
6	G	P	Y	6	6	6
7	H	Q	Z	7	7	7
8	I	R		8	8	8
9				9	9	9

4. REGISTRATION NUMBER (Copy from your Admission Ticket.)

0	0	0	0	0	0	0
1	1	1	1	1	1	1
2	2	2	2	2	2	2
3	3	3	3	3	3	3
4	4	4	4	4	4	4
5	5	5	5	5	5	5
6	6	6	6	6	6	6
7	7	7	7	7	7	7
8	8	8	8	8	8	8
9	9	9	9	9	9	9

5. YOUR NAME

First 4 letters of last name				First Init	Mid Init
A	A	A	A	A	A
B	B	B	B	B	B
C	C	C	C	C	C
D	D	D	D	D	D
E	E	E	E	E	E
F	F	F	F	F	F
G	G	G	G	G	G
H	H	H	H	H	H
I	I	I	I	I	I
J	J	J	J	J	J
K	K	K	K	K	K
L	L	L	L	L	L
M	M	M	M	M	M
N	N	N	N	N	N
O	O	O	O	O	O
P	P	P	P	P	P
Q	Q	Q	Q	Q	Q
R	R	R	R	R	R
S	S	S	S	S	S
T	T	T	T	T	T
U	U	U	U	U	U
V	V	V	V	V	V
W	W	W	W	W	W
X	X	X	X	X	X
Y	Y	Y	Y	Y	Y
Z	Z	Z	Z	Z	Z

6. DATE OF BIRTH

Month	Day		Year	
Jan.				
Feb.				
Mar.	0	0	0	0
Apr.	1	1	1	1
May	2	2	2	2
June	3	3	3	3
July		4	4	4
Aug.		5	5	5
Sept.		6	6	6
Oct.		7	7	7
Nov.		8		8
Dec.		9		9

7. SEX

- Female
- Male

8. TEST BOOK SERIAL NUMBER

Start with number 1 for each new section. If a section has fewer than 50 questions, leave the extra answer spaces blank.

SECTION 1

1	A	B	C	D	E	26	A	B	C	D	E
2	A	B	C	D	E	27	A	B	C	D	E
3	A	B	C	D	E	28	A	B	C	D	E
4	A	B	C	D	E	29	A	B	C	D	E
5	A	B	C	D	E	30	A	B	C	D	E
6	A	B	C	D	E	31	A	B	C	D	E
7	A	B	C	D	E	32	A	B	C	D	E
8	A	B	C	D	E	33	A	B	C	D	E
9	A	B	C	D	E	34	A	B	C	D	E
10	A	B	C	D	E	35	A	B	C	D	E
11	A	B	C	D	E	36	A	B	C	D	E
12	A	B	C	D	E	37	A	B	C	D	E
13	A	B	C	D	E	38	A	B	C	D	E
14	A	B	C	D	E	39	A	B	C	D	E
15	A	B	C	D	E	40	A	B	C	D	E
16	A	B	C	D	E	41	A	B	C	D	E
17	A	B	C	D	E	42	A	B	C	D	E
18	A	B	C	D	E	43	A	B	C	D	E
19	A	B	C	D	E	44	A	B	C	D	E
20	A	B	C	D	E	45	A	B	C	D	E
21	A	B	C	D	E	46	A	B	C	D	E
22	A	B	C	D	E	47	A	B	C	D	E
23	A	B	C	D	E	48	A	B	C	D	E
24	A	B	C	D	E	49	A	B	C	D	E
25	A	B	C	D	E	50	A	B	C	D	E

SECTION 2

1	A	B	C	D	E	26	A	B	C	D	E
2	A	B	C	D	E	27	A	B	C	D	E
3	A	B	C	D	E	28	A	B	C	D	E
4	A	B	C	D	E	29	A	B	C	D	E
5	A	B	C	D	E	30	A	B	C	D	E
6	A	B	C	D	E	31	A	B	C	D	E
7	A	B	C	D	E	32	A	B	C	D	E
8	A	B	C	D	E	33	A	B	C	D	E
9	A	B	C	D	E	34	A	B	C	D	E
10	A	B	C	D	E	35	A	B	C	D	E
11	A	B	C	D	E	36	A	B	C	D	E
12	A	B	C	D	E	37	A	B	C	D	E
13	A	B	C	D	E	38	A	B	C	D	E
14	A	B	C	D	E	39	A	B	C	D	E
15	A	B	C	D	E	40	A	B	C	D	E
16	A	B	C	D	E	41	A	B	C	D	E
17	A	B	C	D	E	42	A	B	C	D	E
18	A	B	C	D	E	43	A	B	C	D	E
19	A	B	C	D	E	44	A	B	C	D	E
20	A	B	C	D	E	45	A	B	C	D	E
21	A	B	C	D	E	46	A	B	C	D	E
22	A	B	C	D	E	47	A	B	C	D	E
23	A	B	C	D	E	48	A	B	C	D	E
24	A	B	C	D	E	49	A	B	C	D	E
25	A	B	C	D	E	50	A	B	C	D	E

I.N. 574006—110VV25P3015

COLLEGE BOARD — SCHOLASTIC APTITUDE TEST and Test of Standard Written English Side 2

Use a No. 2 pencil only. Be sure each mark is dark and completely fills the intended oval. Completely erase any errors or stray marks.

Start with number 1 for each new section. If a section has fewer than 50 questions, leave the extra answer spaces blank.

	SECTION 3	SECTION 4	SECTION 5	SECTION 6
1	A B C D E	A B C D E	A B C D E	A B C D E
2	A B C D E	A B C D E	A B C D E	A B C D E
3	A B C D E	A B C D E	A B C D E	A B C D E
4	A B C D E	A B C D E	A B C D E	A B C D E
5	A B C D E	A B C D E	A B C D E	A B C D E
6	A B C D E	A B C D E	A B C D E	A B C D E
7	A B C D E	A B C D E	A B C D E	A B C D E
8	A B C D E	A B C D E	A B C D E	A B C D E
9	A B C D E	A B C D E	A B C D E	A B C D E
10	A B C D E	A B C D E	A B C D E	A B C D E
11	A B C D E	A B C D E	A B C D E	A B C D E
12	A B C D E	A B C D E	A B C D E	A B C D E
13	A B C D E	A B C D E	A B C D E	A B C D E
14	A B C D E	A B C D E	A B C D E	A B C D E
15	A B C D E	A B C D E	A B C D E	A B C D E
16	A B C D E	A B C D E	A B C D E	A B C D E
17	A B C D E	A B C D E	A B C D E	A B C D E
18	A B C D E	A B C D E	A B C D E	A B C D E
19	A B C D E	A B C D E	A B C D E	A B C D E
20	A B C D E	A B C D E	A B C D E	A B C D E
21	A B C D E	A B C D E	A B C D E	A B C D E
22	A B C D E	A B C D E	A B C D E	A B C D E
23	A B C D E	A B C D E	A B C D E	A B C D E
24	A B C D E	A B C D E	A B C D E	A B C D E
25	A B C D E	A B C D E	A B C D E	A B C D E
26	A B C D E	A B C D E	A B C D E	A B C D E
27	A B C D E	A B C D E	A B C D E	A B C D E
28	A B C D E	A B C D E	A B C D E	A B C D E
29	A B C D E	A B C D E	A B C D E	A B C D E
30	A B C D E	A B C D E	A B C D E	A B C D E
31	A B C D E	A B C D E	A B C D E	A B C D E
32	A B C D E	A B C D E	A B C D E	A B C D E
33	A B C D E	A B C D E	A B C D E	A B C D E
34	A B C D E	A B C D E	A B C D E	A B C D E
35	A B C D E	A B C D E	A B C D E	A B C D E
36	A B C D E	A B C D E	A B C D E	A B C D E
37	A B C D E	A B C D E	A B C D E	A B C D E
38	A B C D E	A B C D E	A B C D E	A B C D E
39	A B C D E	A B C D E	A B C D E	A B C D E
40	A B C D E	A B C D E	A B C D E	A B C D E
41	A B C D E	A B C D E	A B C D E	A B C D E
42	A B C D E	A B C D E	A B C D E	A B C D E
43	A B C D E	A B C D E	A B C D E	A B C D E
44	A B C D E	A B C D E	A B C D E	A B C D E
45	A B C D E	A B C D E	A B C D E	A B C D E
46	A B C D E	A B C D E	A B C D E	A B C D E
47	A B C D E	A B C D E	A B C D E	A B C D E
48	A B C D E	A B C D E	A B C D E	A B C D E
49	A B C D E	A B C D E	A B C D E	A B C D E
50	A B C D E	A B C D E	A B C D E	A B C D E

9. SIGNATURE: ______________________

FOR ETS USE ONLY	VTR	VTFS	VRR	VRFS	VVR	VVFS	WER	WEFS	M4R	M4FS	M5R	M5FS	MTFS	
	VTW	VTCS	VRW	VRCS	VVW	VVCS	WEW	WECS	M4W		M5W		MTCS	

FORM CODE 4X

SECTION 1

Time—30 minutes

45 QUESTIONS

1

For each question in this section, choose the best answer and blacken the corresponding space on the answer sheet.

Each question below consists of a word in capital letters, followed by five lettered words or phrases. Choose the word or phrase that is most nearly opposite in meaning to the word in capital letters. Since some of the questions require you to distinguish fine shades of meaning, consider all the choices before deciding which is best.

Example:

GOOD: (A) sour (B) bad (C) red (D) hot (E) ugly   Ⓐ ● Ⓒ Ⓓ Ⓔ

1. MEANINGFUL: (A) solitary (B) theoretical (C) insignificant (D) incomplete (E) familiar

2. ADAPTABLE: (A) selfish (B) unwholesome (C) inflexible (D) irritable (E) suspicious

3. DISBAND: (A) obey (B) reverse (C) ascend (D) assemble (E) confess

4. EVAPORATE: (A) provide (B) sparkle (C) cleanse (D) devastate (E) condense

5. OBSTINATE: (A) intermittent (B) yielding (C) uncertain (D) careless (E) despairing

6. COMMUNAL: (A) merciful (B) partial (C) neutral (D) liable (E) individual

7. EON: (A) short time (B) polite refusal (C) valuable article (D) vague impression (E) abrupt explanation

8. LUSH: (A) incisive (B) unvarying (C) barren (D) miniscule (E) solid

9. POLARIZATION: (A) incineration (B) consolidation (C) eradication (D) regeneration (E) validation

10. FLAUNT: (A) drift (B) devote (C) interrupt (D) hide (E) sicken

11. AFFINITY: (A) coarseness (B) limit (C) repulsion (D) angularity (E) uniformity

12. MITIGATE: (A) hesitate (B) receive (C) identify (D) review (E) aggravate

13. EVANESCENT: (A) descriptive (B) causal (C) detrimental (D) protective (E) permanent

14. EXPUNGE: (A) degrade (B) relieve (C) command (D) press (E) record

15. HEDONIST: (A) atheist (B) heretic (C) ascetic (D) renegade (E) novice

Each sentence below has one or two blanks, each blank indicating that something has been omitted. Beneath the sentence are five lettered words or sets of words. Choose the word or set of words that best fits the meaning of the sentence as a whole.

Example:

Although its publicity has been ----, the film itself is intelligent, well-acted, handsomely produced, and altogether ----.

(A) tasteless. .respectable (B) extensive. .moderate (C) sophisticated. .amateur (D) risqué. .crude (E) perfect. .spectacular   ● Ⓑ Ⓒ Ⓓ Ⓔ

16. She was ---- success and eager to create a name for herself.

(A) deprecatory toward
(B) impatient for
(C) querulous about
(D) sated by
(E) impassive to

17. Since what constitutes a proper diet remains a ---- subject on which few experts agree, additional research is ----.

(A) controversial. .required
(B) neglected. .deplored
(C) popular. .unexpected
(D) favored. .prohibited
(E) complex. .redundant

18. Although the Civil War ---- much of the South's railroad network, it ---- the growth of railroads in the North and West.

(A) eliminated. .decreased
(B) accounted for. .encouraged
(C) displaced. .dismantled
(D) destroyed. .stimulated
(E) depended on. .established

19. Diversity is essential in spite of the fact that it ---- universal acceptance of a single doctrine.

(A) underlies (B) reserves (C) presupposes (D) entails (E) precludes

20. He makes his attack with a massive display of scholarship but no great ----; all too often the ---- rather than the rapier is his chosen weapon.

(A) pedantry. .bomb (B) elaboration. .ax (C) emphasis. .pen (D) discrimination. .dart (E) subtlety. .bludgeon

GO ON TO THE NEXT PAGE

Each passage below is followed by questions based on its content. Answer all questions following a passage on the basis of what is stated or implied in that passage.

For the artist in the Black Art movement there is no separation between art and the oppressive conditions of society. Art is meant to be removed from the museums and displayed on tenement and playground walls, in schools and recreational centers, in storefront galleries, and on corner lots. Much of the work is collective; therefore, the personality of the artist is of secondary importance to the message or the content. The paintings are deliberately naïve, the forms simple and bold, and there is little subtlety in color relationships. Many movement murals have been painted by neighborhood children or young adults as storefront art center projects; others have been executed by college students under the direction of an artist-in-residence. Frequently, the murals are designed to teach the young about Blacks who have contributed to the growth of the United States. In institutions attended by Black children the murals thus become history lessons, and the Black leaders portrayed, men and women to be emulated.

The American flag is a recurrent theme in the paintings of many movement artists. In this respect and in others, their work resembles that of the Pop artists of the fifties and sixties. Pop Art attempted to erase the boundaries between "fine art" and the messages communicated by the mass media. Its images are large and bold, and there is some suggestion, at least in spirit, of a type of painting practiced by early colonial artists. Pop embraced the objects constituting the most public, everyday facts of modern life and used them in such a way as to criticize that style of life. There is one great difference, however, between Pop Art and the Black Art movement. While the Pop artists tended to objectify their images, stripping them of their original significance, the movement artists are deeply committed to the images and forms of their work.

A group of Chicago movement artists issued a statement about their goals. In the statement, the members of the group declare that because the Black artist and the creative potential of the Black experience have been excluded from the full spectrum of American arts in the past, they want to provide a new form and context for Black artists in which they can work out problems and pursue aims unhampered and uninhibited by the art establishment. The work of the group members is part of the movement effort to strip art of overrefinement and overemphasis on traditional museums; it supports the effort to create a kind of Black museum in the inner city. In essence these artists are saying to their people, "Our art is yours, you are us, and we are you."

The reading passages in this test are brief excerpts or adaptations of excerpts from published material. The ideas contained in them do not necessarily represent the opinions of the College Board or Educational Testing Service. To make the text suitable for testing purposes, we may in some cases have altered the style, contents, or point of view of the original.

21. All of the following statements about movement murals are supported by the passage EXCEPT:
    (A) They are often communal efforts.
    (B) They are seldom displayed in museums.
    (C) They are usually abstract.
    (D) They may have a historical subject.
    (E) They are concerned with standards and values.

22. The author discusses Pop Art primarily in order to
    (A) discredit the importance of Pop Art
    (B) imply that all art shares the same ideals
    (C) propose that movement artists must refer to earlier trends in art
    (D) predict that movement art will gain greater acclaim
    (E) illustrate some distinctive qualities of movement art

23. According to the passage, movement and Pop artists are similar insofar as both
    (A) refuse to exhibit their work in the traditional manner
    (B) employ a vivid communicative style
    (C) preserve their subjects' initial meaning
    (D) propose to supervise social projects
    (E) consider art to be a group enterprise

24. It can be inferred from the passage that movement artists of the Chicago group believe that museums are
    (A) aesthetically inadequate to display their work
    (B) representative of exclusive social practices
    (C) useful only as a means of acquiring recognition
    (D) potentially useful for educational purposes
    (E) responsible for informing Blacks of their past

25. Which of the following most accurately states the artists' position as implied by the last sentence of the passage?
    (A) All art is equally worthy of praise.
    (B) All innovative art is attractive to the general public.
    (C) Art is an activity that supersedes all others.
    (D) Art and society influence each other.
    (E) Socially aware artists must disguise their real objectives.

In 1834 the chemist Jöns Jakob Berzelius analyzed a peculiar meteorite that had fallen near Alais in France. He found that it contained carbonaceous material and he wondered: Does it contain humus or traces of other organic compounds? Does it possibly indicate the presence of organisms on extraterrestrial bodies? Studying the meteorite, Berzelius noted its resemblance to hardened clay. He established the presence of carbon compounds, but the state of organic chemistry in 1834 precluded further analysis. On the basis of his findings Berzelius decided that the presence of "organic" compounds in the meteorite did not "justify the conclusion that organisms existed in its original locality."

Meteorites in which organic compounds have been identified are called carbonaceous chondrites. These are a subgroup of the large family of stony meteorites known as chondrites because they contain small round bodies–chondrules–of the magnesium-iron silicates olivine and pyroxene. Sooty, black, friable objects, they do not look at all like other meteorites. They are characterized by the presence in small quantities (usually less than 1 per cent of the total weight of the sample) of carbonaceous material other than free carbon. Most of the carbon is neither volatile nor soluble, and it is present in fine-grained sooty material that defies precise analysis even with modern techniques. The smallness of carbonaceous chondrites (the largest on record is about the size of a human head: other stony meteorites weigh as much as a ton) is a reflection of the great amount of ablation, or vaporization, they suffer in their fiery passage through the atmosphere and of the readiness with which they break up. The fireballs accompanying their fall are extremely brilliant even when only a few small stones are recovered.

From about 1890 to 1950, little was published on the carbonaceous chondrites and nothing at all on the organic compounds in them. Then a renewal of interest in meteorites once again focused attention on these remarkable objects. The first modern investigation of the organic compounds was that of George G. Mueller, who analyzed the carbonaceous material in the Cold Bokkeveld meteorite. With organic solvents he extracted 1.1 per cent of the sample as a resinous material consisting of organic compounds mixed with free sulphur. A solution of the material in benzene did not rotate the plane of polarized light, which indicated that the material contained no optically active compounds. This finding was significant because optically active compounds are universally present in living organisms. The optical activity of hydrocarbons that have originated in biological material is low, however, and the level of activity could have been less than the sensitivity of Mueller's instrument.

26. The tone of the author's discussion of the work of Berzelius can best be described as

(A) skeptical (B) impersonal (C) apologetic (D) enthusiastic (E) indignant

27. The author's mention of "the state of organic chemistry in 1834" (line 10) indicates that

(A) Berzelius was unable to pursue his analysis further
(B) Berzelius jumped to an unwarranted conclusion
(C) Berzelius should have carried his experiments further
(D) Berzelius' findings should be disregarded
(E) Berzelius' findings were accurate

28. The author mentions the fireballs accompanying the fall of carbonaceous chondrites in order to emphasize

(A) the great amount of carbon in their makeup
(B) the ease with which they can be identified
(C) the improbability of their containing organic substances
(D) the amount of ablation they undergo in the atmosphere
(E) their similarity to other meteorites

29. Mueller's determination that his sample contained no optically active compounds suggests that

(A) the sample was too old to allow an accurate determination
(B) the experiment had not been performed properly
(C) the carbon compounds in the sample probably had not been present in living organisms
(D) living organisms in his sample probably did not contain such compounds
(E) there were no carbon compounds in the sample with which he was working

30. According to the author, one possible reason for Mueller's failure to detect optically active compounds in his sample is that

(A) such compounds cannot be analyzed by any known method
(B) their activity is so slight as to be very difficult to detect
(C) the compounds being studied were insoluble
(D) the presence of sulfur in the meteorite interfered with the analysis
(E) the meteorite being studied was not a carbonaceous chondrite

GO ON TO THE NEXT PAGE

1

Select the word or set of words that best completes each of the following sentences.

31. Her sense of time was oddly ----: ten minutes sometimes seemed like an hour.

(A) credible (B) distorted (C) idealized (D) consistent (E) formidable

32. Narrowing the eyes when startled by a sudden noise or a noxious stimulus is ---- response, serving to reduce the exposure of sense organs to injury.

(A) an imaginative (B) a protective (C) a corrective (D) a therapeutic (E) an impaired

33. As a people, the Aztecs were full of contradictions: ---- and yet prizing humility, ---- and yet obliging and kind.

(A) arrogant. .benevolent
(B) pious. .gallant
(C) provincial. .sullen
(D) tolerant. .competitive
(E) proud. .implacable

34. His brilliant prose style is sometimes ---- by his lapses into ---- reflection and pretentious language.

(A) achieved. .facile
(B) extended. .whimsical
(C) disrupted. .understated
(D) anticipated. .personal
(E) marred. .banal

35. The study of crowds and groups is more than ---- in an age characterized by interdependence and ---- action.

(A) academic. .collective
(B) difficult. .intellectual
(C) vigorous. .assertive
(D) erudite. .formal
(E) general. .specific

Each question below consists of a related pair of words or phrases, followed by five lettered pairs of words or phrases. Select the lettered pair that best expresses a relationship similar to that expressed in the original pair.

Example:

YAWN : BOREDOM :: (A) dream : sleep (B) anger : madness (C) smile : amusement (D) face : expression (E) impatience : rebellion

Ⓐ Ⓑ ● Ⓓ Ⓔ

36. GOGGLES : EYES :: (A) thumbs : fingers (B) noises : ears (C) stilts : legs (D) gloves : hands (E) dimples : cheeks

37. PARAGRAPH : SENTENCES :: (A) cover : pages (B) book : chapters (C) grammar : errors (D) directory : graphs (E) summary : comments

38. PAW : BEAR :: (A) tail : monkey (B) gill : fish (C) wing : bird (D) cub : lion (E) hoof : zebra

39. IMPLY : PROFESS :: (A) propose : negate (B) vacillate : pause (C) hint : announce (D) contemplate : deliberate (E) invite : accept

40. CALLOUS : SENSITIVITY ::
(A) bold : timidity
(B) faultless : perfection
(C) melodramatic : agitation
(D) discriminating : brevity
(E) detrimental : effectiveness

41. FLOE : ICE :: (A) dune : sand (B) bridge : river (C) wake : vessel (D) desert : water (E) blight : plant

42. AMORPHOUS : SHAPE :: (A) aimless : purpose (B) infamous : wealth (C) ambiguous : obscurity (D) stoic : philosophy (E) experimental : idea

43. SOPORIFIC : SLEEP :: (A) antidote : disease (B) narcotic : stupor (C) sedative : tension (D) tonic : immunity (E) liniment : vigor

44. DABBLE : SUPERFICIAL ::
(A) explain : confused (B) repudiate : angry (C) surmise : impartial (D) deter : intelligent (E) invent : resourceful

45. JINGOIST : NATION :: (A) fool : ridicule (B) manager : personnel (C) braggart : self (D) expert : contestant (E) artist : portrait

S T O P

IF YOU FINISH BEFORE TIME IS CALLED, YOU MAY CHECK YOUR WORK ON THIS SECTION ONLY. DO NOT WORK ON ANY OTHER SECTION IN THE TEST.

SECTION 2

Time—30 minutes

25 QUESTIONS

In this section solve each problem, using any available space on the page for scratchwork. Then decide which is the best of the choices given and blacken the corresponding space on the answer sheet.

The following information is for your reference in solving some of the problems.

Circle of radius r: Area $= \pi r^2$; Circumference $= 2\pi r$
The number of degrees of arc in a circle is 360.
The measure in degrees of a straight angle is 180.

Definitions of symbols:

$=$	is equal to	$\leq$	is less than or equal to
$\neq$	is unequal to	$\geq$	is greater than or equal to
$<$	is less than	$\parallel$	is parallel to
$>$	is greater than	$\perp$	is perpendicular to

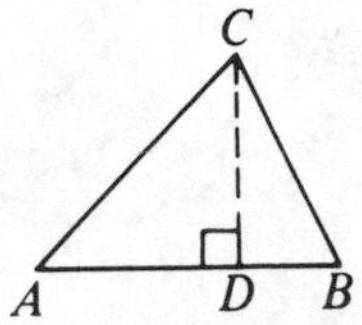

Triangle: The sum of the measures in degrees of the angles of a triangle is 180.

If $\angle CDA$ is a right angle, then

(1) area of $\triangle ABC = \frac{AB \times CD}{2}$

(2) $AC^2 = AD^2 + DC^2$

Note: Figures which accompany problems in this test are intended to provide information useful in solving the problems. They are drawn as accurately as possible EXCEPT when it is stated in a specific problem that its figure is not drawn to scale. All figures lie in a plane unless otherwise indicated. All numbers used are real numbers.

Day	Number Absent
Mon.	7
Tues.	3
Wed.	2
Thurs.	5
Fri.	8

1. What is the average daily absentee rate for the period shown above?

(A) 2 (B) 3 (C) 5 (D) 7 (E) 25

2. A photograph album contains exactly 25 pages numbered consecutively beginning with 1. There are exactly 4 photographs on each even-numbered page and exactly 5 on each odd-numbered page. What is the total number of photographs in the album?

(A) 108 (B) 112 (C) 113
(D) 117 (E) 118

3. If $x = -1$, of the following, which is greatest?

(A) x^2 (B) x^3 (C) $\frac{1}{x}$
(D) $1 + x$ (E) $1 - x$

4. If $v = 3w$, which of the following is equal to $12w - 4v$?

(A) 0 (B) w (C) $2\frac{2}{3}w$ (D) $8w$ (E) $32v$

$$\begin{array}{r} P \\ \times\ Q \\ \hline 15 \end{array} \qquad \begin{array}{r} S \\ \times\ Q \\ \hline 21 \end{array}$$

5. In the multiplication problems above, if P, Q, and S are single digits, then $P \times S =$

(A) 6
(B) 9
(C) 18
(D) 35
(E) 105

GO ON TO THE NEXT PAGE

6. A movie cartoon consists of 4,500 drawings. The animation artist did the first drawing, the sixth, and every fifth drawing thereafter. Of the following drawings in the sequence, which one did the artist produce?

(A) 31st (B) 24th (C) 20th
(D) 15th (E) 14th

7. $\frac{1}{3} \div \left(\frac{1}{3} \div \frac{1}{3}\right) =$

(A) $\frac{1}{9}$ (B) $\frac{1}{3}$ (C) 1 (D) 3 (E) 9

8. For what value of x does a triangle with sides $x + 2$, $3x + 1$, and $7 - 4x$ have a perimeter equal to 11 ?

(A) 0 (B) $\frac{1}{4}$ (C) 1 (D) 7

(E) For no value of x

9. If one week a merchant's income is $160 greater than his weekly rent and the following week his income is $80 less than the rent, what is the difference between the incomes for the two weeks?

(A) $40
(B) $80
(C) $160
(D) $240
(E) It cannot be determined from the information given.

10. The expression "x squide y" is defined as follows: first, square x and then divide the result by the least integer greater than y that will produce an integer solution. The quotient obtained is x squide y. If $x = 12$ and $y = 5$, what is x squide y ?

(A) 2
(B) 12
(C) 24
(D) 29
(E) 36

11. Which of the following CANNOT have more than 2 points in common?

(A) A circle and a triangle
(B) A circle and a rectangle
(C) A line and a circle
(D) Two triangles
(E) A line and a triangle

12. If p, q, and r are the degree measures of the three angles of an isosceles triangle and $p = 100$, then $p - q =$

(A) 20 (B) 40 (C) 50 (D) 60 (E) 80

13. If $6x - 1$ is an odd integer, which of the following represents the next greater odd integer?

(A) $7x + 1$
(B) $7x$
(C) $7x - 1$
(D) $6x + 1$
(E) $6x$

14. A person receives $405 for the first month's work and a $10 a month raise at the beginning of each month thereafter. What will the person's total salary be for the first 6 months?

(A) $2,760
(B) $2,580
(C) $2,480
(D) $2,440
(E) $2,430

GO ON TO THE NEXT PAGE

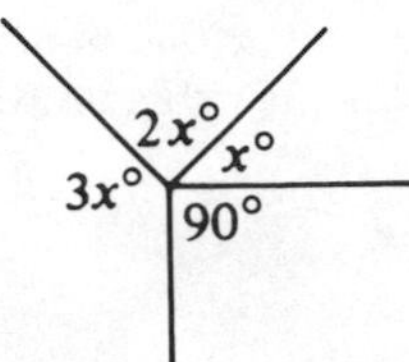

15. In the figure above, the degree measure of the largest of the four angles is how much greater than that of the smallest?

(A) 30 (B) 45 (C) 60 (D) 90 (E) 135

16. If $x^2 + 5x + 6 = (x - 1)(x + 6) + r$, then $r =$

(A) −12 (B) −6 (C) 0 (D) 6 (E) 12

17. In a certain class, on their report cards 10 students received no A's and no B's, 17 students received at least one A, and 13 received at least one B. If 5 students received both A's and B's, how many students are there in the class?

(A) 32
(B) 35
(C) 37
(D) 40
(E) 45

18. On a number line, if point Y is at a distance 3 from point P and point X is at a distance 4 from P, what is the length of XY?

(A) 1 (B) 4 (C) 5 (D) 7
(E) It cannot be determined from the information given.

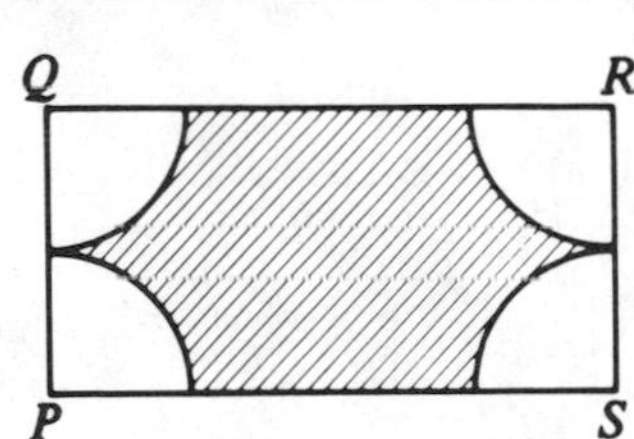

19. In the rectangle above, the shaded region is bounded in part by 4 equal arcs with centers at P, Q, R, and S. If $PQ = 6$ and $QR = 10$, what is the area of the shaded region?

(A) $60 - 9\pi$
(B) $60 - 4\pi$
(C) $32 - 9\pi$
(D) $32 - 4\pi$
(E) $30 - 6\pi$

20. Today Jack is twice as old as Mary was 10 years ago. How old is Mary today if Jack is now y years old?

(A) $\frac{y}{2} - 10$

(B) $\frac{y}{2} + 10$

(C) $y + 10$

(D) $2y - 10$

(E) $2(y - 10)$

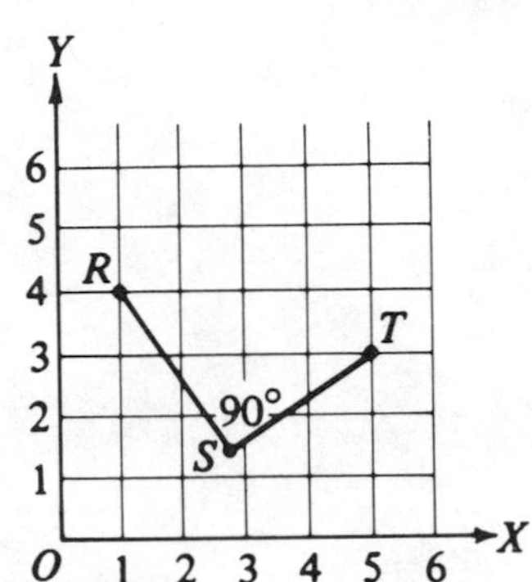

21. In the graph above, $(RS)^2 + (ST)^2 =$

(A) 4 (B) 17 (C) 26 (D) 32 (E) 41

22. If $x = \sqrt{18} + \sqrt{32}$, then $x^2 =$

(A) 48
(B) 50
(C) 64
(D) 82
(E) 98

GO ON TO THE NEXT PAGE

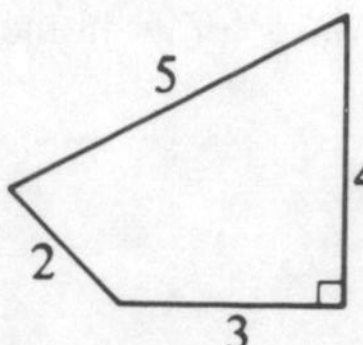

23. In the figure above, what is the area of the quadrilateral?

(A) $6 + 2\sqrt{6}$ (B) $2\sqrt{30}$ (C) 11 (D) 13

(E) It cannot be determined from the information given.

24. For how many 3-digit whole numbers is the average value of the digits equal to 1 ?

(A) 1
(B) 3
(C) 4
(D) 5
(E) 6

25. On a map, 1 centimeter represents 4 kilometers. A circle on the map with a circumference of 3π centimeters represents a circular region with what area?

(A) $6\pi\,km^2$
(B) $12\pi\,km^2$
(C) $36\pi\,km^2$
(D) $72\pi\,km^2$
(E) $144\pi\,km^2$

S T O P

IF YOU FINISH BEFORE TIME IS CALLED, YOU MAY CHECK YOUR WORK ON THIS SECTION ONLY. DO NOT WORK ON ANY OTHER SECTION IN THE TEST.

SECTION 4

Time—30 minutes

40 QUESTIONS

For each question in this section, choose the best answer and blacken the corresponding space on the answer sheet.

Each question below consists of a word in capital letters, followed by five lettered words or phrases. Choose the word or phrase that is most nearly opposite in meaning to the word in capital letters. Since some of the questions require you to distinguish fine shades of meaning, consider all the choices before deciding which is best.

Example:

GOOD: (A) sour (B) bad (C) red (D) hot (E) ugly

Ⓐ ● Ⓒ Ⓓ Ⓔ

1. LICENSED: (A) unnoticed (B) unwritten (C) unstable (D) not formally authorized (E) not properly trained

2. PREDICAMENT: (A) dignified greeting (B) untroubled situation (C) unexpected increase (D) probability (E) disposition

3. SERENE: (A) persistent (B) unreliable (C) nervous (D) shrewd (E) artificial

4. ARTICULATE:
   (A) state honestly
   (B) affect adversely
   (C) ascribe incorrectly
   (D) speak indistinctly
   (E) admire indiscriminately

5. PERIPHERY:
   (A) inner region
   (B) loose connection
   (C) logical arrangement
   (D) hypothetical relationship
   (E) symmetrical placement

6. OSCILLATING: (A) becoming connected (B) gaining sensation (C) swelling quickly (D) remaining steady (E) opening in stages

7. DISPUTE: (A) dispose (B) answer (C) qualify (D) befriend (E) concede

8. UNWIELDY:
   (A) foreseeable
   (B) vulnerable
   (C) of placid disposition
   (D) of manageable size
   (E) of indeterminate nature

9. ACQUIESCE: (A) disagree (B) depart (C) verify (D) distort (E) persuade

10. CORPULENT: (A) lofty (B) dull (C) spare (D) patient (E) courageous

GO ON TO THE NEXT PAGE

4

Each sentence below has one or two blanks, each blank indicating that something has been omitted. Beneath the sentence are five lettered words or sets of words. Choose the word or set of words that best fits the meaning of the sentence as a whole.

Example:

> Although its publicity has been ----, the film itself is intelligent, well-acted, handsomely produced, and altogether ----.
>
> (A) tasteless. .respectable (B) extensive. .moderate (C) sophisticated. .amateur (D) risqué. .crude (E) perfect. .spectacular
>
> ● Ⓑ Ⓒ Ⓓ Ⓔ

11. My suggestion was not so casual as it appeared; I ---- mentioned the election because I knew that she wanted to discuss it.

    (A) ineptly (B) incessantly (C) inadvertently (D) intentionally (E) inconsiderately

12. Bureaucratic squabbles can tie up the government for years and ---- domestic and international problems to the point of ----.

    (A) magnify. .manageability
    (B) reduce. .indignation
    (C) intensify. .crisis
    (D) weaken. .nonexistence
    (E) simplify. .triviality

13. Though there was much ---- among critics over whether or not the play portrayed the "real" Paul Robeson, James Earl Jones's performance was ---- deemed outstanding by audiences and critics.

    (A) commentary. .silently
    (B) controversy. .unanimously
    (C) harassment. .evasively
    (D) disappointment. .instructively
    (E) discussion. .privately

14. Today science, like philosophy, has been ---- in scope: each has ---- its claim to survey all existence and has accepted a province which, if great, is yet smaller than the whole.

    (A) limited. .reiterated (B) narrowed. .resigned (C) expanded. .repudiated (D) fluctuating. .denied (E) receding. .amplified

15. Extremist advocates of the occult claim that existing systems of scientific thought must at least be modified, if not ----.

    (A) evaluated (B) supplemented (C) incorporated (D) implemented (E) overturned

Each question below consists of a related pair of words or phrases, followed by five lettered pairs of words or phrases. Select the lettered pair that best expresses a relationship similar to that expressed in the original pair.

Example:

> YAWN : BOREDOM :: (A) dream : sleep (B) anger : madness (C) smile : amusement (D) face : expression (E) impatience : rebellion
>
> Ⓐ Ⓑ ● Ⓓ Ⓔ

16. VEIN : BLOOD :: (A) wire : cord (B) bone : membrane (C) nose : scent (D) pipe : water (E) tunnel : car

17. REFEREE : CONTEST :: (A) judge : trial (B) defendant : lawsuit (C) noncombatant : war (D) member : union (E) spectator : game

18. SYNONYM : THESAURUS :: (A) date : card catalog (B) definition : dictionary (C) list : roster (D) quotation : novel (E) script : playbill

19. CLASP : HAND :: (A) shoe : foot (B) blink : eye (C) embrace : arm (D) crutch : leg (E) shake : head

20. FIDGET : RESTLESS :: (A) beckon : busy (B) quibble : content (C) ponder : lazy (D) obey : impudent (E) bustle : hurried

21. HOMING PIGEON : BIRD :: (A) balloon : rocket (B) boomerang : missile (C) dirigible : kite (D) fledgling : sparrow (E) bullet : revolver

22. INKLING : CERTITUDE ::
    (A) portent : omen
    (B) hope : despair
    (C) skepticism : dubiety
    (D) misgiving : dread
    (E) pomposity : courtesy

23. FLORID : EMBELLISHMENTS :: (A) candid : ideas (B) verbose : words (C) blatant : voices (D) chimerical : facts (E) monotonous : rhythms

24. HOMELESS : DOMICILE :: (A) childless : orphan (B) impregnable : fortress (C) thirsty : hunger (D) insolvent : money (E) alien : journey

25. DICTUM : AUTHORITATIVE :: (A) libel : defamatory (B) proverb : ethical (C) oath : laudatory (D) accusation : punitive (E) tenet : educational

GO ON TO THE NEXT PAGE

Each passage below is followed by questions based on its content. Answer all questions following a passage on the basis of what is stated or implied in that passage.

Crete was settled about 5000 B.C. by migrants from Greece who journeyed across 60 miles of open sea to reach this island in the Mediterranean. From the beginning the land was too poor for cultivation. To survive, the people had to take advantage of their geographic location. Situated halfway between Egypt and Greece, the Cretans were the first people to develop a modern commercial economy based predominantly on seafaring and trade.

Using evidence from various sources, we can reconstruct some of the details of Cretan life. Archaeological digs support the legend that the people of Crete were ingenious artisans. We know, for example, that shipbuilding was a high point in their technology. The island was well forested, providing timber for ships. Their vessels were seaworthy and must have required careful preliminary designs and expert joinery. They had high, sharply upcurved bows and sterns, and keels plated in bronze that projected some distance beyond the prow, a design which suggests that the boats were intended for ramming. This naval tactic, developed in Crete, dominated sea warfare in classical times.

Because of the inventiveness of the people of Crete, their communities were more prosperous than those of other early civilizations. Trading left the populace with leisure time; bullfights are known to have been a popular diversion. Frescoes show figures dressed in colorful clothes, large gaily decorated hats, and elaborate jewelry. The remains of open-patterned villages suggest an essentially middle-class society. The palace of the priest-kings, the Minos, was as much a commercial center as a palace, reflecting the importance of trade in the Cretan culture.

26. The primary purpose of the passage is to

(A) describe an early culture
(B) explain the technology of shipbuilding
(C) comment on the origin of the settlers of Crete
(D) analyze the advantages of a trade-oriented economy
(E) speculate about the relationship between geography and culture

27. According to the passage, all of the following statements about Crete are true EXCEPT:

(A) The land was not especially suitable for the development of an agricultural economy.
(B) The location of the island enabled the settlers to make a good living by trade.
(C) The island had a well-developed civilization before migrants from Greece arrived.
(D) The island provided an abundant supply of timber.
(E) The island was about as far from Greece as it was from Egypt.

28. The tone of the passage can best be described as

(A) whimsical (B) argumentative
(C) contradictory (D) impatient
(E) objective

GO ON TO THE NEXT PAGE

Mr. Casaubon spent a great deal of time at the Grange during the weeks of his courtship, and the hindrance which this occasioned to the progress of his life's work—*The Key to All Mythologies*—naturally made him look forward the more eagerly to the happy termination of courtship. But he had deliberately incurred the hindrance, having made up his mind that it was now time to adorn his life with the graces of female companionship, to irradiate the gloom which fatigue was apt to cause with the play of female fancy, and to secure in this, his culminating age, the solace of female tendance for his declining years. Hence he abandoned himself to the stream of feeling, and was surprised to find what an exceedingly shallow rill it was. As in droughty regions baptism by immersion could only be performed symbolically, so Mr. Casaubon found that sprinkling was the utmost approach to a plunge which his stream would afford him; and he concluded that the poets had much exaggerated the force of masculine passion. Nevertheless, he observed with pleasure that Miss Brooke showed a submissive affection which promised to fulfill his most agreeable provisions for marriage. It had crossed his mind that possibly there was some deficiency in Dorothea to account for the moderation of his abandonment, but he was unable to discern the deficiency or to figure to himself a woman who would have pleased him better, so that there was clearly no reason to fall upon but the exaggeration of human tradition.

29. Which of the following best expresses Casaubon's principal reason for wanting to be married?

(A) He is passionately in love with Dorothea.
(B) He desires present cheering and future comforting.
(C) He wants to make both Dorothea and himself happy.
(D) He thinks marriage will improve the quality of his scholarship.
(E) He feels it is time to regulate his life and raise a family.

30. It can be inferred that Casaubon views courtship primarily as

(A) an irksome sacrifice to Dorothea's whims
(B) a joy that one should experience before old age sets in
(C) an essential part of the symbolism of marriage
(D) a tradition based on foolish prohibitions
(E) a convention to be observed

31. Which of the following best sums up Casaubon's reasoning about his dissatisfaction with courtship?

(A) Dorothea is deficient in affection; hence, I am disappointed.
(B) I am no longer young; therefore, I must try to moderate my passions.
(C) I simply do not have the temperament for courtship; it can therefore only be disappointing.
(D) People overstate the pleasures of courtship; it cannot live up to its reputation.
(E) Courtship does not take strong emotions into account; it is an outdated tradition.

GO ON TO THE NEXT PAGE

During the 1960's and 1970's, brain researchers developed the very useful, though provisional, "amine hypothesis": depression results from a chemical imbalance of neurotransmitters in the brain. Neurotransmitters are chemicals that carry messages from one nerve cell to the next at lightning speed, telling it to fire or resist firing. Over a dozen neurotransmitters have been identified, but the three most closely studied with respect to mental illness are norepinephrine, dopamine, and serotonin, amines derived from essential amino acids.

The first clue to the role of these three amines came in the late 1950's, when physicians noted that patients taking the drug reserpine to control hypertension became severely depressed, while tubercular patients treated with a new drug, iproniazid, suddenly felt elated. Biochemists studying the brains of rats then discovered that reserpine depleted their stores of norepinephrine and serotonin, whereas iproniazid had the opposite effect.

The amine hypothesis was temporarily threatened by the discovery of the tricyclic antidepressants, new compounds that proved extremely effective against depression but that did not increase the total level of amines in the brains of laboratory animals. The mystery was resolved a few years later when Dr. Julius Axelrod described the way in which norepinephrine is turned off after it has relayed its message at a nerve synapse (the junction between nerve cells): it is reabsorbed by the nerve endings from which it came, to be conserved for future use. Axelrod showed that the tricyclics interfere with this process, thus increasing the amount of norepinephrine that is available to receptors on the next nerve cell. The same proved true of serotonin, and the amine hypothesis was saved.

32. The author's general purpose is to
(A) illustrate the complexity of nerve cell structure
(B) consider competing theories of mental illness
(C) present a biochemical explanation of depression
(D) evaluate the effectiveness of antidepressant drugs
(E) suggest future possibilities for brain research

33. Which of the following can be inferred from the second paragraph?
(A) The combination of reserpine and iproniazid is effective against depression.
(B) Depression is associated with a deficit of norepinephrine and serotonin.
(C) Laboratory animals are more sensitive to reserpine and iproniazid than are humans.
(D) Certain neurotransmitters are themselves causes of depression.
(E) The effects of reserpine and iproniazid vary with brain size.

34. According to the passage, the tricyclics operate by
(A) obstructing the synthesis of amines
(B) freeing certain neurotransmitters for immediate utilization
(C) acting as substitutes for norepinephrine
(D) reducing the nerve cells' need for neurotransmitters
(E) enabling nonessential amines to be used as neurotransmitters

35. Which of the following statements about the amine hypothesis is LEAST supported by the passage?
(A) It is useful in curing a wide variety of brain malfunctions.
(B) It was suggested by seemingly unrelated medical practices.
(C) It may be modified after further experimentation.
(D) It has on occasion been called into question.
(E) It proposes that certain mental disorders are chemically caused.

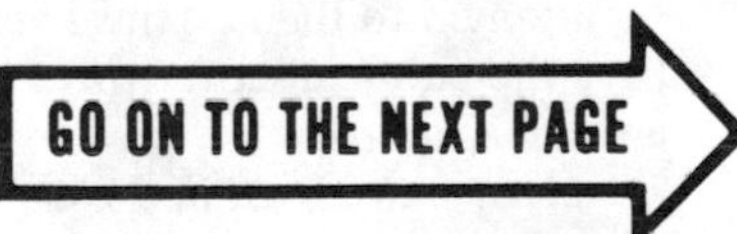

Literary critics have had their go at humor, and I have read some of their interpretations of humorous literature, but without being greatly instructed. Humor can be dissected, as a frog can, but the thing dies in the process and the innards are discouraging to any but the purely scientific mind. Humor has a certain fragility, an evasiveness, which one had best respect. Essentially, it is a mystery.

One of the things commonly said about humorists is that they are really very sad people—clowns with broken hearts. There is some truth in this, but it would be more accurate, I think, to say that there is a deep vein of melancholy running through everyone's life and that a humorist, perhaps more sensible of it than some others, compensates for it actively and positively. Practically everyone is a manic depressive of sorts, with up moments and down moments, and you certainly do not have to be a humorist to taste the sadness of situation and mood. But there is often a rather fine line between laughing and crying, and if a humorous piece of writing brings people to the point where their emotional responses are untrustworthy and seem likely to break over into the opposite realm, it is because humorous writing, like poetical writing, has an extra dimension. It plays, like an active child, close to the big hot fire which is Truth. And sometimes the reader feels the heat.

The world likes humor but treats it patronizingly. It decorates serious artists with laurel and wags with brussels sprouts. It feels that if a thing is funny it is something less than great, because if it were truly great it would be wholly serious. Writers know this, and those who take their literary selves with great seriousness are at considerable pains never to associate their names with anything funny or flippant or nonsensical or "light." They suspect it would hurt their reputations, and they are right. Many poets today sign their real name to their serious verse and a pseudonym to their comical verse, being unwilling to have the public discover them in any but a pensive and sober moment.

Many humorists, in the early stages of their careers, have been asked anxiously by friends when they were "going to write something serious." That occasion is memorable, for it gives them pause to realize that the bright star they are following is held to be not of the first magnitude.

36. The author states that melancholy is a condition

(A) conducive to egotism
(B) universal to humanity
(C) inimical to mystery
(D) caused by insecurity
(E) indicative of sensitivity

37. The author contends that humorists lack

(A) esteem (B) insight (C) emotion (D) popularity (E) subtlety

38. According to the passage, the scientific analysis of humor is

(A) dull but necessary
(B) detailed but obvious
(C) commonplace but misunderstood
(D) possible but inadequate
(E) impressive but difficult

39. Which of the following would the author probably consider most favorable to the future of humor?

(A) More detailed analyses of humorous literature
(B) More frequent use of pseudonyms by humorists
(C) More open-mindedness on the part of the reading public
(D) The curtailment of awards for literary works
(E) The development of a method for treating the manic-depressive personality

40. It can be inferred that the "bright star" mentioned in line 47 of the passage stands for which of the following?

(A) Popularity (B) Wisdom (C) Superiority (D) Wealth (E) Humor

S T O P

IF YOU FINISH BEFORE TIME IS CALLED, YOU MAY CHECK YOUR WORK ON THIS SECTION ONLY. DO NOT WORK ON ANY OTHER SECTION IN THE TEST.

SECTION 5

Time—30 minutes

35 QUESTIONS

In this section solve each problem, using any available space on the page for scratchwork. Then decide which is the best of the choices given and blacken the corresponding space on the answer sheet.

The following information is for your reference in solving some of the problems.

Circle of radius r: Area $= \pi r^2$; Circumference $= 2\pi r$
The number of degrees of arc in a circle is 360.
The measure in degrees of a straight angle is 180.

Definitions of symbols:

$=$	is equal to	$\leq$	is less than or equal to
$\neq$	is unequal to	$\geq$	is greater than or equal to
$<$	is less than	$\parallel$	is parallel to
$>$	is greater than	$\perp$	is perpendicular to

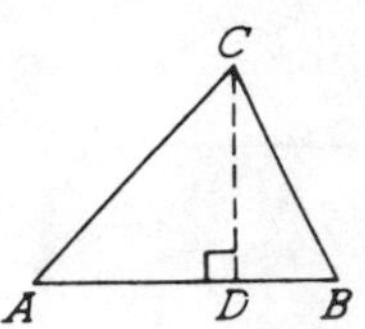

Triangle: The sum of the measures in degrees of the angles of a triangle is 180.

If $\angle CDA$ is a right angle, then

(1) area of $\triangle ABC = \frac{AB \times CD}{2}$

(2) $AC^2 = AD^2 + DC^2$

Note: Figures which accompany problems in this test are intended to provide information useful in solving the problems. They are drawn as accurately as possible EXCEPT when it is stated in a specific problem that its figure is not drawn to scale. All figures lie in a plane unless otherwise indicated. All numbers used are real numbers.

---

1. Which of the following can be divided both by 2 and by 3 with no remainders?

   (A) 56 (B) 63 (C) 76 (D) 81 (E) 96

2. If a synthetic rubber factory can produce 75 pounds of rubber every 30 seconds, how many pounds of rubber can this factory produce per hour?

   (A) 150 (B) 900 (C) 9,000
   (D) 15,000 (E) 135,000

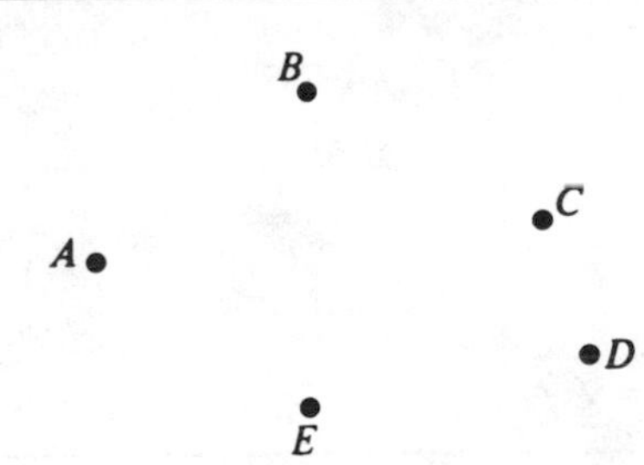

3. How many different line segments can be drawn to connect all possible pairs of points shown above?

   (A) 32 (B) 25 (C) 20 (D) 10 (E) 5

Candy	Cost
A	2 pieces for 5 cents
B	3 pieces for 4 cents
C	4 pieces for 7 cents
D	5 pieces for 6 cents
E	6 pieces for 9 cents

4. According to the table above, which candy costs the least per piece?

   (A) A (B) B (C) C (D) D (E) E

5. Pat rode 5 miles each way from home to the beach at an average rate of 10 miles per hour. If she spent exactly 6 hours at the beach and made no other stops, how many hours was she gone from home?

   (A) $6\frac{1}{2}$ (B) 7 (C) $7\frac{1}{2}$ (D) 8 (E) 10

6. A figure in the plane is said to be "circle-receptive" if a circle touching every side of the figure can be drawn inside the figure, and a circle touching every vertex of the figure can be drawn outside the figure. Which of the following figures is NOT "circle-receptive"?

   (A) 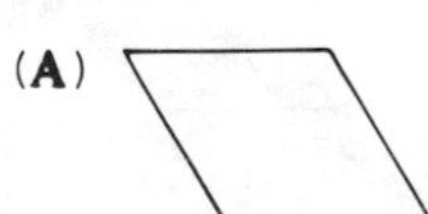
   (B) 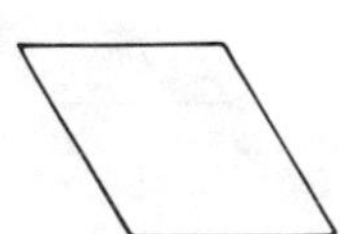 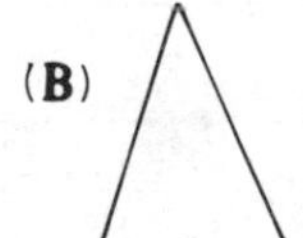
   (C) 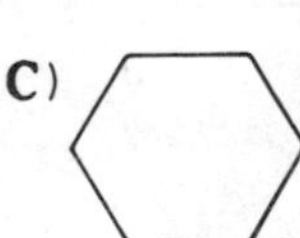
   (D) 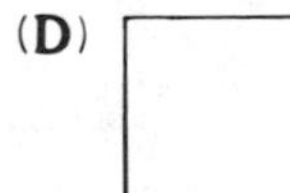
   (E) 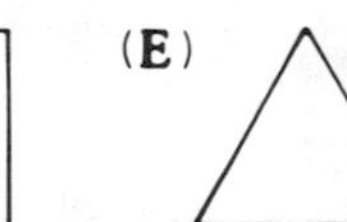

7. If a shirt is priced at $8.50, how much will it cost when its price is reduced by 10 per cent?

   (A) $0.85
   (B) $7.65
   (C) $7.75
   (D) $8.40
   (E) $8.65

GO ON TO THE NEXT PAGE

5

Questions 8-27 each consist of two quantities, one in Column A and one in Column B. You are to compare the two quantities and on the answer sheet blacken space

A if the quantity in Column A is greater;
B if the quantity in Column B is greater;
C if the two quantities are equal;
D if the relationship cannot be determined from the information given.

Notes:
1. In certain questions, information concerning one or both of the quantities to be compared is centered above the two columns.
2. In a given question, a symbol that appears in both columns represents the same thing in Column A as it does in Column B.
3. Letters such as x, n, and k stand for real numbers.

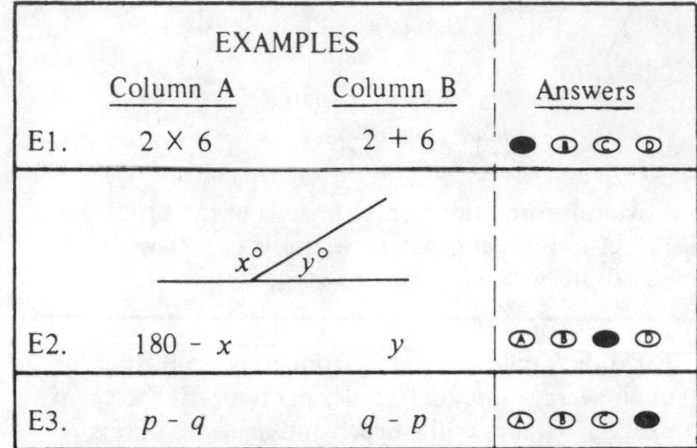

	Column A	Column B
8.	The number of minutes in a day	The number of days in a year
9.	x if $2x - 14 = 0$	y if $y - 7 = 0$
10.	The greatest prime number between 15 and 20	17

A B C D E

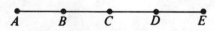

Lettered points are equally spaced.

11.	BD	$\frac{AE}{2}$

If half of N is added to twice N, the sum is 90.

12.	N	32
13.	740 X 0.2	$\frac{1}{4}$ of 740

In $\triangle PQR$, the sum of the degree measures of $\angle Q$ and $\angle R$ is greater than $90°$.

	Column A	Column B
14.	Degree measure of $\angle P$	Degree measure of $\angle Q$
15.	56(842) + 44(842)	84201

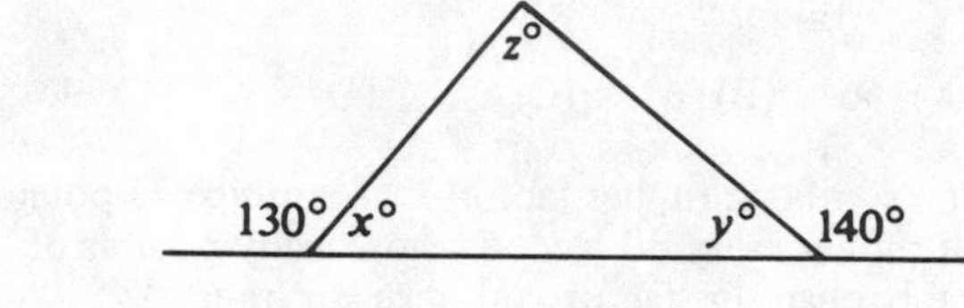

16.	$x + y$	z
17.	x if $11 < x < 17$	y if $12 < 2y < 20$

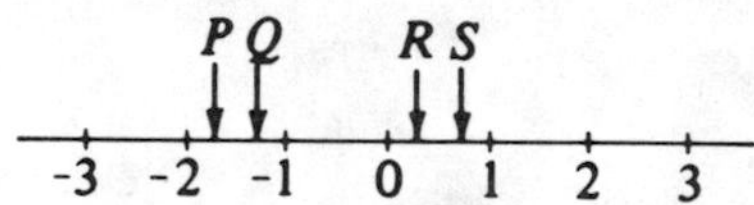

Number Line

18.	$P \times Q$	$R \times S$
19.	$(4^3)^2$	$4^{(3^2)}$
20.	The difference between two numbers each of which is between 2 and 5	The sum of two numbers each of which is between 1 and 2

GO ON TO THE NEXT PAGE

SUMMARY DIRECTIONS FOR COMPARISON QUESTIONS

Answer: A if the quantity in Column A is greater;
B if the quantity in Column B is greater;
C if the two quantities are equal;
D if the relationship cannot be determined from the information given.

	Column A	Column B
	Circle R has diameter 6. Circle S has circumference 4π.	
21.	Area of R	Area of S
	$pq > 0$, $pr < 0$	
22.	qr	0
23.	The volume of a cylinder with height 5	The volume of a cone with height 5
	$x > y > 0$	
24.	(20% of x) + (30% of y)	50% of $(x + y)$
	a and b are positive.	
25.	$\frac{a}{b}$	$\frac{a+1}{b+1}$

	Column A	Column B
	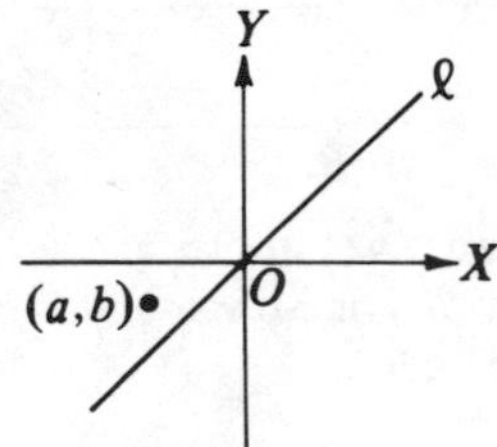 Line ℓ has the equation $y = x$.	
26.	a	b
	S is the set of all integers greater than 0 and less than 100.	
27.	Number of integers N in S such that both $\frac{N}{2}$ and $\frac{N}{5}$ are in S	Number of integers K in S such that $\frac{K}{10}$ is in S

GO ON TO THE NEXT PAGE

5

Solve each of the remaining problems in this section using any available space for scratchwork. Then decide which is the best of the choices given and blacken the corresponding space on the answer sheet.

28. If the present time is 7 a.m., what time was it 40 hours ago?

(A) 3 a.m.
(B) 11 a.m.
(C) 4 p.m.
(D) 3 p.m.
(E) 11 p.m.

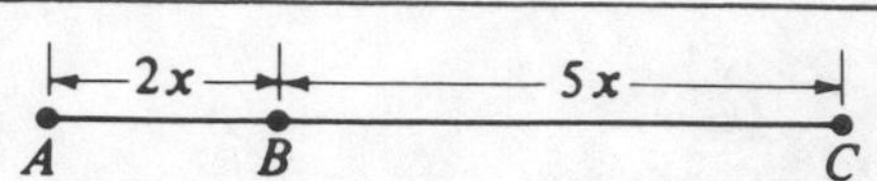

29. If segment AC above has length 35, then segment BC is how much longer than segment AB ?

(A) 7
(B) 10
(C) 15
(D) 21
(E) 25

30. If $x + y = 5$ and $x + 2y = 10$, then $x - y =$

(A) -5 (B) -4 (C) 0 (D) 4 (E) 5

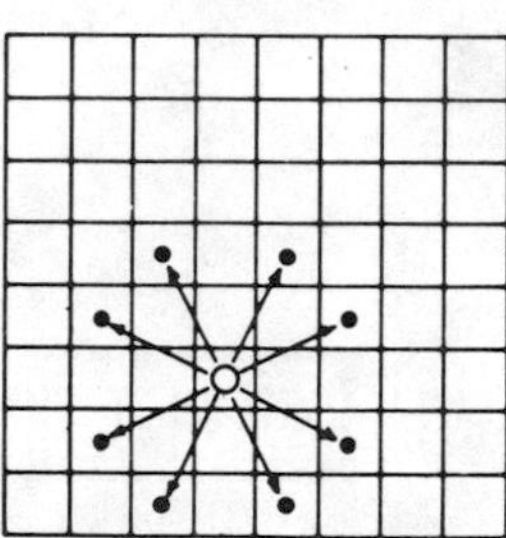

31. In a certain game, a piece is allowed to move as shown by the arrows above. On an empty board, what is the number of spaces from which all 8 such moves are NOT possible?

(A) 16 (B) 24 (C) 32 (D) 48 (E) 56

32. If the sum of three numbers is 3 more than the average of these three numbers, then the sum of these numbers is

(A) $-\frac{9}{2}$ (B) 3 (C) $\frac{9}{2}$ (D) 6 (E) 9

33. In the figure above, five semicircles are drawn on the number line. What is the total shaded area?

(A) $\frac{5\pi}{16}$

(B) $\frac{5\pi}{8}$

(C) $\frac{5\pi}{4}$

(D) $\frac{5\pi}{2}$

(E) 5π

34. The fare schedule for a taxi ride is 75 cents for the first quarter of a mile and 15 cents for each additional quarter of a mile. What is the fare in cents for a ride of x miles, where x is an integer?

(A) $75 + 15x$

(B) $75 + 45x$

(C) $75 + 15(4x)$

(D) $75 + 15\left(x - \frac{1}{4}\right)$

(E) $75 + 15(4x - 1)$

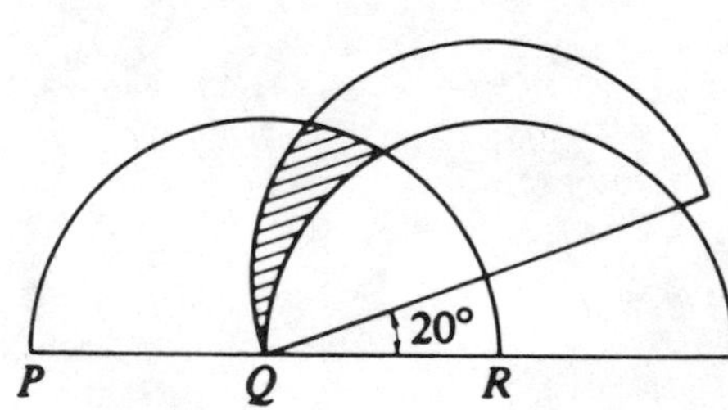

35. If the area of each of the three semicircles shown above is 72 and Q is the midpoint of segment PR, what is the area of the shaded region?

(A) 4 (B) 8 (C) 9 (D) 12 (E) 20

S T O P

IF YOU FINISH BEFORE TIME IS CALLED, YOU MAY CHECK YOUR WORK ON THIS SECTION ONLY. DO NOT WORK ON ANY OTHER SECTION IN THE TEST.

Correct Answers for Scholastic Aptitude Test Form Code 4X

VERBAL		MATHEMATICAL	
Section 1.	**Section 4.**	**Section 2.**	**Section 5.**
1. C	1. D	1. C	1. E
2. C	2. B	2. C	2. C
3. D	3. C	3. E	3. D
4. E	4. D	4. A	4. D
5. B	5. A	5. D	5. B
6. E	6. D	6. A	6. A
7. A	7. E	7. B	7. B
8. C	8. D	8. E	*8. A
9. B	9. A	9. D	*9. C
10. D	10. C	10. C	*10. A
11. C	11. D	11. C	*11. C
12. E	12. C	12. D	*12. A
13. E	13. B	13. D	*13. B
14. E	14. B	14. B	*14. D
15. C	15. E	15. D	*15. B
16. B	16. D	16. E	*16. C
17. A	17. A	17. B	*17. A
18. D	18. B	18. E	*18. A
19. E	19. C	19. A	*19. B
20. E	20. E	20. B	*20. D
21. C	21. B	21. B	*21. A
22. E	22. D	22. E	*22. B
23. B	23. B	23. A	*23. D
24. B	24. D	24. E	*24. B
25. D	25. A	25. C	*25. D
26. B	26. A		*26. B
27. A	27. C		*27. C
28. D	28. E		28. D
29. C	29. B		29. C
30. B	30. E		30. A
31. B	31. D		31. D
32. B	32. C		32. C
33. E	33. B		33. B
34. E	34. B		34. E
35. A	35. A		35. B
36. D	36. B		
37. B	37. A		
38. E	38. D		
39. C	39. C		
40. A	40. E		
41. A			
42. A			
43. B			
44. E			
45. C			

*Indicates four-choice questions. (All of the other questions are five-choice.)

The Scoring Process

Machine-scoring is done in three steps:

- *Scanning.* Your answer sheet is "read" by a scanning machine and the oval you filled in for each question is recorded on a computer tape.
- *Scoring.* The computer compares the oval filled in for each question with the correct response. Each correct answer receives one point; omitted questions do not count toward your score. For each wrong answer, a fraction of a point is subtracted to correct for random guessing. For questions with five answer choices, one-fourth of a point is subtracted for each wrong response; for questions with four answer choices, one-third of a point is subtracted for each wrong response. The SAT-verbal test has 85 questions with five answer choices each. If, for example, a student has 44 right, 32 wrong, and 9 omitted, the resulting raw score is determined as follows:

$$\text{44 right} - \frac{\text{32 wrong}}{4} = 44 - 8 = \text{36 raw score points}$$

  Obtaining raw scores frequently involves the rounding of fractional numbers to the nearest whole number. For example, a raw score of 36.25 is rounded to 36, the nearest whole number. A raw score of 36.50 is rounded upward to 37.
- *Converting to reported scaled score.* Raw test scores are then placed on the College Board scale of 200 to 800 through a process that adjusts scores to account for minor differences in difficulty among different editions of the test. This process, known as equating, is performed so that a student's reported score is not affected by the edition of the test taken nor by the abilities of the group with whom the student takes the test. As a result of placing SAT scores on the College Board scale, scores earned by students at different times can be compared. For example, an SAT-verbal score of 400 on a test taken at one administration indicates the same level of developed verbal ability as a 400 score obtained on a different edition of the test taken at another time.

How to Score the Test

You can verify the College Board SAT scores reported to you recently by using the information in this booklet along with the copy of your answer sheet. *Before you begin, check that the first two characters (number and letter) of the form code you marked in item 3 on your answer sheet are the same as the form code printed on the front of this booklet.* Compare the responses shown on the copy of your answer sheet with the list of correct answers.

SAT-Verbal Sections 1 and 4

Step A: Count the number of correct answers for *section 1* and record the number in the space provided on the worksheet on the next page. Then do the same for the incorrect answers. (Do not count omitted answers.) To determine subtotal A, use the formula:

$$\text{number correct} - \frac{\text{number incorrect}}{4} = \text{subtotal A}$$

Step B: Count the number of correct answers and the number of incorrect answers for *section 4* and record the numbers in the spaces provided on the worksheet. To determine subtotal B, use the formula:

$$\text{number correct} - \frac{\text{number incorrect}}{4} = \text{subtotal B}$$

Step C: To obtain C, add subtotal A to subtotal B, keeping any decimals. Enter the resulting figure on the worksheet.

Step D: To obtain D, your raw verbal score, round C to the nearest whole number. (For example, any number from 44.50 to 45.49 rounds to 45.) Enter the resulting figure on the worksheet.

Step E: To find your reported SAT-verbal score, look up the total raw verbal score you obtained in step D in the conversion table on page 304. Enter this figure on the worksheet.

SAT-Mathematical Sections 2 and 5

Step A: Count the number of correct answers and the number of incorrect answers for *section 2* and record the numbers in the spaces provided on the worksheet. To determine the subtotal A, use the formula:

$$\text{number correct} - \frac{\text{number incorrect}}{4} = \text{subtotal A}$$

Step B: Count the number of correct answers and the number of incorrect answers for the *five-choice questions (questions 1 through 7 and 28 through 35) in section 5* and record the numbers in the spaces provided on the worksheet. To determine the subtotal B, use the formula:

$$\text{number correct} - \frac{\text{number incorrect}}{4} = \text{subtotal B}$$

Step C: Count the number of correct answers and the number of incorrect answers for the *four-choice questions (questions 8 through 27) in section 5* and record the numbers in the spaces provided on the worksheet. To determine the subtotal C, use the formula:

$$\text{number correct} - \frac{\text{number incorrect}}{3} = \text{subtotal C}$$

Step D: To obtain D, add subtotal A, subtotal B, and subtotal C, keeping any decimals. Enter the resulting figure on the worksheet.

Step E: To obtain E, your raw mathematical score, round D to the nearest whole number. (For example, any number from 44.50 to 45.49 rounds to 45.) Enter the resulting figure on the worksheet.

Step F: To find your reported SAT-mathematical score, look up the total raw mathematical score you obtained in E in the conversion table on page 304. Enter this figure on the worksheet.

FORM CODE 4X

SAT SCORING WORKSHEET

SAT-Verbal Sections

A. Section 1:	______ no. correct	− ¼	(______) no. incorrect	=	______ subtotal A
B. Section 4:	______ no. correct	− ¼	(______) no. incorrect	=	______ subtotal B
C. Total unrounded raw score (Total A + B)					______ C
D. Total rounded raw score (Rounded to nearest whole number)					______ D
E. SAT-verbal reported scaled score (See the conversion table on the back cover.)					[ ] SAT-verbal score

SAT-Mathematical Sections

A. Section 2:	______ no. correct	− ¼	(______) no. incorrect	=	______ subtotal A
B. Section 5: Questions 1 through 7 and 28 through 35 (5-choice)	______ no. correct	− ¼	(______) no. incorrect	=	______ subtotal B
C. Section 5: Questions 8 through 27 (4-choice)	______ no. correct	− ⅓	(______) no. incorrect	=	______ subtotal C
D. Total unrounded raw score (Total A + B + C)					______ D
E. Total rounded raw score (Rounded to nearest whole number)					______ E
F. SAT-mathematical reported scaled score (See the conversion table on the back cover.)					[ ] SAT-math score

Score Conversion Table
Scholastic Aptitude Test
Form Code 4X

Raw Score	College Board Reported Score		Raw Score	College Board Reported Score	
	SAT-Verbal	SAT-Math		SAT-Verbal	SAT-Math
85	800		40	450	600
84	780		39	450	590
83	770		38	440	590
82	760		37	430	580
81	750		36	430	570
80	740		35	420	560
79	730		34	410	550
78	720		33	410	540
77	710		32	400	530
76	700		31	390	520
75	690		30	390	520
74	680		29	380	510
73	670		28	370	500
72	670		27	370	490
71	660		26	360	480
70	650		25	350	470
69	650		24	350	460
68	640		23	340	450
67	630		22	330	440
66	630		21	330	440
65	620		20	320	430
64	610		19	310	420
63	610		18	310	410
62	600		17	300	400
61	590		16	290	390
60	590	800	15	290	380
59	580	790	14	280	370
58	570	780	13	270	370
57	570	770	12	270	360
56	560	760	11	260	350
55	550	750	10	250	340
54	550	740	9	250	330
53	540	730	8	240	320
52	530	720	7	230	310
51	530	710	6	230	300
50	520	700	5	220	290
49	510	690	4	210	290
48	510	680	3	210	280
47	500	670	2	200	270
46	490	660	1	200	260
45	490	650	0	200	250
44	480	640	–1	200	240
43	470	630	–2	200	230
42	470	620	–3	200	220
41	460	610	–4	200	220
			–5	200	210
			–6 or below	200	200